EDITOR

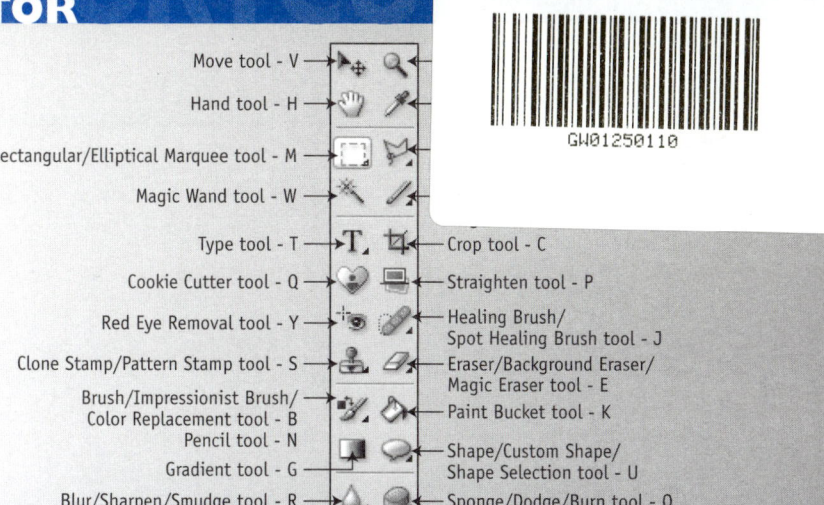

- Move tool - V
- Hand tool - H
- Rectangular/Elliptical Marquee tool - M
- Magic Wand tool - W
- Type tool - T
- Cookie Cutter tool - Q
- Red Eye Removal tool - Y
- Clone Stamp/Pattern Stamp tool - S
- Brush/Impressionist Brush/Color Replacement tool - B
- Pencil tool - N
- Gradient tool - G
- Blur/Sharpen/Smudge tool - R
- Crop tool - C
- Straighten tool - P
- Healing Brush/Spot Healing Brush tool - J
- Eraser/Background Eraser/Magic Eraser tool - E
- Paint Bucket tool - K
- Shape/Custom Shape/Shape Selection tool - U
- Sponge/Dodge/Burn tool - O

EDITOR

File management shortcut keys

New Blank File	Ctrl+N
New Creation	Ctrl+Alt+C
Open	Ctrl+O
Close	Ctrl+W
Save	Ctrl+S
Save As	Ctrl+Shift+S
Print	Ctrl+P
Quit	Ctrl+Q
Photoshop Elements Help	F1
Undo	Ctrl+Z
Redo	Ctrl+Y
Cut	Ctrl+X
Copy	Ctrl+C
Paste	Ctrl+V
Preferences, General	Ctrl+K
Auto Red Eye Fix	Ctrl+R
Levels	Ctrl+L
Adjust Hue/Saturation	Ctrl+U

EDITOR

Layer, selection, and view management shortcut keys

New Layer	Ctrl+Shift+N
Group with Previous	Ctrl+G
Ungroup	Ctrl+Shift+G
Merge Layers	Ctrl+E
Merge Visible	Ctrl+Shift+E
Bring to Front	Ctrl+Shift+]
Bring Forward	Ctrl+]
Send Backward	Ctrl+[
Send to Back	Ctrl+Shift+[
Select All	Ctrl+A
Deselect	Ctrl+D
Reselect	Ctrl+Shift+D
Inverse	Ctrl+Shift+I
Free Transform Shape	Ctrl+T
Zoom in	Ctrl++
Zoom Out	Ctrl+-
Fit on Screen	Ctrl+0
Selection	Ctrl+H
Rulers	Ctrl+R
Last Filter	Ctrl+F

PHOTO BROWSER

File menu shortcut keys

Get Photos From Camera or Card Reader	Ctrl+G
Get Photos From Scanner	Ctrl+U
Get Photos From Files and Folders	Ctrl+Shift+G
Get Photos From Mobile Phone	Ctrl+Shift+M
Catalog	Ctrl+Shift+C
Burn	Ctrl+B
Duplicate	Ctrl+Shift+D
Rename	Ctrl+Shift+N
Move	Ctrl+Shift+V
Export to Computer	Ctrl+E
E-mail	Ctrl+Shift+E
Print	Ctrl+P
Exit	Ctrl+Q

PHOTO BROWSER

Edit menu shortcut keys

Delete from Catalog	Del
Rotate 90º Left	Ctrl+Left
Rotate 90º Right	Ctrl+Right
Auto Smart Fix	Ctrl+Alt+M
Auto Red Eye Fix	Ctrl+R
Go to Standard Edit	Ctrl+I
Adjust Date and Time	Ctrl+J
General Preferences	Ctrl+K

PHOTO BROWSER

View menu shortcut keys

View Photos in Full Screen	F11
Compare Photos Side by Side	F12
Refresh	F5
Go To: Back	Alt+Left
Go To: Forward	Alt+Right

Window menu shortcut keys

Photo Browser	Ctrl+Alt+O
Date View	Ctrl+Alt+C
Tags	Ctrl+T
Collections	Ctrl+Alt+L
Properties	Alt+Enter

the Unofficial Guide® to Photoshop® Elements 4

Donna L. Baker

Wiley Publishing, Inc.

The Unofficial Guide® to Photoshop® Elements 4

Copyright © 2006 by Wiley Publishing, Inc., Hoboken, NJ

Published by Wiley Publishing, Inc.
111 River Street
Hoboken, NJ 07030-5774
www.wiley.com

No part of this publication may be reproduced, stored in a retrieval system or transmitted in any form or by any means, electronic, mechanical, photocopying, recording, scanning or otherwise, except as permitted under Sections 107 or 108 of the 1976 United States Copyright Act, without either the prior written permission of the Publisher, or authorization through payment of the appropriate per-copy fee to the Copyright Clearance Center, 222 Rosewood Drive, Danvers, MA 01923, (978) 750-8400, fax (978) 646-8600, or on the web at www.copyright.com. Requests to the Publisher for permission should be addressed to the Legal Department, Wiley Publishing, Inc., 10475 Crosspoint Blvd., Indianapolis, IN 46256, (317) 572-3447, fax (317) 572-4355, or online at http://www.wiley.com/go/permissions.

Wiley, the Wiley Publishing logo, Unofficial Guide and all related trademarks, logos, and trade dress are trademarks or registered trademarks of John Wiley & Sons, Inc. and/or its affiliates. Photoshop is a registered trademark of Adobe Systems Incorporated in the United States and/or other countries. All other trademarks are the property of their respective owners. Wiley Publishing, Inc. is not associated with any product or vendor mentioned in this book.

The publisher and the author make no representations or warranties with respect to the accuracy or completeness of the contents of this work and specifically disclaim all warranties, including without limitation warranties of fitness for a particular purpose. No warranty may be created or extended by sales or promotional materials. The advice and strategies contained herein may not be suitable for every situation. This work is sold with the understanding that the publisher is not engaged in rendering legal, accounting, or other professional services. If professional assistance is required, the services of a competent professional person should be sought. Neither the publisher nor the author shall be liable for damages arising here from. The fact that an organization or Website is referred to in this work as a citation and/or a potential source of further information does not mean that the author or the publisher endorses the information the organization or Website may provide or recommendations it may make. Further, readers should be aware that Internet Websites listed in this work may have changed or disappeared between when this work was written and when it is read.

For general information on our other products and services or to obtain technical support please contact our Customer Care Department within the U.S. at (800) 762-2974, outside the U.S. at (317) 572-3993 or fax (317) 572-4002.

Wiley also publishes its books in a variety of electronic formats. Some content that appears in print may not be available in electronic books. For more information about Wiley products, please visit our web site at www.wiley.com.

Library of Congress Control Number: 2005937346

ISBN-13: 978-0-471-76323-9

ISBN-10: 0-471-76323-3

Manufactured in the United States of America

10 9 8 7 6 5 4 3 2 1

Page creation by Wiley Publishing, Inc. Composition Services

Acknowledgments

Thanks to my husband Terry for his unending support and acceptance. Special thanks to my supporters — Abby and Rave, Erin and Deena.
Thanks to Cricket Krengel, my uncomparable editor at Wiley, for keeping this book on the right path, and to Jody Lefevere for the opportunity.
And of course, thanks as always to Tom Waits.

For Mom and Dad
—Donna L. Baker

Credits

Acquisitions Editor
Jody Lefevere

Project Editor
Cricket Krengel

Technical Editor
Ron Rockwell

Copy Editor
Gwenette Gaddis Goshert

Editorial Manager
Robyn Siesky

Business Manager
Amy Knies

Vice President & Group Executive Publisher
Richard Swadley

Vice President & Publisher
Barry Pruett

Project Coordinator
Maridee Ennis

Graphics & Production Specialists
Elizabeth Brooks
Carrie Foster
Lauren Goddard
Denny Hager
Barbara Moore
Lynsey Osborn
Melanee Prendergast
Heather Ryan
Amanda Spagnuolo
Ron Terry

Quality Control Technicians
Laura Albert
John Greenough
Susan Moritz

Proofreading
Tricia Liebig

Indexing
Johnna VanHoose

Book Interior Design
Lissa Auciello-Brogan
Elizabeth Brooks

Introduction xxi

I First You Find Some Images 1

1 All Together Now 3
Making your opening move 3
   Pick a task, any task *4*
   Pick the same task *5*
Specifying camera and card reader settings 6
Downloading images from your digital camera 7
Downloading and sorting 10
Scanning photos 12
   Basic scan *13*
   TWAIN scans *14*
Creating new documents 15
Adding existing photos 18
Storing phone images 19
   Creating a watched folder *19*
   Adding phone images *20*
Grabbing images from video clips 20
Just the facts 23

2 Your Digital Shoebox: The Organizer 25
Getting into the Photo Browser 26
   Speeding it up *26*
   What you see *27*
Using the Organizer's catalog 30
   Adding a new catalog *30*
   Moving files *31*
   Deleting files *32*
Sorting your image files 33
   Sorting by date *33*
   Sorting by batch *34*
   Sorting by folder *34*
It's about time 35

Paying attention to details 37
   Understanding icons *37*
   Hiding details *38*
Using special views 39
   Viewing at full screen size *39*
   Working the special views control bar *41*
   Viewing images side by side *42*
   Marking prints *42*
Working with video 43
Working in the Date View 44
   Year by year *45*
   Days and months *46*
   New events *47*
Set another date and time 48
Reconnecting files 49
   Correcting potential problems *49*
   Tips for maintaining connections *50*
Fixing it yourself 51
   Making a reconnection *51*
   Relocation options *52*

   Just the facts 53

3 Tidying Up Your Files **55**
   For the collector 56
      Starting a new collection *56*
      Changing the icon *57*
      Adding images to a collection *58*
   Grouping collections 59
      Defining a group *59*
      Viewing your collection *60*
   Editing collections 62
      Reorganizing the palette *62*
   Organizing options 64
   Stacking images 64
      Shuffling the stack *65*
   Stacking versions of an image 67
      Dealing with versions *68*
      Editing choices *68*
      Viewing the contents *69*
      Editing an image in a version set *70*
   Tag — you're it 71
      Working with the Tags palette *72*
      Exceptions to the rule *73*

Creating categories and tags 75
    Creating a new category or subcategory *75*
    Creating a new tag..*77*
    Attaching tags to images *78*
Making changes to tags...78
    Revising a category or tag *79*
    Reorganizing the Tags palette *79*
    Removing tags from images *80*
Instant tags 80
Tagging faces 82
    Searching for faces...*82*
    Other tagging tricks *84*
Searching photos 85
Checking out properties 86
Just the facts 88

II Image Editing 101 89

4 Seeing What You Have 91

Zzzzzoom 92
    Using default magnification settings *93*
    Setting custom magnifications *93*
    Choosing Zoom options..*94*
    Using the Navigator palette *95*
Make a match 96
    Organizing for quick decision-making...*96*
    Organizing for orientation *98*
Line it up...99
    Showing rulers..*100*
    Using the grid *100*
    Adjusting ruler and grid settings *101*
Just the facts 103

5 Shaping Up Your Images 105

Developing a plan...105
Understanding file size...106
    Image math..*107*
    Calculating pixels *107*
Resizing an image 108
    Changing the dimensions of an image..*108*
    Changing an image's document size...*111*
Resampling an image 111
    Resampling options *111*
    Applying interpolation methods *112*

Cropping images 113
  Visually cropping an image 113
  Quick crops 114
  Changing resolution while cropping 115
Changing canvas size 116
  Modifying the canvas size 116
  Clipping the image 117
Straightening an image 118
  Tips for straightening 119
  Automatically straightening an image 120
  Adjusting the canvas 121
Working with shapes 122
  Viewing shapes 122
  Finding the right shape 124
Cropping into shapes 125
  Cutting out a shape 125
  Tips for choosing Cookie Cutter settings 126
  Adjusting the cutout 126
Drawing with shapes 128
Selecting and transforming shapes 131
  Quick transformations 132
  Common transform commands 132
  Using transformation commands 133
Combining multiple shapes in one layer 135
Just the facts 137

6 Color Inside the Lines 139
Setting foreground and background colors 140
  Changing color swatches 140
  Changing color in the toolbox 140
Defining color using models 141
  What we see 142
  What the monitor sees 142
Working in the Color Picker 143
  Tweaking a color choice 143
  Defining specific color values 144
  Looking for colors 145
  Using a different Color Picker 146
    Adding custom colors 147
      Windows Color dialog box tips 148
  Choosing Web colors 148
  Selecting a color from an image 149
Working with swatch libraries 150
  Adding color swatches 152
  Deleting color swatches 153

Managing color swatch libraries 154
   Saving new libraries *154*
   Resetting a library *155*
Fills 156
   Filling shapes *156*
      Selecting the fill 156
      Specifying fill properties 156
   Filling with patterns *158*
      Applying a pattern fill 158
      Creating a custom pattern 159
Making a splash with the Paint Bucket 160
   Filling with the Paint Bucket *160*
   Understanding the Paint Bucket fill options *162*
Stroking lines 163
Groovin' with gradients 164
   Gradient types *165*
   Choosing gradient options *167*
   Varying the gradient's path *167*
   Defining a gradient *168*
   Add some noise *170*
   Several gradient tips *171*
Just the facts 172

7 Hands-Off Image Correcting 173
Getting into a fix 174
   Protecting images *174*
   Changing the program's startup window *175*
Quick Fix mode's workspace 176
Quick Fix tools 177
Correcting red eye 178
Enhancing images automatically 179
   Selecting auto adjustments *180*
   A quick processing workflow *180*
Adjusting adjustments 182
   General fixes *183*
   Lighting fixes *184*
   Fixing color *185*
   Sharpening the image *186*
Just the facts 187

8 All in the Details 189
Improving image detail 190
   Adjusting highlight and shadow *190*
   Changing brightness and contrast *193*

Finding information 194
Adjusting image color using a graph...195
   When to use levels *196*
   Preparing your workspace *197*
Viewing levels..198
   Orienting yourself..*199*
   Reading the graph..*200*
Fixing the image 200
   Adjusting tones manually *201*
   Adjusting tones automatically *201*
   Tweaking midrange tones *204*
Specifying exact colors..204
Previewing clipped areas...206
Using individual color channels 207
Quick color cast corrections 208
Just the facts 209

9 In Living Color 211

Managing color 211
Calibrating your monitor...212
   Setting your monitor *213*
   Preparing the profile..*214*
Managing color in the program 216
   Embedding color profiles in an image.....................................*216*
   Assigning a program color space *217*
Describing color modes 219
   Color modes *220*
   Channels and bit depth *221*
Converting to shades of gray 222
Bitmapping 223
Indexing color 225
   Converting the image...*226*
Adjusting image color 227
Improving skin tone...228
Dealing with a color cast 230
   Identifying a color cast *230*
   Automatically changing a color cast *230*
Color correction using variations...231
Photo filters 233
Reading color information...235
   Selecting content *235*
   Understanding image statistics *237*
Just the facts 238

III Pick What You Want to Work With 239

10 Choosing Parts 241

Tools for selecting 241
Making geometric selections 243
   The selection's composition 244
   Edge treatments 246
   Sizing the marquee 247
Selecting with Lasso tools 248
   Selecting with the basic Lasso tool 250
   Multi-sided selections with the Polygon Lasso tool 250
   Detecting shapes with the Magnetic Lasso tool 251
Waving your magic wand 255
More or less 256
Brushing a selection 257
   Painting a selection 258
   Painting a mask 259
Magic Selection Brush 261
Magical extractions 262
   Adjust the window's display 263
   Tweaking the selection 265
Using the Move tool 266
   Copying a selection 268
   Copying selections to other images 269
   Pasting a selection into another selection 269
Reselecting selections 271
   Adding feathering 271
   Modifying selection edges 272
Saving and revising selections 273
   Saving the selection 273
   Revising selections 274
Managing the selections 276
Just the facts 276

11 It's Like a Layer Cake 277

What is a layer? 277
Starting in the background 281
   Deleting a selected area on a Background layer 281
   Converting a Background layer 283
   Duplicating the layer 284
Adding layers 285
   Choosing new layer settings 286
Naming and organizing layers 288

Configuring appearances..289
  Setting the transparency appearance 289
  Specifying the layer characteristics 291
Managing layer locks...292
  Locking layer contents 294
  Troubleshooting layer locking 296
Linking and unlinking layers 296
Merging layers 297
  Merging choices 297
  Merging layers into new layers..298
Flattening an image..300
Taking a shortcut..301
Opacity settings 302
Blending modes 304
  Darken blending modes..305
  Lighten blending modes 307
  Using the Overlay blend...309
  Shining a light 310
  Subtracting for effect..313
  Blending color settings...315
Just the facts 320

12 Fun with Layers..321
Adjusting layers 321
  What's in a name?...325
  Applying an adjustment layer..327
  Targeting layers 328
  Grouping shortcuts 329
Masking a layer 331
  Applying a mask to an adjustment layer...................................331
  Shades of gray...333
Masking with text...334
Clipping images...337
Styling options 339
  Opening the palette..339
  It's a matter of style...340
  Scaling the effect..342
Using simple styles 346
Working with complex styles 347
  Layer style behaviors 350
  Reusing a style 351
  Layering with style 353

Picking an effect 354
    Effect categories *354*
    Applying an effect *356*
Just the facts 358

IV Not-So-Basic Image Editing 359

13 Manually Correcting Images 361

Designing a workflow 361
Digging for artifacts 362
A blooming nuisance 363
Removing moiré patterns 365
Turning off the noise 366
JPEG artifact 369
Removing image fringing 370
    Defining the fringed areas on a layer *372*
    Adding and masking the adjustment layer *375*
    Knocking out the fringe *376*
Defringing a selection 378
Removing hot spots 380
    Finding hot spot info *381*
    Adding the adjustment layer *382*
    Tweaking the hot spot *382*
Sharpening up the image 383
    Specifying filter options *384*
    Unsharp Mask tips *386*
Looking for confusing content 387
Just the facts 390

14 Retouching Magic 391

Taking off the pounds 391
    Creating the first shadow *392*
    Adding a new layer *393*
    Blurring the new shadow *395*
Removing strange eye colors 397
Making touchups 399
Fixing spots 399
    Correcting a single spot *400*
    Defining correction color *401*
Fixing bigger problems 403
    Healing an image *404*
    Choosing healing options *405*

Cloning pixels on an image 406
Digital eye enhancements 408
    Setting up the correction *408*
    Erasing the circles *409*
    Fixing extra highlights *410*
Fine-tuning tools 411
Tweaking contrast 411
    Painting contrast changes *412*
    Smudging content *413*
Tweaking light 413
    Lightening and darkening *414*
    Soaking up the color *415*
Replacing color 416
    Making selections *416*
    Replacing the color range *418*
Adding some color 419
Just the facts 421

V From an Image to a Work of Art 423

15 Getting to Know Filters 425

Starting out 425
Applying a filter 426
    Applying a filter from the Styles and Effects palette *427*
    Using menus to apply filters *428*
    Identifying filter categories *429*
Using the Filter Gallery 430
    Adding filters *431*
    Working in the Filter Gallery *431*
    Managing filters *433*
Using Adjustment filters 434
Blurring image content with filters 436
Managing noise with filters 440
Sharpening using filters 441
Changing images using video filters 442
    De-Interlace filter *442*
    NTSC Colors filter *442*
Working with other filters 443
    Applying a High Pass filter *444*
    Replacing pixel brightness with filters *445*
    Offsetting image content *446*
    Building a custom filter *447*

- Detecting watermarks 449
- Rendering content with filters 450
  - *Making it cloudy* *451*
  - *Texturing with fibers* *453*
- Placing an image in a 3D shape 454
  - *Bending an image into shape* *455*
  - *Reshaping the wireframe* *459*
  - *Using a lens flare* *460*
  - *Adding lighting effects* *462*
  - *Choosing a lighting style* *464*
  - *Specifying a reflective surface* *465*
  - *Tips for adjusting lights* *466*
  - *Using texture* *467*
- Just the facts 468

16 Finessing with Filters 469

- Before you start 469
- Basic Distort filters 470
- More complex Distort filters 474
  - *Wrapping an image with a sphere* *475*
  - *Bending an image* *476*
  - *Catching a wave* *478*
- Using a displacement map 481
  - *Applying the filter* *483*
  - *Combining filters* *485*
- Liquifying an image 486
- Pixelating images with filters 490
- Sketching with filters 492
- Stylizing filters 499
- Texturizing with filters 503
- Texture options for other filters 506
- Adding Brush Stroke filters 507
- Applying Artistic filters 509
- Using filters for specific purposes 513
  - *Producing a piece of art* *513*
  - *Adding quick (and cool) backgrounds* *515*
  - *Unifying a number of images* *518*
  - *Creating a sense of motion* *519*
- Just the facts 520

17 Say It with Words *and* a Picture 521

Type tool options 521
Typing text 523
   Adding a line of text *524*
   Adding text blocks *524*
   Committing text *525*
Selecting text and text blocks 526
Resizing a text block 527
Finding fonts 529
   Changing font previews *530*
   Using multiple fonts *531*
   Multiple spacing *532*
Masking text 532
   Creating the selection *532*
   Unmasking your mask *533*
Warping type 534
   Getting warped *534*
   Getting extremely warped *535*
Converting text 536
Liquifying type 537
Just the facts 539

18 Are You the Next Picasso? 541

Sampling image content 541
Types of brush strokes 543
Choosing brush settings 544
Selecting a brush library 545
   Viewing brushes *546*
   Specifying a default brush category *547*
Painting with a brush 549
Customizing brush tips 549
Managing brushes 553
   Saving a custom brush *554*
   Deleting brushes *555*
Using images as brushes 555
Painting in specialized modes 558
Drawing with a pencil 559
Creating an impression 560
Replacing image colors 562
   Sampling color *562*
   Replacing color *564*

Stamping patterns 564
    Creating a new stamp *564*
    Applying a Pattern Stamp *566*
Erasing pixels 568
    Erasing pixels magically *569*
    Erasing backgrounds *572*
Just the facts 574

VI Now That the Images Look Great 575

19 I'll Take a Dozen Copies 577
Printing photos 577
    Printing from Editor mode *578*
    Color managing printing *581*
Printing multiple images 582
    Creating contact sheets *584*
    Using a picture package *584*
    Printing specialized labels *586*
    Modifying image order *587*
Ordering prints online 588
Sending e-mail images 590
    Configuring message contents *590*
    Specifying the layout *591*
Shared collections 593
    Creating a shared collection *593*
    Uploading the collection *594*
    Notifying and viewing *596*
    Working in the gallery *597*
Just the facts 597

20 Creating Fun Stuff 599
Managing creations in the Organizer 599
Setting up a creation 600
Creating photo albums 603
Online ordering 605
Making greeting cards or calendars 606
Designing a photo gallery for the Web 607
    Creating an HTML Photo Gallery *607*
    Customizing the HTML Photo Gallery Web page *609*
    Saving the site *610*
Building panoramic images 611
    Preplanning tips *611*
    Creating the panorama *612*
    Adjusting the images *614*
Just the facts 616

21 On with the Show 617
Slide show basics..617
Setting slide show preferences...618
Getting around the Slide Show Editor....................................620
Making common edits 621
Quick edits...622
Reordering the slide show 623
Adding sound and music..623
Adjusting music clips 624
Narrating a slide show 624
Adding graphic enhancements 625
Attaching labels and text..626
Customizing text appearance..626
Fun with text 627
Transitioning slides..628
Using pan and zoom effects 630
Applying a pan and zoom 630
Adding a second effect...631
Sharing a slide show 632
Burning discs...632
Just the facts 633

22 Managing Image Distribution 635
Displaying your work online 635
Preparing images 636
Choosing a file format..637
Optimizing Web images 637
Optimizing an image automatically.......................................640
Understanding 24-bit color files...642
Managing transparency in 24-bit images..............................645
Simulating matting in a JPEG image.....................................645
Matting a PNG-24 image..646
Indexed color images 648
Checking the image's features..649
Choosing color palettes 651
Customizing an indexed image...654
Choosing matte and transparency options............................656
Creating color with dithering 657
Editing a color table 661
Previewing Web images..663
Previewing an image in a browser 663
Previewing different color displays.......................................666
Previewing dither 666
Building an animated GIF 669

Batch processing files 673
    Specifying file locations *673*
    Processing images *675*
    Applying edits *677*
    Labeling images..*678*
Looking at embedded data 679
Importing and exporting tags..680
    Importing tags with a photo *682*
Creating a copyrighting template 684
    Configuring the template...*685*
    Applying the template..*687*
Watermarking..688
Securing files...689
Just the facts 690

23 Cooking with Raw Images..691
Working with a raw file...692
    The Camera Raw dialog box...*692*
Developing an image adjustment plan..695
Examining the image..696
    Position and zoom *696*
    Viewing clipping in your image *697*
Taking out color casts 698
    Balance the white *698*
    Tint it..*700*
One-click adjustments 700
Modifying an image's tone 702
    Set exposure and shadows *702*
    Previewing the clipped areas *702*
    Brightness and contrast adjustments *703*
    Saturation adjustments..*704*
Taking care of the details...705
Saving digital negatives 706
    Choosing the storage location..*708*
    Defining image names *708*
    Choosing digital negative options..*709*
Using your own settings 710
Just the facts 710

Glossary..711

Appendix A: Resource Guide 731

Appendix B: Useful Real-World Worksheets 735

Index..747

About the Author

Donna L. Baker is an author, graphic designer, and instructor. She has been a writer and contributing editor for an online graphics magazine since 1998. She has experience training graphic and business software users in both corporate and classroom settings.

Donna is the author of many books covering a variety of graphics and Web software, ranging from Acrobat to Photoshop. More information and samples of her work and book projects are available at www.donnabaker.ca.

Introduction

Back in the early 1990s computer programs built for image editing and manipulation were the new kids on the digital block. One of the first programs, and the one that serves as a standard to which other image manipulation programs are compared, is Adobe Photoshop. Adobe Photoshop Elements 4 is the consumer version of Adobe Photoshop CS2. Many people have the idea that Photoshop Elements is a lightweight version of Photoshop. While it is true that Elements is a subset of its parent program, there's nothing lightweight about it.

Crystallizing the program into its most basic functions, Photoshop Elements is designed to:

- Serve as a download agent to transfer images from a camera and other sources such as camera phones to specified storage locations on your computer.
- View images on your computer.
- Sort, order, organize, and manage the contents of your photo catalog using a variety of different tools and methods.
- Create and manage metadata, which is information associated with images.
- Work with the raw camera data and process the files yourself.
- Carry out basic corrections on images quickly and easily.
- Perform extensive image corrections using a range of advanced editing features.
- Use text in association with image elements for composite images.

- Add a wide range of filters to enhance and add artistic treatments to the appearance of images.
- Export images in a range of file formats.
- Create an array of different sorts of products from presentations to calendars.

Wow! That's a lot of functionality for one program, isn't it?

How Elements is designed

If you consider the amount of functionality and types of work you can do in Photoshop Elements, it's not surprising that there are a number of windows and views. Finding what you want and knowing where to look can be a daunting task. For that reason, I have outlined the main components of the program and additional areas you can access from these windows or views.

- **Welcome Screen.** You can access all sections of the program from this dialog box. Click respective buttons to open the Organizer, the Quick Fix mode or Standard Edit mode of the Editor, and the Creation Setup window for constructing photo projects. Click Tutorials to open your browser and access tutorials and tips from Adobe's Web site.
- **Organizer.** The Organizer is used to import, sort, organize, and view images. Your images are shown as thumbnails in the Photo Browser or on a calendar grid in the Date View.
- **Photo Browser.** This view of the Organizer shows you your images according to different sorting arrangements, and you can customize the thumbnail size as desired. Choosing a particular group, version set, or stack opens the selected images in an expanded view within the Photo Browser.
- **Full Screen View.** The program's interface is hidden in the Full Screen View, which is accessible from the Photo Browser. You see one or two images (depending on your choice) and a control toolbar to manipulate the content.
- **Date View.** This is an alternate arrangement of the content of the Organizer, arranged in calendar grids rather than as thumbnails.

- **Face Tagging.** From either the Photo Browser or Date View of the Organizer, choose Find ⇨ Find Faces for Tagging to open the Face Tagging window. The results of the search can be used to attach tags for searching and organizing your photo collection.

- **Creation Setup.** Open the Creation Setup window from either the Organizer or the Editor windows. Choose from a number of options to build interesting output ranging from slide shows to greeting cards.

- **Quick Fix.** The Quick Fix mode of the Editor window is designed to do simple photo corrections. This mode uses a subset of the tools and palettes available in the full Standard Edit mode of the Editor. Access the Quick Fix mode from the Organizer's shortcuts bar or from the Standard Edit mode's shortcuts bar.

- **Standard Edit.** The Standard Edit mode of the Editor window offers the full range of Photoshop Element's correction and image manipulation tools and palettes. Access the Standard Edit mode from the Organizer's shortcuts bar or from the Quick Fix mode's shortcuts bar.

- **Photoshop Elements Help.** Choose Help ⇨ Photoshop Elements Help from any menu in the program, or click the Help light bulb icons at the right of palettes in the Editor views. The Help files open in Adobe Help Center, which is a uniform control program for displaying help files from Adobe products installed on your computer.

What's new?

Opening a new version of software is like unwrapping a birthday gift in my mind. You often have an idea of what you are getting, but it isn't real until you see it with your own eyes.

There are some nice improvements and new features in Photoshop Elements 4 that you are sure to find interesting and useful. Table In.1 shows a list of new features divided into sections according to their function.

Table In.1. New features in Photoshop Elements 4

Program Area	New and Improved Features
Organizer: display	Import contacts from Microsoft Outlook, Outlook Express, or vCards.
	Fix red eye automatically on import; the feature is selected by default.
	Show images in full screen view without the program window.
Organizer: searching and organizing	Search by metadata and by version sets.
	Work with image files in the Folder Location view.
	Locate people in your catalog using the Find Faces for Tagging command.
Organizer: managing PDF files	Import a PDF file as a single file, rather than separate files for each page.
	Extract images from the PDF file.
	Import selected pages from a multi-page PDF; specify resolution, color mode, anti-aliasing.
Organizer: output	Use the Order Prints pane to order photos and send them to specific people.
	Make a collage to use as desktop wallpaper. Choose Edit ⇨ Set as Desktop Wallpaper.
Organizer: slide show editor	Add text and graphics to slides.
	Add and edit photos from within the slide show window.
	Use Pan and Zoom effects.
	Add audio and music files.
Editor: image correction	Noise reduction filters available to remove JPEG noise.
	Use Magic Selection Brush tool to identify areas for automatic selection.
	Use Magic Extractor tool to removes the background from an image.

Program Area	New and Improved Features
Editor: color management	Convert a color profile in an existing image or remove the profile entirely.
	Adjust skin tones automatically.
Editor: image manipulation	Change cropping sizes using aspect ratios.
	Defringe command for removing halo artifacts around selections.
	Display Photoshop Smart Objects: You can move them, but they can't be edited in Photoshop Elements.
Editor: text functions	Construct paragraphs and text boxes using the Text tool.
	WYSIWYG font previews for the Text tool.

How the book is organized

The book's chapters are separated into several areas that correspond to your workflow or a type of function. For example, Chapter 6 describes how to work in the Quick Fix mode, which is one of the Editor's display windows that lets you make a range of corrections at the click of a button. The features you choose for corrections in Chapter 6's discussion are described in much more detail in Chapters 7 and 8 and use the Standard Edit mode, the Editor's complete editing window.

Part I: First You Find Some Images

In the first part, you learn how to get started. Take a tour through the program and see how to collect and bring images into Elements' control window, the Organizer. You also learn about using the main views — the Photo Browser and Date View.

Part II: Image Editing 101

One of Elements' principal uses is image editing. In this first part of image editing, learn to manipulate an image and the view to see what you need to see. Learn about different types of image correction and how to correct color and contrast problems. You also learn about color profiles and different ways to manage color.

Part III: Pick What You Want to Work With
Many times you don't want to make an edit or change to a whole image. In this part, learn how to select and specify a segment of the image for editing, either a portion of the image, or its layers. You see how to use one of numerous tools to select content on an image and how to use, manipulate, and control layers in an image.

Part IV: Not-So-Basic Image Editing
This part of the book is designed for the tweakers in the crowd. See how to repair and retouch images, from removing dark circles under your subject's eyes to removing a tree branch that seems to be coming out of Uncle Joe's head.

Part V: From an Image to a Work of Art
In this section of the book, learn how Elements can help you unleash your imagination. Use filters, text, paint brushes, and other sorts of painting tools to add impact. The dozens of filters in the program let you simulate anything from a stained-glass window to a watercolor.

Part VI: Now That the Images Look Great . . .
Once your images are perfect, learn different ways to distribute them in this section. You learn about printing and creating a number of products, ranging from slide shows to Web sites.

If you use images extensively for business or as an advanced hobbyist, you are sure to find ways to make your work more efficient in this final section of the book.

Tear Card
Take the oh-so-handy tear card that is filled with useful shortcuts out of the book and keep it close by as you learn to work with Photoshop Elements and use it as a quick reference when looking for a shortcut for a new skill or one that is not familiar.

Special features
Every book in the Unofficial Guide series offers the following four special sidebars that are devised to help you get things done cheaply, efficiently, and smartly.

1. **Hack:** Tips and shortcuts that increase productivity. They don't necessarily pertain strictly to Photoshop Elements but sometimes refer to other programs or your operating system.
2. **Watch Out!:** Cautions and warnings to help you avoid common pitfalls.
3. **Bright Idea:** Smart or innovative ways to do something; in many cases, this will be a way that you can save time or hassle.
4. **Inside Scoop:** Useful knowledge gleaned by the author that can help you become more efficient.

Your need to have quick information at your fingertips has been recognized, and we have provided the following comprehensive sections at the back of the book:

1. **Glossary:** Definitions of complicated terminology and jargon.
2. **Resource Guide:** Find listings of sites at Adobe, as well as addresses for technique and discussion sites, and online resources.
3. **Useful Real-World Worksheets:** A number of "how to" checklists you can use for everything from evaluating an image for correction to creating a presentation to what to look for in a new digital camera.
4. **Index**

Welcome to your Unofficial Guide

I wrote this guide with two groups of people in mind — the avid hobbyist and the business user.

The guide is designed to appeal to those of you who are keen hobbyists, whether your hobby is photography, scrapbooking, or creating other types of artwork. Many hobbyists are becoming increasingly sophisticated when it comes to manipulating digital images and more willing to experiment and tweak files.

The second group is business users. In many areas of business, graphics and images are of more significance than in years past, due to our general level of exposure to all things visual. Whether you are creating presentations for sales meetings, designing artwork for your company Web site, or assembling photos from a construction site, you find many ways to help you get the job done.

Whichever group you belong to — or if you belong to both — be sure to check out the different areas in the book. You may be surprised at what you find and how it can work for you!

PART I

First You Find Some Images

GET THE SCOOP ON...
■ Getting started ■ Downloading photos from a camera ■
Ways to start a new image file ■ Adding images from
mobile phones ■ Capturing frames from a video clip

All Together Now

You can start up Photoshop Elements in a number of different ways, depending on your preferences and the task at hand. You can start in the Organizer window, the program component used for organizing and assembling images. If you want to work with an image immediately, choose from one of two different editing modes — Quick Edit or Standard Edit, either of which open in the Editor window. If you want to create a product such as a calendar or slide show, you could also open the program in the Photo Creation window. This chapter concentrates on the Organizer.

The Organizer, as you might guess from the name, is used to organize your photos. Of course, before you can organize them you need to get them into the program. You can import images in several ways. Some methods can be found in the Organizer, while other options are located in the Editor window.

Making your opening move

Select the Photoshop Elements 4.0 icon or program name from the Start menu to open the program. By default, you see the Welcome Screen (referred to generically as the splash screen) shown in Figure 1.1. From here, you can choose the next program area you need for your task.

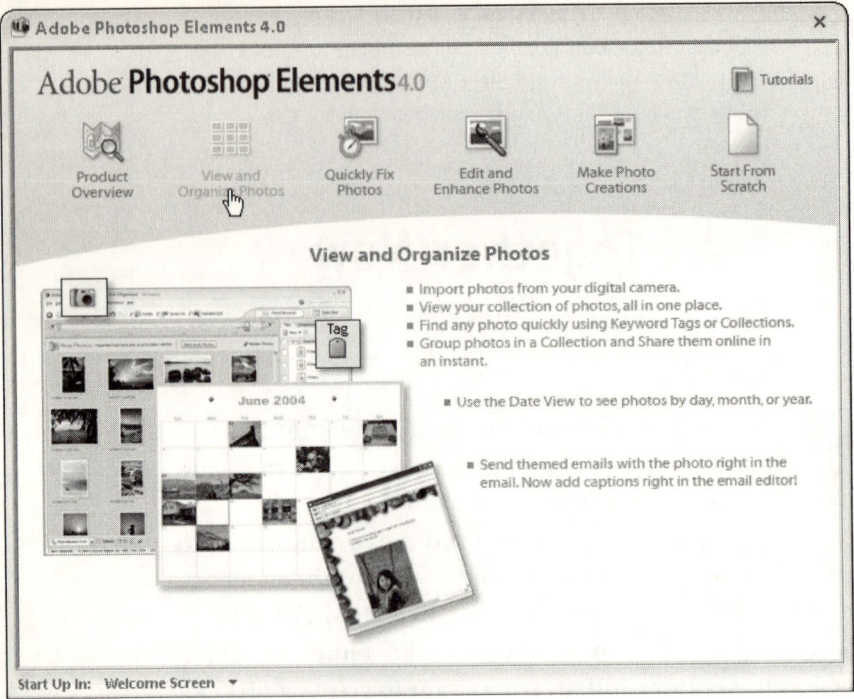

Figure 1.1. The initial view of the program is the Welcome Screen.

Pick a task, any task

The icons along the top of the Welcome Screen dialog box name a set of tasks that you can read about and then initiate the task in the program. Move your mouse over the icons to display more information about that particular function or area of the program. The different task areas are described in Table 1.1.

Table 1.1. Welcome Screen task information

Task Name	What It Describes	Click To...
Product Overview	Key functions and areas in the program about organizing, correcting images, and photo creations	No further action in the program. You can click links to go to the program's Web site for more information
View and Organize Photos	Importing, viewing, and organizing photos into collections; viewing photos as collections or by date	Dismiss the Welcome Screen and open the Organizer window

CHAPTER 1 ■ ALL TOGETHER NOW

Task Name	What It Describes	Click To...
Quickly Fix Photos	Highlights of the photo correction process such as using the Skin Tone Adjustment tool and the Magic Extractor	Dismiss the Welcome Screen and open the Quick Edit window
Edit and Enhance Photos	Some of the key editing features available such as working with layers and creating a panorama	Dismiss the Welcome Screen and open the Standard Edit window
Make Photo Creations	Several of the ways in which you can organize and customize photo distribution such as slide shows and greeting cards	Dismiss the Welcome Screen and open the Photo Creation window
Start From Scratch	How to start a new project from a blank page without specifying an image to use on the page	Dismiss the Welcome Screen and open the Standard Edit window
Tutorials	No description; moving your mouse over the icon shows the program's splash screen	Open the program's Web site and display a list of tutorials to learn about program functions and tasks

Pick the same task

Instead of using the Welcome Screen, you can specify that a program window be displayed automatically. At the lower left of the Welcome Screen, click the Start Up In drop-down arrow and choose an option. You can:

- Open the program in the default Welcome Screen
- Open the program in the Editor window
- Open the program in the Organizer window

I usually switch between using the Editor and Organizer windows as the default opening view, depending on what's going on at the moment.

Inside Scoop

If you are new to the program, using the Welcome Screen is a good way to figure out what you want to do. Be sure to read the short descriptions of each area as you move your mouse over the Welcome Screen's options.

For example, if I have just returned from traveling or shooting images for my collection, I set the program to open in the Organizer. After the images are safely in the Organizer and sorted to my liking, I reset the program to open automatically in the Editor.

Regardless of the view you are using, it's a simple matter of clicking one of the viewing options at the top of the program window to change the active area of the program. In Figure 1.2, the active working area is the Photo Browser in the Organizer, indicated by the highlighted area. Clicking any of the other options or choosing an option from the Edit drop-down menu opens that view of either the Organizer or Editor windows. For example, clicking Go to Quick Fix in the Edit menu opens the Quick Fix view of the Editor window.

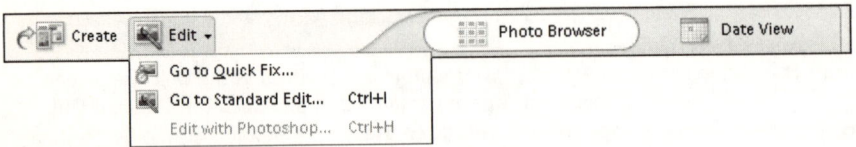

Figure 1.2. The options for opening different program windows are always available from the view in which you are working.

Specifying camera and card reader settings

Streamline your image downloads by setting camera and card reader preferences in the Organizer. You can customize storage locations and other recurring settings that save you time later.

Follow these steps to check out the preferences and make any changes:

1. Choose Edit ➪ Preferences ➪ Camera or Card Reader.
2. Click the Camera drop-down arrow, and choose the name of your camera. If you don't have a specific camera listed, leave the default named "Adobe Photoshop Elements" as shown in Figure 1.3.
3. Deselect the default import option if you use a program other than Adobe Photo Downloader or another method for importing files. The import option Use Adobe Photo Downloader to get photos from Camera or Card Reader is checked by default. When a camera is attached to your computer the Adobe Photo Downloader launches.
4. Click Browse to open the Browse for Folder dialog box. The default location where files are saved on your hard drive is shown in the Files section of the dialog box, but you may not want to save your images there.

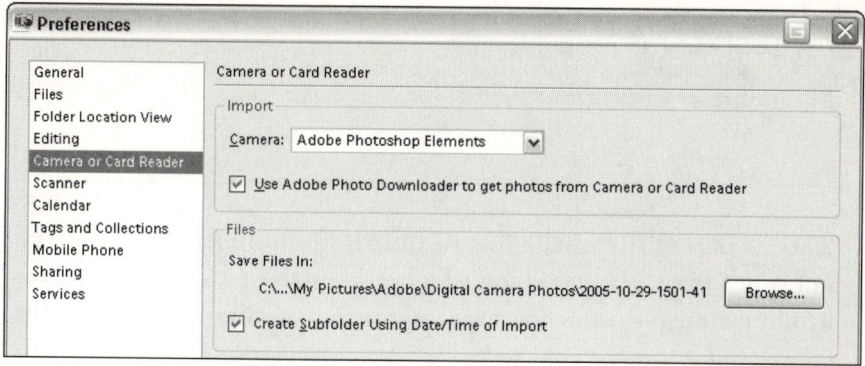

Figure 1.3. Select your camera from the Camera drop-down menu; the options vary according to the devices configured on your computer.

5. Locate the folder you want to use or click Make New Folder and name the folder; click OK to close the dialog box and return to the preferences.

6. In the Preferences dialog box, leave the check box Create Subfolder Using Date/Time of Import selected. This puts each imported group of files in its own folder, which is named using the date and time the photos were imported.

7. Click OK to close the dialog box and apply the changes.

If you make changes to the import and storage preferences and then later change your mind, reopen the Preferences dialog box and click Restore Default Settings to reset the preferences. The defaults are used in the book's discussion and examples.

Downloading images from your digital camera

Can you remember what it was like when you had to actually take a roll of film to a store for processing? And then sort the prints to find the one or two decent shots? Fortunately, that's becoming a distant memory.

You can tap into numerous sources to collect images and photos to work with and add to your image bank. One of the most common methods these days is to download files from your digital camera.

Hack

There's no law that says you need to use the Adobe Photo Downloader to manage and control downloads of files from your camera. You may have another utility you are more comfortable working with, or your camera may include its own download software.

>  **Inside Scoop**
>
> Sometimes when you just want to get the images off of your camera's memory card but don't need to make any changes such as renaming the files, it is quicker to work from the desktop rather than opening Photoshop Elements and activating the Photo Downloader.

And, as part of the installation of the Photoshop Elements program, you also get Photo Downloader, which is a separate program used for controlling image downloads to your computer's hard drive or other storage device.

If you have opened Photoshop Elements in the Organizer window, you can open the Photo Downloader by choosing one of these options:

- Choose File ⇨ Get Photos ⇨ From Camera or Card Reader.
- Press Ctrl+G (a shortcut key combination).
- Click the Camera icon on the Organizer's toolbar, and choose From Camera or Card Reader from the drop-down menu.

After installing Photoshop Elements, the Photo Downloader is included as an icon in the taskbar, shown in Figure 1.4. So, even when you do not have Photoshop Elements open, you can click the icon to open the Adobe Photo Downloader as a separate program.

The Photo Downloader is shown in Figure 1.5. After the window is open (regardless of how you opened it), follow these steps to identify and download images to your computer:

Figure 1.4. Use the taskbar's icon on the desktop for quick access to photo download and storage settings.

1. Click the Get Photos from drop-down arrow in the upper-right corner, and select a camera from the list. If you don't have a camera interface active with your computer, no options are available and the field reads <None Detected>.

2. The images on the camera or card are shown in thumbnails; each is selected automatically. If you don't want to download a particular image, deselect its check box.

3. Click the Browse button, and locate the folder you want to use to store your new image files if the default name doesn't show the desired folder.

>  **Watch Out!**
> Think before deciding to customize image file or folder names or store your files in a custom location. Don't keep changing your options; that can lead to confusion, frustration, and long searches for images. When in doubt, leave the default settings.

4. You can create and name subfolders within your default file storage area and rename the files as they are imported.
5. Select or deselect the Automatically Fix Red Eyes option.
6. Click Get Photos to start the import process. You see a dialog box showing a thumbnail of the image and its import status. If you have chosen the Automatically Fix Red Eye check box, the Auto Red Eye Fix examines the images and makes corrections.
7. After the files are downloaded, the Delete Files on Device? dialog box asks if you want to delete the files from your camera. Click Yes to remove the files.

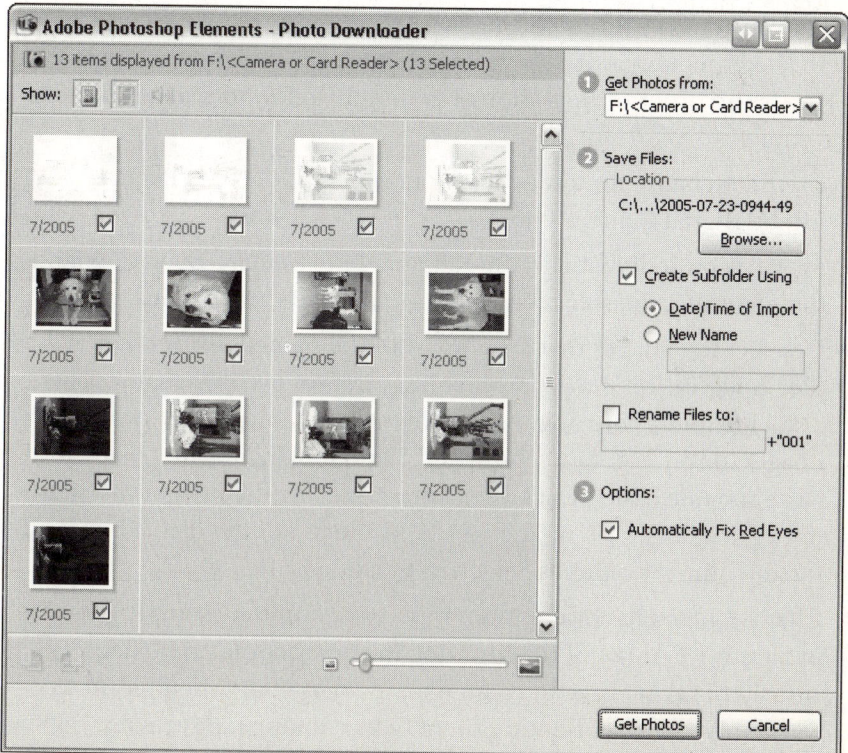

Figure 1.5. The Photo Downloader shows you the images and lets you specify import settings before downloading to your hard drive.

Bright Idea

If you don't have images of faces, you don't have to worry about red eye correction. Save some time when importing by deselecting the option.

Downloading and sorting

Depending on the number of images you work with and how tightly you have to control the access to your images, you should consider using a naming system.

You can start from the Photo Downloader window by choosing several different settings to customize both the folder and file names. For example, you can choose a date/time of import as a name for a subfolder to hold the files you are downloading. You can also name the folder and its images with custom names.

After you have connected your camera and the thumbnails of the images are displayed in the Photo Downloader window, decide how you want to extract the files from your camera. For example, when the images you want to download include many different subjects, a good way to keep them organized is to download them in groups by subject.

Here's the order of operations I generally follow to make downloading a straightforward situation:

- Use the default file storage location, which is: C:\...\My Pictures\Adobe\Digital Camera Photos.
- Specify a custom name in the Rename Files to field. Choose a name that describes the subject of the shots as much as possible.
- Deselect the images that aren't part of the named subject. For example, in Figure 1.5, I was downloading shots of two main subjects — a still life and a cute dog. As you might guess, I intend to use the images for different purposes, and I find looking for files using a custom name easier. Click the check boxes for the images you want to exclude, as shown in Figure 1.6. At the top of the dialog box, you see the number of items Selected/Excluded.
- Change the image orientation, if necessary. In the example shown in Figure 1.5, three of the four dog images are rotated 90 degrees. Instead of taking time to change their orientation when I want to work with them, reorienting them before importing is easier.

Ctrl+click to select the images for rotation. Then click the Rotate Left or Rotate Right icons at the bottom of the thumbnail area to change the images. Figure 1.6 shows the set of images after they are oriented correctly.

- Deselect or select the Automatically Fix Red Eyes check box, depending on your subjects.

After the images are downloaded to your hard drive, return to the Photo Downloader window to select and name another batch of images for import, or close the Photo Downloader window and move on to another task.

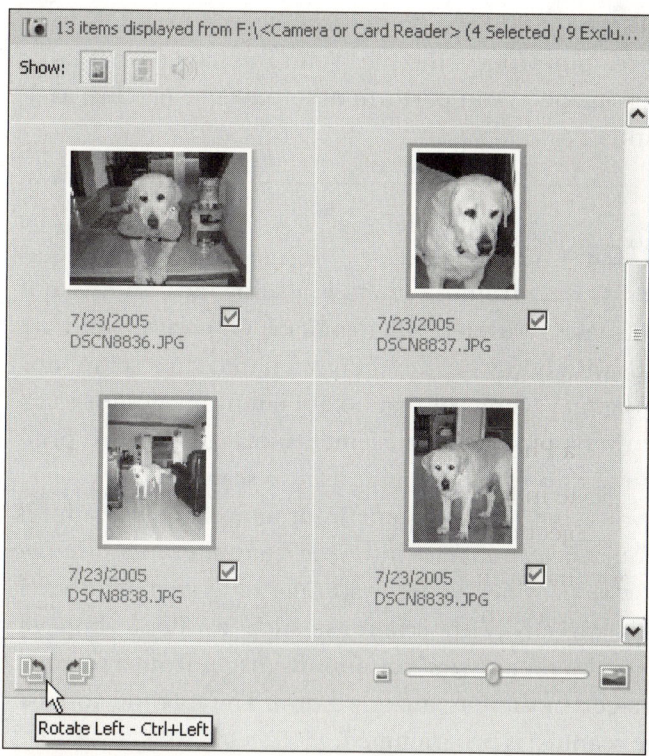

Figure 1.6. Separate the contents of a camera or card into conveniently named groups of images.

Hack
If you like to save files with their capture date, be sure to check the date when importing images into Photoshop Elements. The program uses the date you bring the file into your system, not the date the image was captured.

> **Rotating raw image files**
>
> An image captured in raw format can't be rotated as is. If you select a raw file and click one of the rotation icons, the Cannot Rotate Original File dialog box opens explaining that the image has a format the Photoshop Elements can't write. Click Yes to proceed with making a copy, or No to close the dialog box and return to the Photo Browser.
>
> If you want to show a rotated image in the Photo Browser, which is simpler for reviewing thumbnails, click Yes to open the Select Output Format for Edited File dialog box. Select the format for the copy, one of JPEG, PNG, TIFF, or Photoshop file and click OK to close the dialog box and process the file. You can change orientation in the original image as you perform other raw image edits, as described in Chapter 23.

Scanning photos

Downloading images directly from a camera is a spiffy idea. But what if you want to use prints taken with a regular camera? Or what if you want to include old photos with newly captured digital photos in a scrapbook montage? Or make digital versions of that box of family images for long-term storage? Not to worry. Photoshop Elements lets you capture print images from any source into your computer using a scanner.

Before starting, you need to know some information about scanners and your options. You can scan images into your computer in a number of ways — using software provided with the scanner or as part of another program that works directly with scanners, such as Photoshop or Acrobat. In Photoshop Elements, you can import images from a scanner using a process managed in the Organizer window. The method you use depends on how the scanner is programmed.

Bright Idea

Are you always making the same setting changes when importing images through a scan? Take a minute and change the preferences. Choose Edit ⇨ Preferences ⇨ Scanner. Specify a scanner, the file quality and format, and the storage location. Click OK to close the dialog box and apply the changes.

Basic scan

If you have a simple scanner that was installed as part of a pre-configured system, you may not know whether it is a TWAIN scanner. Before investigating, follow these steps. If you are successful, that's all you need to do to scan and import images into your Photoshop Elements program:

1. Click the Get Photos button on the Organizer window's toolbar to open the menu, and choose From Scanner. The Get Photos dialog box appears (see Figure 1.7).

2. In the Get Photos from Scanner dialog box, click the Scanner drop-down arrow and choose your scanner. The default is named Adobe Photoshop Elements. If your scanner menu shows only the "None Detected" label, check that you have installed your scanner correctly and that it is turned on.

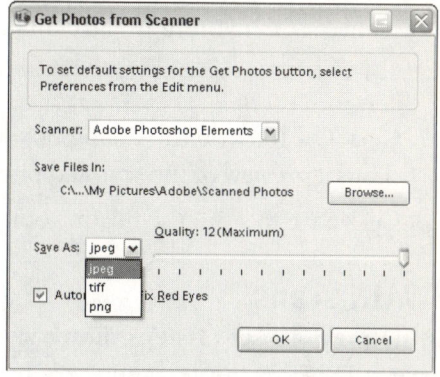

Figure 1.7. Select a scanner, storage location, and file format for scanning images directly into Photoshop Elements.

3. Use the default location for storing scanned images, or click Browse and locate the folder location you want to use. By default, scanned images are stored on your hard drive at C:\...\ My Pictures\Adobe\Scanned Photos.

4. Choose a file format from the Save As drop-down list, shown in Figure 1.7. You can select from JPEG, TIF, or PNG files.

5. For JPEG files only, drag the slider to specify the image quality. The higher the number, the higher the image quality and the larger the file size.

6. Deselect or select the Automatically Fix Red Eyes setting. Your choice depends on the image you are scanning.

 **Inside Scoop**

Plan to set aside some time to scan and digitize your printed images. That way, you can create a digital collection to use for different presentation formats or to burn onto DVD or CD for safe long-term storage.

> ### What is TWAIN?
>
> TWAIN is a standard software protocol and application programming interface (API) for communicating between software applications and image acquisition devices such as cameras and scanners. The term *TWAIN* has many suggested meanings ranging from "technology without an interesting name" to "toolkit without an interesting name" in the context of image scanning, to a more generic "thing without an interesting name." The term isn't an acronym for anything in particular.

7. Click OK to close the dialog box and start the scan. The Organizer shows a preview of the scanned photo in the Getting Photos dialog box.
8. Click Save to store the file on your computer using the chosen settings.

TWAIN scans

If the previous set of steps didn't work for you or if you know that you have a TWAIN scanner, then you have to work from within the Editor window rather than the Organizer window. Follow these steps to import a scan in Photoshop Elements:

1. Click Edit on the Organizer's toolbar to open the drop-down menu, and choose Standard Edit (or press Ctrl+I to open the Editor window).
2. Choose File ⇨ Import, and select your scanner from the list of available devices and formats.
3. Follow the prompts and dialog boxes offered by your particular scanner, which may look similar to Figure 1.8.
4. Click Scan (or the equivalent on your interface) to scan the file.
5. The image opens as an untitled image in the Standard Edit window.
6. Choose File ⇨ Save to open the Save dialog box.
7. Name the file, select its file format, and choose a storage location. Then click Save to save the file and close the dialog box.

> **Hack**
> I prefer not to scan into Photoshop Elements because I use several programs for scanning images and documents. Instead, I use the Microsoft Office Document Imaging program that interfaces with my scanners using TWAIN drivers and lets me choose different methods for saving scanned files.

Figure 1.8. Follow your scanner's instructions and dialog boxes for capturing a scanned photo.

Creating new documents

You may want to create a composite image using several images or portions of images as well as other graphics and text. Although you could start from an existing image and then change its canvas size to make it large enough to hold other content, the quickest way is to start from a blank file.

Add a blank file from within the Editor window by following these steps:

1. Open the Editor window. If you are in the Organizer, click Edit on the Organizer's toolbar to open the drop-down menu, and choose Standard Edit, or press Ctrl+I to open the Editor window.

2. Choose File ⇨ New ⇨ Blank File, or press Ctrl+N to open the New dialog box.

3. The image is named Untitled-1 by default; click the name field and type a name for the image, as shown in Figure 1.9. You can also name the file later.

4. Click the Preset drop-down arrow, and choose an option to use a preconfigured group of settings. The many different selections are explained in Table 1.2. Use this table to help you make the best choice for your task.

5. If you prefer, manually specify the Width, Height, and Resolution for a custom setting. Click the appropriate drop-down arrows and choose settings, or type values in the fields. Values shown in the New dialog box are based on the values used by any image copied to the clipboard or those you chose for the last image you created.

6. Pick a Color Mode from the drop-down list. The list includes RGB Color, Grayscale, or Bitmap options.

7. Click the Background Contents drop-down arrow, and choose the color for the background layer if you don't want to use the default white background. You can select Background Color to use the color set as the background in the toolbox. Choose Transparent if you don't want the background colored.

8. Click OK.

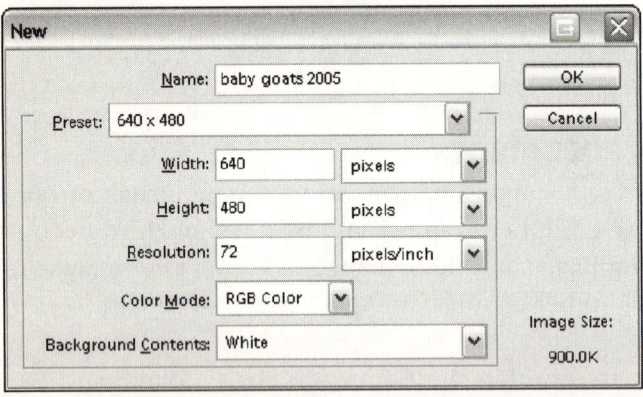

Figure 1.9. Name the new image and choose settings in the dialog box.

Inside Scoop

Have a look at the lower right of the New dialog box when choosing settings for a new image. You see that the size of the image is listed; as you make changes to settings or choose another preset, the image size value changes. Read about resolutions and file sizes in Chapter 5.

Table 1.2. New image file configuration options

Preset Name or Group	About the Preset
Custom	Use the Custom preset if you want to use settings other than those offered by the existing presets. If you select any of the fields on the dialog box and type different values, the Custom preset is selected automatically.
Clipboard	If you have selected an image from anywhere on your system and copied it to the clipboard, this preset is active. Choosing the Clipboard preset uses the resolution, color, and size of the image on the clipboard for the new image.
Default Photoshop Elements size	The standard image size offered by the program is a 5"×7" size image. It uses a low resolution and a color format suitable for online use. The image has a white background.
Standard paper sizes	Choose from standard print sizes such as letter or legal if you want to build a collage or composite that is being printed on a standard size paper or included in a printed project using standard page sizes.
Dimensions in inches	Choose from several standard image sizes such as 2"×3" or 8"×10" to create a project that can be printed to fit standard sized frames.
Screen resolution sizes	Choose different screen sizes when you want to build an image to use onscreen at a certain resolution with square pixels, such as 640×480 or 1024×768.
Digital video resolution sizes	Choose different screen sizes for digital video in common formats when creating content to be viewed on a TV screen, such as part of a DVD presentation.
High definition video resolution sizes	Choose different screen sizes for HDV when creating content to be viewed on an HDV monitor.
A- and B-sized pages	Choose one of the European page sizes when you want to create a full-page image or collage that is to be printed as part of a project using one of these sizes.
Named image files	Any open images in the Editor are listed at the bottom of the Presets menu. Select one of the image names to base the new image on the size and resolution of the selected image.

Bright Idea

Is it laziness or efficiency? Sometimes I find it much simpler to base a new file on an existing image than to try to remember the specific settings I need for the image.

Adding existing photos

Adding photos to the Photo Browser of the Organizer is easy. You can import files one by one from your hard drive or another drive. If you have a lot of files you want to include, you can select groups of images or even entire folders.

Follow these steps to add new image files:

1. In the Organizer window, click the Get Photos button on the toolbar to open its menu and choose From Files and Folders.
2. In the Get Photos from Files and Folders dialog box, locate the folder and files you want to import. Click the name of the file to show a preview on the dialog box, shown in Figure 1.10.
3. Select the file or files. Ctrl+click to select non-contiguous files, or Shift+click to select a group of contiguous files in a folder's list.
4. Click Get Photos. The dialog box closes, and the image files are added to the Organizer window.

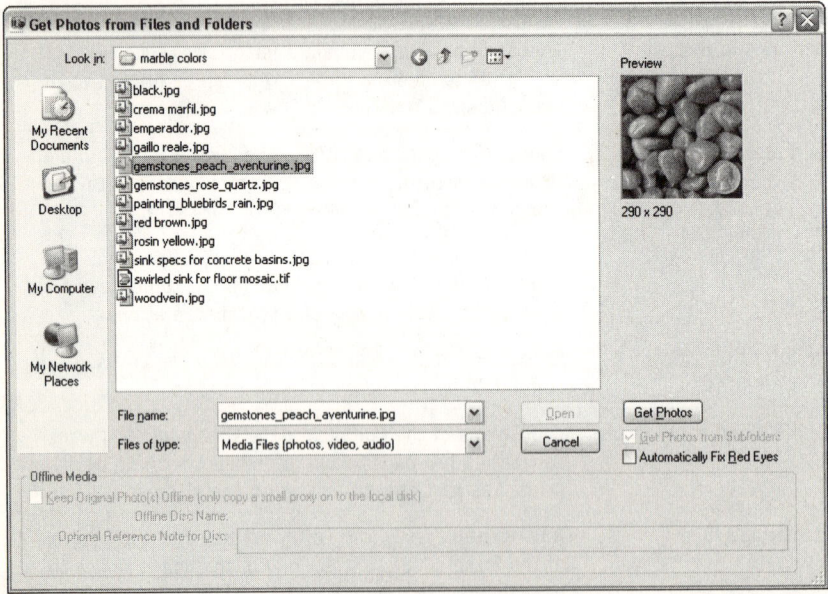

Figure 1.10. Preview files you want to import by selecting them in the Get Photos from Files and Folders dialog box.

Hack
Save yourself some time by moving files visually. Open the Organizer window showing the Photo Browser. Locate an image file that you want to add from the desktop or an open folder, and drag it to the Photo Browser.

Storing phone images

Images can be downloaded from your mobile phone in a number of ways, depending on the phone and its capabilities. Photoshop Elements takes care of downloaded phone images using a watched folder, meaning a folder that is monitored by the program. You have to set up the folder initially in Photoshop Elements. After that, each time the program opens, it checks for images in the folder and imports them into the Photo Browser.

Creating a watched folder

The simplest way to remember where you are storing mobile phone pictures is to create a folder using the same storage location and naming structure as the other image folders that Photoshop Elements creates automatically. That way, you won't misplace the folder or forget what it's called.

If you decide to follow this method, create a new folder named Mobile Phone Photos (or something similar). Store the file as C:\...\My Pictures\Adobe\Mobile Phone Photos as shown in Figure 1.11.

Follow these steps to set up the watched folder:

1. In the Organizer window, click Get Photos on the toolbar and choose From Mobile Phone in the drop-down menu.

2. The first time you use the command, the Specify Mobile Phone Folder dialog box appears. Click Browse, and select the folder you created for use as the watched folder.

3. Click OK to dismiss the dialog box. If you see an information dialog box that explains nothing was imported, don't worry — you're just setting up the folder at this point.

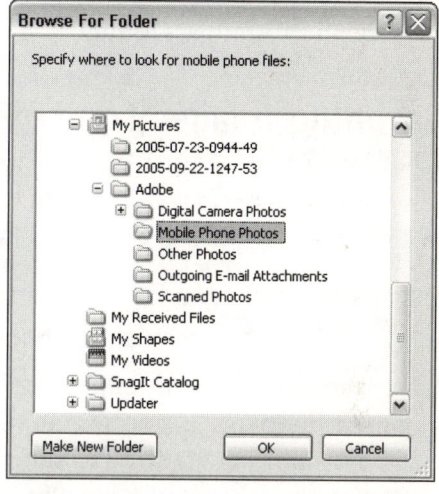

Figure 1.11. Store a folder for holding images imported from a mobile phone with the other Photoshop Elements storage folders.

Bright Idea

To quickly create a new folder, go to the folder where you want to add a new folder. Right-click and choose New ➪ Folder. A new folder appears. Simply begin typing to rename the folder; otherwise, it is named New Folder.

Adding phone images

After a watched folder is set up, getting files into the Organizer window couldn't be easier. Transfer the images to your computer according to your phone's instructions, and store the files in the folder you created as a watched folder.

The next time you open Photoshop Elements, the Organizer window displays a dialog box telling you that new files were found in the watched folder. Follow these steps to choose and add photos from the watched folder to the Organizer window:

1. In the initial dialog box, click Yes to add the files to the Photo Browser.
2. The Add New Files from Watch Folder dialog box opens and shows thumbnails of the images you moved to the watched folder from your phone.
3. All the images are selected by default; you can toggle the check box for each image to choose only those you want to import into the Organizer window, or you can leave them all selected.
4. Click OK to close the dialog box and add the photos to the Organizer window's listing.

Grabbing images from video clips

What if you have a super piece of video that you shot on vacation and would like to have frames from the video to use for your desktop wallpaper, or maybe to send to a friend? Photoshop Elements gives you a great

---

Other phone options

The discussion on importing images from a phone describes generic methods. If your phone stores photos on a removable card or you have a NOKIA PC suite 6.2-compliant phone, you can import photos directly into Photoshop Elements using the From Camera or Card Reader command on the Get Photos menu.

For those whose mobile phone carrier is an Adobe service partner, you may be able to use Online Sharing Services to transfer the photos to your computer using the From Online Sharing Service command on the Get Photos menu.

method for capturing single frames from digital video in a variety of media formats, including ASF, AVI, MLV MPG, MPEG, and WMV.

Before you can convert a single frame to an image, you need to capture the video. Consult the documentation for your system, software, and digital camera to see how you can import video to your computer.

After the video has been captured on your hard drive, import single frames through the Editor window following these steps:

1. From the Editor window, choose File ⇨ Import ⇨ Frame From Video to open the Frame From Video dialog box.
2. Click the Browse button, and locate the video clip from which you want to copy frames.
3. Click Open to dismiss the dialog box and load the video clip into the Frame From Video dialog box, shown in Figure 1.12.

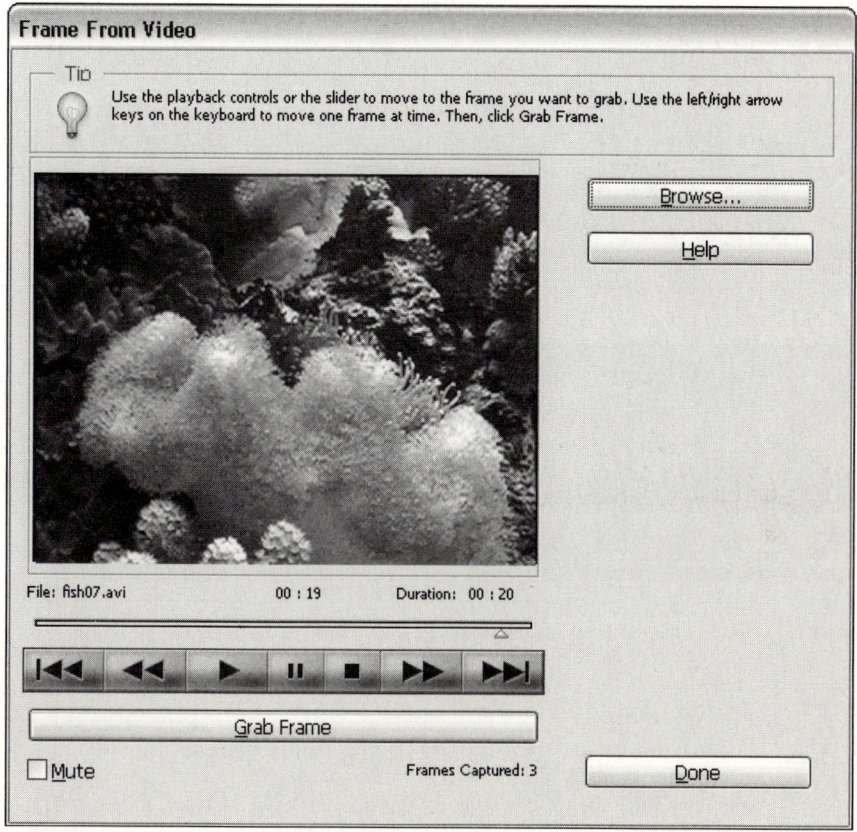

Figure 1.12. Select one or more frames from a video clip to use as still images.

4. Use the playback controls below the clip's preview area on the dialog box to locate the frame you want to use as an image.
5. Click Grab Frame when you find the image you want to capture. It will become a still image.
6. Identify and capture as many frames as you need, and then click Done when you are finished to close the dialog box.

Each of the images is captured in a separate file in the Editor window. The files are named according to the name of the video clip and the frame capture sequence. For instance, the four images shown in Figure 1.13 are captured from a video clip named "backyard path kittys." The images are numbered 01 through 04, indicating the order in which the frames were captured.

Figure 1.13. Grab as many frames as you need to convert them to still images.

Inside Scoop
You can make yourself crazy using the playback controls in the Frame From Video dialog box to identify a precise frame. Instead of using the controls, use the left and right arrow keys on the keyboard to move one frame backward and forward, respectively.

Follow these steps to save the captured frames:

1. Select one image in the Editor and choose File ⇨ Save to open the Save As dialog box.
2. Rename the image if you like, and locate and select the folder in which you want to save the image.
3. Click Save to save the image and close the dialog box.
4. Repeat with other captured frames.

Just the facts

- Choose a task from the Welcome Screen or configure the program to open to a specified window every time.
- Import files directly from your digital camera into Photoshop Elements and customize the file name and storage locations.
- Scan printed photos to include with your digital collection and preserve them for long-term storage.
- Use a watched folder to store images downloaded from your mobile phone.
- Start new images from scratch, and specify the size and resolution of the image as well as its color.
- Capture individual frames from a video clip to use as still images in your projects.

GET THE SCOOP ON...
■ Viewing images and video clips in the Photo Browser ■
Working with catalog files ■ Viewing files with
special screen views ■ Organizing in Date view ■
Reconnecting missing files

Your Digital Shoebox: The Organizer

When you work with digital images, you can still end up with shoeboxes holding your images. Rather than piles of photos, your images are now in folders scattered throughout your hard drive and on removable media such as CDs or DVDs. What are you going to do?

Programs designed to organize and store images have been around for a few years, as has the ubiquitous *My Pictures* folder in Windows. Photoshop Elements is composed of two separate functions, including an editing function that lets you manipulate images in numerous ways, and an image management function, called the Photo Browser, which is controlled by the Organizer. An image management program such as the Photo Browser in Photoshop Elements is designed to organize, correlate, and collate your images in sophisticated ways.

If you are new to digital photography and image editing, keeping track of your images may not seem like a big deal. After being on the loose with your spiffy new camera for a few months and discovering the ease with which you can capture and store images, you need a system of organizing. Trust me. You'll thank me later.

Getting into the Photo Browser

The Photo Browser is displayed by default when you open the Organizer window. You use the Photo Browser much like a visual database to organize, correlate, and keep track of your images. The images are not physically moved when you include them in the Photo Browser, so you can store them where you like, such as with other content used to create a presentation.

In addition to the Photo Browser, the Organizer also houses the Organize Bin, which contains palettes used for organizing and sorting your images and controls access to the Create with Your Photos component of the program that lets you make different print and visual projects.

You can open the Organizer in several ways, depending on your workflow and what you are presently working with.

Here are your options:

- Click View and Organize Photos from the Welcome Screen when you open Photoshop Elements.
- Click Make Photo Creations from the Welcome Screen when you open Photoshop Elements.
- Select Organizer from the Start Up In menu at the lower-left corner of the Welcome Screen to set the program to open automatically showing the Photo Browser.
- If you are working in either the Quick Fix or Standard Edit windows, click Photo Browser on the toolbar to open the Organizer and display the Photo Browser.

Speeding it up

If you are organizing your photo collection for the first time, or you have just returned from vacation with a few hundred pictures to organize and sort, set Photoshop Elements to open automatically in the Photo Browser to save yourself some time.

Hack

If you are having problems with slow screen redraw, decrease the quality of the thumbnails shown in the Photo Browser. In the Organizer window, choose Edit ➪ Preferences ➪ Files, and then click the check box for Use lower quality thumbnails from files in the grid to improve scrolling performance. Click OK.

CHAPTER 2 ▪ YOUR DIGITAL SHOEBOX: THE ORGANIZER

Bright Idea
Plan your tasks ahead of time. If you have already imported all your files and want to do some editing for the next few sessions, change the startup option to the Organizer following the same steps.

Follow these steps to set the Photo Browser as the opening view for the program:

1. Click the Photoshop Elements icon on your desktop, or choose it from your Program list.
2. When the Welcome Screen displays, click the Start Up In drop-down arrow at the bottom left. Choose Organizer from the menu (which also includes the Welcome Screen and Editor as options).
3. Close the Welcome Screen.
4. The next time you open the program, the Organizer automatically opens.

What you see

The Photo Browser gives you lots of options for organizing and showing detail and information about your images. You can hold and store video and sound clips, too. The Organizer window has several standard components.

Here's what you see at the top of the Organizer window (shown in Figure 2.1):

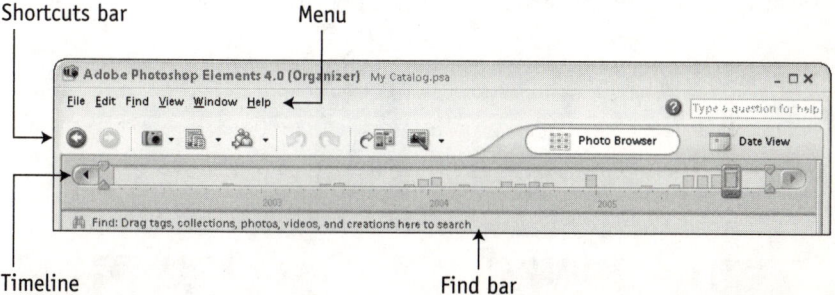

Figure 2.1. The Organizer window controls access to several program elements and ways of organizing images.

- **Menu.** You find commands for controlling common program functions in the Menus.

- **Shortcuts bar.** You find tools and buttons for accessing submenus on the Shortcuts bar.
- **Timeline.** The Timeline shows you both relative numbers of images — indicated by the height of the vertical bar — and a date scale.
- **Find bar.** Use the Find bar to search for items on your hard drive and in your collections.

The images are displayed in thumbnails. You can control the arrangement and view of the thumbnails as shown in Figure 2.2. Control the display of the images in these ways:

- **Thumbnails view.** The images stored in the Photo Browser are shown as thumbnails; drag the vertical scrollbar to move through the thumbnails.
- **Arrangement menu.** The Arrangement menu contains several options you can choose to order the contents of the Photo Browser.
- **Thumbnail size slider.** Drag the slider left to decrease the thumbnail size or right to increase the thumbnail size. Click the icon to the left of the slider to decrease the thumbnails to their smallest size; click the icon to the right of the slider to increase the size of the thumbnails to fit the Photo Browser viewing area.

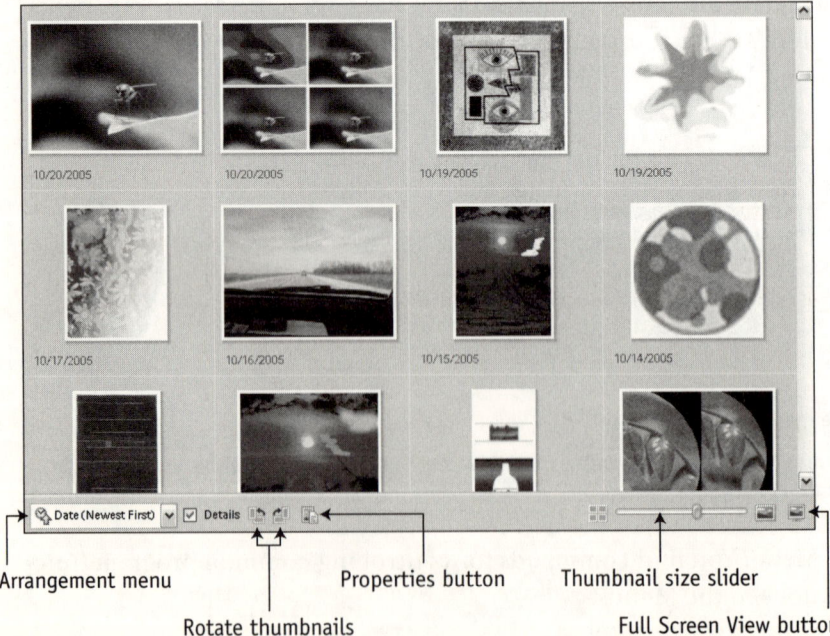

Figure 2.2. The Photo Browser proper contains thumbnails and controls for viewing and organizing.

CHAPTER 2 ■ YOUR DIGITAL SHOEBOX: THE ORGANIZER

- **Full Screen View button.** This option displays the active image on the screen against a black background, removing all program windows.
- **Rotate thumbnails.** Click the Rotate Left button to rotate a selected thumbnail 90 degrees counterclockwise; click the Rotate Right button to rotate a selected thumbnail 90 degrees clockwise.
- **Properties button.** Click the Properties button to toggle the Properties palette view on and off.

The Organize Bin at the right of the Organizer window houses several palettes used for managing information about the images in your collection, shown in Figure 2.3. This section of the window includes:

- **Organize Bin.** View information and palettes to the right of the program window in the Organize Bin.
- **Tags and Collections palettes.** Information about the images can be defined as tags and displayed in the Tags palette; use the Collections palette to organize your images into groups for ease of access.
- **Properties palette.** The Properties palette contains details about the active image such as its name and storage location, history, tags, and camera information.

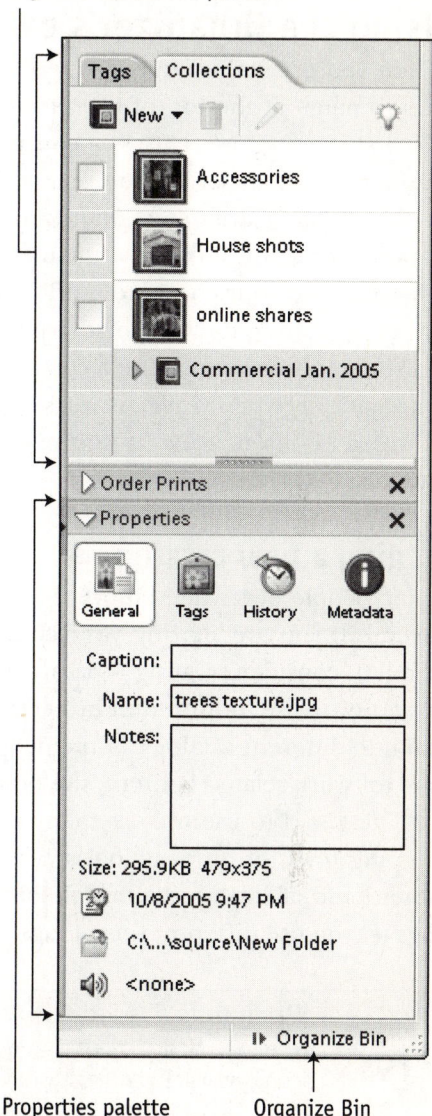

Figure 2.3. Attach information for sorting and organizing in the Organize Bin.

Inside Scoop

You need all the screen real estate you can get for searching thumbnails. Click the Organize Bin label or the arrow to the left of the label at the bottom right of the program window to close the palettes. Click again to reopen the Organize Bin.

Using the Organizer's catalog

When you open the Organizer, you see *My catalog.psa* next to the program's name at the top of the program window. This file is the catalog file that the Organizer uses to control your media files which it displays in the Photo Browser as thumbnails.

The catalog doesn't contain any image files. Instead, it works as a database creating links to your images, creations, and audio and video clips, both on your computer and on removable media such as CDs. The links are listed in the Organizer as thumbnails.

You don't have to create a catalog file yourself because one is started automatically when you start working with the program. As you add and download content to your computer, file information is added to the catalog.

Adding a new catalog

Some people never need more than one catalog, while others may need several. If you are sharing your computer with someone (or the whole family!), consider creating separate catalogs for each person. If you have content you use for different projects, you may want to separate the material into different catalogs. Some people sort content into two catalogs — one for work-related content, the other for personal material.

The key is to use only as many catalogs as necessary simply because keeping track of one catalog is easier than tracking multiples. On the other hand, if you need alternate organization structures, different catalogs let you use different sets of tags and photos in each catalog.

Watch Out!

If you delete an original file, the link is broken and you can't restore the image through Photoshop Elements.

>  **Bright Idea**
> You can use music files shipped with Photoshop Elements as background music for a Full Screen view or slide show creation. Choose File ⇨ Catalog, and check the Import free music into all new catalogs option.

Follow these steps to create a new catalog:

1. Choose File ⇨ Catalog to open the Catalog dialog box and then click New to open the New Catalog dialog box.

2. Name the catalog and specify the storage location. Keep all the catalog files in the same location so you don't lose track of them. By default, the catalog files are stored at C:\\Documents and Settings\All Users\Application Data\Adobe\Catalogs.

3. Click Save to save the new catalog file and close the dialog box.

The Catalog dialog box is shown in Figure 2.4. You can click:

- **New** to create a catalog.
- **Open** to open an existing catalog.
- **Save As** to resave the current catalog with another name.
- **Recover** to check out and repair any problems that may have occurred with a power failure or similar catastrophe.

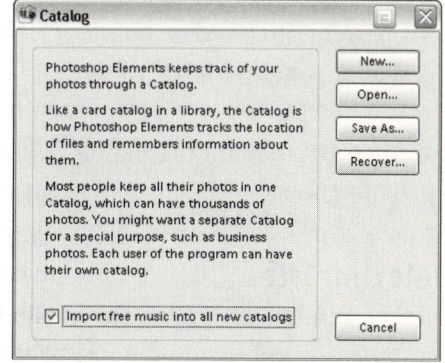

Figure 2.4. Work with Catalog options in the dialog box.

Moving files

The Organizer's catalog is a database containing links between Photoshop Elements and the files' storage locations. To make sure that you don't damage the links, work from within the Photo Browser to move files or change file names.

Follow these steps to move files within a catalog:

1. Select the file or files you want to move in the Photo Browser.

2. Choose File ⇨ Move to open the Move Selected Items dialog box, shown in Figure 2.5. The selected items are shown in thumbnail view.

> **Inside Scoop**
> If you move files by mistake, the simplest way to restore them is to move the folder back to its original location, and then proceed with the steps above.

3. Click the Add button at the bottom of the Items to Move list to select additional images that you want to include in the move. If necessary, click to select a thumbnail, and then click the red minus (-) to remove an image from the group being moved.

4. Click Browse in the Move Selected Items dialog box to open the Browse For Folder dialog box. Select the folder you want to use, or create a new folder.

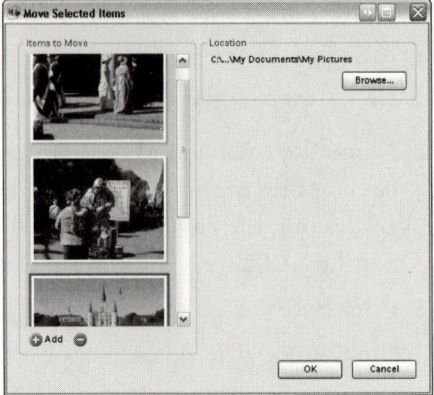

Figure 2.5. You can choose and define new locations for files in your catalog.

5. Click OK to close the dialog box; click OK again to close the Move dialog box.

Deleting files

You can remove files from the catalog and even delete them from your computer entirely using the Organizer.

Follow these steps to delete items from your catalog:

1. Select the thumbnail or thumbnails in the Photo Browser.
2. Press Delete on the keyboard or right-click and choose Delete from Catalog or Delete Selected Items from Catalog. (The command differs based on whether you have selected one or more items.)
3. The Confirm Deletion from Catalog dialog box opens. If you want to remove the original file from your computer, click the Also delete selected item(s) from the hard disk check box.
4. Click OK, close the dialog box, and remove the file listings.

These steps work for deleting all media files you are cataloging in the Photo Browser, but they don't apply to deleting a creation.

> **Inside Scoop**
> Open a specific catalog by holding down the Shift key while launching the Organizer. In the Editor, hold down the Shift key and click the Photo Browser button. Photoshop Elements prompts you to open a catalog.

Creations are types of projects you build using wizards and dialog boxes, and are identified in the Photo Browser with an icon at the upper right of the thumbnail shown in Figure 2.6. As you can read in Chapters 19 and 20, creations can include everything from birthday cards to slide shows to Web page image galleries. If you delete a creation, it is permanently gone.

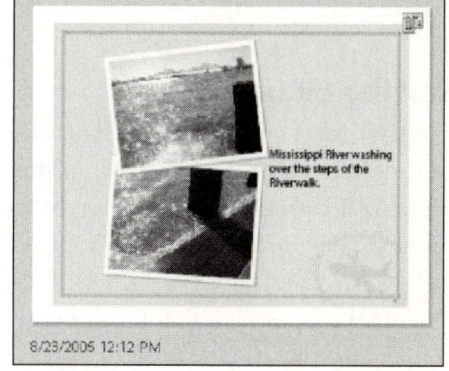

Figure 2.6. A creation displays a distinguishing icon over its thumbnail.

Sorting your image files

When you work in the Photo Browser, the image thumbnails are sorted by default according to the date you brought them into the catalog, showing the newest to the oldest entries. You can also sort in other ways. Take a few minutes to experiment with the different displays.

You can select a sort option by choosing View ⇨ Arrangement ⇨ Option. Or you can click the Arrangement menu's drop-down arrow below the thumbnail display and then select the arrangement from the menu.

Sorting by date

By default, images are sorted newest to oldest. If you have imported numerous images on the same date, they are listed chronologically in the order in which they were captured from the oldest to the newest.

> **Watch Out!**
> Here's how catalogs behave: If you have multiple catalogs, you can open only one catalog at a time. You can't search across multiple catalogs, and you can't move photos or tags between catalogs.

You can reverse the order and display the date from the oldest to newest images. Suppose that your collection started with the cool shots you took with your new camera at Uncle Jerry's birthday party last summer at the lake. Fast forward to today; Uncle Jerry has decided to sell the cottage. You remember that you have some good images of the property, and you want to send him copies. Instead of scrolling through quantities of thumbnails to find the best party pictures, simply change the display of the thumbnails to sort them by date, go to the date of the party, and select the best image.

Sorting by batch

Another method is to sort by batches. Photoshop Elements defines each unit of images you imported into the Photo Browser as a separate batch. Figure 2.7 shows thumbnails sorted by Import Batch. You see the files are separated according to their source, such as a camera or hard disk, as well as the date they were imported. When sorted by batch, you see the Import Batch icon, which looks like a roll of film, to the left of the batch's information line.

Sorting by import batch is a quick way to locate and select a group of images quickly, if you remember the approximate date when the images were imported. The source and the batch's date are displayed next to the film icon. You can select all the files imported in one batch by clicking the Import Batch icon above a group of thumbnails.

Sorting by folder

The final method for sorting is by Folder Location. Your drive's folders are listed in a panel at the left of the program window. Images from your folders included in the Photo Browser are identified in a tooltip and in the thumbnails, as you can see in Figure 2.8.

Inside Scoop

Choose Edit ⇨ Preferences ⇨ Folder Location View, and select the Only Folders Containing Organized Files radio button to see only the folders you need. To save more screen space, choose the Show Files option Only Files in a Selected Folder, rather than the default All Files Grouped By Folder.

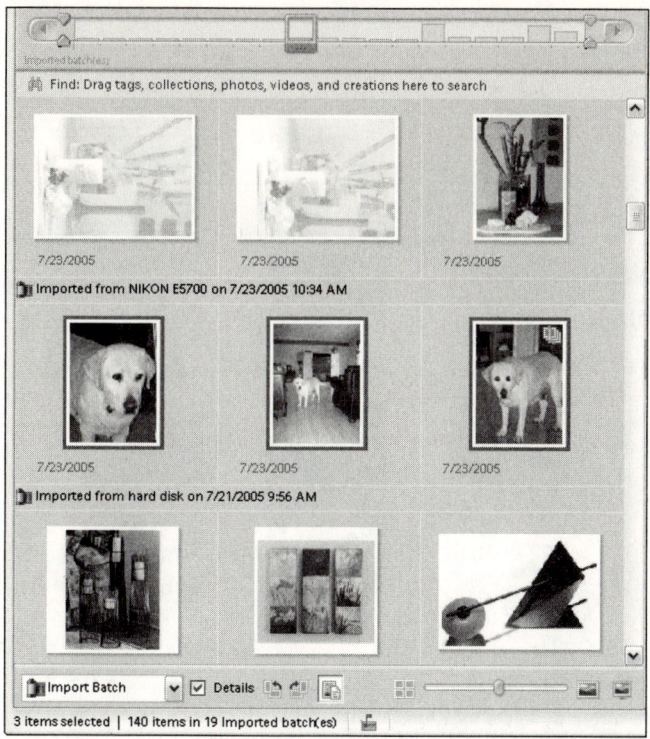

Figure 2.7. Sorting images by batch divides the thumbnails according to the source and date each group of images is imported.

It's about time

Take a look again at the images of the Organizer window shown in this chapter. In each figure, you see that a Timeline stretches across the window above the thumbnail display area.

The Timeline contains basic information about your images including the time of capture or import and their storage location. When you choose an arrangement option based on the different sort criteria, the Timeline's appearance changes as well.

For some people (me included), using the Timeline is a quick way to zero in on images. After you have a handle on how the Timeline works, experiment with using it to help locate content.

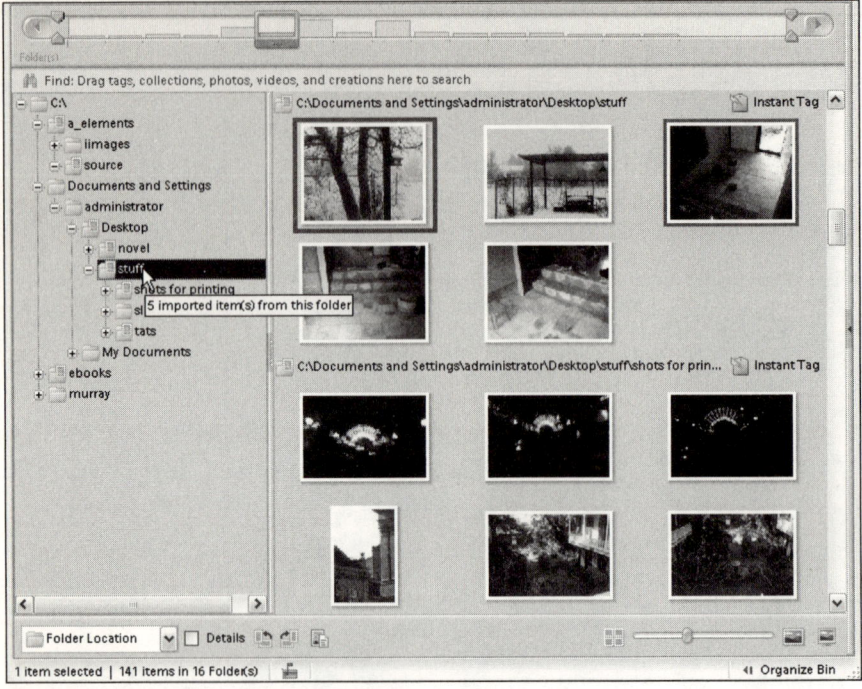

Figure 2.8. Images can be sorted by folder location.

If you are using the Photo Browser and don't see the Timeline, you've toggled it off. Choose View ➪ Timeline to display it. Use these details and tips about how the Timeline works to help you search, seek, and sort:

- The divisions on the Timeline vary according to the Arrangement option being displayed. For both Date arrangements, the Timeline's ruler shows years and months. The Imported Batches option shows numbers of images per imported batch, and the Timeline ruler has no units of measure. The Folder Location option shows numbers of images per each folder; again the Timeline ruler has no units of measure.
- The height of each bar on the Timeline corresponds with the number of images at that location or time.
- Click a bar on the Timeline or drag the indicator box to select a group of images, by date, folder, or batch import date.

Bright Idea

You don't have to see all the types of media files by default. Choose View ⇒ Media Types to open the Items Shown dialog box. Select the types of media you want to include, and click OK. All types are selected by default except Audio files.

- If you have stored lots of images in the Photo Browser, click the arrows at the extreme left and right of the Timeline to scroll the range.
- Narrow down the number of thumbnails displayed by dragging the end points from either end of the Timeline. The end points indicate the range displayed in the Photo Browser; you see that items excluded from the range are shown in gray on the Timeline, as shown in Figure 2.9.
- If you aren't sure what you need to select, hover your mouse over a bar on the Timeline to read basic information such as date or file location, also shown in Figure 2.9.

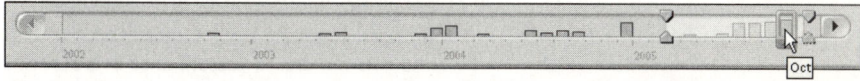

Figure 2.9. Decrease the range for displaying thumbnails by resetting the Timeline's end points.

Paying attention to details

The Photo Browser shows you an image's date as well as its thumbnail image by default. Click the Details check box below the thumbnails view to toggle the display on and off.

Understanding icons

Several icons can also be shown on or next to an image thumbnail in the Photo Browser to indicate other activities or details. Icons are based on a file's format, type of content, or how the file is stored. Understanding the icons in Table 2.1 will be useful.

Table 2.1. Icons used to identify thumbnail features

Icon Name	How It Looks	What It Represents
Stack icon		The Stack icon overlaying the image means the thumbnail is the example chosen for a stack of photos.
Version Set icon		The Version Set icon indicates that a number of versions of an image are stacked with one thumbnail as an example of the edited image.
Video icon		Video clips stored in the Photo Browser are indicated by a Video icon.
Disc icon		Thumbnails representing files stored offline show the Disc icon.
Audio icon		An image or file that includes a recorded audio caption shows the Audio icon.
Tag icon		A Tag icon is shown below the thumbnail of an image that contains sorting labels, called tags. You don't see the Tag icon unless the Details are shown in the Photo Browser. There are several default icons, and you can create custom ones as well; images can have multiple tags attached.
Collection icon		One way of organizing images is to create collections. When an image is assigned to a collection, it shows the Collection icon. Move your mouse over the icon to show the collection name in a tooltip.
Creation icon		A photo or file that has been used in a creation shows the Creation icon.

Hiding details

Why bother hiding the details? If you are looking for an image and can't remember when it was taken, but it is very distinctive in appearance, toggle the Details off. That way, you can show more thumbnails at one time and find your image faster.

Inside Scoop

I prefer to use thumbnails at a small size so I can review files quickly. To instantly find detail about a selected image, choose Window ⇨ Dock Properties in Organize Bin to keep the Properties palette open. When you click an image, you see its details in a consistent location onscreen.

Pick what you want to see in the Photo Browser's details in the program preferences. Choose Edit ⇨ Preferences ⇨ General Preferences, and select an alternate date format or include the file names in the details for each image.

Using special views

Thumbnails can be sized from very small to filling the thumbnail area of the Photo Browser. But what if you want to compare two images? Or suppose you want to view an image without the distraction of the program interface? Photoshop Elements has both these situations covered with the Full Screen view and Side by Side view. You access the Side by Side View command from the interface that displays after the Full Screen view is active.

Viewing at full screen size

The specialized viewing options let you see the images without any program distraction, and they offer a control bar to use for manipulating the images. The control bar and options are the same regardless of which viewing method you use, and you can swap between views.

Follow these steps to view images in Full Screen view:

1. Select the photo or photos you want to work with in the Photo Browser.
2. Click the Full Screen View button at the bottom of the Photo Browser next to the thumbnail size slider.
3. Choose selections in the Full Screen View Options dialog box, shown in Figure 2.10. (Options range from background music to resizing images to specifying how long a page is viewed and applying a fade transition.)

Inside Scoop

Many of the options you choose for the Full Screen view are the same as those used for building presentations, described in Chapter 20. In fact, you use the options selected in the dialog box if you decide to export a slide show.

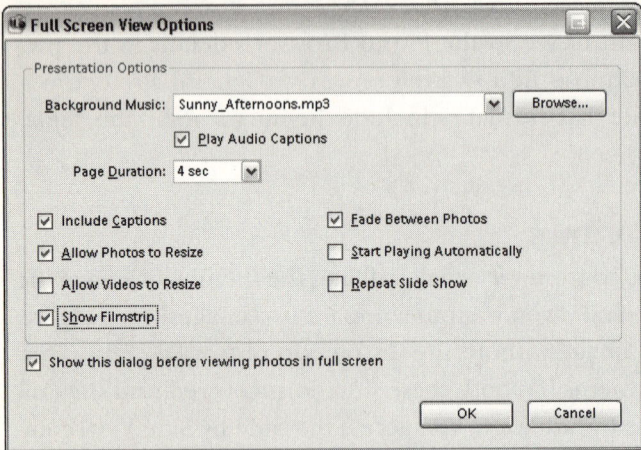

Figure 2.10. Choose options for displaying selected images at full screen size.

4. For ease of use in viewing, click Show Filmstrip on the Full Screen View Options dialog box. When you view the selected image or images, the remaining images in your catalog are shown in a strip of thumbnails along the edge of the screen that you can select to view at full size as well, as shown in Figure 2.11.

5. Click OK to close the Full Screen View Options dialog box and display the image. The special view control bar appears across the top of the screen, as shown in Figure 2.12. The control bar hides itself if the mouse isn't moved for several seconds. To restore the control bar, move the mouse on the screen.

6. When you have finished viewing images, return to the regular program interface by pressing the Esc key or clicking the X playback button on the control bar.

Figure 2.11. Show the selected images as a filmstrip along the side of the screen for easy viewing.

Hack

Instead of viewing hundreds of thumbnails when you are weeding out files, open the Full Screen view and display the thumbnail filmstrip. View the images one by one at full size, and remove those you don't want from the catalog using the Delete button on the control bar.

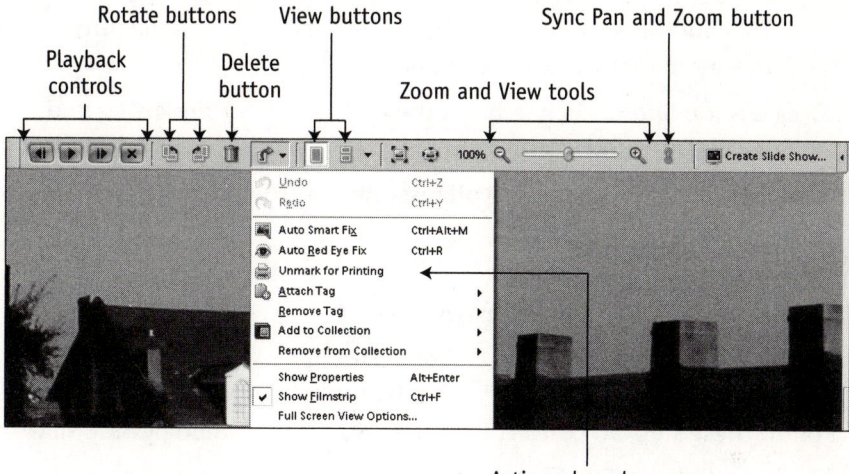

Figure 2.12. Control playback, display, zoom, and assign commands to images viewed at full screen size.

Working the special views control bar

The special views control bar seems complex at first glance. Although it has many buttons, it is made up of several groups of tools. The groups of tools, from left to right on the control bar, include:

- **Playback controls.** These four controls allow you to move through a group of selected thumbnails, forward and backward.
- **Rotate buttons.** With these two buttons, you can rotate a selected thumbnail 90 degrees counterclockwise or clockwise.
- **Delete button.** Click to delete the selected image from your catalog; you can also delete the image from your hard drive.
- **Action menu.** Choose options to apply to a selected image such as tagging it, marking it for printing, applying auto fix options, and more. This menu is shown in Figure 2.12.

- **View buttons.** Switch back and forth from Full Screen view of a single image to Side by Side view of two images; click another image to replace one in Side by Side View mode.
- **View and Zoom tools.** Specify Full Size view of the image, actual pixel size, or drag the slider, or use the Zoom tools to change the magnification of the view.
- **Sync Pan and Zoom tool.** Click this button to move and magnify two images viewed side by side simultaneously.
- **Create Slide Show.** Click to open the dialog box for designing and creating a slide show presentation.
- **Collapse.** Click the arrow to collapse the control bar to just the set of playback tools.

Viewing images side by side

When you are viewing an image at screen size, it's simply a matter of toggling a control in the control bar to change to viewing a pair of images.

Follow these steps to convert from Full Size view to Side by Side view:

1. Click the Side by Side View button to display the current image at one-half screen size at the left of the screen. The image following the active image in the thumbnail view is shown automatically at the right side of the screen.
2. Click the Side by Side View drop-down arrow to open a list shown in Figure 2.13, and select the orientation for the image display.
3. Replace one of the displayed images by selecting it onscreen and then clicking the thumbnail of the image you want to replace it. The two images are numbered 1 and 2, as are the thumbnails of the images displayed.

Marking prints

In Figure 2.13, you may notice the small Printer icons overlaying the three larger thumbnails at the right. The icon indicates that the image is marked for printing.

To identify an image you want to print, select the image or its thumbnail, and choose Mark For Printing from the Actions menu. When the view is closed, returning to the Organizer displays an information dialog

> **Bright Idea**
> If you are looking at two similar images that you want to compare for a project or printing, click the Sync Pan and Zoom tool on the control bar. As you zoom in or out of one image, or drag it to view different areas, the other image automatically follows along.

box listing the number of marked images. Read more about printing images in Chapter 17.

Figure 2.13. Show images side by side or above and below by choosing the images from the thumbnails.

Choose from three commands including:
- Cancel to delete the print mark references.
- Print to send the marked images to your printer.
- Online Print to send the marked images to an online print service.

Working with video
Another type of media to look at from the Photo Browser is video. Video clips stored in your catalog show the first frame of the clip as the thumbnail image.

>  **Bright Idea**
> Use the playback controls and the position slider to locate frames you want to capture as images.

Double-click the video clip's thumbnail in the Photo Browser to open the Photoshop Elements Media Player, shown in Figure 2.14. You can handle the video in a number of ways, including these:

- Use the controls below the video to control the playback.
- Jump among frames by dragging the position slider.
- Check the video's run time and the location of a section of the video using the time indicator shown on the dialog box.
- Drag the audio volume slider left or right to decrease or increase volume for the clip's soundtrack.
- Click the Close button to close the dialog box.

Figure 2.14. Use playback controls to view video clips added to your catalog.

Working in the Date View

Although the Photo Browser shows your images in thumbnails sorted in different ways, the Date view shows your images chronologically in a calendar-like layout.

Most of the operations available in the Photo Browser are also accessible in the Date view. You can view a date's photos as a slide show or create a new event to add to the calendar, such as a birthday or anniversary.

Click the Date View button on the Organizer window, and choose a layout, such as the catalog files for 2004 shown by Year in Figure 2.15.

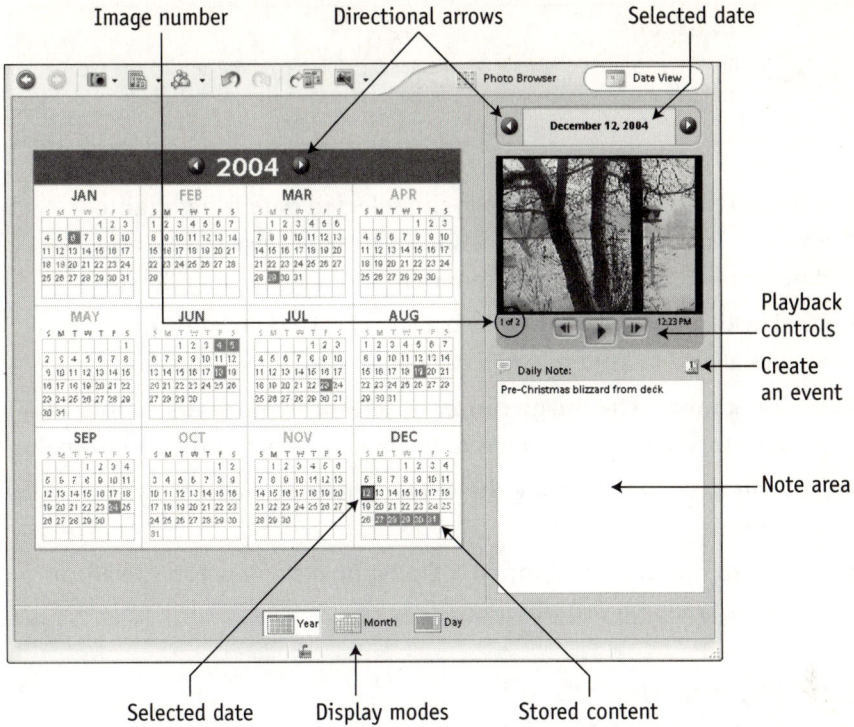

Figure 2.15. Use the Date view to see the dates on which images are added to your catalog.

Year by year

Spend a few minutes experimenting in the Date View. Check the commands available in the menus and in the control bar; click the different buttons and options on the dialog box.

Here's a quick rundown of the window's workings in all display modes. The areas are identified on Figure 2.15:

- **Display modes.** The content of the catalog is shown by Year, by Month, or by Day.
- **Directional arrows.** Click to move to a previous block of time or a subsequent block of time from that currently displayed. You can use the arrows on the calendar or in the preview area.
- **Stored content.** Dates and months on which images were added to the catalog are shown in color on the calendar.

Watch Out!

Don't try to print the Date View calendar: It isn't printable. Use the Create button's wall calendar option to build a calendar for printing.

- **Selected date.** On the calendar, the selected date is highlighted. The first image for that date is shown in the Preview area, and its date displays above the thumbnail.
- **Playback controls.** Use the playback controls to move through the images added for the selected date.
- **Image number.** The image displayed as well as the total number of images stored for the selected date are shown below the thumbnail.
- **Note area.** Click to activate the cursor and type a note for the selected date.
- **Create an event.** Click to open a dialog box that lets you specify an important date on the calendar.

Days and months

If you are showing the Year calendar view, switch to the Month or Day views by clicking the corresponding display buttons on the Date View, or by double-clicking a month's label or a day's label on the calendar to open the month or day respectively.

The month display mode works very similarly to the year calendar display. The day display mode also allows you to locate a selected image in the Photo Browser. Click the Show In Photo Browser button under the photo, shown in Figure 2.16. Click the Full Screen View button to view the date's images without the surrounding program interface.

Hack

Photoshop Elements displays the regional options chosen in your computer's operating system. To change the settings in Windows XP, choose Start ⇨ Control Panel ⇨ Regional and Language Options, and select the appropriate date structure.

CHAPTER 2 ▪ YOUR DIGITAL SHOEBOX: THE ORGANIZER 47

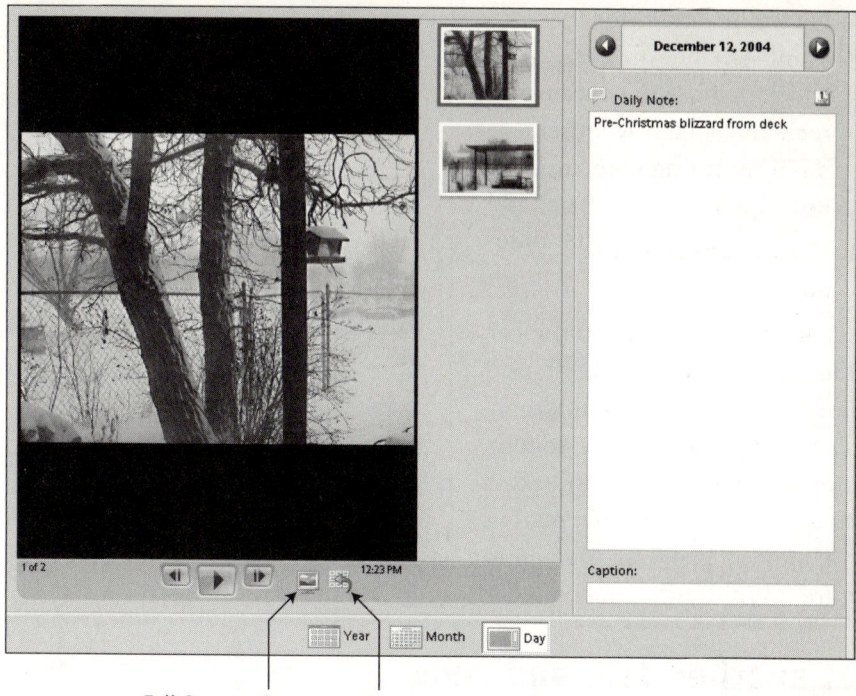

Figure 2.16. Check out the images added to the catalog on a single day in the Day view.

New events

The calendars in Date view show annual events such as holidays. You can add more notices as well, such as birthdays or anniversaries. The nice thing about using some personalized dates on the calendar is that you can quickly search for and locate the images you may have captured from a particular event. It's simply one more way to organize and locate content in your image collection.

Follow these steps to add a new event to the Organizer:

1. Select a date. Click the date in the Year or Month view, or open the date you want to use in the Day view.
2. Click the Event button at the top right of the Daily Note area in all views, or right-click a date and choose Add Event from the shortcut menu to open the Create New Event dialog box.

3. Fill in the details for the event — name the event, check that the date is correct, and specify whether it is a repeating date and its frequency.

4. Click OK to close the dialog box.

The events you add to the calendar are shown using a different color than those added automatically through the system calendar. Move your mouse over an added event, and you see its information in a tooltip, like that shown in Figure 2.17.

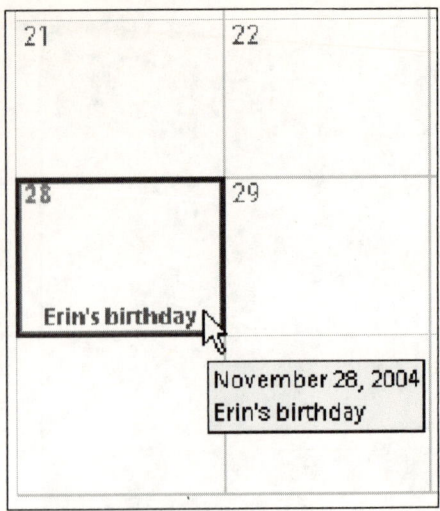

Figure 2.17. Add events and notices as needed to your calendar.

Set another date and time

Information for your media files includes the date and time the content was captured or saved. If you realize that you have set the date incorrectly on your camera or on your computer, or you want to use the image capture date rather than a scanned date, you can adjust the data in either the Photo Browser or Date view.

Follow these steps to adjust the date from either the Photo Browser or Date view:

1. Select one or more files.

2. Choose Edit ⇨ Adjust Date And Time (or choose Edit ⇨ Adjust Date And Time Of Selected Items when you select more than one file).

3. In the Adjust Date and Time dialog box, choose a date and time option.

4. Click OK to close the dialog box. The Timeline automatically adjusts to reflect the changes in the file's date information.

If you do lots of scanning and prefer to use the capture date rather than the scanned date, here's a neat preference for you: Choose Edit ⇨ Preferences ⇨ General, and click the Adjust Date And Time By Clicking On Thumbnail Dates check box. Click OK to close the Preferences dialog box. Now all you need to do is click a date to change the information.

> **It's a date**
>
> Fix the configuration of the calendar according to your own requirements. Choose Edit ⇨ Preferences ⇨ Calendar to display the options. Weeks start on Sunday by default, if you prefer, you can start the week on Monday by selecting the option. In the Holidays listing, uncheck any check boxes that you don't want to include on your calendar. Finally, to add new events to the calendar through the preferences, click New and add the details in the Create New Event dialog box. Click OK to close the Preferences dialog box and make the changes.

Reconnecting files

The Organizer calendar works like a database. If you move, rename, or delete a file outside of Photoshop Elements, the connection to the database is broken and a file-missing icon shows over the thumbnail in the Photo Browser, shown in Figure 2.18.

When you select a thumbnail for a missing image to work with, an information dialog box opens and Photoshop Elements automatically starts searching for the missing file. The search is based on a hunt for files having the same name, modification date, and size as the missing files.

Figure 2.18. Broken links are easily identified in the Photo Browser.

Correcting potential problems

A file that has been deleted from your hard drive is going to result in a file-missing icon in Photoshop Elements. If you do all your image work through Photoshop Elements, you are likely going to maintain your connections.

> **Watch Out!**
>
> Occasionally, you may see the missing icon when you know the file isn't missing, nor is its connection broken. You see the icon if you have file versions in formats that Photoshop Elements doesn't recognize or the file is too large to create a thumbnail.

On the other hand, if you work with several programs and manage images through Windows Explorer, you are bound to run into some problems once in a while. Moving files from within Windows Explorer, for example, means the link created by the Photo Browser catalog is invalid. The same invalidation occurs if you resave an image in another location from a different program.

Sometimes you see a file-missing icon automatically in the Photo Browser, while other times you don't see it until you try to select and work with an image file. You can run through your entire catalog and update it using program commands.

Tips for maintaining connections

I don't always manage files through Photoshop Elements, and then I have to do some serious catalog updating every once in a while.

Here are some tips and actions that I find useful:

- If possible, open Photoshop Elements and select files for deletion rather than using Windows Explorer. I forget to do that sometimes because I prefer to work with image files using their name, not thumbnails. But I pay for it later! Deleting files from outside the Organizer results in broken links; deleting files from within the Organizer lets you get rid of the unnecessary images, but maintain the integrity of the database.

- If you want to reconnect a specific image or group of images, select the thumbnails showing the file-missing icon in the Photo Browser and then choose File ⇨ Reconnect ⇨ Missing File.

- If you are doing a major overhaul and want the entire catalog rechecked, choose File ⇨ Reconnect ⇨ All Missing Files. This command doesn't need any thumbnails selected beforehand.

- Not all my images are edited in Photoshop Elements. If you use other editing programs too, you can maintain a connection to the catalog by setting a preference. Choose Edit ⇨ Preferences ⇨ Editing. Click the Use a Supplementary Editing Application check box. Then click Browse, locate the application's .exe file in the Choose Supplementary Editing Application dialog box, and click Open. The program is listed in the Preferences dialog box; click OK to close the dialog box. Now the program is included in the Edit menu as you can see in Figure 2.19; making changes to the file maintains the connection in the catalog.

>
> **Inside Scoop**
>
> When you have the Organizer open, working on an image in another program that results in changes doesn't automatically update the Photo Browser's thumbnail. Select the image or images you've changed, and choose Edit ⇨ Update Thumbnail or Edit ⇨ Update Thumbnail for Selected Items.

- Don't include images in the catalog if you don't need them there. Not everything needs to be included in a particular catalog. When you save a file in Photoshop Elements, pay attention to the check boxes. The check box Include in the Organizer is selected by default. For files that I don't want in a catalog, I try to remember to deselect this check box before saving the file.

Figure 2.19. Add other programs you use regularly for image editing to the Edit menu.

Fixing it yourself

When you work with a lot of images on a regular basis, you generally remember whether you have done something substantial such as moving folders of images from one location on your hard drive to another. Photoshop Elements tries to reconnect to missing files by checking through your entire file system, but you don't have to wait for the program to do the search for you.

Making a reconnection

You can quickly reconnect by taking matters into your own hands. When you click a thumbnail that's been disconnected from its source file, an information dialog box opens and a search starts automatically. Simply click Browse to stop the automatic search and display the Reconnect Missing Files dialog box. Now you can find the file or files.

The Reconnect Missing Files dialog box, shown in Figure 2.20, shows a list of missing files as well as a Browse list.

Follow these steps to reconnect a file manually:

1. Select the missing file or files in the Files Missing from Catalog list. Information about the file and a thumbnail display at the bottom left of the dialog box. If you have deleted a file from your hard drive or want to remove the thumbnail from the catalog, click Delete from Catalog.
2. Locate the source file in the Locate the Missing Files section of the dialog box, using one of the methods that follow these steps.
3. Click Reconnect to restore the database connection between the thumbnail and the source file.
4. Click Close to dismiss the dialog box.

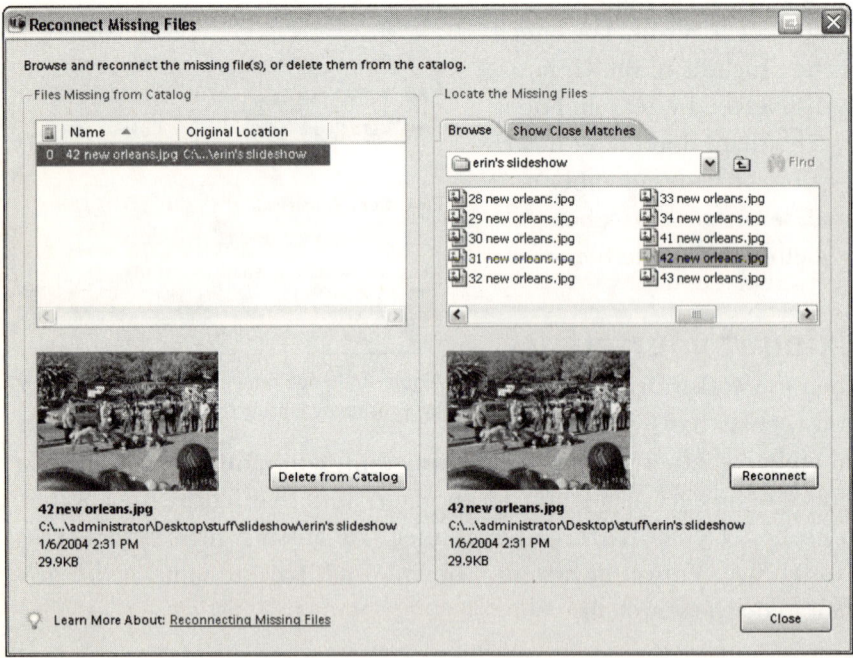

Figure 2.20. Reconnect missing files to restore your catalog's integrity.

Relocation options

You have several ways to find missing files and restore their database connections in the Reconnect Missing Files dialog box. Some ways are more obvious than others. In all cases, after you find your file, click Reconnect to restore the database connection:

> **Hack**
> Turn off automatic searching entirely. Choose Edit ➪ Preferences ➪ Files, and uncheck the Automatically Search for and Reconnect Missing Files check box. Click OK to close the Preferences dialog box.

- On the Browse tab, select a folder or drive and click Find to search that folder or drive. Select the file when it is displayed in the Browse list.
- On the Browse tab, select the folder you know contains the file and then select your file.
- Click the Show Close Matches tab. Files matching the original file's modification date and size are listed. Select your file.

Just the facts

- Use the Photo Browser to look for images added to your system's catalog.
- Add a new catalog to organize images for different uses or different users.
- Sort image files by date, folder, or batch, depending on your particular task.
- Use the Timeline to organize and locate image and other media files.
- Check out images and video using specialized view options.
- Use the Date view for an alternate way of locating and browsing files.
- Customize the Date view options to use your list of events and holidays.
- Use either automatic or manual methods for restoring links to images from the Photo Browser.

GET THE SCOOP ON...
■ Creating and managing collections ■ Stacking images and versions ■ Tagging images and faces ■ Searching images ■ Looking at properties

Tidying Up Your Files

For some folks, working with digital images is a pleasurable pastime or a hobby. For others among you, images are your livelihood. Combining your images into catalogs in the Organizer is a great start to keeping things organized no matter what you reason.

You can organize, sort, and manage your image files in numerous ways within the Organizer. You can use collections, which are like a digital photo album stored within your catalog; you can even group those collections into similar groups for convenience. For example, you may have three or four collections of still images captured from different underwater video clips. To keep them all together, you can easily make a group of the collections.

What if you have several versions of the same image? No problem. You can select the images and create a stack to prevent showing eight similar shots of your baby's first experience with birthday cake in the Photo Browser, yet still access the set of images when you need them.

If you prefer a more detailed method of identifying your images than visual identification, for example if you have large collections of similar images, Photoshop Elements offers a system of tagging images that lets you assign values to images in a range of default and custom options — just the thing for organizing, searching, and managing large numbers of images.

For the collector

If the Photo Browser is like a digital shoebox you use for storing images, then a collection is like an envelope holding a set of images within the shoebox. And like printed images in an envelope, you can shuffle the order of the images in a collection.

It's not always easy to figure out when or if you should use a particular feature. I find collections useful if I am trying to collect images for a new project, for example, or have captured some still images from video clips and haven't decided what to do with them.

Starting a new collection

Collections are created and stored in the Collections palette and tabbed with the Tags palette in the Photo Browser. If you can't see the tab, choose Window ⇨ Collections to open it in the Organize Bin at the right of the Organizer window.

Follow these steps to start a new collection:

1. Click the New drop-down arrow on the Collections palette to open the Create Collection dialog box, and choose New Collection to open the New Collection dialog box.

2. Click the Group drop-down arrow and choose an existing collections group (if you have created one in the past) or leave the default None (Top Level) choice selected.

3. Click the Name field to make it active, and type a name for the new collection, shown in Figure 3.1.

4. Type a note in the Note field to remind yourself (and others working with the catalog) what the collection holds. This note can be found later by clicking the pencil icon when a collection is selected in the menu.

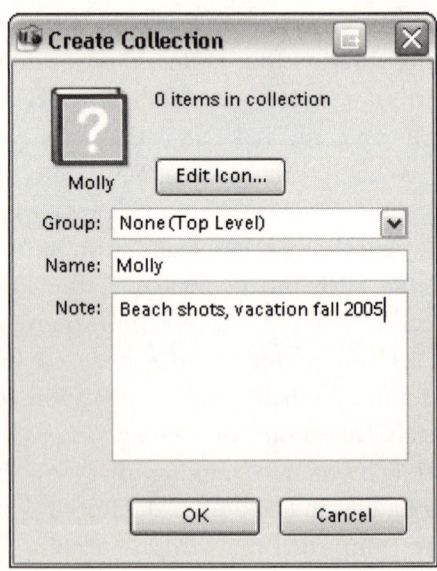

Figure 3.1. Create collections to organize your images.

CHAPTER 3 ▪ TIDYING UP YOUR FILES

Inside Scoop

To read, edit, or add a note, select the collection in the Collections palette, and click the pencil icon to display the Note field.

5. Click OK to close the dialog box and add the collection to the Collections palette.

Changing the icon

A collection's icon shows the first photo to which it is attached. Sometimes that's good, but sometimes it's not really representative of the collection or category. Changing the icon is simple.

Follow these steps to use a different image:

1. Select the collection in the Collections palette.
2. Click the Edit button at the top of the palette to open the Edit Collection dialog box.
3. Click Edit Icon in the Edit Collection dialog box.
4. Click Find to display all the photos having the selected tag, or click the arrows to show the images in the collection. Choose a photo to use for the icon. Or you can click Import in the dialog box, select another image, and click OK.
5. Click OK to close the dialog box, and click OK again to close the Edit Collections dialog box. Now you see the selected image used as your custom icon for the collection, like the upper Molly collection in Figure 3.2.

Sometimes, you may prefer to use only a section of an image for an icon. In that case, when the dialog box is open, do one or both of these actions:

Figure 3.2. Create collections to organize your images. Customize the icon for the collection or leave the default.

> **Watch Out!**
> You can only use images for icons that are in these formats: JPG, BMP, PNG, GIF.

- Drag the dashed outline to show the part of the image you want to reuse.
- Drag one of the corners on the outlined box to surround the content you want to use as the icon, as shown in Figure 3.3.

Click OK, and then click OK again in the Edit Collections dialog box to close it and make the change to the collection's icon.

Adding images to a collection

When you create a new collection, it is listed in the Collections palette using the name you specified. Until you add content, its icon shows only a question mark, like that in the active collection shown in Figure 3.2.

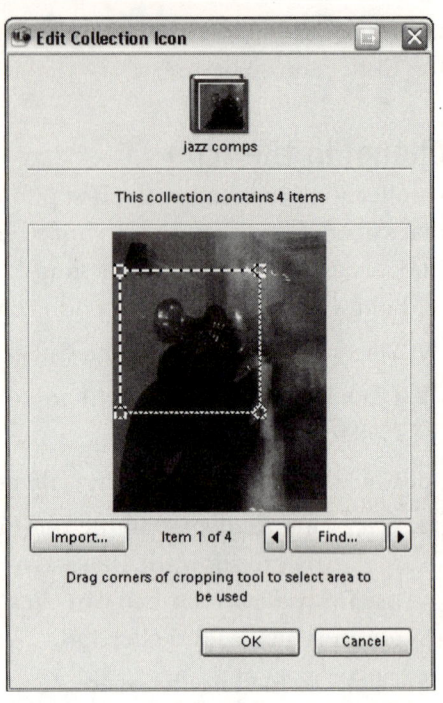

Figure 3.3. Select and specify part of a different image to use for a tag's icon.

Right-click an image, choose Add to Collection, and then choose from your current list of collections to add an image to a specific collection, as shown in Figure 3.4. If you want to remove an image from a

> **Inside Scoop**
> Cropping and resizing the icon's image only works when you are using the default method of using the first image added to the collection as the icon. When you use a custom image, it is automatically cropped and resized when you select it.

 **Watch Out!**
You can't group a collection that is shared online. Read about sharing online in Chapter 19.

collection, right-click the image, choose Remove from Collection, and then select the collection from the thumbnails.

Figure 3.4. Add an image to an existing collection in your catalog.

Grouping collections

You can create as many or as few collections as you like. Over time you may find you have lots of collections listed in the Organizer. Although it may be useful to keep your images in collections, they take up a fair bit of room in the program window.

Defining a group

A group is simply a way to gather your various collections together into a bigger category. Creating groups cleans up your Collections tab; you can open a group to see the collections listed within it.

To organize your content more cleanly, consider grouping similar collections together following these steps:

1. Click the New drop-down arrow in the Collections palette to open its menu, and choose New Collection Group.
2. In the Collection Group Name text box, type a name for the collection group.
3. Click OK to close the dialog box and add the group to the Collections palette.
4. Click OK to close the dialog box and add the collection group to the Collections palette.

When the collection group is created and named, you can add your collections to the group as desired. Simply drag the collection's label in the Collections palette over the group's name. Release it to add it to the group.

As you can see in Figure 3.5, the collection group named *Commercial Jan. 2005* contains three collections with a fourth collection being added.

Viewing your collection

Whether a collection stands alone or is part of a group, you can see only one collection at a time; the group's contents aren't displayed. For example, in Figure 3.6, the collection named *jazz comps* is displayed in the Photo Browser.

You can activate the display of the collection's contents in numerous ways, but the easiest is just to double-click the collection's name in the Collections palette. You can also click the box to the left of the collection's name to display the Find icon.

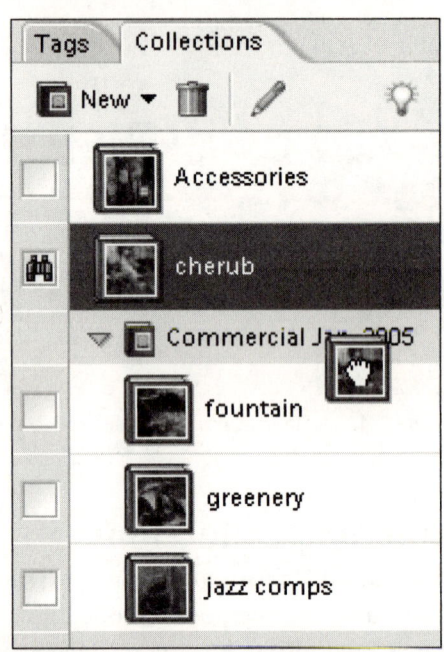

Figure 3.5. Combine similar image collections into a group for ease of organizing.

Inside Scoop

You can also drag the collection from the Collections palette to the Find bar, but I don't advocate this method because of its unnecessary mouse dragging.

Each photo in a collection is numbered in the Photo Browser display showing its order. In Figure 3.6 you can see the numbers in the upper left of the thumbnails. You can change the order of images in your collection by dragging a thumbnail into another location within the collection. The images are automatically renumbered.

When you are finished with the collection, click Back to All Photos to return to the Photo Browser. Your changes are saved automatically.

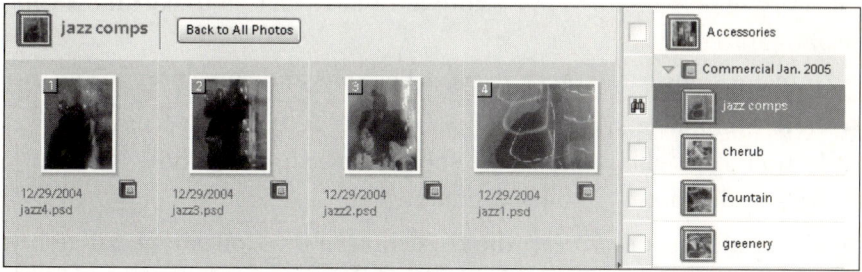

Figure 3.6. Reorder the images in a collection by rearranging their thumbnails.

Reusing a collection structure

You can spend a fair amount of time building and naming collections and groups and their relationships. If you want to set up the same structure on another computer or share it with colleagues or family, you don't have to start from scratch. Instead, save and export the collection structure from your catalog — not the images, just the structure.

Click the New button's drop-down menu, and choose Save Collections To File to open the dialog box. Select the Export All Collections radio button to export the entire structure from your catalog. If you want to export just a part of it, select the Export Specified Collection Group radio button and choose the collection group you want to export. The file is exported and saved as an XML (Extensible Markup Language) file.

To import a collection structure into another catalog, click the New button's drop-down arrow and choose From File. In the browse dialog box that opens, locate the XML file containing the collection structure and click Open. The group and collection structure are loaded, and you can assign your images to the collections.

Inside Scoop

Many Edit commands let you delete content from the catalog. Choose the Also Delete Photos from the Hard Disk option to delete the image from your computer.

Editing collections

Some of the ways in which you edit collection and collection group information is self-explanatory, but a couple of tasks can be tricky unless you know what to do.

Here are some ways you can edit collections and collection groups:

- **Delete an image.** Select the photo or photos to remove from a collection, right-click to open the shortcut menu, and choose Remove from Collection ⇨ [collection name].

- **Delete a collection.** Select the collection in the Collections palette, and click the Delete icon; then click OK in the confirmation dialog box to remove the collection. You can also press the Delete key on the keyboard.

- **Merge collections.** Select the collections you want to combine in the Collections palette. Right-click and choose Merge Collections. In the list that displays, select the collection you want to keep; it will contain all the content after the merge. Click OK to close the dialog box and finish the job.

- **Take a collection out of a group.** You can't drag a collection from its position within a collection group back into the Collections palette. Instead, right-click the collection, or click the Edit button on the Collections palette to open the Edit Collection dialog box. Click the Group drop-down arrow, and choose None (Top Level). Click OK to close the dialog box and move the collection.

Reorganizing the palette

By default, collections and collection groups are listed in the palette in alphabetical order. Change one program preference, and you can set the order of the palettes as you like.

From the Organizer, follow these steps:

1. Choose Edit ⇨ Preferences ⇨ Tags and Collections to open the Preferences dialog box, shown in Figure 3.7.
2. Click the Manual check boxes for Collections and Collection Groups.
3. You can also specify the size of the icon, choosing either the name alone, or the name with a small- or large-sized icon.
4. Click OK to close the dialog box. Now you can move the content in the Tags palette.

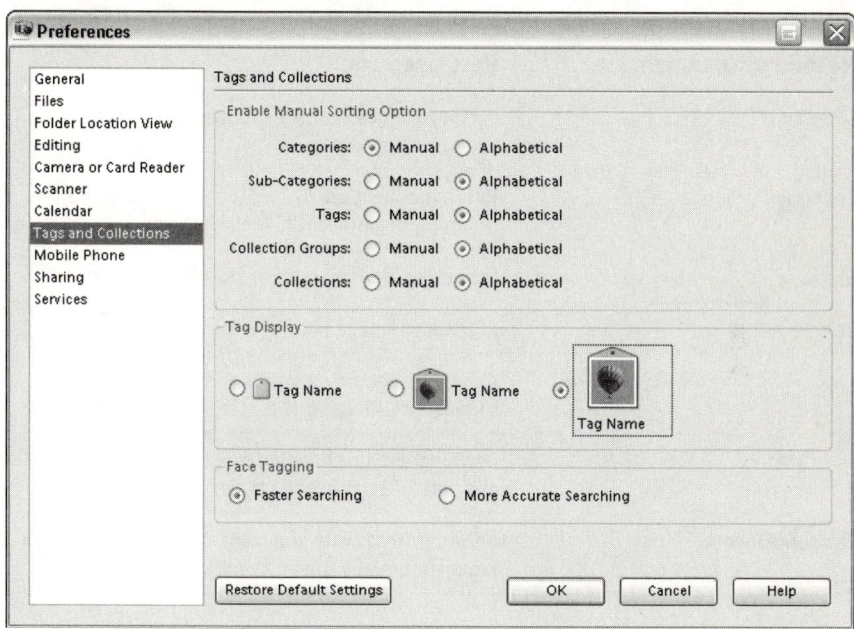

Figure 3.7. Specify characteristics for tags and collections such as how they are sorted and their display options.

When the preference is reset to allow manual ordering, select one or more tags, categories, or subcategories, and drag the item or items to the new listing location. When you move a category or subcategory, the tags it contains move with it.

Bright Idea

Select the manual sorting options for the Tags palette while the preferences are displayed. These options include Categories, Sub-Categories, and Tags radio buttons.

Organizing options

The Organizer offers several ways to organize image files. Some of the options are visual and designed to make working in the Photo Browser simpler, while other are data-oriented, and designed to help organize images by searchable topic or subtopic.

Before you get into the nitty-gritty of the different features available in the Organizer, check out Table 3.1. This table is a quick guide to the available organizing methods and why they should be used.

Table 3.1. Organizing image files

Method of Organizing	Best Used For...
Collection	Sorting images that are grouped by subject, event, or purpose
Collection group	Holding collections sorted according to content grouping or purpose
Stack	Collecting similar shots of the same subject
Version set	Storing an image and its edited versions
Tags	Applying specific keywords to images to use for sorting and locating files
Tag category	Defining a major heading for storing subdivisions and sets of tags in the catalog
Tag subcategory	Defining items within a main category used to organize tags by giving them a label

Stacking images

If you are like me, you enjoy the luxury of using a digital camera to capture multiple versions of a subject in a quest for the perfect shot. The problem is that you can end up with a dozen shots of your prize roses that are very similar.

Save time working in the Photo Browser by stacking a number of photos. Instead of seeing 12 shots of your rose, you see just one with a Stack icon overlaying it.

Use commands from the Edit menu or from the right-click shortcut menu. Follow these steps to create the stack:

1. Ctrl+click to select the images you want to stack in the Photo Browser.
2. Choose Edit ⇨ Stack ⇨ Stack Selected Photos, or right-click and choose Stack ⇨ Stack Selected Photos.
3. The selected images are replaced by one image showing an icon at the top right of the thumbnail, shown in Figure 3.8.

Figure 3.8. Stacked images, like that in the upper left of the figure, display a stacking icon over the top image in the stack.

Shuffling the stack

There are a few handy stack actions that you can take only when the stack is collapsed in the Photo Browser. While the stack is collapsed showing the default Photo Browser view, you can do these things:

- **Flatten the stack.** Right-click the stack thumbnail and choose Stack ⇨ Flatten Stack if you want to delete all the images in the stack except the top one; the remaining image won't display the Stack icon in the Photo Browser.

- **Unstack the photos.** If you change your mind about the stack, right-click and choose Stack ⇨ Unstack Photos. The images then display individually in the Photo Browser. By the way, you can also unstack from the expanded view.

- **Merge two or more stacks.** Select the stacks and choose Edit ⇨ Stack ⇨ Stack Selected Photos. An information dialog opens telling you that the selected photos are already in a stack and will be added to the selection. Click OK. The newest image in the new stack is shown as the thumbnail at the top of the stack.

You have to expand the stack to use other actions. Right-click the stack, and choose Stack ⇨ Reveal Photos in Stack. The images within the stack display in the Photo Browser, as shown in Figure 3.9.

Watch Out! Most actions applied to a collapsed stack such as printing are applied to the top item only; unstack the photos to apply actions to all the photos.

Figure 3.9. Show the images that make up the stack and define some of the stack characteristics.

In Figure 3.9, you see that each image has a small flat icon, indicating it is part of a stack. The middle image also has another icon that looks like a different-shaped stack. This icon indicates the image has more than one version stacked within it.

After the stack is expanded, you can do these things:

- **Remove a selected image.** Right-click an image, and choose Stack ➪ Remove Photo From Stack. The image is pulled out of the stack, but it remains in the catalog. If you want to delete an image from the catalog, select it and press Delete on the keyboard.

- **Pick a new top photo.** The newest image is placed at the top of the stack and is used as the thumbnail. If you want to use a different image as the thumbnail, right-click the image you want on top and choose Stack ➪ Set as Top Photo.

- **Edit a photo.** Select an image, and choose an editing option from the Edit button's drop-down menu on the shortcuts bar. If you edit a photo that's in a stack, the photo and its edited versions become a version set nested inside the stack.

Click the Back to All Photos button to display the Photo Browser's default view.

Stacking versions of an image

When you take the stacking idea to the next level, not only can you stack a collection of images, but you can also stack one image and its edited versions in a type of stack called a *version set*. Instead of having seven variations on the same theme, one thumbnail is shown and the rest are included in the version set, uncluttering the Photo Browser.

To create a version set, follow these steps:

1. Open the image you want to edit in either the Standard Edit or Quick Fix modes, and make your edits.
2. Choose File ⇨ Save As to open the Save As dialog box.
3. Select characteristics for the saved version of the file.
4. Click the Save In Version Set With Original option on the dialog box, shown in Figure 3.10.
5. Click Save to save the image and create a version set.

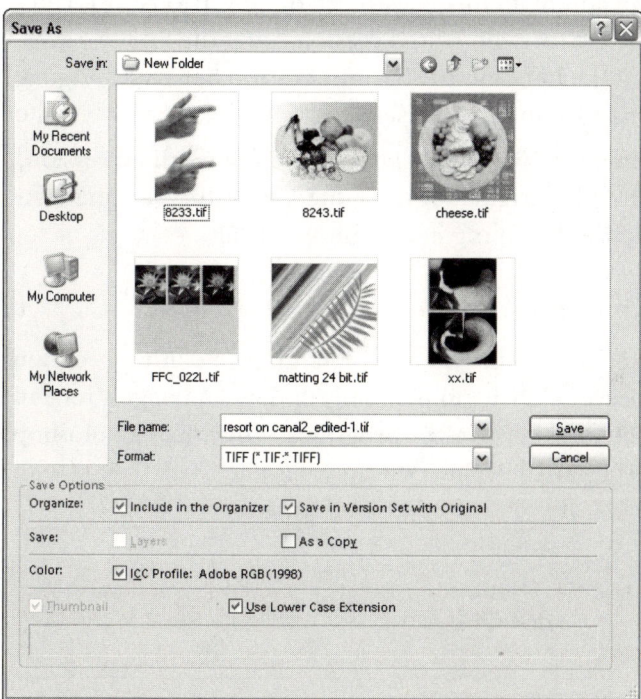

Figure 3.10. Show the images that make up the stack and define some of the stack characteristics.

Hack

Using the Edit ⇨ Auto Smart Fix command automatically saves an image and its edited version as a version set.

Dealing with versions

Several concepts are useful when you're using version sets. After you read the list here, try building and disassembling a couple of version sets to see how they work.

Keep these ideas in mind as you experiment:

- If you edit a photo that's in a stack, the photo and its edited versions become a version set nested inside the stack automatically when you save the image.

- One version stack can contain only one original image and its edits — you can't nest version sets within version sets. If you want to save an edited version of an image with its edited versions (this can get pretty complex!), save the edited version using the File ⇨ Save As command and then choose the Save In Version Set With Original option. Name and save the new version set.

- In a version set that contains the original and a single-edited version, if you delete either the original or the edited copy, the stacking icon is removed from the remaining image automatically.

Editing choices

You have many choices for editing images. Each image-editing program has its benefits. To prevent having to manually update an image's version set when you have created versions in programs other than Photoshop Elements, simply specify an alternate editing program.

Inside Scoop

The last edited version of a photo is visible at the top of the stack. If you want to use a different image, you have to right-click the image you want on top and choose Stack ⇨ Set as Top Photo.

> **Watch Out!**
> The only non-photo thumbnail that can be included in a stack is the result of using the Edit ➪ Edit 3GPP Movie command that saves an edited movie as a copy stacked with the original in a version set. Make a collection if you want to group different file formats together.

Follow these steps to identify an alternate editing program:

1. Choose Edit ➪ Preferences ➪ Editing to open the Preferences dialog box.
2. Select the Use a Supplementary Editing Application check box.
3. Click Browse and locate the .exe file for the program you want to add.
4. Click Open to select the program and return to the Preferences dialog box. The additional editing program is now listed, as shown in Figure 3.11.
5. Click OK to save the preference and close the dialog box.

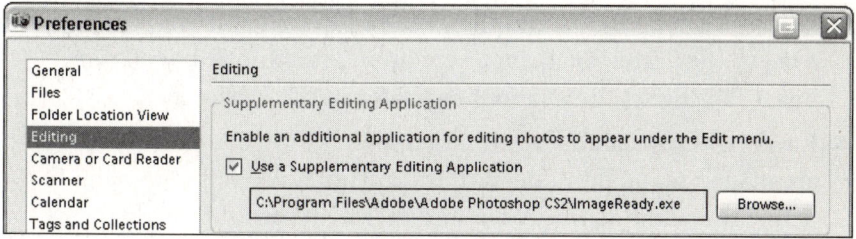

Figure 3.11. Specify an additional editing program to use for editing images.

Viewing the contents

The point of using a version set is to make your Photo Browser less cluttered and easier to manage. When it comes to managing, access commands for working with the files from the Edit menu, or right-click the version set's image in the Photo Browser to open the shortcut menu. The options for managing and viewing the entire set include the following:

- **Reveal Items in Version Set.** This command opens the version set in the Photo Browser, as shown in Figure 3.12. Use it to check out the version set's contents.

>
> **Inside Scoop**
> Any dialog box that allows you to remove an image from the Photo Browser also offers the Also Delete Photos From The Hard Disk option because deleting edited versions of an image from the Photo Browser doesn't delete them from your hard drive automatically.

- **Flatten Version Set.** The version set designation is removed, and only the image showing as the top item remains. You may use this command if you are sure you have finished working with an image and don't need to save any more edit versions.

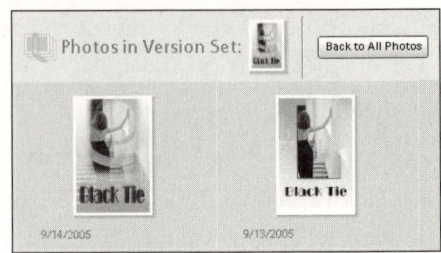

Figure 3.12. Open and modify the contents of a version set in the Photo Browser.

- **Convert Version Set to Individual Items.** The version set connection is removed; you may want to use this command to apply a tag to a specific edited version and then rebuild the version set. If you apply a tag to the visible image in a version set, it is applied to all the images in the set. Read about tags later in the chapter.

- **Revert to Original.** If you aren't happy with the edited versions of an image, or you don't need them anymore, use this command to delete the additional versions and maintain only the original.

After the content of the version set is expanded in the Photo Browser, you can access more commands, again from the right-click shortcut menu or the Edit menu:

- **Remove Item(s) from Version Set.** Select one or more edited images, and choose this command to delete them.

- **Set as Top Item.** If you want a different image to represent the version set as the thumbnail, choose the image and then select this command.

Click the Back to All Photos button to return to the default Photo Browser view when you are finished.

Editing an image in a version set

Editing an image in a version set is one of these little tasks that can make you crazy at the beginning, and then can't believe you didn't think of it before.

If you want to edit the top photo in a version set, click the thumbnail to select it, click the Edit button on the shortcut bar, and then choose an editing mode from the drop-down menu. Make your changes, and then use the File ⇨ Save As command. Choose the Save In Version Set With Original option. The copy is saved and added to the version set.

What if you want to edit a different version of the file? Select the version set and right-click to open the shortcut menu. Choose Reveal Photos In Version Set. Then select the image you want to edit, and proceed with your edits. Again, be sure to specify the Save In Version Set With Original option in the Save As dialog box.

When you return to the Photo Browser, the newly edited copy becomes the top photo of the version set.

Tag — you're it

Photoshop Elements users generally come in two varieties: those that like to organize visually and make collections and stacks, and those that like to organize image data using labels called *tags*.

Tags are another way of organizing files in the Organizer, although they can be used for searching and indexing instead of using a visual function such as stacking or creating version sets. A tag is a label that is attached to an image. You can attach the default tags included with Photoshop Elements, or create your own custom tags.

Tags are created within a category or in a subcategory. Use one or more tags in addition to any other organizing structures for your images. That is, one image can have one or more tags and can be part of a collection or a version set or stack. In Figure 3.13, you see an image with a tag attached, identified as the icon to the bottom right of the tag. Notice also that the image is a stack.

Opening the stacked image in Figure 3.13 reveals three images. The three images in the stack are tagged, and the image at the right of the figure has two tags attached, indicated by the two icons shown

Figure 3.13. One image can be categorized and labeled in a number of ways.

in Figure 3.14. That image also is part of a version set, which can be opened.

Figure 3.14. Opening a stack reveals more levels of images using different tags and structures such as version sets.

Working with the Tags palette

You can create and work with tags in the Tags palette of the Photo Browser. Before you start into a tag-building and applying process, take a few minutes to check out the palette. Open the collapsed categories; try attaching tags to images. I'll wait here.

Ready? Take a look at Figure 3.15 for reference.

Here's what you find in the Tags palette:

- Six default tag categories are available, including Favorites, People, Places, Events, Other, and Hidden.
- Spin-down arrows show subcategories within the Favorites, People, and Places categories.

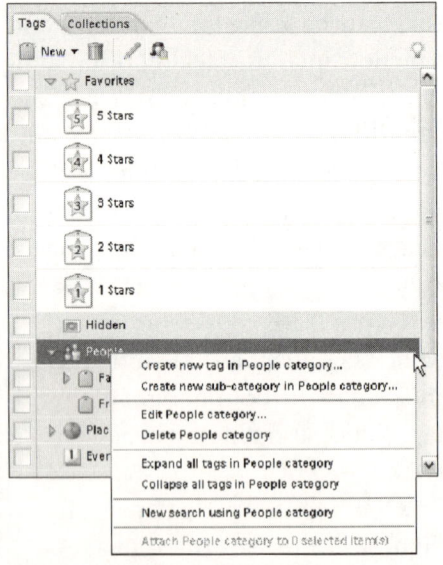

Figure 3.15. Opening a stack reveals more levels of images using different tags and structures such as version sets.

- The tag categories are listed alphabetically by default.
- Each tag, category, and subcategory contains a right-click shortcut menu with commands for editing, deleting, searching, and managing the tag hierarchy with two exceptions: the Favorites and the Hidden categories.

Exceptions to the rule

The Favorites and Hidden categories are different from the other default tags and any tags or categories you create yourself because they are the only ones you can't delete or rename.

The Favorites category contains a set of five "star ratings" tags that can be assigned to an image. If you apply a star rating to an image that already has been rated, the new rating replaces the previous rating tag.

Decide how or if you want to use the Favorites star rating system. You might want to use the Favorites tags if you have a big batch of images to sort through, and you know you only need five or six for a project. For example, follow these steps to sort a batch into categories:

1. In the Photo Browser, scroll through your batch of images and assign a star rating to each image that is a potential candidate for your project.
2. After you have assigned stars, drag the 5 Stars tag from the Tags palette to the Find bar on the Photo Browser, shown in Figure 3.16.

Figure 3.16. Drag the tag to the Find bar to perform a search for the images using the same star rating.

3. The search is performed, and the results are shown in the Photo Browser. As you can see in Figure 3.17, the set of 5 Star tags is short, making it simple to select favorites.

Inside Scoop
Right-click the tag in the Tags palette to open its shortcut menu. You can choose New Search using x Stars tag — the number (x) varies according to the rating tag you right-click.

Figure 3.17. The sorted images — those with the same star rating — are shown in the Photo Browser.

If you attach a Hidden tag to an image in the Photo Browser, it is still in your catalog, but it isn't visible. What's the point? Well, suppose you have a couple thousand images spanning three years or so. Rather than having all those images in the Photo Browser, you can hide the ones you aren't currently working with, such as those added within a certain time frame.

Follow these steps to hide images from a year:

1. Drag the end points on the Timeline to identify the period of time you want to work with. Hold the mouse over the end point to display the date in a tooltip, for example, January 2003 and December 2003. Read about working with the Timeline in Chapter 2.

2. Choose Edit ⇨ Select All, or use the keyboard shortcut Ctrl+A to select all the images in your catalog from your chosen timeframe.

3. Click the Tags tab to display the palette.

4. Attach the Hidden tag by dragging the tag from the palette over one of the selected images and releasing the mouse. You can also right-click the Hidden tag and choose Attach Hidden tag to [number] selected items.

5. Drag the end points back to the edges of the Timeline. You'll see that the images and other files for the specified time period are no longer displayed in the Photo Browser.

Creating categories and tags

You should consider how and why you want to apply the tags. Do you want to rename some of the existing categories and add more tags? Or is it simpler to delete the default categories and start anew? Don't stress too much about making a perfect tagging system; they are simple enough to change.

Creating a new category or subcategory

Instead of trying to make images fit an existing structure, you can add a new category to your catalog, complete with a custom icon chosen from the selection installed with the program.

Follow these steps to create a new category:

1. Click the New button on the Tags palette, and choose New Category from the menu to open the Create Category dialog box, shown in Figure 3.18.

Figure 3.18. Add a new category and even a custom icon to the catalog.

Watch Out!
Make sure you don't have an existing category selected in the Tags palette when you want to add a new category. If you do, the new element is added as a subcategory.

2. Type a name for the category in the Category Name field.

3. Scroll through the Category Icon list and select the icon you want to use to represent the category. You see the icon in the preview at the top of the Create Category dialog box.

4. If you like, click Choose Color to open the Color Picker and select a different color for the tag's tab.

5. Click OK to close the dialog box and add the new category to the list in the Tags palette.

You can use a very similar process to create a subcategory, nested within a category tag, by following these steps:

1. Click the New button on the Tags palette, and choose New Sub-Category from the menu to open the Create Sub-Category dialog box.

2. Type a name in the Sub-Category Name field.

3. Click the Parent Category or Sub-Category drop-down arrow to open a list of the existing categories and sub-categories in your tags listing, and select the appropriate tag.

4. Click OK to close the dialog box and add the new subcategory to the Tags palette, as shown in Figure 3.19.

You don't have an option to select a custom icon because subcategories don't use custom images—just a simple tag icon. The subcategory tag icon's color is based on the parent tag's color.

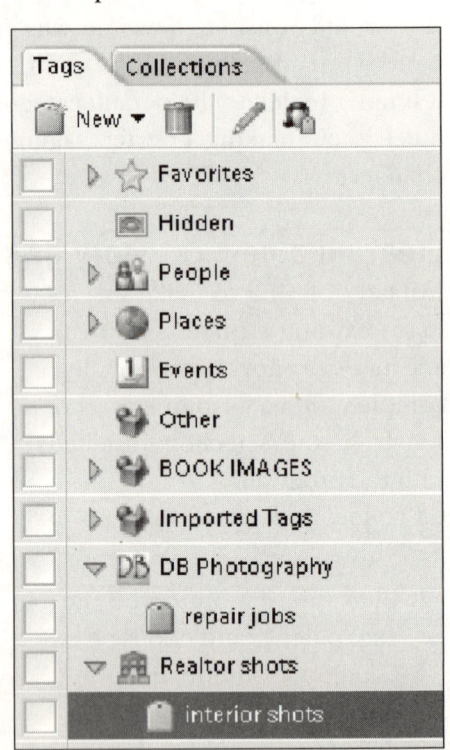

Figure 3.19. Create a tag hierarchy using subcategories.

> **Hack**
>
> You can add your own icons to use for categories in the Organizer. Create an image in any format sized at 20 pixels square. Store the image in this folder: C:\\Program Files\Adobe\Photoshop Elements 4.0\shared_assets\caticons.

Creating a new tag

Use your own tags to identify content in an image. You can create new tags under any category or subcategory. The process is the same whether you are adding a tag to a category or to a nested subcategory; the labels in the dialog box vary for a category or a subcategory although the options are the same.

Follow these steps to create a new tag:

1. Click the New button on the Tags palette, and choose New Tag from the menu to open the Create Tag dialog box shown in Figure 3.20.

2. Click the Category drop-down arrow, and choose an existing category or subcategory from your catalog.

3. Type a name for the tag in the Name field.

4. Add a note, if you like, explaining what the tag represents in your catalog. The note is then visible when you select the tag and click the pencil icon in the shortcut menu.

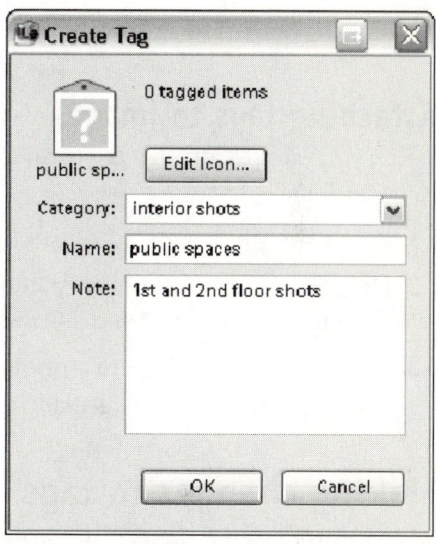

Figure 3.20. Add new tags to your catalog in a specified category.

5. Click OK to close the dialog box and add the tag to the Tags palette.

The tag initially has no image, just a question mark, shown in the Create Tag dialog box in Figure 3.20. When you attach the tag to your files, the image of the first file to which you assign the tag becomes the icon. In Figure 3.21, for instance, the tag "public spaces" uses the image of the kitchen as its icon. In the thumbnail shown at the left of the figure, notice that the parent tag is shown below the thumbnail.

Figure 3.21. The first image that receives the tag is used as an icon for the tag.

Attaching tags to images

When you want to attach a tag to an image, follow these steps in the Photo Browser:

1. Select the photo or photos to which you want to attach the tag.
2. Drag the tag from the Tags palette to the selected photos, or drag the photos from the Photo Browser over the tag on the Tags palette.
3. To add additional tags to a photo or group of photos, repeat these two steps. You can add as many tags as you like to any image.

Making changes to tags

Tag features aren't static. After you have your images tagged, you can modify characteristics such as the tag icon's appearance and the category/subcategory hierarchy.

One of the most visual changes you can make to a tag is to change its icon. The first image to which the tag is applied is set as the icon, which may or may not be the best representation of the tag's subject.

Watch Out!
If you use an imported photo for a tag icon, you have to attach the tag to the image yourself. Although the image and the tag's icon look the same, just as they do when you drag a new tag to its first image, it's not automatically attached.

You can change the tag icon's image using the same method as changing the icon for a collection. Read about using and modifying custom images earlier in the chapter.

Revising a category or tag

Sometimes, you get a system of tags and categories organized, and then you realize that you should have named a category differently or nested a subcategory within a different category.

Making changes to your hierarchy is straightforward. Select the category or subcategory in the Tags palette, and click the Edit button. In the Edit Tags dialog box, you can do these things:

- Rename the category in the Name field.
- Change a category/subcategory relationship by selecting one and dragging it into or out of another.
- Choose a new tag color or icon. Select the color from the Color Picker and an icon from the Category Icon list.

Reorganizing the Tags palette

If you specified manual sorting in the Tags and Collections preferences (shown way back in Figure 3.7), you can select one or more tags, categories, or subcategories, and drag the item or items to a new listing location. When you move a category or subcategory, the tags it contains move with it.

Photoshop Elements shows you in two different ways where reordered content is placed:

- When you drag a tag to reorder it within a category or subcategory, or reorder the list of categories and subcategories, a blue line shows in the list indicating where the content will appear.
- When you move a tag to a new category, or embed a subcategory within a category, the category selected is highlighted indicating where the tag or subcategory will appear.

Watch Out!
You can't move tags, categories, or subcategories into the Favorites category, nor can you move tags from the Favorites or Hidden tag into other categories.

Hack
If you apply a tag to a version set, the tag is applied to all items in the set. If you want the tag attached to only one photo in the version set, remove that photo from the version set and apply the tag individually.

Fortunately, you can undo any modifications you make to your Tags palette's contents. Select a tag and move it back to its original location; if you move a category or subcategory, select the label and click the Edit button to open the Edit Tags dialog box. Specify the correct location using the dialog box's menus, and click OK to restore the structure.

Removing tags from images

A tag isn't a permanent structure. You can easily remove a tag from one or more photos in several ways. Depending on your workflow and how you are viewing the images in the Photo Browser, choose one of these options:

- Right-click a thumbnail, and choose Remove Tag ⇨ [tag name] from the shortcut menu.
- If you are looking at one thumbnail at full size, right-click one of the displayed tags and choose Remove [name] Tag.
- Select the photos you want to modify, and then right-click one of the images and choose Remove Tag From Selected Items ⇨ [category] ⇨ [tag name].

Instant tags

Just add water! Although it's not quite that simple, you can create a set of tags based on a folder location. The tags come in handy if you are the sort of person who likes to organize your work in a folder system. If you need a file from a particular folder, all you do is search for the images using the folder tag.

Follow these steps to create tags from folder names in the Photo Browser:

1. Click the Photo Browser arrangement drop-down arrow at the lower left of the window and choose Folder Location. You can also choose View ⇨ Arrangement ⇨ Folder Location.
2. In the Tags palette, select the category or subcategory in which you want to store the folder tags.

3. Scroll through the folder listing in the Photo Browser, and locate the folder and images to which you want to assign a tag.

4. Click the Instant Tag button to the right of the folder's path name in the Photo Browser, shown in Figure 3.22.

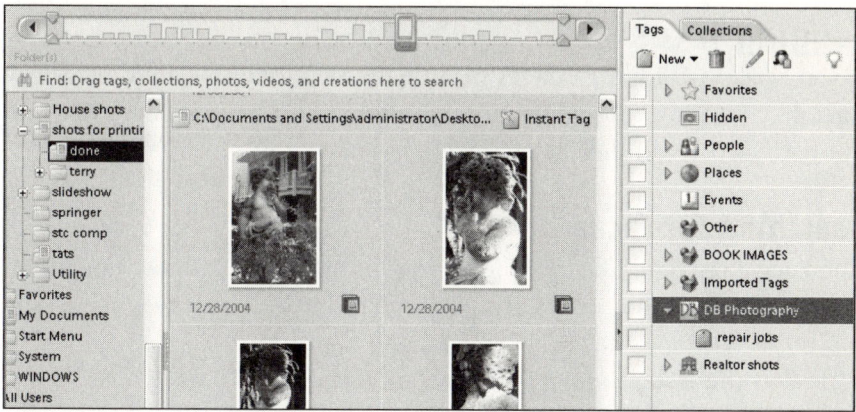

Figure 3.22. Use Instant Tags to apply a new tag to images based on their location on your hard drive.

5. The files in the folder are selected automatically, and the Create and Apply New Tag dialog box opens and shows the name of the folder as the tag's name (see Figure 3.23). Customize the tag as you like — you can change the icon, the name of the tag, or add a note.

6. Click OK to close the dialog box and apply the tags.

Repeat these steps to add tags to more folders' contents. The tags display the first image in the folder as the icon, and can be changed or modified as with other tag and collection icons.

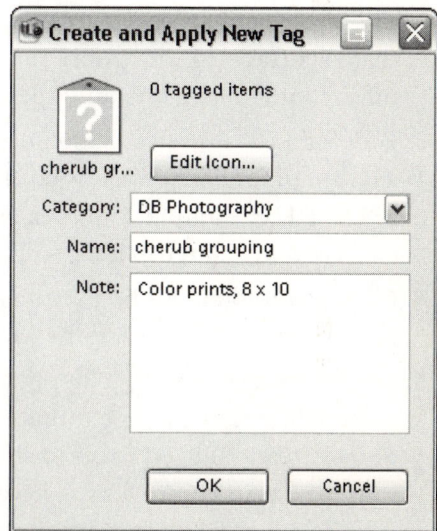

Figure 3.23. Configure the Instant Tags in the same ways as manually created tags.

Watch Out!
Make sure you select the category that you want to hold the folder location tags before you click the Instant Tag button. If not, the tags are nested within whatever category is active.

Tagging faces

If you work with lots of images of humans, you'll appreciate a neat feature in Photoshop Elements. You can automatically find faces in your photos that you can then tag or assign to collections.

Searching for faces

The Face Tagging dialog box helps you locate, select, and tag images of people. Some of the results are not human faces, as you may see when you try searching for faces.

Follow these steps to tag faces in your catalog:

1. Click the Find Faces for Tagging button on the Tags palette, or choose Edit ⇨ Find Faces for Tagging.

2. Only faces in images are tagged. If you have selected any creations or other types of files, you see an information dialog box explaining that Face Tagging will ignore the other files. Click OK to dismiss the information dialog box and open the Face Tagging dialog box.

3. Wait for a few minutes as the images in your catalog are evaluated. The length of time depends on the number of images and number of faces. For example, Figure 3.24 shows the results of face tagging a collection of about 600 images. The search took about three minutes.

4. Click a thumbnail in the Face Tagging dialog box to show its source image in a preview area at the lower right of the dialog box.

5. Select the tag you want to apply, and drag the tag to the image. As you apply tags, the image thumbnails disappear, or you can click Show Already Tagged Faces to show the tagged images below a separator bar, as in Figure 3.24. You can also create a new tag from the Face Tagging dialog box, using the same methods as described earlier in the chapter.

6. Continue with the remaining thumbnails until you have finished tagging them.

Inside Scoop

You don't have to wait for the entire catalog to be searched and thumbnails displayed before you start working on the photos.

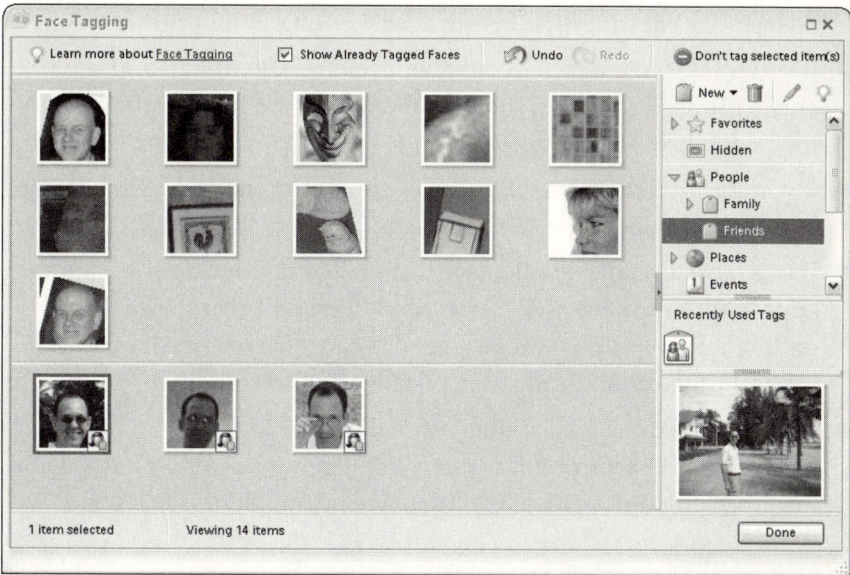

Figure 3.24. The Face Tagging feature locates and lets you assign tags to images of friends and family.

When is a face not a face?

When you use the Face Tagging feature, not all the returned images are human faces, and some seem completely misplaced. In the search I did for the previous set of steps, for example, one of the thumbnails returned was an image of a mask. Technically, that makes sense, as it is a vaguely human face after all.

However, it also returned ceramic cats as a tagged face — they have faces, but certainly not very human faces. You can't always trust this feature to get it right, but it is still a great and quick way to pull out images of that office party or the last family reunion.

Other tagging tricks

You can perform some other tagging tricks in the Face Tagging dialog box, such as

- Create a new tag if you forgot to make one before starting the searching process. Use the same method to create a tag in the Face Tagging dialog box that you use to create a tag from the Photo Browser.
- If you want to see a face in context, click the thumbnail and the entire photo is shown in the preview area at the lower right of the dialog box.
- If you decide not to tag a face, select the thumbnail and click Don't tag selected item(s).
- If you have already added a tag to an image but decide you want to apply another one as well, select Show Tagged Faces to see thumbnails of all the photos you've tagged. Leave this option deselected if you want to automatically hide photos after you tag them.
- If you know you will be adding more than one tag to an image, select Show Tagged Faces when you start the tagging process. That way the images aren't automatically hidden when you add the first tag.

Back and forth

Tags and collections are closely related. You can convert tags to collections, and vice versa, using the structure as a way to select images in the Photo Browser.

If you want to assign some tagged images to a collection, click the Tags tab and then double-click the tag's name to select the images that have the tag assigned. In the Photo Browser, all images using the tag are shown in an expanded view. Choose Edit ⇨ Select All to select all the items in the Photo Browser. Click the Collections palette, and click the box to the left of a collection's name to select it and assign the images to the collection.

To assign tags to a collection, click the Collections tab and then double-click the collection name to display the photos in that collection. Choose Edit ⇨ Select All to select all the items in the Photo Browser. Click the Tags palette and click the box to the left of the tag you want to assign to attach the tag to the images.

Searching photos

You can search for images based on their associated tags using the Find bar, which appears as a horizontal bar above the thumbnails in the Photo Browser, shown in Figure 3.25. When you drag a tag, collection, or other element onto it, the Find bar automatically expands so that you can see the results of the search in the Photo Browser's expanded view.

Customize the search further by dragging more tags to the Find bar, progressively narrowing your search. If you prefer, select two or more tags at one time and drag them to the Find bar to search more quickly. In Figure 3.25, two tags have been added as search parameters, and a third is being added.

Figure 3.25. Drag the tag or tags you want to use for searching to the Find bar.

Search results are shown in an expanded view, like that shown in Figure 3.26.

Figure 3.26. The results of your search as well as the types of matches are shown in the Photo Browser.

Inside Scoop

If you can't remember the contents of a collection or creation, drag its icon to the Find bar to see its components in the Photo Browser's expanded view.

There are three levels of matching possible. You can specify which match results you want to view by clicking the check box or check boxes:

- **Best.** This is what is shown in Figure 3.26 — the seven best matches. This means that all the images match both tags.
- **Close.** In Figure 3.26, the number 12 is next to the Close choice. This means that 12 images had either one or the other of the tags, but not both. If you select this check box, you will see those 12 images along with the seven Best matches.
- **Not.** Next to the Not option in Figure 3.26 is the number 135. This indicates the number of image that do not match either tag. You could select this option to see these images, but if they don't match the criteria at all, I am not sure why you would want to.

When you are finished, click the Back to All Photos button to end the search and go back to the regular Photo Browser view.

Checking out properties

For many of you, keeping track of everything you do to your image collections can be quite a task. If you haven't been working with images for long, you may forget what you have done in the past. Or, if you have been into image-editing mode for some time, you may have dealt with so many images you can't remember the details.

Regardless of which group you fall into, you can check out the history and details of an image quickly using the Properties palette. Choose Window ⇨ Properties to open the palette. Then choose Window ⇨ Dock Properties in Organizer Bin to stack the palette with the Tags and Collections palettes.

The Properties palette shows you information about a selected image in four different panels. Select an image in the Photo Browser or Date view, and select a heading to show the properties. The default panel is the General panel, shown in Figure 3.27.

You can choose from the following options:

- **General.** Click the General button to show the basic settings for the image. These include the name of the file, as well as any caption or notes you have added; you can add a caption and note directly in the palette if you like. You also see the file's size, the date it was captured, its storage location, and whether it has an audio comment attached.

- **Tags.** Click the Tags button to show the tags associated with an image. You can add tags to the selected image while you are viewing the properties, and the palette automatically updates itself.

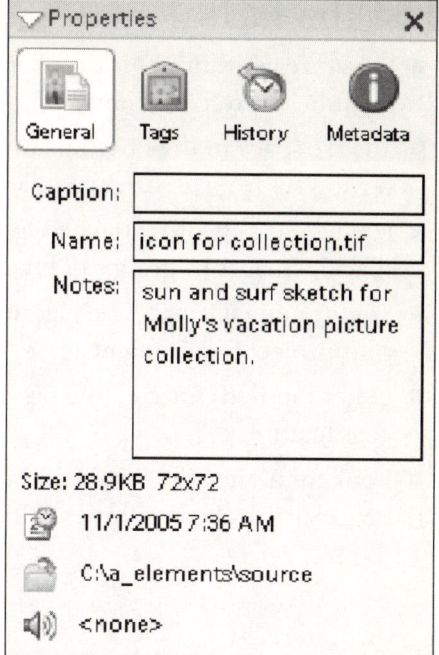

Figure 3.27. Read information about the images in different panels in the Properties palette.

- **History.** Click the History button to show what you have done with the image since you imported it into the Organizer. You can see details such as modification dates, editing dates, or where the image was imported from.

- **Metadata.** Click the Metadata button to show information about the image. The contents of the palette can be very complex, depending on the amount of processing the image has undergone and the type of camera used to capture the image. Metadata is covered in detail in Chapter 21.

Bright Idea

Save yourself time and mouse clicks by docking the Properties palette in the Organizer Bin. After it's docked, it stays open and docked each time you open the program.

Just the facts

- Organize your images into collections or groups of collections when planning a project or importing large numbers of images.
- To save space in the Photo Browser, stack similar images or create a version set from an original image that has several edited versions.
- Use tags as keywords attached to your images to help you find specific images or groups of images.
- Modify and customize the tags and their categories according to your project requirements.
- Other methods for creating tags are the Face Tagging and Instant Tags features.
- Look for an image's details and read about any changes made in its properties in the Properties palette.

PART II

Image Editing 101

GET THE SCOOP ON...
■ Organizing images onscreen ■ Choosing Zoom tools and keys ■ Working with duplicate windows ■ Using visual layout features

Seeing What You Have

Back in the old days when I was teaching in a computer college, I would often see students trying to work with their noses pressed against the monitor screen straining to make out details in a file. Just like kids with their noses pressed against the candy store window, you can't get any closer to the contents in the file that way!

It's simple to forget that you can change the view of your file's contents as you are concentrating on detail, but making the effort to use the best magnification for a task saves time and frustration. You only have two eyes — take care of them.

Speaking of frustration, how often do you find yourself dragging one window out of the way so you can see another one? And then dragging that one out of the way? And then dragging the first one, and then...? And while we are on the subject of dragging, how do you feel about dragging a number of objects around an image trying to lay them out perfectly? Is it irritating, sometimes even annoying?

In this chapter, I describe a number of methods for seeing what you want to see using the Zoom tools and the Navigator palette, and how to use a number of assistive tools such as grids and rulers. You get the inside scoop on how and why to customize the tools for your project, and I show you some time-saving tips.

Bright Idea

When either of the Zoom tools are active, pressing Alt swaps the Zoom In for the Zoom Out tool; the reverse is also true.

Zzzzzoom

Zoom is the term used in Photoshop Elements and most other graphics programs to describe changes in the magnification of an image onscreen. You use the same tools for both Standard Edit and Quick Fix modes, and you can change the magnification of an image from 1 percent to 1600 percent; 100 percent is the actual size of the image. You have two options to activate the Zoom tool:

- Click the Zoom tool on the toolbar.
- Press Z on the keyboard.

The Zoom tool can be either a Zoom In or Zoom Out tool. To change from one tool to the other, click the appropriate tool on the Tool Options bar, or press the Alt key to toggle the Zoom tool.

I try to use shortcut keys whenever I can. Whether you choose to follow my lead depends on how much work you do in the program. For example, if you work with images in Photoshop Elements for hours each day, shortcut keys save you time and mouse clicks. On the other hand, if you work on only a few images each week, or use the program sporadically, locating and clicking the Zoom tool on the toolbar is simpler than remembering shortcut keys.

When you select a tool in the toolbar, its options display horizontally at the top of the program window in the Tool Options bar, shown in Figure 4.1.

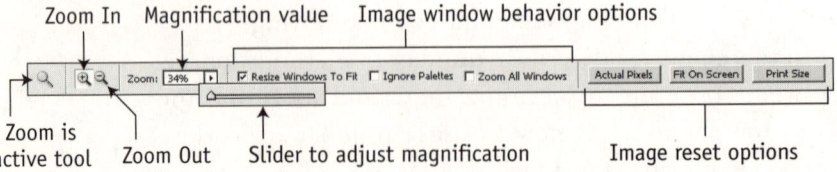

Figure 4.1. Choose options and settings from the Zoom tools and its options.

Hack

Check your mouse's configuration. You may be able to customize a mouse button or wheel to use for zooming in the image window.

>  **Inside Scoop**
>
> I've found using keystroke combinations for changing magnifications is a time- and eye-saver. You won't lose sight of what you are working with because you don't have to take your eyes off your image.

Using default magnification settings

Photoshop Elements provides a group of magnification presets. You can change an image's magnification to an incrementally higher or lower magnification in several ways:

- Click the image window with the Zoom tool.
- Choose View ➪ Zoom In or View ➪ Zoom Out.
- Click the Zoom In or Zoom Out button in the Navigator palette.
- Press Ctrl + = (the equal sign) to zoom in; press Ctrl + − (the minus sign) to zoom out.

Each time you use the tool, the image changes to the next preset percentage. Clicking the image with the Zoom tool centers the image's display around the point you clicked with the tool. If you use any of the other methods, the image is displayed around its actual center point. When the image has reached its maximum magnification level of 1600 percent or a minimum reduction level of 1 pixel, the magnifying glass appears empty.

Of the available options for choosing default settings, probably the least useful are the menu command choices. They take the longest, and if you have to repeat the command, they are even more time-consuming. Which is the best option? It depends on what's handy in the program. If you have the Zoom tool active, try the keystrokes. If your mouse is near the Navigator palette (if it's open) or the Zoom tools on the Tool Options bar, use the tools in those locations.

Setting custom magnifications

Clicking a Zoom tool several times is fine in many circumstances where you just want to take a look at an image's detail, and then zoom out again. However, instead of multiple clicks, you can set custom magnifications in a number of ways:

- Drag a marquee with the Zoom tool to zoom in or out of the area defined by the marquee, depending on which tool is active, shown in Figure 4.2. The amount of magnification applied depends on the size of the window, the size of the marquee, and the existing magnification.

- Click the drop-down arrow on the Zoom toolbar, and drag the slider to set a new Zoom value.
- Click the displayed zoom value on the Zoom toolbar and type a value.

You can use combinations of custom and default magnifications. Suppose I am trying to zoom in on an area for correction in the upper left of an image. I prefer to draw a marquee with the Zoom tool, and then adjust the magnification as necessary using the shortcut keys.

Figure 4.2. Draw a marquee with the Zoom tool to magnify a specific area.

Drawing a marquee with the Zoom tool first tells Photoshop Elements the area to magnify. Using the shortcut keys then lets me increase or decrease the magnification to tweak the view. If I use other combinations of shortcut keys and commands, I still end up with the view I want to see, but it takes more work to reposition the image at my desired magnification.

Choosing Zoom options

Photoshop Elements offers you choices to resize an image with the click of a button. The three options, shown in Figure 4.1, let you quickly see the image at a specific resolution:

- **Actual Pixels.** Click this to show the image at a size of 100 percent, with each image pixel shown by a screen pixel.
- **Fit On Screen.** Click this to resize the image and its window to fit within the Photoshop Elements program window.
- **Print Size.** Click this to see the image at the size specified for printing.

If all you simply want to do is resize the image and its window to fit on the screen, double-click the Hand tool in the toolbox. If you are working with an image and need to change the magnification several times, click the Resize Windows To Fit check box in the Zoom tool's options bar.

> **Automatic window resizing**
>
> The image window doesn't automatically resize if you use shortcut keys to resize your image. You can set a preference to change the behavior. In the Editor, choose Edit ⇨ Preference ⇨ General. Choose the Zoom Resizes Windows preference and click OK to close the dialog box and change the setting.

That way, as you change the size of the image display, you also change the size of the window accordingly, maximizing the view.

Using the Navigator palette

If you are the type of person who wants to see where you are at all times, using the Navigator palette instead of, or along with, Zoom tools is the way to go. If the Navigator palette is closed, choose Window ⇨ Navigator to open the palette. To dock it in the Palette Bin, drag the palette's tab over the Palette Bin and release the mouse.

You can do these things in the Navigator:

- Set the magnification by clicking the value field on the palette and typing a new magnification level.
- Drag the slider left to decrease the magnification or right to increase the magnification.
- Drag the marquee box on the thumbnail view of the image to see different areas of the image in the window, shown in Figure 4.3.

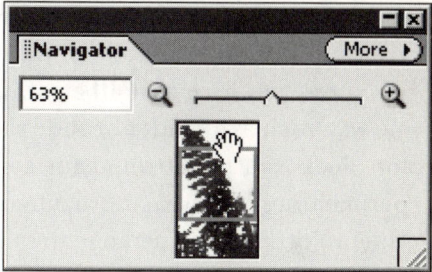

Figure 4.3. Use the Navigator palette to control magnification.

Bright Idea

You can align minimized images along the bottom of the program window by choosing Window ⇨ Images ⇨ Arrange Icons.

Make a match

You can save yourself lots of time and make editing images simpler if you learn to use the View menu commands along with the Zoom tools. You have a number of ways to organize the windows for two or more images on your screen, as described in Table 4.1.

Table 4.1. Organizing and viewing multiple image windows

Command	Window Arrangement
Window ⇨ Images ⇨ Cascade	Displays windows stacked and cascading from the upper left to the lower right
Window ⇨ Images ⇨ Tile	Displays windows edge to edge; closing one image window resizes the remaining windows automatically
Window ⇨ Images ⇨ Match Zoom	Changes the magnification of all open windows to the same value
Window ⇨ Images ⇨ Match Location	Changes the displayed area of all open windows to the same locations

Organizing for quick decision-making

You may be asking yourself, "What is the point? Why bother organizing and arranging and setting up image windows?" These are very good questions. Consider two examples of when these commands can be handy.

Suppose you have a number of images that you'd like to assemble in some way, such as a binder or slide show, and you want to use a consistent color block as a background for some text on each page. Rather than experimenting and tweaking arrangements, colors, and text placement to fit the project, you can arrange the images onscreen and eyeball it first.

Be sure to start with the right image. For both the Match Zoom and Match Location commands, Photoshop Elements resets the windows based on the active image's location and magnification.

Bright Idea

Whether you drag the horizontal and vertical scrollbars on the image window, drag the image with the Hand tool in the image window, or drag the marquee box in the Navigator, you produce the same results. Choose the viewing method that is most convenient and efficient for you.

In the example shown in Figure 4.4, a dark orange semi-transparent rectangle was added behind black text. Estimate how the background rectangle would look on several of your other images. This way you know quickly if your plan is likely to be successful or not.

Figure 4.4. Match the zoom and location shown in several images to estimate the appearance of similar objects.

Follow these steps to do a preliminary layout check for several images:

1. Choose Window ⇨ Navigator to open the Navigator palette, and drag it to dock it in the Palette Bin at the right of the program window.
2. Add the content you want to evaluate to one of the images.

Inside Scoop

You may find that there are times when organizing images in tiled and sized formats comes in very handy. For example, comparing images to one another in terms of content and color matching is much easier to do if the images are all displayed.

> **Convenient tiling**
>
> Photoshop Elements offers automatic image tiling at the click of a button. Click the Automatically Tile Windows button at the upper right of the program window in Standard Edit mode. After you click the button, the display of image windows tiles on an ongoing basis during your session; click the button to deselect the function.

3. With the layered image active, adjust the zoom to show the appropriate section of the image by dragging the slider in the Navigator palette or typing the magnification value in the field.
4. Adjust the section of the image that is visible in the image window. Drag the colored box in the Navigator palette, or adjust the view in the image using the horizontal and vertical scrollbars.
5. Choose Window ➪ Images ➪ Match Zoom to set the magnification of all the images the same.
6. Choose Window ➪ Images ➪ Match Location to show the same area of each image in its window.

Organizing for orientation

One additional feature offered by Photoshop Elements that you may find especially useful is working with more than one copy of the same image. Using two copies is a convenient way to show you both detail and the overall effect of your edits at the same time.

Follow these steps to set up the same layout as that shown in Figure 4.5:

1. Open the image file you want to work with in the Editor.
2. Choose View ➪ New window for [file name] to show a second copy of the image in the program window.
3. Deselect the Zoom All Windows check box on the Zoom tool's options.

> **Watch Out!**
>
> If your image windows tile automatically, even though you haven't chosen the command, the Automatically Tile Windows function is enabled; click the button to deselect it.

4. Using a Zoom tool or process of your choice, size one of the images to show the level of detail you need for your task; size the other copy to show you the entire image.

5. Edit as desired. In Figure 4.5, the color of some of the mossy patches on the bricks is being changed. Even when zooming in to work with the paintbrush, you can still see the outcome of the edits on the unmagnified copy of the image.

6. Close one of the image copies when you have finished editing.

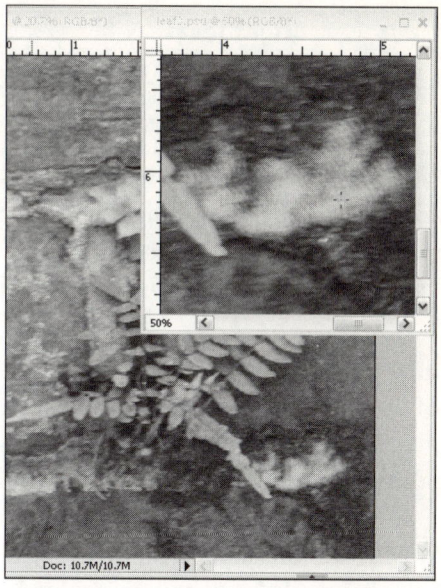

Figure 4.5. Edit at high magnification and see the effects of your edits on the overall image by using two image windows.

Line it up

It's easy to waste lots of precious time nudging and repositioning objects in an image to get them aligned "just right." Fortunately, Photoshop Elements includes a number of placement tools to help you align objects correctly. You can use rulers, gridlines, and arrow keys in Standard Edit mode to organize your masterpieces. The grid is the only placement tool available in Quick Fix mode. If you need to use rulers or change the measurement layout on the image, use Standard Edit mode.

You don't need to use every feature every time you need to adjust the position of content in an image. Aside from being a waste of time, it also can unnecessarily clutter your image. Use what you need depending on what you are doing. For example, if you are adding several rectangular

Bright Idea
Return the ruler origin to its default at the upper left of your image window by double-clicking the upper-left corner of the rulers.

Bright Idea

If you want to change units of measure, say from pixels to inches, right-click the ruler to display a list of measurement options, and then click the measurement unit you want to use.

areas spaced over an image, use the Snap to Grid and grid features. You may find it simpler to reset the ruler origins on the image as well to line up your shapes with features in the image.

Showing rulers

Choose View ⇨ Rulers to display the rules along the top and left side of the active window. In Standard Edit mode, rulers and the grid help you position items such as selections or blocks of text precisely on an image.

The ruler origin is the 0 location on both the top and left rulers. Moving the origin lets you measure from a specific location on the image. You change the rulers' 0 origin by dragging from the upper-left intersection area of the rulers diagonally down and to the right over the image. The 0 locations both horizontally and vertically are reset wherever you release the mouse.

A ruler does more than just show you a divided bar, as you can see in Figure 4.6. The ruler also does these handy things for you:

- Markers on the ruler show the pointer's location when you move it across the image, as you can see in the left image.
- The ruler origin shows the location from which Elements starts measuring your image, shown in the middle image.
- The ruler origin shows the grid's point of origin as well, shown in the right image.

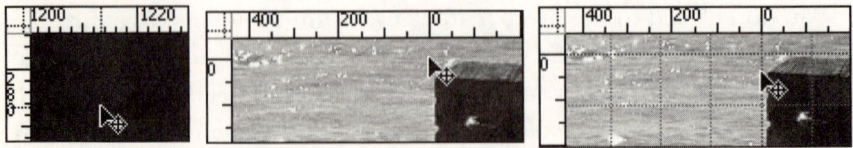

Figure 4.6. The ruler shows points of reference for tool locations (left), the measurement origin locator (center), and the grid's point of origin (right).

Using the grid

Save yourself lots of time and irritation when organizing a number of objects on an image by using Elements' grid feature.

>  **Inside Scoop**
> The Snap to Grid command can be active even when the grid isn't displayed. If moving content on your image window seems jerky, choose View ⇨ Snap to Grid to deselect the command.

The grid, as mentioned earlier, is set according to the 0, 0 origins of the ruler. Adjust the rulers' origins according to how you need to use the grid to make your work simpler. For example, in Figure 4.6, the grid is set up so that the 0, 0 origins are at the corner of the large dark shape. I set the location to start adding text from that position on the image. Instead of eyeballing the layout on the image, or nudging objects pixel by pixel, you can make the content snap to the gridlines' locations. Choose View ⇨ Snap to Grid. Now when you drag a block of text, it jumps or snaps to the gridlines' positions, as shown in Figure 4.7.

When you have finished with your placement, choose View ⇨ Snap to Grid to turn the gridlines off again.

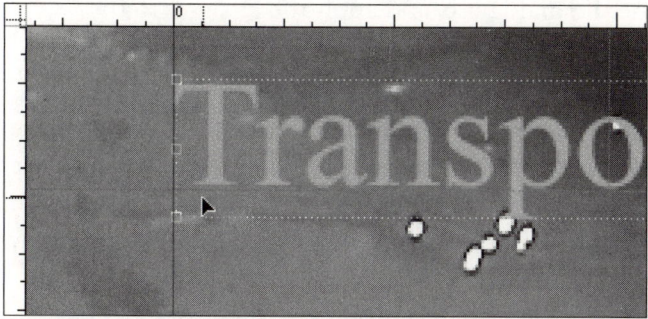

Figure 4.7. The Snap to Grid feature helps place objects quickly and evenly.

Adjusting ruler and grid settings

If you are starting work on a new image and you know you are going to use placement aids, change what you need in the program preferences by following these steps:

1. Choose Edit ⇨ Preferences ⇨ Units & Rulers (Photoshop Elements ⇨ Preferences ⇨ Units & Rulers) to adjust the rulers' unit of measure. Click the Rulers drop-down arrow and choose an option, as shown in Figure 4.8.
2. Click Next in the Preferences dialog box, or click the Preferences options drop-down arrow to show the Grid preferences.

3. Click the Color drop-down arrow, and choose a standard color from the list; or click the color swatch to open the Color Palette, and choose a custom color.

4. Choose a gridline style from the drop-down list. You can use a solid line, a dashed line, or a dotted line.

5. Specify the spacing for the gridline. Type the value in the field, and choose a unit of measure from the drop-down list.

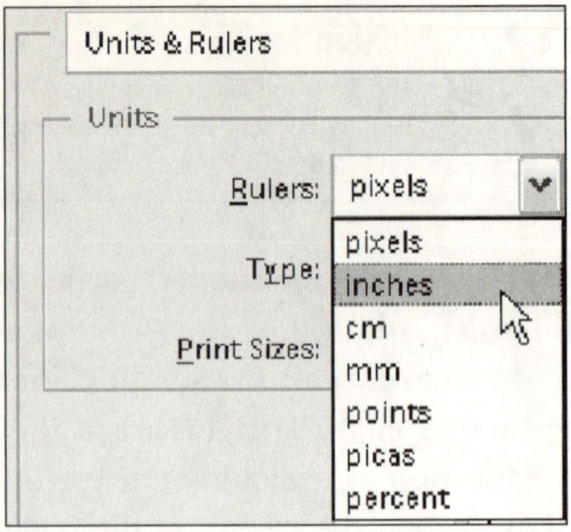

Figure 4.8. Change the rulers' unit of measurement.

6. Change the number of Subdivisions if necessary by typing the value in the field. Subdivisions are used to further divide up grid squares.

7. Click OK to close the dialog box and apply the changes to the image.

How does it look? Figure 4.9 shows the image window using the values specified in the steps. The image includes a marquee to show you more clearly how the settings translate to the window — you can see how the grids' squares are set every 50 pixels. Because the settings are chosen in the program preferences, the grid options remain as specified until they are changed again.

There is no right or wrong time to do preparatory work such as setting grids. I prefer to make adjustments to preference settings as part of the tasks I do prior to starting an image project. I find it less distracting.

Inside Scoop

You wouldn't find a red-dotted grid very useful over a close up of a juicy red apple, would you? So, choose grid options that are most visible on your image.

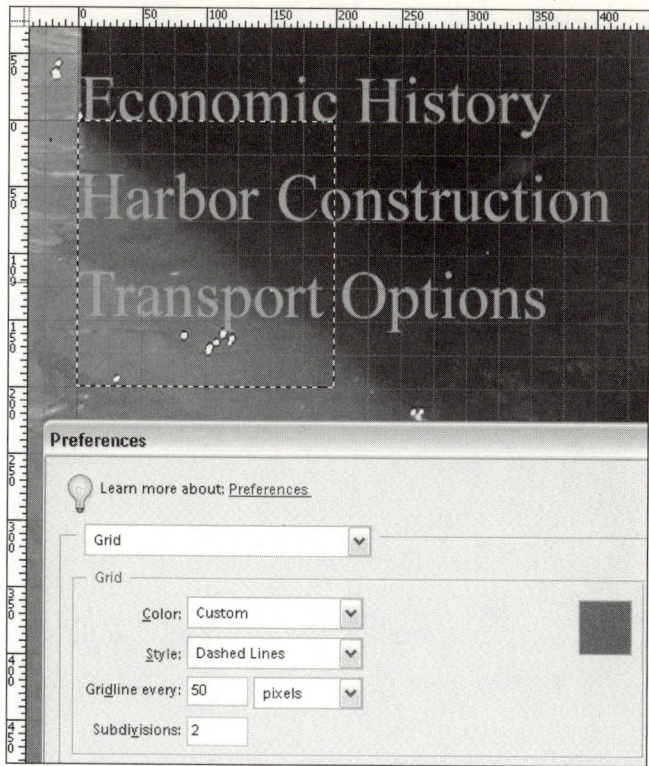

Figure 4.9. The grid is customized for the image and its elements.

Just the facts

- Use the Zoom tools to view what you are working with in detail.
- Unless you are zooming to a specific location or magnification, learn to use the keystroke combinations to save time.
- Use different combinations of the Zoom tool and window settings for different tasks.
- Let rulers and gridlines help you lay out content in an image.
- Remember to change the grid's line color and spacing when necessary to see them clearly against your image.

GET THE SCOOP ON...
■ Understanding the makeup of an image file ■ Resizing and resampling an image ■ Cropping and using cropped shapes ■ Adding drawn shapes ■ Transforming the physical appearance of an image

Shaping Up Your Images

How much time do you spend trying to set up a shot just right, only to have less-than-terrific results or even miss the shot altogether?

Or what about the terrific images of your dream kitchen that you captured at the home show—terrific except for the fact that the camera was tilted, and the kitchen looks like a ship's galley at high sea?

Not to worry! Many of these sorts of image-capturing problems can be corrected. You can even remove content from one or more sides of an existing image to improve the composition. And, did you know that you can enhance your images by using drawn shapes? Photoshop Elements gives you a number of tools for drawing basic shapes such as rectangles and circles, as well as more exotic shapes such as a bunch of grapes or a puzzle piece. Use these shapes as a background for your masterpiece or as added visual elements in an image to punch it up.

Developing a plan

Although there really isn't a right way or a wrong way to approach image restructuring and reshaping, there is a logical way to do it based on two factors—what you need to edit in the image and the image's resolution.

Inside Scoop

If you aren't seeing the dimensions of your image in pixels at the bottom of the image window, drag the window wider; unless it's wide enough, it won't have room to display the information.

Which factors apply in your image, and the method you use will vary. Before you jump in, take a minute to check out the image's characteristics and decide on a plan of action. You will have to answer these questions:

- What is the resolution of the image? What resolution is needed for the project?
- What is the size of the image? What size is required for the project?
- Is the composition correct? Should areas of the image be cut off altogether?
- Do you need to change anything, such as perspective; is the image skewed or crooked? What else is out of kilter?

Understanding file size

If you have two copies of the same image — one used for high-resolution printing, and one used for onscreen display — you'll find that the most notable difference between the two versions of the image is the file size. If your image is intended for online use, check the file size and make any changes necessary before doing any other editing.

At the very least, the image's resolution has to be decreased for displaying online. That way, you don't waste time repeatedly waiting for the monitor to redraw your image. It's interesting to watch the screen redraw a big image pixel by pixel, but the novelty wears off after you've seen it a dozen times or so.

File size is measured in kilobytes (KB), megabytes (MB), and gigabytes (GB). The resolution of the image is a tradeoff between image quality and file size: The higher the number of pixels, the greater the level of detail, but the larger the file size.

You need to keep three values in mind when working with images:

- **Pixel dimensions.** The number of pixels in your image.
- **Pixel resolution.** The number of pixels per inch.
- **Output dimensions.** The size of the printed image based on the printing resolution.

Watch Out!
File format can also affect file size greatly due to the different ways the files are created and compressed. For example, a GIF file is much smaller in file size than the same image using several layers saved as a TIFF file.

Image math

It's time for a quick math lesson — and you thought you left those days behind! Taking the time to understand how an image is displayed and printed can save you lots of time and aggravation.

A *bitmap* image is made of a matrix of square pixels. The image's *pixel dimensions* are the number of pixels that are along the height and width of the image. If you look at the bottom of an image window, you see the image's pixel dimensions, as shown in Figure 5.1. The size is expressed as *x* pixels by *y* pixels; "x" refers to the number of pixels horizontally along the x-axis — 3372 pixels in the example. The "y" refers to the number of pixels vertically, or along the y-axis — 4608 pixels in the example. The amount of detail in an image depends on its pixel dimensions.

Calculating pixels

The number of pixels per inch, or *ppi*, defines the image's resolution. *Resolution* controls how much physical space is used to print or view the pixels. To properly describe an image and determine what you have to do to maximize the efficiency of your images — remember, balancing file size against quality — use the following simple formula:

Pixel dimensions = document output size × resolution

If you look at any image's details at the bottom of the image window in Photoshop Elements, you can see the pixel dimensions and resolution. What isn't so obvious is the size of the image if you are printing it. For example, if an image has a resolution of 300ppi, and pixel dimensions of 1500×1500 pixels, the image will be five-inches square when printed and fit nicely on a standard page. The same image with pixel dimensions of 4500×4500 results in a 15-inch square image and needs modification to fit on a single page.

Bright Idea
Don't decrease the resolution of your only copy of an image if you think you may need to print it at some time, because trying to print a low-quality image at a high resolution produces disappointing results. Instead, use a copy of the image for online use and save the original.

Figure 5.1. The pixel dimensions of the image and its resolution are shown at the bottom of the image window.

Resizing an image

A computer monitor is only capable of showing a small number of pixels per inch, either 72ppi or 96ppi, depending on operating system and version. If the image's resolution is higher than what your monitor can display, you are adding to the file size unnecessarily. For onscreen use, decrease the resolution and adjust the size if necessary in the Image Size dialog box.

Changing the dimensions of an image

Here's a typical situation you may experience: Suppose you are building the Web site for your new company, Tiny Bubbles, a full-service dog grooming and pooch day spa. Now suppose further that your Web site's main page has a large version of your logo, and you want to add smaller copies to other pages in the site.

As you see in Figure 5.2, the logo is slightly larger than a five-inch square, which is far bigger than the petite one-inch square required. You could resize the images on the page by specifying the width and height attributes for the image tag in the pages' XHTML code, but doing so adds to the file processing and downloading times unnecessarily.

Figure 5.2. The pixel dimensions of this image are too large for use as a secondary logo on the Web site.

The simplest way to modify your image is to specify its values in pixels. Follow these steps to change pixel dimensions for an image:

1. Choose Image ⇨ Resize ⇨ Image Size to open the Image Size dialog box.

2. Click Constrain Proportions to automatically update the Width when you change the Height value or update the Height when you change the Width value.

3. Check that the Resample Image check box is selected at the bottom of the dialog box. It's important when resizing an image that the

changes are calculated mathematically; read more about resampling later in the chapter.

4. In the Pixel Dimensions fields in the Image Size dialog box, type new values for either Width or Height. Note that the other value (Width or Height) automatically changes and that the new dimensions in file size are displayed on the dialog box. In the example shown in Figure 5.3, the original file size was 732.4KB. After decreasing the pixel dimensions, the file drops to 29.3KB in size.

5. Click OK to close the dialog box and change the image size.

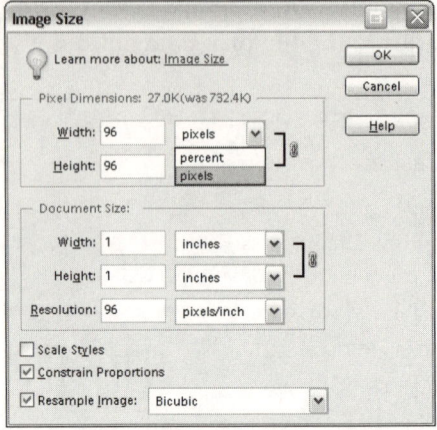

Figure 5.3. Change pixel dimensions to resize the logo image to use on multiple pages online.

If you aren't sure how many pixels you need, click the drop-down arrow for the unit of measurement in the Pixel Dimensions area of the dialog box and choose percent, shown in Figure 5.3. Type a percentage for the dimensions' change, and Photoshop Elements changes the pixel values for you.

Bitmap versus vector images

Bitmap and vector images produce different results when you resize the image. *Bitmaps* are resolution-dependent, and changing the pixel dimensions can degrade the quality of the image.

Vector images are composed of points and curves defined by their geometry and relationship to one another rather than assigning pixel information. Vector images are resolution-independent and can be resized or moved without a drop in quality. You see vector images onscreen as pixels because your monitor display uses a pixel grid. Shapes and text added to your image in Photoshop Elements are in vector format.

Changing an image's document size

If you prefer, adjust the size of an image based on the desired document size rather than specifying pixels. In the Document Size area of the Image Size dialog box, you can directly type the desired Width, Height, and Resolution for your image in the fields.

One additional option lets you choose the unit of measurement directly in the dialog box for both the Height and Width values, shown in Figure 5.4. Choosing a custom unit of measure is terrific if you need to quickly modify an image for a particular job, such as a metric layout.

Following along the metric theme, you can also define the Resolution as pixels/cm rather than the default pixels/in by choosing the other option from the drop-down list, hidden below the open menu shown in Figure 5.4.

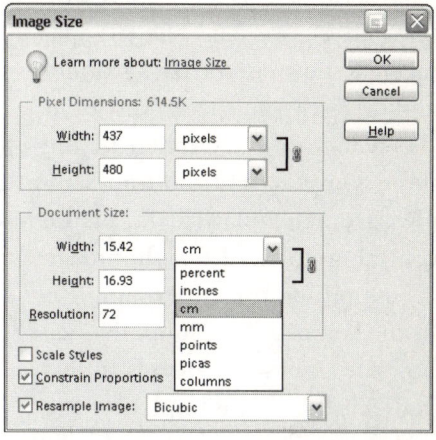

Figure 5.4. Change document sizes and units of measure to modify an image size.

Resampling an image

To change the pixel dimensions and the display size of an image, you work with a process called *resampling*. Resampling means that the program evaluates the pixel information in the image, redraws the pixels, and assigns color to any new pixels added to the image based on the color of the existing pixels.

Resampling options

You can use resampling to *downsample* or decrease the number of pixels, which removes information from the image. *Upsampling*, on the other hand, increases the number of pixels in the image by reading the information

Hack

Resampling can result in rather ugly images if you are trying to upsample an image to larger pixel dimensions. The solution is to capture or scan the image using a higher resolution.

in the existing pixels and assigning color to the new pixels, based on a mathematical formula. The formulas applied to the resampling process are called *interpolation methods*.

You can see examples of resampling in Figure 5.5. The original image is shown in the background, and a circle at the lower right shows the area magnified in the three samples. The bottom sample is from the image at 72ppi; the central sample is from the image at 600ppi, and the upper sample is from the image at 200ppi. Notice how the number of pixels differs between the downsampled image and the upsampled image. You'll also see that pixels become larger as the resolution is lowered.

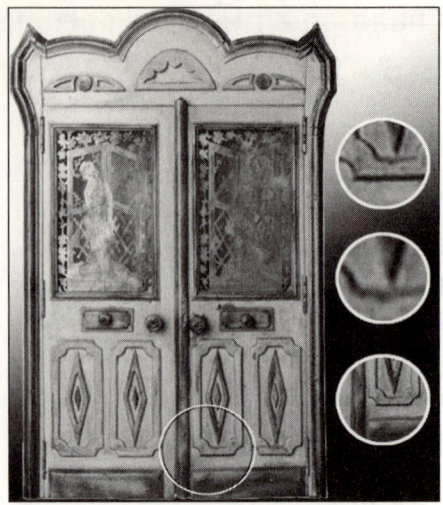

Figure 5.5. Resampling changes the number and size of pixels in an image — from top to bottom — the resolution of the samples are 150ppi, 600ppi, and 72ppi.

Applying interpolation methods

Interpolation is based on one of several algorithms, which are mathematical formulas that Photoshop Elements applies to an image when you are changing the dimensions and size. In addition to image resizing, interpolation is applied to transformations such as skewing or changing perspective in an image.

Choose Image ⇨ Resize ⇨ Image Size to open the Image Size dialog box. Click the Resample Image drop-down arrow (refer to Figure 5.4), and choose a method from the list. These are your choices:

- **Nearest Neighbor.** Use this method for illustrations with hard edges. Nearest Neighbor replicates the pixels in the image; if you use it with anti-aliased images, the result can be quite jagged.

- **Bilinear.** This method adds pixels by averaging color values of surrounding pixels. It's a fairly quick method, but it doesn't create the highest-quality results.

- **Bicubic.** This method is slower than the other methods, but the results are more precise. More complex calculations use the values

>  **Watch Out!**
>
> After you have removed image information from an image and saved the file, the pixels are gone for good. So, test different resolutions using copies of your image first.

of surrounding pixels to produce smoother color gradations than Nearest Neighbor or Bilinear.

- **Bicubic Smoother.** After applying the Bicubic algorithm, the pixels' color is calculated further to produce a more even tonal gradation in the image.
- **Bicubic Sharper.** This method applies Bicubic interpolation and then enhances the detail in the image with enhanced sharpening.

Cropping images

Use the Crop tool to remove part of an image. You can manually draw a cropping marquee on the image or specify a size for cropping in the tool options.

Visually cropping an image

Follow these steps to crop an image manually by drawing with the Crop tool:

1. Open the image you want to crop in Photoshop Elements.
2. Select the Crop tool in the toolbox.
3. Draw a marquee on the image with the tool to select the area you want to retain in the image. The area outside what you selected with the Crop tool is darkened, and the cropping marquee area is framed with a dashed line. You also see a check mark and a cancel symbol below the selected area, as shown in Figure 5.6.

Figure 5.6. Select an area with the Crop tool.

> **Inside Scoop**
> Crop large-sized images twice. Roughly crop to reduce the physical size of the image to the approximate area that you want to use, decreasing file size. When you finish editing, re-crop to the final finished size.

4. Drag the handles at the corners and sides of the cropping marquee to size the cropped area as required.
5. Press Enter or click the green check mark to apply the crop to the image.

Quick crops

Instead of drawing a marquee with the Crop tool and then adjusting its dimensions manually, you can specify an aspect ratio and other Crop tool settings in the options bar, shown in Figure 5.7.

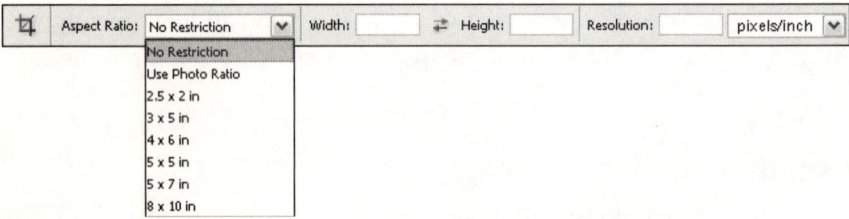

Figure 5.7. Use an aspect ratio for cropping to identify specific cropping sizes.

Click the Aspect Ratio drop-down arrow, and select a setting from the list. Using any defined setting lets you merely click and drag on the image with the Crop tool to display the cropping marquee at the specified size. Your choices include:

- The default choice is No Restriction, which allows you to manually adjust the crop marquee as desired.
- Use Photo Ratio, which sets the ratio for the Crop tool the same as that of the image and automatically adds values in the Width and Height fields on the options bar.

> **Inside Scoop**
> Here are other ways to work with the marqee: Press the Spacebar and drag the marquee to move it; move the cursor outside a corner until you see a double-headed curved arrow, then click and drag to rotate the marquee; double-click inside the marquee to apply the cropping.

Bright Idea

Not sure what you need precisely for a custom size? Pick a size close to what you want and draw the marquee on the image. Its dimensions are shown in the Width and Height fields. Type another value in either field to automatically resize the marquee on the image.

- Select one of the specified sizes, such as 3.5" × 5", which is super for cropping a collection of images that you plan to use in a display of same-sized images.

There are other ways to select sizes as well by specifying values. Options include:

- If you need a specific size that is not included in the list, type values in the Width and Height fields; this size is then defined as a Custom setting.
- If Width and Height values are specified, click the double arrow between the two fields to swap the values.

Changing resolution while cropping

One very neat feature of the Crop tool is the ability to both crop an image and change its resolution at the same time. I use this feature regularly to snip pieces out of high resolution images that I want to distribute online or use on a Web page.

Here's an example, shown in Figure 5.8. The figure shows a closeup of several types of grain. I'd like to have one or two backgrounds for buttons using different grains shown in the image. To create a cropped image using a different resolution follow these steps:

1. Select the Crop tool in the toolbox.
2. Type a Width and Height in the options bar, or choose an existing Aspect Ratio from the list if it is appropriate.
3. Type the desired value in the Resolution field. In the figure, you see the Resolution is set at 72ppi which is fine for online use.

Watch Out!

If you crop and change resolution and then save the image using the original name, you will lose your original image and its information. Save cropped versions using distinct names, or make copies of the original first and then crop them.

4. Click and drag with the tool to create the marquee, also shown in the image. Position the marqee on the image.
5. Press Enter or click the check mark to commit the crop.
6. Save the cropped version of the image with an appropriate name.

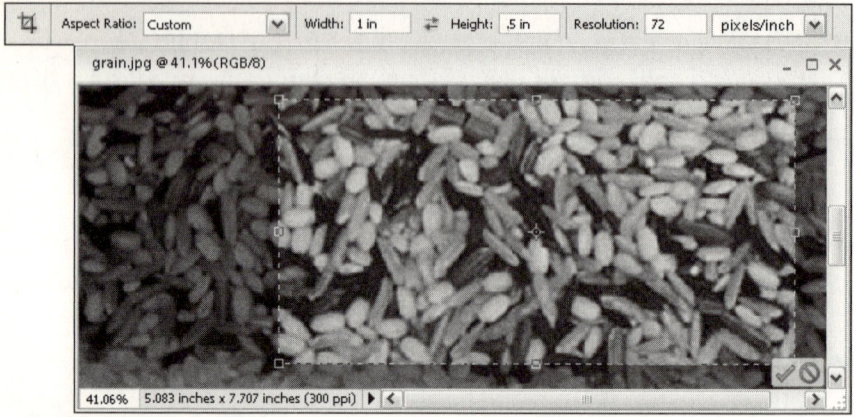

Figure 5.8. Change both resolution and content of an image in one action.

Changing canvas size

The Image Size identifies the dimensions of the image file. The *canvas* is the work surface on which you assemble the components of your image. By default, the Image Size and Canvas Size are the same when you open an image file, but they don't have to remain the same.

Modifying the canvas size

The Canvas Size command lets you add or remove work space around an existing image. You can also use the command to crop an image by decreasing the canvas area.

Follow these steps to adjust the canvas size:

1. Choose Image ⇨ Resize ⇨ Canvas Size to open the Canvas Size dialog box. As with the Image Size dialog box, you can also right-click the top edge of the image window to show the shortcut menu and choose Canvas Size. The dialog box shows the current size and dimensions of your image's canvas.

CHAPTER 5 ▪ SHAPING UP YOUR IMAGES

> **Hack**
> Instead of typing the absolute values in the Height and Width fields, click the Relative check box to set the values at 0 and type the amount of change (increase or decrease) you want for the canvas size in the fields. Negative numbers decrease the size of the canvas; positive values increase the size of the canvas.

2. Type the new Width and/or Height for the canvas in the appropriate fields; click the drop-down arrows to choose a different unit of measurement.

3. Define where the existing image is placed on the new canvas by clicking an Anchor square. For example, if your existing image should be placed at the lower left of a larger canvas, click the lower-left square. You see the arrows on the Anchor illustration change, depending on which square you click.

4. Specify how you want the extra canvas to be colored by choosing an option from the drop-down list shown in Figure 5.9. If your image doesn't contain a background layer, you can't select an extension color.

5. Click OK to dismiss the dialog box and change the canvas size for the image.

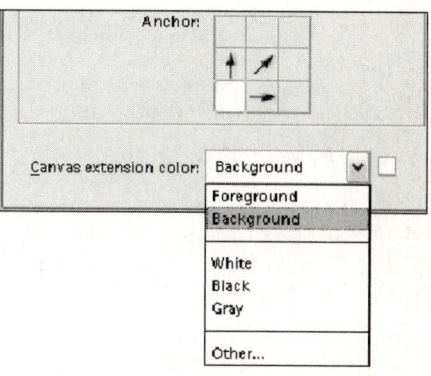

Figure 5.9. Specify where you want the original image placed on the new canvas and the color used for the new canvas area.

Clipping the image

If you specify a smaller size than the original image and canvas size, you see a dialog box telling you that the dimensions will result in clipping, and asking if you want to proceed, shown in Figure 5.10.

Clipping means the image is trimmed to decrease its dimensions depending on its location on the canvas and the amount by which you are decreasing the canvas size. Click Proceed to apply the canvas size change, or click Cancel to dismiss the dialog box without changing the canvas size.

Figure 5.10 shows the Canvas Size dialog box with relative values of -1 in both the Height and Width fields, meaning the image is clipped one inch in both dimensions.

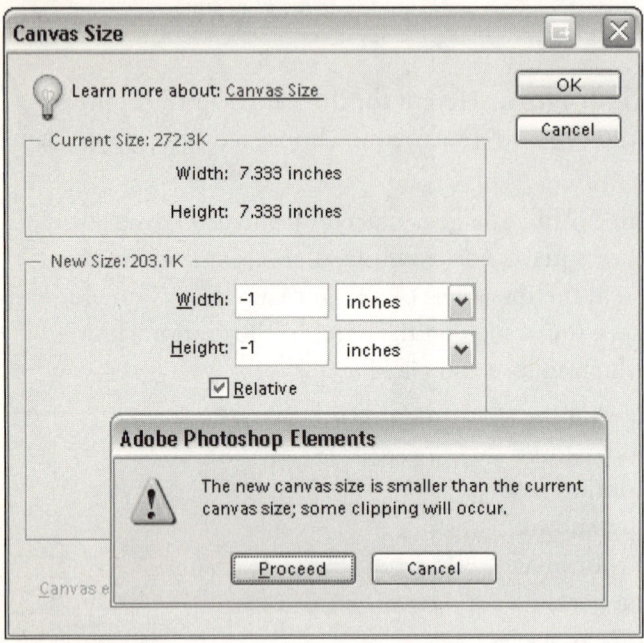

Figure 5.10. When you specify dimensions for the canvas size that are smaller than the image size, Photoshop Elements describes the outcome before trimming the image.

Straightening an image

Sometimes your image's composition looks pretty good, except that you were leaning and objects in the image are off their true axis a bit. Fortunately, you can use the Straighten tool to align objects properly.

Follow these steps to reorient your image:

1. Zoom into an area of the image that is representative of the amount you'd want like to straighten. In Figure 5.11, an area of the building ledge shows how the camera was tilted when the image was captured.

Bright Idea
For some of us, it's important to have a frame of reference. Choose View ⇨ Grid to display the grid overlay on your image. Although you can't use the grid for correction necessarily, you can use it for orienting objects in the image and assessing changes.

2. Select the Straighten tool in the toolbox or press P on the keyboard to activate the tool.

3. Click an area on the image with the tool, and drag to another area of the image to designate the angle for straightening. The path used in the sample image is identified by a large arrow.

4. When the action is applied, zoom out of the image again to see the effect of the tool, shown in Figure 5.12.

Tips for straightening

Here's a very useful tip: if your image looks "wrong" somehow but you can't put your finger on the cause, check to see whether it is slightly crooked. It may not be very obvious, but your eye can pick it up.

Here are some more tips to help when straightening an image:

- In most images, you usually have a selection of areas or elements that you can use as a guide for straightening the image. In Figure 5.11, for example, I could have used one of numerous ledges, frames, or other elements in the buildings.
- When you are trying to straighten an image, use the Straighten tool horizontally

Figure 5.11. Zoom into the image to see the alignment clearly. The arrow in the close up at the top of the image shows the path for the Straighten tool.

Figure 5.12. Use the Straighten tool to correct vertical or horizontal areas in an image.

on the image only. If you drag the tool vertically, you'll flip the image, rather than shifting its axis a degree or two.

- Dragging from left to right has the opposite effect to dragging from right to left. In the example shown in Figure 5.11, the angle and direction of the tool's path are is shown by a large arrow. If the path is drawn the other way, the image is rotated in the opposite direction.

Automatically straightening an image

Rather than zooming in, zooming out, searching for the right angles, and so on, you can automatically straighten and then crop your image in a single step. The results aren't always perfect, but you can save time working with a number of images in many circumstances.

Follow these steps to automatically straighten and crop an image:

1. Open the image in Photoshop Elements.
2. Choose Image ⇨ Rotate ⇨ Straighten and Crop Image. The image is rotated according to an algorithm Photoshop Elements applies to the image.
3. Save the file if the image's modifications are to your liking.

As mentioned, using the automatic features doesn't always work. In Figure 5.11, the image was rotated based on a point of reference chosen visually and the Straighten tool applied manually, with results shown in Figure 5.12. In Figure 5.13, the same figure shows what happens when the automatic feature is used. The image is rotated to align horizontal elements, such as the siding on the building in the background. The image isn't very straight though!

Figure 5.13. Automatically straightening an image may or may not have the desired results.

> **What's the best straighten solution?**
>
> The short answer is that it depends on the contents of the image, and what you are straightening. In my example, straightening manually was the way to go when I wasn't trying to achieve perpendicular lines throughout the image.
>
> On the other hand, if I were assembling a batch of images of buildings for a presentation, I would more likely use an automatic feature to save time because the goal is uniformity rather than artistic sensibility. Also, viewing images in an animated presentation isn't likely to show a slight axis shift like that of the example image.

Adjusting the canvas

Whether the image is straightened using the Straighten tool or using the Straighten and Crop Image menu command, you see blank areas on the edges or sides of the image. You can adjust the canvas separately from the image; if you change the image size, the canvas is adjusted to the new dimensions automatically.

Specify how you want the canvas to behave when the image is adjusted manually to save some steps.

Select the Straighten tool, and then click the drop-down arrow in the options bar, and choose a setting. These are the options:

- **Grow Canvas to Fit.** This option is the default option, and the most useful in many circumstances. The canvas size adjusts automatically to accommodate the larger size of the image when it is rotated, although you see blank areas on each side of the image, like that shown in the left image of Figure 5.14.

- **Crop to Remove Background.** This option produces a cropped image based on the length of the line you draw with the Straighten tool as well as its angle. In the central image of Figure 5.14, you see how much the image is cropped based on the length of the line drawn with the Straighten tool — across the center of the dog's face only.

- **Crop to Original Size.** This option straightens the image within the same size of canvas as that used for the original image, as shown in the right image in Figure 5.14. Use this option if you need to fit an image in a particular location or you only want to use a portion of the image.

The results of the canvas options are shown in Figure 5.14.

 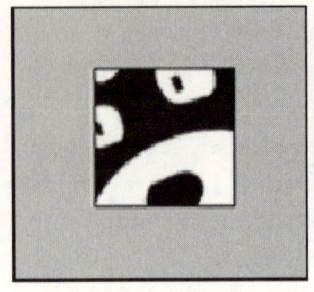 

Figure 5.14. Choose an option for adjusting the canvas when using the Straighten tool. Resize the canvas to the rotated image's size (left), crop and remove the background based on the angle and line length of the Straighten tool (center), or crop the rotated image to fit within the original image's canvas size (right).

Working with shapes

Photoshop Elements offers a number of standard shapes in addition to a large collection of pre-configured shapes that you can use for two different functions.

The available shapes can be used as a drawn shape in your composition, like the quarter-circle shape in the left image in Figure 5.15, or as a template for cutting out an image, such as the quarter-circle shaped crop of the right image in Figure 5.15. (I cover each of these functions in detail later in this chapter.) Although each process uses different options and settings, both draw on the same pool of shapes.

Viewing shapes

Photoshop Elements includes literally hundreds of shapes. To check out the shapes, start by clicking one of two tools. Choose the Cookie Cutter tool to cut the image using a selected shape, like the right image in Figure 15.15 (or use the Q shortcut key). To add a drawn shape to your

Watch Out!
The only Drawing tool that activates the Shapes palette is the Custom Shape tool. Click and hold the displayed Drawing tool to open the submenu, and then click to select the Custom Shape tool.

image, like that in the left image of Figure 15.15, choose the Custom Shape tool (or press the U shortcut key.) When the tool is selected, its options are shown in the options bar on the program window. For either the Custom Shape or Cookie Cutter tool, the Shape command's thumbnail shows the currently selected tool.

Figure 5.15. The same objects can be used both for drawing (as in the left image) and for cutting shapes out of images (as in the right image).

In the Shape palette and menu shown in Figure 5.16, you can organize and view the shapes. You can do these things:

- Click the drop-down arrow to open the palette and view the currently chosen shape collection. In Figure 5.16, the Objects shapes are listed.
- Click to select any shape in the existing list of shapes in the Shapes palette.
- Click the arrow at the right of the Shapes palette to display its menu, a portion of which is also shown in Figure 5.16, and select or deselect shape collections to display on the Shapes palette.
- Choose the layout you want to use to display the shapes — the figure shows the Large List display option.

> **Bright Idea**
> If you are showing all the thumbnails for the shapes, drag the lower-right edge of the Shapes palette to make it larger, showing you more thumbnails at a time.

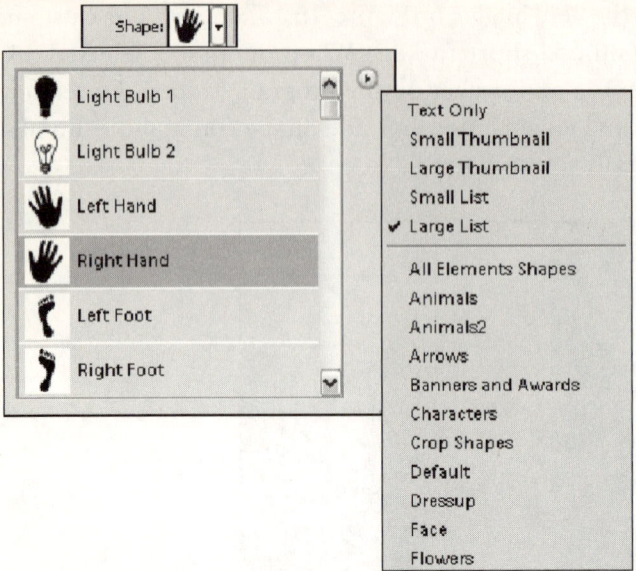

Figure 5.16. Choose the collections and how you want to display the shapes in the menu. The list shown in the figure has been cropped to fit on the page.

Finding the right shape

You have many collections of shapes to choose from for your project. So is it better to have all the shapes showing or just those you want to choose from?

The answer to both questions is "Yes," but for different reasons. If you are new to the program or you aren't sure what sorts of shapes you may be interested in using, show them all. With the Cookie Cutter (or Custom Shape) tool active, click the Shapes drop-down arrow to open the palette, click the spin-down arrow to open the menu, and choose All Elements Shapes.

If you know what shapes you want to work with or you have explored the possibilities and found some likely options, deselect the collections other than the ones you want to work with. This way, you save time scrolling through the Shape palette and redrawing the contents on the screen.

Inside Scoop

When hunting for a shape, I often reset the view in the menu to Large Thumbnails, which enables me to scroll at my leisure. After I have settled on a shape or shapes, I simply deselect the collections.

Cropping into shapes

If you've ever trimmed an image into a custom shape, you have probably used a combination of Selection tools to achieve your goal (Selection tools are described in Chapter 10).

In Photoshop Elements, you can use the prebuilt Shapes as forms for cutting out an image. You can choose from a number of ways to configure the Cookie Cutter as well.

Cutting out a shape

Start your editing process by opening the file you want to use in Photoshop Elements. If you want to cut a shape out of a specific layer, select it in the Layers palette; if not, the Cookie Cutter cuts the entire image into the selected shape. Follow these steps to configure and apply a cutout shape to either an entire image or a selected layer:

1. Click the Cookie Cutter tool in the toolbox to select it. You see its configuration settings display in the options bar.
2. Click the Shape palette's drop-down arrow, and choose your shape. (Refer to the preceding section for details.)
3. Click the Shape Options drop-down arrow, and define how you want the Cookie Cutter to behave. As shown in Figure 5.17, you can use a variety of options.
4. Enter a value in the Feather field if you want the edges of the image to blur rather than appear sharp.

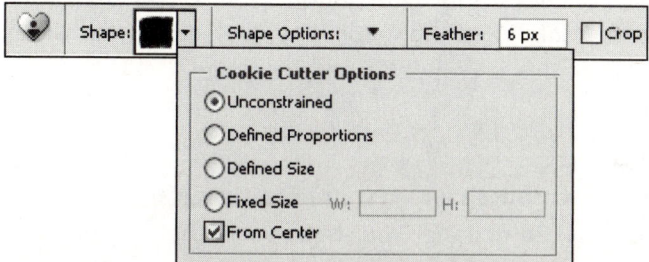

Figure 5.17. Define the Cookie Cutter tool's characteristics for the cutout.

Inside Scoop

If you have multiple layers in your image, be sure to select the layer to which you want to apply the cutout. The Cookie Cutter tool is applied to the active layer even if it isn't visible.

5. Click the image with the tool, and drag in any direction to draw the cutout shape on the image.

6. Release the mouse to finish sizing the shape and delete the content outside the shape's area. The remaining content is displayed within the frame of the selected shape, and the shape is surrounded by a bounding box. Click within the shape and drag to reposition it if required; you see the contents change as the shape is moved.

7. Make adjustments to the shape as necessary.

8. Click the green check mark shown on the options bar, or double-click the image to apply the cutout and deselect the bounding box.

Tips for choosing Cookie Cutter settings

Here are a few ideas to consider as you are working with Cookie Cutter tool shapes:

- Try using the From Center choice in the Cookie Cutter options. The point where you click the image with the tool is the center, rather than an edge, making it easier to estimate the size and location of the shape.

- If you aren't sure whether to use a Cookie Cutter at its default height/width ratio, select Unconstrained from the Shape Options drop-down list. You can see how a constrained version of the image looks by pressing the Shift key.

- If you plan to crop the image after the shape is applied, save yourself one step and click the Crop check box on the options bar when you are configuring the tool. When the shape is applied, content outside the shape's bounding box is cropped from the image.

Adjusting the cutout

After you have drawn the cutout shape on your image, you can modify the shape to your liking. You can't change the shape itself; that is, you can't

Bright Idea
One of the best habits to develop is to use simple shortcuts where possible. Double-clicking the image is much easier than moving the mouse to click an icon on a toolbar.

change a 5-point star to an 8-point star, but you can transform its shape by rotating, scaling, or skewing.

After the shape is drawn, the options bar displays the Transformation tools and information about the shape's size, as shown in Figure 5.18.

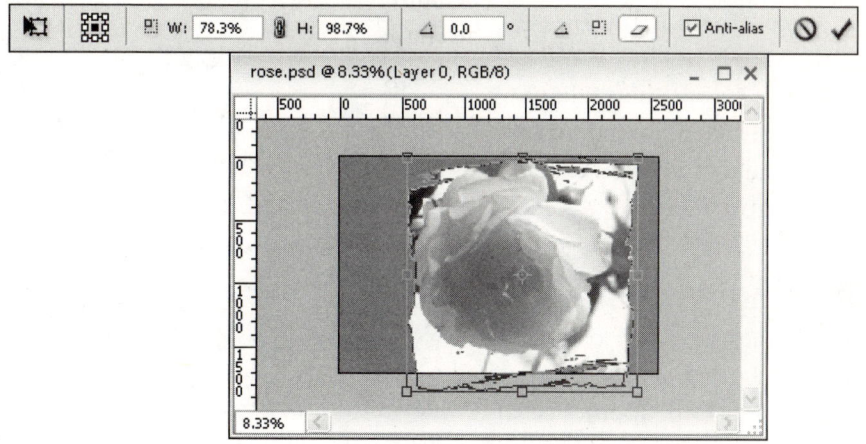

Figure 5.18. Modify the shape before committing the change in your image.

The best way to learn how to work with program features such as cutouts is by experimenting. Here are some configuration tips to get you on your way:

- Drag the edges of the bounding box to resize the shape; drag from within the bounding box to reposition the entire shape over the image.

- Drag from one of the corner resize handles on the bounding box to resize the shape proportionally.

- If you want to modify the shape's characteristics, use the Transformation tools that display on the options bar. Click the Rotate, Scale, or Skew tool to activate it, and then drag the arrows to define the transformation on the shape.

- You can apply more than one shape cutout to an image. For example, apply a frame shape cutout and then apply another cutout shape that removes all but a part of the first cutout. You could use this sort of configuration for a title page or an invitation, such as the example shown in Figure 5.19.

- You don't have to use the entire cutout. For example, if you want to have a decorative edge on only two sides of an image, scale the cutout shape larger than the image size and apply it. Only those areas of the cutout shape that overlay your original image layer are cut away, as you can see in Figure 5.20.

Drawing with shapes

The Shapes palette's objects are used for both cutouts and drawings. Photoshop Elements also includes a set of basic shape tools that you can use in combination with one another or with pre-configured shapes in your image or project. You may want to add a repeating shape behind content or create items such as buttons and menu bars for Web pages (see Figure 5.21).

Use the shape tools to draw lines, rectangles, rounded rectangles, polygons, or ellipses. Shapes are created in shape layers, which can contain one or more shapes depending on the options you choose. Each of the tools has configuration options. Experiment with the different options to see what you like.

Figure 5.19. Use more than one cutout to configure a shape for your project.

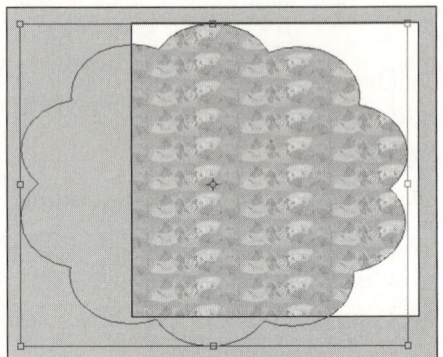

Figure 5.20. The cutout shape doesn't have to match the size of the image.

Watch Out!
You can't step back through any modifications or tweaks you made to the shape after applying it to the image. Instead, you return to the state of the image before you applied the Cookie Cutter tool, and you have to start again.

CHAPTER 5 ▪ SHAPING UP YOUR IMAGES

For example, suppose that you want to add a rounded rectangle shape to use under a block of text. Follow these steps to select the tool and options and add the shape to your image:

1. Click the existing shape tool in the toolbox, and then click the Rounded Rectangle tool in the options bar. The rounded rectangle is shown at the far left of the option bar, indicating that it is the active tool.

2. Click the drop-down arrow next to the Custom Shape tool's icon to open a list of options, shown in Figure 5.22, and described in Table 5.1.

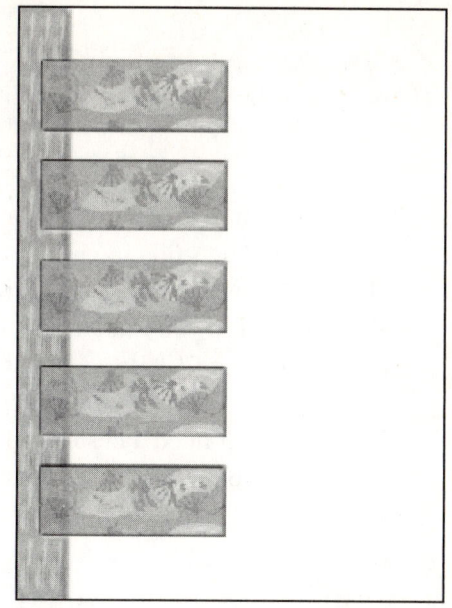

Figure 5.21. Simple shapes can be used for buttons or menu bars.

(Figure 5.22 is a composite. In the real world, you can't display more than one drop-down menu at a time.)

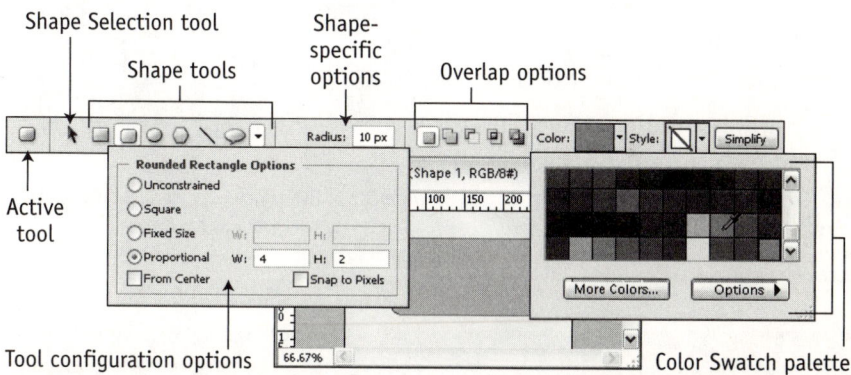

Figure 5.22. Choose and configure shape tools and settings in the options bar.

3. Choose the options and settings you want for your shape.

4. Click the Radius field, and type a value for the curve on the corners of the rectangle. This option isn't available with all tools, of course.

>
> **Watch Out!**
> If you want to apply a Cookie Cutter cutout to a vector drawing layer, you have to simplify the layer first by converting it to a bitmap layer. Read more about layers in Chapters 10 and 11.

5. The color swatch shows the existing foreground color that is used for the rectangle's fill. To choose a different color, click the drop-down arrow next to the color swatch to open a simple palette and choose a color. If you want a custom color, click More Colors to open the Color Picker. Choose your custom color, and click OK to close the Color Picker and change the foreground color. Save an extra click if you know you need a custom color. Click the visible color in the color swatch to go directly to the Color Picker, bypassing the Color Swatches palette.

6. Click the image with your configured tool, and drag to add the rounded rectangle. When you release the mouse, the shape is complete.

7. The finished simple shape is added to the image, shown in Figure 5.23. In the Layers palette, the rectangle is added to a new layer called Shape 1.

If you want to move or adjust the shape's position on the canvas, click the Shape Selection tool in the options bar and click the shape to select it.

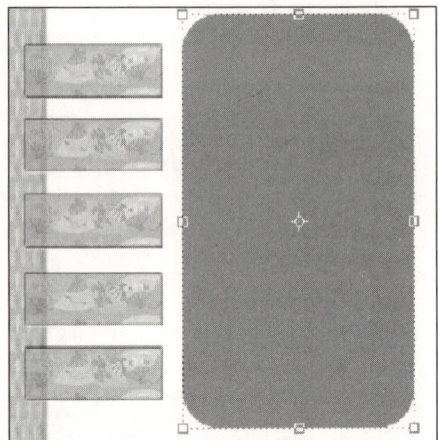

Figure 5.23. Use simple shapes such as rounded rectangles as backgrounds for other content on the image.

Table 5.1. Configuration options for shape tools

Option	Setting	For These Tools
Unconstrained	Height and width are based on how you drag the tool.	Rectangle, Rounded Rectangle, Ellipse
Square	Constrains a rectangle to a square.	Rectangle, Rounded Rectangle

Option	Setting	For These Tools
Circle	Constrains an ellipse to a circle.	Ellipse
Fixed Size	Draws the shape using the values typed in the Height and Width fields.	Rectangle, Rounded Rectangle, Ellipse
From Center	Draws the shape from the center outward.	Rectangle, Rounded Rectangle, Ellipse
Proportional	Draws a proportional shape using the values you type in the Width and Height fields.	Rectangle, Rounded Rectangle, Ellipse
Snap to Pixels	Snaps edges of a rectangle to the pixel boundaries.	Rectangle, Rounded Rectangle
Radius	Specifies the distance from the center of a polygon to the outer points.	Polygon
Smooth Corners	Renders a polygon with smooth corners.	Polygon
Star	Turns a polygon into a star.	Polygon
Indent Sides By	Specifies the depth of the star's indentations.	Polygon
Smooth Indents	Renders a star-shaped polygon with smooth indents.	Polygon
Sides	Specifies the number of sides in a polygon.	Polygon
Arrowheads Start and End	Renders a line with arrowheads. Select Start, End, or both to specify on which end of the line arrows are rendered. The shape options appear in the pop-up dialog box.	Line
Arrowheads Width and Length	Specifies the proportions of the arrowhead as a percentage of the line width (10% to 1000% for Width, and 10% to 5000% for Length).	Line
Concavity	Defines the amount of curvature on the widest part of the arrowhead, where the arrowhead meets the line. Enter a value for the concavity of the arrowhead (from -50% to +50%).	Line
Weight	Determines the width of a line in pixels.	Line

Selecting and transforming shapes

You can adjust drawn shapes in a number of ways. First, select the drawn shape using the Shape Selection tool, identified on Figure 5.22.

When you click the shape with the tool, you see it framed by a set of points and curves and a center anchor. The number of points and curves depends on the drawn shape. Rectangles and ellipses have four points and four curves; a line has two points and one curve, a custom shape varies according to the selected shape, and so on.

You can select and transform an image layer in the same ways as the methods used for transforming shapes. Either click to select the image layer in the Layers palette, or select the Move tool in the toolbox and click the image with the tool.

Quick transformations

After you select the shape, drag it to reposition it on the page. You can transform the shape quickly in the following ways:

- Drag a square on one of the sides of the image to increase or decrease its height or width.
- Drag one of the corner squares to increase or decrease the size of the shape proportionally.
- Move the pointer away from one of the corners until you see the curved double-ended arrow pointer, and then drag to rotate the shape.

Common transform commands

The program commands for transforming an image, drawing, or Custom Shape are listed in the Image menu. Most of the commands are the same whether you are applying the change to an image or a drawing.

You have these choices of commands:

- Select Image ⇨ Rotate, and then choose one of several commands for rotating, flipping, or straightening the selected image or layer.
- Select Image ⇨ Transform, and then select the Skew, Distort, or Perspective command.
- Select Image ⇨ Resize ⇨ Scale.

Inside Scoop
My strong preference is to use the shortcut key for activating the Free Transform command. You don't have to choose any commands, and it doesn't matter whether you are selecting with the Shape Selection tool or the Move tool.

Unless you need a specific setting, such as specifying a rotation value numerically or flipping an image or shape, or you need to use the Perspective or Distort commands, use the Free Transform Shape command to save lots of time selecting and clicking menu items.

Access the Free Transform command in these ways:

- Click a shape with the Shape Selection tool, right-click to open the shortcut menu, and choose Free Transform Shape, shown in Figure 5.24.

- Select a shape or image with the Move tool, and then choose Image ⇨ Transform ⇨ Free Transform.

- Select a shape or image with the Move tool, and then use the shortcut keys Ctrl+T.

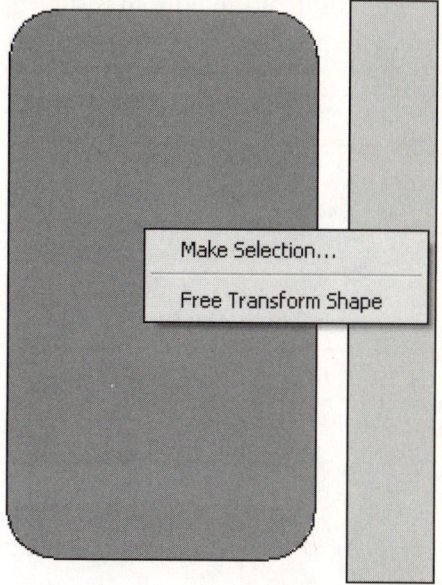

Figure 5.24. The Shape Selection tool lets you access transform commands from the shortcut menu.

Using transformation commands

Whether you choose the commands from the menus or apply them using pointers on the image activated by the Free Transform command, the best way to understand how the different processes work is to use them.

To assist you, Figure 5.25 shows examples of how the different transformations can be applied. From left to right and top to bottom, the images in the figure are as follows:

- The image before modification is shown at the upper left.
- The image rotated 30 degrees is shown at the upper right.
- The image scaled 50 percent smaller in width and 25 percent smaller in height is shown in the middle left image.
- The image skewed left horizontally and downward vertically is shown in the middle right image.

- The image distorted with the left edge upward and the right edge downward is seen in the lower-left image.
- Perspective added by decreasing the width at the top and increasing the width at the bottom is shown in the lower-right image.

After you have made a modification, double-click the selection to apply the changes.

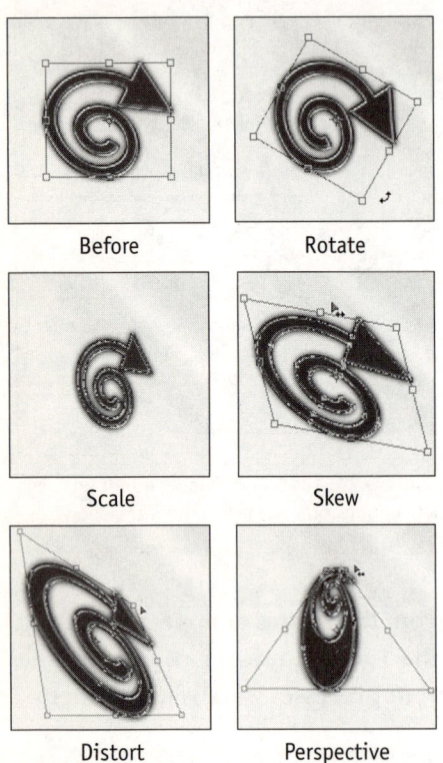

Figure 5.25. Use the transformation commands to modify the appearance of a shape or image.

 **Hack**

If you are going to use multiple transformations, start with the resize and rotate actions because you don't have to select menu commands. After you have made basic changes, you see all the transformations listed when you open the shortcut menu.

Combining multiple shapes in one layer

You can use several shapes in the same layer and combine them in a number of ways. I use this method to create some quick and swanky shapes such as a set of intersecting rectangles for the background shown in Figure 5.26.

You can work faster and more efficiently by adding more shapes to the same shape layer. The combination shape becomes one unit, which is simpler for moving on the canvas or applying a color, a style, or effects.

Figure 5.26. Simple repeating shapes can make an attractive background for an image.

Follow these steps to add and configure multiple shapes in the same shape layer:

1. Create the first shape, or select a shape layer in the Layers palette.
2. Select the shape tool you want to use for the second shape.
3. Select an option for overlapping the shapes on the image.
4. Drag in the image to add the new shape, and continue adding other shapes if you like, as shown in Figure 5.27.

Of course, if you want to add more shapes, you need to repeat these steps. Remember to select how the shapes should overlap, as noted in Step 3. Choose from four options (see Figure 5.28):

- **Add.** This overlap setting adds the new shape to an existing shape, shown in the left example.
- **Subtract.** This setting removes the area where the shapes overlap and works opposite to the Add overlap option. The second example from the left shows the Subtract setting.
- **Intersect.** This setting shows only the area where the shapes have been overlapped; the rest of the areas are removed as shown in the second image from the right.
- **Exclude.** Use this setting to remove the overlapped area as seen in the right image; this is the opposite effect to the Intersect option.

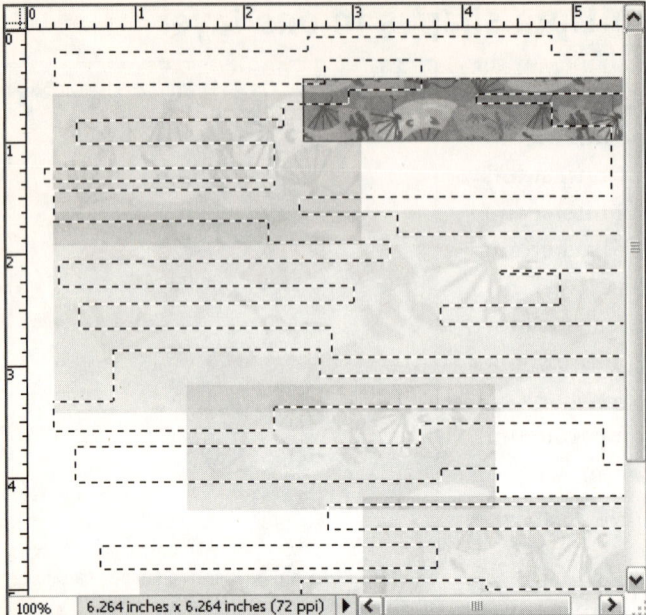

Figure 5.27. Draw and overlap multiple shapes on the same layer to save time.

In Figure 5.28, you can see how the different overlap settings affect two objects. The first shape is a polygon; the cloud shape is added to all images using different overlap methods.

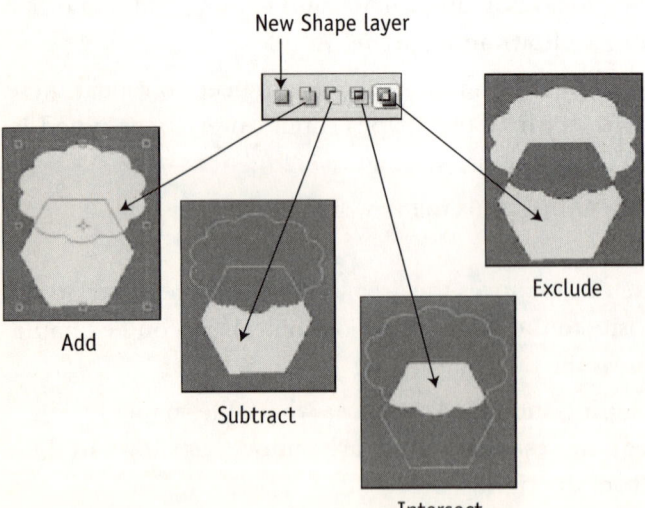

Figure 5.28. Choose an overlap method before drawing the second and subsequent shapes.

CHAPTER 5 ▪ SHAPING UP YOUR IMAGES   137

Inside Scoop
Here's the way I keep the various overlap options straight — the Add and Subtract are opposites of one another and refer to the existing shapes while the Intersect and Exclude settings are also opposite and refer to the overlapped areas.

Just the facts

- Files can be modified based on pixel dimensions, image dimensions, and resolution.
- Alter the canvas on which the image's layers are applied by changing sizes, straightening, or cropping.
- Select, configure, and apply pre-configured shapes as cropping objects in an image.
- Use pre-configured shapes and basic shapes as drawn vector objects in an image.
- Select shapes or images and visually transform their dimensions in several ways.

GET THE SCOOP ON...
■ Using the Color Picker for precise color ■ Setting default colors in the program ■ Saving and editing color swatches ■ Filling shapes or layers with color ■ Adding patterns or gradients ■ Creating your own patterns and gradients

Color Inside the Lines

If you think of a grassy meadow on a sunny day, a big bowl of berries, or a "Welcome Home" banner, one of the first descriptions you think about is the color. Understandably, color is a significant topic in Photoshop Elements.

You can choose and apply color in a number of ways. For convenience, you can use a palette of color swatches to quickly pick from a standard selection of colors. If you need a custom color, on the other hand, specify the custom color from a continuous-tone display or define the color using different color models. Custom colors can be specified for either the foreground or background of an image.

You can color any shape you draw or text you type in Photoshop Elements. Instead of adding a solid color to a shape, apply a number of colors that blend together, called a *gradient*.

Many of the book's chapters deal with color in some regard, whether it is adjusting the color of shadows and highlights, which is covered in Chapter 8; adding text to an image, which is discussed in Chapter 17; or learning how to calibrate a monitor to display the same colors as those printed, which is described in Chapter 9.

Setting foreground and background colors

The foreground color is applied to any new element, text, or painting you add to an image. To change the color, use the Eyedropper tool or click the foreground color to open the Color Picker.

The color defined as the background color is used for filling deleted content on the Background layer or in a flattened image, that is, one that has no transparent layers. The background color can be specified as the background color for a new image or an extended canvas, or even show in areas where you use the Eraser tool on your image. Read about flattened and layered images in Chapter 11, and see how the Eraser tool works in Chapter 18.

Changing color swatches

Color swatches of the foreground and background colors are shown in the toolbox and shown in Figure 6.1. Here's what you can do in the toolbox:

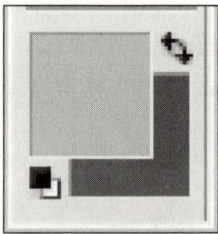

Figure 6.1. Specify foreground and background colors used by default.

- Click either the foreground color swatch on the left or the background color swatch on the right to open the Color Picker to choose a custom color.
- Click the double-ended arrow to the right of the swatches to swap colors, making the current foreground color the background, and vice versa.
- Click the black/white icon at the lower left of the swatches (or press the D key) to reset the color swatches to their default black foreground and white background.

Changing color in the toolbox

You can use the Eyedropper tool to sample color directly from the document window to change the color in the toolbox, rather than clicking

Bright Idea

Instead of using the Eyedropper tool as the cursor, press Caps Lock on your keyboard to convert the shape of the cursor to a circle and crosshairs cursor. Identifying the area you are sampling is easier with the circle if you aren't familiar with the program.

a color swatch to open the Color Picker and then using the Eyedropper tool.

Follow these steps to pick custom background and foreground colors, starting with the color you want to specify for the background:

1. Select the Eyedropper tool in the toolbox.

2. Move the mouse over the image to locate the color you want to use and click the mouse. The sampled color is shown in the toolbox as the foreground color swatch, shown in Figure 6.2.

3. Click the double-ended arrow to swap the background and foreground colors.

4. Repeat Steps 1 and 2 to sample the image again, this time selecting the foreground color.

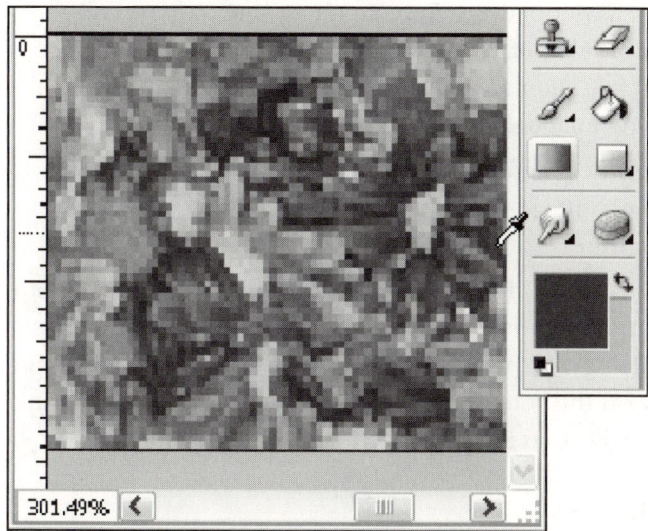

Figure 6.2. Use the Eyedropper tool to select foreground and background colors from an image.

Defining color using models

Color is identified numerically using different methods called *color models*. Photoshop Elements uses two models — one based on human perception of color and the other on a computer monitor's perception of color.

What we see

A human eye perceives color using three descriptions called Hue, Saturation, and Brightness (HSB) color. In Photoshop Elements HSB color can be used for choosing colors, but you can't use the color model for editing images.

The Color Picker in Photoshop Elements displays color using the HSB color model:

- **Hue.** Objects have a color, known as *hue*, whether we are talking about grass green or honey yellow. An object's color is measured in degrees from 0 to 360 on a color wheel, like the ones you see in your local paint store. The color spectrum flows around a color wheel from red through yellow and green to blues and finally back to reds.
- **Saturation.** The strength of a color is its *saturation*. Saturation, also known as *chroma*, is defined as a percentage of hue to gray. Fully saturated color has a value of 100 percent, meaning the color you see contains no gray; *desaturated* color is pure gray with a value of 0 percent, meaning the image shows only gray and no color tint.
- **Brightness.** Brightness defines the lightness or darkness of a color measured as a percentage — from 0 percent brightness (or black) to 100 percent brightness (or white).

Hue extends from left to right across the HSB color graph from 0 to 360 degrees. Saturation is shown vertically in the graph, from 0 percent at the bottom of the graph to 100 percent at the top of the graph. Brightness is shown on the color bar to the right of the graph, extending from 0 percent at the bottom to 100 percent at the top of the bar.

What the monitor sees

Computer monitors display color based on displays of red, blue, and green (RGB) colored light using a visible light spectrum. Most of the colors we see — and all those shown by a computer monitor — are created by mixing red, green, and blue light. The three colors of light are called *additive primaries:* If all three are mixed at full intensity, the light is white.

Each color of light is shown with an intensity numbering from 0 to 255; the lower the value is, the less intense the color of light. White, for example, has an RGB value of 255/255/255, while black has an RGB value of 0/0/0.

If you mix two colors of light together, you see cyan, magenta, or yellow. These three colors are called *subtractive primaries*, meaning that each is made up of two of the three colors of light. Of course, the image is shown in grayscale on the page, but you can see the relationships among the intersecting colors.

Color separations, which are separate plates sent to a printer for color printing, use a color model called CMYK. The CMYK model is based on the subtractive primaries plus black (called K in the acronym). Photoshop Elements doesn't support CMYK.

Working in the Color Picker

Choose a color based on color model values, or select a color visually in the Color Picker, which is shown in Figure 6.3. You access the Color Picker by clicking a color swatch in many locations in the program, including: Windows, dialog boxes, Option bars, and palettes.

To pick a color for a specific purpose, such as coloring text or changing part of a gradient, follow these steps:

1. Click either the Foreground or Background color swatches in the toolbox to open the Color Picker, and select a basic foreground or background color in the program. In Adobe Color Picker, the color array is laid out in a spectrum like that used to display HSB color.

2. Click a color to select it from one of the spectrum displays. You can also enter the color value numbers, or you can type the actual hexadecimal number for a Web color in the # field.

3. Click OK to close the dialog box and apply the color.

Tweaking a color choice

Suppose you know that you want a color that is a "perfect" shade of orange. You can define "perfect" in quite a few ways, both visually and numerically. Depending on the type of person you are, you may prefer to use visual methods to pick colors, or you may want to rely more on color numbers.

View the color graph and color bar in a different way by clicking one of the color values. Each color value shows a corresponding color spectrum graph, as well as different content in the continuum slider:

- **Hue (H).** The default Color Picker display shows the Hue for a selected color, and the color bar shows the full spectrum of colors on the color wheel.
- **Saturation (S).** Adjust the saturation by dragging the slider on the color bar up to make the color more intense or down to make the color less intense. In the color graph, the indicator circle remains stationary while the saturation percentage increases or decreases at that point, depending on which way you move the slider.
- **Brightness (B).** Drag the slider on the color bar up to make the color brighter or down to make the color darker. In the color graph, the indicator circle remains stationary as the entire graph is darkened or lightened.
- **Red (R).** The red end of the color spectrum is shown in the color graph with the orange color identified. The color bar shows a segment of the color spectrum that includes the selected orange color. Drag the slider on the color bar to move through yellow to green; click on the color graph to select an orange that is more red, yellow, or magenta in color.
- **Green (G).** The green end of the color spectrum is shown in the color graph with the orange color identified. The color bar shows a segment of the color spectrum from yellow to red, which includes the selected orange. Drag the slider on the color bar to move through yellow or red tones. Click a color on the color graph that is more green, cyan, or magenta in color.
- **Blue (B).** The color graph shows the orange color with some of the blue end of the color spectrum. Because blue and orange are opposites on the color wheel, only a limited number of blue tones are shown on the color graph. Drag the slider on the color bar to move through orange and magenta tones.

Defining specific color values

Colors in the Color Picker can be defined using HSB, RGB, or hexadecimal color, which is a simple model used for defining Web colors. Each different color model has its own method of defining colors numerically by assigning values to the model's components. To define an RGB color, for example, you need to specify a color value for each of the red (R), green (G), and blue (B) components of the model in the corresponding fields.

For example, you can select the same bright orange color in three ways, as shown in Figure 6.3.

- Type **36/100/100** in the H/S/B fields.
- Type **255/153/0** in the R/G/B fields.
- Type **ff9900** in the # field to show the hexadecimal color.

As you make adjustments in one set of fields or click another area on the color display, note how the different color models' values change automatically.

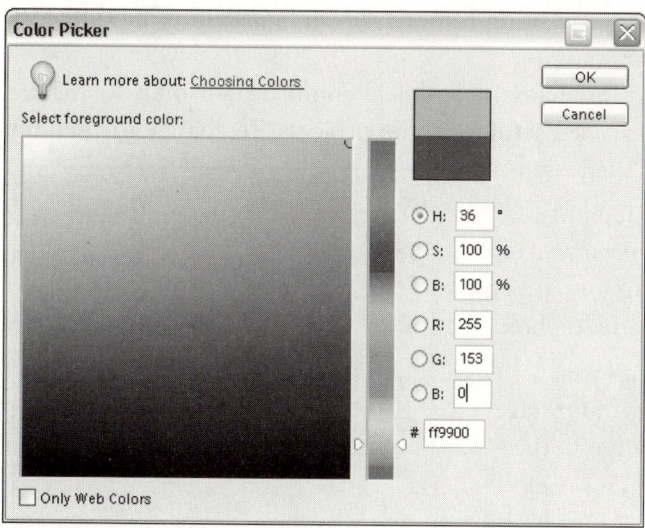

Figure 6.3. Choose colors in different ways in the Color Picker.

Looking for colors

Finding the perfect color for a graphic element to accompany an image can be frustrating. But when you find that just-right color, it's like the sun coming out on a cloudy day.

Aside from typing values in the color models' value fields, you can identify colors in the Color Picker in these other ways:

- Click anywhere inside the color graph to show the color and its values in the appropriate fields. Compare the new color you clicked to the previous color picked; both colors are shown in the swatches to the right of the color bar.

- Drag the color slider on the color bar up or down to display varying color ranges in the color graph.

- Click at an approximate location on the color bar to show the general range of color in which you are interested.

Using a different Color Picker

Photoshop Elements uses the Adobe Color Picker by default, but you can also use the Windows Color Picker or others you may have installed on your computer. For some people, using the same Color Picker regardless of which program they are using is more convenient than using different ones in different programs.

The Windows Color dialog box is less sophisticated than its Adobe counterpart, but it can be useful for some projects. To change the default Color Picker, follow these steps:

1. In Photoshop Elements, choose Edit ⇨ Preferences to open the General panel of the Preferences dialog box.

2. Click the Color Picker drop-down arrow, and select Windows to change to the Windows Color Picker. If you have other color pickers installed on your system, they are also listed in the drop-down menu.

3. Click OK to close the dialog box and set the preference. Now when you click a color swatch, the Color Picker you've chosen as your new default opens, as shown in Figure 6.4.

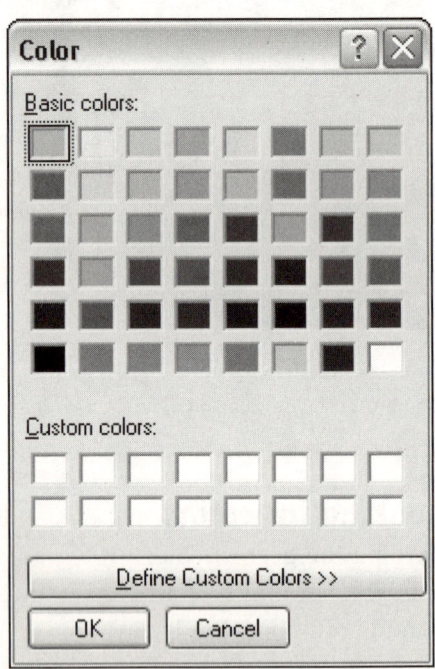

Figure 6.4. The Window Color Picker shows 48 basic colors when you open the Color dialog box.

Adding custom colors

To choose and add a custom color to the Color dialog box, follow these steps:

1. Click a color swatch anywhere in Photoshop Elements to open the default Color dialog box.

2. Click Define Custom Colors to open the expanded view of the dialog box, as shown in Figure 6.5.

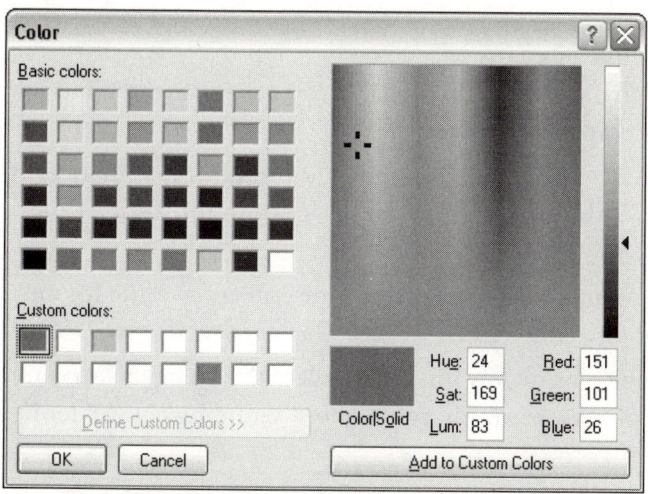

Figure 6.5. Specify custom colors in the expanded view of the dialog box.

3. Select the custom color. You can do this a variety of ways:

- Click the color spectrum graph in the general area of the color you want to define to start choosing your color.
- Drag the slider at the far right of the dialog box to increase or decrease the luminance of the color.
- Type values in the different fields on the dialog box instead of selecting a location on the spectrum graph.

Watch Out!
Color produced by the Windows Color Picker is not identical to that defined by the Adobe Color Picker, in spite of using the same RGB values.

>  **Inside Scoop**
> The Windows Color Picker can be too restrictive, so after using it for a specific project, I always switch back to the Adobe Color Picker.

4. Click Add to Custom Colors to fill one of the swatches in the Custom colors area of the dialog box.
5. Click OK to close the dialog box.

Windows Color dialog box tips

Here are some tips that can come in handy if you are using the Windows Color dialog box as your Color Picker:

- The Windows Color dialog box uses Hue/Saturation/Luminance instead of Hue/Saturation/Brightness as shown in the Adobe Color Picker. They are the same color model.
- You don't have an option for specifying a hexadecimal value for an image designed for online use.
- You can't sample color on any images to select the color, as you can in the Adobe Color Picker (read more about sampling color later in the chapter).
- You can define which swatch is used by a custom color. Notice in Figure 6.3 that there are custom colors scattered throughout the swatches. Before you start configuring a new color, click the swatch in the Custom colors area to select it; when you define the color and click Add to Custom Colors, the selected swatch is used.
- You don't see any comparison of colors in the Windows Color dialog box like those seen in the Adobe Color Picker, nor is there an out of gamut indicator.
- Reopen the Edit ⇨ Preferences ⇨ General dialog box to switch back to the Adobe Color Picker, or use another color picker.

Choosing Web colors

The Color Picker has a number of features specifically designed to make it simpler to choose colors for online use. As mentioned earlier, you can type a hexadecimal value for a color into the # field on the Color Picker.

Web safe colors are a uniform group of 218 colors that can be viewed correctly regardless of browser or operating system. If you are looking for colors to use online and want them to be Web safe, the Color Picker offers some assistance:

- If you choose a color that isn't a Web safe color, you see an indicator next to the color samples at the upper right of the Color Picker, shown in Figure 6.6. Click the indicator, and the Color Picker selects the closest Web safe color.

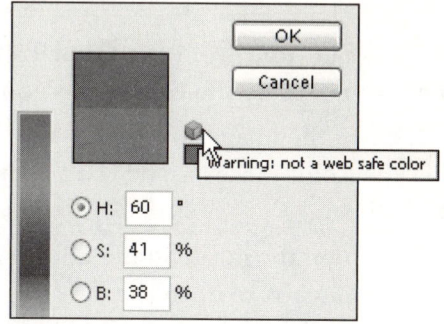

Figure 6.6. You can force a color to its closest Web safe color.

- Instead of picking colors at random or typing a hexadecimal value for a Web color, click Only Web Colors at the lower left of the Color Picker as shown in Figure 6.7. You see the color spectrum graph simplify to display just the Web safe colors. To quickly change the display, click the basic color range you want to choose from in the vertical continuum to the right of the color spectrum graph.

You can read more about working with color in indexed color images and using color tables in Chapter 22.

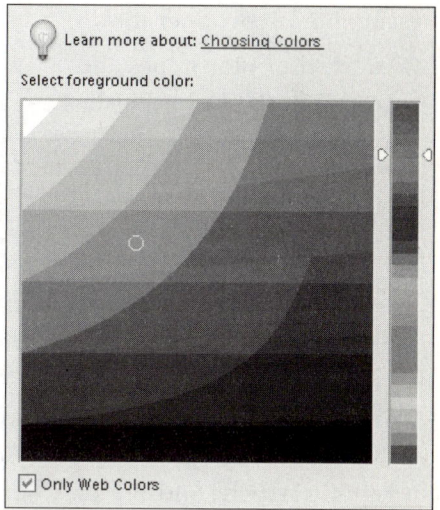

Figure 6.7. Pick from just the Web safe colors by changing the color spectrum view.

Selecting a color from an image

One of the best features of the Color Picker is the ability to pick, or *sample*, a color directly from an image. Sampling the correct color for a graphic such as a frame around an image is so much easier than trying to match a color sample to what you hope is the image's color.

Hack

You can configure the Eyedropper tool in several ways depending on the purpose of the samples and what is best for the way you work. Read more about setting Eyedropper tool options in Chapter 8.

You can work from the Color Picker to sample a color in an image rather than using the Eyedropper tool. Follow these steps:

1. Open the image you want to use for sampling color before opening the Color Picker — you can't open an image while the Color Picker is open.

2. Position the image in the Editor window and click a color swatch in the toolbox to open the Color Picker.

3. Move the mouse over the image to automatically activate the Eyedropper tool.

4. Watch the color values and sample in the Color Picker as you move the mouse. Click where you would like the sample of the color.

5. The color is selected in the Color Picker's color graph and displayed in the color values, shown in Figure 6.8.

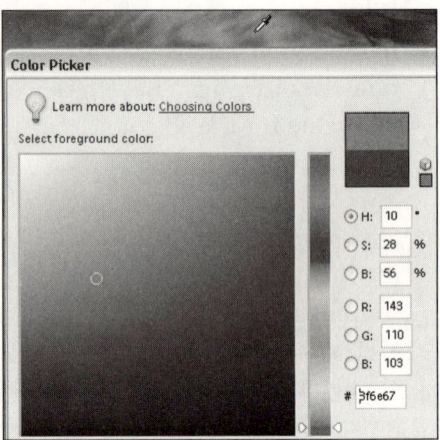

Figure 6.8. Sample color directly from the image to display its values in the Color Picker.

You can't open or close images while the Color Picker is open, but if you want to see your image more closely to sample its color, use the shortcut keys Ctrl+ (Ctrl and the plus sign) to zoom in or Ctrl- (Ctrl and the minus sign) to zoom out. You can also reposition the image using the vertical and horizontal scrollbars.

Working with swatch libraries

You are bound to ask yourself these three questions at some point in your Photoshop Elements experience:

1. Isn't there a simpler way to pick basic purple or green than specifying a custom color?
2. Do I have to keep picking custom colors when I am working with a number of them?
3. What if I want to use a set of colors in a different program or on a different computer?

Regardless of which of these three questions you ask, the answer is the same: Use Swatches instead of the Color Picker. Choose Window ➪ Color Swatches to open the palette, or click any color swatch used in a tool, such as one of the brushes or the Text tool to display the Color Swatches shown in Figure 6.9.

The Color Swatches palette shows one of the swatch libraries installed as part of the Photoshop Elements program; you can display more than one library if you like. Photoshop Elements offers seven palettes, described in Table 6.1.

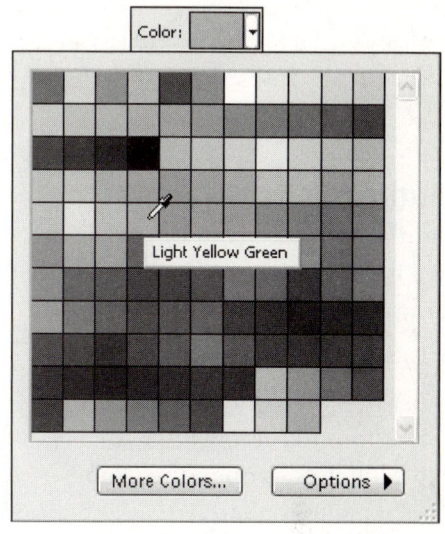

Figure 6.9. Common colors are listed in the Default color swatch, one of the available color libraries.

Table 6.1. Available color swatch libraries

Library	Palette Contents
Default	Common colors, including primary, secondary, and tertiary colors and shades of gray.
Mac OS	256 basic colors used in Mac OS; the color table runs from Black to White.
Photo Filter Colors	Colors available from the Photo Filter.
Web Hues	Colors shown on a Web page arranged in the library in order of hue.
Web Safe Colors	216 colors used on both Mac OS and Windows that display predictably on Web pages.

continued

Table 6.1. *continued*

Library	Palette Contents
Web Spectrum	Colors shown on a Web page arranged in the library ordered by location on the color wheel.
Windows	256 basic colors used in Windows; the color table runs from White to Black.

Adding color swatches

Add a color to any of the existing color libraries. How you add the color is a matter of personal working style and what you are viewing in the program. Follow these steps:

1. Sample or create a new foreground color.
2. Choose Window ⇨ Color Swatches to open the Color Swatches palette.
3. Move the mouse over a blank area of the palette. If there is blank space on the palette, the cursor changes to a paint bucket, shown in Figure 6.10. Click to open the Color Swatch Name dialog box, type a name for the color, and click OK to add it to the palette.

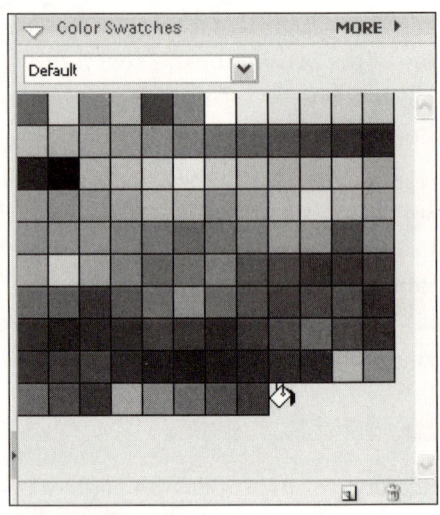

Figure 6.10. Add custom colors to your Color Swatches palette.

Hack

The Color Swatch library files are stored at this path: Program Files/Adobe/ Photoshop Elements/ Presets/Color Swatches. New libraries that you create or import are shown in the Color Swatches menu if you store them in the correct folder.

CHAPTER 6 ▪ COLOR INSIDE THE LINES

Bright Idea
You don't have to state the obvious when naming a color. Instead, if I construct a palette for a job, I often name a color according to its use in a particular project, such as "border edge" instead of dark blue.

There are other ways to add color to the Color Swatches palette depending on what you are working with in the program, such as:

- If you prefer, or if the palette displays only a portion of the color swatches, click New Swatch at the bottom of the Color Swatches palette to add the swatch to the end of the existing palette. Double-click the swatch to open the Color Swatch Name dialog box, shown in Figure 6.11, type a name for the color, and click OK.

- If the Color Swatches panel is already open, select the Eyedropper tool and pick a color from your image; follow Step 3 to add the custom color to the Color Swatches.

- If the Color Swatches panel is already open, click More to open the menu and choose New Swatch to open the Color Swatch Name dialog box. Type a name for the new color, and add the foreground color to the panel.

Figure 6.11. Add and name additional colors to your Color Swatches when the palette is open.

Deleting color swatches

Some colors may not be ones that you ever use. You can remove colors from an existing library, for example, in preparation for saving a custom library. Drag the color from the swatches to the Delete icon (the trashcan) at the bottom of the palette. A confirmation dialog box opens, asking if you really want to delete the color. Click OK to close the dialog box and remove the color from the library.

Watch Out!

New colors are saved in the Preferences file so that they persist between editing sessions. If the Preferences file is deleted, so are the custom colors. To permanently save a color, save it in a library.

Managing color swatch libraries

The Default color palette is sufficient for many Photoshop Elements users. But for other users, creating custom color swatch libraries can save time and confusion. For example, if you are a Web designer, your clients likely require custom color palettes as part of their product branding and marketing. Creating a color swatch library file that you use for each client can be an efficient way to keep track of colors.

Saving new libraries

You aren't limited to the number of palette library files provided by Photoshop Elements. You can save new color swatch library files by:

- Adding or removing color swatches in an existing library in the Color Swatches palette. The program asks if you want to save the palette.
- Clicking the More button on the Color Swatches palette to open the menu, and choosing Save Swatches.

In either case, the Save dialog box opens; name the file and save it. A new color swatch library file is stored in its default location on your hard drive with the other color swatch palette files, using the default Color Swatches ACO file format.

Perhaps you have deleted several gray shades or swapped some of the blues for more brown shades in a default color swatch library. If the colors are a palette that you use regularly, save the file using its default name. Otherwise, save it with a logical name, such as the project you are working on or your client's name, like the one I used in Figure 6.12.

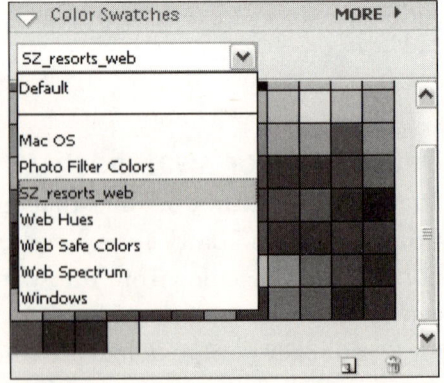

Figure 6.12. Saved custom color swatch libraries are included in the palette's menu.

Bright Idea

Some people like to see what they are working with clearly. If you are that sort of person, delete colors you never use from the color swatch library, leaving only those that appeal to you. It takes a few minutes, but finding the color you want is easier later.

A custom color palette that you create and save isn't shown in the program until you close and reopen Photoshop Elements.

To replace the current swatch library with a different library, choose Replace Swatches from the More menu in the Preset Manager and select a library file.

Resetting a library

If you change one of the libraries by mistake, you can reset it to its original configuration. Follow these steps, working from the Color Swatches palette:

1. Click More on the Color Swatches palette, and choose Preset Manager from the menu.
2. In the Preset Manager dialog box, click More to open its menu and choose Reset Swatches.
3. Click Done, and your colors are reset.

What's in a color swatch?

Photoshop Elements can use three file types as color swatch libraries. The basic swatch files are in the Swatches format, which is an Adobe COlor (ACO) file.

A collection of color swatches that you create and save, such as indexed color or for storing custom colors, is saved as an Adobe Color Table (ACT) file.

You can exchange color swatches with Adobe CS2 application users, or load an Adobe CS2 application's custom color palette when it is saved in the Adobe Swatch Exchange (ASE) format. ASE files can store and exchange basic color swatches only, not tints, gradients, or mixed inks that may be created in an program such as InDesign CS2.

Fills

The appearance applied to the inside of the shape is its *fill*. There are several different types of fill, including color, gradients, and patterns. Applying a single color is called a *solid fill*. You use much the same methods for applying fills to objects that you do to layers. Read about using layers in Chapters 11 and 12.

Filling shapes

A shape may be open or closed. A pencil scribble or a perfect arc is an *open* shape, having definite starting and end points and not enclosing any space, such as that shown on the left in Figure 6.13. A *closed* shape, on the other hand, has a continuous margin surrounding space, and indefinable start and end points, such as that shown on the right in Figure 6.13. Custom shapes available in the Custom Shape Tool's palettes are defined as closed shapes automatically.

The foreground color shown in the toolbox is applied automatically to a closed shape.

Figure 6.13. While both open and closed shapes can have a stroke, only closed shapes can be filled.

Selecting the fill

The basic process for filling an object follows these steps:

1. Draw an object, create a selection, or select an area on your image using the Select tools and features (described in Chapter 10).
2. Choose Edit ⇨ Fill Selection to open the Fill dialog box.
3. Select the options for the fill, including the color you want to use, the opacity, and the blending mode. Check out Chapter 11 for descriptions and examples of blending modes.
4. Click OK to close the dialog box and add the fill.

Specifying fill properties

You have to define two choices in the Fill dialog box before applying the fill: the type of fill and the blending characteristics for the fill. In the Fill dialog box, click the Use drop-down arrow and choose the type of fill option from the menu:

- **Foreground.** Apply the foreground color specified in the toolbox to the object.
- **Background.** Apply the background color specified in the toolbox to the object.
- **Color.** Open the Color Picker, specify a color for the fill, and click OK to return to the Fill dialog box.
- **Pattern.** Fill the object with either a custom or predefined pattern, described in the next section.
- **Black, White, 50% Gray.** These are three separate choices; each is self-explanatory.

You also have to define blending settings:

- **Mode.** Click the Mode drop-down arrow, and choose an option from the list that defines how the fill blends with existing image pixels.
- **Opacity.** Type a value in the Opacity field to define how transparent the filled object should be in relation to the rest of the image.
- **Preserve Transparency.** Click this check box to fill only opaque pixels in the object. The pixels that are transparent remain transparent. In Figure 6.14, the image at the top is filled using the Preserve Transparency option. Because the selected area is transparent, choosing the Preserve Transparency option doesn't add any fill to the selected areas. The identical image shown at the bottom uses the same options without the Preserve Transparency setting and displays filled areas.

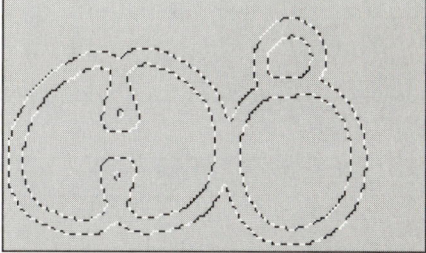

Figure 6.14. A fill can be excluded from transparent pixels, as in the top image, or applied to transparent pixels, as in the bottom image.

Filling with patterns

Filling with a pattern is one of the choices available in the Fill Layers dialog box. You can use one of Photoshop Elements' patterns from one of several pattern libraries, or you can create and use your own patterns.

Patterns can be used by a number of tools, such as the Paint Bucket, Brush, and the Pattern stamp tool. See Chapter 18 for more details.

Applying a pattern fill

To use a pattern for a fill, follow these steps:

1. Draw an object, create a selection, or select an area on your image using the Select tools and features (described in Chapter 10).
2. Choose Edit ➪ Fill Selection to open the Fill Layer dialog box.
3. In the Fill Layers dialog box, choose Pattern from the Use drop-down menu.
4. Click the Custom Pattern drop-down arrow and choose a pattern from the displayed library as shown in Figure 6.15. If you prefer, click the arrow in the displayed library to open a menu of pattern libraries and select an alternate library.
5. After you select the pattern, specify the blend mode and opacity as required, as with a solid fill.
6. Click OK to close the dialog box and add the fill.

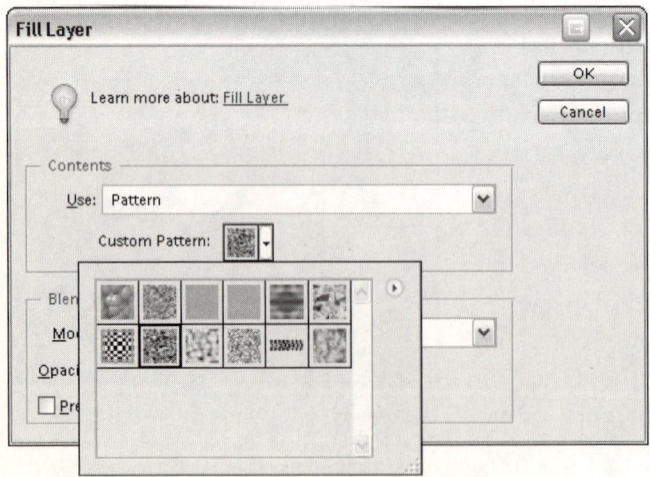

Figure 6.15. Fill an object with a repeating pattern rather than a color.

Creating a custom pattern

You can add your own patterns and construct custom libraries of patterns. You may want to build custom patterns to use for client projects, or you may choose to design your own patterns to use for page layouts or scrapbook pages.

The content you use as the source of the pattern can be from any source or file. For example, you might have an image of a rocky beach, or a picture of you wearing your favorite red sweater that can be used as the basis for the pattern. You can also create a drawing in Photoshop Elements using any of the many drawing and painting tools, or apply effects to an existing image or drawing to create the basis for an interesting pattern. Follow these steps to create a custom pattern from content on an image:

1. Open the image you want to use as the basis for the pattern in Photoshop Elements.
2. Select the Rectangular Marquee tool in the toolbox, and drag a rectangle around a sample area of the image you want to use for the custom pattern.
3. Choose Edit ⇨ Define Pattern From Selection to open the Pattern Name dialog box, shown in Figure 6.16.
4. Type a name for the custom pattern in the Name field, and click OK to close the dialog box.
5. Choose Select ⇨ Deselect to deselect the marquee.

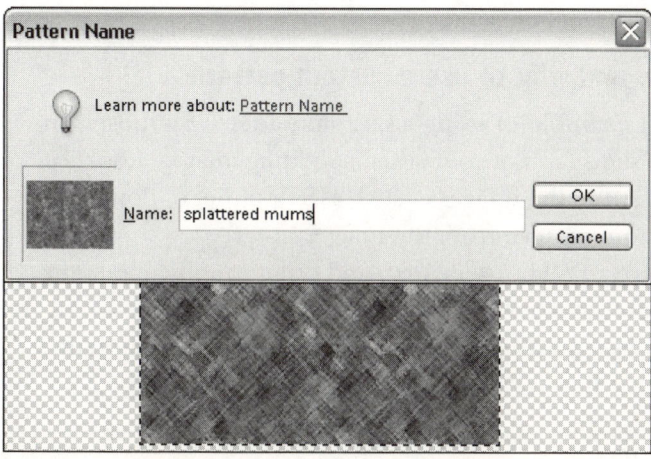

Figure 6.16. Save selected content as a custom pattern.

Watch Out!

A custom pattern is added to whichever pattern library was chosen last, regardless of the tool used to select the pattern library. Check the active pattern library in the Fill dialog box or through the options bar for tools such as the Paint Bucket or Brushes.

You can also use an entire image as a pattern following nearly the same process. Open your image, and choose Edit ⇨ Define Pattern. In the Pattern Name dialog box, name the new pattern and click OK.

Making a splash with the Paint Bucket

For quick color changes, you can't beat the Paint Bucket tool. Instead of having to specify any sort of selection, Photoshop Elements automatically applies the color to a range of pixels similar in color to the one you click. The tool works with foreground or background material on an image equally well.

Filling with the Paint Bucket

Follow these steps to specify settings and apply a fill:

1. Select the Paint Bucket tool in the toolbox.
2. Choose options for the fill in the options bar; the options are shown and described in Table 6.2.
3. Click the area on the image that you want filled.

How and why to use a custom pattern

Here's a neat example of using a custom pattern: Suppose you are assembling a slide show of your sister's wedding images. Look for a recurring element in the images — such as a bouquet of flowers — and create a custom pattern from the image.

Use the pattern to fill borders, text, and other graphic elements in your pages. Sample a few colors from the bouquet to use as custom color swatches, and use the colors for backgrounds, gradients, text fills, and shape fills.

Table 6.2. Paint Bucket tool filling options

Tool	Option	Your Choices
Fill: Pattern	Fill	Choose either the foreground color or a pattern.
Pattern:	Pattern	If a pattern fill is selected, choose the pattern from the appropriate library.
Mode: Normal	Mode	Define how you want the fill pixels to blend with the underlying image pixels.
Opacity: 100%	Opacity	Specify how transparent the fill appears by dragging the slider or typing a number.
Tolerance: 10	Tolerance	Define how close pixels must be to one another in color value. Low tolerance refers to similarly colored pixels; high tolerance expands the range of color.
☑ Anti-alias	Anti-aliased	Select to smooth the edges of the selection.
☑ Contiguous	Contiguous	Select to have similarly colored pixels that are in contact with one another filled only. Deselect to have all pixels in the image of the similar color filled, whether or not they are touching.
☑ Use All Layers	Use All Layers	Pixels on any visible layer within the Tolerance and Contiguous options' settings are filled.

Watch Out!

A shape added with the Custom Shape tool is filled automatically regardless of the area you click on the image, unless the shape layer is simplified. Read about simplifying layers in Chapter 11.

Understanding the Paint Bucket fill options

A couple of the options you can apply to a Paint Bucket fill, listed in Table 6.2, may be difficult to understand just by reading.

The best way to see how the different settings work is to experiment; the second-best way is to look at these examples. In Figure 6.17, I show three versions of the same image after applying the Paint Bucket tool using the same color, and three different tolerance levels.

The other concept that may be difficult to visualize is whether the fill is contiguous. Figure 6.18 shows the same image using opposite settings. In the left image, the Contiguous check box is selected. When the image is clicked with the Paint Bucket tool, in the location shown in the left image, the area of the wood surrounding the Paint Bucket's location is filled within the specified Tolerance of 25 pixels. In the right image, using the same 25 pixel Tolerance, but with the Contiguous option deselected, all the similar shades in the entire image are filled.

Figure 6.17. The amount of fill applied varies according to the tolerance level; the top image uses a tolerance of 5 pixels; the middle 25 pixels, and the bottom image 50 pixels.

Figure 6.18. Specify whether or not the fill is applied to contiguous pixels. In the left image, clicking the image with the Paint Bucket filled the contiguous areas around the Paint Bucket's location. In the right image, clicking the image with the Paint Bucket filled all similar pixels in the entire image with the color.

Stroking lines

Some objects look better with an outline, also called a *stroke*. For example, text filled with a pattern often looks better if the letters have a finishing stroke applied for emphasis.

To add strokes, go to the Edit menu and follow these steps:

1. Select the object using one of the Select tools, described in detail in Chapter 10. An entire layer can also have a stroke applied to its outer edge, like a frame.
2. Choose Edit ⇨ Stroke (Outline) Selection to open the Stroke dialog box.
3. Select options for the stroke, including the width and color of the stroke, its location, and blending choices. A stroke width can be set from 1 to 250 pixels.
4. Click OK to close the dialog box and apply the stroke.

The settings for applying a stroke are much the same as for applying a color or pattern fill, with the exception of the Location choices. You can specify whether a selection is stroked using an Inside, Center, or Outside location in relation to the selection or layer boundaries. An example of each option is shown applied to the same image in Figure 6.19.

Although the three circles appear to be different sizes, they are actually the same size — the difference is based on the stroke location. In the left image, the stroke is within the circle's boundary, the middle circle has the stroke centered over the circle's edges, and the right circle has the stroke applied outside the circle's boundary.

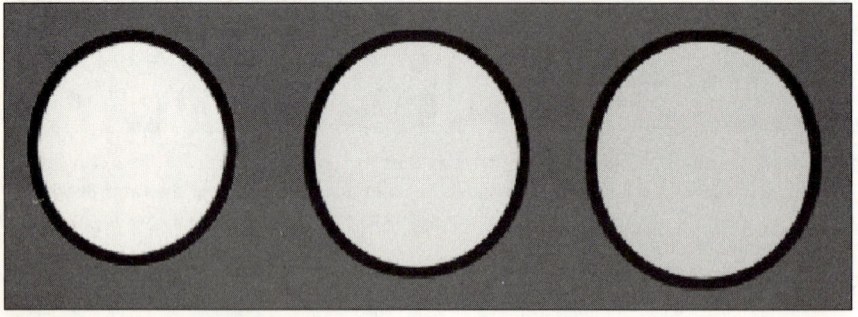

Figure 6.19. Specify where the stroke is applied in relation to the selection's edge — inside the selection, centered over the selection, or outside the selection.

Groovin' with gradients

A gradient is a type of fill that uses two or more colors, or transparency, and gradually blends from one color to another within the fill. The gradient can take on different forms, such as linear or radial.

Photoshop Elements gives you a raft of ways to work with gradients. You can use a gradient from one of several libraries, edit existing gradients, create your own, or apply the same gradient in very different ways depending on the type and how you indicate the gradient on the image.

Follow these basic steps to apply a gradient in your image:

1. Select or specify the layer for filling in the image.
2. Select the Gradient tool in the toolbox.

3. Click the Gradient Picker drop-down arrow and choose a gradient from the existing library, or choose one from another gradient library.
4. Choose the gradient type in the options bar.
5. Select a blend mode, set the opacity, and choose other options as needed.
6. Click the location on the image or the workspace where you want to start the gradient (the start point).
7. Drag across the image and release the mouse where you want the gradient to end (the end point).

Gradient types

The same color configuration can look very different depending on the type of gradient you select in the options bar. Figure 6.20 shows a sample of each type of gradient. The gradient types are listed in Table 6.3, along with a tip about using the different gradient type.

Table 6.3. Gradient types

Option	Description
Linear	A Linear gradient is shown in the upper-left image in Figure 6.20. Shading is in a straight line from start to end point. Probably the most common type for a background.
Radial	The Radial gradient shown in the upper-right image in Figure 6.20 shades from start to end points in a circle. Drag the start and end points beyond the image's edges to produce a curvilinear gradient. This is nice when used for a background and is softer than a Linear gradient.
Angle	The Angle gradient, shown in the middle-left image of Figure 6.20, produces a sharp line between the start and end colors around a starting point. It looks good for angular types of images such as hard-edged buttons or shapes.
Reflected	The Reflected gradient, shown in the middle-right image of Figure 6.20, applies two Linear gradients at either side of the starting point. This gradient produces an interesting fill in sharp-edged linear graphic elements like bars.
Diamond	The lower-left image of Figure 6.20 shows a Diamond gradient, which is applied from the start point outward with the end point defining one corner of the diamond. Create an interesting chevron pattern by adjusting start and end points.

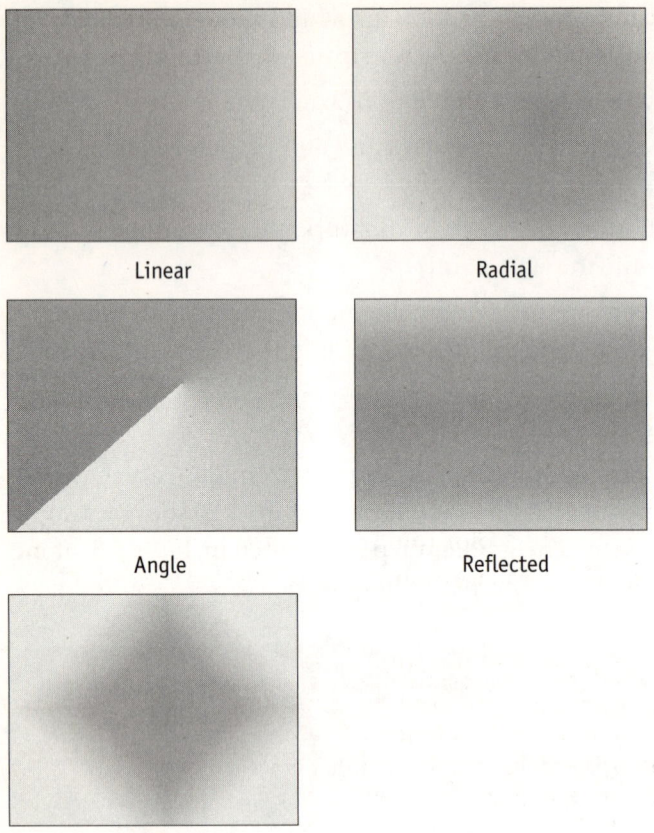

Figure 6.20. Choose from five types of gradients.

 **Bright Idea**
If you want to constrain the gradient's angle, hold down Shift as you drag. If you try to reorient the angle, it jumps 45 degrees at a time.

Choosing gradient options

After selecting the type of gradient you want to apply, choose other options from the options bar if desired:

- **Mode.** Select a blend mode from the drop-down menu to define how the gradient blends with the rest of the image. If the gradient is on its own layer, you could choose a mode on the Layers palette.
- **Opacity.** Click the Opacity drop-down arrow, and drag the slider or type a value in the field to define the gradient's level of transparency.
- **Reverse.** You can reverse the order of colors in the fill. I never use this option, because reversing can be done just by changing the start and end points when the gradient is applied.
- **Dither.** This smoothes the color transitions in the gradient. Make sure it is selected in low-resolution images for a softer appearance.
- **Transparency.** Don't confuse this with opacity! Some gradients use transparency as a color point in the gradient. Click Transparency to use the transparency in the gradient rather than any underlying transparency in the image.

Varying the gradient's path

Filling an area with a gradient is simple. Click the mouse where you want to set the start point of the gradient, and drag to define the end point. You can start within the margins of an image, from edge to edge, or go beyond the image to set the start or end points on the workspace.

The same radial gradient can look very different depending on how the gradient is indicated on the image. Examples are shown in Figure 6.21. In each image, you can see the spread and direction of the gradient.

> **Inside Scoop**
>
> Rather than working directly on your image, use a Fill Layer to apply a gradient. The added layer lets you change the properties and apply the gradient to a specified area on the image. Read about layers in Chapters 10 and 11.

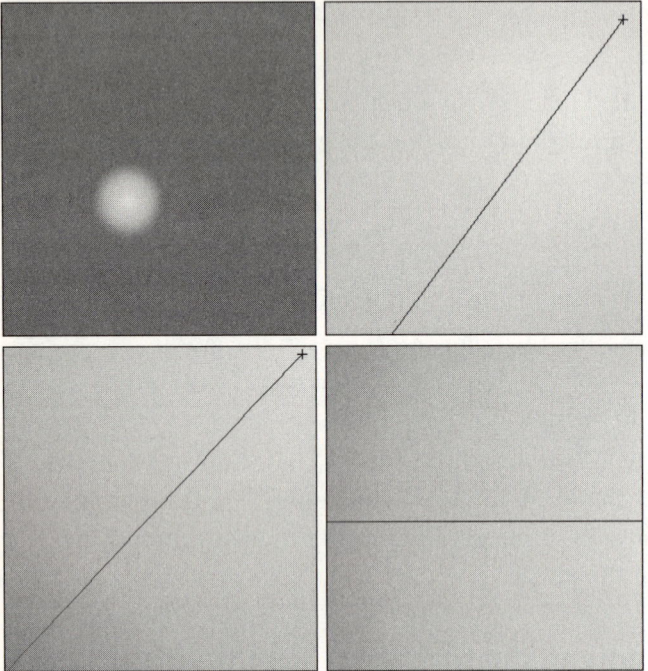

Figure 6.21. Specify where the stroke is applied in relation to the selection's edge.

Defining a gradient

Photoshop Elements comes with nine gradient libraries. For some of us, and in some circumstances, nine libraries just aren't enough. Fortunately, you can modify existing gradients or build your own in the Gradient Editor.

There really are no rules for building a gradient, except that it must include two or more colors, or use a single color that fades to transparency.

In the Gradient Editor, shown in Figure 6.22, define the colors and opacity, and their locations on the gradient's continuum.

> **Loading gradients**
>
> Gradients are stored in libraries, like color swatches and patterns. Click the drop-down arrow on the Gradient Picker, and click the arrow on the displayed library to open a menu listing other libraries. Select a library to load its gradients.
>
> You can create and save your own gradients and libraries, and load gradient libraries. Work with gradients either through the options bar when the Gradient tool is active or through the Preset Manager.

Follow these steps to create a new Solid gradient:

1. Select the Gradient tool in the toolbox.
2. Click the Edit button next to the visible gradient sample to open the Gradient Editor.
3. Select one of the existing gradients in the Presets area of the dialog box to edit or use as a starting point for a new gradient. You can also click More to load a different gradient library, and then select a gradient from that group.
4. Adjust the color. Click one of the existing Color Stops and drag it to reset its location, or type a new value in the Location field. Click the Color drop-down arrow, and choose whether to apply the Foreground or Background color set in the toolbox. Double-click the Color Stop or the color swatch to open the Color Picker, and select a custom color.
5. Add more Color Stops by clicking below the color continuum; remove existing Color Stops by dragging the stop beyond the margins of the dialog box.
6. Specify the Color Midpoint — the center point between two colors on the continuum — by dragging the diamond along the continuum.
7. Modify the opacity of the gradient. Each gradient has a start and end Opacity Stop. Select an Opacity Stop, change the value in the Opacity field, and drag the stop along the continuum to adjust its location if you like. Add another Opacity Stop by clicking above the continuum bar.

8. Type a name for the new gradient if you are creating a custom gradient.
9. Click New to add the gradient to the displayed presets in the Gradient Editor.
10. Click OK to close the Gradient Editor.

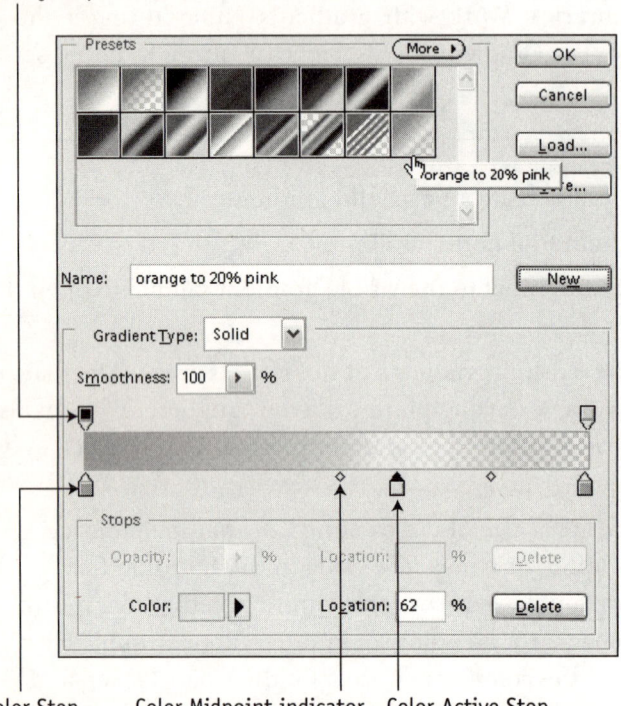

Figure 6.22. Define a new or modified gradient's color and opacity settings.

Add some noise

Gradients come in two basic types: smooth and noise. If you want to apply a gradual color to an object, use a Solid gradient. If you want something that is much punchier and shows definite bands of color, use a Noise gradient. Choose either option from the Gradient Type drop-down list in the Gradient Editor.

Watch Out!
Don't bother naming the gradient until you are finished with its configuration. Each time you change any of the values or adjust anything on the dialog box, the name reverts to "Custom."

Specify whether to use RGB color or HSB color in the Gradient Editor settings, as well as whether to use transparency. Adjust the Roughness as a percentage from 0 to 100 percent, with 0 percent very smooth and 100 percent highly banded, as shown in Figure 6.23.

Figure 6.23. The same gradient looks much different depending on how noisy it is. The upper band uses 0 percent noise, the middle band uses 50 percent noise, and the lower band uses 100 percent noise.

Several gradient tips

Keep these tips in mind when you are building or editing a gradient:

- Moving a color midpoint close to a Color Stop produces a sharper and more defined color change in the gradient; placing it about midway creates a very smooth gradient.
- The active Color Stop or Opacity Stop shows a black fill for its pointer. Make sure to select the right one before adjusting opacity and location settings in the Stops area of the dialog box.
- If you can't see a color midpoint diamond on the continuum, click one of the Color Stops bordering the color midpoint you want to adjust.
- If you use a gradient that has a transparency setting, make sure the Transparency check box is selected in the options bar.

> **Locating libraries**
>
> There are several program locations where you can find the pattern, color swatch, and gradient libraries, such as in the Fill and Stroke dialog boxes, Paint Bucket, and Paint tools. In each case, tools that use the library contents display library selections on the options bar. For example, the Pattern libraries are available from the options bar for the Pattern Stamp tool and the Paint Bucket tool.
>
> You can also use the Preset Manager to organize, add, load, and save libraries. Choose Edit ⇨ Preset Manager, and select the appropriate library. Store additional library files in the same hard drive location as the program's defaults in order to include your custom choices in the menus.

Just the facts

- Choose and use a color model that corresponds with what you are creating.
- Select and customize colors to match your project in the Color Picker.
- Specify default foreground and background colors that Photoshop Elements applies automatically to elements such as text or new layer fills.
- Save custom colors in a color swatch library; manage existing and new color swatch libraries in the Preset Manager.
- Fill shapes using colors or patterns.
- Create custom patterns or use existing patterns to fill objects in your images.
- Add an outline to objects such as text for more definition.
- Create and use gradients for more color interest in your images.

GET THE SCOOP ON...
■ Opening the program for editing ■ Using Quick Fix for quick corrections ■ Correcting red eye in images ■ Using Auto adjustments to correct lighting and color

Hands-Off Image Correcting

Taking pictures with a digital camera is a way of life for many of us. Now, it's easier than ever to shoot and print hundreds and hundreds of images because cameras and printing materials have decreased in price.

Even with your best efforts and a quality camera, you may need to make some small corrections or changes that improve an image. Perhaps the lighting is too dark or too light, or the entire image may look too red or green. And, you certainly want to fix red eye to prevent your photos of the family picnic from looking like a bunch of demonic white rabbits in wigs.

For the many Photoshop Elements users who don't need to make extensive image correction, work with layers, or use filters, the Quick Fix editing mode is tailor-made for you. However, if you find over time that you develop more interest in the particulars of the corrections, begin experimenting with the options, and start using different sequences of correction, bypass the Quick Fix window altogether. Instead, open images directly in Standard Edit mode to both customize enhancements and use other features such as layers.

Getting into a fix

Quick Fix mode can perform different types of image correction and enhancement, automatically fix common image problems, and apply calculations to determine how much an image needs to be repaired.

In the Quick Fix program window, you choose from a number of automatic corrections and other features to quickly process and correct images. Although it isn't quite "hands-off" as the chapter's name implies, working in Quick Fix mode comes pretty close!

You can open Quick Fix mode from several areas in the program, depending on what window is showing in the program. Open Quick Fix mode using one of these methods:

- From the Welcome Screen, move your mouse over the Quickly Fix Photos selection at the top of the dialog box to show an overview of the functions. The dialog box lists basic information features such as adjusting skin tones and selecting and extracting content from an image. Click to open the Quick Fix window.
- From the Organizer, choose Edit ⇨ Go to Quick Fix, or click the Edit button on the shortcut bar and choose Go to Quick Fix.
- From the Standard Edit window, click the Quick Fix button on the shortcut bar.

Protecting images

If you are in the Organizer and want to open a particular image, click the image to select it, click the Edit button, and choose Go to Quick Fix.

The image opens in a separate window in the Quick Fix editing view. If you display the Organizer window, you see a red bar and a lock on the image's thumbnail, shown in Figure 7.1. This means the image is open for editing.

By the way, if you select Standard Edit instead of Quick Fix, you see the same indicator on the thumbnail view in the Organizer.

Bright Idea
You may run into a circumstance when you're using Quick Fix mode that requires more editing power. You can easily change to the Standard Editing mode by clicking the Standard Edit button above the Palette Bin at the right of the program window.

CHAPTER 7 ■ HANDS-OFF IMAGE CORRECTING

Figure 7.1. The Organizer displays an Edit in Progress indicator when an image is open in an editing mode.

Changing the program's startup window

If you are new to image editing, then starting in the Quick Fix window makes the most sense. So, instead of opening Photoshop Elements in the Organizer window, you can have the program automatically start in the Quick Fix mode. Follow these steps to reset the program:

1. From the Organizer or Editor window, choose Window ⇨ Welcome to open the Welcome Screen.

2. Click the Start Up In drop-down arrow at the lower left of the dialog box, and choose Editor from the drop-down menu, shown in Figure 7.2.

Figure 7.2. Choose a different view to display when the program opens.

3. Close the Welcome Screen. The next time the program is closed and reopened, the Editor is opened automatically.

The last editing mode used — either Standard Edit or Quick Fix — displays the next time you open the program.

Quick Fix mode's workspace

Quick Fix mode is basically a subset of the full Standard Edit mode that includes some of the same tools and commands, as well as the same basic window organization.

In Quick Fix mode, you find these items:

- **Menu.** The menu bar in Quick Fix mode includes many commands common to both Quick Fix and Standard Edit modes.

- **Shortcuts bar.** Use the buttons shown below the menu to perform basic functions such as saving and printing, or to open other program components such as the Organizer or Creation Setup dialog boxes. In this area of the window, you also find a field for accessing help and the buttons to toggle between Quick Fix and Standard Edit modes.

- **Toolbox.** The toolbox offers several basic manipulation tools, such as Zoom and Hand tools, as well as some basic editing features such as cropping and removing red eye.

- **Toolbar.** The toolbar shows the commands available for a selected tool and lets you configure the options. In Figure 7.3, the Zoom tool is selected and shows the options in the toolbar.

- **Document window.** The area on the window where your image is displayed is called the document window. By default, the After Only view is shown; you can display both before and after views of the image in different orientations using the options in the View drop-down menu, like the example in Figure 7.3.

- **Photo Bin.** The images open in the program are shown in thumbnails at the bottom of the Quick Fix window. The active image is highlighted in the Photo Bin. Collapse the Photo Bin when not selecting images to give you more screen space for the document window.

- **Palettes.** Quick Fix mode shows a set of four stationery palettes at the right of the program window. You can collapse or open each palette by clicking the spin-down arrow, but you can't collapse the palette area, called the Palette Bin in the Standard Edit mode. If you aren't sure how to use a palette's commands, click the light bulb icon at the right of each palette heading to open the Help file for advice and instruction. Those commands are covered in detail elsewhere in the book as noted later in this chapter.

>  **Hack**
>
> When you work with several files at a time, you usually choose them from the list in the Windows menu. The Photo Bin serves the same purpose; you see thumbnails instead of file names — super when using cryptic camera image names!

Document window

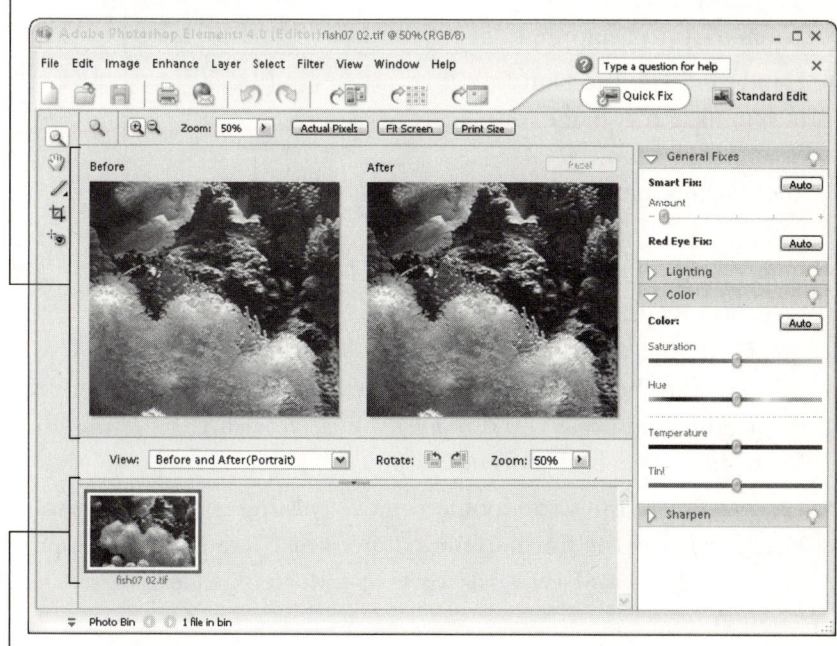

Photo Bin

Figure 7.3. Quick Edit mode offers a collection of features to speedily enhance and correct images.

Quick Fix tools

The contents of the palettes in Quick Fix and Standard Edit modes differ. Both Quick Fix and Standard Edit modes include a toolbox, but the Quick Fix versions contain Auto buttons, and generally fewer controls to modify than their counterparts in the Standard Edit mode. With the exception of the Red Eye Removal tool, the tools are covered in other chapters according to their general purpose.

In Quick Fix mode, you can select from these tools shown in Figure 7.4:

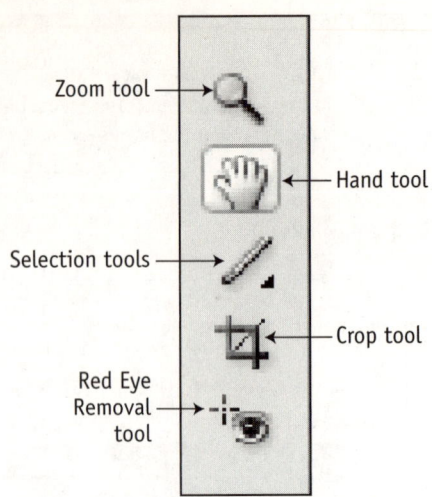

Figure 7.4. The toolbox contains several tools used for editing and viewing your image.

- **Zoom tool.** Use the Zoom tool features to magnify and view different areas of your image. Read about using Zoom tools in Chapter 4.
- **Hand tool.** Use the Hand tool to drag the image in the document window. Read about using the Hand tool in Chapter 4.
- **Selection tools.** The Magic Selection Brush tool lets you quickly define an area on your image, such as a background. Use the Selection Brush tool to select an area on an image by painting it or to paint over areas you don't want to select using the Mask mode. Read about selection tools in Chapter 10.
- **Crop tool.** Use the Crop tool to remove existing content from your image, resizing the finished file's dimensions. Read about cropping using the Crop tool as well as working with Cookie Cutters in Chapter 5.
- **Red Eye Removal tool.** Snapping a picture of Aunt Sally or Rover using a flash often reflects the light from the retina as a red circle. Use this tool to automatically correct the image error.

Correcting red eye

You can correct red eye in an image using the tool in the toolbox or the Auto Red Eye Fix button in the General Fixes palette.

Hack
If your camera has an automatic Red Eye Reduction feature, but you forget to use it, you have the option to have the Organizer automatically correct red eye as images are imported.

Follow these steps to use and adjust the Red Eye Removal tool:

1. Select the Red Eye Removal tool in the toolbox.
2. Click a red area of the eye, or drag a marquee over the red eye in the image.
3. Release the mouse to process the image and correct the error.

You may find that the eyes aren't always corrected enough for your image. The pupil may be larger than the default size, or the color may need darkening further. If either of these conditions is true, click the Pupil Size or Darken Amount arrows on the Red Eye Removal's toolbar to display sliders and adjust the levels, as shown in Figure 7.5. Then click the eye again to reapply the command.

Figure 7.5. Adjust the sliders on the toolbar to modify the size and darkness of the corrected area.

Enhancing images automatically

Simplify your decision-making by using the automatic correction options in Photoshop Elements. Quick Fix mode shows four palettes by default and offers you commands for adjusting the settings in the palettes. Automatic options include the most commonly made corrections, adjusting lighting, adjusting color, and sharpening an image to make its contents more clearly visible.

It's not easy to understand what you need to do when you first start working with images. You may think the photo is "off," but you aren't sure what "off" means or how to fix it. Maybe it's a question of adjusting the contrast or modifying the saturation, but if you haven't worked with image editing before, how are you supposed to know?

Fortunately, Quick Fix mode lets you experiment and make corrections without damaging your original image. Quick Fix mode has been designed as you should use it. By that I mean the set of palettes at the right of the program window are presented in the general order you should look at an image. Virtually all images can use a bit of tweaking.

Selecting auto adjustments

You can make six different auto adjustments in Quick Fix mode:

- **Smart Fix.** The simplest of all fixes is the Smart Fix. Use this option to adjust color balance and basic shadow and highlight details.
- **Red Eye Fix.** Click the Auto Red Eye Fix button to repair red eye automatically.
- **Levels.** Auto Levels adjusts the contrast of an image and often affects the color.
- **Contrast.** Auto Contrast adjusts the distinction between light and dark areas in a photo.
- **Color.** Auto Color Correction adjusts both the contrast and the color in an image.
- **Sharpen.** Auto Sharpen increases the amount of contrast at the edges of objects to make the details stand out.

A quick processing workflow

The auto adjustments you need to apply depend on the characteristics of each image. For example, if you don't have subjects with eyes, you aren't going to have to make a Red Eye Fix correction; if you have a yellow cast to the image, you don't necessarily need to make any changes to the contrast.

For the most part, however, you can always improve the appearance of an image with a bit of correction. Here's an example workflow you can follow to correct an image in Quick Fix mode:

1. If the image looks good overall, click the Smart Fix Auto button to see if a bit of correction tweaks the image, making it a bit clearer with crisper detail.
2. Does the amount of shadow and highlight seem right for the subject and the lighting used? If not, click the Auto button on the Levels

Inside Scoop

Use the Red Eye Fix Auto button in the General Fixes palette to automatically find and fix the problem; use the Red Eye Removal tool in the toolbox, dragging a marquee with the tool to define the repair area. Both produce the same outcome.

> **Watch Out!**
> Use the Undo command if you are going back one step; if you click the Reset button on the document window, the image returns to its original settings.

palette to adjust the contrast. If adjusting Levels changes the color, click the Auto button on the Contrast palette instead to change the contrast in the overall image without changing any colors in the image. If you prefer, drag the sliders on the Lighting palette to change the image's appearance, as shown in Figure 7.6.

Figure 7.6. Use the Auto buttons on the palettes for quick correction, or drag the sliders to control the amount of change, like the large amount of contrast shown in the After image in the figure.

3. Now check the color. The Color Auto button makes several changes to the image, depending on the positions of the sliders in the Color palette.

4. When the other adjustments are made, click the Auto button on the Sharpen palette to increase the definition of the edges of your image. Sharpening should be the last enhancement applied so it doesn't affect application of other modifications.

Regardless of the Auto button you use, undo the action by clicking the Undo button on the shortcuts bar, choosing Edit ⇨ Undo, or pressing the Ctrl+Z keystroke combination.

Inside Scoop

Choose portrait or landscape view for the Before and After image display. Portrait view crops the side edges of the preview images to display them side by side; landscape view crops the top and bottom edges to stack the display vertically.

Adjusting adjustments

Sometimes the auto correction doesn't work for the image, or the amount of change isn't correct, being either too much or too little. If that happens, you can adjust the settings using either the sliders in the palettes or using menu commands.

Take a look at each correction, how it can be adjusted, and the impact of changing the settings. Like many things, the best way to learn how to correct an image is by experimenting. You aren't going to see the effects in color in this book, of course, because it's printed in black and white.

Follow these steps to make a correction using custom settings in Quick Fix mode:

1. Open the image for correction in the Quick Fix mode of the Editor.

2. Click the View drop-down arrow below the document window, and choose the Before and After display to let you easily compare the changed image to the original.

3. Click the spin-down arrow for the palette to display its slider or sliders.

4. Drag the slider to make the adjustment to the correction. As you move the slider, icons display on the label bar for the palette, shown in Figure 7.7.

Figure 7.7. Adjust the sliders on the palettes to specify the amount of correction to apply to the image.

5. Click the check mark to apply the correction using the setting you specified, or click the cancel icon to reset the correction's slider to its default setting without applying the correction to the image.

General fixes

The Smart Fix makes basic color and contrast tweaks. You can increase the amount of correction by dragging the slider in the General Fixes palette. In the image shown in Figure 7.8, for example, adjusting the slider to increase the amount of correction applied through the Smart Fix command makes the texture of the rock behind the fish much more distinct.

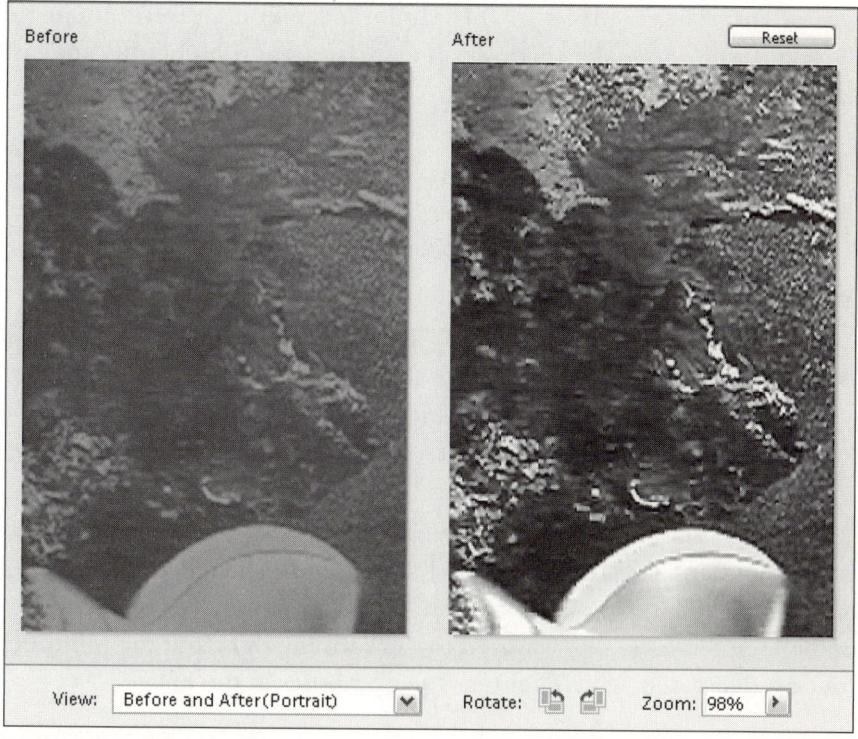

Figure 7.8. The Smart Fix command can quickly correct an image.

Lighting fixes

The two different auto commands in the Lighting palette can be confusing to understand. In very simple terms, use the Levels adjustment to change the contrast in an image that also has a distortion in the overall color. Use the Contrast adjustment to change the strength of the shadows and highlights when the image's color is correct.

The color distortion, called a *color cast*, occurs when an image is shot in less than optimal conditions. You can sometimes find a yellow color cast in indoor shots taken without a flash, or a blue cast when images are taken under fluorescent light.

Contrast refers to the areas of shadow and highlights in an image. If you adjust the sliders for the Contrast Auto fix, the command finds the lightest and darkest pixels in the whole image and converts them to black and white to make shadows appear darker and highlights appear lighter.

Reposition the three Contrast sliders to correct an image by adjusting the sliders:

- **Lighten Shadows.** Drag the slider to the right to lighten the darkest areas in the image; pure black pixels aren't affected.
- **Darken Highlights.** Drag the slider to the right to darken the lightest areas in the image; pure white pixels aren't affected.
- **Midtone Contrast.** Use this slider to adjust contrast in the gray tones between white and black; drag the slider left to lighten the midtones and right to darken the midtones. An example of adjusting Contrast is shown in Figure 7.6.

You can adjust all three sliders in combination. It's best to move a slider incrementally and watch what happens in the image. In Figure 7.9, for example, the image at the right shows the lightening effects of having the Lighten Shadows slider moved to the extreme right and the Midtone Contrast decreased, which lightens the gray tones in the image.

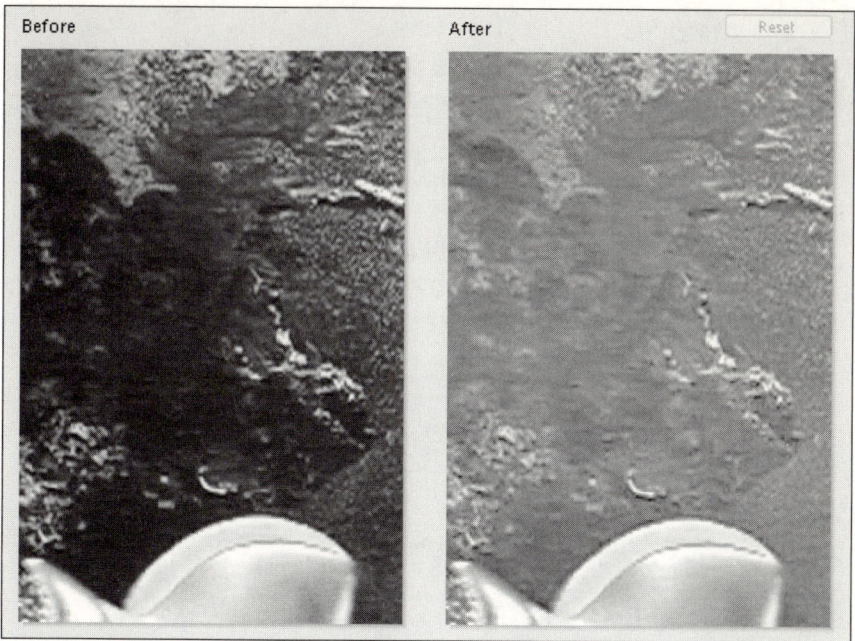

Figure 7.9. Lowering the amount of contrast applied flattens the image dramatically.

Fixing color

Click the Auto Color button on the Color palette to adjust the color in your image. You can adjust the four Color sliders to modify color, which is defined using these four values:

- **Saturation.** Drag the slider left to make the color more muted; drag right to make the color more vibrant.
- **Hue.** The color you see — red or blue or purple — is its hue. Drag the slider left to adjust the color in the image through the red to blue shades; drag the slider right to adjust the image's color through the yellow to blue shades.
- **Temperature.** Drag the Temperature slider left to make colors in the image cooler, or more blue; drag right to make the colors warmer, or more red.
- **Tint.** Drag the Tint slider left to make colors in the image more green; drag right to make the colors more magenta.

>
> **Watch Out!**
> Don't adjust all the sliders in the Color palette at one time because you will never know what effect each change is making in the overall image. Instead, make the changes one by one. For example, make any Tint changes after Temperature changes to moderate the blue or red added.

If you drag the Tint slider you can produce an image that is predominantly one color, like that shown in the After image in Figure 7.10. Choose a color by moving the Hue slider.

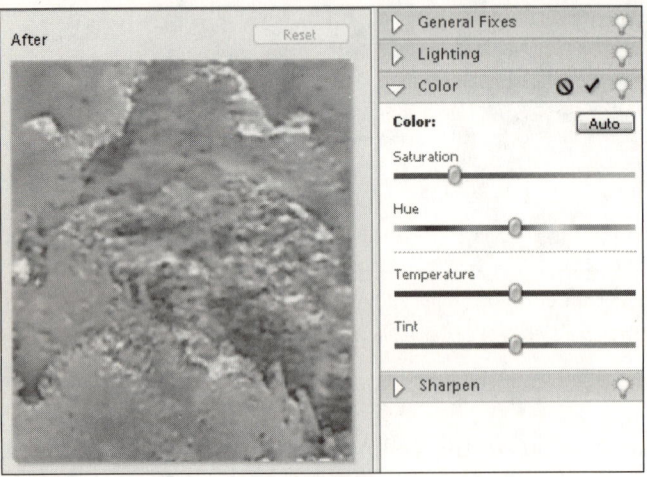

Figure 7.10. Lowering the amount of contrast applied flattens the image dramatically.

Sharpening the image

Sharpening increases the contrast at the edges of objects in your image, making the image look crisper and more defined. Click the Auto Sharpen button to apply default sharpening to your image.

Like other auto corrections, drag the slider to increase the amount of sharpening applied. As you can see in Figure 7.11, too much sharpening produces too much overall emphasis on the details at the edges of objects, making it difficult to identify the objects clearly. Zoom your preview to actual size to get a more accurate view of the amount of sharpening you are applying.

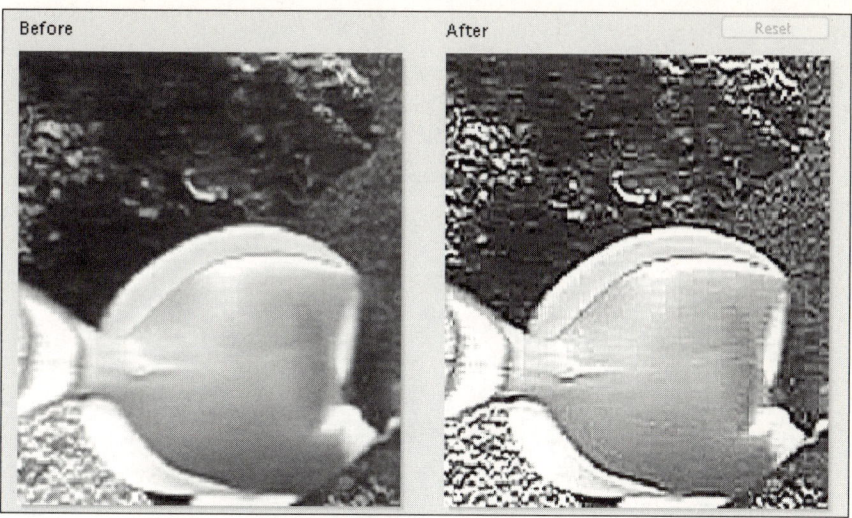

Figure 7.11. Too much sharpening makes the image's objects difficult to define.

Just the facts

- Start the program in Quick Fix Edit mode automatically by changing the settings in the Welcome Screen.
- Use the tools and palettes in Quick Fix mode to make simple corrections to your images.
- Choose either of two methods for correcting red eye.
- Use the Auto adjustments to make quick fixes to lighting and color in your image.
- Adjust the values to increase or decrease the effect of using an auto adjustment.

GET THE SCOOP ON...
■ Changing highlights and shadows ■ Showing contrast and detail ■ Using image information ■ Understanding image intensity ■ Adjusting tonal ranges graphically ■ Fine-tuning levels

All in the Details

Has this ever happened to you? You notice something odd in the back corner of your closet. There's your cat sleeping in a shoebox, looking as cute as a cheesy calendar picture.

My first reaction, and probably yours too, is to grab the camera and capture the moment. Because it has to be a quick shot before the cat moves, it may not be very distinct. Maybe your ankles still bear scars from the last time you woke Fluffy by surprise, so you decide against using the flash and the image is dark. Or perhaps you did use the flash, and washed the image out completely.

Of course, we would prefer to shoot the perfect image, but that doesn't happen very often. Fortunately, Photoshop Elements can help you adjust the appearance of the image to show the detail more clearly.

Aside from making corrections to the overall image, you can also work with selected areas of the image or make corrections on a special type of layer called an Adjustment layer.

You may be wondering just what *detail* is and how you can improve it. I'm not referring to an image of an open book that doesn't show any text, to which you magically add text using some sleight-of-hand in Photoshop Elements. Instead, I am referring to ways you can adjust the levels of shadow and highlight, for example, to reveal more detail that may be hidden in too-dark shadows or washed out in too-bright highlights.

> **Hack**
> If you do lots of editing, make sure to choose camera settings with a high resolution so you have plenty of pixels to work with. Read about setting resolution in Chapter 5.

Improving image detail

You can use the automatic settings in the Quick Fix or Standard Edit modes to make a variety of corrections as described in Chapter 7. Sometimes your results may not be as precise as you'd like, or maybe you want to tweak the image a bit. Photoshop Elements gives you a number of ways to configure details manually.

Adjusting highlight and shadow

Sometimes lots of detail is hidden in dark and light areas of your image. Follow these steps to adjust shadows and highlights:

1. With an image open, choose Enhance ⇨ Adjust Lighting ⇨ Shadows/Highlights to open the Shadows/Highlights dialog box.
2. Make sure the Preview check box is selected so you can see the effects of your adjustments as you make them.
3. Adjust the sliders in the dialog box, or type values in the fields, as shown in Figure 8.1.

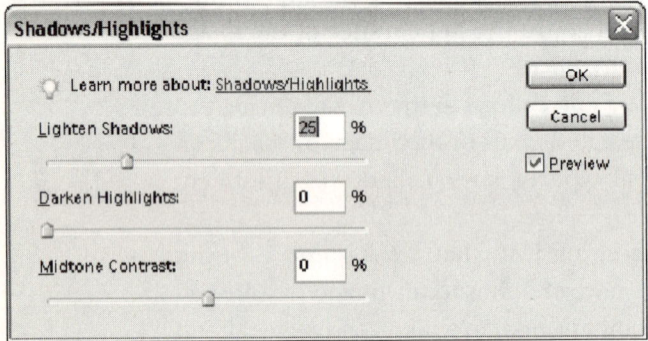

Figure 8.1. Bring out details using the Shadows/Highlights dialog box.

4. Watch the preview as you adjust the values. The adjustments are made in percentages of the original image's tonal values. Lightening shadows by 25 percent in one image may result in much more or

much less lightening in one image than in another. In Figure 8.2, for example, lightening the shadows by 25 percent made a significant difference in terms of showing detail. In the figure, the image at the left shows a pair of cowboy boots on a shelf. By lightening the shadow, you see the intricate stitching in the leather in the right image.

5. Click OK to close the dialog box and make the changes to the image.

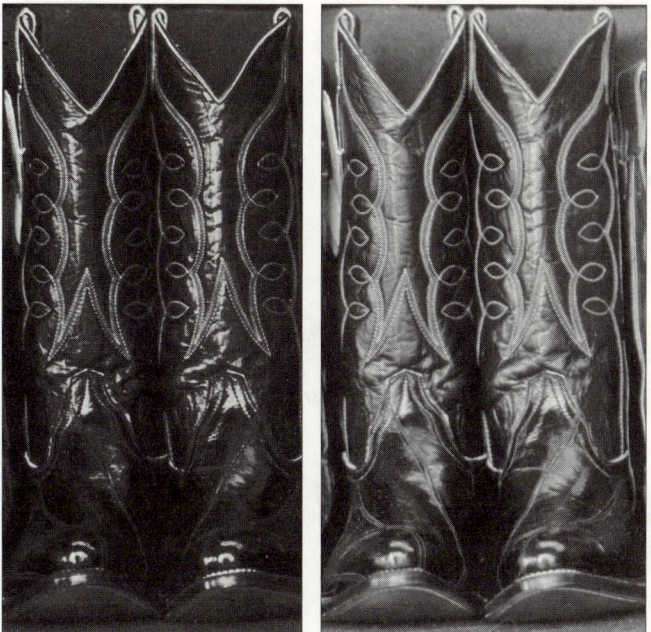

Figure 8.2. Lightening shadow can produce a significant change in some images, showing much more detail such as the stitching in the boots in the right image.

Figuring out the best combination of changes to make to your image's tonal values is not always easy. You can use the following options to make adjustments in the Shadows/Highlights dialog box:

- **Lighten Shadows slider.** Use the Lighten Shadows slider if the dark areas are too dark. By lightening the shadows, you can show more of the detail in the dark areas of the image, like the right image in Figure 8.2.
- **Darken Highlights slider.** Use the Darken Highlights slider when the light areas are too light; darkening the highlights shows more detail

in the light areas of the image. You can see an example of the 'before' and 'after' in an image with highlights that are too light in Figure 8.3.

- **Midtone Contrast slider.** The midtone contrast in the image may be either too dark or too light, causing the image to appear muddy overall. Use the Midtone Contrast slider to add or decrease the amount of contrast in the middle tones of the image. In Figure 8.4, the image at the right has 35 percent more contrast added to the midtones than in the original at the left.

Figure 8.3. Darkening highlights can reveal more detail. In the left image, it's hard to tell what the shapes are; darkening the highlights shows the contents of the image clearly.

 Watch Out!
Pure black and pure white areas in images don't have any details, so adjusting the shadow and highlight sliders has no effect in those areas.

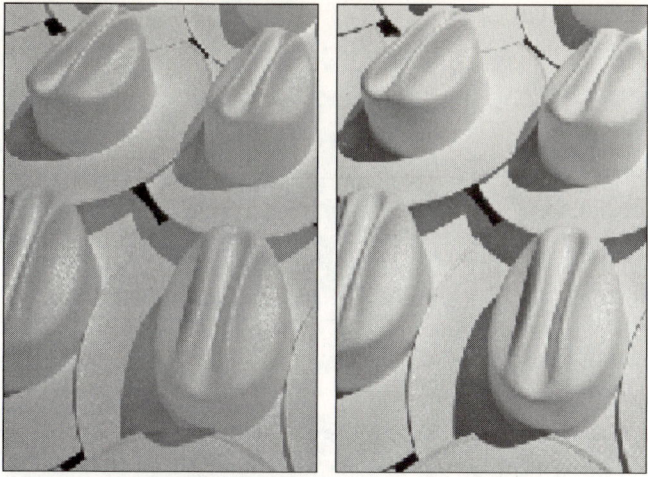

Figure 8.4. The image may be muddy if the midtone contrast is incorrect (left). Adjusting the Midtone Contrast image brings out the detail (right).

Changing brightness and contrast

What if you adjust the shadows and highlights in an image, and you still think the quality is less than stellar? Move on to the next tool in your arsenal.

Apply Brightness/Contrast changes to help improve the quality of detail in an image, but not for making overall changes in shadows and highlights. When you experiment with the Brightness and Contrast controls, you see that changes are made in highlights and shadows. However, because these changes are quite indistinct, make changes first in the Shadows/Highlights dialog box and then move into the Brightness/Contrast controls.

Follow these steps to adjust brightness and contrast in an image:

1. Choose Enhance ➪ Adjust Lighting ➪ Brightness/Contrast to open the Brightness/Contrast dialog box, shown in Figure 8.5.

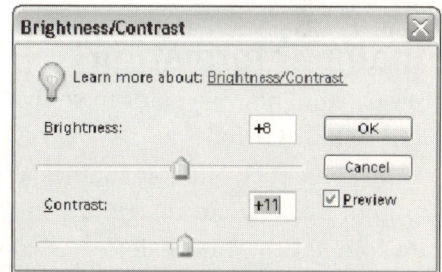

Figure 8.5. Easily tweak detail quality by making adjustments in the Brightness/Contrast dialog box.

2. Make sure the Preview check box is selected so you can see the effects of your adjustments as you make them.

3. Adjust the sliders in the dialog box, or type values in the fields. The original positions of both the Brightness and Contrast sliders are at the central 0 point. Drag left to decrease the value of the setting, or drag right to increase the value of the setting. Both Brightness and Contrast values range from –100 to +100, although the values aren't a unit of measurement *per se*. Drag the slider to the far left to reach –100 and to the far right to reach +100. You see in Figure 8.6 that the image's appearance changes dramatically as you drag the sliders.

Figure 8.6. Sometimes, small changes make a big difference. By increasing both the Brightness and Contrast settings, the detail in the lower image is enhanced from the original image (top).

4. Click OK to close the dialog box and make the changes to the image. As you can see in Figure 8.6, if you compare the original image shown at the top of the figure to one with simple brightness and contrast adjustments, you see how much clearer the detail becomes, such as the leaves on the trees.

Finding information

How do you know if a color in your image is really white? Or white with a bit of yellow? Or red?

You can check out color values as you are selecting a specific pixel or group of pixels in an image. This is called *sampling*. Choose Window ➪ Info to open the Info palette. As you move a tool over your image, the color values of the sample area below the tool are shown in the Info palette.

Figure 8.7 shows an image where the Eyedropper tool is over a white pixel. In the Info palette, notice that the RGB values are 255/255/255, which is pure white. Read more about color and color values in Chapter 6.

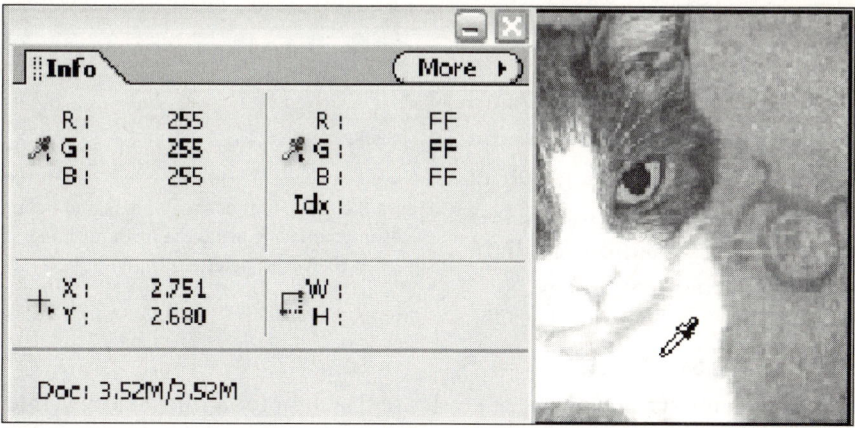

Figure 8.7. Find the color value for a point on an image in the Info palette.

When you are using the eyedroppers for sampling colors in the program's dialog boxes, such as the Layers or Color Picker dialog boxes, viewing the color information in the Info palette lets you sample colors more accurately and quickly.

Adjusting image color using a graph

Some people — and we know who we are — aren't happy unless they're digging deep into the innards of something to find out how it works.

The Levels dialog box is a way for you to "see" the innards of an image and quantify the intensity of its color on a graph called a *histogram*. In addition to the histogram used to configure tonal range in the Levels palette, Photoshop Elements includes a separate Histogram palette.

Watch Out!

Histograms force you to correlate what your eyes see in an image with numerical and graphically plotted information on the histogram. Take your time and watch the image closely as you make adjustments to the histogram.

You find Levels palettes in Photoshop Elements as well as other Adobe products, such as Photoshop, Premiere Pro, and After Effects.

The histogram graph in the Levels dialog box, shown in Figure 8.8, is used to read and adjust the areas of darkness and light in an image. The graph at the upper part of the dialog box shows the distribution of light and dark values in an image.

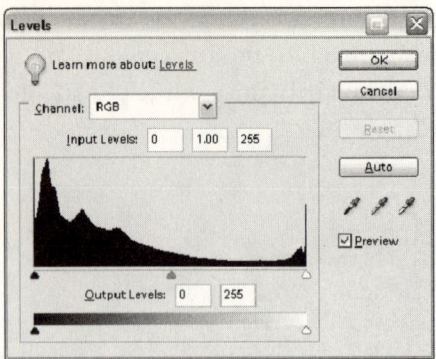

Figure 8.8. Specify the range of dark and light colors in your image using the histogram and sliders in the Levels palette.

When to use levels

There are some situations where levels are the right tools for the job. While it is true that adjusting levels is more complex than clicking an "Auto Fix Something" button, you maintain much more control over the image.

These are some situations in which you may want to consider using levels:

- You want to make sure your image uses a full range of tones and consequently the right amount of contrast.
- You want to adjust the mid-range gray tones without changing the shadows or highlights.
- You want to control a *color cast,* or slight color tint, manually by neutralizing or adding color in the grays in your image.
- You want to send images to a commercial printer and need to specify color values for shadow and highlight areas.

My example image is a shot of rooftops in New Orleans at sunrise, shown in Figure 8.9. It's a nice photo, but there is too much contrast, it's hard to make out details, and the highlights don't cover enough range.

Inside Scoop

When you work with levels, you can work directly on the image pixels or through an Adjustment layer. Read about using separate layers to make corrections in Chapter 11.

Also, the image was shot in winter, and it would be nicer if the sunlight were slightly warmer.

Figure 8.9. This image is interesting, but it could be improved.

Preparing your workspace

Make some changes to the Eyedropper tool's settings, and change the image view before adjusting levels in an image. You work with very precise corrections, and need correct sampling and view settings.

For the most accurate results, set the Eyedropper tool's sample size settings in the Standard Edit mode before opening the Levels dialog box. Like several other processes in Photoshop Elements, the Levels dialog box uses eyedroppers. By default, the eyedroppers in a dialog box use the tool settings specified in the program.

Click the Eyedropper tool in the toolbox to select it and display its configuration options in the tool options. Click the Sample Size drop-down arrow, and choose 3 by 3 Average. When you use the Eyedropper tool on the image, the sample is made from combining the values of a block of nine pixels, rather than a single pixel.

Figure 8.10 shows the Info Palette color values for a pixel sample. The eyedropper is set for sampling a single pixel. When the eyedropper's sample is increased to a 3 by 3 Average sample, the Red and Green values of the sampled area decrease slightly. Over the course of a project and multiple edits, that small change can make a difference.

> **Watch Out!**
> If your image has a very high resolution, you may want to experiment with the 5 by 5 Average sample size to compensate for the large number of pixels and color variations in the image.

Set the view in your image next. Choose View ⇨ Actual Pixels to display the range of tones and colors in your image at a 1:1 ratio of image to screen pixels. You can instead set the magnification to 100 percent using one of the Zoom tools. Displaying the image at 100 percent lets you make more accurate samples.

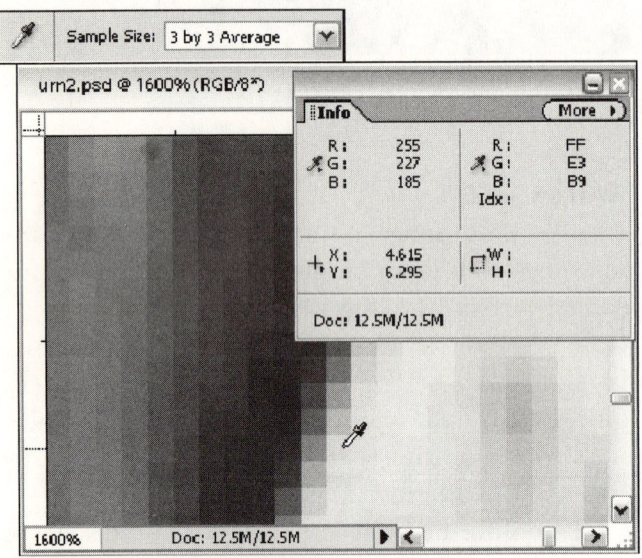

Figure 8.10. The Eyedropper tool's settings affect how the eyedroppers in the Levels dialog box sample color on the image.

Viewing levels

Drum roll, please: You need some leveling action. Choose Enhance ⇨ Adjust Lighting ⇨ Levels, or use the shortcut keys Ctrl+L to open the Levels dialog box, shown in Figure 8.11 with a sample image.

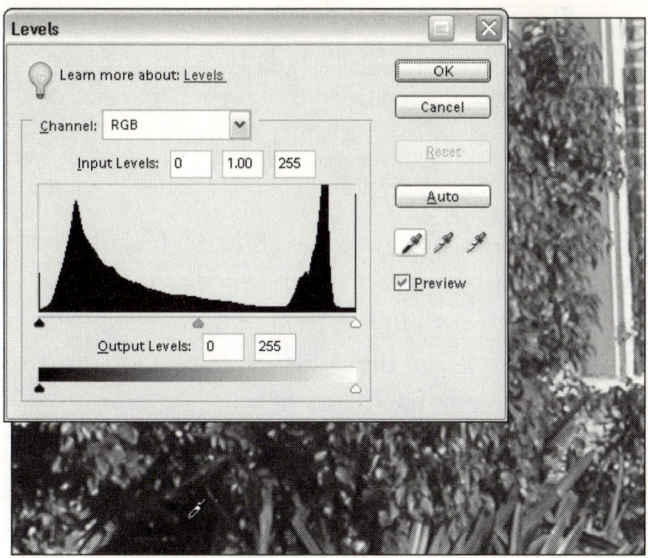

Figure 8.11. Examine and adjust an image's tonal range in the Levels dialog box.

Orienting yourself

Before you see how to modify an image using the controls, take at look at what the Levels dialog box shows:

- The Channel drop-down menu lets you see the levels for the default RGB image, or choose separate red, green, or blue color channels from the drop-down menu.
- Input levels list the brightness values along the x-axis (horizontal axis) from dark (0) at the left to medium (1.0) in the center to bright (255) at the right.
- Three triangles along a slider correspond to the dark, medium, and light values shown in the Input Levels fields above the graph.

Watch Out!
If you are working with a grayscale image, you won't have any options in the Channel drop-down menu as grayscale images have only one channel.

Inside Scoop

When the Levels dialog box is open, you can position and change the view of the image using the scrollbars, keyboard shortcuts, and mouse. In Figure 8.11, adjustments are made at 100 percent zoom and captured at 15 percent zoom to show you the full image in the screenshots.

- The y-axis (vertical axis) shows how many pixels in the image use a particular brightness value. The higher the spike is, the more pixels that use a particular level of brightness.
- Output Levels and the slider below the fields are adjusted to distribute brightness in the processed image.
- Three eyedroppers are used to sample the image to specify dark, medium, and light tones.

Reading the graph

My sample image, shown full-size in Figure 8.9, uses dark to medium brightness with no lightness at all, which is why the image is rather dark. Look at the graph in the Levels dialog box shown in Figure 8.11 to see how the description of my image translates into the graph's appearance.

In the graph, note that the pixels are distributed in the greatest numbers in two locations along the x-axis — the very dark pixels and a patch of fairly bright pixels. In numerical terms, the peaks are in the 15-25 range and again in the 197-200 range. Therefore, of the possible 255 levels of brightness available, my image is using only about 220 levels, missing out on 30 or so levels.

Remember that I said my image had too much contrast? Bunching up the pixels in the dark areas and having no pixels in the lightest areas results in far too much contrast in the image because the image isn't using the full range of tones available.

Fixing the image

The sample image needs fixing in three ways:
- The overall range needs adjusting to display more detail.
- The midrange tones need more distribution to show more contrast.
- The lightest tones need a bit of yellow to warm up the sunshine (although you can't see the color version of the image of course).

All of these things can be done through the Levels dialog box, and coincidentally using all the Layer dialog box's features. You'll be able to see the outcome of the first two fixes in the images coming up. Unfortunately, you can't see the improvement in changing the color of the sunshine in a grayscale image.

Adjusting tones manually

First up, you need to remap the Input Levels. These levels are shown on the graph in the Levels dialog box when you start working with the image. Adjusting the sliders changes the distribution of dark, medium, and light tones more evenly.

Moving the sliders readjusts the intensity of each pixel in the image. Drag the black triangle below the graph right to remap the intensity of the darker pixels. All pixels that are darker than the new value you set are adjusted, or *remapped*, to darker values. Drag the white triangle left in the third Input Level field to decrease the range of intensity, which remaps some of the medium pixels into the lighter value range. The midrange gray triangle slides along as you move either the black or white triangles.

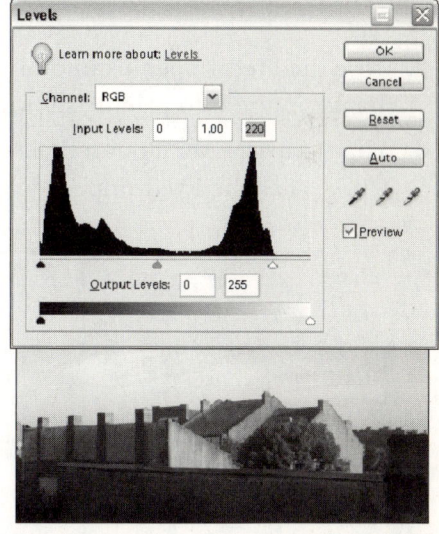

In the example shown in Figure 8.12, the third Input Level field shows a value of 220, and you can see below the graph that the white triangle is moved to the left. In the sample, also shown in the figure, the overall image is now lighter.

Figure 8.12. Adjust the Input Levels to coincide with the image's actual tonal distribution.

Adjusting tones automatically

Rather than using the sliders or typing values in the fields, you can also use the eyedroppers and sample the image directly, letting the program take care of adjusting the graph. Follow these steps:

> ### It's not as scary as it looks
>
> Some people have a knee-jerk reaction to anything graph-like because it reminds them of math class, not everyone's fondest memory. Working with levels is really not that bad.
>
> You can either work from the graph and its values numerically, or you can use the eyedroppers, or you can do both. When you sample an image with an eyedropper from the Levels dialog box, the levels in the graph are automatically adjusted.
>
> However, you have to work from the graph at the left side of the dialog box if you want to modify Output Levels.

1. Click the Set Black Point eyedropper, which is the left eyedropper below the Auto button on the Levels dialog box shown in Figure 8.13.
2. Move the eyedropper around on the image, and watch the values change in the Info palette, shown back in Figure 8.10.
3. When you are over a point that shows RGB values close or equal to 0/0/0, click the Eyedropper tool.

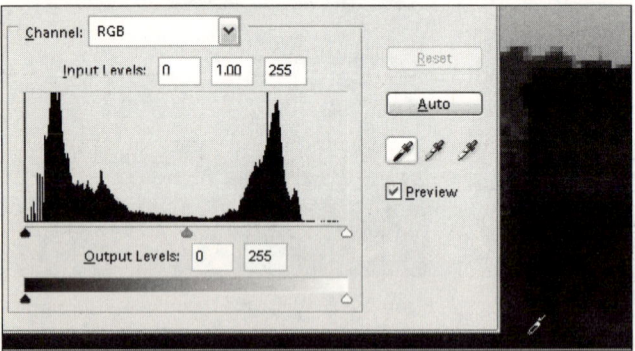

Figure 8.13. Moving the eyedropper around the image gives you lots of color information.

Bright Idea
The gray triangle on the slider moves along as you adjust positions for either the black or white triangles. Drag the gray triangle itself to expand the range of darker or lighter midtones in your image, enhancing the detail.

The eyedroppers are used to select specific values, or points. These include:

- **Black point.** The preceding steps describe how to sample the black point for the image, that is, the darkest pixel in the image. All other pixels in the image are remapped to correspond with the selected sample. Depending on your image, you may not have any pixels close to black at all, but choose the darkest pixels you can find. You are aiming for the lowest values in the RGB listings on the Info palette.

- **White point.** To choose the brightest area on the image, click the Set White Point eyedropper, the right eyedropper in the Levels dialog box, and repeat the steps above. This time, you are looking for the closest RGB value to white, or 255/255/255. Depending on the brightness of your image, you may or may not find a value close to white — sample the lightest value in your image with the eyedropper. The example image has a slightly blue tinge, so its lightest RGB value is about 230/206/168. The remapped levels are shown in Figure 8.14. You see the spikes in the graph are distributed much more evenly across the graph than they were before resampling, shown in Figure 8.11.

- **Gray point.** The Set Gray Point eyedropper is the middle eyedropper in the Levels dialog box. You can click the eyedropper and sample the image to specify the midrange tones on the image. In the Info palette, look for RGB values in the midrange, somewhere in the 128/128/128 value.

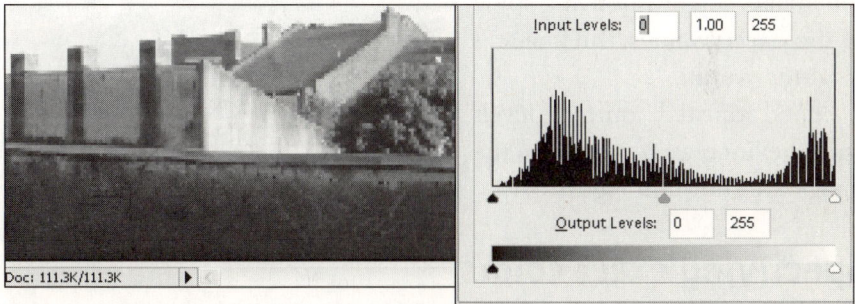

Figure 8.14. Redefining the black and white points on the image distributes the levels of darkness and lightness across the image.

Tweaking midrange tones

The total pixel range in the rooftops at dawn image was decreased to 220 levels in the Input Levels histogram to distribute dark and light better by shifting pixels to brighter values. The next step is to improve the detail and contrast by adjusting the midrange tones.

The midrange can be handled in a number of ways, including these:

- Sample the image using the Set Gray Point eyedropper. As explained earlier, this method may or may not be very accurate.

- Adjust the gray point on the Input Levels slider. Dragging the gray triangle below the graph on the Levels dialog box to the left moves dark pixels into the midtone range, providing more midrange detail. Dragging the gray triangle below the graph on the Levels dialog box to the right moves light pixels into the midtone range, again providing more midrange detail.

- Adjust the black Output Level slider. Dragging the black triangle under the Output Levels gradient to the right decreases the amount of black in the image, lightening the midtones and overall lightening the image. In the opposite way, dragging the white Output Levels triangle below the gradient to the left sets a darker color as white and makes the image darker overall.

In the sample image, the black triangle under the Output Levels gradient is moved to the right 15 levels. Nothing is changed in the input levels for the image, but by removing some of the darker values, the image is brighter overall.

The adjusted output levels and the increased detail in the image are shown in Figure 8.15.

Figure 8.15. Adjusting the gray point shows more detail, such as the mortar on the brick wall and the clusters of leaves on the trees.

Specifying exact colors

Suppose you have a picture taken in winter and you'd rather create the illusion of summer sun. You could go about creating this illusion in a number of ways, such as using Photo Filters (read about them in Chapter 9) or

CHAPTER 8 ■ ALL IN THE DETAILS

Inside Scoop

I seldom use the Set Gray Point eyedropper for simply mapping the color range because it takes too much time to choose a sample accurately. Instead, I make adjustments to either the Input Levels or the Output Levels sliders in the Levels dialog box.

working with an Adjustment layer (more in Chapter 11). Or you can make the adjustment right in the Levels dialog box, which applies the changes directly to the image's pixels.

Coincidentally, I just happen to have an image that needs a final touch. Let's go back to the example photo shown in Figure 8.15 one last time. Follow these steps to adjust the color values for highlights:

1. Move the Set White Point eyedropper over the image, reading the values in the Info palette.
2. When the Info palette identifies a very light value, double-click the Set White Point eyedropper to open the Color Picker.
3. Type the color values you want to assign to the lightest level in the image, or adjust the sliders and click a color in the Color Picker, shown in Figure 8.16.

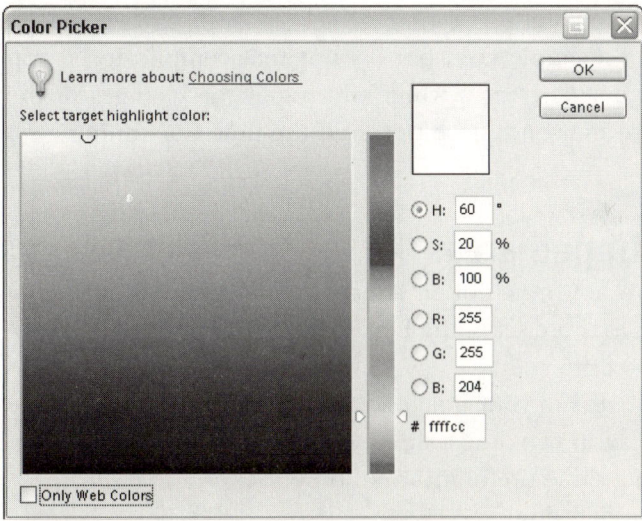

Figure 8.16. A soft yellow color was selected to make the highlight in the image simulate warmer sunshine.

>  **Hack**
>
> The next time you open the Levels dialog box, you won't see the image's original histogram because the file has been saved with the adjusted tonal range. Make a habit of saving a copy of the original file.

4. Click OK to close the Color Picker and return to the Levels dialog box.

5. When all adjustments are made, click OK to close the Levels dialog box. Be sure to save the edited image.

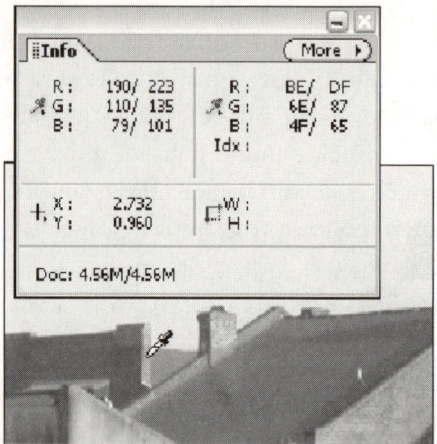

Figure 8.17. The Info palette lists the color at a sample point before and after modification.

The pixel values throughout the image are adjusted proportionately to the new highlight values. The Info palette shows the values both before and after the color adjustment. In Figure 8.17, for example, a sample area showing an area on the brick chimney where light is being reflected shows two color values in the Info palette.

Using levels isn't a simple task, but it's not that complicated if you experiment with the sliders for a while and watch the changes in the image. Of course, you may not have to spend the time fine-tuning each and every image.

Previewing clipped areas

You may not be sure how much of an effect you can create by adjusting lighting levels, such as those set in the Levels dialog box or the Shadows/Highlights dialog box.

Check out what areas of your image will be clipped to black or white by pressing the Alt key as you drag a slider. It's a rather interesting effect, aside from displaying some useful information.

You discover the following:

- Black patches show areas that are clipped to black when using a Shadow or Black Point slider, as shown in Figure 8.18.

- White patches show areas that are clipped to white when using a Highlight or White Point slider.
- Colored patches show clipping in individual color channels.

Figure 8.18. Preview the clipping areas, such as the areas clipped to black.

Using individual color channels

One final task you can perform in the Levels dialog box is to work with individual color channels to remove a color cast, an abnormal color tint such as blue or yellow.

Modifying color casts by adjusting a channel's levels is a fairly advanced activity. You need to understand color theory and how color values interrelate. For example:

- Choose the Red channel to add either red or cyan to the image.
- Choose the Green channel to add either green or magenta to the image.
- Choose the Blue channel to add either blue or yellow to the image.

Here's an example using the Blue channel. To make adjustments to an image using a single color channel, follow these steps:

1. Click the Channel drop-down menu at the top of the Levels dialog box and choose an individual color channel for alteration; the examples shown in Figure 8.19 result from shifting color in the Blue channel.
2. Drag the middle input slider left to add more of the channel's blue color, or right to subtract color, moving the color to the opposite

side of the color wheel, such as yellow, shown in the lower image in Figure 8.19.

3. Choose RGB from the Channel drop-down menu to return to the full image.

4. When all adjustments are finished, click OK to close the Levels dialog box.

Figure 8.19. Select a single channel and drag the input slider left to increase the channel's color (top) or decrease the channel's color (bottom).

Quick color cast corrections

If you have a color cast in your image, you can remove it quickly in the Levels dialog box. Using the Gray Point eyedropper, click a location on the image that should be neutral gray without any other color. When you click the eyedropper, you specify the color that should be neutral and the rest of the image is remapped and the abnormal color cast disappears.

If the area you sample isn't correct, the image shifts into very bright and strange colors, such as bright purple. Click the Reset button and sample another area.

Read about color casts and how to remove them using several other methods in Chapter 9.

Just the facts

- Enhance an image by adjusting highlights and shadows visually using sliders.
- Adjust the brightness and contrast in a photo to show more detail.
- Use the Info palette to show color information for a point or a sample on the image.
- The histogram in the Levels dialog box shows the distribution of dark, medium, and light tones in an image.
- Use the sliders and fields in the Levels dialog box to adjust tonal values numerically.

- Specify White, Black, and Gray Points in the image using the appropriate eyedroppers to adjust the levels visually; you can also choose an exact color for one of the sampled points from the Color Picker.
- Previewing the clipped areas in the Levels dialog box gives you an indication of how much adjustment is needed in the image.
- Use separate color channels in the Levels dialog box to adjust individual colors.

GET THE SCOOP ON...
■ Color management and calibration ■ Using color profiles ■ Converting color modes ■ Modifying and improving color ■ Removing color casts

In Living Color

What does robin's egg blue really look like? Or how about canary yellow? Or leaf green? You may be able to answer these questions, but I doubt your computer can.

Humans are often very sensitive to color, and use it as a means of expression in many industries and walks of life. Reliance on color to such a large extent is both good and bad. Technology has developed that manipulates color in very sophisticated ways. On the other hand, interpreting color can be very difficult for electronic devices, especially when communicating with each another.

Managing color

Look around your office for a moment and what do you see? Don't eye that set of matching wicker baskets you added after watching another home improvement program; I am referring to the equipment. In my office (aside from my own set of matching wicker baskets), I have a couple of scanners, two flat-screen LCD monitors, one analog monitor, a printer, and a shelf holding several digital still and video cameras.

What ties all these things together (aside from cables)? They all capture or manipulate data using color. Unfortunately, each device reproduces color in a different way because of its characteristics. A computer monitor and a printer both interpret color, but they do it using different

Chapter 9

> **Inside Scoop**
> Don't bother using the Adobe Gamma calibration method with a flat-screen monitor or a laptop. The colors on LCD monitors change dramatically based on your viewing angle. Instead, use your monitor's color profile.

ranges of color, called *color gamuts*. A monitor, for example, can display millions of colors, while a printer has much less range.

An example of the differences between the two gamuts is shown in Figure 9.1. If you look at the overlapped triangle and oval shapes, you see that some areas are within one shape that aren't within another. These are called *out-of-gamut* colors, and the colors that must be interpreted between color models.

Each time digital information is transferred from one device to another, the colors in the file shift because each device uses a different color gamut. Different devices and systems use different methods of *color management*, which is a method of examining and translating image color.

In many devices, you can find a way to calibrate the color, comparing the existing settings against an established standard and modifying the settings to match the standard. In this way, transferring data from one device to another — such as from a camera to computer monitor to printer — can be more predictable.

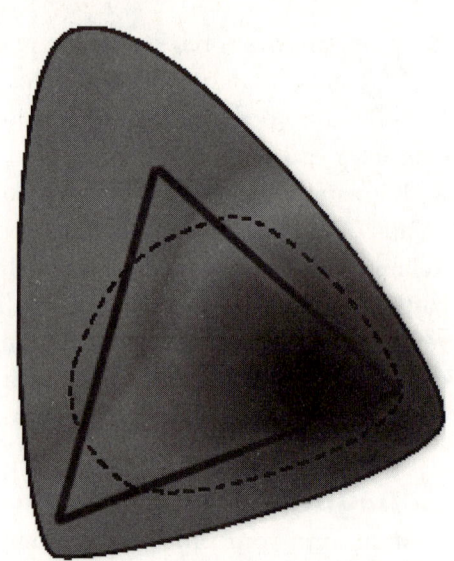

Figure 9.1. Monitors and printers display different ranges of color.

Calibrating your monitor

Photoshop Elements provides a color management tool for displaying monitor color accurately based on International Color Consortium (ICC) device profiles, the industry standard for reproducing colors accurately across devices such as scanners, monitors, and printers. ICC profiles are

> **What kind of monitor are you using?**
>
> You are likely working with either an analog or an LCD monitor. The difference lies in the technology used to display the image, which makes the two types of monitors radically different in terms of physical size.
>
> An analog monitor, like a traditional television, is based on cathode ray tube (CRT) technology. To display color, the monitor uses a coating on the inside of the screen that shows color in response to electronic stimulation. The monitor requires a specific distance to stimulate the screen's coating, resulting in the traditional deep (and heavy) monitor.
>
> A digital display uses LCD (Liquid Crystal Display) to display color. The diodes are stimulated electronically as well, but because they are arranged on a flat plastic sheet, the monitor can be sleek and flat.

an example of Image Color Matching (ICM), a technique that uses color profiles for images and devices such as scanners or printers.

Calibration involves two processes for the monitor: The first is setting up your computer's monitor for testing, and the second is applying the profile.

Setting your monitor

If you are working with an analog monitor, follow these steps to set it up for calibration:

1. Right-click the desktop, and choose Properties from the shortcut menu to open the Display Properties dialog box.

2. Click the Desktop tab. Scroll through the Background menu, and select None to remove any background image you may have set.

Watch Out!
Don't calibrate your monitor immediately after turning it on. Monitors may not show color accurately until they are warmed up, which takes about 30 minutes.

3. Click the color swatch at the lower right of the dialog box to open a small color palette, and choose the neutral gray at the top right of the palette, shown in Figure 9.2.

4. Click Apply to reset the desktop color and click OK to close the Display Properties dialog box.

Preparing the profile

Now that the desktop is set, you're ready to do the calibration. Again, you start from the desktop. To calibrate the monitor, you have to be logged on to the computer as Administrator. Check the Help files to learn how to log in as Administrator. The method used to specify the login depends on how your system is set up.

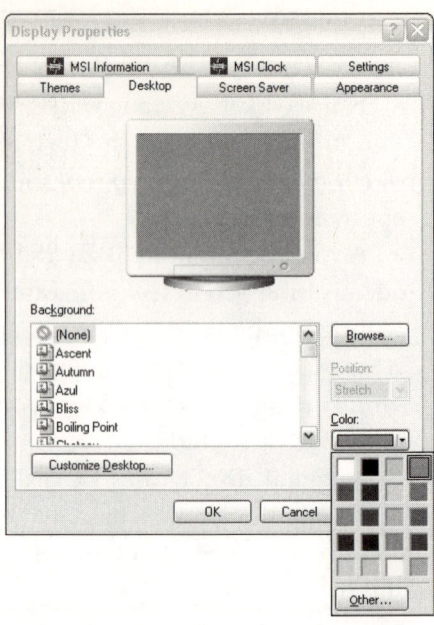

Figure 9.2. Change the desktop color to a neutral gray for calibration.

Makeup of a monitor profile

When you create a monitor profile, information about how color is generated by both your video card and monitor is stored in a file. The profile includes brightness, contrast, and *gamma*, the brightness of the midtone values. Also included in the profile is information about the monitor's *phosphors*, the elements that emit color on the screen. Finally, data about the monitor's white point is stored. *White point* refers to the coordinates on a color chart where the red, green, and blue phosphors create white when fired at full intensity.

Inside Scoop

If you are unsure or don't have much experience in monitor calibration — and let's face it, it's not really a common skill — follow through the Wizard's panels. I usually don't recommend that anyone take the long way to do anything, but a calibration profile is one exception.

Follow these steps to set up the calibration:

1. Choose Start ⇨ Settings ⇨ Control Panel ⇨ Adobe Gamma.

2. In the Adobe Gamma dialog box, choose one of two ways to calibrate the monitor and create its profile. You can choose either Step by Step (Wizard) or Control Panel.

3. Follow through the remaining dialog boxes. Using the Wizard option, you pass through seven panes, making choices and adjusting settings. Perhaps the biggest advantage of using the Wizard is the final pane that lets you toggle the Before and After views to see the changes. Very helpful if this is your first foray into calibration.

If you choose the Control Panel option, you choose the same options, but they are collected in one dialog box, shown in Figure 9.3.

4. After you have made changes to the settings using either method, click Finish in the Wizard or OK in the control panel. A Save As dialog box opens.

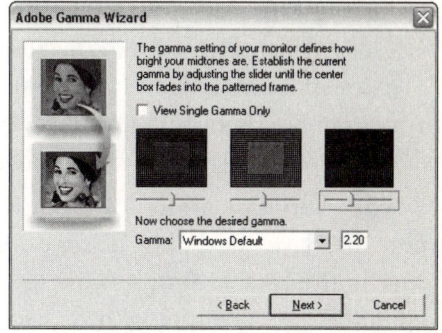

Figure 9.3. Specify a range of settings to produce a monitor profile.

5. Name the monitor profile and click Save to store the file on your computer as an ICC profile. Storing a copy of the profile means that you can reinstall the same profile quickly when you need to, for example, if you move the monitor to another computer.

Hack

If you are not using Windows XP, check that the Color quality in the Settings tab of the Display Properties dialog box is at least 16-bit color. If not, choose the setting from the drop-down menu. In Windows XP, the lowest color quality available is 16-bit color.

Managing color in the program

In Photoshop Elements, you can apply color management profiles to individual images or assign a color profile to the entire program.

Embedding color profiles in an image

Assigning a color profile to an image means that you will be working with it in the same color space, making sure the image displays colors correctly and consistently when it's opened.

When your file is opened in the Standard Editor mode, choose Image ⇨ Convert Color Profile and select a profile choice from the submenu. To remove an existing color profile from an image, choose Image ⇨ Convert Color Profile ⇨ Remove Profile.

In Photoshop Elements, you can choose from two profiles:

- **sRGB.** Most monitors are capable of displaying the range of colors in the sRGB color space only. The sRGB color space is calibrated specifically for use online and is now a Web standard.

- **AdobeRGB.** Adobe Systems created the AdobeRGB color space, used for its suite of programs that manage color and images. This color space includes a large color gamut that can be used for converting documents to CMYK (Cyan-Magenta-Yellow-Black color, a color space designed for printing).

When you have added or modified an image's color profile and you open the Save As dialog box, you see that the ICC Profile choice is active in the Save Options in the lower part of the dialog box. As shown in Figure 9.4, the dialog box also specifies which profile has been applied.

Bright Idea

You certainly don't need to embed color profiles for images that are used casually, such as your kid's school picnic photos. On the other hand, if you are preparing images for your online catalog, you want the color to be as accurate as possible.

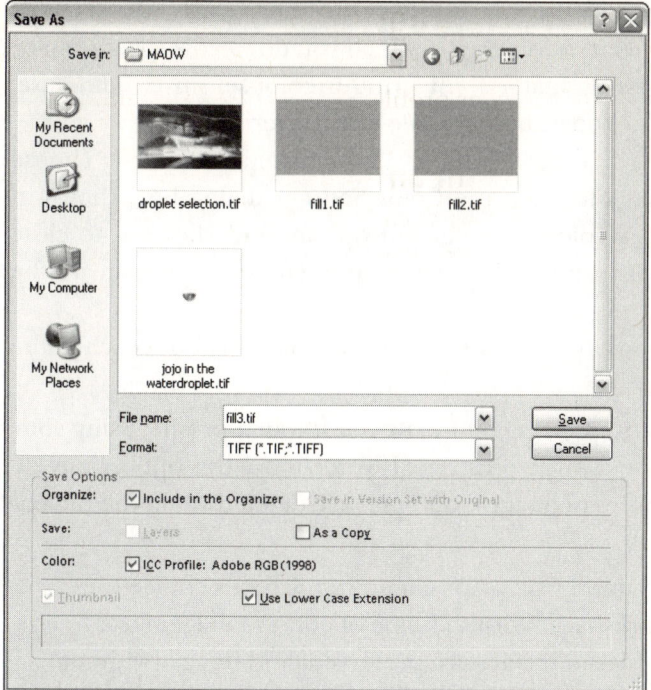

Figure 9.4. The available color profile is shown in the dialog box.

Assigning a program color space

Instead of manually choosing color spaces for each image, you can specify that Photoshop Elements apply a color space automatically.

Depending on the work I am doing, I may choose one of the available profiles, or I may specify no color management. It's not a big deal for many of us most of the time, but it is one more thing to consider and choose, so it is helpful to understand the choices.

If you have chosen a color space for the program and then you open an image using another embedded color space, you have to respond to a dialog box asking how you want to manage the image's color. Although you can click the Don't Show Again check box that prevents the dialog box from displaying in the future, that's not necessarily a good idea either. You may have circumstances in which you do need a specific color space, such as preparing material for print or color-sensitive online use, and it's important to know about the file's characteristics.

From either the Standard Edit or Photo Browser window, choose Edit ⇨ Color Settings to open the Color Settings dialog box, shown in Figure 9.5. Choose a color management option, and click OK to close the dialog box. The settings are maintained in the program as the default.

The Color Settings dialog box includes information about each of the choices:

- Choose No Color Management to work without a profile, using your monitor's profile as the workspace. If you choose this option, any embedded profiles in images you open are deleted when the file is saved.

- The Always Optimize Colors for Computer Screens choice uses sRGB as the workspace. With this type of color management, embedded profiles in images are preserved, and images without embedded profiles are tagged as sRGB files when opened.

- Choose the Always Optimize for Printing choice to use AdobeRGB as the workspace. This choice preserves embedded profiles and assigns AdobeRGB when opening untagged files.

- Select Allow Me to Choose to pick a profile to attach to files that have no embedded profile when they are opened in Standard Edit mode; the program's workspace is sRGB.

Inside Scoop
To find out which profile is attached to an image in the Photo Browser, click the Metadata button in the Properties palette, and find the Color Profile listing in the File Properties. Read more about metadata in Chapter 21.

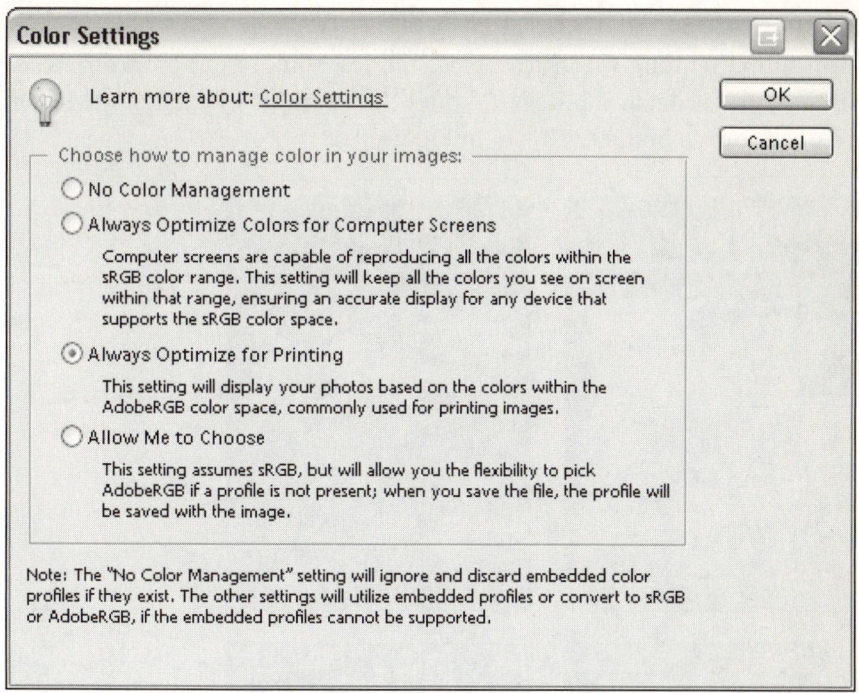

Figure 9.5. Select a method for handling color in an image from the Color Settings dialog box.

Describing color modes

Color, besides coming in all sorts of actual colors, also comes in a variety of models, modes, depths, and channels. Color *models* are systems that define the attributes of color. As described earlier in the chapter, models are standards defined and maintained by various organizations and manufacturers to allow devices to specify color in a certain way. Models include RGB, HSB, and CMYK color.

A color *mode* describes how the colors in an individual image are defined. Common color modes are RGB and grayscale.

Channels and color or bit depth go hand in hand. A *channel* is a description for color data. Different types of images have different numbers of channels. For instance, a grayscale image has one channel — gray — and an RGB image has three channels — red, green, and blue. The *depth* of the color depends on the number of bits of information stored in each channel.

Color modes

Photoshop Elements offers four color modes. You can choose from **RGB**, bitmaps, grayscale, and indexed modes. An example of each mode using the same source image is shown in Figure 9.6.

Figure 9.6. Clockwise from top left are RGB, indexed, grayscale, and bitmap color. The same image looks quite different depending on the color mode (although in this grayscale image, both grayscale and RGB color examples look the same).

RGB color, as described elsewhere, refers to color that uses a grid arrangement of red, green, and blue pixels in varying depths to create color.

Bitmap images are composed of rows and columns of colored dots. When you see a bitmap onscreen, each dot is shown as a pixel; when you

Inside Scoop

You can't save all image modes in all file formats. Some formats are specific to certain formats. For instance, the WBMP format (wireless bitmap) is available only if the image is a bitmap; the Photoshop RAW and JPEG 2000 formats are available only if the image is RGB or grayscale.

see a printed bitmap, each dot is printed as an ink dot. Bitmaps are *resolution-dependent*. That is, changing the size of a bitmap changes the size of its pixels, causing distortion in the image.

A *grayscale* image displays relative lightness and darkness that you see as shades of gray. Grayscale images can be saved in the same file formats as RGB images, such as TIFF or JPEG.

Indexed color contains limited color information. Indexed color files, such as GIF image files you often see on the Web, are designed in an interesting way. Indexed color uses a specified number of colors, ranging from 2 colors to 256 colors. Rather than pixels that are shaded different colors, the pixels in an indexed color image are *indexed*, or referenced, to a palette of colors that define the colors you see in the image.

Channels and bit depth

Images have channels. Not as many as your TV, fortunately, but common image modes have varying numbers of channels.

A *channel* is a description for color data. Different types of images have different numbers of channels. For example, grayscale, bitmap-mode, or indexed-color images all have one channel. RGB images have three channels, and CMYK images have four channels — one each for cyan, magenta, yellow, and black (the K in CMYK).

Bit *depth* ranges from 1-bit to 48-bit color depth and describes the number of bits per channel. The numbers identify how much color information can be stored in the image. The higher the number, the more color information is stored, as you can see in Figure 9.7.

Hack

If you have images in other formats such as CMYK, you have to change their mode to use them in Photoshop Elements. When you try to open the file, a dialog box opens explaining the problem. Click Convert mode, and the file opens as an RGB file.

Figure 9.7. Even though this image isn't printed in color, the difference between the 4-bit image on the left and the 16-bit image on the right is very noticeable.

The higher the color depth, the more color information is available for displaying or printing. As a result, the image displays a larger number of colors and produces a more accurate image. It also results in a larger file size.

Converting to shades of gray

Photoshop Elements gives you two commands and a third option for removing color, or desaturating an image. One method produces an actual color mode change, while the others simply adjust the RGB values of the image. These are your options:

- Convert an image to grayscale mode to change the color information in the image. Choose Image ⇨ Mode ⇨ Grayscale. A dialog box opens asking if you want to discard the color information. Click OK to close the dialog box and change the image.

- Strip the color from an image to display it in shades of gray. Choose Enhance ⇨ Adjust Color ⇨ Remove Color. The color in the image is removed, leaving the shades of gray only.

- Choose Enhance ⇨ Adjust Color ⇨ Adjust Hue/Saturation. Drag the Saturation slider to -100 to desaturate the image's color.

The file size is substantially different between an image converted to grayscale and the other two options. In the latter cases, the RGB color information remains in the file, but values for red, green, and blue are

>  **Inside Scoop**
>
> A very interesting effect can be produced in an image using the Remove Color command. Select an area of an image with one of the selection tools, and then apply the Remove Color command. The selected area is desaturated while the rest of the image remains colored. Read about selection tools in Chapter 10.

changed to the same value that is seen as a shade of gray. Removing the color and desaturating the color in an image are the same thing.

When a grayscale image is created, the color channels are removed, leaving one channel to hold the gray information.

Bitmapping

A bitmap image is a very efficient type of image file because it contains very little color information. On the down side, only certain types of content work well as images saved in bitmap mode. The best candidates for converting to bitmap mode are simple line drawings or text.

You can experiment with any sort of image to see if it will work as a bitmap. The graininess of the bitmap mode adds an interesting effect to the image in Figure 9.8 while decreasing file size substantially. Converting an image from an RGB file to a bitmap file decreased the file size from more than 11,000KB to 567KB, while using the same size and resolution.

Bitmap mode can be used to create some interesting images, although they are nothing like the originals. Experiment with the options in the Bitmap dialog box for different outcomes.

Figure 9.8. Experiment with an image to see how it looks converted to bitmap mode.

Follow these steps to convert an image to a bitmap:

1. Choose Image ⇨ Mode ⇨ Bitmap.
2. A bitmap can be generated only from a grayscale image, but you don't have to do that manually. A dialog box opens asking if you want to convert the image to grayscale. Click OK.
3. The Bitmap dialog box sets the original file's Input resolution as the Output resolution as identified in Figure 9.9; click the field, and type an alternate value if you want to change the converted image's resolution as part of the overall conversion process.

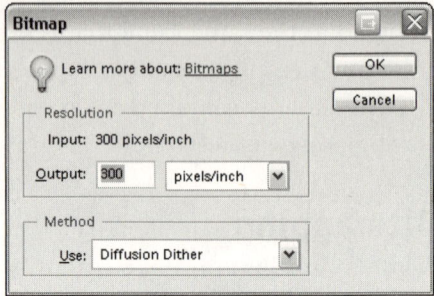

Figure 9.9. Specify the resolution for your converted image and the type of dithering to apply.

4. Choose a conversion method from the Use drop-down menu. The methods available include 50% Threshold, Pattern Dither, or Diffusion Dither. The outcomes are quite different, as you can see in Figure 9.10. Differences between the options are described in Table 9.1.
5. Click OK to close the dialog box and finish the conversion.

Table 9.1. Bitmap conversion options	
Setting	**Effect**
50% Threshold	The outcome is a very high-contrast image because the pixels are assigned to either black or white. Pixels with a gray value of 128 or more convert to white; pixels with a gray value less than 128 convert to black.
Pattern Dither	The gray levels in the image are arranged into geometric configurations of black or white dots.
Diffusion Dither	This method applies a mathematical process starting with the pixel at the upper-left corner. If the pixel is above mid gray, with a value of 128 or more, the pixel converts to white; pixels below 128 convert to black. The amount of error calculated between the selected pixel and pure black or white is diffused through the image, causing a grainy texture.

CHAPTER 9 ■ IN LIVING COLOR

Inside Scoop
To make your image more interesting, consider using something in the background, such as a simple linear gradient like that used in the example shown in Figure 9.10.

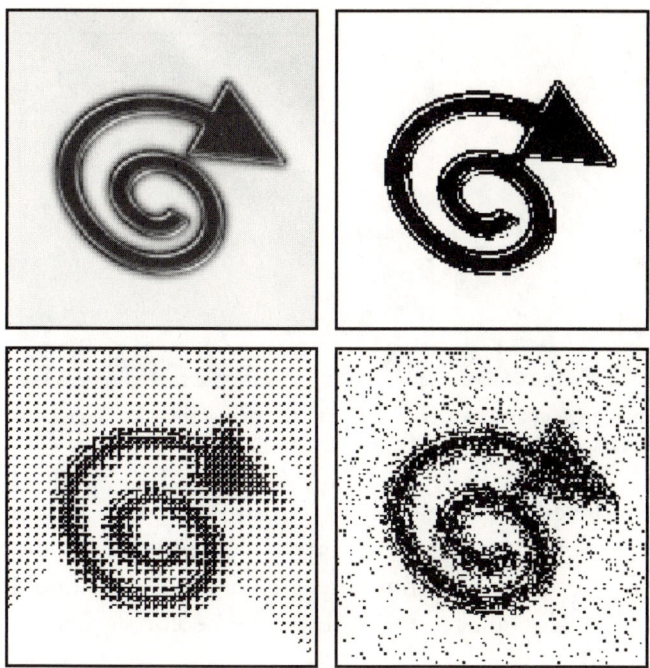

Figure 9.10. The conversion method used to create a bitmap can produce very different results. Clockwise from the top left are grayscale, 50% Threshold, Diffusion Dither, and Pattern Dither.

Indexing color

Indexed color produces efficiently sized images, ideal for use online when the image contains the right sorts of content. Large blocks of color, no gradients, and simple shapes like text are best for indexed color.

The files are small because of the limited amount of color information stored in the file. If you compare a sketch or line drawing of a sunset with a photograph of a sunset, you can understand the difference. You can also understand why an image with the amount of detail like that used in a photograph isn't a good candidate for indexed color. If you zoom into a high-resolution photograph, you can easily find a few hundred shades of a color like that shown in the top image in Figure 9.11. An image in indexed mode can have only 256 colors in total—converting the photo to an indexed image produces blocks of color, like the lower image in Figure 9.11.

 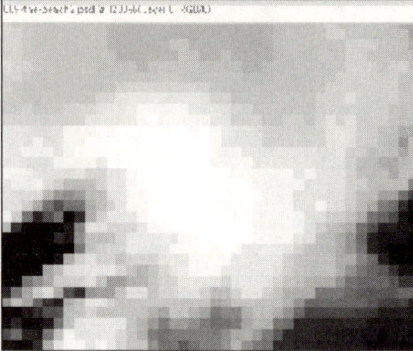

Figure 9.11. High-resolution photographs have hundreds of shades of one color (left), making them poor candidates for indexed color mode (right).

The color in an indexed color image is derived from a color lookup table (CLUT), created when the file is converted. The table stores and indexes the colors in the image. To condense the colors to the limited number in an indexed color image, either the closest color or a simulated color is substituted.

You can read about working with indexed color and color tables in Chapter 22.

Converting the image

If you are converting a grayscale image to indexed color mode, selecting the command converts the file automatically and that's all there is to it.

However, to convert an RGB image to indexed color, you need to follow these steps:

1. Open the RGB image, and choose Image ⇨ Mode ⇨ Indexed Color to open the Indexed Color dialog box.

2. By default, the Preview check box should be selected. Check to make sure it is selected, because it is helpful to see previews when setting the conversion options.

3. Choose a Palette from the list of 10 palettes in the drop-down menu. The palette you select determines the remaining options available in the dialog box.

4. Choose other options as required and available. You can specify a transparency, choose a matte color for transparency, specify a dithering option, and determine how much the original colors are affected by the applied dither.

5. Click OK to close the dialog box and convert the file.

Adjusting image color

One common way to adjust color in an RGB or indexed color image is by modifying Hue/Saturation/Lightness values, known as HSL. Color can be adjusted using these three factors in a variety of dialog boxes in the program or through the Hue/Saturation command.

To change the color of an image, choose Enhance ⇨ Adjust Color ⇨ Adjust Hue/Saturation. In the dialog box shown in Figure 9.12, you can choose to edit one color range by selecting it from the Edit drop-down menu, or you can leave the default Master option selected, which edits all color in the image.

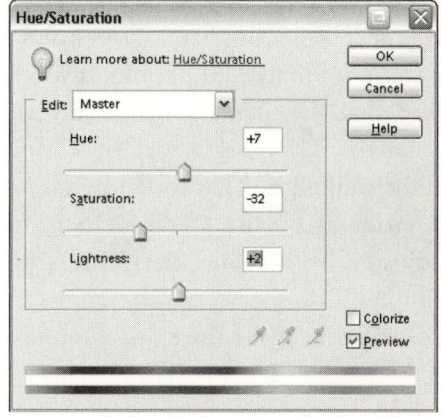

Figure 9.12. Adjust color in the Hue/Saturation dialog box, available for indexed and RGB color modes.

Adjusting the sliders in the dialog box produces these effects:

- Drag the Hue slider right to change color through blue to red, using values from 0 to +180; drag the Hue slider left to change color through green to red, using values from 0 to -180.

Watch Out!
If you are using a bitmap or grayscale image, you don't have color to adjust, and therefore the command isn't available.

>
> **Inside Scoop**
>
> Customizing the range for individual colors in the Adjust Hue/Saturation dialog box can produce interesting color shift effects. Select a color from the Edit drop-down menu and drag the sliders at the bottom of the dialog box, or use the eyedroppers to sample color in the image.

- Drag the Saturation slider left to decrease the intensity of the color, in a range of 0 to -180, which is desaturated, or drag it right to make the color brighter, in a range of 0 to +180.

- Drag the Lightness slider left to darken the image and right to brighten the image. At the far left, with a value of -100, the image is solid black; at the far right, with a value of +100, the image is solid white.

Improving skin tone

If you look through many peoples' image collections, you see a large number of images of people. If you look closely at those images, you may find that the skin coloring isn't quite right. Although you can adjust color for skin using a variety of tools, Photoshop Elements offers a special tool designed for touching up skin color.

Your image isn't edited in isolation, however. As the skin tone is adjusted, so are the other colors in the image. Correcting the color is simpler if the person in the image is the main subject. When you set the color correctly for the skin, the rest of the image follows suit.

> ### Hue/Saturation effects
>
> Aside from making improvements to the color in your image, you can use the Hue/Saturation sliders for some interesting effects. For example, try selecting different areas in an image and desaturate them to make other areas of the image stand out because of their color.
>
> You could also flip the Hue, dragging the Hue slider to the opposite end of the slider so the image's contents are colored opposite to what you might expect.

> **Bright Idea**
> Make a selection if you need to make corrections to certain areas instead of applying a skin tone correction to an entire face or body. Read about selections in Chapter 10.

Choose Enhance ⇨ Adjust Color ⇨ Adjust Color For Skin Tone to open the dialog box shown in Figure 9.13. To make the basic adjustment, move your mouse over the image and click the skin.

Sometimes the changes are slight, while other times they are quite dramatic. In Figure 9.13, the top image, which is the before picture, was far too red and almost blotchy; the corrected image, shown in the bottom image, is much more realistic.

If you aren't satisfied with the change, drag the sliders to change brown or red levels in the skin, or adjust the Ambient Light slider to change the overall color in the image. You can reset the image using the Reset button; click OK when your adjustments are made.

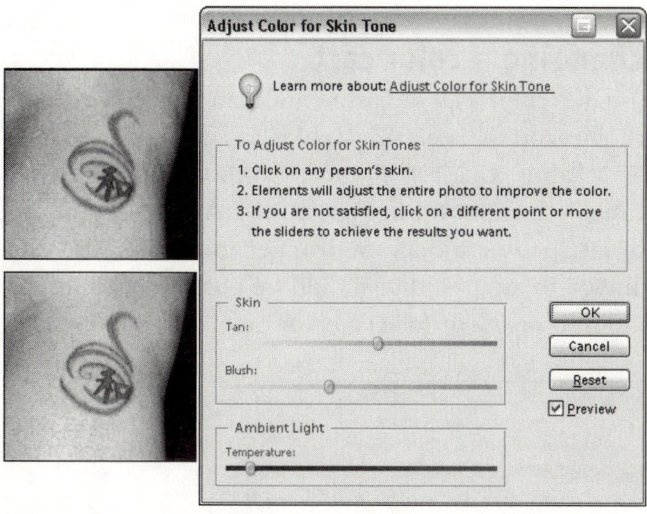

Figure 9.13. The color in the image is adjusted automatically based on modifications to the skin tone.

Dealing with a color cast

Our eyes see neutral tones as neutral, regardless of the color of the light under normal lighting conditions. A camera, not being human, doesn't "see" in the same way and captures neutral grays as they exist and not as they are interpreted.

Identifying a color cast

When you take a photograph, your camera uses the light that is available. Different types of light have different color casts. For example, pictures shot indoors without a flash often show a yellow color cast, although you may not notice any extra color at all. On the other hand, a daytime image on an overcast day, again without flash, may have more of a bluish cast.

What does that mean for your editing? Take a good look at your images, and search for areas that are or should be neutral. When you make adjustments, keep track of how the neutral areas look.

If you are the hands-on type, you can correct color casts, highlights, and shadows using the Variations window, described a bit later.

Automatically changing a color cast

You don't have to make color cast adjustments manually. Photoshop Elements provides a command for removing a color cast with a single click.

Choose Enhance ⇨ Adjust Color ⇨ Remove Color Cast to open the Remove Color Cast dialog box shown in Figure 9.14. All you see in the dialog box is a bit of instruction and an eyedropper tool. Move the eyedropper over your image to an area that should be pure gray, white, or black, and click the tool to *sample* or select a color pixel for analysis.

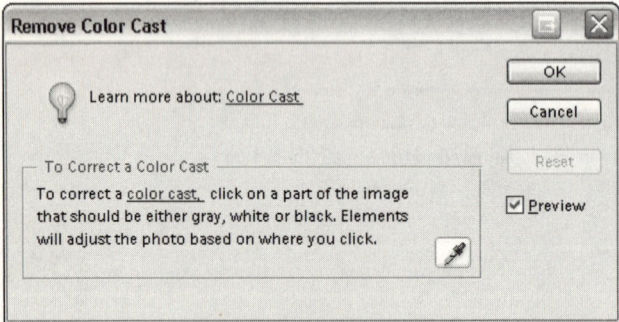

Figure 9.14. Use the single eyedropper in the Remove Color Cast dialog box to sample the image and adjust its color automatically.

Inside Scoop

Instead of one-click color cast removal, you can manipulate color casts as part of working with Levels. Read about using levels in Chapter 8.

Photoshop Elements interprets the sampled pixel as white, black, or gray, and adjusts the color in the image automatically. If you sample an area and the image changes to some bright and obviously incorrect color, click Reset in the Remove Color Cast dialog box to return to your original color and start again. Click OK to close the dialog box and return to the freshly colored image.

Color correction using variations

Since I was an eager young design student, one of my favorite Photoshop (and now Photoshop Elements) activities has been using the Color Variations dialog box to play with color and tone in an image.

Unlike other commands that apply changes to your image as you modify settings in the dialog box, the Color Variations dialog box shows a collection of thumbnails. The really neat thing is that each time you make a change in the dialog box, all the thumbnails are updated. It's a very dynamic way to work.

If your image needs lots of color adjustment, you may want to use the Levels dialog box instead, which is described in Chapter 8.

Choose Enhance ⇨ Adjust Color ⇨ Color Variations to open the Color Variations dialog box, shown in Figure 9.15. The dialog box describes the order you use to choose each type of adjustment:

1. Select the adjustment option by clicking the radio button. You can adjust the Midtones, Shadows, Highlights, or Saturation.
2. Drag the Adjust Color Amount slider to control the amount of change applied to the image per mouse click.
3. Click a thumbnail to apply the change illustrated. If you are adjusting Saturation, you only see two thumbnails.

Watch Out!
If you can't choose the Color Variations command from the menu, check the image mode. Variations can't be adjusted for images using indexed color.

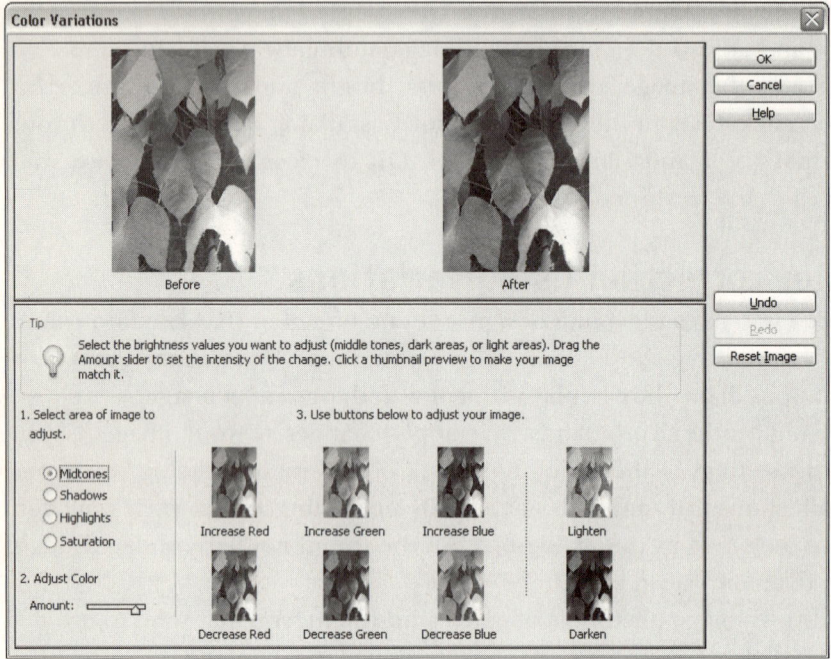

Figure 9.15. Adjust color and tone dynamically in the Color Variations dialog box.

There isn't a specific path that you must follow through the dialog box to make changes to a photo, just their recommended order of operations. Here are some pointers and tips to consider:

- Keep an eye on your changes using the previews at the top of the dialog box. You see both the original image and the edited image.
- Choose a tonal range you want to adjust by clicking one of Shadows, Midtones, or Highlights to adjust dark, medium, and light areas, respectively.
- Use the Adjust Color Intensity slider to make changes. Drag the slider to the left to decrease the intensity or right to increase the intensity.
- Add color to your image by clicking the Increase color thumbnail; remove color by clicking the Decrease color thumbnail.

- Undo your changes by clicking Reset Image to return to the original image.
- Use Undo to return to previous adjustments. You can click Undo repeatedly, but you can't undo Reset Image. To track back, click Redo, which you can also apply repeatedly until you get to the final adjustment made to the image.
- For adjusting color saturation, click Less Saturation or More Saturation and watch the changes in the preview; you can click the button as many times as necessary, of course.
- When the image is perfect, click OK to close the dialog box and apply the adjustments.

Photo filters

Photoshop Elements includes some specialized filters called Photo Filters that simulate different types of camera filters as well as specific colors. The advantage of using a filter rather than making changes in the Color Variations dialog box, for example, is the amount of control you have over how the color is applied. In addition to choosing a filter color, you can also specify the density, or how intense the filter is shown over the image. Preserve the brightness in the image by selecting the Luminosity check box.

Each image shown in Figure 9.16 uses the same Orange Photo Filter, and each has the same density setting of 100%, meaning the filter is applied at full strength. You see the bottom version is much darker, resulting from

Figure 9.16. Both versions of the image use the same filter and density; the bottom image doesn't have luminosity preserved, resulting in a much darker image.

deselecting the Luminosity setting in the Photo Filter dialog box. Maintaining the luminosity prevents the color added by the filter from darkening the image by applying the color to the image without affecting the brightness levels. The groups of photo filters and how they appear are listed in Table 9.2.

Follow these steps to use a photo filter on your image:

1. Choose Filter ➪ Adjustments ➪ Photo Filter to open the Photo Filter dialog box. The Preview and Preserve Luminosity check boxes are selected by default as shown in Figure 9.17.

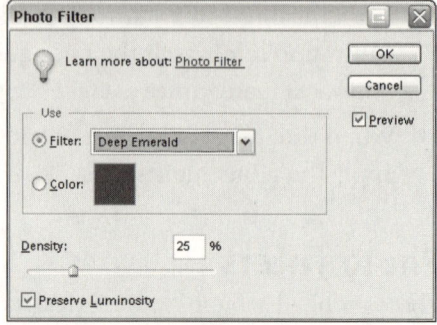

Figure 9.17. Specify the named filter or a color in the dialog box.

2. Select a type of filter, either a named filter or a color:

   - Select the Filter radio button, click the drop-down arrow, and choose a filter from the menu.
   - Select the Color radio button, and then double-click the color swatch to open the Color Picker. Select the color you want to apply, and click OK to close the Color Picker and return to the Photo Filter dialog box.

3. Drag the Density slider to adjust the amount of color added to the image, or type a value in the percentage field. The color is defined as a percentage.

4. Click the Preserve Luminosity check box to prevent the image from being darkened, like the lower sample in Figure 9.16.

5. Click OK to close the dialog box.

Inside Scoop

Instead of applying the filter directly to your image, you can use an Adjustment layer. Read about Adjustment layers in Chapter 11.

Table 9.2. Types of photo filters

Group of Filters	Produce This Effect
Warming	Adjusts white balance making the image warmer (more yellow)
Cooling	Adjusts white balance making the image cooler (more blue)
Colors	Adjusts hue based on selected color
Underwater	Displays a greenish-blue color cast like that seen underwater

Reading color information

In Chapter 7, a histogram was shown in the Layers dialog box to show how to adjust areas of darkness and light in an image. In Chapter 23 a histogram is used in the Camera Raw dialog box to show you how to manipulate the unprocessed camera data. If you like, you can display a separate histogram that displays data for any image, except for bitmaps.

Working with histograms isn't for everyone. They are complex, and require that you correlate what your eyes see in an image with numerical and graphically plotted information on the histogram. For some people, using a histogram is a useful tool to help quantify what you are correcting in an image.

Selecting content

Choose Window ⇨ Histogram to open the Histogram palette. If you don't have an image open, all you see is ø in a blank space.

The contents of the histogram describe an image, separate channels, or layers in the image. First click the Source drop-down menu and pick an option. The contents in the menu vary according to what's in your file. If you have a single layer, the menu isn't available; if you have other components, you can select specific layers or an Adjustment layer and its underlying content from the menu. In Figure 9.18, for example, the histogram for the layer of the image showing just the blue sky is shown. In the histogram, notice that all the pixels are shifted to the right of the graph because there is very little range of color information in the sky color's layer.

To examine what's what in your image, click the Channel drop-down arrow and choose RGB, Red, Green, Blue, Luminosity, or Color.

When you make a selection, the histogram display varies according to what is selected:

- **RGB.** You see a histogram of each color channel stacked in a single display, like that shown in Figure 9.18.
- **Red, Green,** or **Blue.** You see the histogram for the selected color channel.
- **Luminosity.** You see a histogram of the intensity values of the entire image.
- **Colors.** The colors in the RGB histogram display as separate color overlays showing areas of red, green, and blue. Where the histograms of two color channels overlap you see cyan, magenta, and yellow. Gray represents areas where all three color channel histograms overlap. Figure 9.19 shows the Colors histogram; unfortunately you see it in shades of gray on the page.

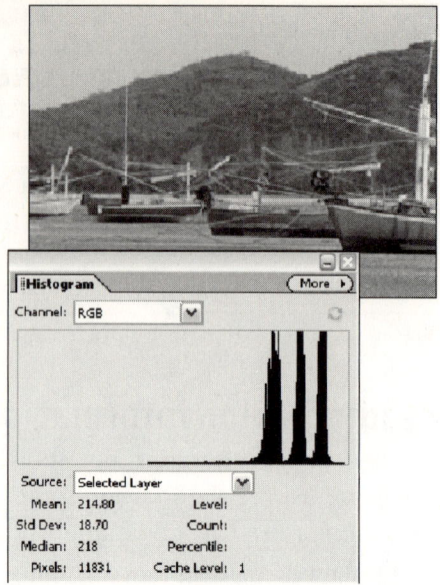

Figure 9.18. Show the histogram for a layer or selected image to evaluate its color information.

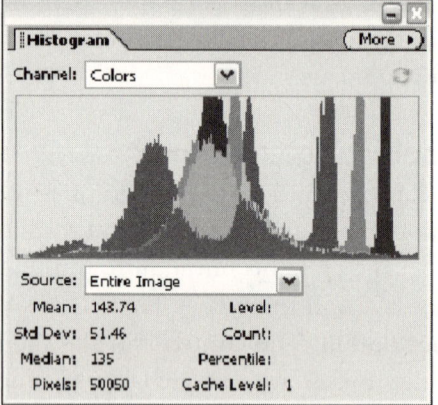

Figure 9.19. You can see and evaluate the range of colors used in the image by showing the Colors option from the Channel menu.

Bright Idea
If you have an area in an image that you aren't sure about, you can select it using one of the selection tools and then check out its information in the Histogram palette. Read about selections in Chapter 10.

Understanding image statistics

Beyond what you see in the histogram's graph, you can read image statistics at the lower part of the Histogram palette. Either move the mouse over the histogram's graph or drag across a part of the graph to highlight a range. Data types and descriptions are listed in Table 9.3.

Table 9.3. Data shown in the Histogram palette

Data Label	Value
Mean	Mean represents the average intensity value.
Std Dev	Standard Deviation defines how much the intensity values vary.
Median	Median shows the middle value in the intensity range.
Pixels	The Pixels value lists the total number of pixels calculated in the histogram.
Level	Level displays the intensity level of the sampled area under the mouse pointer.
Count	Count shows the total number of pixels at the specified intensity level under the mouse pointer.
Percentile	Percentile identifies the percentage of pixels at and below the intensity level of the sample pixel under the mouse pointer; all pixels in the image equal 100 percent.
Cache Level	The Cache Level shows the setting for the image cache that stores data in the program before refreshing the display.

Watch Out!
As you make changes to an image, they are stored in the file but the display in the Histogram palette doesn't update automatically. When a change is made that isn't reflected in the histogram's graph, a triangular caution icon displays on the palette. Click it to refresh the display.

Just the facts

- Color management processes are necessary to allow different devices and systems to communicate color information correctly.
- Calibrate your monitor to make sure it is displaying color correctly.
- Color profiles can be embedded in an image file or assigned to the program.
- Work with a number of color modes, including bitmap, indexed color, and grayscale.
- Modify an image's color using Hue, Saturation, and Lightness settings, or apply specialized color modifications to make alterations to a person's skin tone.
- Remove a color cast from an image for more accurate color using different methods such as specifying variations or applying photo filters.
- Reveal in-depth information about an image's color using the Histogram palette.

PART III

Pick What You Want to Work With

GET THE SCOOP ON...
▪ Making simple geometric selections ▪ Selecting pixels using several tools ▪ Creating a selection based on color ranges ▪ Selecting foreground and background areas ▪ Extracting content from an image

Choosing Parts

One word is becoming more and more common in the media: *Photoshopping*. The term refers to using Photoshop to modify an image in some way while retaining an authentic appearance. Photoshopping is also something you can do equally well with Photoshop Elements.

One of the key processes that contribute to the phenomenon that is Photoshopping is the ability to select precise content on an image and modify it or use it elsewhere, which of course explains how a supermarket tabloid cover can show irrefutable proof that Elvis is actually an alien.

You can select an editable area in an image using one of a number of tools and commands included in Photoshop Elements. For example, one tool selects a perfect circle, and one can select all the blue in the sky.

Tools for selecting

Selection tools can be based on pixel selection such as the Rectangular Marquee tool shown in Figure 10.1, while others are based on color selections, such as the Magic Wand tool. And then there is the Magic Selection Brush tool, which bases selections on both color and texture.

Figure 10.1. Selection tools can be simple rectangles, such as the one selecting the tile in the image, or very complex shapes.

You can combine selected areas and use different tools to make pixel-perfect selections. Table 10.1 lists the available tools and their basic uses.

Creating a selection can be a lengthy process, but fortunately you can save selections for reuse either in the same image or a different image.

Table 10.1. Selection tools

Tool	How It Looks	Type of Selection
Rectangular Marquee		Draws a rectangular or square selection.
Elliptical Marquee		Draws an elliptical or round selection.
Lasso		Draws freehand selection borders. This tool is great for making very precise selections.
Polygonal Lasso		Draws straight-edged segments of a selection border. You can create as many segments as you need to draw a selection border.
Magnetic Lasso		Draws a selection border that automatically snaps to edges you drag over in the photo. This makes drawing precise selection borders easy.

Watch Out!

A selection is used only with the active layer in an image. Flatten the affected layers in the image if you need to apply or create a selection using content on multiple layers. Read about flattening and layers in Chapters 11 and 12.

Tool	How It Looks	Type of Selection
Magic Wand		Selects pixels of similar color with one click. You specify the color range, or tolerance, for the tool's selection. Use the Magic Wand tool when you have an area of similar colors, such as a blue sky.
Magic Selection Brush		Identify the area you want to select by scribbling or drawing on the image. The selection border is drawn automatically.
Selection Brush		Makes selections in two ways: paints the area to select in Selection mode, and paints over areas you don't want to select in the Mask mode.

Making geometric selections

The simplest selection tools to use are the geometric Rectangular Marquee and Elliptical Marquee selection tools. Use the Rectangular Marquee tool to draw a rectangular or square selection; use the Elliptical Marquee tool to draw an elliptical or round selection.

Select the tool in the toolbox, and drag to draw a marquee on the image; hold the Shift key as you drag to constrain the marquee to a perfect square or circle.

Selecting either tool in the toolbox displays the same set of configuration choices in the options bar, shown in Figure 10.2. The options bar's choices vary according to the tool you select, but include these sections:

- **The selected tool and the other options available.** In Figure 10.2, the Rectangle Marquee tool is active, and shown at the left of the options bar, as well as shown selected next to the Elliptical Marquee tool, the other selection tool available through the same toolbox icon submenu.

- **Selection types.** The four icons indicate how selected areas are managed in relation to existing selections.
- **Feather settings.** Feathering defines the softness of the edge of the selection and how it blends with the background or underlying content.
- **Mode.** Choose a mode from the list to specify how the marquee is drawn on the image; if a fixed size or fixed aspect ratio is selected, the Width and Height fields are activated.

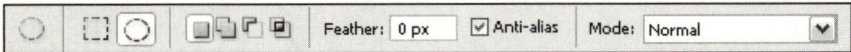

Figure 10.2. Configure selection tool options in a number of ways in the options bar.

The selection's composition

The selection tools offer four methods for making selections. To use any composition except for the new selection option, you need an existing selection in the image.

Follow these steps to make the initial selection:

1. Select the Rectangular or Elliptical Marquee tool from the toolbox.
2. In the Selection Mode area of the options bar, click the New Selection option (the furthest to the left), shown active in Figure 10.3.
3. Click and drag the image to select an area.
4. Release the mouse. You see the marquee outline around the selected area, shown in Figure 10.3.

When the initial selection is made, you can modify it easily

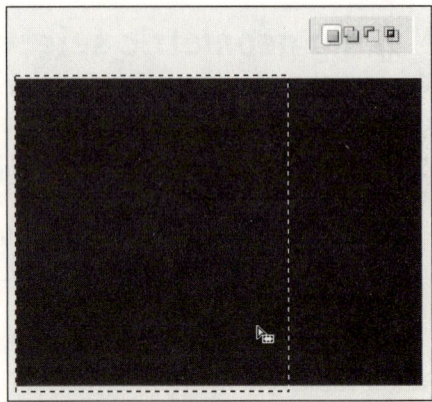

Figure 10.3. Draw a simple selection area on the image using the Rectangular Marquee tool.

using the remaining selection options. The multi-segmented selection shown in Figure 10.4 results from using the Add to selection option. The option is the active icon at the top of the image. In the figure, you see the original rectangle has another rectangle selected to its right, as well as an additional rectangular area currently being added. The ability to add more pixels to an existing selection is very useful when making complicated selections.

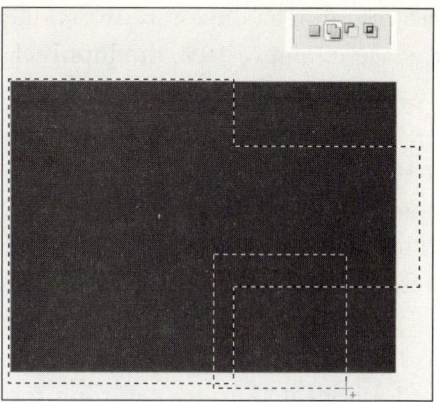

Figure 10.4. Add more pixels to an existing selection to make more complex selections.

Also to help you make more complex selections, you can subtract content from an existing selection by choosing the Subtract from selection option before using a selection tool on the image. In Figure 10.5, a large central rectangle was selected and removed from the existing selection, shown in Figure 10.4. Pressing Delete on the keyboard removes the content from the selected area, leaving the transparent outline of the complex angular selection, shown in the figure.

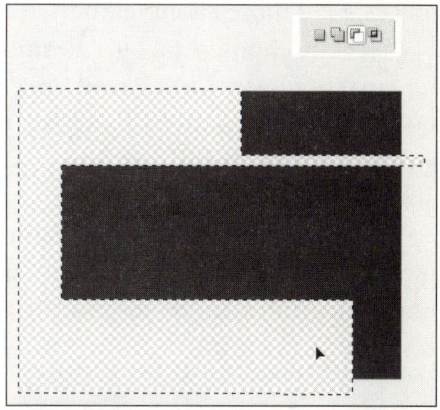

Figure 10.5. Select pixels to remove from an existing selection using the Subtract from selection setting.

Instead of adding or subtracting from a selection, you can select just the areas that intersect, as in the example shown in Figure 10.6. Choose the Intersect with selection option on the options bar and draw a second marquee. Only those areas that

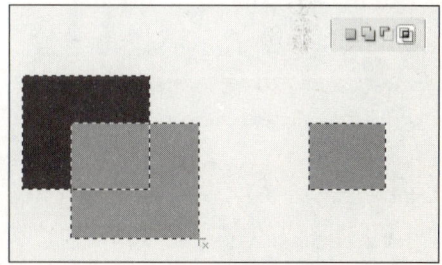

Figure 10.6. The Intersect with selection options selects only overlapped areas of existing selections.

are common to the entire selection are left in the new selection. As you can see in Figure 10.6, the intersected selection is only the small square area that overlaps both shapes.

Edge treatments

Sometimes you want the edges of a selection to be sharp and crisp, while at other times you want the edges to be soft, and gradually blend with the underlying content in the image.

The Feather option is available for most selection tools you can work with in Photoshop Elements, including both the Rectangular Marquee and Elliptical Marquee selection tools. Feathering blurs the edge of the selection for smoother transitions between areas of the foreground and background, such as for blends or pasting content to other layers or images; read more about feathering later in this chapter.

Likewise, choose Anti-alias to smooth the jagged pixels that make up the curved edges of a selected area when using the Elliptical Marquee tool. Anti-aliasing softens the color transition between edge pixels and background pixels without loss of detail because only the edge pixels change.

You can see two examples in Figure 10.7. Both are Elliptical selections filled with a solid color. Using the Anti-alias feature makes the left shape much smoother than the one at the right drawn without aliasing.

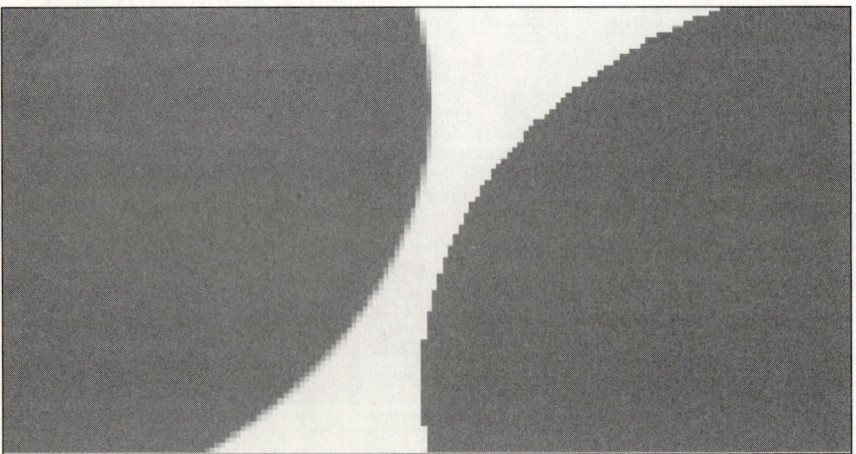

Figure 10.7. The edges of a curved shape appear much smoother when anti-aliasing is used (as in the left shape) than when it is deselected (as in the right shape).

Inside Scoop

The Magic Wand tool and Selection Brush tools are the only selection tools that don't offer feathering as an option.

Sizing the marquee

Choose an option from the Mode drop-down list shown in Figure 10.8 to help you draw a marquee.

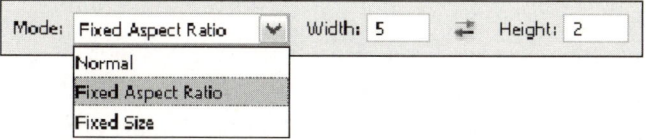

Figure 10.8. Specify how a marquee is sized using one of the available modes.

You can specify the sizing of the marquee in one of three ways:

- **Normal.** The Normal mode is the default mode, which lets you draw the selection frame's size visually using any size you wish.
- **Fixed Aspect Ratio.** An aspect ratio refers to the relationship between the width and height of an object. For example, a marquee that is two inches wide by three inches high has an aspect ratio of 2:3. For Fixed Aspect Ratio, type values in the Width and Height fields corresponding to the ratio you want applied. For example, typing **5** and **2** results in a marquee using a 5:2 ratio. The ratio is fixed, which means that any marquee you draw is sized at 5 units in width and 2 units in height, whether it is a 5 inch × 2 inch selection or a 20 inch × 8 inch selection.
- **Fixed Size.** Choose the Fixed Size mode, and type values in the Width and Height fields for precise selection marquees. The default unit of measure is pixels. If you want to use another unit of measure, type its abbreviation into the field. For example, type **100pt** if you want either the Width or Height of the marquee to be measured in points; type **3.2in** to measure the selection in inches, and so on.

Bright Idea

If you draw a marquee and realize it should be moved, press and hold the spacebar and drag the marquee with the selection tool. Release the spacebar when the marquee is in the right location.

Name that tool

Do you sometimes forget which tool you have active? It can happen, especially if you are using Caps Lock to display crosshairs instead of a tool cursor.

To specify that the active tool is shown on the image's window, first set the image window to Maximize mode to fill the program window. You see a label next to the magnification value on the image window's status bar.

Click the arrow to open a drop-down menu showing a variety of settings such as Document Sizes, Document Dimensions, and Efficiency. Click Current Tool. Now any tool that you activate is shown by name at the bottom of the image's window.

Selecting with Lasso tools

Many selections in an image aren't confined to a geometric shape. After all, you don't find many perfectly square trees or circular flowers. Photoshop Elements offers three variations on a Lasso tool to help you make odd-shaped selections, including a simple Lasso tool, a Magnetic Lasso tool, and a Polygonal Lasso tool.

A Lasso tool, as the name suggests, is used to encircle an area. On releasing the mouse, the identified area is converted to a selection.

Watch Out!

Deselecting a selection by clicking outside the selected area anywhere on the image is handy when you want to start over. The problem is that if your active tool is one of the selection tools that work by mouse clicks, such as the lasso tools, you start a new selection. So to deselect a selection in these circumstances, press Ctrl+D.

A triangle at the bottom-right of a tool icon means that there are other tools that can be accessed in the toolbox. Click the visible tool on the toolbox, and hold the mouse button pressed for a few seconds until a submenu appears, such as the one shown in Figure 10.9; all the tools in the submenu will be applied to the options bar until you change tools.

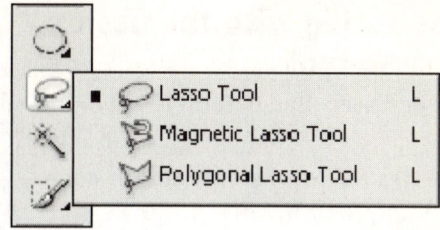

Figure 10.9. Choose one of several Lasso tools from the submenu on the toolbox.

The tools share some common options:

- Each offers the same four selection modes shown in Figures 10.2, 10.3, 10.4, 10.5, and 10.6. Choose a mode to determine the selection's purpose: create a new selection, add to an existing selection, subtract from an existing selection, or select an intersected area.

- Specify a Feather value in the options bar for any of the three tools to soften the selection border. In Figure 10.10, the left image isn't feathered, while the right uses a 20px feather.

- Define whether the curved edges of the selection edges are smoothed by selecting the Anti-alias check box.

Figure 10.10. The left image shows sharp edges, while the right image uses feathering to soften the edges of the selection.

Inside Scoop

When you select a Lasso tool, all three Lasso tools appear in the options bar above the document window; you can click a different tool from the options bar instead of waiting for the subtoolbar to open on the toolbox.

Selecting with the basic Lasso tool

The basic Lasso tool is used to draw a freehand selection. It works well on its own and in conjunction with other tools to add or delete pixels from existing selections. Select the tool, and drag to create a selection, returning to overlap the starting point as shown in Figure 10.11. Release the mouse button to complete the selection.

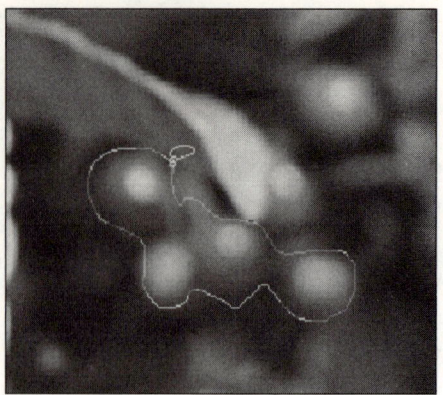

Figure 10.11. The Lasso tool lets you make a freeform selection shape; overlap the starting point to complete the selection.

Multi-sided selections with the Polygon Lasso tool

Use the Polygon Lasso tool to make multi-sided selections. The Polygon Lasso tool lets you make very precise selections and maintain mouse control.

Follow these steps to make a selection:

1. Select the Polygonal Lasso tool in the toolbox or from the options bar.
2. Click at a location on the margin of your proposed selection to add an *anchor point*. The next segment of the selection continues in the direction you move your mouse based on the anchor point's location, letting you control the direction in which the line segments are added.
3. Move the mouse, and click at the next location where you want to place a point.

Bright Idea

If the mouse isn't over the starting point but you want to close the selection using either the Polygonal or Magnetic Lasso tools, double-click the mouse. The selection is completed by adding a straight line from your cursor location to the starting point.

4. Continue until you have identified the area you want as a selection.

5. Move the mouse over the starting point, and when you see a circle next to the tool's icon, click to complete the selection.

Figure 10.12 shows an example of the Polygon Lasso in action.

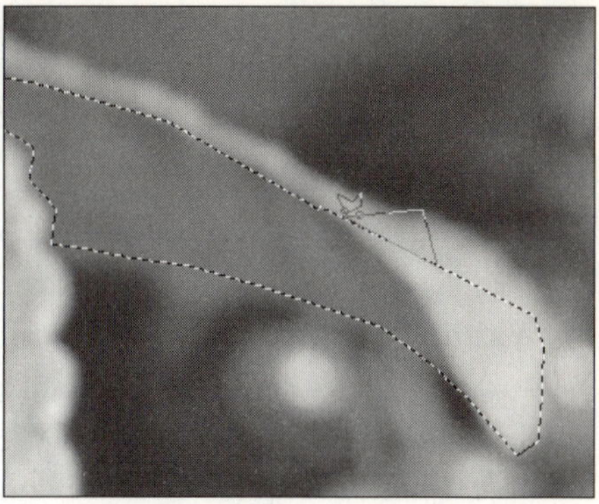

Figure 10.12. The Polygonal Lasso tool lets you draw segments of a selection to control the shape precisely; you see a small circle next to the tool when you move it over the starting point.

Detecting shapes with the Magnetic Lasso tool

The Magnetic Lasso tool, when used skillfully, can be a very accurate selection tool. In addition to the same selection modes and feathering that you can specify with the other two tools, the Magnetic Lasso also lets you customize several other features.

Follow these steps to draw a selection using the Magnetic Lasso tool:

1. Select the Magnetic Lasso tool in the toolbox or in the options bar if another Lasso tool is active in the program.

2. Press the Caps Lock key to use the crosshairs cursor instead of the tool cursor. The Magnetic Lasso tool shows you the width within which the tool will select edges for drawing the shape as a circle around the crosshairs.

3. Click the location on the image at which you want to start drawing the selection.

4. Slowly move the cursor around the edges of the shape or area you are selecting.

5. When the tool reaches the starting point, you see a small circle at the edge of the tool's cursor; click to complete the selection and display the finished selection marquee.

The Magnetic Lasso tool draws a selection shape as you move the tool. Its precision is based on several settings, in addition to how precisely you move the tool along the edges of the area you want to select. You can specify the sensitivity of the tool and the precision of its selection using several settings that display in the options bar when you select the tool:

- **Width.** Type a value in pixels in the Width field to define how wide an area the tool will detect. The value can range from 1 to 256; 10 is the default value. Figure 10.13 shows two examples of the same object being selected by the Magnetic Lasso too. In the left image, the Width is set at a value of 3px, while the Width of 15px is used for selecting the right image. Using lower-width values results in a poor selection as the tool checks for edges only within three pixels of the tool's location on the image. At a width of 15px, it's much more likely the tool will find an edge.

The tool isn't magic — it follows where you move the mouse. If you look at the lower right of the left leaf or the lower left of the right leaf selections in Figure 10.13, notice the areas of the leaf omitted from the selection. That is operator error.

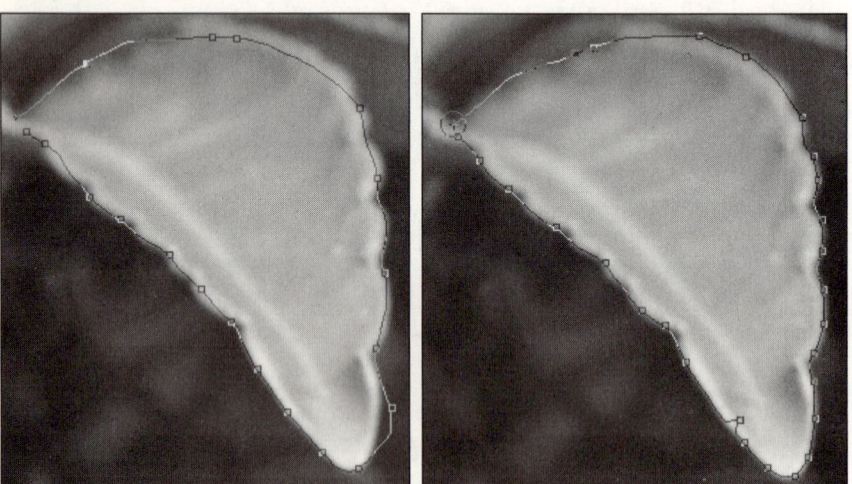

Figure 10.13. The Magnetic Lasso tool can make very imprecise selections (left) or more accurate selections (right) based on the specified detection width. Using the Caps Lock feature to display crosshairs shows the selected Width value as well.

Bright Idea

The steps include using the Caps Lock feature to show the tool as crosshairs. Although that isn't necessary, it gives you much more information, showing the diameter of the area the tool is checking for edges.

Changing the Magnetic Lasso tool's edge detection settings and adding manual points would make the selection more precise.

- **Edge Contrast.** Change the value from 1 to 100 percent for Edge Contrast depending on the differences in contrast between what you want to select and the rest of the image. The lower the value, the more likely lower-contrast edges are detected. In an image, such as the leaf shown in Figures 10.13 and 10.14, some areas of the leaf are very similar in color and contrast to other content in the image. In other words, they have *low edge contrast*. In Figure 10.14, the leaf is shown as it is being selected with the Magnetic Lasso tool. The Width used is the default 10px, and the Edge Contrast is decreased to 1 percent. You can see how closely the tool follows along the edge of the leaf in the image, even in areas where it overlays a similarly colored background.

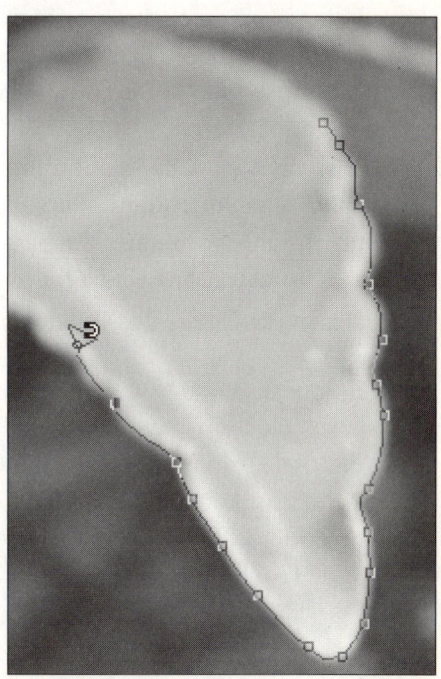

Figure 10.14. The Magnetic Lasso tool can make precise selections, even in an edge that has little contrast, by decreasing the Edge Contrast value.

Inside Scoop

Using 100 percent as the Edge Contrast can only be used for extreme contrast, such as selecting black on a white background. The only way to define what is ideal for a selection is to test the Edge Contrast percentage values.

To Magnetic Lasso or not to Magnetic Lasso?

As your experience with the tools expands, you may find you prefer one Lasso selection tool over the others. Spend a few minutes getting the feel of the tools, especially the Magnetic Lasso tool, and try selecting content on an image by adjusting the tool's settings and adding points manually.

The Magnetic Lasso tool is not the tool for everyone — some people don't like the drawn marquee edge that follows along behind the cursor or find it time-consuming to make all the setting adjustments.

I use the tool occasionally, but not that often. Because I learned to make selections many years ago when the first Lasso tool was invented, I most often use the basic Lasso and Polygonal Lasso tools with the image zoomed to a high magnification.

- **Frequency.** The Magnetic Lasso tool adds points and line segments to your selections automatically. As you can see in the leaf selections in Figures 10.13 and 10.14, each time the tool moves in a different direction an anchor point is added to the selection's outline. Adjust the frequency from 0 to 100 to define how many anchor points are added. The higher the number, the more frequent the points.

  When you draw a selection using the Magnetic Lasso tool, you can also click when you want to add a point manually. If you are drawing and see the line start to veer off your required selection's path, click to place a point and redirect the tool.

Watch Out!

The Magnetic Lasso tool can easily add points you don't want. Luckily, you can press Delete to go back to the previous point along the selection's edge. Pressing Delete repeatedly removes points until you get to the most recent point you want to maintain.

Waving your magic wand

Photoshop Elements contains tools that select pixels based on color, including the Magic Wand tool, the Selection Brush tool, and the Magic Selection Brush tool. Click an image using the Magic Wand tool to select pixels that have a similar color range.

Select these options for the Magic Wand tool in the options bar:

- Type a value from 0 to 255 in the Tolerance field of the options bar. The lower the value you choose, the smaller the range of colors selected at the cursor location on the image, as you can see in the left image in Figure 10.15. By using a tolerance of 10 and clicking the center of the shape, only the central diamond is selected. Increasing the tolerance increases the range of color selected by the Magic Wand when you click the image, as shown at the left of Figure 10.15. Here, using a tolerance of 100, the interior three diamonds are selected when the center of the shape is clicked.

- Select Anti-aliased to smooth the edge of the selection.

- Select Contiguous to select only adjacent areas of the same color; deselect the option to select the same color range in the entire image.

- Select Use All Layers to select color from all layers visible in the image. The setting is deselected by default, and the tool selects color only in the active layer.

Figure 10.15. The Magic Wand tool selects areas of similar color based on the tolerance level you select.

More or less

Use commands in the Select menu to modify a selection. You can apply several commands from the Select menu to any existing selection in your image or apply more than one command.

Follow these steps to modify your selection:

1. Make your selection using the Magic Wand tool. A selection using a tolerance of 25px is shown in the upper-left image in Figure 10.16.

2. Choose Select and select one of the modification commands:

   - Choose Select ⇨ Grow to add to the selection all pixels adjacent to your selection that fall within the Tolerance range. As shown in the upper-right image in Figure 10.16, numerous pixels of similar color are included. Using the Grow command is similar to increasing the Magic Wand tool's Tolerance level in the options bar.

   - Choose Select ⇨ Similar to add pixels throughout the image that are within the color tolerance range, shown in the bottom-left image in Figure 10.16. Using the Similar command is the same as deselecting the Contiguous check box in the options bar.

   - Choose Select ⇨ Modify ⇨ Smooth, and type a value for the Sample Radius from 1 to 100. The command looks around each selected pixel in your image and adds to the selection any pixels within the same color range, or decreases pixels depending on the size of the initial selection. As you can see in the lower-right image in Figure 10.16, using a Sample Radius of 3 shrinks the selection. Smoothing is similar to using the Anti-alias option available from the tool's options bar.

3. Save your selection (read about saving selections later in the chapter), apply other commands such as Fill or Delete, or modify it using another of the selection tools as required.

Watch Out!
Use the Grow and Similar commands carefully. Each time you use the command the selection's tolerance increases. After using the command a few times, you might select the entire image! Instead, save time deselecting and starting again using a slightly larger tolerance.

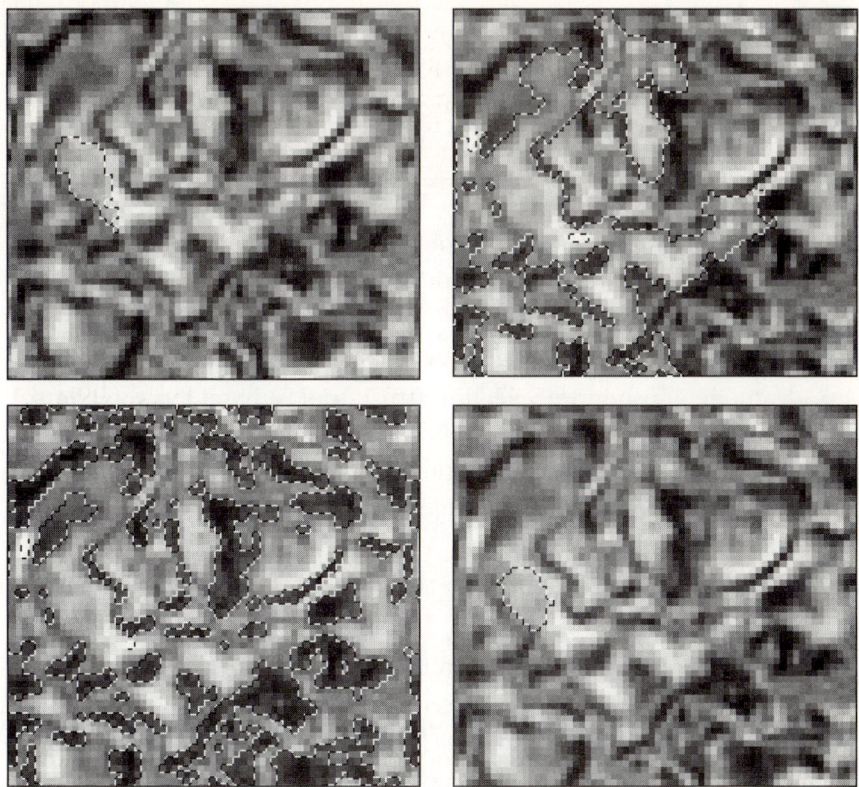

Figure 10.16. Use Select commands to modify an existing selection. Clockwise from upper left are original selection, the Grow command, the Smooth command, and the Similar command.

Brushing a selection

The Selection Brush tool is made for both the half-full and the half-empty crowds: the tool can either select the area you want to use in Selection mode or select the areas you don't want to use in Mask mode. If you have ever applied a stencil to a wall or a book, you have worked with a mask: only the areas you want to receive paint or ink are exposed, and the rest of the area is hidden by paper or tape.

You are already familiar with using the Selection mode as it has been the subject of this chapter so far. Mask mode specifies just the opposite. Instead of identifying the areas you want affected by commands and actions in Photoshop Elements, you *mask*, or hide all but the areas you

> **Inside Scoop**
>
> Both the Selection Brush and the Magic Selection Brush tools are used for selections, but their brush characteristics are the same as those used by painting, erasing, and clone tools in the program. Read about Brush options in Chapter 18.

want affected in Mask mode. You specify either a selection or a mask in an image — you don't work with both modes at the same time.

Painting a selection

The advantage of using the Selection Brush tool is that it lets you control the hardness or softness of the edges of the selection by using a brush tip. The other selection tools, such as the Lasso and Rectangular/Elliptical Marquee tools let you modify the edges only by adjusting Feather or Anti-alias settings.

Follow these steps to configure the Selection Brush tool to use in Selection mode:

1. Click the Selection Brush tool in the toolbox.

2. Choose a selection mode in the options bar, shown in Figure 10.17. Click the Add to selection icon or Subtract from selection icon. In the example in Figure 10.17, Add to selection is selected in the options bar.

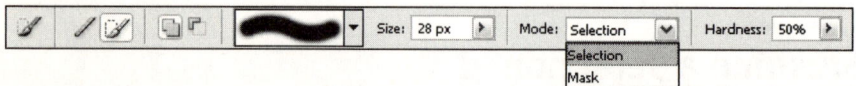

Figure 10.17. Define the Selection Brush's settings in the options bar, including specifying whether you will paint a Selection or a Mask.

3. Click the Brush presets drop-down arrow, and choose a brush from the list. You can also just leave the default solid brush selected as in the options bar shown in Figure 10.17.

4. Click the Size arrow, and drag the slider that appears to change the brush's diameter. If you know the exact size you want to use, type a value directly in the Size field.

5. Choose Selection from the Mode drop-down list. Selection will select content in the image, while Mask subtracts from the selection.

6. Set the Hardness value for the brush, which defines how much of the brush's stroke is hard. The default is 100 percent, meaning the brush stroke is solid; you can set anywhere from 1 to 100 percent hardness. The lower the percentage, the less sharp the brush stroke and the softer the edges.

7. Paint on the image to add to the selection using the brush's characteristics. You can see an example of adding to an existing selection in Figure 10.18. In the figure, the shadow to the right of the window has been partially selected using other selection tools. Applying the Selection brush adds more pixels using a soft edge.

Figure 10.18. Paint with the Selection Brush tool to add or remove content from a selection.

Painting a mask

Sometimes seeing what's selected on an image is simpler using a mask than viewing the Selection mode. For example, in Figure 10.19, you see the same image from Figure 10.18, except that the Selection Brush tool is in Mask mode now. When you paint over a stencil, the mask areas that you don't want to affect are covered by paper, tape, or other solid material. In Photoshop Elements, the mask is a semi-transparent red color that covers everything in the image except your selected area.

Figure 10.19. Paint with the Selection Brush in Mask mode to add or remove content from a selection; all but the selected areas are masked with a semi-transparent red overlay.

Painting with the Selection Brush in Mask mode gives you a different way to see what you are trying to select. In Figure 10.19, for example, you see the Selection Brush in Mask mode was dragged across part of the earlier selection.

In addition to the selection mode and brush settings listed for painting in the Selection mode, and shown in Figure 10.17, you can adjust settings for the mask, as shown in Figure 10.20.

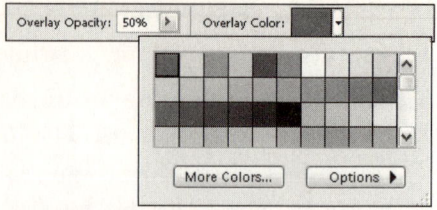

Figure 10.20. Configure the mask's appearance according to your image's requirements.

Modify the overlay for the mask using these settings when in Mask mode:

- Specify an Overlay Opacity for the mask's red color between 1 percent and 100 percent. The image in Figure 10.19 uses 50 percent. The higher the percentage, the more of the image is hidden by the red overlay; of course, the lower the percentage, the more transparent the red overlay becomes.

- Click the Overlay Color swatch and select a color in the Color Picker shown in Figure 10.20 to change the mask color from its default bright red. If your image uses similar red colors, change to a different mask color.

You can work with the same selection, using the Selection tool to add to a selection, and the Mask mode to remove pixels from the selection. In Figure 10.21, the same image of the window and shadow is shown, but now back in Selection mode. The doodle painted with the Selection Brush in Mask mode, shown in Figure 10.19, is now deleted from the selection.

Figure 10.21. Displaying the image using the Selection mode for the Selection Brush tool shows the area painted previously in the Mask mode deleted from the selection.

> **Bright Idea**
> To switch between adding to and subtracting from a selection, press Alt as you paint.

Magic Selection Brush

The Magic Selection Brush tool is similar in some ways to the Magic Wand in that it also considers color when making the selection. However, unlike the Magic Wand tool, the Magic Selection Brush tool makes its selection primarily based on texture.

Painting on an image provides information for the program so it can define the texture you are trying to select. Because the Magic Selection Brush tool works with texture, it isn't always easy to predict what the brush will select. When you use the Magic Selection Brush tool, it redraws the selection, compared with the Magic Wand tool that adds to the selection.

Some subjects that are very difficult to select based on color, such as animals or flowers, are selected quite well using the Magic Selection Brush tool.

Follow these steps to make a selection:

1. Select the Magic Selection Brush tool in the toolbox.

2. Choose a selection option in the options bar. The default choice is New Selection, which starts a new drawing. As you are working with the image, choose Indicate Foreground to add to an existing selection or Indicate Background to subtract from an existing selection.

3. Click the Color swatch, and choose a color for the brush stroke if the default red is too close to your subject's color. In the example shown in Figure 10.22, the big red bug is very close to the default red color, so the tool's color was changed to blue.

Figure 10.22. Identify areas of texture and color for selection.

4. Click the Size arrow, and drag the slider to set a size for the brush. For making smaller, more precise selections, decrease the size of the brush. You can also type a value directly into the field.

5. Click the image, scribble over an area, or encircle an area you want to select. In the left image in Figure 10.22, you can see a scribble on the back of the bug.

6. Release the mouse. The image is processed, and the selection outline displays on the image, shown at the right in Figure 10.22.

After creating your selection, you can adjust the brush size, and choose alternative selection options to add content to and remove content from the selection, if it isn't as accurate as you need.

Magical extractions

Haven't had your fill of magic yet? Try the Magic Extractor for even more selection magic. It's not a tool, it's a program command with its own window. Choose Image ➪ Magic Extractor to open the Magic Extractor window. Your active image is shown in the window.

The Magic Extractor is designed to remove a foreground subject from an image's background. It works by extrapolating selections based on defined foreground and background areas. No pixels are hurt or damaged in the application of the Magic Extractor command because the processed image opens as a new file in the Editor.

Within the Magic Extractor dialog box, shown in Figure 10.23, you make several adjustments to how you view an image and to the image itself.

There are also several tools you can use to make your adjustments. They are located to the left of the image window (see Figure 10.23) and are, from top to bottom: Foreground Brush tool, Background Brush tool, Point Eraser tool, Add to Selection tool, Remove from Selection tool, Smoothing Brush tool, Zoom tool, and Hand tool.

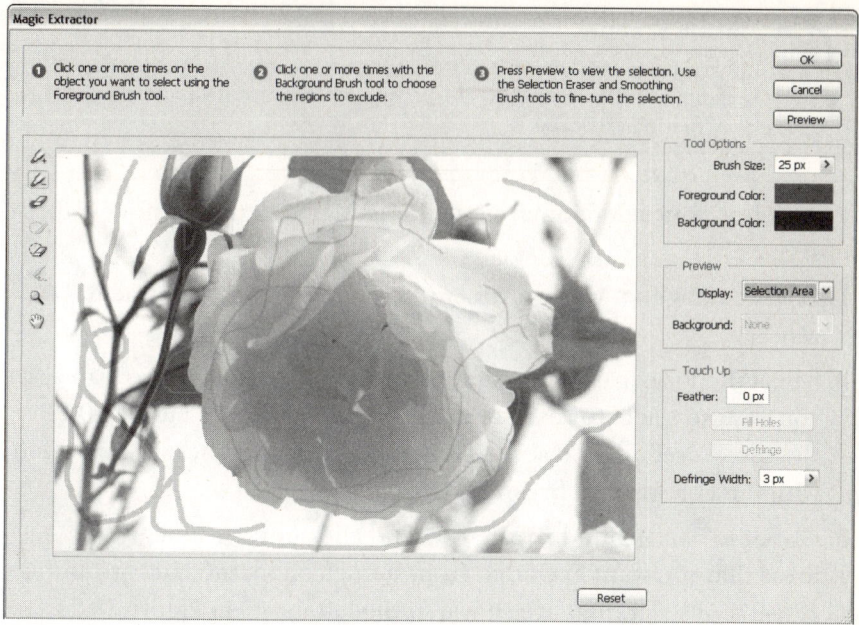

Figure 10.23. The basics of the Magic Extractor dialog box.

Adjust the window's display

Like all other areas of Photoshop Elements, you have access to both a Zoom tool and a Hand tool for showing and viewing different areas in the image as you are working.

In addition, you can make a few other adjustments to improve your view and extraction accuracy, including these:

- **Tool Options.** Change the color and size of either the Foreground or Background Brush tools. The default is a red foreground and a blue background. Select the brush and choose a new size from the Brush Size drop-down menu, or click the color swatch for either tool to open the Color Picker. Choose a color, and click OK.

- **Preview.** Change what is shown in the Preview. Click the Display drop-down arrow, and choose either Selection Area or Original Photo. If you choose the Selection Area option, click the Background drop-down arrow and choose a Black, White, or Gray Matte or Mask option from the list.

>
> **Inside Scoop**
>
> If your image uses lots of colors and textures, the more areas and colors you indicate with the Foreground and Background Brush tools, the more accurate your finished extraction.

To define your selection areas with the Magic Extractor, follow these steps:

1. Choose Image ⇨ Magic Extractor to open the Magic Extractor window.
2. Select the Foreground Brush tool, and click or drag to mark areas you want to select for extraction. In the left image of Figure 10.24, the rose, rosebud, and several leaves are identified by marking them with the Foreground Brush tool.
3. Click the Background Brush tool, and click or drag to mark the areas that you want excluded from the selection; the Background Brush tool's markings are shown in the left image in Figure 10.24, drawn through the blurred background of the rose.

Combining tools

The basic idea of making a selection and then adding or deleting from it applies regardless of whether you are using a Rectangular/Elliptical Marquee tool, a Lasso tool, or a color selection tool such as the Magic Wand or Selection Brush tool. When a selection you want to make is going to be tricky, use as many choices as you need to create the final selection.

Unfortunately, there are no hard and fast rules for selection nirvana. Some people like to start with a general selection and then peel bits away until the final selection is complete; others prefer to add pieces to an initial rough selection. The most important thing to remember is that you *can* and should use multiple tools in many circumstances.

You can use many different tool combinations to achieve the same outcome. It all depends on your preferred way of working and your level of comfort with the different tools.

> **Hack**
> If you want to extract something from an image, such as a person standing in a group, make a rough selection of that person in the file before opening the Magic Extractor window. Using only the selected image segment speeds up the processing.

Figure 10.24. Mark the areas in the image you want to preserve and those you want to remove (left image); the Preview shows you the extraction based on your selections (right image).

4. Click Preview to process the image and display the extraction preview, shown in the right image of Figure 10-24.
5. Click OK to process the image and close the window.

Tweaking the selection

After the basic selection is made, you can make more adjustments in the Magic Extractor. Your options include several tools and options:

- **Point Eraser tool.** Use the Point Eraser tool to erase unwanted dots or lines that you added to define foreground or background areas.
- **Add to Selection tool.** Use the Add to Selection tool by dragging over additional areas to add them to the selection.
- **Remove from Selection tool.** Use the Remove from Selection tool by dragging over areas you want removed from the selection.
- **Smoothing Brush tool.** Smooth the edges of the foreground by clicking the Smoothing Brush tool and dragging it over the areas you want smoothed.
- **Feather.** Click the Feather field, and type a value for edge softening. Feathering is explained in greater detail later in the chapter.

> **Bright Idea**
> If you want to remove custom settings from a tool, click the tool's icon at the far left of the options bar to open a Reset menu. Click Reset Tool to revert to the default settings for the active tool; click Reset All Tools to revert to default settings for all tools.

- **Fill Holes.** Click Fill Holes to fill holes in the main selection. You can see an example in Figure 10.25. The image at the left shows a segment of a petal that has the center cut out. After Fill Holes is applied, the petal is refilled.

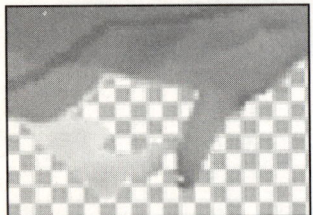 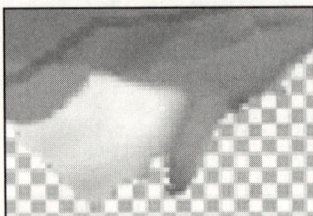

Figure 10.25. Fill in holes to complete image elements that were extracted by mistake.

- **Defringe Width.** If there are marked differences in color between foreground and background colors, you often see colored or *fringed* edges. Click Defringe, and specify a value in the Defringe Width field to remove more areas of color.

Using the Move tool

After you have made a selection, you can use it or reuse it in a number of ways working with the Move tool. The Move tool isn't just for moving. Yes, a selection can be moved on the image with this tool, but you can also use it to copy the image, or copy and paste it to another image or another layer.

> **Bright Idea**
> You don't have to click the Move tool in the toolbox to select it. If you have another tool active (except for the Hand tool) press the Ctrl key and the tool changes to the Move tool. Move the object and then release the Ctrl key to return to your previously active tool.

When you select the Move tool in the toolbox, you can choose two options in the options bar, both of which are active by default. The choices include:

- **Auto Select Layer.** The Auto Select Layer option is a very handy feature. Clicking or selecting any pixels on the image automatically selects their layer in the Layer palette.

- **Show Bounding Box.** The Show Bounding Box option is also selected by default, meaning a bounding box is shown around a selected object or objects. Click and drag from anywhere within the margins of the bounding box to move the selection anywhere on the image. If you resize, move, or transform the object or objects, the bounding box adjusts as well, you can see a before and after in the left and right images in Figure 10.26.

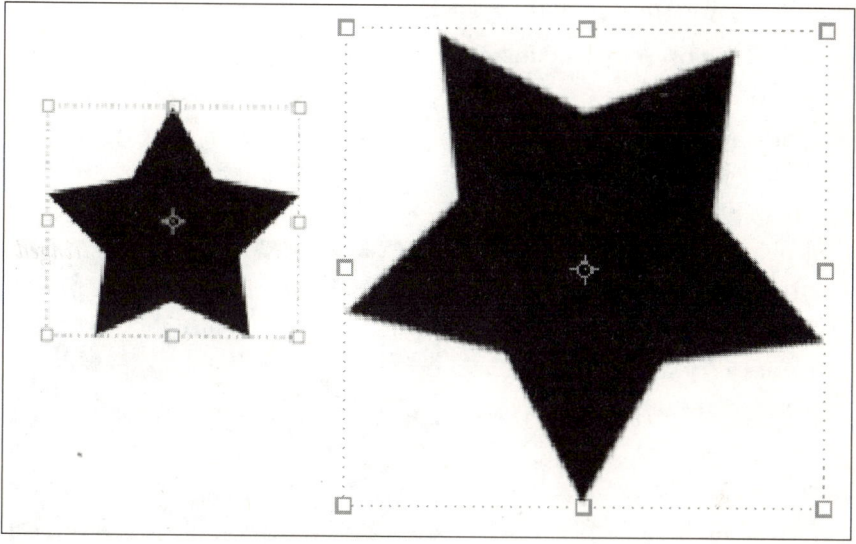

Figure 10.26. Adjusting an object also adjusts its bounding box. In the right image, after rotating and resizing the object, the bounding box still frames the shape, as it did in the original image shown at the left.

Copying a selection

Sure, you can use Edit menu commands to copy and paste selections, but if you simply want to add a duplicate of a selected area to your image or to another open image, don't bother with menu commands. Instead, select the Move tool.

Place the Move tool over the selection and then press and hold the Alt key as you drag a copy of the selection away from the original selection. You can repeat this as many times as you like. The last copy you create is the active selection.

Suppose you want to stack some copies of a selected object, such as the body of the big bug shown in Figure 10.22. Don't laugh: The outcome is far more interesting than you might imagine. You can offset the copies by different numbers of pixels to produce different effects ranging from blurring to a stacked appearance.

Follow these steps to make a stacked arrangement of objects:

1. Select the object in the image.
2. Press the Alt key and click one of the keyboard arrows. A copy is made and added to the image offset by 1 pixel from the original in the direction of the key you pressed. That is, pressing the right arrow places the offset copy 1 pixel to the right of the original, and so on.
3. Continue adding other offset copies as desired. In Figure 10.27, eight duplicates of the image were offset one pixel left, and another eight were offset one pixel upward, and create an interesting edge effect.

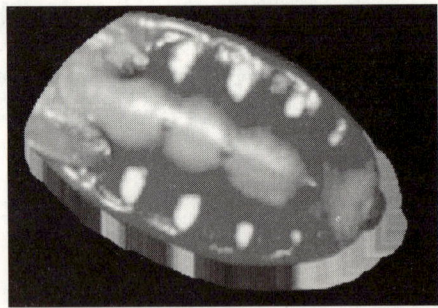

Figure 10.27. Numerous duplicates of an object offset by one pixel create a blurred edge effect.

4. To offset the duplicate by 10 pixels, press Alt+Shift, and then press an arrow key to create a duplicate. In Figure 10.28, seven duplicates of the original are shown; each offset 10 pixels, creating an interesting scalloped edge, reminiscent of scalloped flower petals.

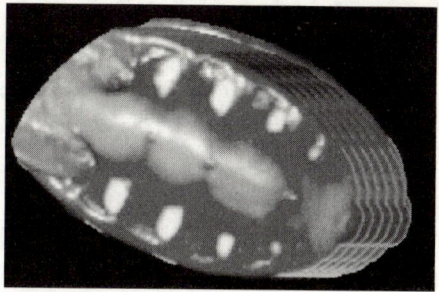

Figure 10.28. Duplicates made using different directional arrow keys create different effects.

Copying selections to other images

You can easily add copies of selected content from one image to another using the Move tool. Follow these steps:

1. Open both the source image and receiving image. Arrange the images in the Editor window so you can clearly see the sections you want to work with.

2. Select the Move tool, and drag the selection from the source image window to the receiving image window. You see a darkened border when the receiving window is active.

3. Release the mouse, and the copy is added. The content is placed on its own layer in the receiving image, and the original image is unaffected. Read about layers in Chapters 11 and 12.

Pasting a selection into another selection

What if you want a picture of your cat's face in a droplet of water? Or your dog's face reflected in a mirror? Or...? The point is that combining content from different images is a slick process and not too difficult if you do it the right way.

Watch Out!

A selection added to another image retains its original pixel dimensions, which can make the pasted content look out of proportion. Fix this by making the source image and receiving image the same resolution. Choose Image ⇨ Resize ⇨ Image Size, as discussed in Chapter 5.

>  **Inside Scoop**
>
> If the image you want to copy from is already open in another program, you can copy your selection to the clipboard from the program in which it is open, instead of reopening the image in Photoshop Elements.

You work with the selection tools, the Paste Into Selection command, layers, and the Move tool to build a very interesting image. You can read about layers in Chapters 11 and 12 if you have trouble completing the steps.

Follow these steps to combine a selection from one image into another image in Photoshop Elements:

1. Open the images you want to work with in the Editor.
2. Select and copy the part of the source image you want to paste. The pasted content is placed on your system clipboard. You are finished with the source image now.
3. Create the selection in the receiving image that you want to use to paste into the selection you copied in Step 2.
4. Choose Window ⇨ Layers to open the Layers palette.
5. Click New Layer to add a new layer to the receiving image. It is automatically the active layer in the image, and the selection is active for the new layer.
6. Choose Edit ⇨ Paste Into Selection. The content you copied to the clipboard is shown within the selected area and is placed on the new layer. In Figure 10.29, the cat's face, copied from the original image, is pasted into a selected water drop.
7. Use the Move tool to adjust the position of the pasted content within the selection as necessary.
8. Deselect the pasted image to complete the job.

Figure 10.29. Paste content from one image into selected areas on another image for interesting compositions.

CHAPTER 10 ■ CHOOSING PARTS

> **Watch Out!**
> If you copied content to the clipboard, you must choose Edit ⇨ Preferences and select Export Clipboard in the General Preferences; otherwise, the content is gone when you close the program.

Reselecting selections

After you have created a selection, you can modify it in Photoshop Elements in numerous ways, using commands in the Select menu.

Adding feathering

Most selection tools allow you to specify feathering. But, it's simple to create a selection and use it in an image without feathering, only to decide that it needs to be feathered. You don't have to start from scratch, redoing the selection with modified feather options for the tool.

You often don't see the impact of the feathering until you manipulate the selection in some way such as filling or moving it. If the feathering is significant, you will see a difference in the selection border itself, as shown in Figure 10.30. In the figure, although the entire central black area was selected, the dotted border for the selection is rounded at the corners, indicating feathering.

Figure 10.30. Feathering rounds the edges of the selection.

Follow these steps to add feathering to an existing selection:

1. Choose Select ⇨ Feather to open the Feather Radius dialog box, shown in Figure 10.31.
2. Type a value in the field between 2 and 250. The value defines the width of the feathering in pixels.
3. Click OK to close the dialog box. In the example shown in Figure 10.30, the feathering is set at 25 pixels. You can see that the borders

>  **Inside Scoop**
> If you aren't sure whether you need feathering when you intend to use a selection, don't set a feathering value in the selection tool's options. It's faster to feather an existing selection than to reset the tool and start selecting again.

are rounded as a result of the feathering. The feathering is centered on the dashed line; half of the feather amount is inside the line letting the image stay dark, and the other half is outside, feathering to transparency.

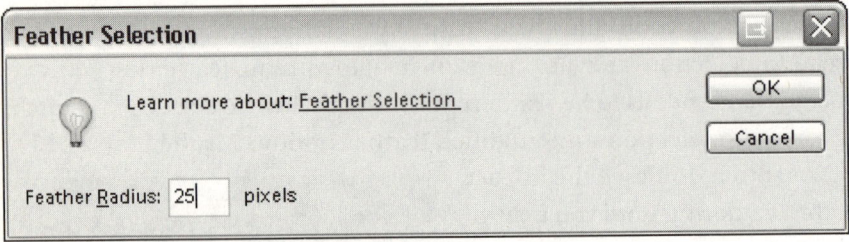

Figure 10.31. Specify the amount to feather an existing selection in the dialog box.

Modifying selection edges

For more adjusting options, select one of four ways to adjust the edges of an existing selection. Examples of each type are shown in the following figures. In each case, a small dialog box opens displaying a text field for you to type a value for the modification in pixels.

Choose Select ⇨ Modify and select one of these choices:

- **Border.** The border is shown as a separate framing selection that can be filled for a different effect (shown in Figure 10.32).

Figure 10.32. A 10-pixel border has been added.

- **Expand.** The border of the selection is expanded (shown in Figure 10.33).
- **Contract.** The border of the selection is shrunk (shown in Figure 10.34).
- **Smooth.** The border of the selection is simplified (shown in Figure 10.35). The original selection in the figure included all the angled areas. Smoothing the selection simplified the path of the selection, but also deselected some of the content.

Saving and revising selections

After you have made a tricky (or even not-so-tricky) selection, you can save it for reuse later.

Saving the selection

The advantage of saving a selection is that you can reload it into the image at any time, use it on another layer, or even use it on other images. You can also combine or change selections. But you can't do any of this if you didn't save your selection in the first place.

So start from the initial selection, following these steps:

Figure 10.33. The border has been expanded by 10 pixels.

Figure 10.34. The border has been contracted by 10 pixels.

Figure 10.35. A 10-pixel smoothing has been added.

Hack
If you want to use a selection from one image in another, copy the content between the images. In the second image, save the selection. You can then use the selection as you like in the image (or any other image once it is saved).

1. Choose Select ⇨ Save Selection to open the Save Selection dialog box (see Figure 10.36).
2. Click the Selection drop-down arrow, and choose New.
3. In the Save Selection dialog box, choose New from the Selection drop-down menu if you have any other selections saved for the image. If not, the default option is New and there are no other options in the drop-down list.

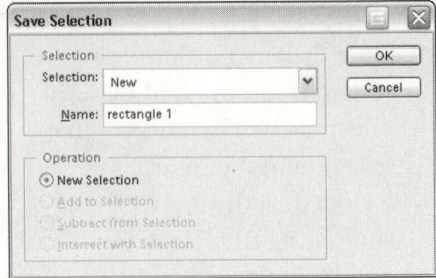

Figure 10.36. Save a selection in your image file for future use.

4. Type a name in the Name field, and click OK to close the dialog box and save the selection.

Revising selections

After the selection is saved, you can continue creating and saving other selections, following the same steps as described earlier.

You can also revise selections by combining them with previously created selections. To revise saved selections, follow these steps:

1. Make the selection using any combination of selection tools.
2. Choose Select ⇨ Save Selection to open the Save Selection dialog box.
3. Click the Selection drop-down arrow and choose the selection you want to revise.
4. Select an Operation radio button on the dialog box, shown in Figure 10.37. Notice

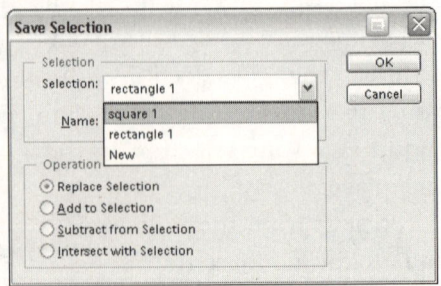

Figure 10.37. Revise selections you are saving in an image.

that the four operations are the same as those you use from the options bar when working with selections.

5. Click OK to close the dialog box and save the revised selection.

When you need to work with your selections at a later time, you can easily reload them and perform different selection operations. Follow these steps to reopen a selection:

1. To open the Load Selection dialog box, choose Select ⇨ Load Selection.

2. Click the Selection drop-down arrow, and choose your saved selection. If you have only one selection, it is shown automatically. If you've saved several selections, select the one you want.

3. Click OK. The dialog box closes and displays the selection on the image.

You can also modify saved selections after loading them on your image. You can create, add to, subtract from, or create an intersected selection. Simply open your saved selection, and use one of the choices on the options bar. The choices can be seen back in Figures 10.2, 10.3, and 10.4, and are listed in Table 10.2.

Table 10.2. Selection operations

Command	Effect
Replace Selection	Replace the saved selection with the current selection.
Add to Selection	Add the current selection to the saved selection.
Subtract from Selection	Subtract the current selection from the saved selection.
Invert	Reverse the areas selected.
Intersect with Selection	Replace the saved selection with the intersection between the current selection and the saved selection.

Bright Idea

If you are creating a fairly complex selection, save it in stages with different names. The image in Figure 10.18 is a good example. To control changes easily, I have one selection for the main shadow, one for the deeper shadows, and another for the shadow details.

Finally, if you no longer want or need a selection you've saved, choose Select ⇨ Delete Selection to open the Delete Selection dialog box. Click the Selection drop-down arrow, and choose one of your selections from the list. Click OK to remove the selection permanently and close the dialog box.

Managing the selections

Regardless of the tool you are using, you can tell the program what you want selected in several ways, including these:

- Select all the pixels on a layer by selecting the layer in the Layers palette and pressing Ctrl+A.
- Deselect an active selection by pressing Ctrl+D.
- Reselect your last selection by pressing Shift+Ctrl+D.
- Hide the selection marquee by pressing Ctrl+H; show the marquee again by using Ctrl+H.

Although you can choose the command from the Select menu for each of the selection methods listed, save yourself dozens of mouse clicks by learning and using the shortcut keystroke combinations.

Just the facts

- Many tools and commands are available to create precise selections.
- Selections can be combined with other selections in several ways.
- Geometric marquee tools and the Lasso tools select pixel areas on the image.
- Combine the use of several tools to perfect a selection if necessary.
- The Magic Wand tool selects pixels based on a specified color range.
- Select pixels using a brush, either by painting the pixels for selection or by painting a mask area for exclusion.
- Extract content from an image that is saved as a separate file.
- Use selections in other images and layers.
- Adjust the characteristics of a selection, such as its feathering or border.
- Save selections for future use, and revise or modify saved selections.

GET THE SCOOP ON...
▪ Understanding types of layers ▪ Modifying background layers ▪ Adding and configuring layers ▪ Adjusting layer opacity ▪ Blending layers

It's Like a Layer Cake

You sit down to sort through some pictures of your beloved dog when the phone rings. You leave the room to answer it and when you return, the resident child in your household has decided that Fido would look better with a beard and goofy glasses. How irritated would you be?

If the "artwork" is done with permanent ink on the surface of the photo itself, the irritation factor could be substantial. On the other hand, if the image is sitting in a protective plastic sleeve and the art is on the plastic cover, there's no real harm done.

Perhaps you are wondering what this has to do with Photoshop Elements. In fact, being able to edit content without affecting the integrity of the original file is a cornerstone of image manipulation software. In Photoshop Elements, you easily make all sorts of changes to an image without touching the original content by using layers in Standard Edit mode — the Photoshop Elements equivalent of a plastic cover.

What is a layer?

Simply put, a layer is a part of an image that is stored in a stack. Each layer in the stack is transparent (except for the background layer) and holds image content. One layer can hold different items, such as a copy of the entire image, a selection, a solid color, or a gradient. Every image has at

Chapter 11

least one layer, the Background. By default, an image's background isn't transparent.

Building an image can involve several layers and they can all be different types of layers. All the layers in an image appear in the Layers palette, shown in Figure 11.1. This image has a number of layers and several types of thumbnails, indicating different types of layers. The layers in the figure are described briefly in Table 11.1. You can read a description of the type of layer shown in the figure, as well as where to find information about that particular type of layer.

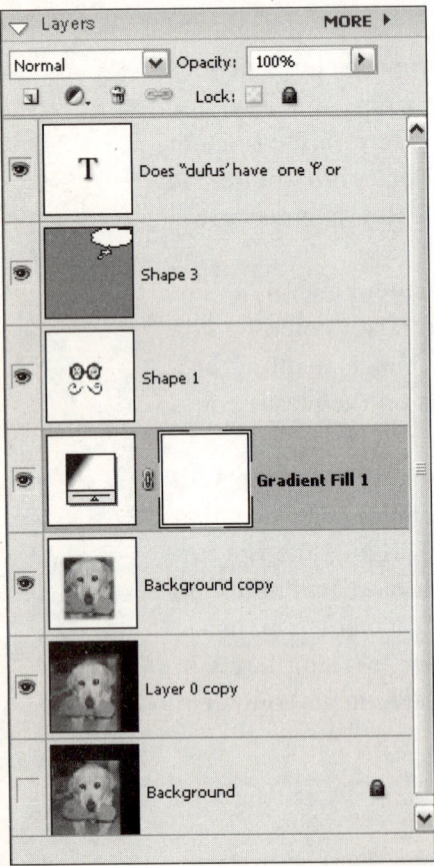

Figure 11.1. The Layers palette lists the types and sequence of layers added to an image file.

Table 11.1. Layer thumbnails shown in Figure 11.1

Thumbnail	Type of Layer	More Information
Text Vector layer	The default type of layer added when you type text on the image using the Type tool.	Read about using text in Chapter 17.
Shape Vector layer	The default type of layer added automatically when you draw with a Custom Shape tool on the image.	Read about working with shapes in Chapter 5.
Rasterized Shape layer	A shape or text layer can't be modified in many ways, such as using effects, unless the format of the layer is changed. A rasterized layer can accept effects, but it can no longer be edited by the tool used to create it originally such as the Text tool or a Custom Shape tool.	Read about working with shapes in Chapter 5.
Fill layer using a gradient	Use one of several different types of Adjustment layers, special layers that apply changes to the underlying content in the image without permanently affecting the image's contents.	Read about Adjustment layers in Chapter 12.
Cropped Image layer copy	A copy of the original image placed on its own layer and cropped to allow underlying content to be visible. In Figure 11.1, note the background for the row in the palette is darker gray, indicating this is the active layer.	Read more in this chapter.
Image layer copy	A full copy of the original image.	Read more in this chapter.
Original Image layer	The original image is the Background. Notice that the Eye icon to the left of the thumbnail is off, meaning the layer is hidden. Also notice a Lock icon to the right of the layer's name. The Background is locked by default, meaning it can't be changed or altered.	Read more in this chapter.

Inside Scoop

One file can contain up to 8,000 layers, but you would likely run out of processing power long before that. Each layer can have its own opacity and blending mode.

Layers are stacked on top of the original image called the Background layer, which is shown at the bottom of the Layers palette. The layers' visibility is affected by their stacking order. Everything on the very top layer is always visible regardless of what type of layer it is.

Some types of layers are added automatically by the program when you perform certain functions, such as copying and pasting or typing text. The different types of layers are listed in Table 11.2.

Table 11.2. Types of layers

Layer Type	Description
Image	This is the basic layer type. The content is pixel-based. Add image layers manually, or add them automatically by pasting content into your image.
Fill	These are special types of layers used to hold color — solid color, a pattern, or a gradient. Figure 11.1 uses an example of a Gradient Fill layer. Read about Fill layers in Chapter 12.
Adjustment	This is a type of layer that lets you modify an underlying image layer without permanently changing the layer's content. Read about Adjustment layers in Chapter 12.
Vector	These types of layers are use to add text and shapes. Read about Text Vector layers in Chapter 17, and about Shape Vector layers in Chapter 5.
Background	This is the default layer of an image. Each image always begins with a Background layer.

Starting in the background

When you open an image in Photoshop Elements for the first time, you see a single layer in the Layers palette. This layer is named Background, as shown in Figure 11.2.

The Background layer always has these features when you open an image:

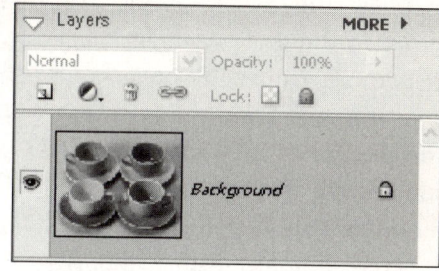

Figure 11.2. The Background layer is locked and visible.

- A thumbnail of the starting image is shown to help identify the layer.

- The layer is visible, indicated by the Eye icon to the left of the thumbnail. You can hide the layer by clicking the Eye icon to toggle it off.

- The layer is locked, indicated by the Lock icon to the right of the thumbnail. It can only be unlocked by changing the Background to a common image layer.

- The background area of the thumbnail in the Layers palette is highlighted in darker gray, indicating it is the active layer when you open the image file initially. Of course, because it is also the only layer, it must also be the active one.

- None of the controls affecting transparency or blending (at the top of the Layers palette) are available.

Deleting a selected area on a Background layer

You can perform most program functions on a Background layer. For example, all the selection tools are functional, as are the drawing, text, and shape tools. However, the settings and controls you can apply to other types of layers — such as specifying a blending mode, changing opacity, or even completely deleting — aren't available to a Background layer.

One of the biggest differences between the Background layer and an ordinary layer in an image is its transparency. If you make a selection on a regular image layer and then press the Delete key, the content in the selected area is removed and becomes transparent, revealing any visible underlying content, or transparency if there is nothing below the deleted area. As shown in Figure 11.3, deleting the leaf shape from the mottled layer reveals both some content on an underlying area as well as areas of transparency where there is no content on the underlying layer.

Figure 11.3. Deleting some content from a regular image layer shows areas of transparency and content on the underlying layer.

On the other hand, in a Background layer, making a selection of any type and pressing the Delete key to delete it, fills the area with the background color specified in the toolbox. You won't see any areas of transparency as long as the Background layer uses its default characteristics. Figure 11.4, for example, shows a mottled orange Background layer and a leaf shape. Deleting the leaf shape from the Background layer fills the selection with the background color.

Figure 11.4. Deleting selected content on a Background layer fills the selection with the background color specified in the toolbox.

By the way, if you want to use the foreground color instead of the background color shown in the toolbox to fill a deleted selection, click the double-ended arrow in the toolbox to swap the color swatches.

Hack
Instead of swapping colors in the toolbox, save some time by pressing Alt+ Delete to delete the content of a selection and fill it with the foreground color automatically.

Converting a Background layer

Because a Background layer can't be altered to display transparency, there are a few ways you can make your Background layer into a "regular" image layer so you can do fancy tricks with it (especially using transparency or blending modes, which are discussed later in the chapter). So, if you know that you intend to do more with the Background layer than just filling in selected areas, go ahead and convert the Background layer.

There are a few ways to convert the Background layer to a regular image layer. The method I find the quickest follows these steps:

1. Double-click the name of the layer to open the New Layer dialog box. The layer is named Layer 0 by default, as shown in Figure 11.5.

2. Click the Name field, and type a different name for the layer if you like.

3. Click OK to close the dialog box and change the layer format.

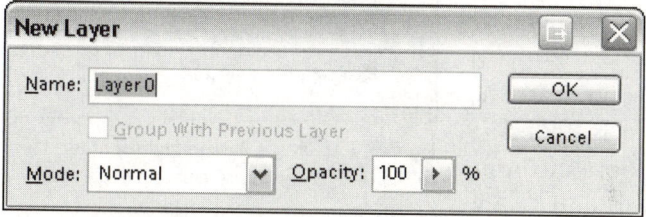

Figure 11.5. Rename the Background layer when converting it to a basic image layer if you prefer.

Watch Out!
If you convert the Background layer, make changes, and then resave the file, your original image is gone. Save a copy, rename the file, or save it in another format to preserve the original.

> **Bright Idea**
> The converted layer is named Layer 0 by default, and I usually leave the default name. It saves a bit of time, and by following the same method all the time, I know automatically that Layer 0 is the previous background.

Other ways you can convert a background to a layer include:

- Right-click the Background layer to open a shortcut menu, and choose Layer from Background to open the New Layer dialog box.
- Choose Layer ⇨ New ⇨ Layer from Background to open the New Layer dialog box.

In either case, name the layer if you like in the New Layer dialog box, and click OK to close the dialog box and change the layer's format.

Duplicating the layer

As a safer alternative to converting the Background layer, you can duplicate it. The quickest way to duplicate a layer doesn't require using dialog boxes at all. Instead, drag the Background layer from the Layers palette to the New Layer icon at the top of the palette. When you release the mouse, a new layer is added to the Layers palette above the original named Background copy, shown in Figure 11.6. The duplicate layer isn't locked.

Figure 11.6. Drag a Background (or other) layer to the New Layer icon to create a duplicate.

> **Inside Scoop**
> You can duplicate any type of layer in your image by dragging it to the New Layer icon — not only Background layers.

Inside Scoop

I rarely use the Background layer. Instead, I make a duplicate or a copy, leave the original Background layer in the file for safekeeping, and click the Eye icon to hide it from view. It adds one more layer to the file, but you won't misplace or modify the original.

If you prefer, you can duplicate the Background layer following these steps:

1. Click More on the Layers palette to open its menu and choose Duplicate. You can also right-click the layer in the Layers palette and choose Duplicate from the shortcut menu. The Duplicate Layer dialog box opens and the layer is listed on the dialog box as a Background copy.
2. In the Destination section, click the Document drop-down arrow and select an open file's name if you want to add a copy of the layer to a different file. Otherwise, click OK to close the dialog box.
3. The Layers palette lists a copy of your layer, called Background copy.

Adding layers

My friend Peter is a European designer who works with lots of layered images for Flash-enabled Web sites. He says he's never shy about using lots of layers because they always come in handy, which is great advice.

And, adding layers to your image is a simple task so you shouldn't be shy about it either. In any image, a new layer is inserted above the active layer in the palette's listing. So if your image has just the background, a new layer is added above the background. If your image has 10 layers, the new layer is added above whichever layer is active in the Layers palette.

There are many ways to add layers to an image, including a few methods I use consistently depending on the layer's characteristics. The most common reasons for adding new layers and my favorite methods are listed in Table 11.3.

Watch Out!

Remember that with every layer you add, the file size increases accordingly. Bigger images are slower to open and eat up storage space on your hard drive.

Table 11.3. Adding layers for different purposes

Purpose of New Layer	Quickest Way to Add It
Duplicating an existing layer	Drag from the layer to the New Layer icon and release the mouse to add a new layer.
Adding content from another file	Select the content in the source file, then drag it to the image you are working on (if both image files are open) or select and copy the content in the source file, then press Ctrl+V to paste it into the image as a new layer.
Copying a layer's content to a new layer	Select the layer in the Layers palette, and then press Ctrl+J to add a copy.
Copying a layer	Drag an existing layer to the New Layer icon on the Layers palette. The layer and its contents are copied to a new layer, the name of which has "copy" appended to the name.
Adding a blank layer	Click the New Layer icon, or use the shortcut Shift+Ctrl+N.

Choosing new layer settings

When you've added a new layer in some way, such as using any of the methods listed in Table 11.3, the New Layer dialog box opens, as shown in Figure 11.7.

Choose from these options to configure the new layer:

- You can give the new layer a name — it starts to get confusing when you've added a few layers, but haven't named them, so it is a good idea to do this when you create the layer. You can always change the name later if you need to.

Bright Idea

The new layer can have settings established before it is added to the Layers palette. But, if you aren't yet sure how you plan to use the layer, leave the defaults and make adjustments as you work with the layer later on.

Inside Scoop

Content that is cut and pasted to a new layer is placed in the same position relative to the image's boundaries as its original location as long as the selection marquee is active. When the marquee is deselected, the selection is pasted to the center of the image.

- If you want to group this new layer to the previous layer, click the check box to select that option. Use grouped layers for building clipping groups, a method of showing and hiding content within the group. Read about clipping groups in Chapter 12.

- You can specify a blending mode in the New Layer dialog box. Click the Mode drop-down arrow and choose one of numerous ways to define how the new layer will blend with its underlying layer or layers. Modes can be based on many different image components, such as types of light, saturation, color, hue, and differences between pixels in the overlying and underlying layers.

- Depending on the Mode you choose from the drop-down list in the New Layer dialog box, a check box may appear below the drop-down list. If you select the option, the new layer is filled with the neutral color that applies to the mode. Not all modes have neutral colors; read about modes later in the chapter.

- Specify how transparent the new layer appears by setting the Opacity for the layer. Type a value in the field or drag the Opacity slider. Again, you can change the opacity at any time from the Layer's palette as you are working.

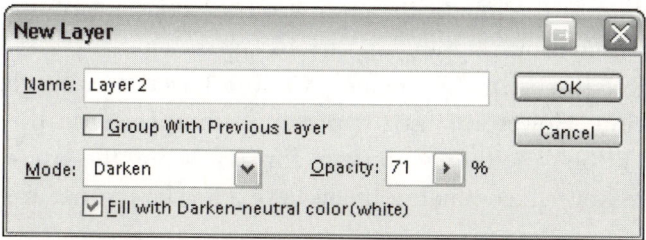

Figure 11.7. You can specify characteristics for new layers before adding them to the file.

Naming and organizing layers

New layers are named according to the method used for adding them. When you add a layer using commands from the Layer menu or via shortcut keys, the new layer is named "Layer X" (where X is a number) and added to the Layers palette. For example, if you add three new layers in a row, they will appear in the Layers palette as Layer 1, Layer 2, and Layer 3.

If you copy a layer it is named using the source layer's name with "copy" appended to it. Duplicated layers are also named using the original layer's name with "copy" appended to the name. If you add several duplicates, each is numbered as well as using the word "copy" in the name.

If you copy and paste or cut and paste content from one image into another, the new content uses the name "Layer" and is numbered according to the existing numbering in your receiving image.

Because it can be complicated to keep track of a project using lots of layers with cryptic names such as Layer 2 Copy 2, renaming your layers as you work on them is a good idea. To rename a layer, double-click the existing name in the Layers palette and type a new one. Click off the name field to change the layer's name.

Layers are organized in a stack. The bottom layer is the Background layer, the first layer that was added to the image file. All other layers are stacked on top of the first layer, both in the Layers palette and on the image.

If you need to rearrange your layers at any point, you can simply drag the layers in the Layers palette. Click a layer to highlight it, and then drag it up or down in the stack to change its position. You may see a difference in the content of the image, depending on the contents of the layer you move and what is overlapping on various layers.

You can also use Layer menu commands. Choose Layer ➪ Arrange and choose an option. However, I usually prefer to drag layers in the Layers palette, and I don't use the menu items for reordering the layers at all, except for the Reverse command. If you have a few layers that are

Inside Scoop

If you double-click the layer's name, you activate the name field. If you double-click the thumbnail, you open the Layer Properties dialog box, which shows the Name field. Either way, you have the same outcome.

Bright Idea

Regardless of where the layers come from, or how they are ordered, it is good practice to take a few minutes and organize the naming for your project. It's not a big deal when working with two or three layers — 20 or 30 is another matter.

out of order and would like to reverse their stacking order, select the layers in the Layers palette and then choose Layer ➪ Arrange ➪ Reverse.

If you were wondering about shortcut keys for these commands, Table 11.4 lists them. Many people find these better for a speedy workflow.

Table 11.4. Ways to arrange layers

Command	Layer Movement	Shortcut Keys
Bring to Front	Moves the selected layer to the top of the stack in the image and the Layers palette	Shift+Ctrl+]
Bring Forward	Moves the selected layer one step up the stack in the image and the Layers palette	Ctrl+]
Send Backward	Moves the selected layer one layer down the stack in the image and the Layers palette	Ctrl+[
Send to Back	Moves the selected layer to the bottom of the stack in the image and the Layers palette	Shift+Ctrl+[
Reverse	Swaps the order of selected layers	Sadly, there isn't one

Configuring appearances

When working with layers, you might want to modify one of the program preferences or adjust the Layers palette's options to suit how you work. You can redefine the default appearance for transparency in an image to suit your eyesight. You might also want to change the way the layers are displayed in the Layers palette.

Setting the transparency appearance

Understanding what is and isn't transparent can be confusing, especially if you aren't familiar with transparency. The default for the program shows a pale gray and white checked grid identifying transparent areas. For some people, that checkerboard appearance can be very distracting.

Bright Idea

My preference is to use white and a pale peachy-beige color with a large-sized grid. It's not distracting, and although the color is very pale, the large size of the checkerboard squares clearly differentiates the transparent areas.

Depending on the quality of your monitor, its settings, and your eyes, the checkerboard can seem to vibrate.

You can modify the transparency appearance (and save your eyes!) by following these steps:

1. Choose Edit ➪ Preferences ➪ Transparency to open the Preferences dialog box, shown in Figure 11.8.
2. Choose an option from the Grid Size drop-down menu. You can select None, Small, Medium, and Large.
3. Click the Grid Colors drop-down arrow, and choose an option. Choices include the level of darkness from gray/white to gray/dark gray or select from several colors and white. You can also click the color swatches below the Grid Colors and pick your own checkerboard colors.
4. Click OK to close the dialog box and adjust your setting.

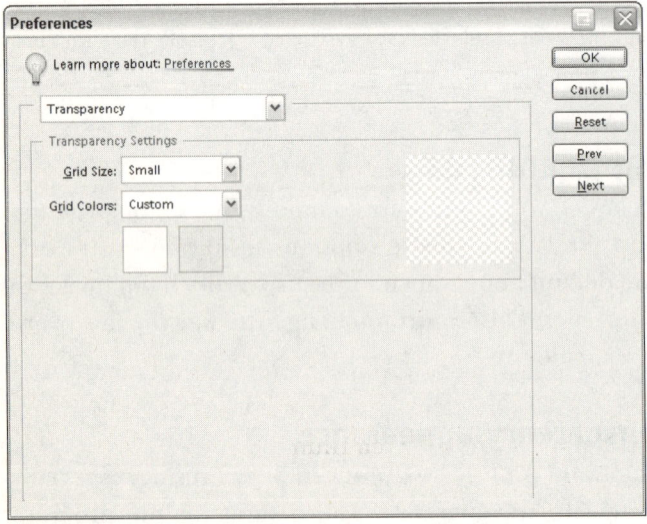

Figure 11.8. Pick custom colors or grid size for showing transparency in an image.

Watch Out!

If you choose None in the Grid Size list, the transparency is shown as white. It isn't a problem when working with colored image content, but if your image also contains layers or areas of white, it can be difficult to tell what's white from what's transparent.

Specifying the layer characteristics

You can also define how you want to see the content of your image displayed in the Layers palette. Pick thumbnail characteristics as well as the extent of view.

Follow these steps to configure the Layers palette's appearance:

1. Click More on the Layers palette to open the menu, and choose Palette Options. The Layers Palette Options dialog box opens, shown in Figure 11.9.
2. Select a Thumbnail Size radio button, ranging in size from no thumbnail to large ones.
3. Select an option for the Thumbnail Contents. Choose either Layer Bounds or leave the default Entire Document option. In Figure 11.10, the left example shows the Layer Bounds option, which shows just the content on the layer if it uses less than the full layer's dimensions, while the right shows the same Layers palette using the Entire Document display option, showing the full image layer dimensions in each thumbnail.
4. Click OK to close the dialog box and make the changes.

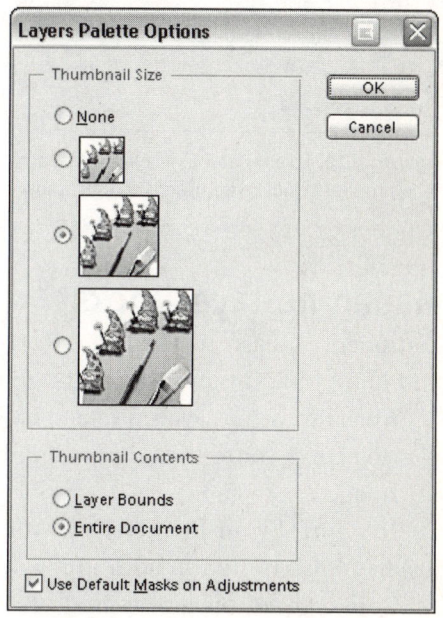

Figure 11.9. Select display options for the Layers palette in the dialog box.

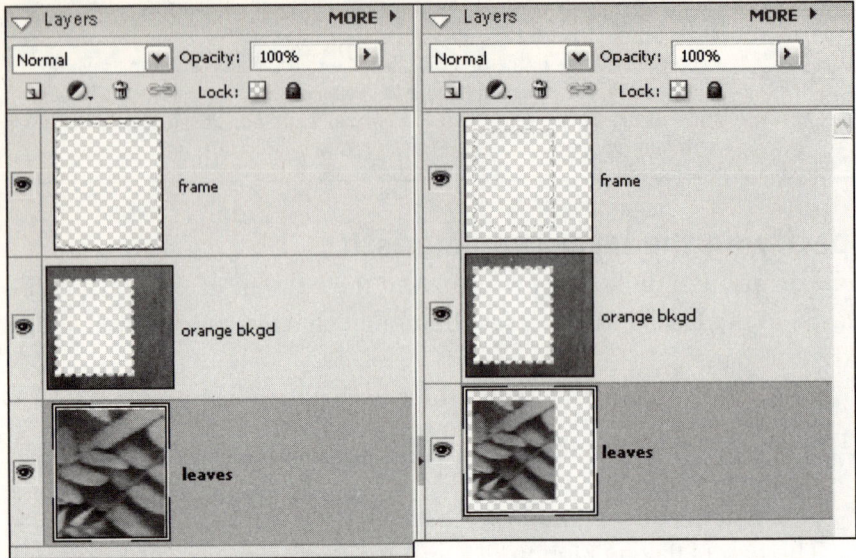

Figure 11.10. Specify how the layer's content is shown in the Layers palette. The left example shows the Layer Bounds option; the right shows the default Entire Document display option.

Managing layer locks

You need to learn to use layers correctly. If not, they can be confusing and more of a nuisance than a boon to your productivity.

Working with a layered image isn't an intuitive process. Not only are you selecting content on an image, but you are also selecting a layer in the image.

To control your image layers, you can lock either the entire layer or just its transparency. In addition, you can link and merge layers.

Unlike some programs that are layer-specific, Photoshop Elements lets you select content by clicking it in the image without having to select the layer first, which is a terrific feature!

The layer containing the selected material is active automatically. However, the auto selection works only for content that is uppermost in

Inside Scoop

Use the Layer Bounds option when you have numerous small elements added on different layers to more easily identify the content on each layer.

> ### Can't decide on a thumbnail size?
>
> Keep in mind that you can easily change the size and appearance of the thumbnail depending on your image's layers. You may want to make changes in any of these situations:
>
> - You have quite a few layers. Decreasing the thumbnails' sizes shows more layers on the Layers palette.
>
> - You have several similar layers. Increase the thumbnails' sizes to show you the differences more clearly.
>
> - Also for similar layers or objects copied from other files or layers, choose Layer Bounds to display just the content in the thumbnail.
>
> - When similar layers are arranged in a sequence on the image, using the Entire Document option can show which layer is which, based on position.

the image's layer stack. That is, you can't select a background layer by clicking the image if it is covered by other layers. In that case, select the layer in the Layers palette.

The content that is uppermost in an image isn't necessarily on the top layer. Figure 11.11 shows the three-layered image represented by the Layers palette examples shown in Figure 11.10. In the image, the uppermost layer is a black frame, the central layer is the mottled pattern, and the bottom layer is the image of leaves. Clicking the leaves selects them, even though they are on the bottom layer because there is no overlying content.

Figure 11.11. Click to select content automatically — the uppermost object is selected whether or not it is on the top layer.

Locking layer contents

You can protect the integrity of finished layers in your image by locking them. Or, you can lock those layers that you don't want to disturb when working with other layers.

You can choose to lock the transparency of the layer or the entire layer. Select the layer you want to protect, and click either the Lock Transparency or Lock All icons at the top right of the Layers palette. When you lock the transparency, the layer can be repositioned on the image or reordered in the layer stack, but you can't add a fill, pattern, or paint with any tool within transparent areas. When you lock the entire layer using Lock All, you can move the layer in the layer stack, but you can't reposition it in the image, nor can you select or edit the content of the layer in any way.

It isn't necessary to always lock a layer, but locking is a good idea in these circumstances:

- You have layers composed of selections smaller than the full image size. Locking those layers prevents them from being selected and moved accidentally.
- You are finished working with upper layers, but want to make changes on the lower layers in the image. Lock the layers in the Layers palette that you don't want to disturb in the document window. The example in Figure 11.12 shows the Layers palette and an image with three layers named Layer 1, Layer 2, and Layer 3, with Layer 1 at the bottom of the stacking order. As you can see in the image at the top of Figure 11.12, locking Layer 2 and Layer 3 means clicking the image selects Layer 1's content.
- You want to protect the transparent areas of a layer and don't need to lock the layer's position as you are filling or painting. Choose Lock Transparency, which prevents color being applied to transparent pixels in the layer.

It's all well and good that you can lock transparency or lock a layer altogether, but the real use is for showing you the image as you are working on it, without affecting any of the transparent areas.

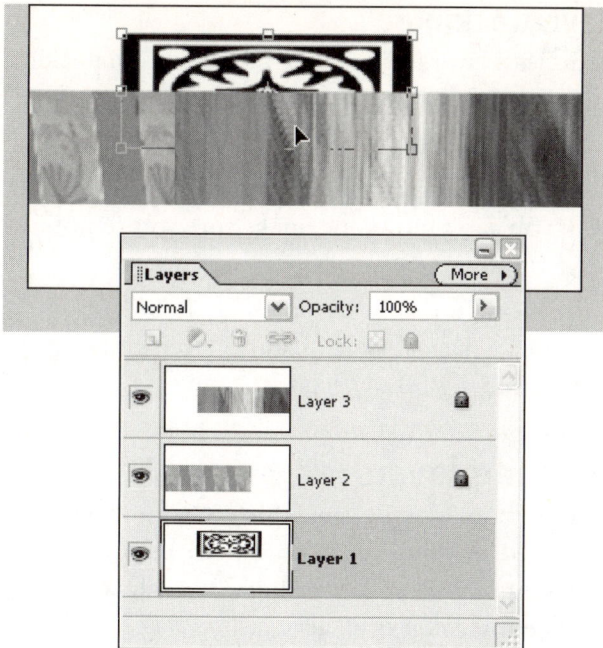

Figure 11.12. Locking upper layers lets you select a lower layer by clicking the image.

Figure 11.13 shows a three-layered image and its Layers palette. The bottom layer, named Layer 0, is locked, and can't be moved or edited. Layer 1 and Layer 2 contain similar shapes filled with a pattern. Each shape also includes transparent areas. Layer 1 has locked transparency, while Layer 2 has no locks applied. The transparent areas of the border surrounding the shape on Layer 2 is filled with the pattern, while Layer 1 maintains its transparent areas.

Read about border selections and other types of selection in Chapter 10. Filling with patterns and color is discussed in Chapter 6.

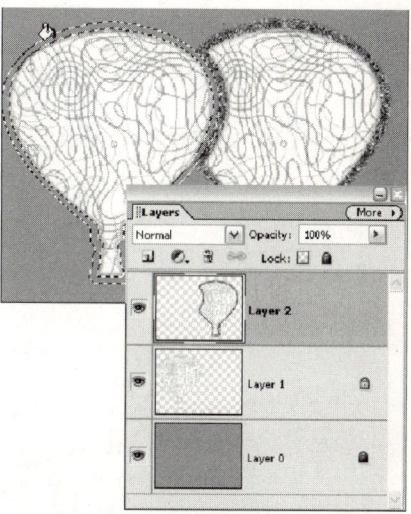

Figure 11.13. Locking transparency prevents the transparent areas from being colored by painting or filling while letting you see the entire composition.

Troubleshooting layer locking

If you are having problems with layer locking, one of these tips may help:

- If you have locked a layer and can't remove the lock, make sure the layer is visible.
- Layers can be moved in the stacking order regardless of whether or not they are locked. If you can't move one, make sure you're not trying to move the Background layer.
- Check the color of the lock if the layer doesn't seem to be working right; a locked layer shows a dark Lock icon, and a layer with only transparency locking shows a light Lock icon.

Linking and unlinking layers

Suppose you have four or five copies of the same thing in your image and decide they should be moved on the image, or should be a different color, or need some other edit. Rather than working with each layer individually, link them and make the changes all at once.

Follow these steps to link layers in the Layers palette:

1. In the Layers palette, unlock any locked layers you want to include with the grouped of linked layers. Although you can link a layer with other layers while it is locked, you can't make any edits, which defeats much of the purpose of the activity.

2. In the Layers palette, click to select the first layer for the group.

3. Ctrl+click to select additional layers.

4. Click Link Layer at the top of the Layers palette. You see the Link Layers icon shows to the right of each linked layer in the Layers palette, shown in Figure 11.14.

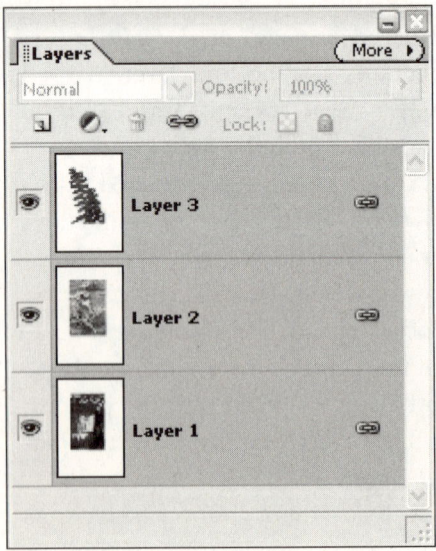

Figure 11.14. Link layers to apply commands to them simultaneously.

> **Watch Out!**
> Clicking a layer that isn't part of the linked set hides the Link icon on the Layers palette and none of the linked layers show the icon.

When you want to unlink a layer, select the linked layer in the Layers palette and click the Link Layers icon. The Link icon disappears from the layer's listing. Other layers in the linked set remain linked.

Merging layers

It takes time to scroll through a long list of layers in the Layers palette. Not only that, but layers can greatly increase the size of a file. However, it is important to make sure you have finished all the work you want to do with an individual layer before merging it with other layers.

To save time and file size, look for layers that can be merged. For example, you may have content on several layers that you have finished working with, or you would prefer to have all the content from several layers on the same layer for convenience.

Merging choices

Choose from one of several ways to merge content in your image file depending on what you are merging. In all cases, the visibility of the layer plays a part in the merge. As a general rule of thumb, make sure the layers you want to merge are visible (they display the Eye icon), and those you don't want to merge are hidden (the Eye icon is toggled off).

There are different types of merges for different circumstances. As often as possible I try to use the Merge Visible choice because I don't have to try to remember what I want to merge! Merge visible layers following these steps:

1. Click the Eye icons to the left of the names of layers that you want to merge to make them visible; any hidden layers aren't included in the merge.
2. Press Shift+Ctrl+E to merge the layers. If you prefer, choose Layer ⇨ Merge Visible, or click the Layers palette's More menu and choose Merge Visible.
3. Click the Eye icons to make the layers visible that you want to work with next. These are the other types of merges:

> **Bright Idea**
> Be sure all the layers you want to include in the merge are visible. Hide the rest to help you keep track and prevent them from being included in the merged layers.

- **Merge Layers.** Select two or more layers in the Layers palette. Choose Layer ⇨ Merge Layers, or click the palette's More menu and choose Merge Layers. The layers are combined into a single layer using the name of the first layer selected.

- **Merge Down.** Select the layer you want to be on top of the pair. Choose Layer ⇨ Merge Down, or click the Layers palette's More menu and choose Merge Down. You can also use the Ctrl+E shortcut combination.

- **Merged Linked.** Click the Eye icons to the left of the linked layers that you want to merge. Choose Layer ⇨ Merge Linked, or click the Layers palette's More menu and choose Merge Linked.

Merging layers into new layers

Merging layers is a good way to create "batches" of similar images, like the examples shown in Figure 11.15. In each of the examples, a background layer, an image, and a text label are merged into a new layer without affecting the original layers because they still exist. And, because they still exist, you can reuse them in different combinations to make other merged layers.

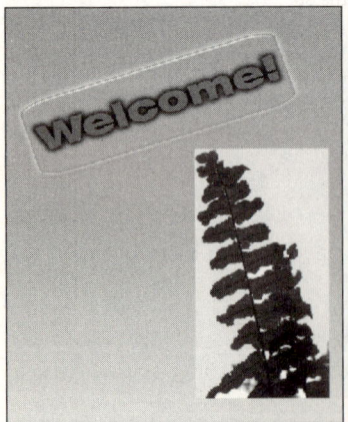

Figure 11.15. Combine selected layers into different images while preserving the originals for further use.

CHAPTER 11 ▪ IT'S LIKE A LAYER CAKE

After layers are merged you can't make any changes to the contents of the components in the merged layer. If you need to make changes, you must change the original layer and then re-create the merged layer again. Both examples use layers from the same image with different selections in the Layers palette, shown in Figure 11.16, combined for each.

Follow these steps to merge selected layers into new layers:

1. Add a new layer for each merge group you want to create in the Layers palette. In the example, you see two layers named "Merge 1" and "Merge 2".

2. Make sure the layers you want to merge are visible, showing the Eye icon, and unlocked.

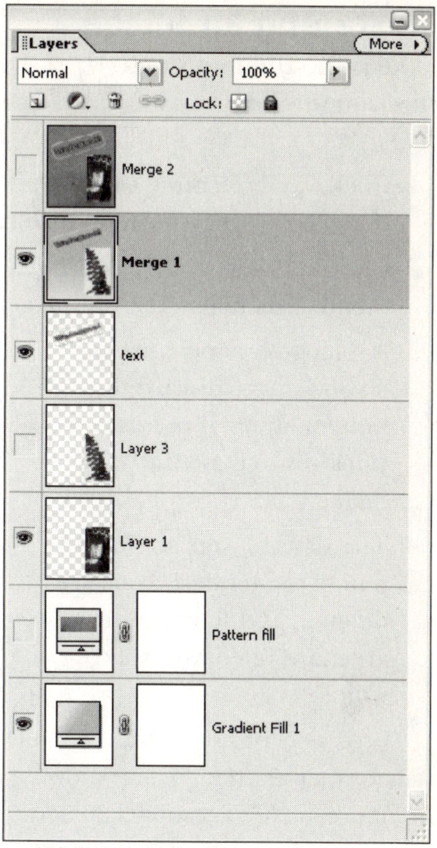

Figure 11.16. Store different options for an image in the same file and mix and match as necessary.

3. Select the layer you want to receive the merged layers. In the figure, the Merge 1 layer is the active layer, and it holds the contents from the visible layers.

4. Press Alt+Shift+Ctrl+E. Copies of each visible layer are placed into the active layer; the original layers are not affected.

5. Repeat as necessary. In the figure, the Merge 2 layer group is similar, except it includes a different image layer.

Hack

If four keys are too much for one shortcut for you, press the Alt key and choose Layer ⇨ Merge Layers, or click More on the Layers palette and choose Merge Layers from the menu.

Flattening an image

Flatten the file to a single layer if you are finished with it and you're sure you won't be making any changes. Follow these steps to flatten the file:

1. Click the Eye icon to toggle the visibility of the layers you want to show in the final image to visible.
2. Choose Layer ⇨ Flatten Image, or click the Layers palette's More menu and choose Flatten Image.
3. A dialog box opens asking if you want to discard the hidden layers, if present. Click Yes to close the dialog box.
4. The visible layers are flattened, the hidden layers are deleted, and transparent areas are filled with solid white.

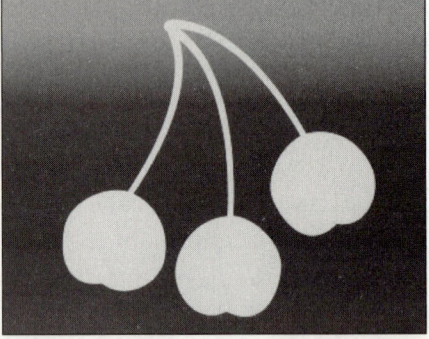
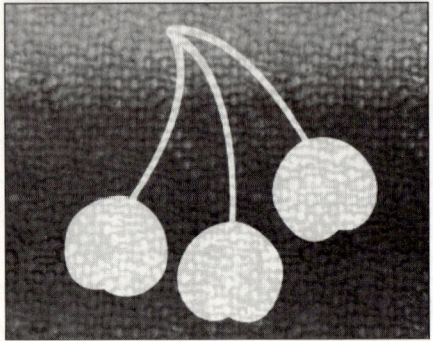

Two versions of the same image after flattening are shown in Figure 11.17. The upper image shows a shape against a gradient background. In the lower image, you see a texture that looks like woven cloth. The texture layer, hidden in the upper image before flattening, is discarded and not used in the final composition.

Figure 11.17. Only visible layers are included in a flattened image.

Inside Scoop

The flattened version can't be edited in the same way as the original multi-layered file. If you need to make changes such as text or opacity, you have to open the full original file.

Taking a shortcut

Layered image files can be very large, but if you may make changes in the future you need to preserve the layers. Instead of opening the entire file when you want to take a quick look, you can open a flattened, single-layer version of the file.

Opening a flattened version lets you use the content of your original image in a single layer. In Figure 11.18, the left Layers palette shows the many layers of the image; the file's total size is nearly 3.5MB. The right Layers palette shows the same image opened as composite data; this version is under 1MB, and contains a single layer named Layer 0. If you make changes, be sure to save the file with a new name.

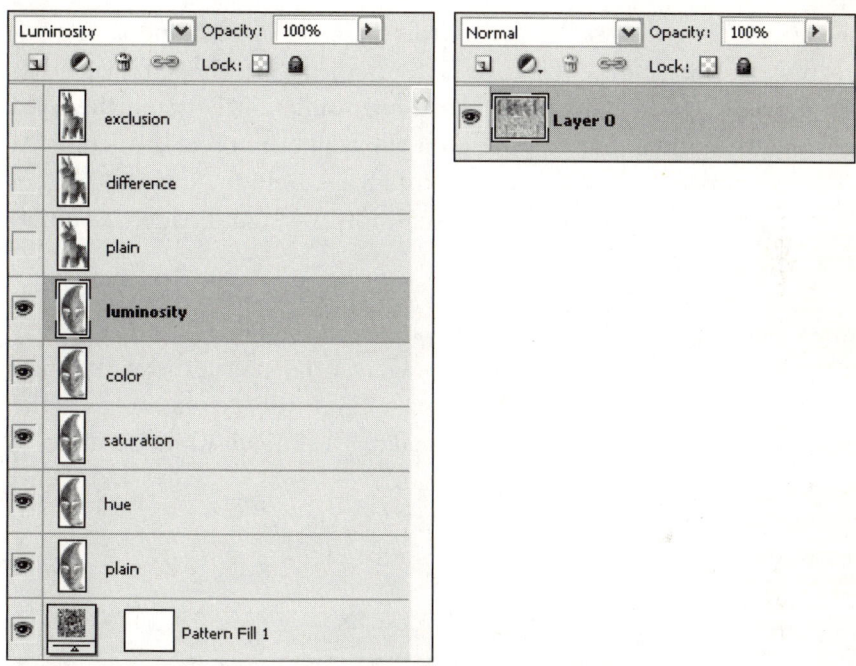

Figure 11.18. Use a shortcut to open a flattened version of a layered file.

>  **Watch Out!**
> If the bottom layer in a selected pair or group of layers is a shape or type layer, it must be simplified. Fortunately, Photoshop Elements asks you if you want to simplify the layer, so you don't have to worry about the command not being applied correctly. When it's simplified, the image is flattened.

Opacity settings

Each layer in your image, including the Background layer, can have a specified opacity. Click the Opacity arrow at the top of the Layers palette to reveal the Opacity slider and drag it to decrease opacity from its default 100 percent. If you prefer, click the Opacity field to activate it and type a value.

Change the opacity of a layer to create a blending with underlying layers, such as those shown in Figure 11.19. In the figure, the left image uses 100 percent opacity, and there is a clear distinction between the solid color background and the upper layer showing bright blocks of color. At 50 percent opacity, shown in the center image, both the top and bottom layers have the same importance visually. In the right image, at 10 percent, the color blocks are very faint.

Changing the opacity of the layer also changes the opacity of the transparency checkerboard, as you can see in Figure 11.20. It's usually difficult to see how the layer appears against the checkerboard because as you decrease the opacity of the image layer, you increasingly see the checkerboard through your image, making it difficult to judge the true color and effect in the image. If a semi-transparent image displays against a white background, you see the impact of changing the opacity much more clearly, like the right image in Figure 11.20.

Figure 11.19. The simplest way to blend content on one layer with the underlying layer is to change its opacity.

Figure 11.20. The content in a layer with some transparency can be hard to see clearly against the checkerboard pattern.

There are a few ways to clearly see what's going on in your image when changing opacity settings. These include:

- Choose Edit ➪ Preferences ➪ Transparency and choose None from the Grid Size drop-down list, check out the image, and then restore the checkerboard grid from the same command path.

- Add an extra layer to your image, fill it with white and store it at the bottom of the layer stack. When you want to preview opacity, make the layer visible.

- Choose Layer ➪ Flatten Image to flatten all layers in the image to a solid white background. This is my favorite method, but it is also the most dangerous method. After you have seen how the changed opacity looks, choose Edit ➪ Revert or use the Ctrl+Z shortcut keys to restore the layers to your image.

Blending modes

The list of blending modes is available at the top left of the Layers palette. To apply a blend to layers, follow these steps:

1. Click the layer to which you want to apply the blend to make it active.
2. Click the Blend drop-down arrow at the top left of the Layers palette to open the list and select the mode from the list.
3. The list closes, and the mode is applied to the layer.

The key to understanding blending modes is to understand that the name of the blend always refers to what's happening to the active layer blending with the one (or more) below it. Remember that, and you are on your way to blending stardom. The example in Figure 11.21 shows the impact of using the Dissolve mode on the text. You see it has fuzzy spotted edges that mix with the background's pixels.

Figure 11.21. The blending mode is applied to the selected layer and affects how it blends with its underlying layer.

There's more to understanding blending than my little pearl of wisdom. Like other concepts, you have to take the time to figure out how each affects an image and how different colors and combinations react differently. You don't configure blend modes. They are applied or they aren't.

The two blends that don't really belong to another group are listed at the top of the Blend Mode list. Normal is the mode assigned to any layer by default. Dissolve produces a scattering of effects at the edges of the layer to which it is applied.

Bright Idea

You can use both opacity changes and blending modes on the same layer. You must experiment with the appearance, because applying a blend looks different depending on the opacity.

>  **Inside Scoop**
>
> The discussions on blending modes include images showing the active layer, the underlying content, and the outcome of the blend.

- **Normal.** The default mode is Normal. In this mode, each pixel is painted or adjusted to produce the final color. There isn't any blending with underlying pixels. When you paste content from another image into your working image, or create a new image, the layer uses a Normal blend. If you don't need to use any blending to create a specific look or make underlying content visible, leave the default Normal mode selected.
- **Dissolve.** Each pixel is modified to produce the resulting color, which is randomly assigned to the base color or the blend color, depending on the opacity. The color is calculated and assigned by the program, like the scattered pixels surrounding the letters in Figure 11.21.

The rest of the blending modes fall into several basic categories. There are modes that darken the content, lighten the content, simulate different sorts of light, calculate pixel values, or affect the components of the color, such as its hue or saturation.

Darken blending modes

Several of the blending modes darken the combined pixels by applying different mathematical formulas to the pixel information.

These are your choices for darkening modes:

- **Darken.** For each pixel, the darker of either the base or blend color is calculated by the program and shown as the result color. In the image of the crayons against a bright blue background, shown in Figure 11.22, you see that in the blended image at the right, the stripes from all the crayons are visible, as the stripes are darker than the blue background. You also see varying amounts of the crayon colors, depending on whether they are lighter or darker than the background. Pixels lighter than the blend color are replaced, while pixels darker than the blend color remain.

Figure 11.22. The Darken mode shows the darker of either the base or blend pixel color. In the image, the parts of the crayons that are darker than the blue background are shown, while those areas lighter than the blue background disappear.

- **Multiply.** The Multiply blend actually does do some multiplication to produce its results, which are always darker than the original colors. The resulting color is the base color multiplied by the blend color. In the image shown in Figure 11.23, the left puzzle piece is magenta, the right is yellow, and the area where they overlap is a rust color. There are some exceptions to the Multiply blend: multiplying any color by black results in black; multiplying any color by white results in no change.

Figure 11.23. Use the Multiply blend to darken color by multiplying color values.

- **Color Burn.** The Color Burn mode darkens the base color. The example shown in Figure 11.24 shows three images of a water lily. The central image is the original — a bright pink water lily surrounded by rich green leaves. The background, or base color for the image, is a slightly lighter shade of pink than the lily. The left version shows the Color Burn mode applied, darkening the base color to reflect the blend color. In other words, the green leaves surrounding the lily take on a dark red color, and the lily takes on some red tones as well. Blending with white results in no change.

- **Linear Burn.** Although Color Burn and Linear Burn are separate blend modes, they work in very similar ways by darkening the base color. An example of how the Linear Burn mode displays is shown in the right image in Figure 11.24. The base color darkens to reflect the blend color by decreasing the brightness. In the example, the lily is a dark pink, and the surrounding leaves and stems are very dark, almost black, with the exception of highlights which remain the pink of the background. Blending with white results in no change, as with the Color Burn.

Figure 11.24. Burn blends darken the base color. The Color Burn (left) produces less dramatic changes than the Linear Burn (right).

Lighten blending modes

Several of the blending modes result in lighter outcomes. When you select the mode, the program compares color information in the pixels of each layer and adjusts the appearance.

You have these lighten modes choices:

- **Lighten.** The Lighten blend mode looks at the color information in each of the Red, Green, and Blue color channels. The color you see after the blend is applied is the lighter of either the base color (the underlying color) or the blend color (the color in the pixels). Pixels darker than the blend color are replaced, and pixels lighter than the blend color do not change. In the example shown in Figure 11.25, both the man's shirt and the background behind him are darker (left) than the color of the leaves in the underlying layer (middle). As a result, the colors in the shirt and the background blend with the leaves' colors (right).

308 PART III ■ PICK WHAT YOU WANT TO WORK WITH

Figure 11.25. Pixels are compared, and the lighter pixel in each layer is shown after applying different formulas in each blending mode.

- **Screen.** The Screen blend always results in a lighter color. In Figure 11.26, the original image of balloons is shown at the left, and the effect in the middle is using the Lighten mode for comparison. A Screen blend, shown in the right image of Figure 11.26, is calculated by multiplying the inverse of the blend and base colors. What this means is that regardless of how dark the two layers are, the resulting blend is always lighter because the inverse of a dark color is a light color. Screening with black results in no change; screening with white produces white.

Figure 11.26. Pixels are always lighter in the Screen blend, shown at the far right, than they are with other similar blends, such as the Lighten mode, shown in the middle image.

- **Color Dodge/Linear Dodge.** The Color Dodge blend brightens the base color to reflect the blend color, shown in the middle image in Figure 11.27. Because of the background color's similarity to some of the blend colors, areas of the image become very translucent. For example, in the original image, shown at the left of the figure, the uppermost balloon is red, and the upper right balloon is green.

When the Color Dodge mode is applied both of those balloons become translucent. Blending with black produces no change.

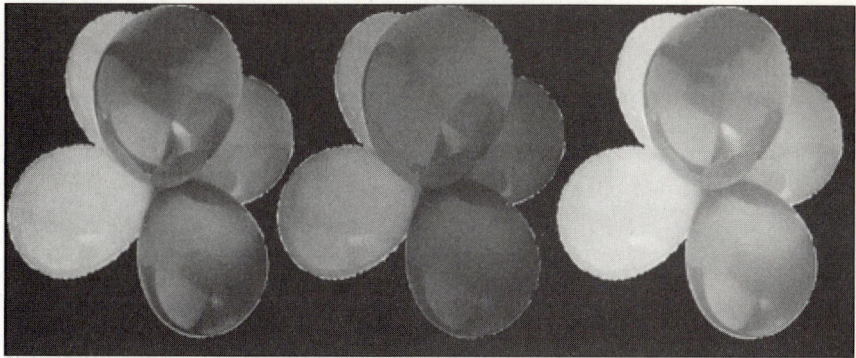

Figure 11.27. Both the Color Dodge mode (center) and the Linear Dodge mode (right) result in brighter images than the original (left).

- **Linear Dodge.** The Linear Dodge blend brightens the base color to reflect the blend color by increasing image brightness, shown in the right image in Figure 11.27. In terms of the balloon image, that means the green balloon at the upper right of the bunch becomes almost transparent green, and the lower right balloon, a deep blue, becomes light purple. The red and dark yellow balloons become bright pink and pale peach, respectively. As with the Color Dodge, blending with black has no effect.

Using the Overlay blend

The Overlay mode is a true combo blend. It either multiplies (darkens) or screens (lightens) the color, depending on the base color. The example shown in Figure 11.28 shows both of the Overlay mode's effects. The sunglasses' layer is the uppermost layer, and uses the Overlay blend mode on top of a multi-hued blend of gradients, shown next to the sunglasses.

The color in the sunglasses is mixed with the blend colors to reflect the base color's lightness or darkness, without changing the shadow or

Bright Idea

Taking the time to experiment with a set of images, such as those used in this discussion, are worth every minute. You not only see the effect of the different blends, but you can compare the differences in color.

highlights in the base layer. Of course, because the example is a pattern and not an image, there isn't much concern for highlights or shadows.

When the mode is applied, you see in the right image that there are areas where the sunglasses are lighter, and other areas where they are darker, in response to the colors in the pattern. Highlights and shadows are covered in Chapter 8.

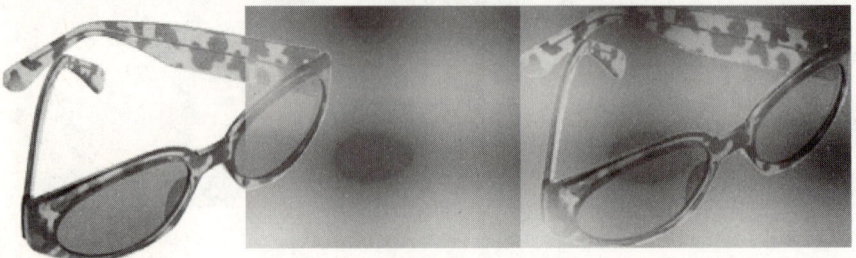

Figure 11.28. An Overlay blend both lightens and darkens, depending on the base color.

Shining a light

You can apply several different types of light as a blending mode. Sometimes, the differences are subtle, while others are dramatic. To illustrate how the various Light blending modes work, I'm using the two images shown in Figure 11.29. Each background in this example uses the same set of three layers — a solid color burgundy layer; a layer with a hatched pattern in dark red, gold, and a blue middle layer. The image that is placed on top is on the right of the figure; it shows four cups and saucers in bright gold, red, blue, and green.

Figure 11.29. The Light blend examples use the same set of layers.

The different light blending modes are shown in Figure 11.30. In each case, notice the differences in the blend outcomes.

Figure 11.30. The Light blend modes produce significantly different results. The top row shows Soft Light and Hard Light; the middle row is Vivid Light and Linear Light; finally, the bottom row is Pin Light and Hard Mix.

These light modes are available:

- **Soft Light.** Soft Light, shown in the top left of Figure 11.30, looks like a diffused spotlight. The resulting colors depend on the blend color, which is calculated by the program. When Photoshop Elements does the calculations, if the blend color is less than 50 percent gray, the image is lightened; if the color is more than 50 percent gray, the image is darkened. Pure black produces a dark area that isn't pure black, while pure white produces a light area that isn't pure white. In the figure, you can see the soft areas of light at the edges of the cups. You also see the differences in how the stripes in the underlying layers are shown based on the cups' colors.
- **Hard Light.** Hard Light looks like a sharp spotlight and can be seen in the upper-right image in Figure 11.30. If the blend color is less than 50 percent gray, the image is screened, or lightened. When the blend color is more than 50 percent gray, the image is multiplied, or darkened (and, using pure black or white results in pure black or white). Highlights created with Hard Light blend modes are much harsher and brighter than those created with the Soft Light blend mode. Use Hard Light for adding highlights and shadows.
- **Vivid Light.** Vivid Light, shown in the middle-left of Figure 11.30, increases or decreases the contrast depending on the blend color. In the figure, you can see that Vivid Light produces a sharp, edgy appearance, both in how the cups appear against the background and how the stripes' texture is shown. If the blend color is less than 50 percent gray, the contrast is decreased and the image is lightened. If the blend color is more than 50 percent gray, the contrast is increased and the image is darkened.
- **Linear Light.** Linear Light increases or decreases the brightness depending on the blend color. It is shown in the middle-right of Figure 11.30. When the blend color is less than 50 percent gray, the lightness of the colors increases. When the blend color is more than 50 percent gray, the lightness decreases. In the figure, the Linear Light mode example is similar to the Hard Light example at the upper right of the figure, except the contrast is much stronger. You can especially see the difference if you look at the edges of the cups and saucers.

- **Pin Light.** The Pin Light mode, shown in the lower-left of Figure 11.30, uses the result of the blend color to define what is replaced. If the blend color is less than 50 percent gray—so we are talking about the lighter colors in the image—pixels darker than the blend color are replaced and the rest of the pixels don't change. If the blend color is more than 50 percent gray (the darker colors), pixels lighter than the blend color are replaced and the rest of the pixels don't change. This means the colors in the image layer are blended based on how the gray levels assign the colors. For example, the lower-right cup is red on a bright green saucer, and shown against a burgundy background. With the Pin Light blend is applied, most of the saucer disappears because the amount of gray in the image and the background are similar, leaving the highlight areas around its rim.
- **Hard Mix.** The Hard Mix mode, shown in the lower-right of Figure 11.30, takes things down to the basics. The resulting colors in an image are based on the base and blend colors. It is a straightforward mode, there aren't any special conditions. It just works like this: After the colors in the layers are blended, all color is reduced to red, green, blue, yellow, cyan, magenta, white, and black. You see in the example that the effect is extremely sharp and the color areas are dense.

Subtracting for effect

Many blending modes increase the color, but there a few that actually take away color. The Difference and Exclusion blends are two such modes; they are both based on subtraction. The main difference between Exclusion and Difference is contrast; Exclusion has less.

For each of the Red, Green, and Blue color channels that make up an image, either the blend color is subtracted from the base color or the base color is subtracted from the blend color, depending on which color is brighter. Blending with black has no change; blending with white inverts the base color values and "flips" the appearance of the blend.

> **Inside Scoop**
>
> If your image has a pale fringing around it like that in the left image of Figure 11.31, you can use the Difference or Exclusion modes to reverse the color to black, which looks like you've added an outline.

In the example shown in Figure 11.31, the far left piñata uses the Normal blend. The middle image has the Difference mode applied, and the intensity of color is brighter than the original, as well as having the colors shift from the red-blue to green-blue realm. The most obvious change is in the eye. The original eye is white with a black pupil, while the blended versions both show a green eye based on the light green background color in the image. The far right image, using the Exclusion blending mode, is very similar in color to the middle image but it has less contrast. Again, its colors are green-blue, but more subdued than the central image.

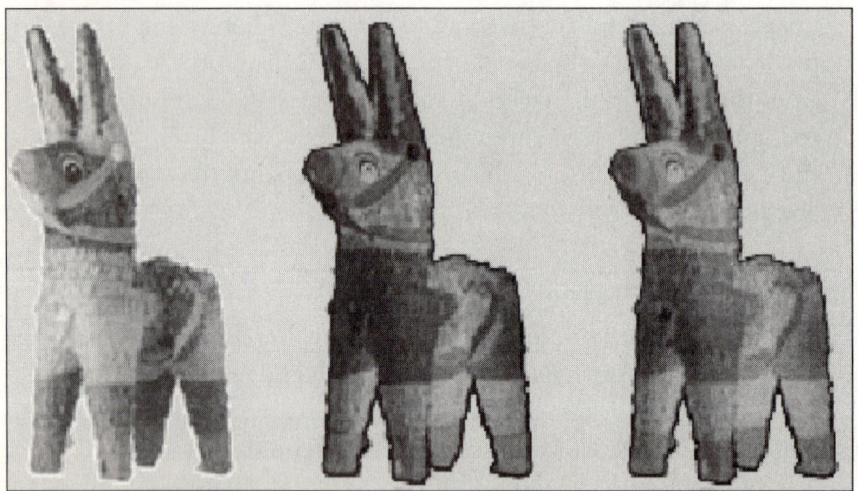

Figure 11.31. Use subtraction blends for different effects based on brightness comparisons.

Blending color settings

The last group of blending modes deals with color values. You can choose blends that affect an image's hue, saturation, color, or luminosity. Figure 11.32 shows the Normal blend of this ghostly looking mask. All examples overlay the same pastel patterned background.

You are likely to find a good use for these blending modes in your work; my favorite has always been the Luminosity blend, probably because it shows detail of the underlying layer so well. You can choose from these blends:

Figure 11.32. The Normal blend shows the wooden mask overlaying the pastel patterned background.

> **Inside Scoop**
> Because some of the color setting blends are subtle, experimenting with the blending modes to see how they vary is your best bet.

- **Hue.** In the Hue blending mode, show in Figure 11.33, the resulting color is created from the hue of the blend color plus the luminance and saturation of the base color. The mask in the example is in the brown-yellow range and overlays the colors of the pattern on the background base layer.

Figure 11.33. The Hue blend shows the wooden mask much darker where it overlays darker areas of the background.

- **Saturation.** The resulting color in the Saturation blending mode is created from the saturation of the blend color plus the hue and luminance of the base color, as shown in Figure 11.34. The mask is fairly saturated in color, and you see the blend results in much darker tones in the underlying base layer's patterns. Unsaturated areas that are neutral gray don't have any changes.

Figure 11.34. The Saturation blend shows the mask in quite dramatic saturated colors based on the pale pastel colors in the background pattern.

- **Color.** The resulting color in the Color blending mode is created from the luminance of the base color and the hue and saturation of the blend color. In Figure 11.35, the color is stripped from the background pattern, and the areas of dark and light in the pattern are shown in the mask's color range. In effect, the Color mode tinted the Background layer.

Figure 11.35. The Color blend tints the background color with the range of color in the mask.

- **Luminosity.** In the Luminosity blending mode, the resulting color is created from the luminance of the blend color and the hue and saturation of the base color. In Figure 11.36, the luminosity of the mask is retained and overlays the colors and pattern in the background, intensifying their depth to show the details of the mask.

The Color and Luminosity modes produce inverse effects.

Figure 11.36. The Luminosity blend maintains the characteristics of the mask's features, highlights, and shadows, and intensifies them with color from the pastel patterned background.

Just the facts

- Copy or duplicate existing layers or add new layers for manipulating images.
- The Background layer in an image has different characteristics than other layers.
- Use a naming and organizing method that helps you keep track of content in an image.
- Use locks for transparency in a layer, or lock the entire layer.
- Select more than one layer and link them to apply edits to several layers simultaneously.
- Merge layers in a file based on the selected, active, or visible layers both to decrease file size and keep track of an image's contents.
- Adjust opacity settings in layers for simple blending.
- Apply one of many blending modes to apply calculations to a layer to combine its content with underlying layers based on characteristics such as color, luminosity, the amount of gray, and other options.

GET THE SCOOP ON...
■ Using Fill layers for color and pattern ■ Editing with Adjustment layers ■ Using masks to control edits ■ Masking with text ■ Picking styles ■ Working with multiple styles

Fun with Layers

There are many ways to add a new layer to an image as described in Chapter 11. You can add text or a shape to an image, copy and paste content from one image into another image, or copy and paste content within an image to add a new layer to an image's file.

In this chapter, you read about a species of layer used for controlling and adjusting other layers. The process is designed to let you experiment to your heart's content with the appearance of an image without permanently affecting the original image.

And, speaking of experimenting, you can choose from an entire category of styles designed specifically for layers, called — you guessed it — *layer styles*. After you start to use layer styles and understand how they work, your ability to create impressive output is limited "only by your imagination."

Adjusting layers

Chapter 11 described the ins and outs of using layers in a Photoshop Elements image. *Adjustment layers* are another form of layer that does as their name implies — the layers are added to your image to modify the underlying content in a specific way. You can choose from numerous types of adjustment layers that fall into four categories including:

■ **Fills.** Use the Solid Color, Gradient, or Pattern Fill layers to add a colored layer to your image, the Gradient Fill layer's thumbnail is active in the Layers palette, shown in Figure 12.1.

Inside Scoop

Adjustment layers are separate commands and submenus. On the Layers palette, both types are selected from the same menu, which is displayed when you click the Adjustment Layer icon on the Layers palette.

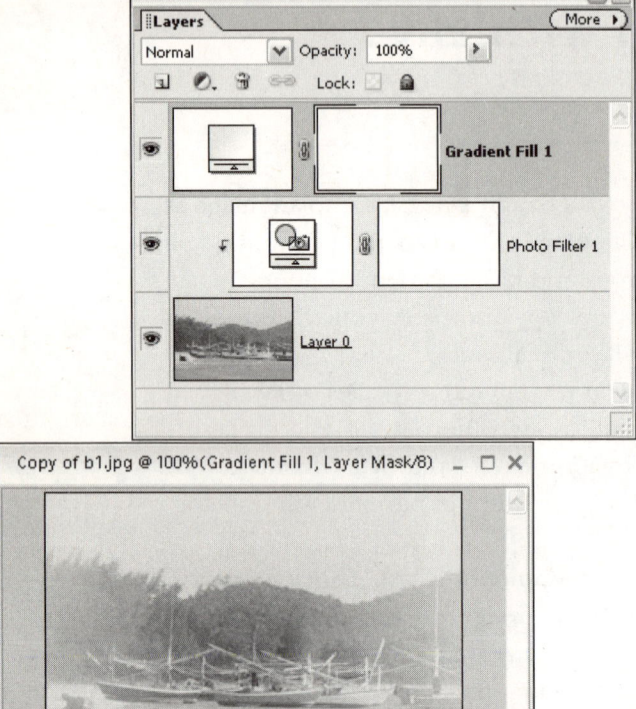

Figure 12.1. Two of the adjustment layers are used for adding different types of fill to an image, such as the Gradient Fill, shown as the active layer in the Layers palette.

- **Lighting.** Use the Levels or Brightness/Contrast adjustment layer types to modify the light and dark characteristics in a layer. When a Levels adjustment layer is added to the image file, the Levels dialog box opens to configure the levels settings, and the layer is added to the Layers palette, shown in Figure 12.2.

CHAPTER 12 ■ FUN WITH LAYERS

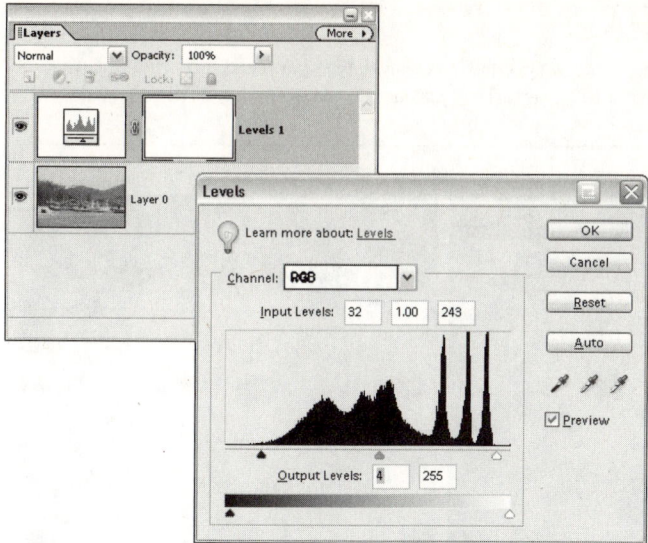

Figure 12.2. Lighting adjustment layers affect the light and dark characteristics of an underlying layer. The original layer (left) shows much more contrast after a brightness/contrast adjustment layer is added.

- **Color.** Change color in different ways using Hue/Saturation, Gradient Map, or Photo Filter adjustment layers (see Figure 12.3).
- **Tone.** Make tonal changes in a layer using Invert, Threshold, or Posterize adjustment layers to change the shadows, highlights, and midtones in an image. Figure 12.4 shows the original image at the left, and the image after adding a Posterize adjustment layer. The finished image, used at a low opacity, makes a terrific background for a collection of photos assembled into a slide show.

Figure 12.3. Color in an image (upper image) can be changed by using a color-based adjustment layer, such as the Gradient Map shown in the lower image.

> **Bright Idea**
> If you aren't sure what adjustment layer type you need, just think of what you are trying to achieve. The types are named according to what they do.

Figure 12.4. Change the shadow and highlight in an image (left) using an adjustment layer, such as the Posterize adjustment layer (right).

Brief information about each type of adjustment layer is listed in Table 12.1.

Table 12.1. Types of adjustment layers

Adjustment Layer Type	What It Does
Solid Color	Fills the layer with the foreground color; opens the Color Picker automatically.
Gradient	Fills the layer with the default gradient using the foreground color; opens the Gradient Fill dialog box. Read about gradients in Chapter 6.
Pattern	Fills the layer with the last pattern used; opens the Pattern Fill dialog box. Read about pattern fills in Chapter 6.
Levels	Adjusts the tonal values in the image; opens the Levels dialog box. Read about levels in Chapter 8.

Adjustment Layer Type	What It Does
Brightness/Contrast	Lightens or darkens the image; opens the Brightness/Contrast dialog box. Read about working with brightness and contrast in Chapter 8.
Hue/Saturation	Adjusts the image's color; opens the Hue/Saturation dialog box. Read about adjusting hue/saturation in Chapter 9.
Gradient Map	Applies a gradient map to change the image's pixel colors to those in the selected gradient; opens the Gradient Map dialog box. Read about gradient maps later in this chapter, and also in Chapter 16 where gradient maps are used for filters.
Photo Filter	Applies one of numerous program filters; opens the Photo Filter dialog box. Read about using photo filters in Chapter 9.
Invert	Produces a photo-negative effect by creating a negative based on the brightness values of the image. Read about the Invert effect in Chapter 15.
Threshold	Simplifies the image to black and white only, without gray, so you can define lightest and darkest areas; opens the Threshold dialog box. Read about the Threshold effect in Chapter 15.
Posterize	Reduces the number of brightness levels in the image, reducing the number of colors. Read about the Posterize effect in Chapter 15; see an example in Figure 12.4.

What's in a name?

Using adjustment layers gives you lots of design power. You can experiment freely without damaging or degrading your original image, such as the example shown in Figure 12.5. In this figure, one image layer uses three adjustment layers to achieve the final, rather ethereal effect. In the example image:

- A Gradient Fill adjustment layer overlays the background image of a butterfly on a flower. Grouping the Gradient Fill layer with the image layer affects the color of the image.

- Over those layers, a Pattern Fill adjustment layer using a basketweave pattern is added.
- Finally, a Posterize adjustment layer is added to decrease the number of color levels in the Pattern Fill adjustment layer. Grouping the Posterize adjustment layer with the Pattern Fill adjustment layer confines the effect to the layer with which it is grouped.

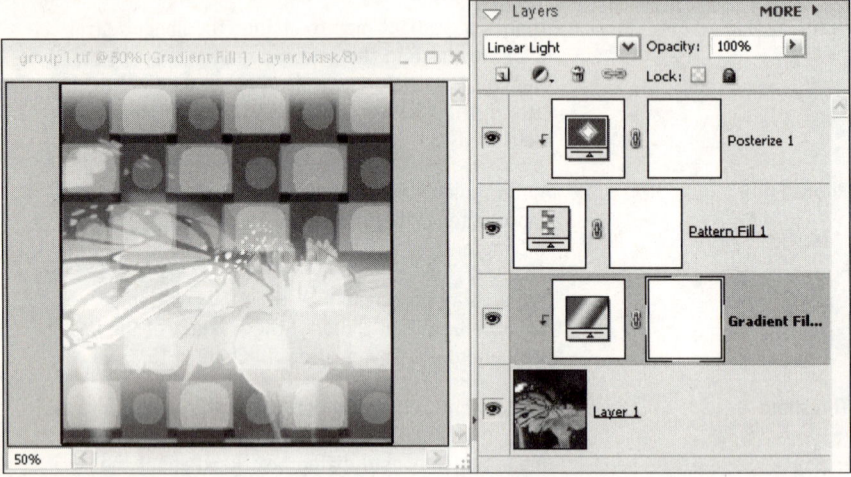

Figure 12.5. Adjustment and fill layers can be used in combination for interesting effects without damaging the original image. The example starts with a simple image which is then modified by adding a gradient and a pattern, and decreasing the levels of color in the image.

The three Fill adjustment layer types — Solid Fill, Gradient Fill, and Pattern Fill, work in slightly different ways than the other types of adjustment layers. These are the similarities and differences:

- Opacity and blending mode settings apply to all adjustment layer types equally.
- Adjustment layers can be moved and repositioned like regular layers.
- All adjustment layer types include a mask that can be painted on.
- Fill adjustment layers don't affect the layers below them in the stacking order in the same way as other adjustment layer types. That is, adding a fill type of adjustment layer doesn't modify the underlying layer, while adding another adjustment layer type automatically affects the underlying layer or layers.

- Adjustment layers affect the content on all layers below them in the stacking order or group.
- A fill type of adjustment layer can be simplified to convert the layer from an adjustment layer to a regular layer; the other adjustment layers can't be simplified.

Applying an adjustment layer

Adjustment layers can be applied from the Layers palette or the Layer menu; using the Layers palette saves mouse clicks. Here's an example showing how to apply a Hue/Saturation adjustment layer to an image file:

Follow these steps to apply an adjustment layer from the Layers palette:

1. Select the layer below the position in the stacking order where you want the adjustment layer added. The image in the example uses only one layer, which of course is the selected layer.

2. Click the Adjustment Layer icon on the Layers palette to open the menu shown in Figure 12.6, and choose a layer type. In the example, the Hue/Saturation adjustment layer is chosen.

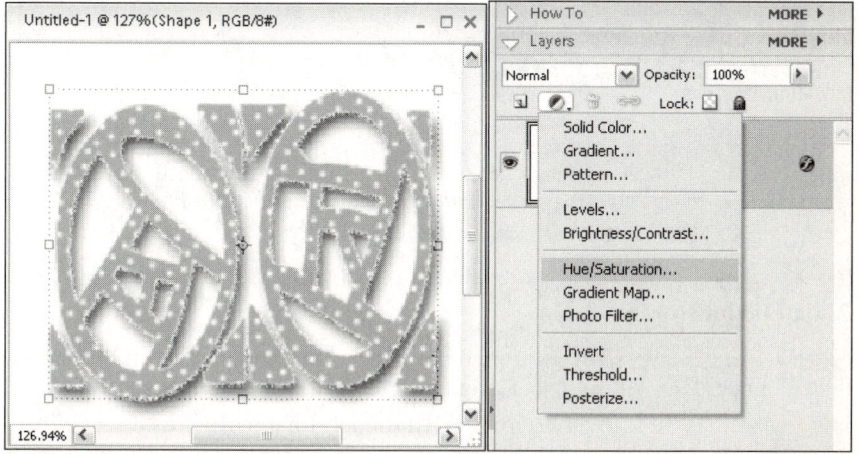

Figure 12.6. Choose the layer to which you want to apply the adjustment layer and select the type from the list.

3. The dialog box opens that controls the settings for the chosen adjustment layer type, as noted in Table 12.1.

>  **Bright Idea**
>
> After you add an adjustment layer, you can make adjustments to the Blend and Opacity settings in the Layers palette. Read about layer blending and transparency in Chapter 11.

4. Adjust or modify settings for the layer in its dialog box. You can observe the effects on the image as you adjust the settings. In the example, the Hue and Lightness were both adjusted.

5. Click OK to close the dialog box. The layer is added to the Layers palette above the originally selected layer, as shown in Figure 12.7.

Figure 12.7. The adjustment layer is added to the Layers palette and its effects are seen in the image window. In the example, the image's Hue and Lightness were modified.

Targeting layers

Before you start the adjustment layer process, consider what you want it to affect. Figure 12.8 shows the Layers palette for two versions of the same image, as well as their finished images. In the left image, the Posterize adjustment layer is applied to both the Pattern Fill and the image layer showing the flower and butterfly. In the Layers palette, shown at the upper right of the figure, you see a normal Layer arrangement showing the three layers.

Contrast the left image and its Layers palette with the right image and its Layers palette shown in Figure 12.8. The same two adjustment layers—Posterize and Pattern Fill—are applied to both images, but the Posterize layer is grouped with the Pattern Fill layer in the right image which restricts its effect to that layer.

You see the basketweave pattern in both images, while the butterfly and flower's colors are much smoother in the right image because they aren't affected by the Posterize effect.

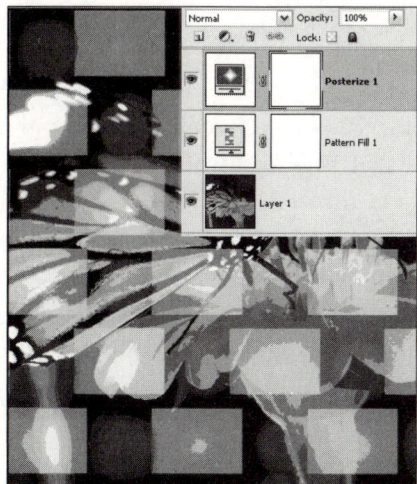

Figure 12.8. Group layers in the Layers palette to restrict adjustment effects to specific layers. In the left image, both adjustment layers are applied to the image; in the right image, one adjustment layer is applied to the image, and a second adjustment layer is applied to the first.

Grouping shortcuts

Images can look very different depending on how the layers are grouped. If you are learning about adjustment layers, go ahead and choose Layer ⇨ New Fill Layer or Layer ⇨ New Adjustment Layer. When the New Layer dialog box opens for you to confirm the new layer, shown in Figure 12.9, you can click the Group With Previous Layer check box to make a grouping automatically. You can also select a blending mode and opacity right from the dialog box.

Inside Scoop

In the Layer menu, fill and adjustment layers are separate commands and sub-menus. On the Layers palette, both types are selected from the same menu, which is displayed when you click the Adjustment Layer icon on the Layers palette.

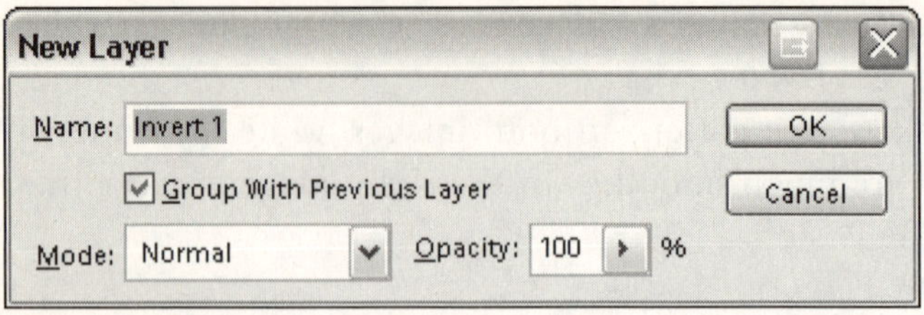

Figure 12.9. Using menu commands lets you apply grouping, blending, and opacity settings in the dialog box.

You can save yourself a fair bit of time when you become more comfortable with the process by using shortcut keys and working from the Layers palette exclusively. Add the layers through the Layers palette's menu. Select the layer above the one you want to group with, and press Ctrl+G to group or Shift+Ctrl+G to ungroup an existing group.

Personally, I like the most direct route using shortcut keys. At any time, whether you are using adjustment, fill, or regular image layers, use the Group shortcut in the Layers palette. You don't even have to select anything first!

Press Alt, and move the cursor over the edge of a layer label's listing in the Layers palette. When you see the Group icon, which looks like a pair of overlapping rings as you can see in Figure 12.10, release the mouse to finish the grouping; repeat the process to ungroup layers.

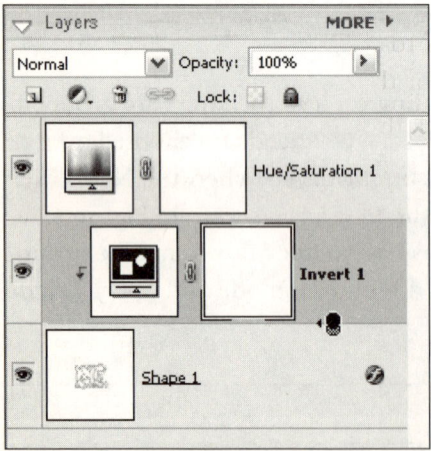

Figure 12.10. Group and ungroup layers using shortcut keys in the Layers palette.

Masking a layer

Suppose you have some wonderful pictures from your family reunion, but the best shot of your Aunt Sadie shows her dressed in her best, posed in front of some less-than-lovely trash cans. There are different ways you can take care of the problem and blur or even paint out the trash cans, one of which starts with a layer mask.

When an adjustment layer is added to an image, you see the layer listed in the Layers palette. Have you noticed that extra thumbnail in the Layers palette to the right of adjustment layer's thumbnail? The extra thumbnail represents the *layer mask*. A mask is used to constrict an effect to a specific area, or to show or hide content in the image, like the aforementioned trash cans.

Applying a mask to an adjustment layer

If you look at the adjustment layer mask's thumbnail in the Layers palette, you see it is white, meaning there's nothing constricting the display, and the effect or color is applied to all underlying layers. Check out any of the images in earlier parts of the chapter that show the Layers palette — they all show the default adjustment layer's mask.

You can use any painting or editing tool to customize the mask layer by painting any areas you don't want affected by the adjustment or effect. Read a full discussion on designing and constructing layer masks in Chapter 10.

Follow these steps to apply a mask to an adjustment layer:

1. Select the layer you want to use for the mask.
2. Press Alt+Shift, and click the mask thumbnail in the Layers palette. You see all the layers' Eye icons are grayed out, which means you are working in *mask mode*.
3. Select the painting or editing tool you want to use for the mask and draw or paint the mask. In Figure 12.11, the mask is simply a rectangle drawn with the Custom Shape tool and filled with the foreground

Inside Scoop

Read about different methods to take care of distracting content in an image, including making and using selections in Chapter 10, and touching up flaws in your images in Chapter 14.

Inside Scoop

The default red masking color is a holdover from manual masking days when red film, called Rubylith, was used as an overlay on images. Areas of the Rubylith that were cut away were shown in the final output, and masked areas remained hidden.

color set in the toolbox, which is black. When you start painting or drawing, the image is overlaid with a red semi-transparent layer color, indicating you are working on a mask, not on the image layer.

Figure 12.11. Use a mask to constrain an effect to a specific area.

4. Continue drawing or painting on the mask. As you paint or draw you erase parts of the red overlay, showing the areas on the image that will be revealed by the mask. You want the areas that will reveal the effects of the adjustment layer to be painted black.

5. Press Alt+Shift, and click the mask thumbnail again to deselect the mask and display the image's layers.

When you look in the Layers palette, you see the black rectangular masking shape on the mask thumbnail. The masked area is transparent and allows the gradient fill in the layer to display within the boundaries

Bright Idea

If you have used a layer mask and think you may need to use it in the future in the same or a similar image, save the selection. You can use it at a later time and also add or subtract from the original selection. Read about using and saving selections in Chapter 10.

of the rectangle. The rest of the mask is white which defines opaque areas. In the example, the white area blocks the gradient fill in the adjustment layer, constraining the effect.

Shades of gray

To add another layer of intricacy to the mix, you can also paint with shades of gray. The darker the shade of gray, the more transparent the mask is and the less the effect is masked. Of course, the lighter the shade of gray, the more opaque the mask is and the more the effect is masked.

Viewing the mask

There are two different methods for working with masks. The method described in the previous set of steps is more clearly visible, and the method I generally use. A second method lets you see just the mask without the underlying image.

In the preceding section, Steps 2 and 5 instruct you to press Alt+Shift as you click the mask thumbnail to show the red mask overlay on the image. If you prefer, you can show just the mask layer. Press Alt and click the mask thumbnail; press Alt and click the thumbnail again to toggle the mask mode off and make the image's layers visible.

If you are having difficulty with the masking process and it's not making much sense, try showing just the mask layer. Figuring it out that way is often easier, although you don't see the underlying image content, which can make it more difficult to position the mask.

If you are using a paintbrush or pencil, click the Foreground color swatch and choose a gray shade from the Color Picker. If you prefer, use any combination of painting or editing tools to create the mask.

For example, the mask shown in the left image in Figure 12.12 looks fairly complex, but it was actually very simple to make from two objects:

- The mask started as a rectangle with feathering applied to blur its edges (read about feathering selections in Chapter 13).
- The rectangle is filled with a radial gradient.

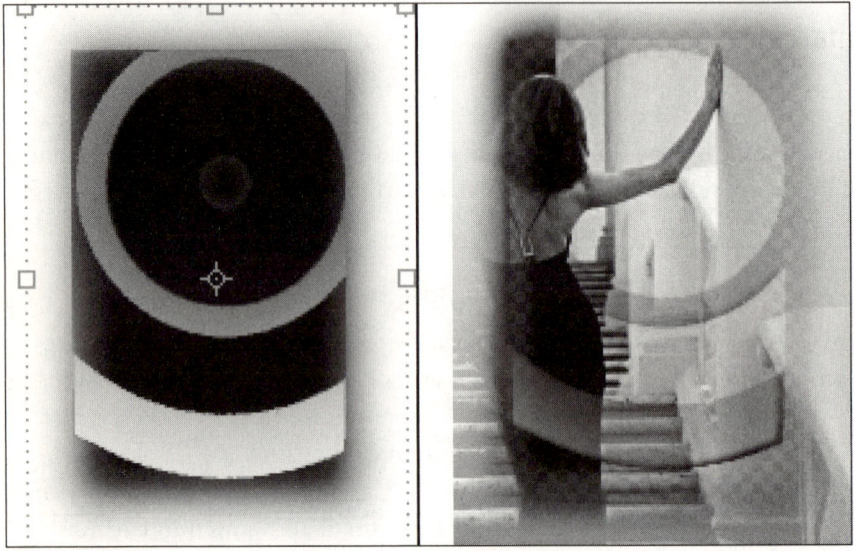

Figure 12.12. Shades of gray produce various levels of masking.

In the right image, you see how the concentric circles in the mask are used to define areas in the image. The lighter areas in the mask layer show less of the underlying image, and the darker areas of the mask show more of the underlying image.

Masking with text

You can use text for creating interesting masks, like the decorative text shown in Figure 12.13.

Figure 12.13. Use Type Mask tools to create interesting text effects in your image.

Follow these steps to add a text mask to an image:

1. Select the layer you want to use for the selection. Don't use an existing text layer because the new mask becomes a part of the existing text in a text layer.
2. Select either the Horizontal Type Mask tool or the Vertical Type Mask tool in the toolbox; or click the displayed Text tool to make it active and choose the mask tool on the options bar. In Figure 12.14, the Horizontal Type Mask tool is active.

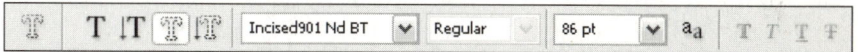

Figure 12.14. Choose a Type Mask tool from the Type tools' options bar.

3. Click the image with the tool at the location where you want to add the text. You see the image is overlaid with the red mask layer.
4. Type the text, and configure it as desired. Read about using text in Chapter 17.
5. Fill the text with black, white, or gray as required for the mask effect you are trying to achieve:
   - Black areas are transparent and show the underlying image.
   - Gray areas are semi-transparent depending on how dark or light they are, either more or less of the underlying image is shown.
   - White areas are opaque and block out the underlying image.

To duplicate the example, follow these steps, illustrated in Figure 12.15:

1. Add a Pattern Fill adjustment layer to the image file. In the example, the pattern is a wavy dark pattern.

2. Type the text on the pattern fill layer, shown in the upper image of Figure 12.15. The red mask overlay displays when you click the image with the Text Mask tool.

3. The text mask shape is shown on the default white of the layer mask, as in the middle image of Figure 12.15.

4. Press Ctrl+Alt+I to invert the selection, selecting all the content on the mask layer except the structure of the letters, and press Delete. The rest of the mask is filled with black, shown in the lower image of Figure 12.15.

Figure 12.15. Define the portion of the pattern you want to see in the image by masking it.

5. Press Alt+click the mask thumbnail to return to the regular image view.

6. Add layer styles and effects if you like, such as the inner and outer shadows used in the sample text, shown in Figure 12.13.

In the example's Layers palette shown in Figure 12.16, the text on the Pattern Fill adjustment layer's mask is painted white. The letters are the only part of the pattern you want to show on the image. Because the rest of the mask is black, it makes the remainder of the pattern in the Pattern Fill layer transparent.

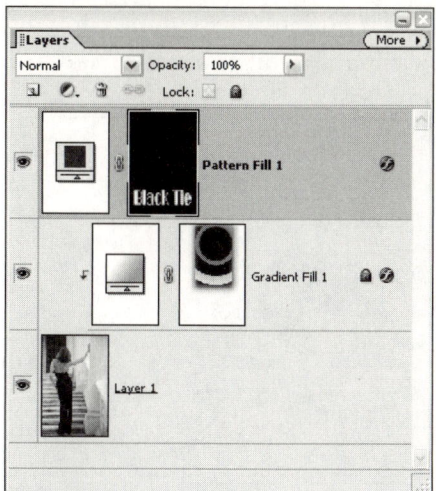

Figure 12.16. The Pattern Fill adjustment layer's mask defines the areas of the pattern that are visible in the image — in this case, just the text is seen.

Clipping images

You've seen how an adjustment layer can use a mask to define where its effect is shown in the image, and how an adjustment layer can be grouped with another layer.

Grouping layers isn't restricted to adjustment layers and image layers. Any two or more layers can be grouped as long as the layers are arranged in sequence in the Layers palette. A set of layers using a masked layer is called a *clipping group*. The lowest layer in the stacking order, the *base layer*, defines the visible image, which is all visible areas of all layers within the margins of the mask.

Figure 12.17 shows an example of a clipping group using a flower shape drawn with the Custom Shape tool as the clipping mask named Shape 1. The mask sits below an image in the Layers palette named Layer 0. Because the image layer is grouped with the flower shape, its margins are clipped into the shape of the flower.

The base layer's name is underlined, indicating that it's the base layer for the clipping group. The lowest level is a gradient fill layer; because it's below the base layer, it's not included in the clipping group.

Now look at the lower image and its Layers palette in Figure 12.17. In the Layers palette, the Gradient Fill layer is now included in the clipping group. You see that it's now part of the clipped content in the image.

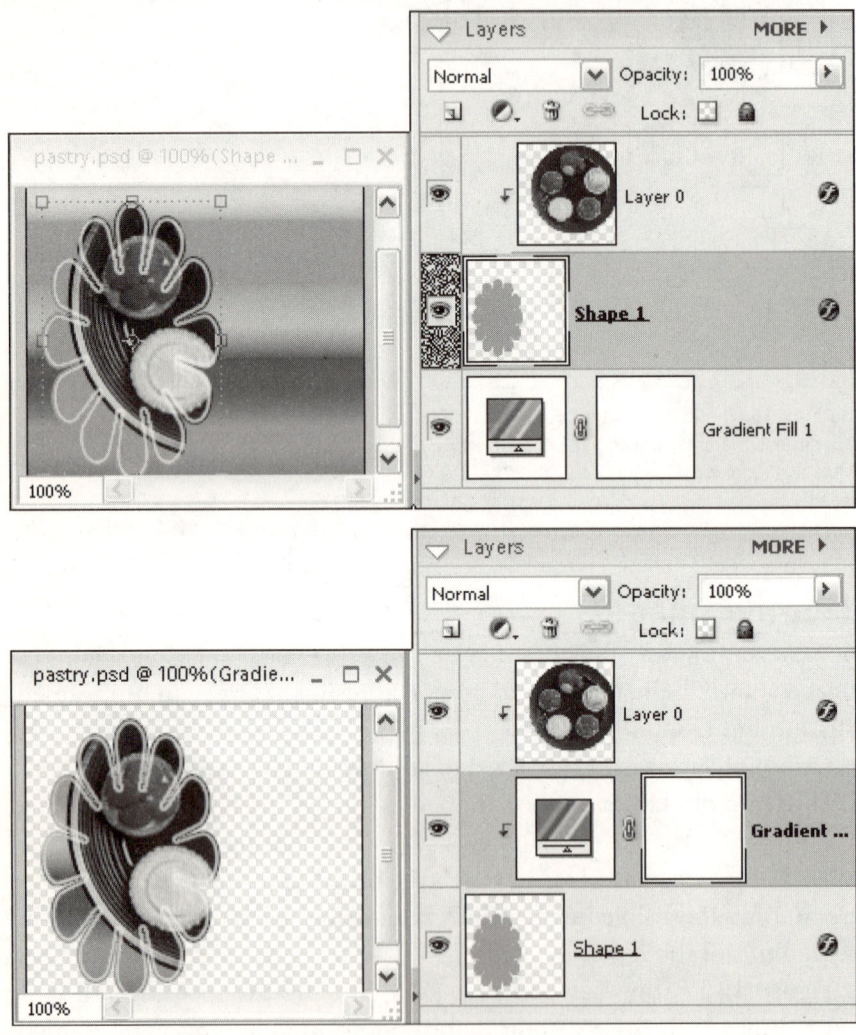

Figure 12.17. The bottom layer of the clipping group defines the displayed area of the image layer.

> **Hack**
> Link the layers in the clipping group if you want to adjust them on the image, such as changing scale or location.

Styling options

If using adjustment layers, fill layers, and blends isn't enough for you, you can always add styles designed specifically for layers. *Layer styles* are a group of effects that modify a selected layer in an image.

With all the different styles and effects at your disposal, it can be extremely difficult to figure out what you want to work with. Instead of opening menus, guessing what an effect looks like, and then applying it to the image, work through the Styles and Effects palette. The styles, effects, and filters you can use with layers are included within their own palette — along with thumbnails to simplify picking the right command.

Opening the palette

If you are in the part of a project's workflow where it's time to start working on the "cool" stuff, save some time and add the Styles and Effects palette to the Palette Bin.

Follow these steps to set up the Styles and Effects palette if it isn't docked in the Palette Bin:

1. Choose Window ⇨ Styles and Effects to open the palette.
2. Drag the palette and drop it in the Palette Bin.
3. Click More at the top of the palette to open the menu and choose Place in Palette Bin when Closed. Now, if you click the arrow to the left of the palette's name to toggle the palette open or closed, it stays in the Palette Bin and is always accessible to you.

Choose your view

Click the More button on the Styles and Effects palette and choose either Thumbnails or List from the menu. The contents are shown as thumbnails by default, which is good for scanning samples quickly. List view shows the full titles and a sample of the selected effect. Use the list if you are more familiar with the options.

The Styles and Effects palette is divided into three sections, available by choosing from the drop-down list at the left of the palette, shown in Figure 12.18. The categories include effects, filters, and layer styles. If you add a filter, the Filter Gallery window opens. Refer to Chapters 15 and 16 for information on using filters.

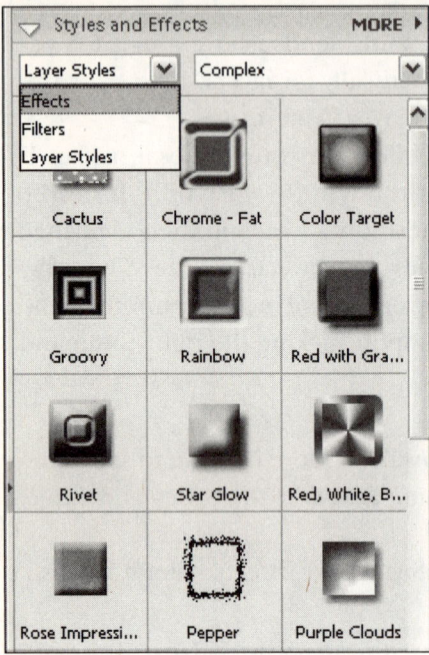

Figure 12.18. Select effects, filters, or layer styles from the palette's drop-down list.

It's a matter of style

Layer styles are applied to a selected layer following these steps:

1. Click the layer in the Layers palette to select it.
2. From the Styles and Effects palette, click the left drop-down arrow to open the menu, shown in Figure 12.18, and choose Layer Styles from the list to load the styles into the palette.
3. Click the right drop-down menu, and choose one of the 14 style categories, shown in Figure 12.19.

>
> **Inside Scoop**
> You can add the same styles when you first draw a shape — available from the Style drop-down menu — as you can add later on by using the styles available in the Styles and Effects palette. They are the same options. Read about shapes in Chapter 5.

4. Click the style you want to apply in the palette, or drag it from the palette to the image.
5. The style is applied to the selected layer in the image, and an icon that looks like a lowercase "f" shows next to the layer's name on the Layers palette. You can see examples of the icon on several images, including Figures 12.16 and 12.17.

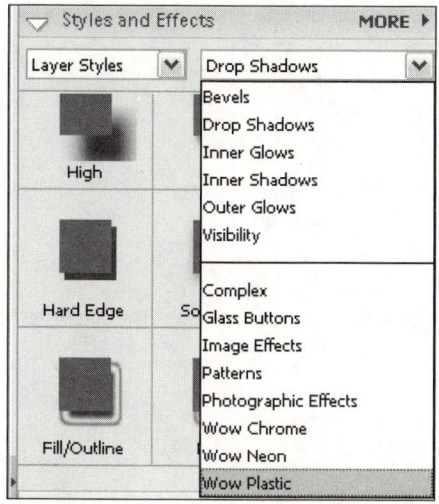

Figure 12.19. Select a style category from the drop-down list.

Most of the layer styles include editable options. Styles that include measurements such as the distance of a shadow or the thickness of a bevel can be customized. Follow these steps to modify a style applied to a layer using an Outer Glow style as an example:

1. Double-click the "f" icon on the Layers palette shown at the right of Figure 12.20 to open the Style Settings dialog box, also shown in the figure.

2. Type a value or drag the Outer Glow Size slider higher to increase the scale of the glow, or lower to decrease the scale of the glow. In Figure 12.20, the image uses an Outer Glow Size of 67 pixels.

3. Click OK to close the dialog box and change the Layer Style setting.

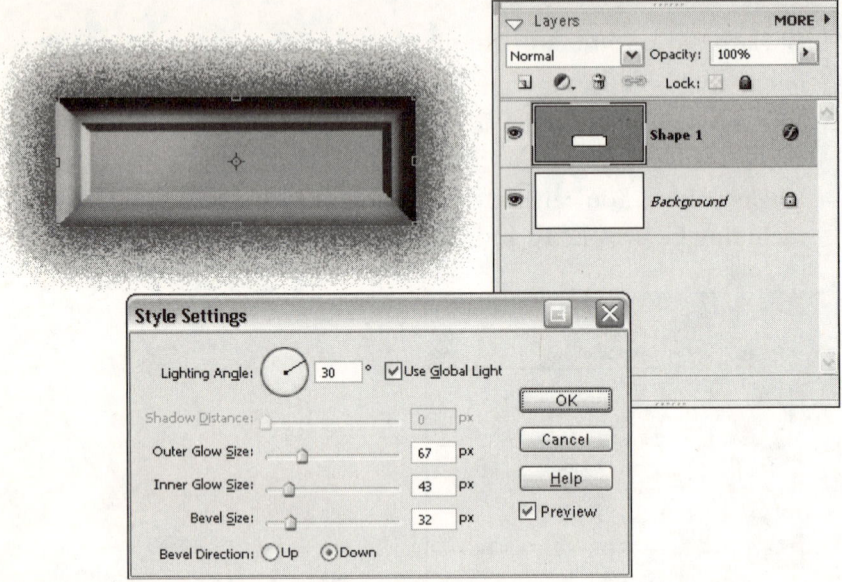

Figure 12.20. The Style Settings dialog box includes options for customizing the characteristics of the Layer Style.

Scaling the effect

If you want to simply change the scale of an effect, follow these steps:

1. Select the layer and choose Layer ⇨ Layer Style ⇨ Scale Effects to open the Scale Layer Effects dialog box, shown in Figure 12.21.

2. Type a scale value in the Scale field. The default size of the effect is set as 100 percent, like the glow surrounding the box in the upper

Hack

I never use the Scale Effects command with a single layer style. Double-clicking the *f* icon on the layer's listing in the Layers palette to open the Style Settings dialog box is much easier. On the other hand, if you have added several layer styles, Scale Effects will quickly change the dimensions of all effects at once.

image in Figure 12.21; increasing the value increases the scale of the effect, as shown in the bottom image in Figure 12.21.

3. Click OK to close the dialog box.

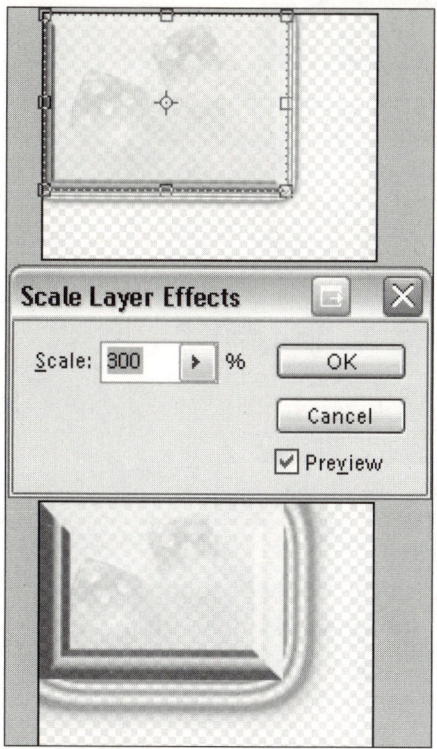

Figure 12.21. Scale the effects applied to the layer by specifying a scale percentage.

The options you can customize depend on the specific style. The customizations fall into four groups of options including:

- **Lights.** Two different style options let you specify the lighting angle for a style. For any style using a light, drag the circular slider to indicate the direction of the light source for the effect in degrees. If you are working with multiple styles in a project, selecting the Use Global Light check box automatically applies consistent shadows or highlights for each style as necessary. Figure 12.22 shows the Toy Layer Style. The default angle for the Light is set at 30 degrees, shown in the figure.

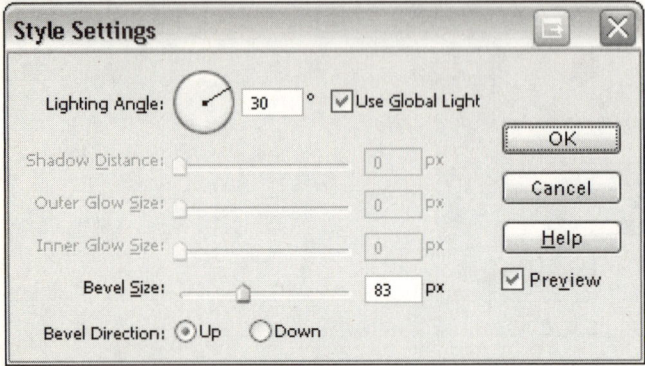

Figure 12.22. Define the angle for lights, as well as whether the same setting should be used for multiple styles using lights.

- **Shadow Distance.** Specify how far a drop shadow extends from the content in the layer. Figure 12.23 shows two examples. In the left example, the Shadow Distance is 52 pixels, while the right example uses a distance of 10 pixels. Both shadows' light angles are set at 30 degrees.

- **Glow Sizes.** Both the Outer and Inner Glow settings can be modified in styles using the effect. The Outer Glow Size defines the size of a glow originating from the outside edges of a layer's content; the Inner Glow Size defines the size of a glow originating from the interior of a layer's content. An example of the Outer Glow style and its settings are shown in Figure 12.20.

- **Bevel Values.** Many styles use bevels as edging or emphasis, like the example shown in Figure 12.24. Specify a Bevel Size in the Style Settings dialog box, also shown in Figure 12.24 to define the width of beveling along the inside edges of a layer or its contents; specify the Bevel Direction to define whether the bevel is shown up or down.

CHAPTER 12 ■ FUN WITH LAYERS 345

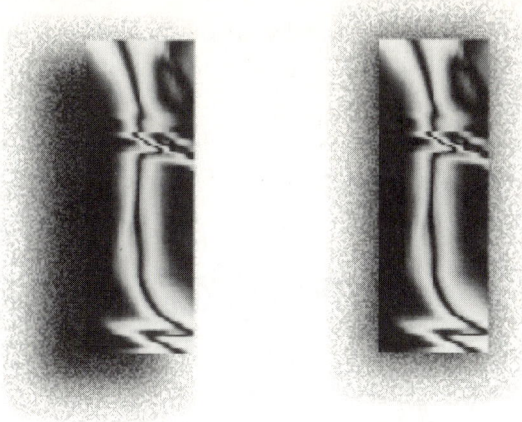

Figure 12.23. Adjust the distance of a drop shadow in pixels; the higher the value, the wider the shadow extends from the image.

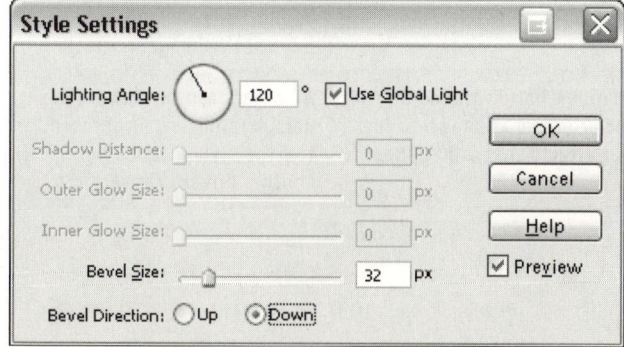

Figure 12.24. Define the direction of the bevel and its width in pixels.

Using simple styles

In the Layers Styles menu, the styles are divided into two sections, shown in Figure 12.19. The first section is made up of styles that apply simple effects, such as glows and shadows.

Table 12.2 briefly explains the Layer Styles categories and the usual types of customizations you can configure for the first grouping of styles.

Table 12.2. Simple layer styles and how they work

Style Category	Characterized By...	Types of Customizations
Bevels	Borders added to an object or layer that simulate a raised button appearance.	Specify the size, direction of the bevel, and location of the light source.
Drop Shadows	Shadow applied to simulate a light shining across the object or layer.	Choose direction, size, density of shadow, and color of light. You can't apply the style to a full-size layer because the shadow would extend beyond the image's size.
Inner Glows	A glow that appears to be within the inside edges of a layer or object.	Choose direction, size, and amount of light.
Inner Shadows	A shadow that appears to be within the inside edges of a layer or object.	Choose direction, size, depth of shadow, and color of light.
Outer Glows	A glow that appears to be outside the edges of a layer or object.	Choose direction, size, and amount of light. The style can't be applied to a full-size layer as the shadow would extend beyond the image's size.
Visibility	Specifies whether the actual layer or object is shown or just other effects that are applied.	An object can be shown (the default), hidden, or ghosted. Use the style after applying another effect or filter.

> **Try the visibility style**
>
> At first glance, applying a style to hide or ghost a layer seems a bit pointless. You can achieve the same thing by just turning off the layer's visibility or changing its opacity in the Layers palette. Or can you?
>
> No, you can't. When you hide a layer, it's completely gone. When you adjust its opacity, the entire layer's opacity changes. Using the visibility style hides the content of the layer itself; any other styles you've applied are unaffected. It's a neat style. Give it a try.

Working with complex styles

Aside from the simple, but very effective, shadow and glow-type layer styles, a second category of layer styles exists. And, although still applied with a single mouse-click, they are much more complicated.

The more elaborate layer styles produce interesting, complex, and sometimes downright wild effects. The complex style categories include:

- **Complex.** The Complex layer styles include a variety of different patterned and shaded or highlighted fills or borders, such as the Sunset Sky style shown in the left image in Figure 12.25, or the White Grid on Orange style, shown in the right image in Figure 12.25. Set the angle for the light or shadow, as well as sizes for the glow and bevel to customize the effect.

Figure 12.25. Complex layer styles.

- **Glass Buttons.** Add a beveled solid color overlay with a glass-like appearance using the Glass Button style, shown in Figure 12.26. To customize the effect, set the angle for the light, as well as sizes for the glow and bevel.

Figure 12.26. Create the appearance of colored buttons that look like glass.

- **Image Effects.** The Image Effects apply overlays that simulate different natural or designed effects. The effects are applied as-is without customizations. Both examples in Figure 12.27 were filled with a rippled satiny texture; the left example in Figure 12.27 shows a Circular Vignette effect, which fades out the edges of the shape; the right shows the Snow effect.

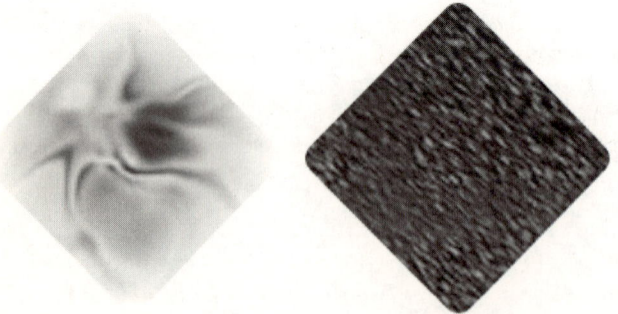

Figure 12.27. Select a style category from the drop-down list.

- **Patterns.** Select a Pattern effect to add an overlay, usually solid, using a pattern such as marble, a texture such as stucco, or a gradient such as copper. The pattern fills are applied as-is, and can't be customized. The shape at the left of Figure 12.28 uses a pattern named "abstract fire;" the right image uses a fill resembling diamond plate steel.

Figure 12.28. Apply a layer style using an abstract Pattern effect (left) or one that mimics a product such as steel (right).

- **Photographic Effects.** Apply a color tone for a quick change of image color such as sepia or purple using the Photographic Effects style. There are no customizations: the effect either is or isn't applied.
- **Wow Chrome.** The Wow Chrome effect adds a solid overlay using different fill or stroke styles simulating chrome, shown in the left image in Figure 12.29. Set the angle for the light, and specify the size for the glow and bevel to customize the effect.
- **Wow Neon.** The Wow Neon effect adds a border that looks either like a neon strip turned off or lit; the lit strip is outside the margins of the layer's objects, while the strip shows within the margins if the light is "off." The effect adds several versions to make a multi-bordered effect like that shown in the center image in Figure 12.29. Specify the angle of the light and the distance for the shadows, glows, and bevel.

> **Bright Idea**
> If you want to check a before and after of your image, choose Layer ➪ Layer Style ➪ Hide All Effects to toggle the effects off; repeat and select Show All Effects to toggle the effects on.

- **Wow Plastic.** The Wow Plastic effect produces a solid colored fill with areas of highlight and drop shadow creating the look of shiny plastic, shown in the right image in Figure 12.29. You can set the angle of the light and the distance for the shadows, glows, and bevel.

Figure 12.29. The Wow categories of layer styles apply overlays to make the image look like chrome (left), neon light (center), or plastic (right).

Layer style behaviors

Layer styles have some interesting behaviors. After you apply a style to a layer, it belongs to the layer. That is, the style is linked to the contents, and changing the contents of the layer also affects the style's appearance.

Figure 12.30 shows an example of how a style behaves when its layer is modified. In the left image, layer styles are applied to the two image layers. In the right image, the same layers are scaled and moved to the upper corner of the canvas: you see the layer style changes right along with the content. The Layers palette is shown for reference.

> **Watch Out!**
> Make sure you are finished editing a style before adding the next one. When you add a subsequent style, the only way to return to adjust the settings for a previous style is to Undo the additional styles.

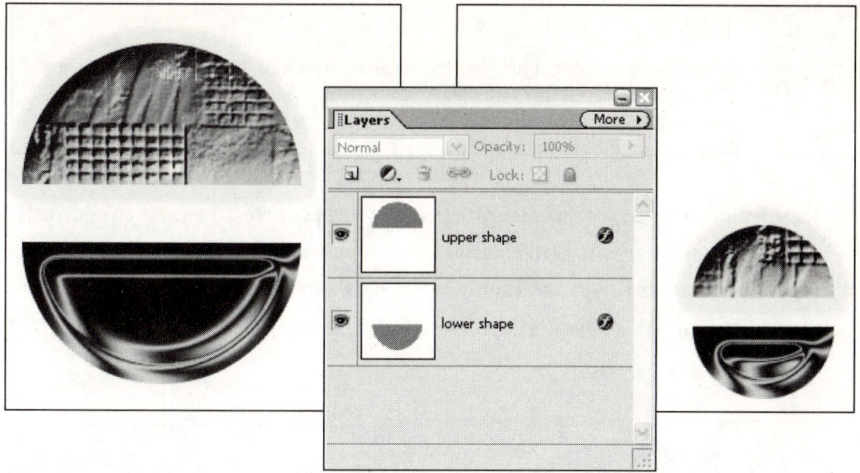

Figure 12.30. Changing a layer also changes its linked style.

Here are more layer style behaviors to keep in mind:

- You can add multiple layer styles to a single layer.
- Only one style from each category of styles can be added to a layer.
- Unless a style is absolute, such as the Photographic Effects, you can adjust the style's settings.
- If you add multiple styles to a layer, you can edit settings only for the last style applied.

Reusing a style

If you have been working with styles for a while and come up with something very attractive, you can copy it and reuse it for another layer or even another image.

Follow these steps to reuse a style:

1. Select the layer containing the style you want to reuse, such as the upper shape image shown in Figure 12.31.
2. Right-click the layer's listing in the Layers palette to open the shortcut menu, and choose Copy Layer Style. Or you can choose Layer ⇨ Layer Style ⇨ Copy Layer Style.
3. Select a layer to which you want to apply the copied style, either in the existing file or another image file.

Hack

If you have custom styles you like, add each one to a separate layer in any old image to use as a storage image. When you need one of the custom styles, open the image, copy the style from its layer, and paste it into your project.

4. Right-click the layer's listing in the Layers palette to open the shortcut menu shown in Figure 12.31, and choose Paste Layer Style. Or you can choose Layer ⇨ Layer Style ⇨ Paste Layer Style. The style is pasted to the new layer, or, as in the lower image in Figure 12.31, to a new image.

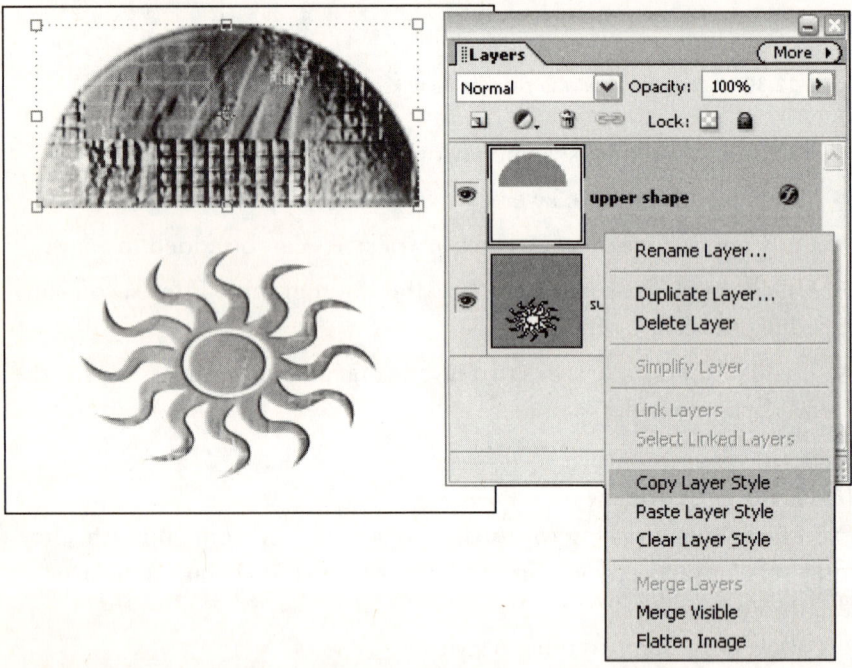

Figure 12.31. Copy styles between layers or files.

Layering with style

You don't have to build sets of layers, create groups, and apply blends and adjustments to produce your goal image effect. In many cases, you can use pre-configured layer styles, either alone or in combination with adjustment layers.

Figure 12.32 shows two versions of the same image on separate layers in an image as well as the Layers palette. Both images use a simple drop shadow style. The upper image also uses Invert and Pattern Fill adjustment layers, that are grouped with the upper image layer.

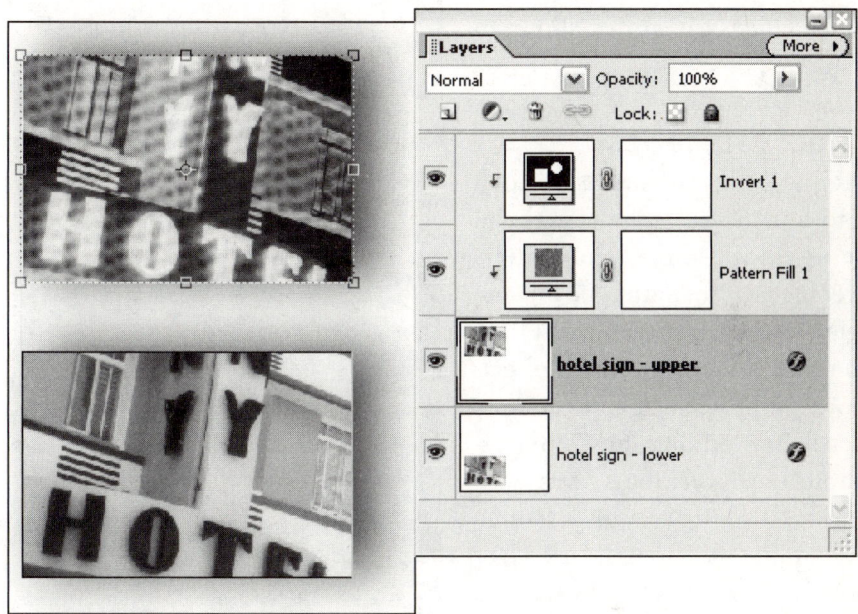

Figure 12.32. Combine both adjustment layers and layer effects for interesting images.

Photoshop Elements includes a multitude of effects of different types. Chapters 15 and 16 are the place to turn to for discussions on the what and why of effects.

Picking an effect

One final category of visual enhancement in the Styles and Effects palette you can add to an image or layer are effects, one of the group of options. Click the left drop-down arrow in the Styles and Effects palette to open a list and choose Effects; click the right drop-down arrow and choose one of the effects categories, shown in Figure 12.33.

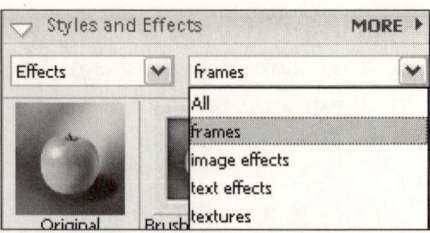

Figure 12.33. Choose options from one of four effect categories to enhance your images.

Effect categories

The Effects category is divided into four types. Many effects can be used with layers, while others are specific to flattened images, selections, or text. You don't have to try to remember which effects work with what image component. Try adding any effect—Photoshop Elements lets you know if the effect requires flattening an image, that is used for text only, or that you need to make a selection, as shown in the information dialog box in Figure 12.34.

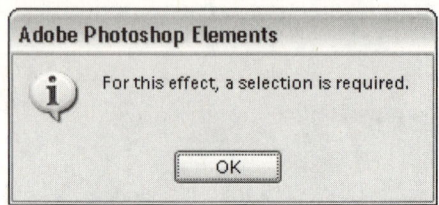

Figure 12.34. Photoshop Elements lets you know if you have to use a particular type of object to apply an effect.

These are the options:

- **Frames.** The frame effects are specific to flattened images, or in some cases, selections. The example frame shown in Figure 12.35 is used with a flattened image only.

Figure 12.35. The Foreground Color Frame effect adds a frame to the image using the foreground color specified in the toolbox.

- **Image effects.** Most of the image effects are designed for flattened images or selected elements. Experiment with adding two effects to the same layer — the first effect is added to the Background layer, and the second added to a copy of the Background. Two effects can be applied to a layer to simulate fluorescent chalk and quadrant color, as seen in Figure 12.36.
- **Text effects.** Text effects are used for text only. You can only apply one text effect at a time, such as the Sprayed Stencil effect shown in Figure 12.37.
- **Textures.** The texture effects can be applied to various objects in one image. For example, in Figure 12.38, a Rusted Metal effect is added to the text layer, a Metallic Gold effect is added to a rectangle shown behind the text, and a Marbled Glass effect is added to the image on Layer 0. Only the effect applied to Layer 0 adds an additional layer to the image file.

Figure 12.36. One or more image effects, such as the Fluorescent Chalk and Quadrant Color can be applied to the same image.

Figure 12.37. The Foreground Color Frame effect adds a frame to the image using the foreground color specified in the toolbox.

> **Inside Scoop**
>
> When an effect is applied to text, the text layer is changed to a regular image layer, and the program no longer recognizes it as text. As a result you can't add more than one effect to the same piece of text. Read more about text layers in Chapter 16.

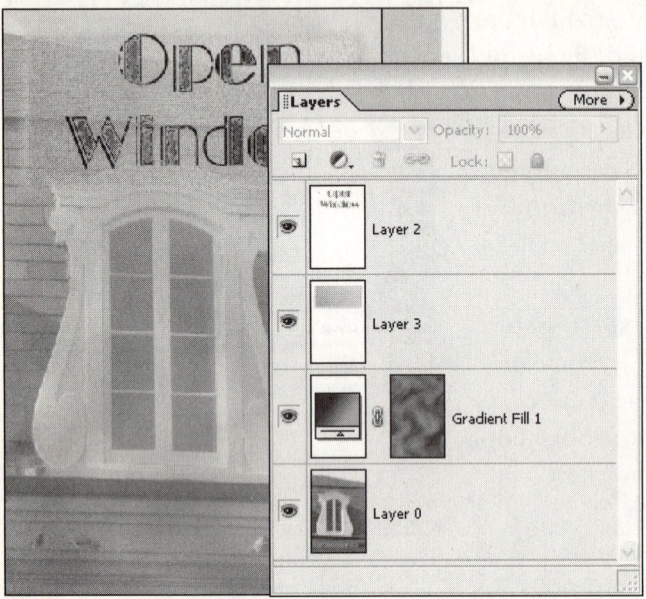

Figure 12.38. Texture effects can be added to selections, layers, or text.

Applying an effect

Some effects add one layer to the image while others add two layers depending on the complexity of the effect. For example, a frame effect, like the one shown in Figure 12.35 adds two layers — one layer is blank and larger than the original image, and the second is used for the frame itself.

Follow these steps to apply an effect:

1. Select the target layer in the Layers palette. Layer effects and styles don't work with background layers, locked layers, or layer sets.
2. Drag the effect from the Styles and Effects palette to the image and release the mouse.

3. The effect is processed and applied. Any additional layers added by the effect are shown on the Layers palette above the selected target layer.

4. Adjust opacity for the new layers if necessary. Figure 12.39 shows an example using a Sunset effect. In the upper image, you see the effect adds a gradient and shape to the image; two layers are added to the Layers palette above the image layer. Adjusting opacity of the effect layers, seen in the lower image and Layers palette, shows the underlying image and the effect.

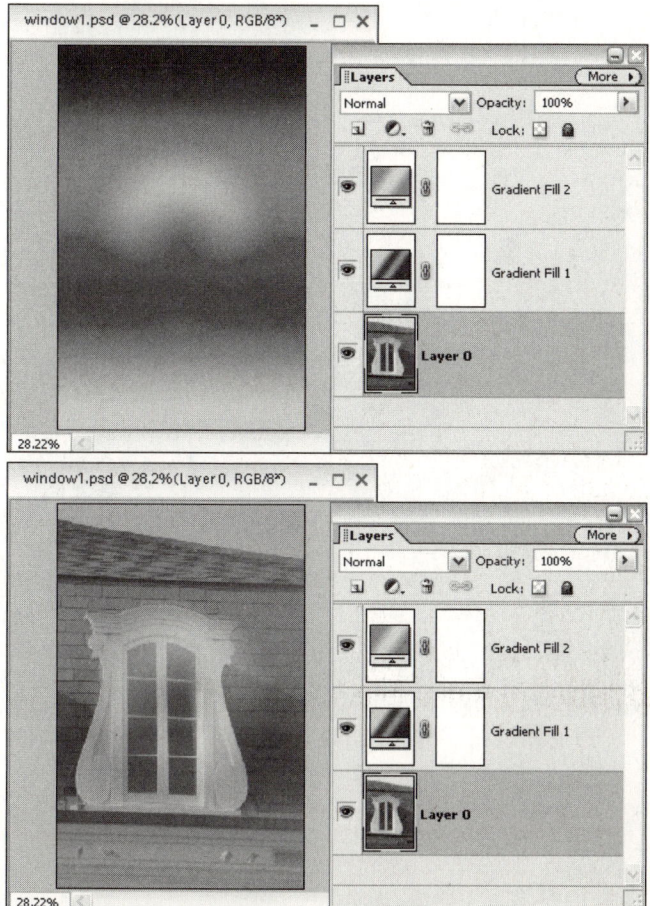

Figure 12.39. Effects designed for layers add one or two layers to the image above the target layer in the image (upper). Rearrange the contents to make best use of the effect (lower).

Just the facts

- Use fill layers for adding different colors and patterns to your image.
- Modify an adjustment at any time by double-clicking the adjustment layer to reopen its settings dialog box.
- Stack adjustment layers to make multiple adjustments without degrading the image.
- Use an adjustment layer's layer mask to confine an adjustment to a portion of the image.
- Text masks can be used in various ways, including showing letter-shaped content in a fill layer.
- Use filters and layer styles to modify the appearance of an image with a single mouse-click.
- More than one layer style can be added to the same layer, but only the last style applied can be modified.

PART IV

Not-So-Basic Image Editing

GET THE SCOOP ON...
■ Identifying and correcting artifacts ■ Handling image noise ■ Removing fringing ■ Correcting hot spots ■ Using sharpening ■ Eliminating distracting objects

Manually Correcting Images

After you have learned to use Photoshop Elements' automated correction and editing features, you are likely going to reach the point where you notice other features and details in your images that you'd like to change.

One area you are likely going to want to work with is correcting image characteristics resulting from how a camera captures your images and interprets the data. Many of these characteristics can be easily handled by Quick Fix mode described in Chapter 7. If you prefer, you can make the edits manually, using options in Standard Edit mode, described in this chapter.

Whether you use Quick Fix mode's options, or adjust settings yourself, another area where you are likely going to explore is making adjustments in response to other corrections you have made to the image. For example, removing dust and scratches from an image can result in blurriness that you might then correct by applying a sharpening filter.

Designing a workflow
Many image corrections are done using filters. Image correction follows different paths, but you want to take care of some tasks before doing others. A basic correction workflow is listed in Table 13.1.

Table 13.1. Image correction workflow

Task	Comments
Correct artifacts	Unnecessary pixels that show on the image can obscure the detail and content of the image that you want to correct. Use one of several different methods of removing or reducing the artifact from the image.
Remove dust	Dust is all around us, including on your images — remove it to show image detail.
Adjust brightness and color	As described in Chapter 8, make adjustments to clearly represent the color and clarity of your subject. You can also read about more tools and options in Chapter 14.
Use the Unsharp Mask filter	This filter makes the image crisper, but it can also produce noise or bright spots that need to be toned down.
Create emphasis	Make changes to depth of field and focus to emphasize the subject matter.

Digging for artifacts

When I say "artifact," I don't mean the ancient, world-changing relics that the dashing hero stumbles across in a movie. In imaging terms, an *artifact* is an unexpected and unwanted change in an image. An artifact can be caused by camera settings, camera quality, or image processing errors.

Artifacts can be managed and corrected using different methods and tools in Photoshop Elements.

These are some common artifact types:

- **Blooming.** *Blooming* refers to color information that bleeds from one pixel to another when the image is captured. You can often see blooming as streaks, outlines, or halos around objects in high-contrast images with very bright edges captured against dark edges, such as the vine tendrils and leaves shown in Figure 13.1.

Figure 13.1. Strong sunlight and contrast can produce streaks and halos in an image.

- **Moiré.** If you look at a piece of folded window screen you often see a wavy pattern of tone on tone color, referred to as *moiré*. A moiré pattern occurs most often in scanned images.

- **Noise.** The most common type of artifact is *noise*. Visual noise is caused by either a camera problem or compression errors. Extra pixels, either in grayscale or color, make the image look grainy and imprecise.

- **Halo.** A *halo* artifact is shown as a bright ring or line at an object's edges, like that shown in Figure 13.2. In the figure, you can see abnormally bright bands of highlights along the edges of the wooden detail of an ornate window frame. Halo can result from high-contrast images naturally, or when the contrast at the edges of objects is increased too much.

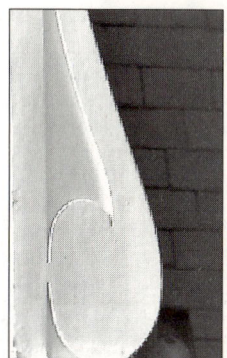

Figure 13.2. Too much sharpening produces unnatural bands of color, like the bright areas along both sides of the curved window frame detail.

A blooming nuisance

The simplest way to see blooming is to use the sun as a strong backlight for an image, such as the image shown in Figure 13.1. In this figure, you see that detail in some of the leaves is virtually gone, and streaks and halos appear at the edges of many of the leaves and tendrils in the vines.

Blooming is a type of artifact that doesn't necessarily need correcting. Because our brains easily understand that the sun produces this brightening effect, this artifact doesn't always detract from the image. But if you do decide that you want to correct the artifact, you can use any of a number of tools and methods to select the artifact area for correction. For example, you can select the area for correction with the Lasso tool if it is an irregular shape, or use a Rectangular or Elliptical Marquee tool for a regular-shaped area.

After the area is selected, apply a Blur filter to correct the artifact. Figure 13.3 shows a selected area of the vines and the result of applying a High Quality Smart Blur filter to the image. The most dominant artifact is the vertical streak between the two vine tendrils; applying a blur removes the streak, as you can see in the Smart Blur dialog box preview area. Adjust the sliders in the dialog box until the artifact disappears. I discuss filter options later in the chapter. For a quick rundown of the filters you can apply to correct blooming as well as settings you can customize, refer to Table 13.2. Read more about the Blur filters and how they are used in Chapters 14 and 15.

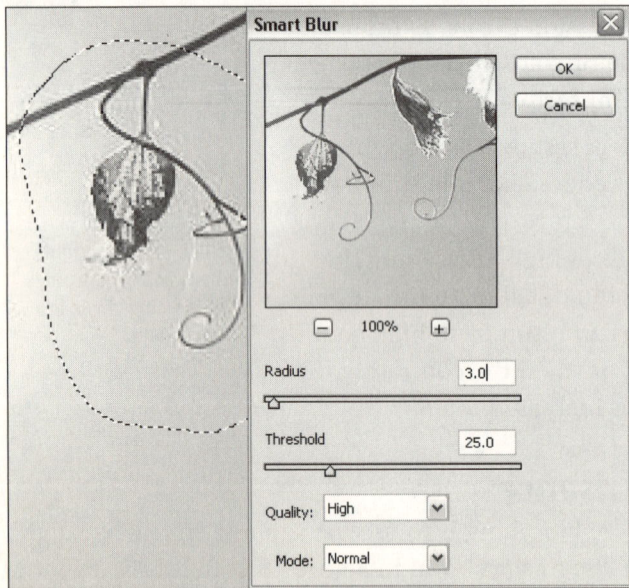

Figure 13.3. Select artifact areas and use blurs to correct them.

> **Hack**
> Blooming can be corrected using blurs, or adjusting contrast, or even painting the image, as described in Chapter 18.

Removing moiré patterns

Moiré artifacts occur most often when scanning, especially when you scan an image that has been previously printed. Technically, the artifact occurs as a result of interference between two or more structures with different frequencies.

You may not know it, but you view and interpret visual frequencies every day. For example, if you walk down a sidewalk where you can view multiple fences at the same time, you see a similar type of effect to that shown in Figure 13.4. The frequency of one pattern superimposes on the frequency of a subsequent pattern to create the effect. Another common appearance is looking at a stack of fine mesh, like a folded window screen or silk stocking.

Figure 13.4. Moiré effects result from frequency interference.

How you repair a moiré pattern depends on its characteristics and the source of the image. Keep these ideas in mind:

- For slight moiré effects, use a blur effect to remove the pattern.
- If you have a scanned image that shows a heavy moiré effect, try rotating the original in the scanner and rescanning it. You may have to experiment with using different angles of rotation. Scan the image at the highest possible resolution.
- After you have an improved scanned image, use blur effects such as Gaussian Blur to further reduce the pattern.

Turning off the noise

Image noise refers to the visible artifacts that make your image seem grainy. Images can have two types of noise — *luminance,* or grayscale noise, and *chroma,* or color noise. You see luminance noise as grainy gray dots; color noise appears as sprinkled dots of different colors.

Noise usually shows in images captured with low-end digital cameras such as cell phone cameras or with images shot with a high ISO setting, usually more than 400 ISO. The image in Figure 13.5 is noisy; the closeup copy of the image shown at the left of the figure shows lots of noise.

Use one of several filters to repair noise in an image. Any filter you use softens the image to some degree, so try to apply the filter only where it is needed.

Photoshop Elements offers four filters for working with noise, in addition to the Blur filters, which can be used as well. Figure 13.6 is divided into six sections, each of which uses a different method for correcting the noise. You can see that some of the options are more useful than others. The key to correcting noise is to experiment. You may find one filter with a particular group of settings works well for one image, yet doesn't correct another image's noise sufficiently.

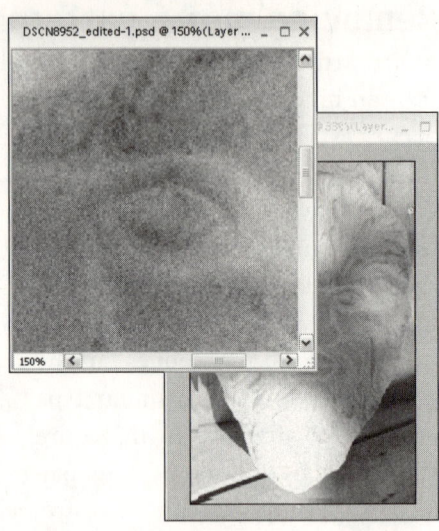

Figure 13.5. Noise artifact shows as grainy dots on the image.

Inside Scoop

After you have repaired the pattern as much as possible, apply a blur effect to finish the correction.

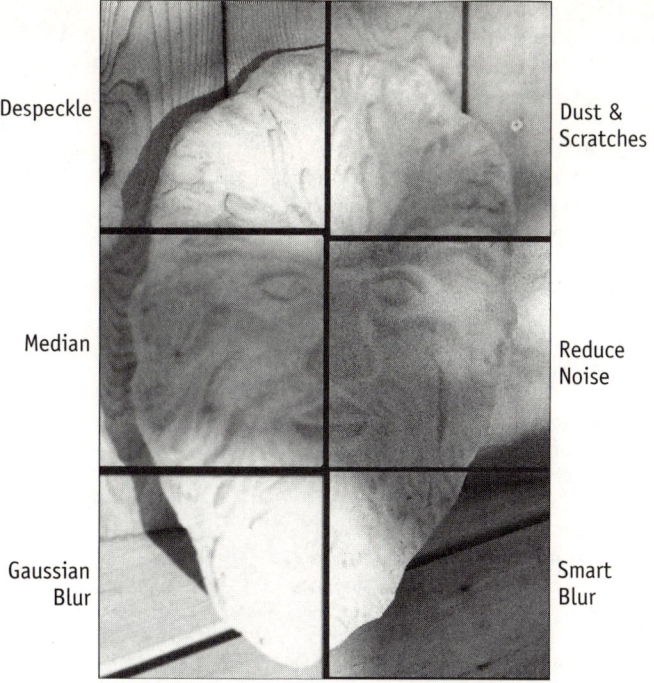

Figure 13.6. Different options produce varying degrees of noise correction.

Table 13.2 lists the common options you can try for correcting noise, as well as the details of the filters as applied to the example image. The settings used for the examples are not necessarily the only values that will work in the image. Each filter adds some degree of blurriness or softness to the image. In all cases, the next step is to look at sharpening the image's edges and features.

 **Hack**

The best way to remove noise is not to create it. Don't use a too-high ISO setting on your camera. Use different types of flashes, such as fill flashes, if the image contrast is high. You can try underexposing your image slightly, although underexposure can create more noise.

Table 13.2. Ways to correct image noise

Filter	What It Does	Settings Used in the Examples
Filter ⇨ Noise ⇨ Despeckle	Despeckle looks for edges in the image and blurs all the content except for the defined edges, removing noise and preserving detail.	No customizable settings
Filter ⇨ Noise ⇨ Dust & Scratches	This filter evaluates pixels and changes dissimilar pixels to match their neighbors according to the radius and threshold levels chosen.	Radius 3, Threshold 16 levels
Filter ⇨ Noise ⇨ Median	The brightness of pixels in different areas of similar brightness is blended.	Radius 3
Filter ⇨ Noise ⇨ Reduce Noise	This filter affects the amount of luminance and chroma noise and allows preservation of detail. The higher the level of detail, the more noise is retained in the image.	Luminance 8, Preserve Details 10%, Reduce Color Noise 100%
Filter ⇨ Blur ⇨ Gaussian Blur	A weighted average is applied to the amount of blurring applied to the image. The radius defines how far the filter looks for dissimilar pixels to blur.	Radius 1.5
Filter ⇨ Blur ⇨ Smart Blur	The image is precisely blurred based on the specified radius, a threshold that determines when a pixel has to be changed, and a blur quality.	Radius 1.2, Threshold 25, Medium quality, Normal mode

You see that many of the filters let you choose Radius and Threshold settings. *Radius* refers to the region you are using for comparing each pixel. The *Threshold* refers to the distance a pixel must be from a surrounding area to be affected by the filter's action. The pixels involved are called *edge* pixels, as they differentiate one item from another in the image.

> **Watch Out!**
> Inexpensive digital cameras tend to produce noisier images. A basic camera is fine for getting your image capture career underway, but keep in mind that as your experience and interest develops, so does your capability and capacity to use better equipment.

JPEG artifact

We have all seen the blocky, clunky artifact that occurs in a JPEG image that has been increased in size beyond its optimal dimensions. Figure 13.7 shows numerous chunky pixels and halos in the image of a woman holding a rose.

The artifact can be fixed using the Reduce Noise filter's settings. The filter's settings include two values that work in opposition to one another—Strength and Preserve Details. The Strength value defines how much smoothing occurs, while the Preserve Details value defines how much detail is retained.

Follow these steps to apply the filter:

Figure 13.7. JPEG artifact shows as blocky pixels and halos.

1. Choose Filter ➪ Noise ➪ Reduce Noise to open the Reduce Noise dialog box.
2. Click the Remove JPEG Artifact check box at the bottom of the dialog box. Instantly, you see an improvement in the image's appearance.

> **Watch Out!**
> An artifact is created every time you save an image in JPEG format. Save a JPEG image from your original file, not from a previous JPEG file to prevent compounding the distortions in the image.

3. Type a value in the Strength field, or drag its slider to set the value. There is no difference in the outcome whether the Strength is set at 1 or at 10 when using a high Preserve Details value as in the example; the setting simply must be active by choosing any value greater than 0 to activate the Preserve Details option.

4. Drag the Preserve Details slider or type a value in the field to specify the amount of detail compared to the amount of smoothing that is shown in the image. In the example shown in Figure 13.8, the Preserve Details setting is 90 percent.

5. Click OK to close the dialog box and apply the filter.

Figure 13.8. The image is smoother and it is easier to identify objects after reducing noise.

Removing image fringing

You may sometimes see a peculiar type of edge color on your images called *fringing*. It is most commonly seen along the edges of backlit subjects such as plants or people. The fringing is a type of *chromatic aberration*, an error that occurs when the camera lens can't focus the different wavelengths of light onto the same spot on the image. Fringing most often comes in purplish tones, but you also see it in blue-green and other colors as well.

Inside Scoop
Image fringing is caused by camera lenses and applies to the entire image. There is also another type of fringing caused by cutting selections from an image that carry along bits of the background color to the selection's new image location. The two types of fringing are managed in different ways.

The example used here has fringing that is a particularly unpleasant shade of greenish-blue, which you see as the strange light-gray highlighted area along the left of the hut's thatching in Figure 13.9. Removing shades of greenish-blue is tricky when the image has so much green foliage, but it's an interesting exercise.

Figure 13.9. Camera lenses can produce fringing, shown along the edges of your subject.

Bright Idea
Some people prefer to have the structure for a mask ready before working with adjustment layers. If you are one of those people, now's the time to create the mask content.

Removing fringing can be more or less complex, depending on whether you have any of the following:

- Similar color ranges for both the image and the fringing. Removing purple fringing is easier in a predominantly green image than removing green fringing in the same image.
- A need for advanced correction. For many common uses of images, such as sharing them with family and colleagues or building online presentations, the fringing may not be relevant.
- Time to work on the image. As you see, masking fringed areas and then adjusting their intensity takes time; decide whether it is worth the effort.

Defining the fringed areas on a layer

Before starting any defringing corrections, make sure that the image has been corrected overall, including removal of any color casts that may interfere with identifying and destroying the color fringing.

For working with a mask, it is important that you can see content on different layers properly, and can easily differentiate what is background from what is transparent, as demonstrated in Figure 13.10.

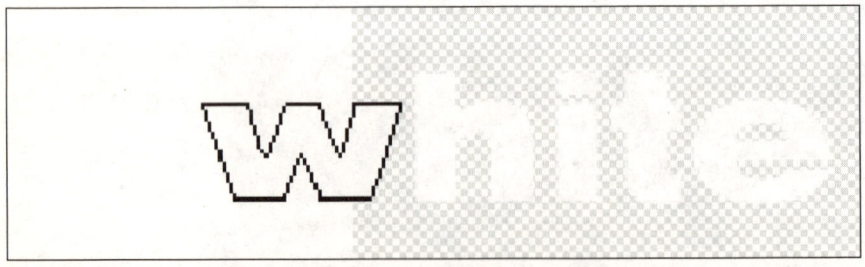

Figure 13.10. Make sure you can identify transparency in uncolored areas. In the figure, using white against a transparent background is clearly visible when the background uses a checkerboard, and impossible to define when image elements are also white.

Inside Scoop

Make sure that the underlying image layer is visible. This way, when you delete content from the masking layer, you see immediately whether you have deleted areas that should be maintained.

Check or change the Transparency preference following these steps:

1. Choose Edit ⇨ Preferences ⇨ Transparency to display the Transparency settings. Click the Grid Size drop-down arrow and choose any size (select from Small, Medium, or Large) except None.
2. Click OK to close the Preferences dialog box.

Now when you work on layer content, you see transparent areas as a checkerboard, easily differentiating transparency from white. There is much more to transparency than specifying a checkerboard size. Read about transparency issues in Chapter 6.

An important task for the correction of the sample image is to define the areas that display fringing, as opposed to general green-blue areas of the image itself. Follow these steps to construct the mask that defines the fringing areas:

1. Click the New Layer icon in the Layers palette to add a new blank layer above the existing image layer. The new layer uses the default transparent background.
2. Select the image layer in the Layers palette.
3. Using any combination of selection tools, select fringed areas from the original image layer. The selected areas to use for the mask are shown at the edges along the top of the image in Figure 13.11.
4. With the pixels still selected, click the new layer and add a solid black color fill to the selection. Continue until you have selected all the areas containing the fringing.
5. Using any combination of painting, selection, or fill tools, add more content to the fringed areas' masks on the mask layer, if required.
6. Complete the masking layer by filling the transparent areas of the new layer with white, shown in Figure 13.12.

Figure 13.11. Start by making selections from the original image for constructing your mask.

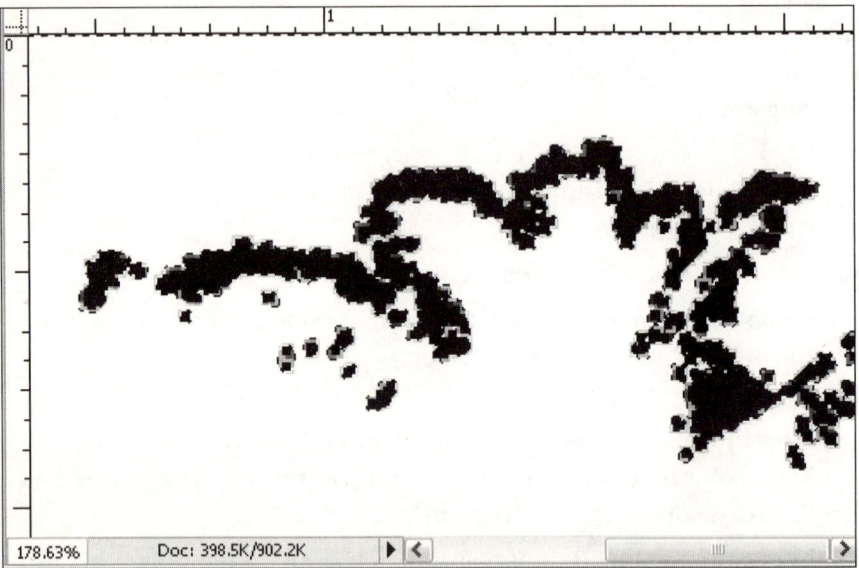

Figure 13.12. Fill selected areas black, and the remainder of the layer white to complete the mask.

Inside Scoop
The instructions for constructing a mask layer don't describe any settings for the selection tools. How you choose to use the tools and their options depends on your personal work preferences as well as the characteristics of your image's fringing. In the example image in Figure 13.12, the mask has a 1px feathering applied.

> ### Starting with levels
>
> Depending on the characteristics of the fringing and your image, you may want to start the mask layer using a copy of the image with adjusted levels. In a copy of the image, choose Enhance ⇨ Adjust Lighting ⇨ Levels or press Ctrl+L to open the Levels dialog box.
>
> Click the Channel drop-down arrow, and select an individual channel. You have to experiment to see which channel shows more of the fringe. Drag the white input slider for the single channel to the left until only most of the fringe is left visible. Close the Layers dialog box. Finish the rest of the fringe selection and coloring as described in the previous steps.

Adding and masking the adjustment layer

In an image, you are likely to have some color similar to the fringing that you don't want to remove, as in the case in the example. You don't want to change the shades of green in the entire image, just those unnatural greenish-blue shades in the areas of fringing. You work with an adjustment layer next.

Follow these steps to add the layer and then mask it:

1. With the image layer selected in the Layers palette, click the Create Adjustment Layer icon to open its menu and choose Hue/Saturation.
2. The adjustment layer is added to the Layers palette, and the Hue/Saturation dialog box opens. Click OK to close it. You'll come back to the dialog box in a minute.
3. In the Layers palette, select the layer you added to hold the mask.
4. Press Ctrl+A, Ctrl+C, and Ctrl+D to select the layer, copy its contents, and then deselect the layer again.

> **Bright Idea**
> Hide the image layer you used to construct the mask's content. When the correction is complete, the layer can be deleted.

5. Press Alt+Shift and click the mask for the Hue/Saturation adjustment layer. You know the mask is active when the eye icons for visible layers in the image are grayed out but visible, shown in Figure 13.13.

Figure 13.13. Visibility icons are locked for regular layers when a layer mask is active.

6. Press Ctrl+V to paste the content you worked with on the mask layer to the actual masking location for use. You see that the mask is now colored in the Layers palette, and of course, it is shown on the image as well.

7. Press Alt+Shift and click the mask for the Hue/Saturation adjustment layer again to deselect the mask and return to the regular Layers palette visibility.

Knocking out the fringe

It's time to banish those strange colors from the edge of the image's trees and building using a Hue/Saturation adjustment layer.

The steps described here are for the particular fringing in my image, which is a bright blue-green. If you are experiencing a purple fringe, use the Magentas channel and settings; similarly use the Yellows channel and settings if your fringe is within that color range.

Follow these steps to customize the adjustment layer:

1. Double-click the adjustment layer's icon on the Layers palette to reopen the Hue/Saturation dialog box.

2. Click the Edit drop-down arrow, and choose the color channel you want to edit. In the example, editing is started in the Cyans channel.

3. Drag the Saturation slider or type the value in the field. The lower the Saturation value, the less saturated the color; in the example the saturation is decreased to −80.

4. Drag the Lightness slider or type the value in the field to adjust the intensity of the color. The higher the value, the lighter the color. In the example, the Lightness slider is set at +20.

5. Click OK to close the dialog box.

When you select a channel from the Edit menu, a gray horizontal slider displays between the two color bars at the bottom of the dialog box, shown in Figure 13.14. When you make adjustments to the Saturation and Lightness values, you see the changes reflected in the colors in the lower of the two color bars. You also see the slider's bar change size when you add or remove color from the defined color range.

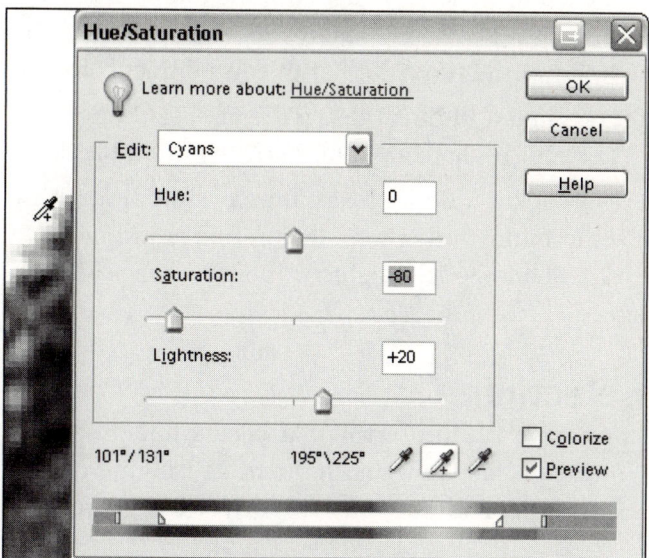

Figure 13.14. Adjust the saturation of some pixel colors using the adjustment layer.

To remove the fringe, the program substitutes the desaturated and lighter tones for those colored pixels you specified in the dialog box that are found within the boundaries of the mask you specified for the layer.

Before you close the dialog box, check out the image to see if the fringe has been taken care of. You may need to do one or more of the following:

- Click the middle Add to Sample Eyedropper tool on the Hue/Saturation dialog box, and click the image with the tool to add more colors to the range of the affected pixels. You see the changes in coloration in the lower of the two color bars if you add more colors.

Inside Scoop

You can zoom in and out of the image while adjusting the sliders and values in the dialog box by using the plus (+) and minus (–) keyboard keys.

- Click the right Subtract from Sample Eyedropper tool on the Hue/Saturation dialog box, and click the image with the tool to remove colors from the range of the affected pixels. You see the changes in coloration in the lower of the two color bars if you subtract colors.

- You may have to experiment with feathering the mask, although the adjustment layer's effect isn't harsh and may not be noticeable.

Your image likely will look a little washed out as a result of applying the mask and need some minor tinkering. Making fine adjustments to the Brightness/Contrast, Shadows/Highlights, or Levels settings will correct these problems.

Defringing a selection

Camera fringing is an image capture error that occurs under specific conditions. Nearly any image can show another type of fringing caused by making selections in an image that you can correct using program commands.

When you make a selection in an image and move it, pixels at the edges of the selection are also included. In the example shown in Figure 13.15, a dark gray border surrounds all the shapes, which is clearly visible when shown against the new background. Depending on the colors of the selection and the original layer's background, these marginal pixels can produce a halo or fringe.

In the image, the central shape is a pale apple green copied from its original layer with a dark plum background. Pasting the object to its new layer shows a fringe of darker pixels against the bright pink of the new layer. To make the copied content blend into the new image, the fringe of dark pixels has to be removed.

Use the Defringe command to replace the aberrant pixels on the selection's edges using pure color from nearby pixels. As a result, the selected areas are increased in size slightly by the specified number of pixels you set in the Defringe dialog box.

> **Watch Out!**
> Make sure that your selections are good ones from the beginning! Be sure that the tolerance of the selection tool or tools used is set to the smallest level possible that lets you make the selection easily while minimizing the amount of background color included. The less background you carry over to the new image, the less defringing required.

Figure 13.15. A selection can include pixels from the original layer's background. In the image, the shapes are surrounded by a dark fringe, which is the background color of the image from which the shapes were copied.

In the example shown in Figure 13.16, the dark pixels are replaced by the pixels of the new layer. In my image, that means the dark plum pixels surrounding the green object are replaced by the bright pink of the new layer.

Follow these steps to defringe the selection:

1. Paste the selection into its receiving layer, either a new or existing layer.

2. Choose Enhance ➪ Adjust Color ➪ Defringe Layer to open the Defringe dialog box.

3. Type a value for the number of pixels to replace around the object; one or two pixels usually works.

4. Click OK to close the dialog box and finish the correction.

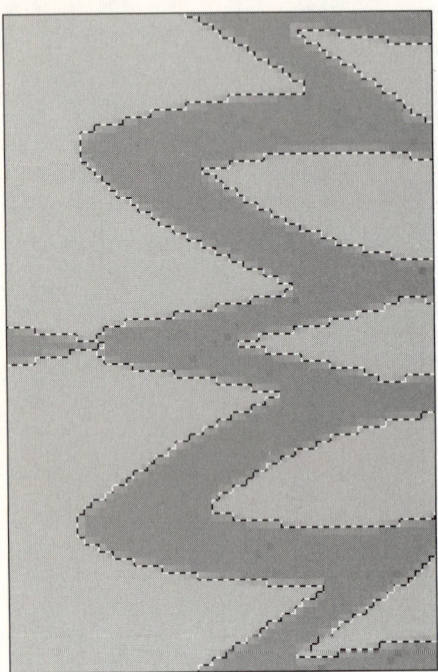

Figure 13.16. The Defringe command removes the pixels and replaces them with the new background's color.

Removing hot spots

A hot spot isn't the latest trendy nightclub. In image correction terms, a *hot spot* is an area of concentrated light on an image. The concentration of light is extensive enough to lose all detail, making the area white. The opposite occurs as well, when there is no light and the area is shown as black. At either extreme, the pixels' colors are said to be blown out to white or black. Unless you are going for a high contrast look, adjust the image's levels to balance the contrast a little better. A better balance is especially important if you plan to send images to a professional print press.

Inside Scoop

Get up close to what you need to see when you are setting levels. When the Levels dialog box is open, you can scroll and change the magnification of the image in the document window using the scrollbars, View menu, Hand and Zoom tools, and keyboard shortcuts.

Use either the Levels dialog box or a Levels adjustment layer to make the corrections as outlined in this discussion. Read about working with Levels in Chapter 8 and using adjustment layers in Chapter 12.

Finding hot spot info

Open the Info palette to use for reference. Whether you use the Info palette's information before or after you add the Levels adjustment layer doesn't make a difference in terms of how you manage the image. The important thing is that you adjust the highlight or shadow to make a better image.

When the Info palette is open, move your cursor over the image. You see the value of the sample area below the cursor shown on the Info palette in different ways. For example, Figure 13.17 shows a sample area over a highlight on an image. In the Info palette, you see that the RGB value for the sampled area is 255/255/255, or pure white. As a result, that area of the image doesn't show any detail, such as ripples in the water.

Figure 13.17. Info about the sampled area shows that it's pure white.

Adding the adjustment layer

Now that you've seen how the image's color information is distributed, follow these steps to add the Levels adjustment layer:

1. Click to select the layer in the Layers palette to which you want to apply the adjustment layer.
2. Click the Create adjustment layer icon on the Layers palette to open its menu, and click Levels. A new adjustment layer is added to the Layers palette above the one you previously selected.
3. The Levels dialog box opens automatically when the Levels adjustment layer option is selected in the Layers palette. As you move the mouse around the image, you see sample values in the Info palette.

Tweaking the hot spot

Follow these steps to adjust the white point value in an image:

1. Double-click the Set White Point tool in the Levels dialog box to display the Color Picker.
2. Type the color values to assign to the lightest area in the image. You can type either RGB or HSB values.
3. Click OK to close the Color Picker. Pixel color values are adjusted according to the new highlight value. Pixels lighter than the area selected become specular white, for example.
4. Move the cursor over the image again. In the Info palette, you see the before and after color values for the level adjustment, as shown in Figure 13.18.

Figure 13.18. After adjusting the white point, a sampled area shows the before and after color values.

Watch Out!
If you sample the wrong spot on the image, click Reset on the Levels dialog box and start again. Don't click Cancel because the dialog box closes and you have to start again.

If you want to adjust the shadows in an image, follow the same steps, using the Set Black Point tool in the Levels dialog box.

Sharpening up the image

Photoshop Elements includes several filters you can use for increasing the clarity in your images and several tools that can increase contrast in specific areas. For virtually any image, however, you should use the Unsharp Mask filter.

Don't let the name throw you off! The Unsharp Mask filter sharpens the edges in an image. Blurring results from virtually all imaging processes, including capturing the image, scanning, printing, resampling, or editing. Figure 13.19 shows an image after it has been manipulated: the leaves aren't as distinct or crisply defined from one another as they should be.

Figure 13.19. Any sort of editing or manipulation can cause blurring in an image.

Inside Scoop
Several other filters and tools can be used for sharpening in different ways. Refer to Chapter 14 for information.

Follow these steps to set the filter's parameters:

1. Choose Filter ➪ Sharpen ➪ Unsharp Mask to open the Unsharp Mask dialog box.
2. Type a value in the field or drag the slider to specify the settings for the filter; settings for the example image are shown in Figure 13.20.
3. Zoom in and out of the preview area, or click the Zoom buttons to view the image preview at different magnifications. Click and drag to reposition the image in the preview area.
4. Click OK to close the dialog box and apply the filter.

Figure 13.20. Specify Unsharp Mask values according to the image resolution and its intended use.

Specifying filter options

You can modify three different settings for the Unsharp Mask filter. In each case, either type a value in the field or drag the slider to specify the setting's value. Adjust these values:

- **Amount.** The Amount value specifies how much to increase the contrast as a percentage. Try a value of 150 to 200 percent for high-resolution print images. My image is low-resolution, and 75 percent is sufficient.
- **Radius.** Define the number of pixels to sharpen around the edges of the subject material by setting the radius. The lower the value, the narrower the band of pixels sharpened around the edges of objects. If your image is high resolution, use a low value of 1 or 2. The effect of the radius isn't very noticeable in a print version of an image. However, onscreen, because you see only 72 or 96 pixels per inch, the radius is much more visible.

- **Threshold.** Establish an area for the program to calculate whether a pixel is considered an edge pixel by setting a Threshold. The difference between an edge pixel and an non-edge pixel is arbitrary, but required for the program to calculate the filter's effect. You generally have to experiment with the Threshold value to see how much sharpening occurs at the edges of the objects, producing the clearest display of your image's contents. The higher the Threshold value is set, the fewer pixels are defined as edge pixels and sharpened. Of course, the lower the Threshold value is set, the more pixels are defined as edge pixels and sharpened.

The "after" image in Figure 13.21 shows the effect of applying the Unsharp Mask filter to the blurred image shown in Figure 13.19. You now see a greater distinction among the leaves in the image that result from sharpening the edges.

Figure 13.21. The Unsharp Mask filter can restore clarity and crispness to your image.

Sharpening last

Be aware that the Unsharp Mask can't be applied to an adjustment layer. You can only sharpen layers containing an image or image selection.

If a high level of precision is required for your project or work, save a copy of the image before flattening and applying the mask. That way, your original image is never touched and you can always make further edits or changes as necessary.

You can also apply the Unsharp Mask filter before making other adjustments, but if the file is saved after sharpening, you won't be able to tweak the sharpening at a later time.

Hack

For the ultimate in image control, finish your image corrections and save the file. Each time you need to print a copy, open the layered file, flatten it, and sharpen it. Close the file without saving the changes.

Unsharp Mask tips

The effects of the Unsharp Mask filter are much more visible onscreen than in print, so if you are creating a presentation or slide show, remember to apply the filter. Regardless of how you intend to use the image, keep these tips in mind:

- A Threshold value of 0, the default value, sharpens all pixels in the image.
- If you see noise appear as you are adjusting the values, lowering the Threshold value may wipe out the noise.
- You can apply the filter in two or more passes. Using lower settings in the Unsharp Mask filter dialog box results in less extreme sharpening each time the filter is applied, letting you control the sharpening more precisely.
- Speaking of preciseness, you can apply an Unsharp Mask filter to just a selected area on the image as well. Make the selection first and then apply the filter for precise modifications.
- If you apply the filter to a selected area, check the margins of the selection. If they are visible, undo the filter and then feather the edges of the selection. Feathering often produces a smoother transition between the sharpened and unsharpened areas of the image.
- To feather the edges and remove extreme sharpness, you can use the Eraser tool with a wide feathered brush to remove a sharp halo. Read about the Eraser tool in Chapter 18.

Looking for confusing content

You can't control some of the subject matter in your images, but you can certainly make changes in Photoshop Elements. Before you send that image off for printing or upload it to a presentation server, check for items that might distract from the subject of your image without contributing anything to its message, such as the shiny mugs in the image in Figure 13.22.

Some of the cups in the upper cupboard in the image are very reflective. Unless the intention is to show how they look on the shelves, it may be more useful to erase them from the image, or add cloned copies of some of the existing crockery. The glow from the coffee mugs competes with the glow from the glass tile. If you contrast the image in Figure 13.22 with the one shown in Figure 13.23, you see that there is no longer competition in the image for importance, and your eye is drawn to the glowing tile as intended.

Objects that are perfectly all right in themselves can cause confusion in how an image is presented. When you evaluate your composition, consider whether you need to make any changes to how the subject relates to the image's background.

Figure 13.22. Have you finished editing the image? Check for content that is taking attention away from the image's subject.

Figure 13.23. Removing competing shiny objects lets the viewer focus on the subject of the image — the glass tiles.

Inside Scoop

Composing the image's subject is the same as making corrections. Use the same tools, such as painting, filling a selection with a pattern or color, using the Clone Stamp tool, and so on. Read about fills in Chapter 6, painting in Chapter 18, and cloning content in Chapter 14.

After an image has been corrected, you can take a number of actions to improve the composition. Here are a few common modifications that you may find useful, as well as examples illustrating the ideas:

- **Remove extraneous content that unnecessarily confuse the image.** In Figure 13.24, you see that the image is very geometric and contains a number of repeating patterns. The telephone poles and utility lines provide unnecessary extra patterns that detract from both the subject and the inherent patterns of the subject. Removing the poles and cables returns the focus to the patterns in the shot.

Figure 13.24. The power lines and poles provide patterns that distract your eye from the image's subject.

- **Darken the background areas of the image slightly.** Darken the background to increase the contrast between the subject of the image and the surrounding content. Make sure that the rest of the image isn't too dark to tell what it is, if that's important to the image. You can also simulate an increased depth of field in the image by adding a blur that increases as the background increasingly darkens. In Figure 13.25, the sky and the section of the building in shadow are both darkened considerably, letting the focus center on the architecture of the building as reflected in the morning sun. To enhance the focus even more, a blur is applied to the darker areas of the building.

Figure 13.25. Darken and possibly blur the background to increase the focus on the image's subject.

- **Lighten instead of darkening the background.** The effect produced by lightening is more artificial than darkening the background often appears, but it certainly can focus your attention on the main subject of the image. In Figure 13.26, there's no doubt that the live oak is the focus of the image.

Figure 13.26. Lighten and even blur the background to emphasize the subject of an image.

Just the facts

- Artifacts are abnormal pixels in an image that occur from camera settings, camera quality issues, image processing errors, or processing in some file formats such as JPEG.
- Noise is the most common artifact, and it can be seen either in color or grayscale.
- Fringing is a type of error that occurs when the camera lens can't focus multiple wavelengths of light on the same spot.
- Fringing can be corrected using a Hue/Saturation adjustment layer and the effect controlled by a layer mask if necessary.
- Fringing can also occur within an image resulting from making selections.
- Hot spots are blown out areas of white (or black) that show no detail; they can be corrected using a number of methods.
- The Unsharp Mask filter is used to sharpen the edges of objects in most images to correct the blurring that occurs from creating or processing the image.

GET THE SCOOP ON...
■ Improving appearances digitally ■ Touching up content
■ Cloning pixels on an image ■ Tweaking brightness and
contrast ■ Replacing colors ■ Colorizing images

Retouching Magic

In the old days, photographers shot portraits with lens filters to soften wrinkles and airbrushed out other imperfections during processing. Although you should strive to capture the best possible image, you can do lots of retouching in Photoshop Elements without special filters.

Aside from wrinkles, other popular retouching jobs you can do to a person's face include removing blemishes, taking off a few pounds, and erasing dark circles from under the eyes.

Several of Photoshop Elements' tools are terrific for making different sorts of corrections, such as the Healing Brush and Cloning tool. Each tool lets you correct problems on an image using content from a different part of the image for consistency. Corrections aren't limited to blemishes or wrinkles: Use the program's tools for removing unwanted objects from an image too.

You can also work with a set of tools that are specific to fine correction tasks, like slightly darkening or lightening shadows or blurring an object's edge.

Taking off the pounds

You have probably heard that a camera adds 10 pounds. How about taking a few off instead? You can use the program features in different ways to alter a person's appearance slightly. One of the simplest is to adjust the appearance of shadows to simulate depth.

If you look at a thin person's face you usually see a shadow just below the jaw line, which your brain interprets as the edge of the jaw. If you look at the face of a heavier person using the same lighting, your brain perceives less shadow and sometimes even sees highlights, because the line of the jaw is shallower in a plumper face.

The shadow's appearance varies according to the light used to capture the image. In general, you can shave off pounds by adding more shadow under the jaw and possibly along the collar as well, depending on the shape of the face and the pose.

Any touching-up process is going to follow these three phases:

- Identify and select the area for modification.
- On a separate layer, change the color and adjust brightness and contrast in the selected area using a variety of methods, such as filling or painting strokes.
- Blend the new pixels with the original image.

Photoshop Elements includes numerous tools and a variety of methods you can use to enhance your images. For the most part, the choice is based on how you prefer to work rather than a specific tool or method for any single job. In the following sections, I have listed the method I use for a simple jaw-slimming process.

Creating the first shadow

First, draw and save a shadow shape to start the process. In the example image shown in Figure 14.1, the young lady has a puffy jaw line that shows a shadow and highlights a ridge above the shadow that adds weight to her face.

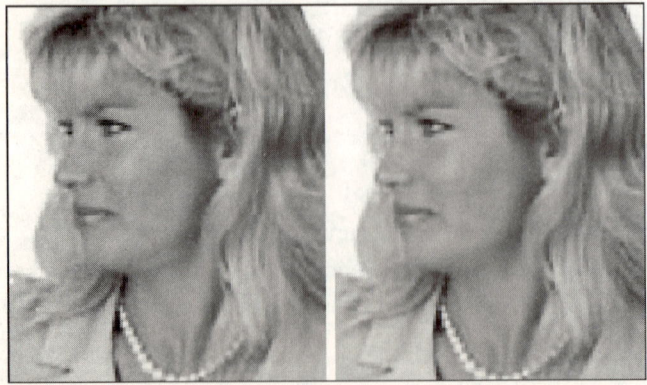

Figure 14.1. The highlighted ridge under the jaw (left image) can be modified to slim the face (right).

> **Watch Out!**
> If you use this method to add a shadow to take some weight off a face, check the person's collar as well. If the collar is touching the skin, add a shadow between the collar and the neck using the same method as the jaw line shadow to make the appearance consistent.

Follow these steps to add the first shadow shape as a selection to the image file:

1. Open the image in the Editor.
2. Select a Lasso tool and specify a feathering value. The example uses the Polygonal Lasso tool.
3. Draw the area where you want to adjust the shadow in the image using the selection tool, as shown in Figure 14.2.
4. Zoom in and out to view your selection against the rest of the image. You may have to add or remove pixels to the selection.
5. Choose Select ⇨ Save Selection to open the Save Selection dialog box. Leave the default New Selection active, and type a name for the selection in the Name field. Use a descriptive name, such as "Shadow."
6. Save the image file, leaving the selection active.

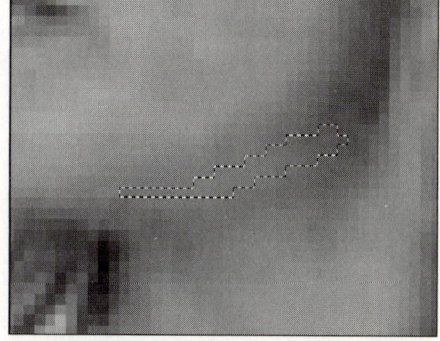

Figure 14.2. Draw the area where you want to adjust the shadow in the image using the selection tool; under the jaw line a selection is likely crescent-shaped.

Adding a new layer

Now that the initial selection has been drawn, you can use it to fill and adjust shadows in different layers.

Follow these steps to add and color the shadow for a new layer:

1. Click the New Layer icon in the Layers palette. Name the new layer something descriptive, such as "shadow."
2. Click the new layer to make it active; the selection is still active as well.

Inside Scoop

Take a few seconds to save a selection. Regardless of how you may deselect and lose it, all you have to do is choose the Select ➪ Load Selection command, choose the selection, and you are back in business.

3. Fill the selection to add a darker shadow to the selcted area. You could choose Edit ➪ Fill Selection and select settings in the Fill Layer dialog box, or click the Fill tool and choose settings on the options bar. As shown in Figure 14.3, the settings chosen in the options bar include:

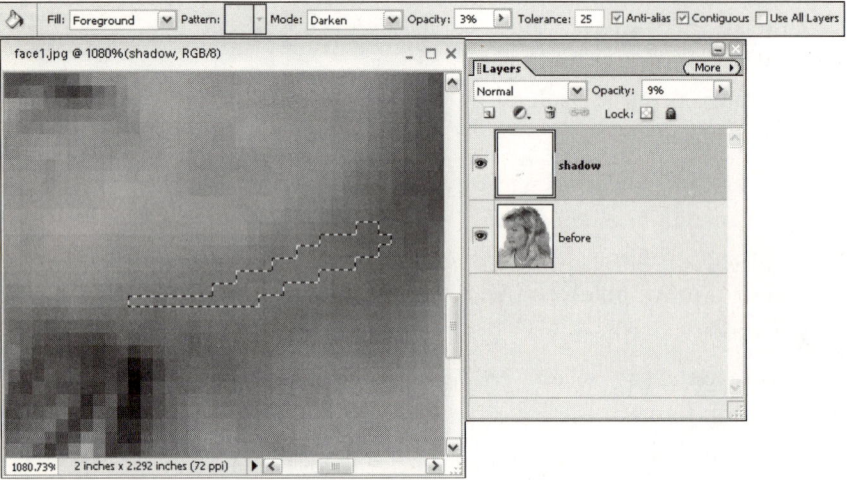

Figure 14.3. Adding a layer to hold the shadow fill lets you control its blending with other layers without affecting your original image.

- Foreground fill; the color set in the foreground color swatch in the toolbox is black.
- A specified mode; the example uses a Darken mode, which means pixels are colored when the pixel to be colored is darker than the fill color.
- Specify an opacity level. The example uses an Opacity of 3 percent, which adds a very small amount of color to the selected pixels with each application.
- Tolerance level refers to the range of color that is affected by the fill; the settings use the default Tolerance of 25.
- Anti-alias is selected to smooth the edges of the fill area.

Inside Scoop

If you prefer, fill the selection with a dark color sampled from the image itself, or use default fill settings. Because the selection is on its own layer, the same blend and opacity values can be set on the Layers palette for the shadow's layer as established for the fill in Step 3.

- Contiguous is selected to fill just the selected area; a non-contiguous fill adds color to similarly colored pixels throughout the image.

4. Adjust the Shadow layer's opacity by dragging the Opacity slider in the Layers palette. The amount of darkness you need in the new shadow area depends on the colors in the image, the depth of color used for the fill, and the amount of color you add. The shadow fill is shown in Figure 14.4. It matches the tone of the surrounding shadow, but is very sharp and noticeable at this point.

Figure 14.4. The pixels used for the fill are darker than the underlying image.

Be sure to toggle the selection on and off to see what you are working with more clearly. Press Ctrl+H to hide the selection, and repeat the keyboard shortcut to show the selection's boundaries again.

Blurring the new shadow

The edges of the new shadow should be blurred near the existing shadows to hide the editing. You can add a blur manually by using the Blur tool or by using one of the program's several Blur filters. Keeping with the method of using a selection for touching up an image, you need to expand the existing selection first to prevent the blur showing boundaries.

Bright Idea

For you shortcut key people, use Ctrl+Shift+N to add a new layer. The New Layer dialog box opens; name the layer, and click OK to close the dialog box and add it to the image.

> ### Brush it out
>
> You can use brushes instead of working with selections and fill tools. Select the Brush tool in the toolbox, and then choose a soft brush. Decrease the brush opacity to 25 percent or less. Sample the color in the darker areas surrounding the lighter ridge being corrected by moving the Brush tool over the pixel and pressing the Alt key. Build up the strokes until the color depth matches the surrounding shadow. An example touch-up using brushes is included later in the chapter. Read about using brushes in Chapter 18.

Follow these steps to modify the selection and apply a Blur filter:

1. Select the Shadow layer and check that the shadow selection is still active, shown in the left image in Figure 14.5.
2. Choose Select ⇨ Modify ⇨ Expand to open the Expand Selection dialog box. Type a value to define how much the selection is increased and click OK to close the dialog box and change the selection, shown in the right image in Figure 14.5. The example image has a low resolution, so using a one-pixel expansion value is large enough.
3. Choose Filter ⇨ Blur ⇨ Gaussian Blur to open the Gaussian Blur dialog box.
4. Drag the Radius slider to increase the value depending on the resolution of your image. The example is low resolution, so setting a one-pixel radius is enough blur.

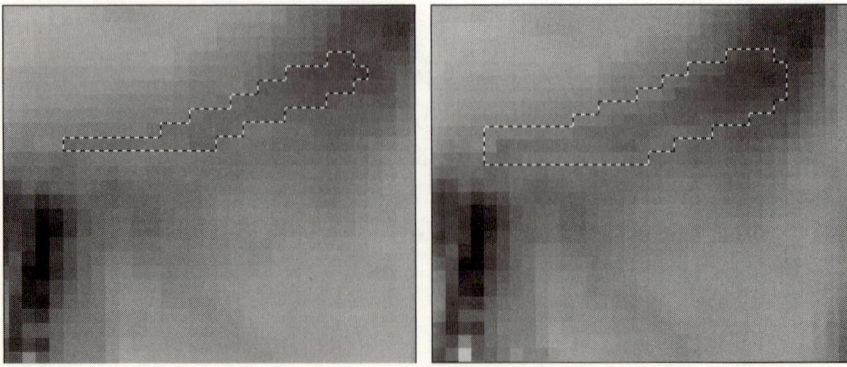

Figure 14.5. Increase the margins of the original selection (left) to a larger size (right) using the Expand command.

> **Watch Out!**
> Keep an eye on the edges! The edges of any sort of painting or touchups are key to making something look "right." If you don't blur the edge of the shadow, the face will look "wrong."

5. Click OK to close the dialog box and apply the blur.

6. For the final touch, tweak the opacity of the shadow layer. The example image uses 9 percent opacity for the shadow. That doesn't seem like very much, but it is enough to create the change we are looking for, which you can see in the "after" image at the right in Figure 14.1. The key is to be subtle.

Removing strange eye colors

The Red Eye Removal tool removes red eye in flash photos caused by a reflection of the camera flash on the subject's retina, as does your camera's red eye reduction feature.

When you are working with an image, you can fix red eye in two ways:

- Use the Automatically Fix Red Eyes command in Photoshop Elements, applied when you bring pictures into the Photo Browser.
- Use the Red Eye Removal tool in Standard Edit or Quick Edit mode.

But what if the eyes aren't red? In some cases, such as the image of the cat shown in Figure 14.6, the eyes may have a different colored reflection, such as green. There isn't a Green Eye Removal tool, but the problem can be corrected simply by painting or filling the eyes on their own layer.

Follow these steps to correct unusual eye color:

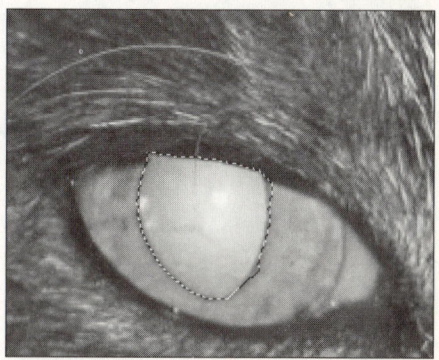

Figure 14.6. The off-colored area of reflection is selected in the eye.

1. Select the areas of the eyes you want to change on the image using any of the selection tools; use a Feather value of 1 or 2 pixels. One eye's selection is shown in Figure 14.6.

Inside Scoop
Read about using the Automatically Fix Red Eyes command in Chapter 1. The Red Eye Removal tool is covered in Chapter 7. Check out painting information in Chapter 18.

2. Add a new layer to the image to hold the edits. Click the Blend mode drop-down arrow in the Layers palette, and choose Color.
3. Double-click the foreground color swatch in the toolbox to open the Color Picker, and select the color for the eye; the sample uses a very dark green.
4. Select the Brush tool in the toolbox.
5. In the options bar, choose a soft-edged brush smaller than the green eye area.
6. Drag the opacity slider to about 30 percent.
7. Gradually paint over the green area in the eyes to add paint to the selection areas, shown in Figure 14.7. Continue applying brush strokes until the eye color is repaired.

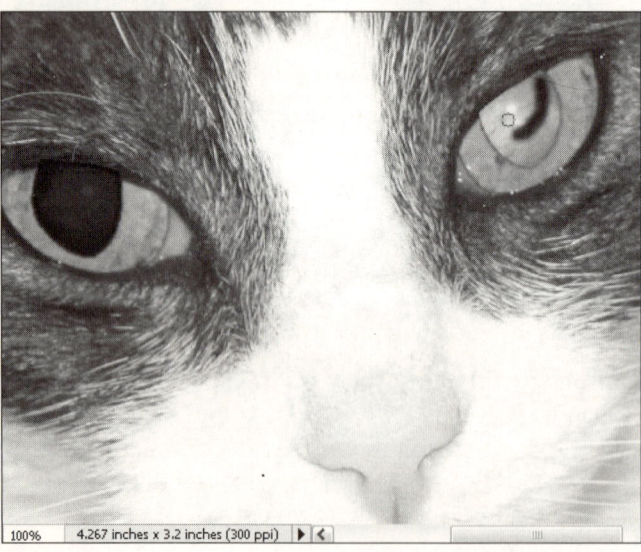

Figure 14.7. Use the paintbrush to fill in the eye's color.

Bright Idea
If you tweak the size of the brush to match the size of the correction area, you don't even need to use a selection.

Watch Out!
Be sure to consider both the brush's and the layer's blend modes. Painting using a blend mode produces different effects on a layer depending on what blend mode is applied to the layer. Read about blend modes in Chapter 11.

Experiment with setting blend modes for the paintbrush or for the layer used to hold the correction. In the example, the paint is applied using a Normal blend at 100 percent opacity, and the layer uses a Linear Burn blend at 90 percent to allow the underlying highlights to show in the corrected tone.

After you are satisfied with the color correction, you can flatten the layers to save storage space — unless, of course, you need a picture of your precious kitty in full-on demon mode.

Making touchups

Photoshop Elements offers some tools that you can use to make touchups of varying degrees of complexity. Fortunately, you don't have to be a digital artist to remove the big zit from your son's prom picture or block out the less-than-lovely trashcans in the background of your otherwise perfect garden photo.

One trashcan peeking over a fence is simpler to repair than a row of them marching along a fence line. The right tool for the job depends on the degree of work involved.

The available options include:

- **Spot Healing Brush.** The Spot Healing Brush tool repairs simple spots and imperfections such as a facial blemish or a spot of dust from the camera lens.
- **Healing Brush.** The Healing Brush tool repairs larger problems in an image. It removes objects from a uniform background, such as a sidewalk or a lawn.
- **Clone Stamp.** The Clone Stamp tool paints with a sampled area of the image. Use this method to duplicate or remove objects or paint over large imperfections in an image.

Fixing spots

The Spot Healing Brush tool removes blemishes, spots, and other imperfections in your photos. It is a good tool to use instead of the Dust & Scratches filter if you find a couple of spots from the lens showing in your image, such as the water spots shown in Figure 14.8. Unlike applying a filter, using the Spot Healing Brush tool affects only those areas that you sample on the image.

Figure 14.8. The Spot Healing Brush tool can repair dust or water spots on the lens, like the ones in the image.

Correcting a single spot

Use the Spot Healing Brush tool either by clicking on a flaw in the image or dragging to correct an area.

Follow these steps to take care of problem spots or blemishes using the Spot Healing Brush tool:

1. In the Editor, select the Spot Healing Brush tool in the toolbox.
2. In the tool's options bar, click the Brush drop-down arrow and choose the brush you want to work with, or leave the default brush selected.
3. Click the Size field and type a brush size, or click the arrow and drag the slider to set the size of the brush.

> **Bright Idea**
> If you choose a brush size that is slightly larger than the area to fix, one click repairs the blemish.

4. Click the spot you want to fix, or click and drag to fix a larger area like the water spots on the lens shown in Figure 14.9. In the image, one of the original four water spots has been repaired and one is partially corrected.

Figure 14.9. Choose a matching brush, and water spots can disappear.

Defining correction color

Photoshop Elements provides two methods to define the color and content of the brush area when you are correcting a spot.

After you select the Spot Healing Brush tool, the options become active in the options bar, shown at the top of Figure 14.10. Along with setting other Brush options, choose the Type of color matching by clicking either the Proximity Match or Create Texture options. These are the two ways the program defines color for the correction:

- **Proximity Match.** Proximity Match is the default program setting and works best in solid color areas. This type matches the pixels at the edge of the area defined by the brush to use as a patch.
- **Create Texture.** The Create Texture option uses all the pixels in the selection area defined by the brush to create a texture, and often works better in corrections made on patterned areas.

Figure 14.10. Using different color definition options for the Spot Healing Brush tool produces variable correction results.

>  **Watch Out!**
> One additional choice in the options bar lets you Sample All Layers, which uses the content of all visible layers in your image. If you are trying to make a correction in a layered image and something doesn't seem quite right, check that the option is deselected.

The left image shown in Figure 14.10 shows a close-up of one of the water spots shown in Figure 14.8 and Figure 14.9; the water spot is highlighted with a black ring to identify it on the image. The center image in Figure 14.10 shows the outcome of using the Proximity Match type of color matching; you see that there is little correction in the water spot. Using the Create Texture type of color matching produces a significant amount of correction, as you can see in the right image in the figure.

Fixing bigger problems

If the area you are correcting is larger than a spot or two, try the Healing Brush tool. The Healing Brush tool works especially well for removing an object from an image such as dead leaves from your garden path or the telephone lines and poles shown in Figure 14.11.

Figure 14.11. Use the Healing Brush to make corrections in an image, such as removing the utility lines and poles that take away from the graphic nature of the image.

Healing an image

Any sort of image having a uniform background can be corrected with the Healing Brush tool, following these steps:

1. Select the Healing Brush tool in the toolbox; the tool's options bar is active.
2. Click the drop-down arrow to open the Brush palette, and choose brush settings, including the diameter, hardness, and spacing; you can also choose whether the brush size can change in response to pen or stylus actions.
3. Select healing options such as the mode, whether the painted strokes are aligned, and so on.
4. Alt+click to sample an image area to use for the painting.
5. Drag over the area you want to correct. As you drag, you see a circle identifying the Healing Brush tool's location as well as crosshairs showing the sample location; both identifying locations are shown in Figure 14.12. Release the mouse to apply the changes.
6. Repeat as required until the correction is complete.

Figure 14.12. Select a location to use as a sample location, and click to substitute the pixels and make the correction. In the figure, the distracting utility lines and poles are in the process of being removed.

Choosing healing options

Using the Healing Brush tool can produce different results depending on the choices you make. Spend a couple of minutes to experiment with the options shown in Figure 14.13 and see how they affect the same image.

Figure 14.13. Specify the mode and other options to define how the new pixels interact with the existing pixels using the Healing Brush tool.

Make your choices from these Healing Brush tool options:

- **Mode.** Define how you want the healing pixels to blend with the original ones by specifying the mode. Normal mode blends the new pixels on the image with the sample pixels; Replace mode replaces the underlying image's texture. With Replace mode, the Healing Brush paints the pattern over the underlying image. Several other modes you can choose include Multiply, Screen, Darken, Lighten, Color, and Luminosity. Read about the blending modes in detail in Chapter 11.

- **Source.** The Source determines where you want the pixels for correction to come from. *Sampled* uses pixels from the image itself as a source; *Pattern* uses pixels from a pattern specified in the Pattern palette.

- **Aligned.** Toggle the Aligned option on or off to specify how sampled pixels are applied. *Aligned* samples pixels following a continuous sampling point. In Figure 14.14, each stroke at the left follows the same path from the point of origin, the center of one of the flowers. If Aligned is deselected, each time you release the mouse and click again

Figure 14.14. The Aligned option determines where pixels are sampled each time the tool is applied.

> **Inside Scoop**
> You can sample from one image and apply pixels to another. Make sure that both images use the same color mode; however, if one of the images is grayscale, sampling also works.

the replacement content continues the pixel replacement at the same distance from the tool's location, relative to the original sampling point, like the example strokes at the right in Figure 14.14.

- **Sample All Layers.** Choose the Sample All Layers setting to copy data from all the layers visible in your image; deselect the option to sample only the active layer. You might want to sample all the layers if you are separating content for editing, but need to use color from different layers for making a correction.

Cloning pixels on an image

Another tool in the arsenal for making touchups is the Clone Stamp tool, which uses a sample of an image to paint on the image. The other Clone tool in the toolbox is the Clone Pattern tool, described in detail in Chapter 18.

Use the Clone Stamp tool to add duplicates of an object to an image or remove objects or content in an image. In Figure 14.15, for example, you can use the Clone Stamp tool to remove the cushion tossed on the floor, while preserving the pattern in the wood floor.

Figure 14.15. The cushion lying on the floor detracts from the sense of order in the image. Take care of the disorder easily using the Clone Stamp tool.

Follow these steps to use the Clone Stamp tool:

> **Inside Scoop**
> You may find it simpler and more accurate to make a selection before starting the correction. When you have an area of high contrast or you need to follow the lines of an object precisely, make a selection to prevent the tool from bleeding content into or out of the shape.

1. Select the Clone Stamp tool in the toolbox; the tool's options are displayed in the options bar.
2. Click the Brushes drop-down arrow, choose a brush tip, and drag the slider to specify the size of the brush in pixels. Read about Brush settings in Chapter 18.
3. Choose other options as necessary.
4. Alt+click the mouse over the area you want to sample.
5. Drag to paint with image pixels on the image layer and replace original pixel content, as shown in Figure 14.16.

Figure 14.16. Define the opacity and other settings for painting with the Clone Stamp tool and use the tool to correct errors in an image, such as the cushion lying on the floor. This figure shows a close-up of a portion of the image shown in Figure 14.15.

The Clone Stamp tool uses the same options as those available for the Healing Brush tool, including the Mode, Aligned, and Sample All Layers options. The Mode settings include the full list of blend choices available in Photoshop Elements, as well as Normal and Replace options, like those offered by the Healing Brush tool.

Which tool is best?

The short answer is that it depends. Each tool is uniquely suited for its own particular group of tasks. If you are a minimalist (I prefer that term to bone-idle lazy), you can use the Clone Stamp tool to perform any of the other tools' functions as well as its own. If you are the "right tool for the right job" sort of person, use the Spot Healing Brush tool for simple corrections where you can just click away a problem, such as spots of dust on a lens. For a larger job, or one where you want to blend the changes into the existing pixels, try the Healing Brush. When the key to success is subtle painting, as that used in the upcoming section on removing the dark circles from under my eyes, the tool of choice is the Clone Stamp tool.

In addition, you can specify the opacity of the paint. Click the Opacity slider in the options bar, and drag to set the value higher or lower. The lower the Opacity value, the more the underlying pixels show through the painted pixels.

Digital eye enhancements

With just a few minutes of work, you can remove the toll time takes on all of us — at least digitally. Fixing dark circles under the eyes is one of the easiest and most noticeable corrections. The tool used for this successful touchup is the Clone Stamp tool.

Figure 14.17 shows the before image of a seemingly tired woman. Barring sufficient quantities of beauty sleep, a little image correction goes a long way in removing the bruise-like circles under her eyes.

Figure 14.17. The dark circles under this woman's eyes look like bruises. Clearly, she needs a vacation, or some expert makeup advice.

Setting up the correction

Retouching images is like any other type of image correction in that it is much safer to work on a new layer. Follow these steps to set up the file and the Clone Stamp tool:

1. In the Layers palette, click New Layer to add a layer for touchups; name it if you like.
2. Click the Clone Stamp tool in the toolbox to activate its options bar.
3. Choose the settings for the Clone Stamp tool.

You want the Clone Stamp tool to do these things:

Hack

As in all corrections, different correction tools can be used to produce much the same outcome. For example, the correction in this discussion could be done using a variety of tools, including the Healing Brush or the Spot Healing Brush tools. It could even be painted. It's your choice.

- Use a brush size that corresponds with the image's resolution and contents. In the example, a 14px brush is used because it allows for sampling in a small area; a smaller area is necessary because of the variations in skin tone in the cheek.
- Use a feathered brush to blend the correction with the image.
- Use a blending mode depending on the areas you are correcting. For example, in the example image using the Lighten Blending mode can ensure that just the darker pixels are affected for a more natural look.
- Set the Opacity to a low level, somewhere in the 15-25 percent range. Paint strokes aren't harshly defined at that level of transparency.
- Use the Aligned feature to make sure the variation in the painted content matches that of the image.
- Use the Sample All Layers option to sample the image on the underlying layer.

Erasing the circles

Now you're set to create the magic. Alt+click the image with the Clone Stamp tool at a point below the darkened area to sample normal-looking skin.

Keep these ideas in mind:

- Click with the tool to add strokes to the image layer, as shown in Figure 14.18. If you see that the color changes are too dark, decrease the Opacity.
- Keep an eye on how the tool's coloring is applied and reset the Align location for the Clone Stamp tool by pressing Alt and clicking a new sample area on the image.

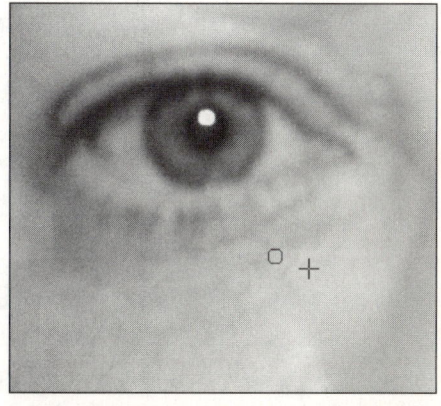

Figure 14.18. Paint with a range of sample areas to remove the dark shadows, as in this magnified portion of the image shown in Figure 14.17.

- Toggle the paint layer on and off in the Layers palette to see your progress.

> **Bright Idea**
> If you are doing only a simple correction, don't bother making separate layers for each element you correct or naming each layer. On the other hand, if you are touching up Miss Universe's publicity shots, use as many layers as there are areas touched up.

Fixing extra highlights

While you are working on an image, check for any unnatural highlight areas. In the example, there's a highlight that runs perpendicular to the nose. This is the sort of highlight that is caused when you press on your skin.

Fixing highlights is similar to working with dark circles. Use the same settings as those for the shadow corrections, but this time use the Darken Blending mode. In the example image, the highlight is ridged, which then requires that the adjoining shadow be lightened as well.

The final results of the repairs are shown in Figure 14.19. Compare the after with the original image shown in Figure 14.17.

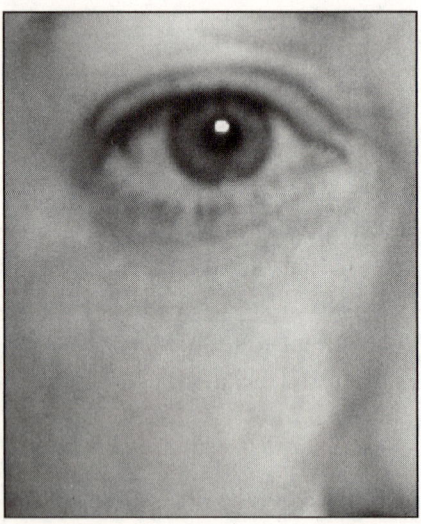

Figure 14.19. All it takes is some subtle painting on a separate layer (left) to improve the eye significantly.

Watch Out!

Humans have eye sockets; eye sockets show shadow. It's normal to have some level of shadowing under the eye to show the contouring of the skull. Too much erasing can make the subject's face look abnormally flat.

Fine-tuning tools

When you think of painting, you naturally think of applying color. You can also use different tools in Photoshop Elements that are like painting with light, contrast, or saturation. The tools are found in the toolbox in two sets of three tools each.

One set of tools includes the Sharpen, Blur, and Smudge tools. Each is characterized by the strength at which the tool is applied with each stroke to your image, as well as the blend type used for applying the effect. These tools modify the contrast in your image one stroke at a time.

The second set of tools includes the Dodge, Burn, and Sponge tools. These tools are characterized by the range they affect in the image: highlights, midtones, or shadows. These tools affect the saturation or light as you use them.

Any of the tools can help in perfecting your image as you control the effect of the change one stroke at a time, blending with the surrounding pixels in the image. This way, you don't have a universal change applied as in applying a command to the image, and you don't have to worry about making and blending selections to hold changed pixels. The advantage to using these tools is the amount of control you have over the edit.

Tweaking contrast

Use the Sharpen, Blur, and Smudge tools to modify the contrast in your image one stroke at a time. Click the visible tool in the toolbox, and choose the tool you want to use from the options bar; or press and hold the visible tool until the subtoolbar displays, and choose the tool you want to use.

For each tool, you can choose similar settings in the options bar, described in Table 14.1.

Table 14.1. Settings available in the options bar

Setting	Available Options
Brushes	Choose from one of hundreds of brush tips.
Size	Choose a size for the brush tip by typing the value in the Size field or dragging the slider.
Mode	Define how the tool blends existing pixels in the image using one of several modes. Options include Normal, Darken, Lighten, Hue, Color, or Luminance.
Strength	Specifies the amount of change that occurs as a percentage with each stroke. Click the field and type a value from 1 to 100, or drag the slider.
Sample All Layers	The tool affects all layers of the image if selected; if deselected, only the active layer is changed.

Painting contrast changes

The Sharpen and Blur tools work in opposite fashions. The Sharpen tool focuses soft edges between objects in an image; the Blur tool softens edges between objects or areas in an image to reduce detail.

Figure 14.20 shows an example of using the Sharpen and Blur tools. The left edge area of the circle is sharpened, while the Blur tool is used at the right of the circle. Both tools were applied in several strokes.

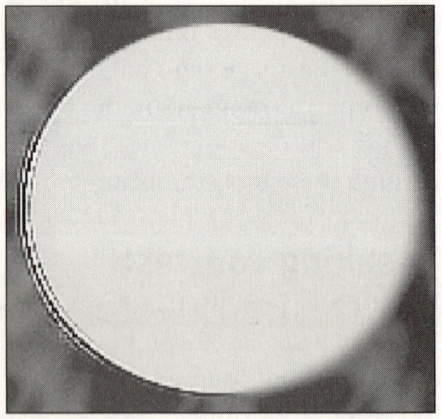

Figure 14.20. Modify contrast one stroke at a time using the Sharpen and Blur tools.

Bright Idea

For the best results and most control, use a low Strength value and stroke the image with the tools several times to build up the effect.

> **Combining tools**
>
> If you want to define the subject of an image more strongly, you can use the Blur tool applied to the image's background content. Earlier in the chapter I discuss how the Blur tool can be used instead of a Blur filter to produce the same outcome, although doing so would take much longer. You could use both: Apply the Blur filter to make the major changes, and then use the Blur tool to tidy up the edges, blending any pixels where the edges of the selection may be visible.

Smudging content

The Smudge tool works like dragging your finger through wet paint, and even simulates the same appearance as dragging through wet paint and gradually lifting your finger to leave a teardrop-shaped modification.

Color is picked up at the start of the stroke and pushed in the direction you drag, shown in the left leaf shape in Figure 14.21. Smudging uses the color in the image by default. If you prefer, you can also use the existing foreground color. Click Finger Painting in the options bar to start each stroke using the foreground color, shown in the right leaf shape in Figure 14.21.

Figure 14.21. Smudge areas on the image using its colors or the current foreground color.

Tweaking light

Use the Dodge and Burn tools to lighten or darken areas of the image one stroke at a time. The Dodge tool can help define detail in areas of shadow, while the Burn tool can help define detail in highlighted areas. The Sponge tool changes the color saturation as you apply strokes to the image.

Watch Out!
Combine any layers that need combining first; the tools don't offer an option for sampling more than one layer.

Click the visible tool in the toolbox, and choose the tool you want to use from the options bar; or press and hold the visible tool until the subtoolbar displays, and choose the tool you want to use.

For each tool, you can choose similar settings in the options bar. The Brushes and Size settings are the same as those listed in Table 14.1.

Lightening and darkening

Use the Dodge and Burn tools to lighten or darken areas of the image one stroke at a time. Follow these steps:

1. Select the tool in the toolbox, and specify the brush tip and size in the options bar.
2. Choose the Range to specify the tonal ranges that are modified with the tool as you apply strokes to the image. Choose from Shadows to change the dark areas, Highlights to change the light areas, and Midtones to change mid-gray tones.
3. Set an Exposure value to specify the depth of the effect applied per stroke. The values range from 1 to 100 percent; type the number in the Exposure field, or drag the Exposure slider to change the percentage.
4. Drag the tool over the image to apply the effect.

The Dodge and Burn tools have opposite effects. Figure 14.22 shows the effects of using the Dodge and Burn tools. The original image is shown at the left; the same image after using both tools is shown at the right. In the right image, the shadow was removed and added to the other side of the figure, simulating a different time of day.

Inside Scoop
The Exposure setting used for the Dodge and Burn tools functions the same as the Strength setting for the Blur, Sharpen, and Smudge tools. The different name is used in association with the darkroom analogy of the Dodge and Burn tools' functions.

Figure 14.22. The Dodge and Burn tools can enhance or change detail in an image by lightening or darkening areas.

Soaking up the color

The Sponge tool works by increasing or decreasing the vividness of color in your image. You can use the tool for very subtle effects, such as slightly desaturating background content in an image to emphasize the subject.

Burn, baby, burn

Dodge and burn are two terms used in traditional photographic darkroom editing. If the subject has more contrast or a greater range of brightness than the film can record, the photograph may not have enough detail in the shadows or highlights.

To prevent too much darkness in the shadows, as an image is exposed, the photographer shades the problem area using a hand or piece of cardboard on a paper clip — a technique known as dodging. The Dodge tool in the toolbox is shown as a piece of paper on a stick.

If an area on an image is too white after exposure, the image can be corrected by adding additional light, or burning, the white area. The extra light is added to the exposure through a hole in a piece of cardboard, or by curving your hand into a cup shape, like the icon shown for the Burn tool.

Depending on the look of an image, you can use oversaturated color as a method of enhancing other characteristics, such as oversaturing the color in an object in a strongly graphical composition.

Replacing color

Suppose you have a picture of your garden shed, and you wonder how it would look in a different color. Or maybe you'd like to change the color of the tie your nephew is wearing in his graduation photos. Photoshop Elements has two different methods you can use to replace colors in your image.

One of the color replacement methods is more like a style of painting, using the Color Replacement Brush. It's described in Chapter 18 with other painting techniques and discussions.

You can also use the Color Replace dialog box to make changes to your image's colors. To start the process, choose Enhance ➪ Adjust Color ➪ Replace Color to open the Replace Color dialog box. You complete two separate processes to replace the color: selecting the range to replace, and then specifying the color range for replacement. It's a very neat tool.

Making selections

First, you have to select the color range you want to replace. In the example described here, a garden shed with a terra cotta color is going to get a new look in sage green.

Click the Eyedropper tool in the Selection area of the dialog box, and click the image to select the color. You see the selected color in the upper color swatch in the dialog box.

Toggle the Preview on or off by clicking the Preview check box at the right of the dialog box; the Preview is shown by default. The area shown in the Preview changes can show either the entire image or a selection.

Bright Idea
If you are working with a grayscale image, the Sponge tool increases or decreases contrast in the image.

The default is the Selection option, which shows the selected content. Click the Image check box to show the entire image, a useful option when the color is being replaced in a variety of areas in a large image.

If you look at the thumbnail showing the selection in the example shown in Figure 14.23, you see that only a portion of the siding is actually selected.

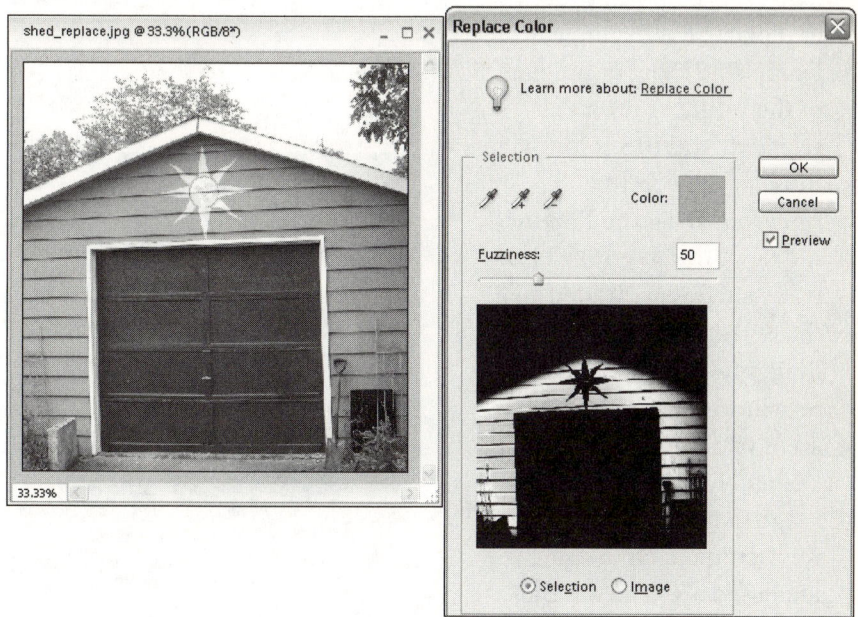

Figure 14.23. The range of colors selected show in the Selection preview as white.

There isn't really a right or wrong way to select the color in your image, although some ways take more or less time. Here are some tips for speeding up the selection process working with a Selection preview in the dialog box:

- Start with a lower Fuzziness setting; I usually start at about 30-50 for an image like my example that has large blocks of color. *Fuzziness* refers to the number of shades similar to the point you sample with the eyedropper. The lower the number, the fewer similar shades are selected with your sample; the higher the number, the more shades are selected with your sample.

- Click with the eyedropper to take the sample and check out the Selection preview. The pixels that have been selected are shown in white on the Preview. This way, you have an idea how much of the image is to be replaced with the new color.

- Drag the Fuzziness slider to increase the selected area, as long as it is the color you want to replace. For example, in Figure 14.23, the upper edges of the building aren't selected, and the color in those areas won't be replaced. Drag the Fuzziness slider higher to control how many shades are added to the Selection preview. Stop dragging the slider when the Selection starts to include areas you don't want to change. Figure 14.24 shows a range that is too extensive. Replacing the color using the identified areas means the shed would be green, but so would most of the trim and the concrete slab in front of the door.

Figure 14.24. When the Fuzziness setting is too high, objects like the trim are also selected, indicating the color range selected is too extensive, as you can see in the Preview.

Replacing the color range

After most of the color range has been specified, define the color you want to use in the Replacement area of the dialog box, shown in Figure 14.25.

Bright Idea

If similar colors appear in different parts of the image that could be selected automatically in the Replace Colors dialog box, you can draw a selection on the image first before using the command. The changes are then restricted to the areas identified by the selection's boundary.

Drag the Hue, Saturation, and Lightness sliders in the Replacement area of the dialog box to display your replacement color. Alternatively, you can double-click the Result color swatch to open the Color Picker, and select your desired color. Click OK to close the Color Picker; the values of the color adjust the Replacement sliders automatically. You see that the selection area is replaced in the image with the new color.

Now it's tweaking time. Click the Add to Sample central eyedropper in the Selection area, and sample one of the colors still to be replaced in the image. Your color is adjusted in the image. Continue using both the Add to Sample and Remove from Sample tools until the color replacement is complete, as shown in Figure 14.25.

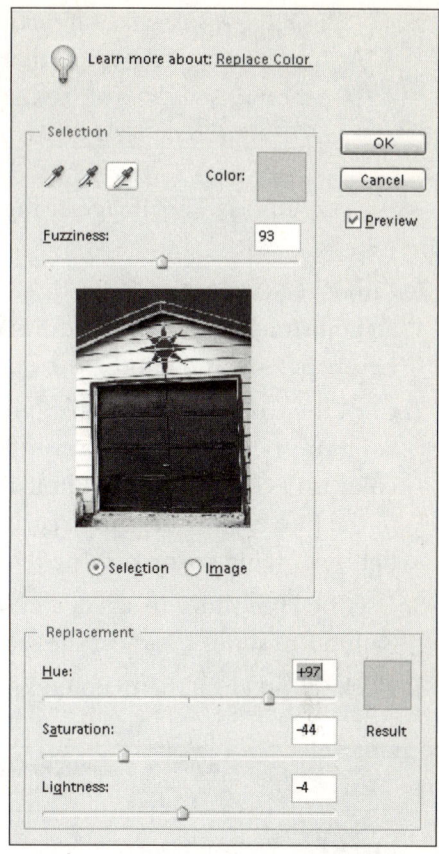

Figure 14.25. Define the replacement color by setting the Hue, Saturation, and Lightness values.

Adding some color

A popular and effective technique for enhancing images is to color specific areas in a grayscale image, a technique called *colorizing*. You can colorize an entire grayscale image, or select areas to colorize with different colors. The point of colorizing isn't to create realistic color, such as skin tones, in the image. Instead, it is designed for emphasizing features in an image.

You can use a number of methods to add some color to a grayscale image. To add color to a specific area, make a selection and then fill it or paint it.

Watch Out!
You can't recolor an image that is in grayscale mode. Convert it to RGB by choosing Image ⇨ Mode ⇨ RGB.

You can colorize an image using an adjustment layer by following these steps:

1. Choose Layer ⇨ New Adjustment Layer ⇨ Hue/Saturation to add an adjustment layer, or click the Adjustment Layer icon in the Layers palette and choose the option from the drop-down list.
2. Click the Colorize check box at the bottom right of the Hue/Saturation dialog box, shown in Figure 14.26. If the foreground color isn't black or white, Photoshop Elements converts the image to the hue of the current foreground color without changing the lightness value of the pixels.
3. Use the Hue slider to select a new color if desired. Use the Saturation slider to adjust the saturation.
4. Click OK to close the dialog box and make the change.

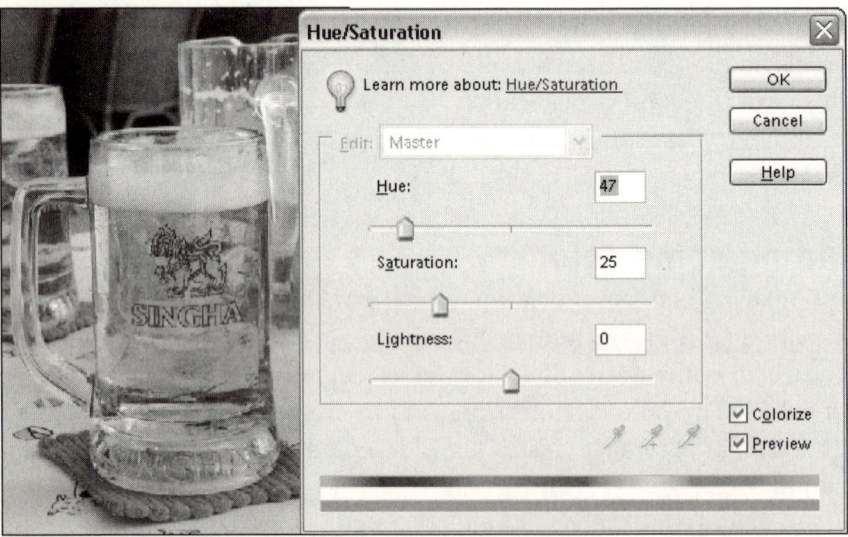

Figure 14.26. The replacement hue is shown in the lower color bar in the dialog box and previewed on the image.

Inside Scoop

The instructions describe adding a tint to an image using an Adjustment layer. You can change the image's color by choosing Enhance ⇨ Adjust Color ⇨ Adjust Hue/Saturation. My strong preference is to use adjustment layers whenever possible to protect the original image.

Just the facts

- Use the Healing Brush tools to repair single spots or larger imperfections.
- Use program features such as the Clone Stamp tool to repair and tweak portraits and other images.
- The Dodge and Burn tools paint lighter and darker areas in the image, great for enhancing detail.
- Use the Sharpen and Blur tools to make fine changes to contrast in your image, or smudge areas with the Smudge tool to control the direction and amount of blurriness.
- Let the Sponge tool increase or decrease saturation in an image's color to highlight areas or make them fade into the background.
- Use fuzziness levels to quickly select and replace color in an image.

PART V

From an Image to a Work of Art

GET THE SCOOP ON...
■ Applying filters ■ Selecting the right filter for the job ■
Working in the Filter Gallery ■ Using common effects ■
Adding 3D effects ■ Lighting an image

Getting to Know Filters

When you think of image editing, what's the first thing that comes to mind? For many people, it isn't the capacity to adjust levels or remove color casts. Instead, it's the ability to add interesting and clever effects to an existing image—such as making a photo look like a delicate watercolor or creating an image from scratch that ends up looking like textured artwork.

The many filters offered by Photoshop Elements are divided into two general categories, which you can read about in both this chapter and the next. Before you move on to the more artistic of the filters, which are covered in Chapter 16, you need to know about the more functional filters—the ones that improve an image's appearance and generally edit the content.

Starting out

Don't confuse filters with effects and styles. Sometimes, you can create the look of a filter with effects and styles, but they affect the image differently than filters do. Although it may seem that the terms are interchangeable, in Photoshop Elements each refers to a different method of image manipulation. You can read more about styles and effects in Chapters 11 and 12.

Inside Scoop

The differences lie in whether the change is configurable or not, what methods are used to apply the change, and the permanence of the change.

Here's what these terms mean:

- **Filter.** A filter changes the appearance of your overall image. For example, a filter may apply special lighting such as a spotlight, or rewrite the image information to sharpen the edges of the image's objects. Filters are the main subject of this chapter.
- **Effect.** An effect is applied to a layer to change its appearance, such as adding shadows, bevels, strokes, and overlays. If you edit the content of a layer after applying an effect, the effect changes as well. For example, if you apply a drop shadow effect to text on a layer and then change the text, the shadow changes automatically and shadows the new characters. Read about using effects with text in Chapter 17.
- **Style.** A style is a pre-configured change applied to a layer. You simply drag the style from the Styles and Effects palette to apply it. Just like effects, when an image is modified, the style changes as well. Styles are described in depth in Chapter 12.

Applying a filter

You can apply a filter in Photoshop Elements in numerous ways. The option you select depends on your preferred method of working and the complexity of the task you are trying to accomplish.

Choose filters from either 15 or 16 categories, depending on whether you are using filters from third-party developers. That seems like lots of categories—and it certainly is—but you are sure to find some filters that will become your favorites.

Watch Out!

If you choose the "All" option for the display of filters in the Filters pane of the Styles and Effects palette, the filters are arranged alphabetically, not by category. If you aren't sure of what you want to use, select an individual category first to narrow the choices.

Applying a filter from the Styles and Effects palette

My preferred method is using the Filters pane in the Styles and Effects palette. Follow these steps:

1. Choose Window ⇨ Styles and Effects, and drag the palette to dock it in the Palette Bin.

2. When you open the palette, the Styles pane is shown by default: Choose Filters from the palette's drop-down menu to display the Filters pane.

3. Click the right drop-down menu in the palette, and choose a filter category, listed in Table 15.1.

4. Scroll through the filters shown in the palette to find the one you want to apply. The Filters pane in the Styles and Effects palette shows all the available filters in the program; the palette is shown in Figure 15.1.

5. Drag the filter's thumbnail from the Styles and Effects palette, and drop it on your image.

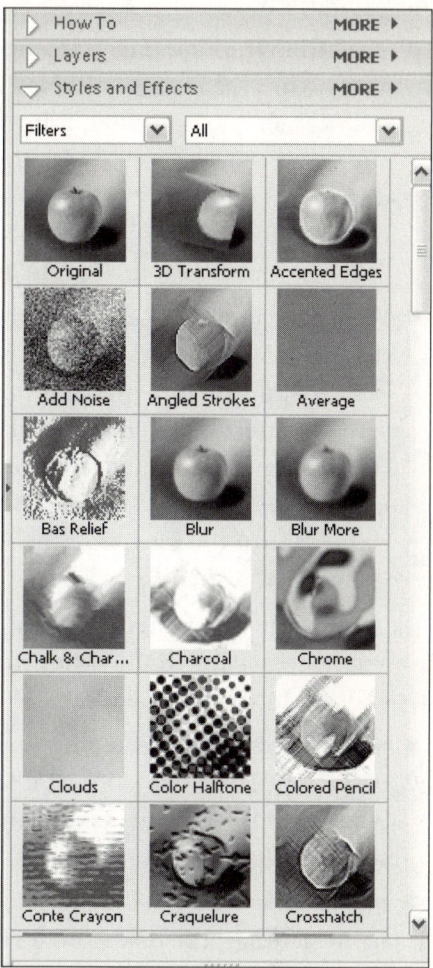

Figure 15.1. All the filters are listed in a pane of the Styles and Effects palette for easy access.

Inside Scoop

The method you choose also depends on how lazy — or efficient — you are. Is it worth the time to use a few mouse clicks to open a palette, for example, or is it easier to work from a menu?

Using menus to apply filters

If you prefer to work from a menu, you can apply a filter in either of these other ways:

- Work from the Filter menu by choosing Filter and then a filter category and the specific filter. For filters that don't have configuration options, such as a simple Blur filter, using the menu is the easiest option. And, after you become familiar with the program's filter options and know what you want to apply, the Filter menu can be a quick way to go. If you work from the Filter menu, you can apply as many filters as you like, but you must return to the Filter menu each time.

- Work from the Filter Gallery by choosing Filter ⇨ Filter Gallery to open the window. You see thumbnail examples of each filter as well as the effect of applying the filter to your image. You can apply filters in a series of effect layers, but not all filters are included in the Filter Gallery. For example, the Noise and Sharpen categories of filters aren't included in the Filter Gallery. The advantage of using the Filter Gallery is the control you have over the sequence of filters you want to apply.

The configuration location for a filter depends on the program's design. Regardless of whether you select a filter from the Filters menu or from the Filters pane in the Styles and Effects palette, what happens next depends on the individual filter.

- Some filters are applied automatically, and you have no configurable options. For example, if you choose Filter ⇨ Sharpen ⇨ Sharpen Edges, the areas of contrast change in the image are intensified automatically, and there are no settings for you to modify.

- Some filters, like the Blur filters, open a dialog box to let you configure settings; the dialog boxes usually have one or two controls for you to customize.

- The rest of the available filters have more complex settings, and are configured in the Filter Gallery. For those filters, dragging and dropping the thumbnail from the Filters pane in the Styles and Effects palette or choosing a filter from the Filters menu opens the Filter Gallery window.

Watch Out!

You can't change where a filter is configured in Photoshop Elements. For example, you won't open a command or a program preference if you want to configure a filter in the Filter Gallery as an option.

Watch Out!
Filters don't work on all images: Some won't work with grayscale images, and no filters work with Bitmap or Index Color images.

Identifying filter categories

The categories of filters and their general uses are listed in Table 15.1. Because the filters are divided into two chapters, the ones discussed in this chapter are listed first. The more artistic filters, talked about in detail in Chapter 16 are indicated by an asterisk (*) after the filter category's name.

Table 15.1. Categories of available filters

Category	Use These Filters For...
Adjustment filters	Adjustment filters offer similar actions to the Enhance menu's or the Adjustment layers' options for changing color, tone, and brightness in an image.
Blur filters	The Blur filters offer different methods of softening an image or a selected area.
Digimarc filter	Automatically read a Digimarc watermark using the Digimarc filter.
Noise filters	Add or remove scattered extra colored pixels using Noise filters. Add noise for further effects or to blend into other areas of an image; remove dust and scratches or other types of artifacts.
Render filters	The Render filters apply algorithms to create different patterns such as clouds, light, and refraction, and they create 3D shapes.
Sharpen filters	The Sharpen filters increase contrast between pixels in different ways, helping to decrease blur.
Video filters	The two Video filters remap an RGB image to the more-restrictive television color gamut or repair the way lines of pixels are drawn on an image captured from video.
Other filters	The Other filters category contains several filters that are used for specific tasks such as offsetting selections and adjusting colors.
Plug-in filters	If you install filters developed by companies other than Adobe, a Plug-in filters category is added to the menu.
Artistic filters*	The Artistic filters simulate the appearance of art created using traditional media, such as watercolor and oil.

continued

Table 15.1. *continued*

Category	Use These Filters For...
Brush Stroke filters*	The Brush Stroke filters produce a painterly look. Choose from a number of brush and ink stroke effects.
Distort filters*	Use the Distort filters to reshape the geometry of an image or create 3D effects.
Pixelate filters*	Clump pixels in different patterns based on color values using Pixelate filters.
Sketch filters*	Sketch filters are a group of artistic filters used to simulate hand drawing or to add texture.
Stylize filters*	The Stylize filters displace pixels and change the level of contrast to produce a painted effect.
Texture filters*	Texture filters add depth to an image by simulating different substances or materials.

Using the Filter Gallery

The Filter Gallery is a separate window provided for many types of filters in Photoshop Elements. The Filter Gallery window opens in response to choosing a filter from the Filters menu or from the Filters pane of the Styles and Effects palette. You can also open it manually by choosing Filter ⇨ Filter Gallery.

After the window is open, you can choose, configure, and preview one or more effects; and apply and reorder multiple effects for the same image. Figure 15.2 shows the preview area of the Filter Gallery showing an image of a water lily.

Figure 15.2. You can watch the preview change as you choose and display filters and their settings, such as the Sharpen Edges and Brush Stroke filters applied to the water lily in the figure.

Inside Scoop

If you add a filter and can't decide if you want to use it or not, leave it in place and hide it in the Filter Gallery. It's not shown in the image itself. If you change your mind later, you can reopen the Filter Gallery and show it again.

Adding filters

The Filter Gallery window allows for applying multiple filters to the same image, each of which can be configured separately in the Filter Gallery window.

Follow these steps to add a second and subsequent filters to an image:

1. Click the New Effect Layer button at the bottom right of the Filter Gallery window. A copy of the active filter is added to the list as a new layer, shown in Figure 15.3.

2. Leave the layer copy active, and choose your filter from the menu or click a thumbnail to change the layer copy to the selected filter.

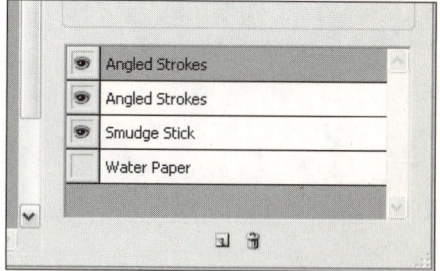

Figure 15.3. When you add a new effect layer, the active effect is copied; in the figure, the Angled Strokes effect was active when the New Effect Layer button was clicked.

3. Choose the settings for the new filter at the right of the Filter Gallery window.

Working in the Filter Gallery

Take your time exploring the Filter Gallery window and see how to effectively choose, configure, and arrange the best effects for your project. Here are some tips I've found helpful when working in the window:

- Drag in the preview area to reposition the image. If you are zoomed into the image, you can also position it using scrollbars.

- Use the zoom buttons under the preview area at the left of the window to change the magnification of the preview image and zoom in for a close look.

- Open the menus and click a thumbnail of a specific filter to apply it to the image, as shown in Figure 15.4.

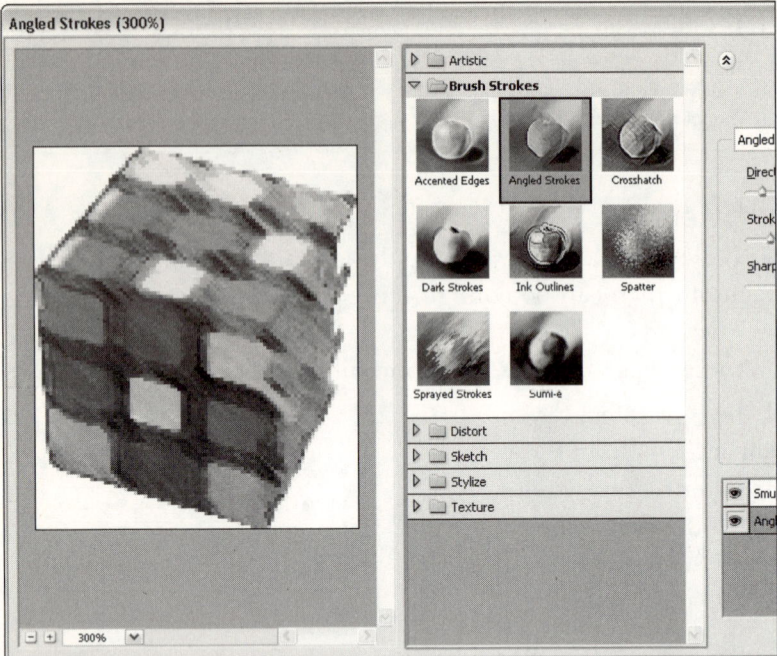

Figure 15.4. Choose a filter visually from the menus in the Filter Gallery window.

- If you are familiar with the filters offered in Photoshop Elements, toggle the Show/Hide button to the left of the OK and Cancel buttons to close the Filter menu and thumbnails view and show a larger preview area. In Figure 15.5, the Show/Hide button is toggled to the closed position.
- Choose filters from the drop-down menu in the filter configuration area at the right of the preview window. The filters are listed in alphabetical order, as you can see in Figure 15.5.
- The configuration settings for the active filter appear at the

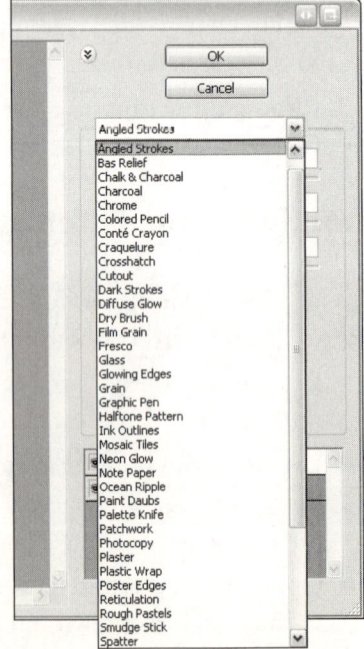

Figure 15.5. Choose and display filters and their settings in the right panel of the window.

right side of the window, shown in Figure 15.6. Drag the sliders or type values in the fields to change settings. The settings vary according to the filter you are working with. In Figure 15.6, the Angled Strokes filter is active, and its configuration settings are shown on the Filter Gallery window.

- Toggle filters off and on to see their effects. In Figure 15.6, notice that only two of the three filters used in the image are active. Active filters are indicated by a visible Eye icon.

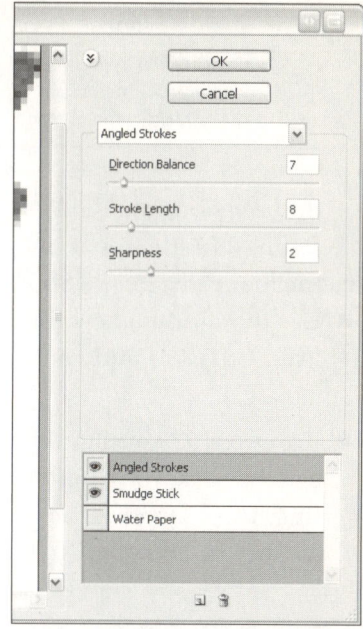

Figure 15.6. Choose and display filters and their settings in the right panel of the window.

Managing filters

One of the Filter Gallery's best features is the ability to experiment with different combinations and orders of effects. These tips may help you make your way through configuring, viewing, and ordering filters:

- Click the Eye icon next to a filter to hide the effect in the preview image.
- To remove a filter from the image, select it in the list and click the Delete Effect Layer button.
- Rearrange filters by dragging the name in the list to another position. Rearranging the order of filters can dramatically change the way your image looks, as you can see in Figure 15.7.

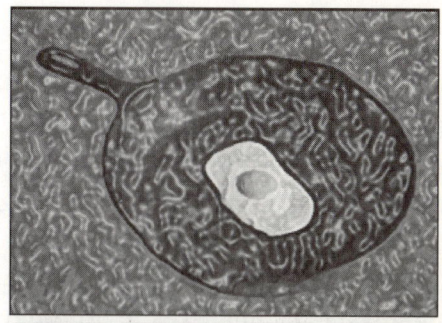

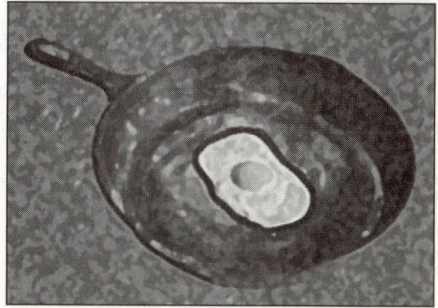

Figure 15.7. The order in which filters are applied makes a big difference in how the image looks.

Inside Scoop

Compare the appearance of the Show/Hide button in Figures 15.4 and 15.5. In Figure 15.4, the button's arrows are pointed upward instead of downward, and the Filter thumbnail menu is open in the Filter Gallery window.

Both versions use the Plastic Wrap and Sponge filters with the same settings. In the upper image, the Plastic Wrap filter is uppermost; in the lower image, the Sponge filter is uppermost.

- Use the shortcut keys for fast work in the Filter Gallery window. Press Ctrl+Z to undo an action; press Ctrl+Shift+Z to redo an action.
- If you realize you should have used a different setting three or four actions back, you don't have to restart the effect to correct the setting. You can move backward one action at a time in your filter settings by pressing Ctrl+Alt+Z.

Using Adjustment filters

The Adjustment filters are a group of filters that perform functions similar to those you can achieve with the Adjustment layer options, which are described in Chapter 12.

The difference between using a filter and applying an Adjustment layer using the same filter lies in how the processes behave with other image content. In the Layers palette, using an Adjustment layer applies the settings in the Adjustment layer to the image layer, letting you modify or change the image without affecting the image itself.

On the other hand, if you are applying an Adjustment filter, it is applied to an entire image or a selection, regardless of image layers. To remove a filter applied as an Adjustment layer, you simply delete the layer. When the filter is applied through the Filter menu, you have to undo the action to remove it.

- **Equalize.** The Equalize filter adjusts the brightness values of the pixels to redistribute the range of brightness levels. The filter distributes pixels either within a selection or for the entire image. This filter has no settings that you can adjust.

- **Gradient Map.** The Gradient Map filter applies a gradient map to change the image's pixel colors to those in the selected gradient. Select a gradient in the dialog box, and configure it as you like. By default, the shadows, midtones, and highlights of the image are mapped respectively to the starting color, midpoint color, and ending color of the gradient fill. You can add noise to smooth the fill by selecting Dither, or you can invert the fill by selecting Reverse.

- **Invert.** The Invert filter creates a negative image based on the brightness values of the image. The Invert filter converts the brightness value of each pixel to its inverse value on a scale of 256 steps. This means a pixel with a brightness value of 50 becomes a value of 156, a white pixel with a value of 256 becomes pure black with a value of 0, and so on. You can use the filter to simulate an image negative or make a positive from a scanned black and white negative.

- **Posterize.** The Posterize filter reduces the number of brightness levels in an image to 16 or fewer, reducing the number of colors and resulting in discrete blocks of color. Specify the number of tone or brightness levels in an image, and the filter maps pixels to the closest matching level producing large blocks of color. A Posterize filter can be set for up to 16 levels. The lower the number of levels, the fewer the colors and the larger the blocks of color. In Figure 15.8, the Posterize filter is applied to the image of the duck decoy (upper) using eight Posterize levels. You see the blocks of similar colors resulting from the filter in the lower image.

Figure 15.8. The Posterize filter decreases the color range in the image. The original image (top) uses a full range of color, which is condensed to blocks of color by applying the Posterize filter (bottom).

- **Threshold.** The Threshold filter simplifies the image to areas of black and white only, without gray. Use the Threshold filter to convert both color and grayscale images to high contrast black-and-white images. The Threshold value defines the level at which a color is mapped to either black or white. All pixels darker than the threshold are converted to black, and all pixels lighter than the threshold are converted to white. In Figure 15.9, the straw hat at the top of the image is remapped to only black and white. Using the Threshold filter applied with a value of 128 evenly divides the pixels in the image between black and white.

Figure 15.9. The Threshold filter maps images, like the straw hat at the top of the figure, to high contrast black-and-white versions, like that shown in the bottom image.

- **Photo Filter.** The Photo Filter applies one of numerous color filters to simulate different color and lighting conditions. The Photo Filter filter is the same as that accessed either through the Layers menu or through the Adjustment Layers options. The filter options include a series of warming and cooling filters as well as a number of different hue adjustment options. The filter applied to the image is the same whether you are using the Photo Filter filter from the Adjustment filters category or adding a Photo Filter Adjustment layer in the Layers palette. In fact, choosing an Adjustment layer or its equivalent Adjustment layer type opens the same dialog boxes to configure the settings.

Blurring image content with filters

The Blur filters don't launch the Filter Gallery window when you select them. Some open their own dialog boxes, while others are applied automatically. The Blurs and basic information about the filters is shown in Table 15.2.

> ### Finding an average
>
> As Table 15.2 explains, Average Blur replaces color with a new color representing the average of all colors in the selection or image.
>
> What's the point of finding an average? In some projects, the Average filter can save you time. Suppose you have an image that you want to use as part of a larger composition and need to find an appropriate color for graphic elements, backgrounds, text, and so on. Make a copy of the image, and apply the Average Blur filter to the copy. Then sample the color in the layer to find the precise color to use for complementing your image.

Table 15.2. Blurring image content

Blur Filter	How It Looks
Blur, Blur More	The image is softened using either the Blur or Blur More filters: The difference between the two is the degree of blurriness. You just select the filter to apply it because there are no settings to configure. Both the Blur and Blur More filters can be added several times to slowly decrease the contrast in the image or selection.
Average Blur	Average Blur replaces the content in an image or a selection with a color that is the average of all colors in the selection or image.
Gaussian Blur	Blur is applied using a Gaussian distribution pattern based on a specified radius setting.
Motion Blur	Blur is specified both by the amount as well as the direction in which it is applied.
Radial Blur	Soften an image by decreasing the contrast based on a specified center point.
Smart Blur	To use the Smart Blur, specify both the amount of blur as well as the amount of difference that must exist among pixels in order for the blur to be applied.

Four of the Blur filters can be customized using settings in dialog boxes. For example, you can configure the Blur filters to specify the amount and directions in which the blurs are applied as shown in the outer images in Figure 15.10. The original image without any filtering is shown in the center of the figure.

- **Gaussian Blur.** Gaussian Blur is probably the most common type of blur used. When you select the filter, the Gaussian Blur dialog box opens, shown in Figure 15.11. Drag the Radius slider right to increase the pixel value or left to decrease the value. The amount of blur refers to the area of pixels that are blurred together: A 10-pixel blur looks far softer than a 2-pixel blur. In Figure 15.10, the upper-left example of the image uses a Gaussian Blur with a 7-pixel blur radius.

- **Motion Blur.** When you apply a Motion Blur, you specify the length of the blur and its direction. In the upper-right image in Figure 15.10, the image is blurred at a distance of 15 pixels and set at −45 degrees. The angle blurs the pixels in the map toward the right bottom of the image.

Figure 15.10. Clockwise from the upper-left corner, the blurs applied are Gaussian Blur, Motion Blur, Smart Blur, and Radial Blur; the original image is shown in the center of the figure.

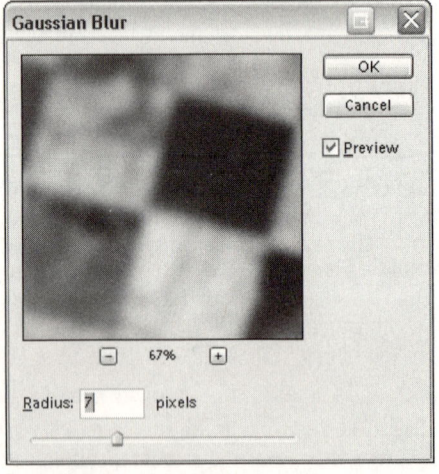

Figure 15.11. Configure the amount of blur by dragging the slider in the dialog box.

- **Radial Blur.** Radial Blur lets you decrease the contrast in an image and move the content around a center point. The filter is applied either as a spin clockwise around the center outward by choosing the Spin option, or from the center outward using the Zoom option. The example at the bottom left of Figure 15.10 uses the Spin Radial Blur at a distance of 30 pixels.

- **Smart Blur.** The Smart Blur filter is actually smart in that it lets you configure how an image will blur by specifying pixel characteristics and quality of blurring in the dialog box, shown in Figure 15.12, rather than simply applying general softening to the entire image or selection. You specify a radius in pixels to define how far the blur will extend and a threshold value to define how much different a pixel must be to be blurred. In the example shown in the lower-right of Figure 15.10, the Smart Blur uses a Threshold of 20 and a radius of 20. Choose a blur quality as well: Low, Medium,

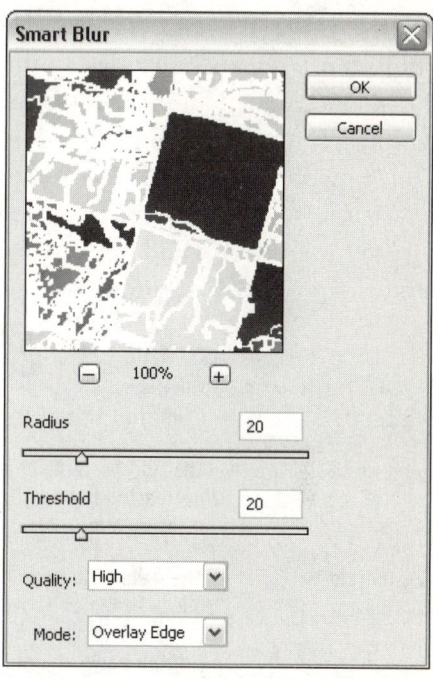

Figure 15.12. Configure the amount of blur by dragging the slider in the dialog box.

or High. You can also choose a mode for applying the blur. The Normal setting applies the blur to all the pixels that meet the other criteria. You can also specify an Edge Only and Overlay Edge option for the edges of color transitions; the example shown in Figure 15.10 uses the Overlay Edge option.

Bright Idea

Take the value of the Average Blur filter one step further by selecting areas in the image first and then sampling them to get a palette of colors for a project.

Bright Idea

For a quick and interesting effect, make two copies of your layer or image. Add a Smart Blur using one of the edge options to one copy and another Smart Blur using the Normal option to the other. Then decrease the opacity of the uppermost layer, and blend them.

Managing noise with filters

Photoshop Elements includes a number of filters used to manage *noise*, the inconvenient and unexpected sprinkle of pixels that can occur in different circumstances, ranging from sampling an image to capture errors. The Noise filters and their use are listed briefly in Table 15.3.

Chapters 13 and 14 describe the use of the Noise filters in depth as they are used to edit and improve the contents of an image; these chapters also include discussions on noise and other artifacts.

Table 15.3. Using Noise filters

Filter	Common Uses
Add Noise	The Add Noise filter adds random pixels to the image. Use it for decreasing banding in gradients, adding noise to touchups, or creating a texture.
Despeckle	The Despeckle filter detects edges and blurs everything but the edges to remove noise and preserve detail. Use it to remove noise resulting from scanning printed pages. In a scanned printed page, the noise results from the halftone dots used to print the page.
Dust & Scratches	The Dust & Scratches filter removes noise by recoloring unusually colored pixels. As a result, the image is slightly blurred as well.
Median	The Median filter blends the brightness of pixels in the selection. Use the filter to reduce artifacts, such as moiré and halos, described in Chapter 13.
Reduce Noise	Use the Reduce Noise filter to remove noise added to images captured by camera phones, like that shown in Figure 15.13. Use the filter to remove JPEG artifacts like blocks and halos created in low-quality JPEG images.

Figure 15.13. The Reduce Noise filter helps improve the appearance of noisy images (left) by smoothing the noise (right).

Sharpening using filters

Photoshop Elements includes a group of Sharpen filters used to increase the clarity and contrast in your images. Sharpen filters are described in detail in Chapters 13 and 14 in discussions on image correction and touch-ups.

Most of the Sharpen filters, listed in Table 15.4, are not configurable, but are automatically applied to the image when selected.

Table 15.4. Filters that sharpen images

Filter	Common Uses
Sharpen, Sharpen More	Neither the Sharpen filter nor Sharpen More filter is configurable. The difference is in the amount of sharpening applied by each application of the filter. Both increase the contrast between light and dark edges in an image.
Sharpen Edges	The Sharpen Edges filter is applied automatically. It finds the areas in the image where significant color changes occur and sharpens them without affecting the smoothness of the rest of the image. Before and after examples of the Sharpen Edges filter are shown in Figure 15.14. The image of the flower in Figure 15.14 shows how an image can be over-sharpened by applying the Sharpen Edges filter multiple times.
Unsharp Mask	The Unsharp Mask filter, described in detail in Chapter 13, is used to correct blurring that occurs from any sort of image processing from the capture itself to resampling. The Unsharp Mask filter lets you specify the characteristics of the edge detail.

Figure 15.14. The Sharpen Edges filter enhances the contrast at color changes without sharpening the rest of the image. The left shows the image before sharpening.

Changing images using video filters

There are two Video filters, each designed to solve a specific problem: De-Interlace and NTSC Colors filter. Sometimes, you have captured video of an event or other subjects, but you don't have any still images. If you extract single frames as still images, you see an unexpected pattern of horizontal lines throughout the image. This is called *interlacing*, and it results from the difference in how an image is drawn on a computer screen versus a television screen.

De-Interlace filter

Use the De-Interlace filter to replace either the odd or even scan lines with duplicated or interpolated image content, as shown in Figure 15.15. *Duplicated* content copies the image content in one scan line and pastes it into the scan line that is being removed. *Interpolation*, on the other hand, looks at two retained scan lines and then "splits the difference" to create content for the scan line that is to be removed.

NTSC Colors filter

When you display images on a television screen, you sometimes see bleeding colors, particularly red. The NTSC Colors filter decreases the color gamut in the image to make it viewable on a television screen without color bleeding. If you apply the filter to an image and compare it to the original, you notice the colors are more muted overall, which occurs because there are fewer colors in the NTSC gamut than the default RGB gamut.

Working with other filters

Photoshop Elements includes a group of filters, listed in Table 15.5, called Other filters. These are filters that don't belong in any specific category so they've been lumped together as Other.

The changes in an image produced by filters in this category can be subtle. Bypassing them on your quest for the perfect image can be easy, but they are a useful collection of filters and well worth the time to experiment with.

Table 15.5. Using other filters

Filter	Common Uses
High Pass filter	The High Pass filter works by removing some general detail while keeping edge detail where sharp color transitions occur.
Maximum and Minimum filters	The Maximum and Minimum filters replace a pixel's brightness with the highest or lowest brightness value of the surrounding pixels.
Offset filter	Use the Offset filter to move a selection or a layer horizontally or vertically according to the value you specify.
Custom filters	Configure and save your own custom filter settings based on pixel brightness levels.

Figure 15.15. A captured frame from a video shows horizontal lines (left) that are corrected using the De-Interlace filter (right).

Applying a High Pass filter

Table 15.5 explains what the High Pass filter does. That is, it leaves edge detail in areas of sharp color transition, but removes other detail. Are you wondering how that would look?

For the best results when applying the High Pass filter, make sure the image you are using has strong color contrast areas, like the collection of globes shown in Figure 15.16. Each globe in the collection is strongly colored and different from those next to it.

Figure 15.16. Apply the High Pass filter to an image with areas of strong color contrast, like this collection of globes.

Here's how to use the High Pass filter for a quick and easy way to add more definition to an image:

1. Open the image you want to work with and make a copy of the image layer. You apply the filter to the copy.

2. Choose Filter ➪ Other ➪ High Pass to open the High Pass dialog box.

3. Define the radius for the detail you want to preserve. To keep just the edge pixels, use a radius of 0.1 pixels. In the dialog box shown in Figure 15.17, the Radius for the example image is set at 10 pixels. In the preview area, you can see that the image is hazy, and there appear to be halos surrounding the objects.

Figure 15.17. Specify how much detail to keep in the image copy by setting the Radius.

4. Click OK to close the dialog box and apply the filter. A magnified area of the image is shown in Figure 15.18.

5. To complete the effect, select the copy in the Layers palette. Click the Blend mode drop-down arrow and choose Overlay.

> **Hack**
>
> High Pass works in the opposite way to the Gaussian Blur filter. You can use it to extract black and white from images, or to add extra information to an image by applying it to a copy of the image and blending it with underlying layers, like the effect described here.

Figure 15.18 shows magnified portions of the picture of the globes. Adding and blending a filtered copy of the image boosts the detail, shown in the right image, when compared to the original, shown in the left image.

Figure 15.18. The detail in the original image (left) is boosted when blended with a layer filtered with the High Pass filter (right).

Replacing pixel brightness with filters

The Maximum and Minimum filters replace a pixel's brightness with the highest or lowest brightness value of the surrounding pixels. You define the radius in which the pixels are compared.

The Maximum filter works like a *choke*, in that it spreads out white areas and chokes in black areas, as you can see in the left image in Figure 15.19. The Minimum filter works like a *spread* in that it spreads out black areas and shrinks white areas, shown in the right image in Figure 15.19.

> **Bright Idea**
>
> If you want to extract black and white from an image, use the High Pass filter first, and then use the Threshold adjustment filter or convert the image to a bitmap.

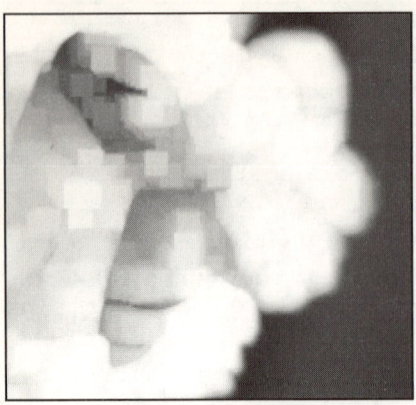 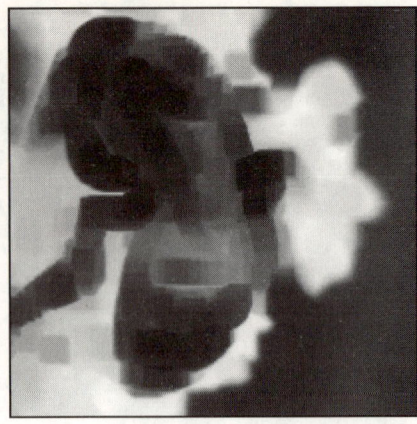

Figure 15.19. Concentrate brightness in an image using the Maximum filter (left); concentrate darkness using the Minimum filter (right).

Offsetting image content

The Offset filter might be one of those filters you don't think you would ever find a use for. It is designed to move a selection or a layer horizontally or vertically according to a specified value.

Here's a way you can use the filter for adding corner elements to an image. Follow these steps:

1. Open the image you want to modify and add a new layer. Move the object you intend to use for the corner element to one corner of your image.

2. Choose Filter ⇨ Other ⇨ Offset to open the dialog box shown in Figure 15.20. Specify a value for offsetting the pixels in the image on both the Horizontal and Vertical sliders. Watch the image as you adjust the numbers until the corners are even.

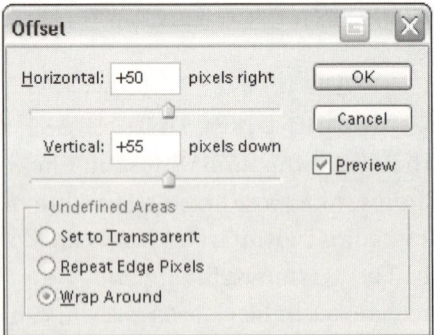

Figure 15.20. Adjust the offset amount and direction and how the offset pixels are handled in the dialog box.

3. Choose an option for the Undefined Areas by clicking one of the radio buttons. When the content is offset, an empty space occurs in

the original location. Use the Wrap Around option to create corner elements. The Set to Transparent option deletes the pixels that are wrapped while the Repeat Edge Pixels duplicates the pixels at the edge of the image and fills the empty space.

4. Click OK to close the dialog box and apply the filter. In Figure 15.21, the left image shows the file before the filter is applied with the group of diamonds set at the lower right of the layer. After applying the filter, the group of diamonds is split, and matching sections are shown at each corner.

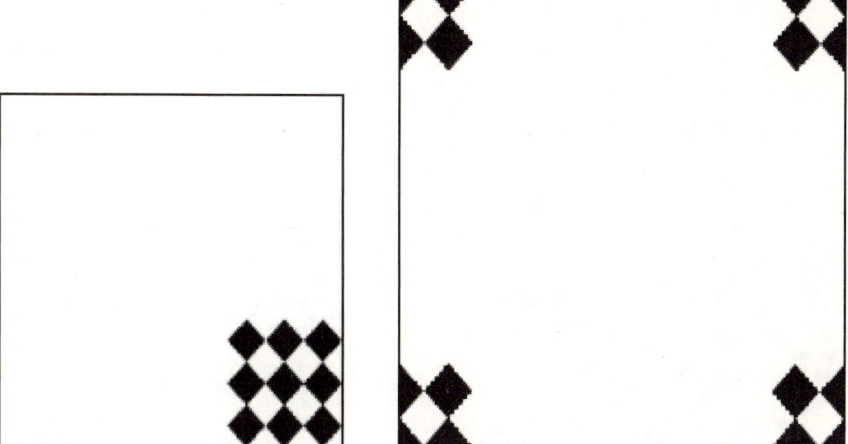

Figure 15.21. The original image (left) uses the Offset filter to split it into matching corner elements (right).

Building a custom filter

Choose Filter ➪ Other ➪ Custom to open a dialog box that lets you design your own effect. You specify brightness in each pixel, which is changed according the values of surrounding pixels by applying a mathematical formula.

Inside Scoop

The process of remapping the image mathematically is called *convolution*; the term is used in some programs to identify a mapping effect.

>  **Watch Out!**
> Be sure to save custom filters with a recognizable name, and in a location you will remember, such as inside the Photoshop Elements folder on your hard drive. There's no point in building and saving a custom filter if you can't find it or recognize it.

Select the layer, image, or selection you want to affect and follow these steps to design your own filter:

1. Choose Filters ⇨ Other ⇨ Custom to open the Custom filter dialog box, or select Custom from the Filters category of the Styles and Effects palette.
2. Type a value in the center text box from –999 to +999, to define how much you want to multiply the brightness of a pixel being tested by the program. The brightness is multiplied by 2 in the example filter shown in Figure 15.22.

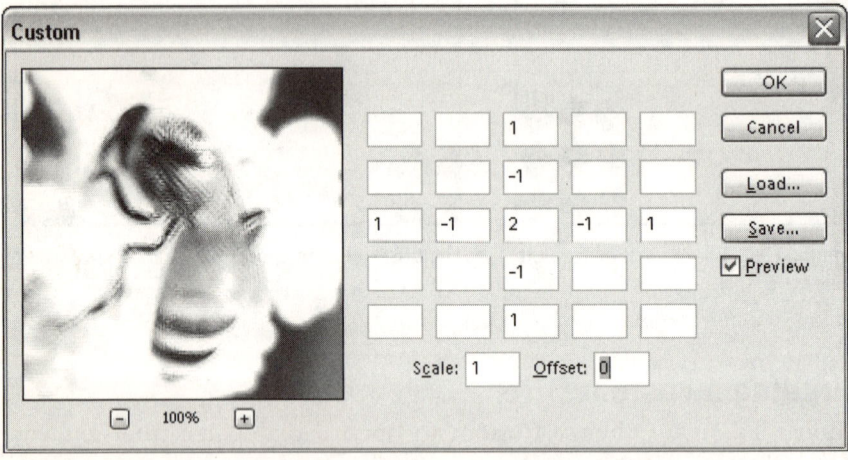

Figure 15.22. Define a matrix of pixel brightness calculations in the Custom filter's dialog box.

3. Click a text box identifying an adjacent pixel, and type a value you want to use for multiplying the pixel in that position. If you want to double the brightness, use 2, for example. In the sample, the brightness is set at –1, which makes the adjacent pixels darker.
4. Continue adding values in fields you want to include in the matrix. In the example, a second set of pixels is considered, using a brightness of 1.

5. Define the Scale for the filter. The brightness values for the pixels defined in the matrix are divided by the specified Scale. The example uses the default 1, which means the values are divided by 1 and won't change.

6. Enter a value to be added to the result of the scale calculation you created in the previous step in the Offset field. The example uses an offset of 0, which means the pixel isn't displaced.

7. Click OK to close the dialog box and apply the filter. Figure 15.23 shows the original image at the left, and the image after applying the custom filter at the right. The filter produces a much brighter image. The filter also results in a boxy hatched effect due to the varying brightness values entered in the filter's matrix in the Custom dialog box.

Figure 15.23. The original image, shown at the left, shows a brightness pattern when a custom pattern is applied, shown in the right image.

Detecting watermarks

Photoshop Elements contains one filter used for detecting a *watermark*, which is a digital way of signing images. Choose Filter ⇨ Digimarc ⇨ Read Watermark. If the image contains a watermark, the Digimarc ID, image attributes, and the year of copyright are displayed in an information dialog box.

Read more about using copyrights and watermarks in Chapter 23.

Rendering content with filters

Photoshop Elements includes a number of filters called Render filters. *Rendering* is different from the processing of other filters in that it isn't simply applying a filter to produce the effect. Instead, rendering is a process that creates something different from what originally existed.

Some of the rendering filters, such as the Clouds, Difference Clouds, and Fiber filters, are applied automatically or have very simple configuration dialog boxes. Others, such as the 3D Transform, Lens Flare, and Lighting Effects filters have much more complex configuration requirements.

For example, there are Render filters for producing clouds that look nothing like the original image, as you can see in the images in Figure 15.24. The left image shows the original picture of the bird, while the right image is the result of applying the Render Clouds filter: The foreground and background colors are combined to form blurry clouds, replacing the original image entirely.

Figure 15.24. Make a cloudy background or texture using Render filters such as the Clouds filter.

Rendering uses a geometric model, a lighting model, a camera view, and other image generation parameters and applies formulas to create images. Basic information about the Render filters offered in Photoshop Elements is listed in Table 15.6.

 **Inside Scoop**
The Digimarc company has a paid subscription service that costs from $79 to $499 per year that allows you to embed your own watermark in images.

Table 15.6. Rendering filter choices

Filter	How It Works
Clouds	Use the Clouds filter to generate a cloudy pattern using a range of values between the foreground and background colors.
Difference Clouds	The Difference Clouds filter uses the same method as the Clouds filter to generate a range of colors. When you apply the filter, some of the image color is inverted in the cloud pattern.
Fibers	The Fibers filter produces the appearance of woven fiber using the foreground and background colors.
3D Transform	The 3D Transform filter map converts your flat image to cubes, spheres, and cylinders that can be manipulated in three dimensions.
Lens Flare	The Lens Flare filter simulates the appearance of shining bright light into a camera lens.
Lighting Effects	The Lighting Effects filter is an advanced filter used to produce lighting effects on an RGB image. Effects can include multiple lights with separate properties and locations, and may include textures as well.

Making it cloudy

Two of the Render filters generate clouds. However, although the clouds are similar, how they are applied to the image is quite different. Both apply random color based on the color values between the foreground and background colors set in the toolbox. The similarity ends there.

The Clouds filter is shown in Figure 15.24; after the filter is applied, the original image is completely obscured. Contrast that with the image shown in Figure 15.25. Again, the bird is the subject of the image, but using the Difference Clouds filter produces an overlay of random colors, again using the range between the foreground and background colors set in the toolbox. In addition, some of the colors are inverted.

Figure 15.25. The Difference Clouds filter combines the rendered content with the original image using the foreground and background colors set in the toolbox.

Applying the Difference Clouds filter several times creates a different effect. Rib and vein patterns develop that resemble a stone texture, like that shown in Figure 15.26.

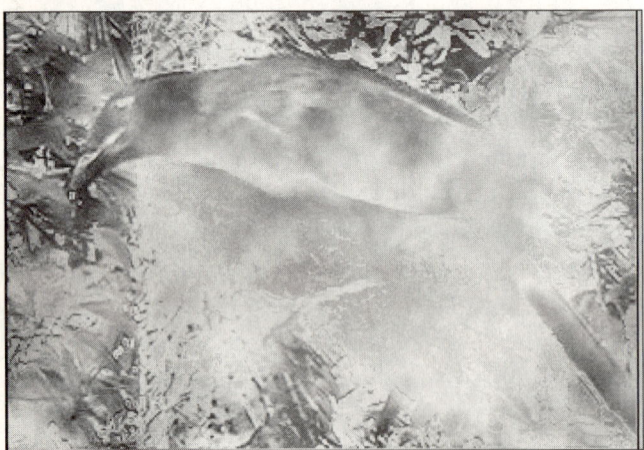

Figure 15.26. The Difference Clouds filter combines the rendered content with the original image.

Use the Difference Clouds filter to create very strong compositions. For example, copies of a repeating element can have sequential Difference Clouds filters added for an array of interesting color ways and color shifts.

> **Inside Scoop**
> You can generate sharper and higher contrast cloud patterns by pressing the Alt key as you apply the filter.

Texturing with fibers

Like the simple Clouds filter, the Fiber filter produces a rendered layer that is unlike the original image. Instead of clouds, the filter generates streaks of color based on the foreground and background colors in the toolbox.

With your image open in the Editor, follow these steps to use the Fiber filter:

1. Set the colors you want to use for the filter in the program's Foreground and Background color swatches on the toolbox. Click each swatch to open the Color Picker, choose the color you want to use, and click OK to close the Color Picker and change the color swatch.

2. Choose Filter ➪ Render ➪ Fibers to open the dialog box shown in Figure 15.27.

3. Adjust the Fiber filter's parameters in the Fiber dialog box as follows:

    - Control the range of colors by changing the Variance value. A low value uses longer color streaks; a high value produces short fibers.

    - Control the appearance of each fiber with the Strength option. A low value produces spread out fibers; a high value produces short clumped fibers.

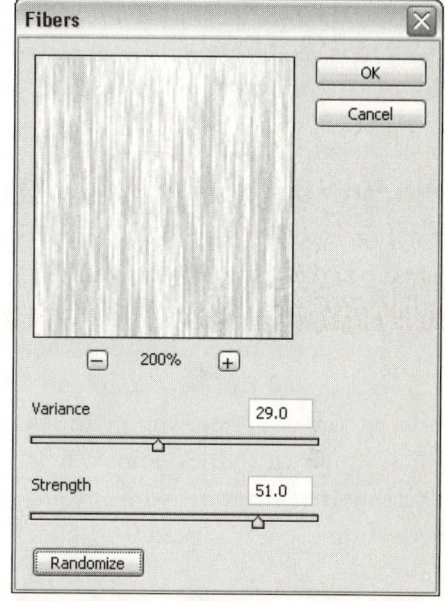

Figure 15.27. Change the content of the image by rendering fibers using the foreground and background colors in the program.

    - Click Randomize to modify the pattern's appearance; click repeatedly to cycle through a range of different patterns.

4. Click OK when you are pleased with the pattern to close the dialog box and apply the filter.

> **Bright Idea**
> Instead of using the foreground and background colors as the basis for the filter, use a gradient map as an adjustment layer to color the fibers. Read about adjustment layers in Chapter 12.

Figure 15.28 shows two examples of Fibers taken to extremes. The left image uses low Variance and Strength values; the right image uses high values.

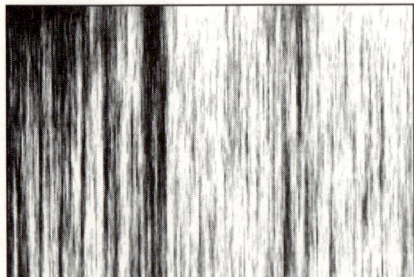 

Figure 15.28. The Fiber filter produces a randomized streaked fiber image. Low settings produce light streaking (left), and high settings produce densely packed, heavy streaking (right).

Placing an image in a 3D shape

You don't need to present your work using a flat, two-dimensional image when you can expand it into a 3D representation using the 3D Transform filter.

The filter represents your image as a three-dimensional shape called a *wireframe* that can be manipulated in a number of ways such as repositioning, resizing, or changing the perspective. Photoshop Elements offers three standard shapes, known as *primitives* that include a cube, sphere, and cylinder. You work with the image's layer in the 3D Transform dialog box using the tools listed in Table 15.7.

Table 15.7. 3D Transform tools

Tool	Tool Name	How It Is Used
▶	Select	Use this tool to select and move the entire wireframe object on the preview.
▷	Direct Select	Use this tool to select individual anchor points on the wireframe for manipulation.

Tool	Tool Name	How It Is Used
	Cube	This tool maps the image to a cubic surface.
	Sphere	This tool maps the image to a spherical surface.
	Cylinder	This tool maps the image to a cylindrical surface.
	Convert Anchor Point	Use this tool to convert a corner anchor point to a smooth anchor point, and vice versa.
	Add Anchor Point	Use this tool to place additional anchor points on the wireframe.
	Delete Anchor Point	Click an anchor point with this tool to remove it from the wireframe.
	Pan Camera	Use this tool to drag the image within the wireframe shape to reposition it.
	Trackball	Use this tool to rotate the image within the wireframe.

The toolbox also includes the Zoom and Hand tools, which aren't included in Table 15.7. If you are working with an advanced feature such as the 3D Transform filter, you should know already how to view an image!

Bending an image into shape

You can configure an image as a 3D form in numerous ways. Follow these general steps to get your image into shape:

1. Open your image and select the layer you want to configure to a 3D shape.
2. Choose Filter ⇨ Render ⇨ 3D Transform to open the 3D Transform dialog box. You see the active layer in the image shown in the dialog box's preview area in black and white.
3. Click one of the 3D wireframe tools in the toolbox, described in Table 15.7, and drag it over the preview to create the basic primitive. The shape is drawn as a series of green lines with connectors or *anchor points* at corners or along the shape's outline. Use the Cube tool to draw a cubic surface; the Sphere tool to draw a globe shape; the Cylinder tool to draw a cylindrical surface. The example starts from a Cylinder shape, shown in Figure 15.29.

Figure 15.29. Use one of the pre-configured wireframe shapes as a starting point.

4. Click the Select tool from the toolbox, and drag the wireframe over the surface of the image to reposition it if necessary. If you size the wireframe shape incorrectly, click it with the Select tool, and press Delete. Then redraw the shape again.

5. Move the object within the wireframe if necessary using the Pan Camera tool. You can drag the wireframe to a different location on the image, as shown in Figure 15.30. Release the mouse to reposition the image.

Figure 15.30. The Pan Camera tool moves the content within the wireframe's margins; drag the wireframe with the tool to reposition it on the image.

Inside Scoop

The 3D Transform filter works on a single layer only. If you want to use more than one layer for the filter, use a flattened copy of your image.

 **Inside Scoop**

You can use the Direct Selection tool to resize the shape by clicking and dragging an anchor point with the tool. Or, you can press Delete to remove the shape and redraw it. Sometimes it's faster to delete and start again, especially at the early stage of the design.

6. Your image is shown flat against the wireframe in the 3D Transform dialog box, but you can reposition it so it is angled by dragging in any direction with the Trackball. In the example shown in Figure 15.31, the image is tipped forward slightly toward the camera.

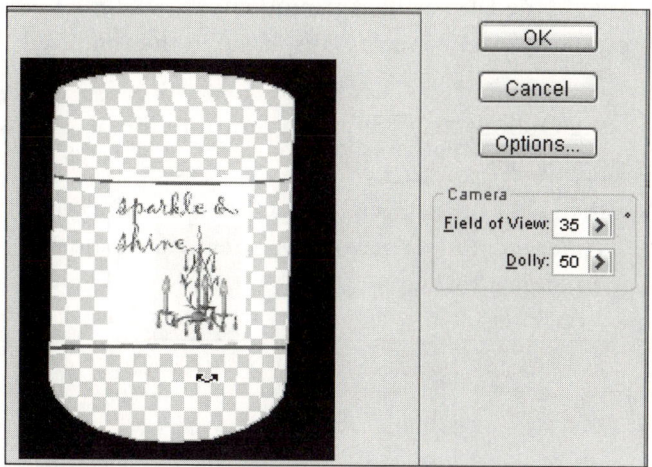

Figure 15.31. Rotate the image inside the margins of the wireframe using the Trackball tool.

7. Make adjustments to how the wireframe is shown in the finished image when the Pan Camera or Trackball tools are active by setting Camera options. The example uses the default values; the two Camera settings include:

- **Field of View.** Click the arrow to display the slider and drag to reset the Field of View in degrees, moving the image closer or farther away from the wireframe, and consequently wrapping more or less of the image on the wireframe. The default view is set at 35 degrees.

- **Dolly.** Click the arrow to display the slider and drag to reset the Dolly value, which defines where the 3D camera is in relation to the image. The default value is 50; set a lower value to move the camera closer to the image, making it appear larger; set a higher value to move the camera away from the image, making it appear smaller.

8. Click Options to open a dialog box to specify rendering options, including:

   - **Resolution.** Click the drop-down arrow and choose Low, Medium, or High resolution rendering. The higher the resolution, the more crisp the rendered image. If your image is very large, a high rendering resolution will take much longer than a low rendering resolution.
   - **Anti-aliasing.** Click the drop-down arrow and choose None, Low, Medium, or High to specify how much smoothing is applied to the image as it is rendered.
   - **Background.** Toggle the Display Background check box to define whether the rest of the layer's image is displayed in the rendered image.

9. Click OK to close the Options dialog box and return to the 3D Transform filter's dialog box.

10. When you are satisfied with the preview, click OK to close the dialog box. The image is rendered and displayed in its new shape, shown in the right image in Figure 15.32.

Figure 15.32. The label (left) takes on the shape of the cylinder wireframe (right).

 **Watch Out!**
You can't save or restore the settings used for the 3D Transform filter. Be sure that you are satisfied with the appearance before closing the filter's dialog box. Otherwise, you have to reopen the dialog box and start again.

Reshaping the wireframe

The example image started out as a cylinder. The cylinder's shape is composed of two vertical line segments connecting two parallel oval shapes. But, say you want to reshape that boring straight-sided cylinder into a bottle? You can — and you can make a multitude of other shapes as well. But, to get you started in the right direction, try my method outlined here.

1. Select the Add Anchor point tool in the toolbox, and click the vertical line at the right side of the cylinder below the upper oval, and again about halfway down the side of the cylinder to add two anchor points, as shown in Figure 15.33. Anchor points are always added as angled nodes.

2. Look closely at the two anchor points you have added. An anchor point that produces a sharp corner uses

Figure 15.33. Add additional anchor points to use for shaping the bottle.

a diamond-shaped node, while one that produces a smooth curve shows a round node. The upper anchor point added should be sharp, and the lower should be round. Change the style of the

 **Inside Scoop**
Remove an unnecessary anchor point you added manually using the Remove Anchor Point tool.

anchor point from a sharp angle to a smooth curve by clicking it with the Convert Anchor Point tool. The anchor points that make up the original cylinder are square, and can't be converted.

3. Click the Direct Selection tool in the toolbox, and drag the anchor points on the wireframe to the left to decrease the width of the oval at the top, and form the neck and body of the bottle (see Figure 15.34).

4. Make any final adjustments to the image — check out the steps for building the basic cylinder in the previous section to read about adjustments to the wireframe and image, such as changing the Camera settings or Render options.

5. Click OK to close the dialog box and apply the filter to finish the bottle's shape, shown in Figure 15.35.

Figure 15.34. Adjust the new and existing anchor points to finish the bottle shape.

Figure 15.35. The image of the label is wrapped over the bottle shape.

Using a lens flare

After you have constructed a 3D representation for your image, add some simple light using a lens flare, which is a rendered filter that simulates the reflected lights you sometimes see in images from camera flashes.

The Lens Flare filter lets you specify the flare brightness, flare location, and flare or lens shape. Follow these steps to apply a lens flare to simulate a highlight in a sphere:

1. Choose Filter ➪ Render ➪ Lens Flare to open the Lens Flare dialog box, shown in Figure 15.36.
2. Choose a type of lens, such as a 35mm or zoom lens. The example shown in Figure 15.37 uses a Movie Prime lens type.
3. Drag the Brightness slider to adjust the amount of light, which can vary from 10 percent to 300 percent. At 10 percent Brightness, the light is barely visible; at 300 percent Brightness, the entire image is replaced by white light. The example uses 150 percent Brightness.

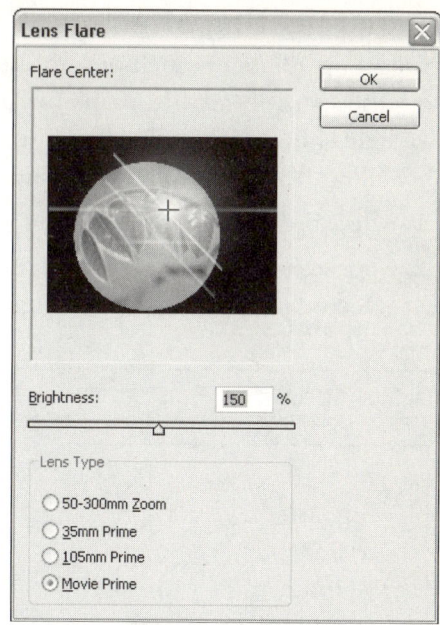

Figure 15.36. Choose a type and strength of flare and its location in the dialog box.

4. Click the image to reposition the lens flare's location, indicated by a (+) marker on the preview area.
5. Click OK to close the dialog box and apply the lighting.

The sphere shown in the left image in Figure 15.37 is interesting, but it could use a bit of light. The image at the right shows the same sphere, but it now sports some lens flares.

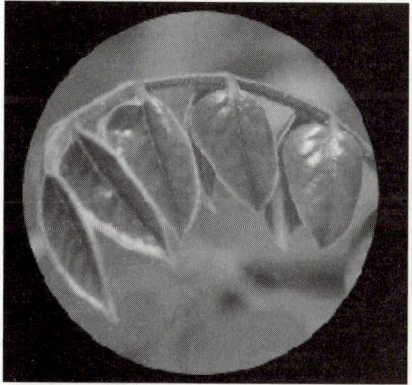 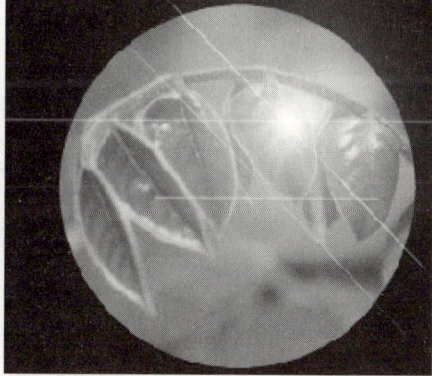

Figure 15.37. Add some sparkle to an image (left) by adding a lens flare (right).

Adding lighting effects

Photoshop Elements includes an advanced lighting filter. In addition, you also can use texture maps for producing more interesting effects, like light shining through a lace curtain or a slatted blind.

Follow these steps to add lighting effects to an image:

1. Select the content to which you want to apply the filter.
2. Choose Filter ➪ Render ➪ Lighting Effects to open the Lighting Effects dialog box, shown in Figure 15.38.

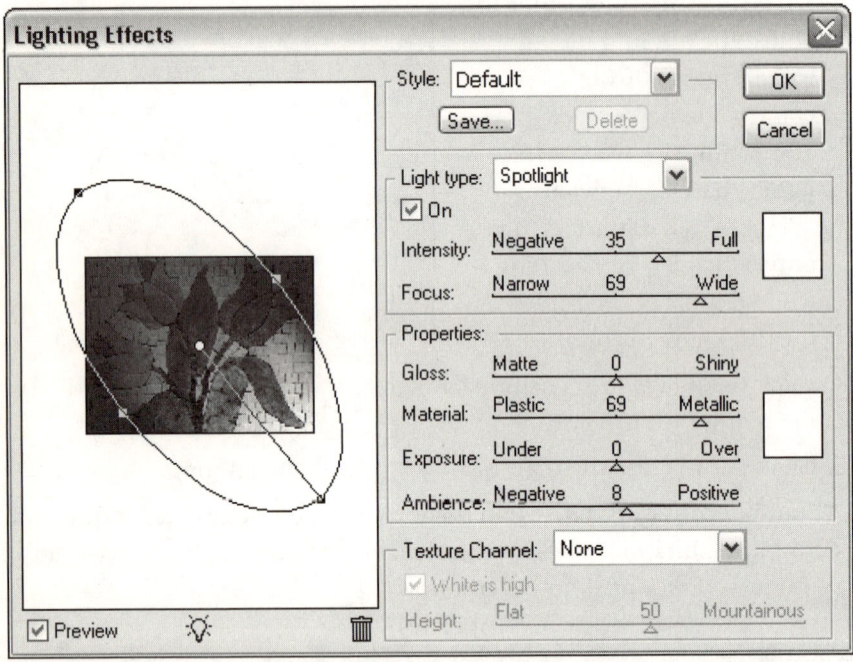

Figure 15.38. Configure rendered lights in the Lighting Effects dialog box.

3. Choose from over a dozen lighting styles in the Style drop-down menu; read about the lighting styles in the next section. The example uses the Soft Spotlight style.
4. Choose a type of light from the Light type drop-down menu. Select from a Spotlight, Directional, or Omni light. The example shown in

Bright Idea

If you make a lighting effect that you think you may reuse at a later time, save it as a new style. It is added to the filter's Style menu. If you change your mind, select the custom style from the menu and click Delete to remove it.

Figure 15.39 uses the Spotlight type of light.

5. Position the light as desired on the image shown in the preview area by dragging from its center point. In the Preview shown in Figure 15.39, you see most of the image is lit, with the focus at the center of the image.

In the Lighting Effects filter, you can use up to 16 lights with different properties and locations for each light.

6. Resize the light or adjust its direction using the handle or handles on the periphery of the light. As you reposition a light, you see both its original location and where it will be placed when the mouse is released.

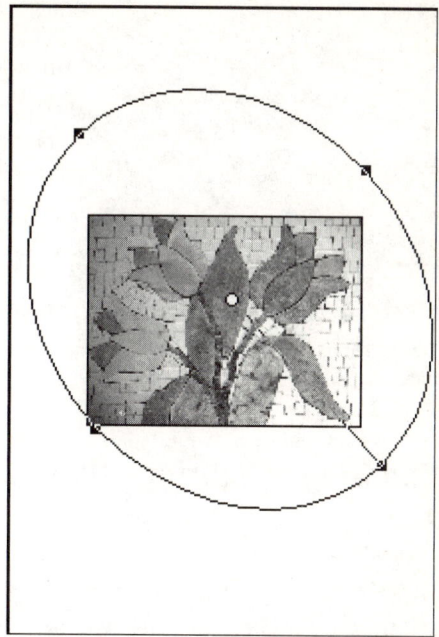

Figure 15.39. Choose options and adjust the light's features in the preview area.

7. Modify the color, intensity, and focus of the light according to the look you are trying to achieve.

8. Depending on the effect you are trying to achieve, change the properties by defining how glossy the image is, how reflective the surface is, the degree of exposure, and how much ambient light is in the image. Read more about properties later in the chapter.

9. Emphasize detail in the image using a Texture Channel that defines areas where the light is intensified or darkened. The Texture Channel options are based on color channels and layers in the image, and used to mimic texture in the subject, like the tile in the example. Select a color channel from the Texture Channel drop-down menu and specify how the light is applied based on the selected color channel. In the example, the Red channel is selected and used to emphasize the tile shapes in the image.

10. Click OK to close the dialog box and apply the lighting. Figure 15.40 shows the original image at the left, and the same image at the right after applying the spotlight and texture.

Figure 15.40. A basic image (left) can be dramatically enhanced by using some customized light effects (right).

Choosing a lighting style

Take some time to experiment with the lighting styles. Photoshop Elements includes more than a dozen styles that range from the default white spotlight, which has a medium intensity and wide focus, to sets of spotlights and sets of groovy little colored lights. Each style can be used as-is, or it can be modified for building custom styles.

Figure 15.41 shows examples of three styles of lights. The left image shows a simple omni light style, the center shows one of the multiple light styles, and the right image shows a sequence of omni lights using different colors.

The Default lighting style is applied when you open the Lighting Effects filter's dialog box. Click the Style drop-down arrow, and choose a style from the menu, which includes several types of spotlights, directional or general lighting, and colored lights.

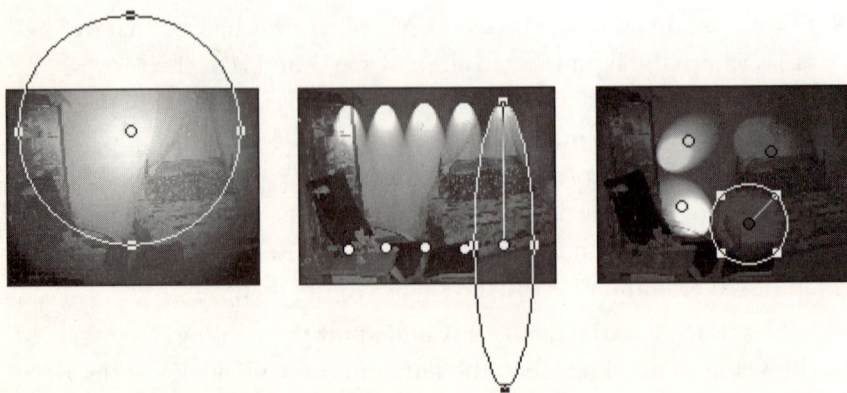

Figure 15.41. Use or start from one of numerous preconfigured Style options. From left to right, the examples shown are the Soft Omni, Five Lights Down, and Four Colored Lights styles.

After you select a basic style, you can modify its characteristics. Choose one of these options to specify the settings for the light's options:

- Click On to toggle the light on or off in the preview.
- Specify the light's brightness using the Intensity value.
- Specify the beam's width using the Focus value, or drag any of the four points making up the beam's area. The omni light type has no Focus option, but can be modified by moving the beam area's points.
- Click the color swatch to choose a custom color in the Color Picker so you can change the color of the light.

Specifying a reflective surface

The surface of your image can be modified in the Properties section of the Light Effects dialog box. By specifying reflection characteristics, you can produce more realistic results. Keep in mind, however, that Photoshop Elements isn't a 3D modeling program, but it does handle basic properties well, such as lighting a glossy surface more sharply than a matte surface.

These choices are used to customize a reflective surface:

- **Gloss.** The Gloss value defines how much light is reflected based on the surface reflection. Drag the slider from Matte to Shiny to change from low to high reflectance. The vases in the left image in Figure 15.42 are matte, while the same vases in the right image are shiny.
- **Material.** Drag the slider between the Plastic and Metallic options. Plastic material reflects the color of the

Figure 15.42. Specify a matte surface (left) or a shiny surface (right) for the selection or image.

light, while Metallic material reflects the color of the object. Using the highest Plastic value looks much the same as using the highest Shiny value for the Gloss property; while using the highest Metallic value looks much the same as using the highest Matte value for the Gloss property.

- **Exposure.** Drag the slider right to increase exposure or left to decrease exposure. At 0, the exposure uses the image's own exposure.

- **Ambience.** General lighting in a space or room is called *ambient* light. Drag the Ambience slider in the Properties area of the Lighting Effects dialog box from its default location at a value of 0 percent to specify how much of the light used in the image is ambient. Drag right to a value of +100, which makes the ambient light a very strong and predominant light source. The lower the value below 0, the more diffused the light until it disappears altogether and the image is black. The example shown in Figure 15.43 uses the default spotlight style. The original image is shown at the left, the center image shows an Ambience value of 50, and the right image shows the effect of using a −20 value.
- **Color.** Click the color swatch to open the Color Picker, and specify an ambient light color other than the default white.

Figure 15.43. Specify the general illumination of the space or image using an ambient light value. The original image (left) is much brighter when a positive Ambience level is applied (center). The image virtually disappears using a negative Ambience value (right).

Tips for adjusting lights

After you have added and colored your lights, you can modify them in a number of ways:

- Drag the center circle to move any sort of light.
- Drag the handle at the end of the line to change the direction of a directional light such as a spotlight. Press the Ctrl key and drag to maintain the height of the light.
- Drag the handle at the end of the line in the direction of the line to change the height of a directional light. Keep the angle constant by pressing the Shift key as you drag.
- Drag one of the handles defining the edges of the light to change the size of an omni light.
- Drag one of the handles to rotate the light or stretch the ellipse of a spotlight.

You can also reuse existing lights using one of these options:

Lighting a group of objects

To light the components of an image more realistically when they are flat images without any reflection, such as sketches, use selections and apply the same light with varying reflective properties. Simplify the task by configuring the light for the first object, saving a style, and then reapplying the style and modifying surface textures.

Inside Scoop

The impact of changing the Ambience setting depends on which light style and type is used.

- Copy any of the lights currently in the preview, and reuse them. Click the light in the preview to select it, and then press Alt and drag a copy of the light into its new position.
- Select a light for deletion in the preview area, and drag it to the Trash or press Delete.
- As you modify lighting, try pressing the Shift or Ctrl keys to maintain one of the light's parameters. For example, press Ctrl and drag to maintain the height of a spotlight as you change its direction.

Using texture

Create interesting texture effects as part of the other lighting configurations working with the pre-existing texture channel menu options in the Lighting Effects dialog box.

Figure 15.44 shows the before and after versions of the same image. Both images use the same lighting style applied in the Lighting Effect filter's dialog box. The right image uses texture applied in the Green channel to control the light in the image The White is High option is deselected with a height of 50. You also see in the right image that light is added to only the brightest areas of the image.

Bright Idea

Adjust a light at any time regardless of whether it is colored correctly or not. Sometimes, I color a light first before resizing its range; other times, I want the lights in the correct locations first. It depends on the image, the impact of the light, and sometimes my mood!

>  **Inside Scoop**
>
> You can also apply texture along with lighting by using a texture map on a separate layer. Read about using textures in Chapter 16; read about using layers in Chapters 11 and 12.

Figure 15.44. Choosing texture in a channel defines what colors in the image are lit. The original image (left) is uniformly lit, while the right image shows the effect of using a Green texture channel.

You have these choices for creating more texture in your image:

- Click the Texture Channel drop-down arrow, and choose the red, green, or blue color channel options. The channel is used to manipulate light reflections.
- Select the White Is High option to raise the lightest parts of the selected color channel from the surface. If you want to lift the darkest areas of the surface, deselect the option.
- Specify the Height by varying the depth of the texture. The range extends from Flat with a value of 0 to Mountainous with a value of 100.

Just the facts

- Apply a filter through one of the filter's dialog boxes, in the Filter Gallery, or by choosing the filter in the Styles and Effects palette.
- Adjustment filters are similar in function to adjustment layer functions.
- Noise and blurs can be managed using a variety of filters.
- Numerous filters produce different rendered effects, ranging from creating clouds to adding a lens flare.
- Wrap an image on a 3D surface by using the 3D Transform filter.
- Construct and configure lighting using the Light Effects rendering filter.

GET THE SCOOP ON...
■ Distorting image geometry ■ Using artistic filters ■
Applying textures ■ Creating and adding backgrounds ■
Simulating action and art with filters

Finessing with Filters

Sometimes the biggest kick for a Photoshop Elements aficionado is stumbling across a combination of filters or settings that makes you sit back and enjoy the view. Your "Wow!" moment can come when the cover of a photo album is tinted the perfect green ocean color you remember from your vacation, or you collaged several family pictures into a neat group gift.

It's all about the "wow." This chapter gives you some simple guidelines with which you can enhance the message in an image, change its appearance, or produce some truly art-like images using one or more Photoshop Elements filters.

Before you start

Decide what you want to do before you start looking for a filter. Different filters applied to the same source material can create vastly diverse outcomes as shown in the four quadrants of the image in Figure 16.1.

Do you want to unify the appearance of several different images? Maybe you want to create a "painting" from one of your favorite images. Or perhaps you want to draw attention to an element in an image. You can achieve these tasks and more using filters.

If you are new to filters, go back a chapter and review Chapter 15. It describes using filters and effects for specific purposes, such as adjusting color, contrast, sharpening, and adding blurs to correct and enhance images.

Figure 16.1. The same image can look very different depending on the filters you apply. The image uses the Watercolor filter (upper left), the Angled Stroke filter (upper right), the Mezzotint filter (lower left), and the Find Edges filter (lower right).

Basic Distort filters

The Distort filters are filters that modify the geometry of an image's objects. Filters such as Spherize and Twirl distort the content around an axis using custom settings. Others distort content using different points such as edges of the image. Figure 16.2 shows the same image using the Glass filter at the left and the ZigZag filter at the right.

The complexity of the Distort filters varies depending on how the filter distorts the structure of the image. The Distort filters using a simple type of structural distortion are listed in Table 16.1.

Watch Out!
Don't let yourself get confused with the filters; the point is that each Distort filter affects the image's geometry. Think of the image as a piece of elastic paper rather than a flat solid substance, and you'll more quickly understand what the filters can do.

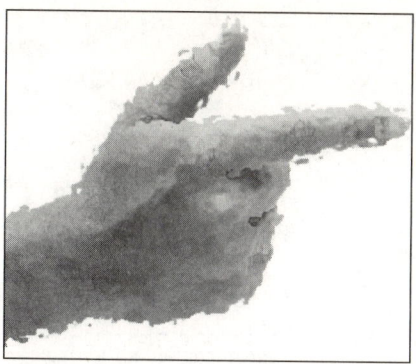 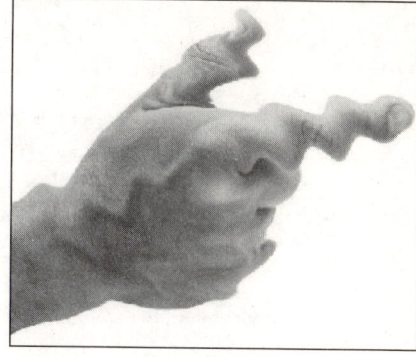

Figure 16.2. Distort filters modify an image's geometry to produce effects such as the glassy appearance in the left image or the creepy alien appearance in the right image.

Many of the Photoshop Elements filters can be configured and applied in combination in the Filter Gallery, a separate window that opens by choosing Filter ⇨ Filter Gallery. Not all filters are included in the Filter Gallery—of the Distort filters, only the Diffuse Glow, Glass, and Ocean Ripple filters are configured in the Filter Gallery dialog box.

Table 16.1. Simple Distort filters

Filter	How It Looks	Configuring the Filter
Diffuse Glow	The Diffuse Glow filter gives the image a soft, glowing appearance, achieved by using white noise and fading the glow from the center of the image outward.	Adjust the graininess, the amount of glow, and how clear the image is overall in the Filter Gallery.
Glass	The Glass filter creates the appearance that your image is behind glass. Several glass textures are available, including glass block or frosted glass.	Adjust the glass appearance further by adjusting the smoothness, scale, and distortion.
Ocean Ripple	Add randomly spaced ripples to the image making it look as if it is under water using the Ocean Ripple filter.	Adjust the magnitude and size of each ripple to simulate more or less turbulence.
Pinch	Use the Pinch filter to put the squeeze on an image, like the example in Figure 16.3.	Drag the slider right to pinch the image inward or left to pull the image outward.

continued

Table 16.1. *continued*

Filter	How It Looks	Configuring the Filter
Polar Coordinates	An image is converted from its default rectangular coordinates to polar coordinates, shown in Figure 16.4, using the Polar Coordinates filter.	Choose whether to wrap the image Polar to Rectangular, or Rectangular to Polar for opposite effects.
Ripple	Create a surface such as ripples on a pond using the Ripple filter.	You can adjust the number and size of the ripples. If you want to configure the ripples more, use the Wave filter instead (see Table 16.2).
Twirl	Use the Twirl filter to rotate an image around a center point. The amount of rotation decreases outward from the center point.	Specify whether the image twirls clockwise or counter-clockwise, and how many revolutions are included in the effect.
ZigZag	The ZigZag filter produces a regular up and down angular pattern. The effects of using the ZigZag filter are shown in the lower image in Figure 16.2.	The filter's appearance is specified as an amount of distortion based on a radius.

Because some of these filters are difficult to visualize just by reading a description, I have included more information and images for a select few:

- **Pinch.** The Pinch filter works well in an image like the one in Figure 16.3 because additional layers blur the detail around the dog, focusing the viewer on her face — and her glasses.
- **Polar Coordinates.** You can see the stunning effect of the Polar Coordinates filter in Figure 16.4 on the right image of the dragonfly and some grasses. At the upper center of the filtered version, you see a line where the left and right edges of the image are wrapped to one another. Instead of the image being mapped to a four-sided rectangle, it is mapped to two poles.

Figure 16.3. With apologies to my dog, use the Pinch filter to squeeze an image inward (as in the left image) or outward (as in the right image).

Figure 16.4. Polar Coordinates remaps the image from a four-sided image (left) to a polar image around a central axis (right).

- **ZigZag.** When you use the ZigZag filter, keep in mind that the filter uses an amount of distortion over a specified area. Set the Amount to define the distortion's level and direction; set the Ridges value to define how many zigs occur from the center to the edge of the

Bright Idea

Consider using a copy of your image with the Polar Coordinates filter applied as a pattern or background when you need something that coordinates with your subject's color range. The more similar the content at both left and right sides, the less able you are to see the edge, which is seen at the upper center of the filtered image.

> **Inside Scoop**
> I can't explain which is the "Zig" and which is the "Zag." One unit is composed of one zig and one zag. Which is up and which is down is an unknown, but because you get equal numbers of each, it's a moot point.

image. The three sets of crayons shown in Figure 16.5 use the same Amount and Ridge values. Their styles (the direction in which the zigs and zags are displaced) are different. From left to right, the Style displacement option used is around the center, out from the center, or toward the upper left or lower right.

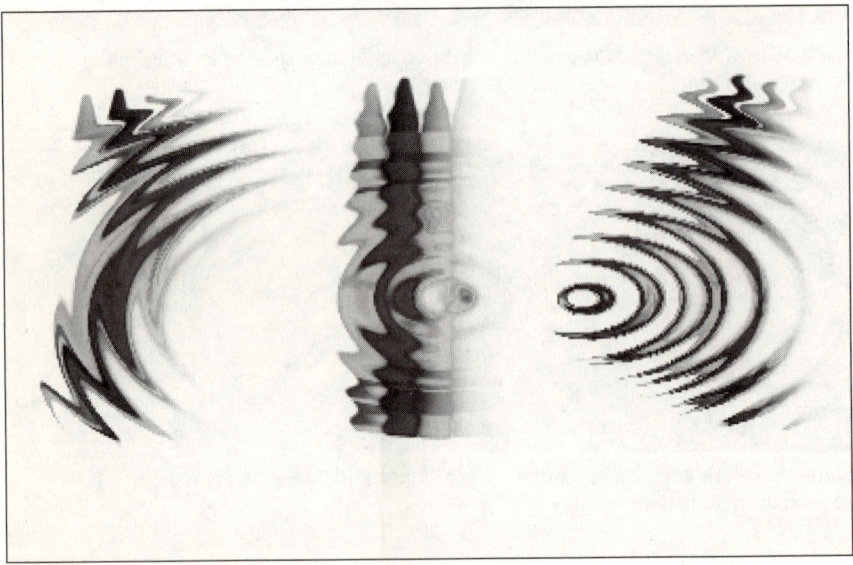

Figure 16.5. A ZigZag filter spreads a specified amount of distortion over a specified area.

More complex Distort filters

One specific group of the Distort filters can involve a considerable amount of configuration. These complex filters are described in Table 16.2. Because the following discussion describes how to use the filters in depth, there aren't any configuring details in the table.

Table 16.2. Complex Distort filters

Filter	How It Looks
Spherize	Use the Spherize filter to warp an image in a convex or concave shape.
Shear	The Shear filter creates a distortion by bending an image along a defined curve.
Wave	The Wave filter creates a wavelike pattern. You can use different types of wave forms and configure them in a number of ways.
Displace	You can precisely control how a layer or selection is displaced or shifted on the image using an image called a *displacement map*.
Liquify	In the Liquify filter's window, your image behaves as if it was soft and malleable, and can be smeared in different ways with the tools.

Wrapping an image with a sphere

For an interesting 3D effect, use the Spherize filter to warp an image in a convex or concave shape. The Spherize filter's dialog box is much less complex and more intuitive than using the 3D Transform filter's window, but creates a simple and quick shape distortion.

Select the content to which you want to apply the effect, choose Filter ⇨ Distort ⇨ Spherize to open the Spherize dialog box shown in Figure 16.6.

Specify the sphere settings doing the following:

- **Specify the Amount.** A positive value stretches the image around a spherical space producing a convex appearance; a negative value compresses the image to the interior of a spherical space, producing a concave appearance.

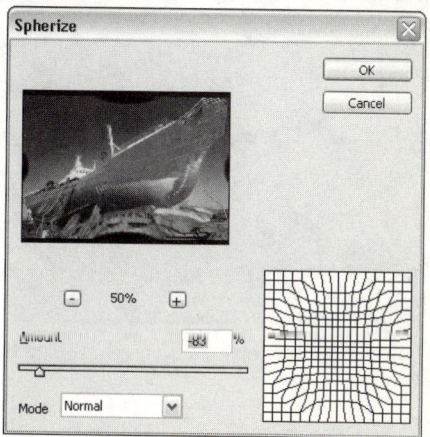

Figure 16.6. Map an image to a 3D sphere shape using the Spherize filter.

- **Specify the Mode.** Choose to apply the filter in both directions, or just vertically or horizontally.

> **Inside Scoop**
>
> If you use an image with a border, like the one in the example, but don't want the spherized effect on the image edges, delete the border before applying the filter, or crop the image after the filter is applied.

After you are pleased with the look, click OK to close the dialog box and apply the filter. Figure 16.7 shows an image of a ship destined to become part of a collage background. If you look at the edges of the image, you see the image is surrounded by a black border, with semi-circular black patches on each side of the image. These bulged areas result from the effect of the filter, which draws the content toward the center of the image.

Figure 16.7. The filter draws content toward the center from all sides.

Bending an image

The Shear filter has nothing to do with scissors. Instead, Shear refers to adding a series of bends to a shape laterally based on points and curves added to a vertical line down the middle of the image. Select the content you want to bend, and then follow these steps to bend the content:

1. Choose Filters ➪ Distort ➪ Shear to open the Shear dialog box, shown in Figure 16.8. When the dialog box opens, the vertical line has points only at the extreme top and bottom.

2. Define the distortion curve by any of these methods:

   - Click beside the vertical line to curve the line segment. In the example, the upper half of the image is curved to the left, while the lower half of the image is curved to the right.

   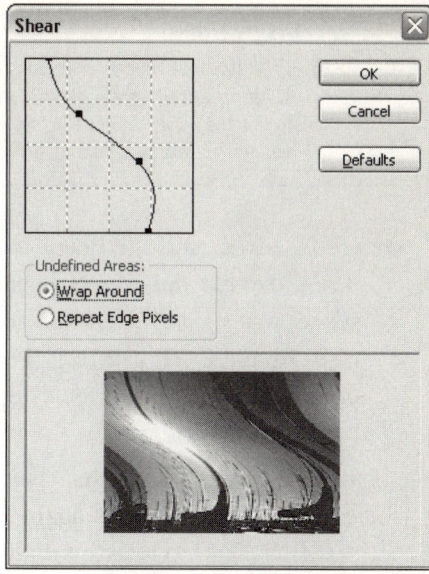

   Figure 16.8. Bend the image according to the points and segments of a distortion curve.

   - Click the line and drag to add a curve point. The example uses two additional points.
   - Drag a point along the curve to adjust it. Click the line anywhere to add a point and slide it along the curve with the mouse.
   - Drag the default upper or lower points left or right along the top or bottom edge of the line's graph preview area.

3. After you define the distortion curve, take care of the Undefined Areas. These are areas that are blank after the filter is applied, resulting from the distortions along the sides of the image. You have these choices:

   - Choose Wrap Around to fill the space with content from the opposite side of the image. You can see an example of the Wrap Around option in the left image in Figure 16.9.

Inside Scoop

It's simple to add too many points to the curve, which can make the changes between segments too abrupt. If you have too many, click a point and drag it; move the mouse beyond the frame of the graph and release the mouse. The point is gone.

> **Bright Idea**
>
> For a seamless image that doesn't make the distorted areas apparent, use either option when the background is a solid color. Wrapping pixels from one side to the other side of the image makes an image background smoother and less distracting in appearance.

- Choose Repeat Edge Pixels to extend the pixel color from the filtered areas to the edges. As each pixel is duplicated to fill the space, you see stripes in the blank spaces to fill them, like the right image in Figure 16.9. The Repeat Edge Pixels option produces very different effects depending on the background of the image, as you can see in the right image in Figure 16.9.

4. If you don't like the results, click the Defaults button to restore the original settings and start again; when you are satisfied with the effect, click OK to close the dialog box and apply the filter.

Figure 16.9. The edges of the image look very different depending on how you choose to fill them. In the left image, the image's content is wrapped to fill the distorted areas, in the right image the edge pixels are repeated to fill the distorted areas.

Catching a wave

The Wave filter creates an undulating pattern from your image. You can use different types of wave forms in the filter and configure them in a number of ways.

Follow these steps to configure and apply a Wave filter:

1. Select the content you want to apply the filter to in the image, and choose Filter ➪ Distort ➪ Wave to open the Wave dialog box, shown in Figure 16.10.

2. Select one of the wave types. You can choose Sine, Triangle, or Square patterns. The patterns roughly translate to their appearance. That is, the Triangle type produces a pointed wave, and the Square type produces a flattened wave. A Sine wave looks like the sort of wave you can produce by repeatedly moving one end of a long rope up and down while the other end remains fixed; or the patterns you usually see on monitors in 1960's science fiction movies.

3. Specify the number of wave generators by dragging the slider. The example uses 10 generators to create the waves.

4. Set the distance between wave crests using the minimum and maximum Wavelength sliders.

5. Set the wave strength by moving the minimum and maximum Amplitude sliders.

6. Set the wave height and width by dragging the Scale sliders. You can use different percentages for the Horizontal and Vertical scale, or use the same values, as in the example.

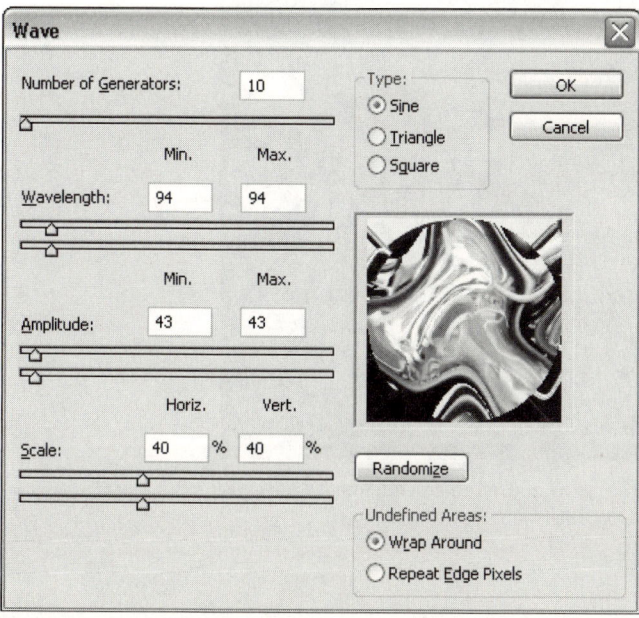

Figure 16.10. Choose settings for generating a wave effect in your image.

Inside Scoop

It's usually simplest to type a value for the Number of Generators rather than trying to adjust the slider as you can use between 1 and 000 waves — a small movement of the slider makes a big difference in the number.

7. Click Randomize to use random results based on the entered values in the dialog box. Click Randomize several times to intensify the variability of the results.
8. Choose a wrapping option for the blank spaces resulting from the effect, as described in other Distort filters' descriptions.
9. Click OK to close the dialog box and apply the filter. In Figure 16.11, you see the results of the settings configured in the dialog box shown in the earlier figure.

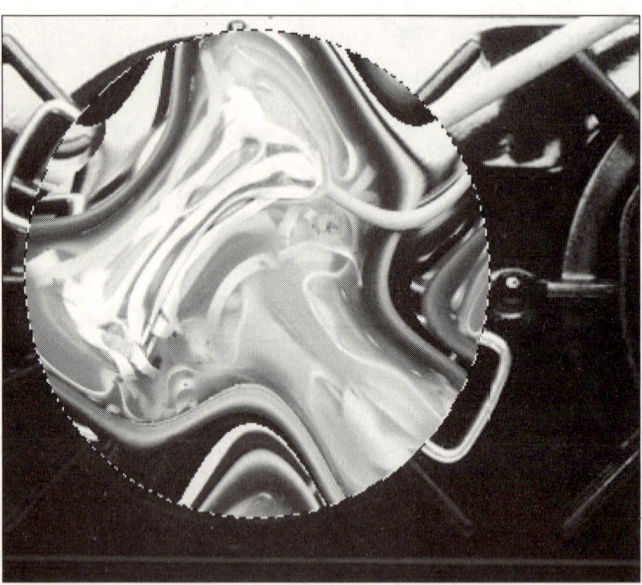

Figure 16.11. A Wave filter can be applied to an entire image or to just a selection, like this pan of noodle soup.

Sometimes, imagining how you actually use a filter in a practical way is difficult. A good example is shown in Figure 16.12, which shows the application of the Wave filter to the selected background in the image. The Wave type is square, which produces the blocked background on the image. The content of the blocks is actually repeated segments of the image, resulting in a fast way to produce a coordinating and interesting graphic background.

Figure 16.12. Using square waves can produce a coordinated background for an image.

Using a displacement map

You can precisely control how a layer or selection is displaced or shifted on an image using an image called a *displacement map*. The displacement map image is used by the Displace filter, and the contents of your image are modified based on the shades of gray in the displacement map image. The amount of distortion varies according to the values you set in the dialog box.

You can use files included with Photoshop Elements or create custom files for use as displacement maps. A displacement map can be either a flattened Photoshop file or a bitmap.

Before you apply the Displace filter, take a few minutes to check out the available displacement map files and find what you want to use for your image.

Open the folder at this location on your hard drive: Program Files/ Adobe/Photoshop Elements 4/Plug-Ins/Displacement Maps. The available map images are shown in Figure 16.13.

Watch Out!
Pay attention to the size of the map file. Figure 16.13 shows some of the map images magnified. They might actually be bigger or smaller than you think. So, you may have to adjust the settings in the dialog box to achieve the right effect.

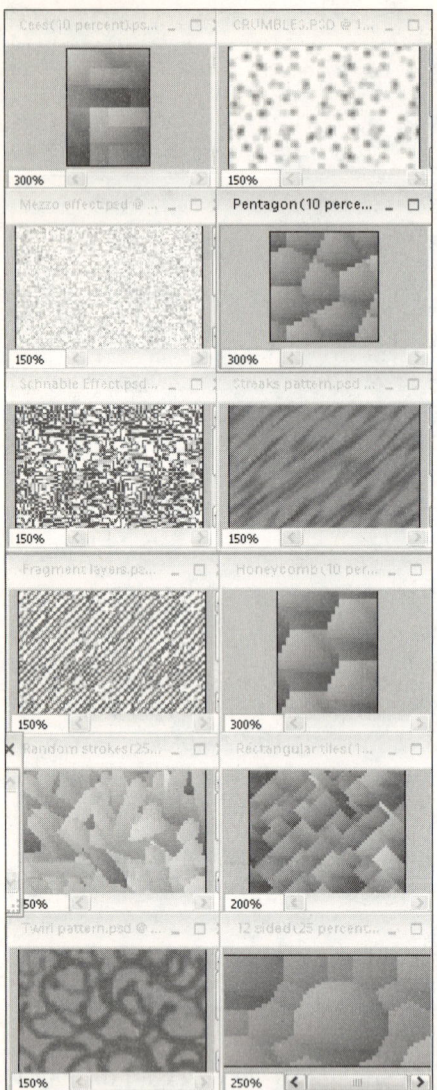

Figure 16.13. You can choose from pre-configured displacement map images that are included as part of the program installation.

You can also use another set of files that are installed as part of the program. From Windows Explorer, choose Program Files/Adobe/Photoshop Elements 4/Presets/Textures folders. Texture images available in PSD format are shown in Figure 16.14.

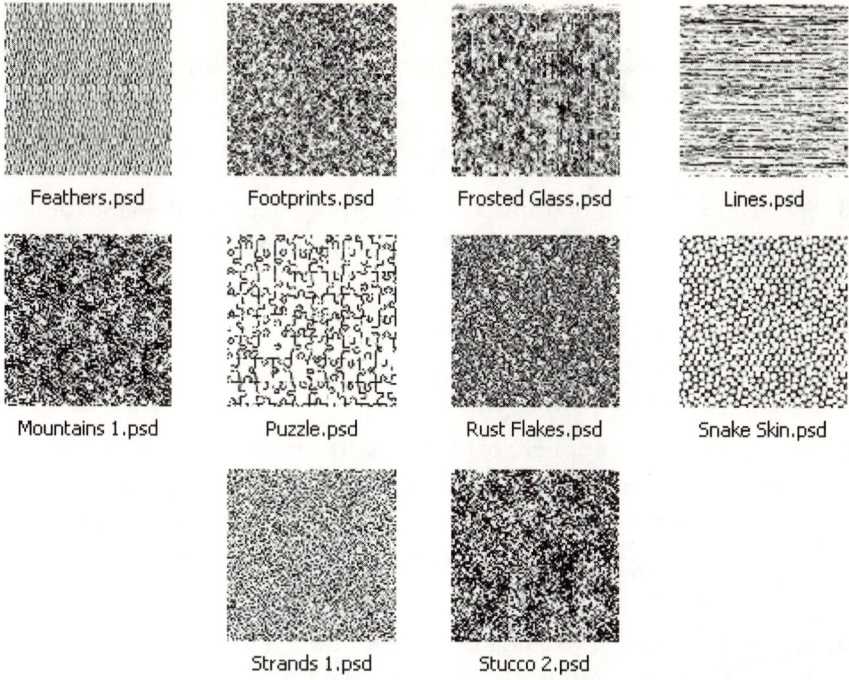

Figure 16.14. The texture images that are installed with the program can also be used as displacement maps.

Applying the filter

After you have decided on the image you want to use for the displacement map, you can start the process. Follow these steps to apply a Displace filter:

1. Select the content in your image you want to affect with the filter.

2. Choose Filter ⇨ Distort ⇨ Displace to open the Displace dialog box, shown in Figure 16.15.

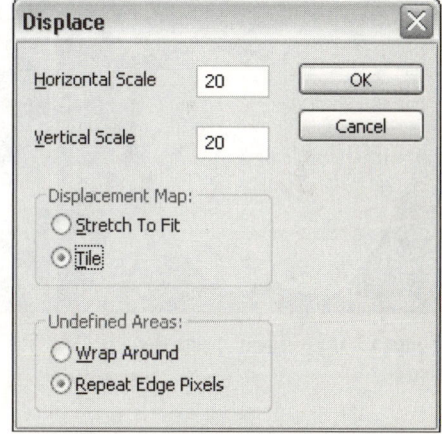

Figure 16.15. The Displace dialog box.

>  **Inside Scoop**
>
> You can use a value between -999 and 999 to scale the displacement. The displacement deflects the image down, up, left, or right using the map's contents.

3. Specify the amount of displacement by typing values in the Horizontal and Vertical Scale text boxes. The example image uses a value of 5 for both scales.
4. Specify how the map should be changed to fit the image. Select either Stretch To Fit to resize the map or Tile to repeat the map in a pattern. In the example, the map is tiled.
5. When the filter is applied, blank areas are created due to the displacement. Select one of two methods for filling the blanks. Choose Wrap Around to fill the empty areas with content from the opposite edge of the image, or choose Repeat Edge Pixels to extend the pixel colors into the blank spaces.
6. Click OK to close the dialog box; the Choose a displacement map dialog box opens automatically. Select the file you want to use, and click Open.
7. The dialog box closes, and the map is applied to the image, as shown in Figure 16.16.

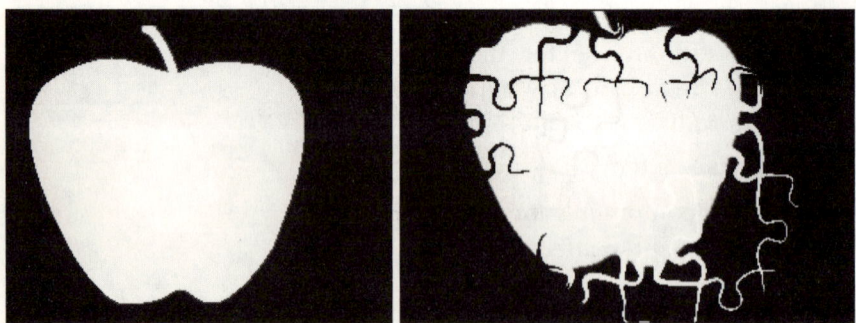

Figure 16.16. A simple image (left) is given a more exotic look by applying a displacement map (right).

In the figure, you can see the outcome of applying the settings described in the steps. The map is the puzzle.psd file, one of the texture

>  **Watch Out!**
> Only Photoshop PSD files and bitmaps can be used for a displacement map.

samples. The displaced content, cut into the shape of the puzzle pieces, is shifted to the right and downward.

When the image layer's opacity is decreased, an image such as the one used in Figure 16.16 makes an attractive background for a collage or under text.

Combining filters

Experiment with using the same image both as a source for a displacement map and as a texture for the same image. Sometimes, the repetition of the effect can result in very interesting images, like the combo shown in Figure 16.17, that started where the image shown in Figure 16.16 left off.

This version of the image includes the Texturizer filter, using the same puzzle texture image file. The second filter adds a sense of depth and light to the image that isn't shown with the basic displacement map. You can read more about the Texturizer filter later in the chapter.

Figure 16.17. Use the same map for more than one filter for interest.

Liquifying an image

Have you ever seen those greeting cards that feature some little critter with eyes bigger than its head? If you have, you may have been looking at an image modified with a Liquify filter.

In the Liquify filter's window, your image behaves as if it were soft and malleable, and it can be smeared in different ways with the tools. Follow these steps to apply the filter:

1. Select the image or area you want to modify.
2. Choose Filter ➪ Distort ➪ Liquify to open the Liquify window shown in Figure 16.18.

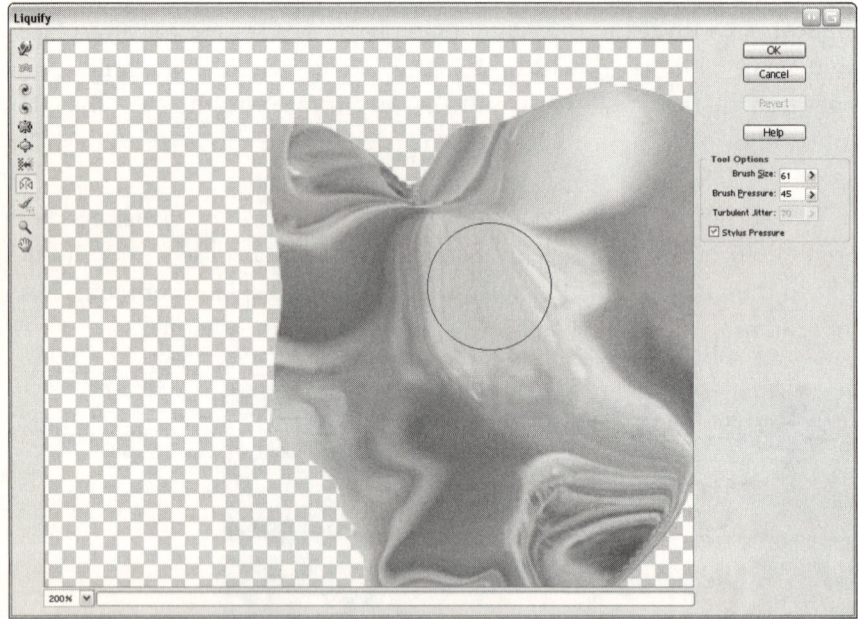

Figure 16.18. The Liquify dialog box.

3. Select a tool from the toolbox. The tools and their functions are listed in Table 16.3.
4. Specify the settings for the selected tool. You can define the Brush Size in pixels from 1 to 600, and the Brush Pressure in percentage. Turbulence Jitter is a value used with the Turbulence tool, described in Table 16.3. The tools shown in the Tool Options vary according to the tool selected in the dialog box.

5. Click or drag on the image to apply the tool.

6. Continue with other tools until the edit is complete.

7. Click OK to close the window and apply the filter to your image.

There are many effects you can create with the filter. Examples of four Liquify processes used on quadrants of the same image are shown in Figure 16.19. The upper left uses the Warp tool; the upper right the Turbulence and Rotate Clockwise tools. The lower-left quadrant shows the effect of the Pucker and Bloat tools, while the lower right uses the Shift Pixels and Reflect tools to give the appearance of a watery reflection. For reference, the original image is shown in the inset at the bottom left.

There is much more that you can do with the group of Liquify tools, including liquifing text, which is explained in detail in Chapter 17.

Going back again

The work done in the Liquify window can become very complex, as you can use multiple tools, and apply them multiple times. Undo some of what you have done without reverting to the original image using the Reconstruct tool.

Select the Reconstruct tool in the Liquify window's toolbox, and move the mouse over the image to the area you want to correct. Press and hold the mouse when you want to make changes in a single area, or drag to correct distortion over a greater area.

If you want to go back to the original image and maintain your tool settings, press Alt and click Revert in the Liquify window. Click Revert to return to the original image and reset the tools.

Inside Scoop

If you are using a tablet and stylus for working on the image, click the Stylus Pressure check box to allow you to modify the strokes.

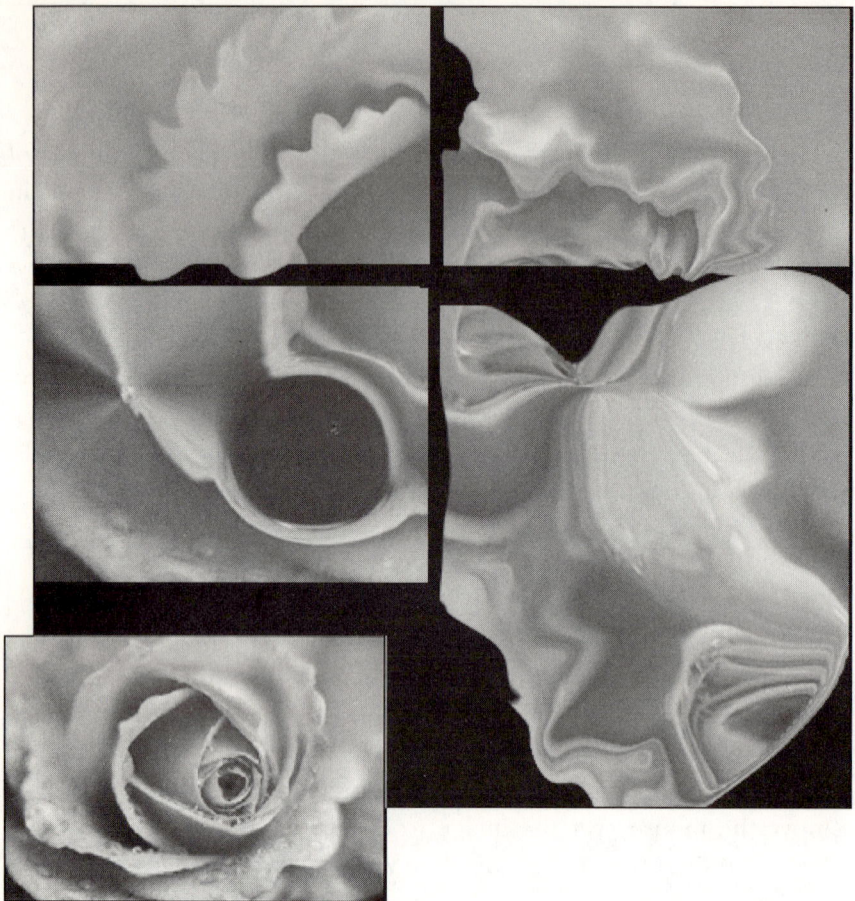

Figure 16.19. Use the Liquify filter's tools to smear the content in an image in interesting ways.

Table 16.3. Liquify tools		
Tool	**Tool Name**	**What It's Used For**
	Warp	Pushes pixels forward as you drag.
	Turbulence	Creates turbulent effects such as fire or weaves. Adjust the smoothness by setting the Turbulent Jitter value in the options from 1 to 100. The higher the value is, the smoother the effect. This tool smoothly scrambles pixels and creates fire, clouds, waves, and similar effects.

Tool	Tool Name	What It's Used For
	Twirl Clockwise	Rotates pixels clockwise as you press the mouse button or drag across the image.
	Twirl Counterclockwise	Rotates pixels counterclockwise as you press the mouse button or drag across the image.
	Pucker	Moves pixels toward the center of the brush area as you press the mouse button or drag.
	Bloat	Moves pixels away from the center of the brush area as you press the mouse button or drag.
	Shift Pixels	Moves pixels perpendicularly to the stroke direction. Drag the mouse to move pixels to the left and Alt-drag to move the pixels to the right.
	Reflection	Reflects pixels perpendicularly to the brush stroke direction. Dragging the tool reflects the area perpendicular to the direction of the stroke, either left or below your stroke direction. Pressing the Alt key while dragging reflects the areas under the brush in the direction opposite to the stroke direction. Overlap strokes to simulate reflections in water.
	Reconstruct	Reverses changes made in the image in specified areas.
	Zoom	Brings your image closer, or allows you to see more of your image. Change the magnification using the Zoom tool, or use the viewing tools under the preview area on the window.
	Hand	Lets you move your image. Drag the visible area of the image using the Hand tool.

Bright Idea

You can create a dragging appearance in a straight line using the Warp, Shift Pixels, or Reflection tools. Shift+click with the tool at the starting point, and again at the ending point of the line.

Pixelating images with filters

Pixelating filters produce some intriguing effects that you can use for adding interest in an image, drawing attention to particular selections, or for backgrounds, textures, or fills. Choose Filter ⇨ Pixelate, and select one of the filters from the submenu that displays, as listed in Table 16.4.

Table 16.4. About Pixelate filters		
Filter	**How It Looks**	**How to Use It**
Color Halftone	This filter simulates a halftone screen. The image is divided into rectangles, and then each rectangle is converted to a circle.	Configure the radius of the dots and the angle of the light.
Crystallize	This filter redraws a layer as polygon-shaped clumps of color. The filter is used in the top image of Figure 6.21.	Select the size and numbers of the cells.
Facet	Produce abstract painterly effects using this filter, which redraws the image in blocks of color, shown in the center image of Figure 16.21.	You can't configure the Facet filter.
Fragment	This filter produces a soft effect by redrawing the image so it appears blurred and offset, shown in the lower image of Figure 16.21.	The Fragment filter also isn't configurable.
Mezzotint	This filter redraws a layer as a random pattern of dots, lines, or strokes. In a grayscale image, the pattern is black-and-white areas, while in a color image the pattern is fully saturated color.	Specify the characteristics of the pattern, including the type, size, and configuration of the dots using the options, in the Mezzotint dialog box. The filter is used in the backgrounds shown in Figure 16.1.

Filter	How It Looks	How to Use It
Mosaic	This filter redraws a layer as square blocks of color.	Specify the cell size by dragging the slider in the Mosaic dialog box.
Pointillize	This filter redraws a layer as randomly placed custom-sized dots, like that in a pointillist painting. See an example of the Pointillize filter in the top image in Figure 16.40.	The filter uses the background color as the canvas color. Drag the slider in the Pointillize dialog box to size the dots.

Follow these steps to apply a Fragment Pixelate filter:

1. Open the image, and then choose Filter ➪ Pixelate ➪ Crystallize to open the Crystallize dialog box shown in Figure 16.20.
2. Adjust the Cell Size for the filter by typing a value in the field or dragging the slider.
3. When the effect looks as you like in the preview area, click OK to close the dialog box and apply the filter.

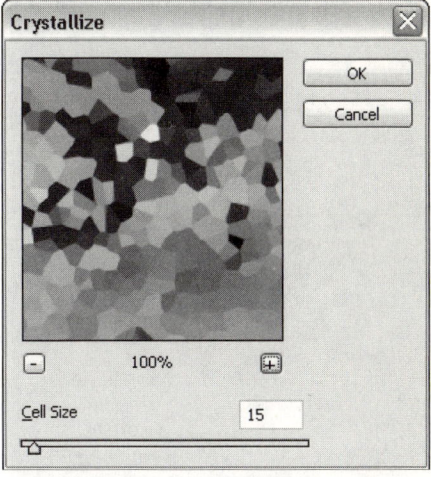

Figure 16.20. Pixelate filters, such as the Crystallize filter, break up the image in certain patterns based on the size you specify.

The finished image is shown at the top of Figure 16.21. Also in the figure are examples of two other Pixelate filters; the Facet filter (middle) and Fragment filter (lower).

 **Inside Scoop**
You don't configure either the Facet or Fragment filters. To increase the effect, reapply the filter.

Figure 16.21. Use a Crystallize filter to fracture the image into a crystal structure (top); make an abstract piece using the Facet filter (center), or a more ethereal piece using the Fragment filter (lower)

Sketching with filters

The Sketch filters imitate different pens and inks, or suggest different sketching surfaces or ways of reproducing images. Table 16.5 describes filters that produce effects such as those produced by different pens, inks, and reproduction techniques.

Table 16.5. Sketch filters: Pens and inks

Filter	How It Looks	How to Use It
Chalk & Charcoal	This filter redraws an image's highlights and midtones with a solid midtone gray background drawn in coarse chalk. Shadow areas are replaced with black diagonal charcoal lines.	The charcoal is drawn in the foreground color and the chalk in the background color. You can set stroke pressure, and the extent of the charcoal and chalk areas. In Figure 16.22, for example, the chalk area is predominant.
Charcoal	Create a smudged effect using this filter. Areas of high contrast are edged with hard lines and midtones and are sketched with diagonal lines.	Choose the charcoal thickness, how much image detail you want to preserve, and the light/dark balance.
Chrome	Use this filter to simulate a polished chrome surface on the image.	The highlights are mapped to high points, and the shadows are mapped to low points; you specify the level of detail and smoothness.
Conté Crayon	This filter replicates the texture of dense dark and pure white Conté crayons on an image.	This filter uses the foreground color for dark areas and the background color for light areas. You can set the level of foreground and background emphasis, and texture options.
Graphic Pen	This filter uses fine, linear ink strokes to capture the details in the original image and is especially striking with scanned images.	The filter replaces color in the original image, using the foreground color for ink and background color for paper. You can set the stroke length and direction, and the light/dark balance.
Stamp	This filter simplifies the image so that it seems made with a rubber or wood stamp. An image like that shown in Figure 16.23 is useful for creating graphic elements for Web pages, publications, and the like.	You can set the smoothness and the balance between light and dark, which is terrific for creating a simplified version of an image.

One of the neatest ways to use Sketch filters is in combination with other layers. Experiment with using a Sketch filter on one layer blended with a blur or other filter that decreases contrast on another layer for some interesting effects.

Figure 16.22 shows an example of this technique. The image uses two copies of the key photo on two separate layers. The lower copy of the photo is untouched, while the upper layer's image uses the Chalk & Charcoal filter. Decreasing the opacity of the filtered upper layer reveals some of the underlying photo; using the Difference blend emphasizes the blockiness of the filtered layer.

Figure 16.22. Combine sketches and images for simple artistic effects.

Sometimes you can compose a very attractive presentation or page mixing images and graphic elements. What if you don't have sketches, or can't draw a sketch to save your life? No matter. The Stamp filter can do it for you.

Here are some examples of mixing images and graphics:

- A graphic to use in a scrapbook identifying the theme of the image.
- Small graphics sprinkled through a presentation identifying the topic.
- A graphic that shows some sort of detail about an event like the day everyone slept in and nearly missed leaving for a family vacation.

I just happen to have an image of an alarm clock that could enhance the message of the third example very well. As you can see in Figure 16.23, the original image at the left is a simple photo of an alarm clock; applying the Stamp filter produces a neat sketch, like the version on the right.

Figure 16.23. Use the Stamp filter to convert a simple image (left) into a very graphical sketch (right) ideal for projects like Web pages or enhancing compositions and layouts.

To change the image's appearance from a photo to a drawing, follow these steps:

1. Choose Filter ➪ Sketch ➪ Stamp to open the image in the Filter Gallery, shown in Figure 16.24. You could also choose Filter ➪ Filter Gallery, and then select the filter from the Sketch category in the Filter Gallery.
2. Drag the Light/Dark Balance slider right to increase the contrast, or left to decrease the contrast.
3. Drag the Smoothness slider left to increase the amount of detail, or right to decrease the amount of detail.
4. When the image in the preview area looks correct, click OK to close the Filter Gallery window.

Inside Scoop

Sketch filters respond well to changes in contrast. Either before applying the filter or after using the filter, adjust Levels to change the contrast in the image.

Figure 16.24. Specify the amount of detail using settings in the Filter Gallery.

Some Sketch filters imitate reproduction techniques and are described in Table 16.6.

Table 16.6. Sketch filters: Reproduction techniques

Filter	How It Looks	How to Use It
Halftone Pattern	This filter simulates the effect of a halftone screen while maintaining the continuous range of tones.	You can set the halftone size, contrast, and pattern type.
Photocopy	This filter simulates the effect of photocopying an image. Large areas of darkness tend to copy only around their edges, and midtones fall away to either solid black or white.	Specify areas of darkness and light. Figure 16.25 shows how the filter produces a high contrast version of the rubber ducky shown in the left of the image.
Torn Edges	This filter reconstructs the image as ragged, torn pieces of paper, and then colorizes the image using the foreground and background color.	You can set the image balance, smoothness, and contrast. This filter is particularly useful for images consisting of text or high-contrast objects.

Another way you can create a sketch-like image from a picture is using the Photocopy filter. If you have seen a poor-quality print from a photocopy machine, you have an idea of how the filter works. In this case, however, you want the high contrast light and dark areas. An example of using the Photocopy filter is shown in Figure 16.25.

Figure 16.25. The Photocopy filter produces a sophisticated version of an image — regardless of how unsophisticated the subject matter!

A final group of Sketch filters are those that simulate paper types. These filters and how they work are listed in Table 16.7.

Table 16.7. Sketch filters: Paper and surfaces

Filter	How It Looks	How to Use It
Bas Relief	This filter simulates a low-relief carving.	Specify the amount of detail, smoothness, and light characteristics.
Note Paper	This filter simulates the texture of handmade paper by combining the effects of the Emboss and Grain filters. Dark areas of the image appear as holes in the top layer of paper, revealing the background color.	You can set the image balance, graininess, and relief.
Plaster	This filter molds the layer into a 3D plaster effect and then colorizes the result using the foreground and background color. Dark areas are raised, and light areas are sunken.	You can set the image balance, smoothness, and light direction.

continued

Table 16.7. continued

Filter	How It Looks	How to Use It
Reticulation	This filter simulates the controlled shrinking and distorting of film emulsion to create an image that appears clumped in the shadow areas and lightly grained in the highlights.	You can set the density, foreground, and background levels, which is used in the image shown in Figure 16.26.
Water Paper	This filter uses blotchy daubs that appear to be painted onto fibrous, damp paper, causing the colors to flow and blend.	You can set the paper's fiber length, brightness, and contrast.

In Figure 16.26, the television screen's area is selected, and the Reticulation filter is applied following these steps:

1. Make the selection for the area you want to filter. Read about making selections in Chapter 10.
2. Choose Filter ➪ Sketch ➪ Reticulation to open the window. You can also choose Filter ➪ Filter Gallery, and then choose the filter from the Sketch thumbnails in the Filter Gallery window.
3. Create the "snowy" test patter by adjusting the filter's settings. Specify the density of the distortion areas, as well as the amounts of foreground and background shown. Drag the sliders left to decrease the amount applied, or right to increase the amount applied.
4. Click OK to close the dialog and apply the filter.

Figure 16.26. Create a 60s-inspired television test pattern using the Reticulation filter.

Stylizing filters

The Stylize filters replace pixels to create specific looks or effects in an image. The filters fall into two groups, that include:

- Filters that affect the edges of the image only
- Filters that affect the overall image

Four of the filters affect the edges of an object or selected area in an image, and are listed in Table 16.8.

Table 16.8. Stylize filters: Edge modifying

Filter	What It Does	How to Use It
Find Edges	This filter outlines the edges of high contrast areas with a dark line against a white background, like the image shown in Figure 16.27.	You don't choose any settings for this filter. If you want to make the effect stronger or less distinct, adjust the contrast before applying the filter.
Emboss	Create the appearance of stamped or embossed paper using this filter.	Specify how much color to leave in the image, as well as how deep the embossing should appear at the edges of objects, and the angle of the light.
Glowing Edges	Use this filter to add a neon, radioactive-like glow to the edges.	Control the amount of glow by specifying the width, brightness, and smoothness of the edges. The image shown in Figure 16.20 includes the Glowing Edges filter as part of its construction.
Trace Contour	Produce an effect similar to a contour map using this filter. The lines are based on brightness levels.	Specify the color level, as well as whether to apply lines to pixels below or above the threshold level. Save some time using this filter. Before you start, identify a color value you want traced in the Info palette. Use the value in the Level field when you are applying the filter.

A filter such as the Find Edges filter identifies areas of contrast in the image, and directly applied to the image. That is, you choose Filter ➪ Stylize ➪ Find Edges and the filter is applied automatically, like the left image shown in Figure 16.27. After the filter is applied, you can adjust the image further by adjusting the lighting. The right image in Figure 16.27 shows the same image after adjusting the brightness and contrast to remove most of the midrange color, leaving the dark outline.

Figure 16.27. Identify just the edges in an image using the Find Edges filter (left); control the color range by adjusting the contrast (right).

The only Stylize filter you find in the Filter Gallery is the Glowing Edges filter; the others are available only through the Filter menu, by choose Filter ⇨ Stylize, and then the filter from the submenu.

The Glowing Edges filter applies neon-bright colors to the edges while darkening the rest of the image. You can see an example of a flower, showing the outlines of the petals and stamens in the image in Figure 16.28.

You can adjust the intensity of the effect by setting the width and brightness of the edge, as well as specifying the edge smoothness in the Filter Gallery window. The lower the Smoothness number, the more detailed edges are displayed in the image.

The remaining Stylize filters apply changes to the overall image, and are described in Table 16.9.

Bright Idea

Filters that find edges are useful for creating a drawing from an image. Increase the contrast to just black and white, and build your own coloring book.

Figure 16.28. Instead of merely highlighting the edges of objects, give them a neon glow using the Glowing Edges filter.

Table 16.9. Stylize filters: Overall effecting

Filter	What It Does	How to Use It
Diffuse	This filter unfocuses an image by shuffling pixels.	Choose Normal to move the pixels randomly, Darken Only to replace light with dark pixels, Lighten Only to replace dark with light pixels, and Anisotropic to soften all pixels regardless of brightness.
Extrude	Use this filter to produce a three-dimensional texture based on the image's structure.	Define whether to use block or pyramid shapes. Then specify the characteristics of the shapes, such as size or depth; the right image in Figure 16.30 uses the Extrude filter.
Solarize	This filter blends a negative and a positive version of the image.	The effect is similar to exposing a photograph to light as it is being developed. Specify the amount of light to control the effect.

continued

Table 16.9. continued

Filter	What It Does	How to Use It
Tiles	Use this filter to break up the image into a number of tiles, each of which is offset slightly.	Specify the number of tiles and the offset amount. Choose to fill the empty spaces between the tiles with the Background Color, Foreground Color, Inverse Image, or Unaltered Image.
Wind	This filter creates a network of horizontal lines in the image to simulate a wind effect.	The line characteristics are based on wind strength and direction options.

Each of the Stylize filters listed in the table is configured in its own dialog box, rather than in the Filter Gallery. Use one of the Stylize filters to make interesting backgrounds or frames for your projects following these steps:

1. Choose Filter ⇨ Stylize ⇨ Extrude to open the Extrude dialog box, shown in Figure 16.29.

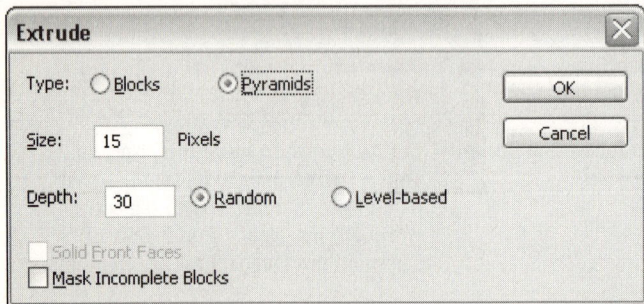

Figure 16.29. Specify settings for the extrusion, such as the size and shape in the dialog box.

2. Choose the extrusion settings by selecting either Blocks or Pyramids. Blocks produce a flat face, while a pyramid extrusion appears triangular.
3. Type a value in the Size field, which defines the amount of the image used in each extrusion shape in pixels.
4. Type a value for the Depth field. The values are relative, that is, the higher the Depth value, the deeper the extrusions appear. You can

also specify whether the depth is random or based on how far a particular extrusion is from the midpoint of the image.

5. If you like, choose Mask Incomplete Blocks to remove partial extrusions from the edges of the image. If you choose the Blocks extrusion type, you can also select to have the front face drawn in a solid color.

6. Click OK to close the dialog box and apply the filter.

Figure 16.30 shows the before view in the left image; the right image shows the same glass on the table, but using the Extrude filter gives it a much different appearance.

Figure 16.30. Use a Stylize filter, such as the Extrude filter, to radically change an image you can use for a background or as part of a composition.

Texturizing with filters

Photoshop Elements includes a selection of filters used for applying specific types of textures, as well as one filter that lets you apply pre-configured filters or custom images called the Texturizer. The texture filters, with the exception of the Texturizer, are shown in Figure 16.31. The filters used in the top row are Craquelure (top left) and Grain (top right); the bottom row shows the Mosaic Tiles filter (bottom left), the Patchwork filter (bottom center), and the Stained Glass filter (bottom right). The basic information is listed in Table 16.10.

Figure 16.31. Use a pre-configured texture filter to add interest to an image or as the basis for a background layer or texture.

Table 16.10. Texture filters

Filter	How It Works	How to Use It
Craquelure	This filter simulates the appearance of painting on plaster, complete with cracks following the image's contours as shown in the top left of Figure 16.31.	The filter gives an embossing effect; set the spacing, depth, and brightness of the cracks.
Grain	This filter simulates grain textures by fracturing the image into specks and spots overlaying the background color as shown at the top right of Figure 16.31	Set the background color in the toolbox before using this filter. Select the intensity, contrast, and type of grain. Figure 16.31 shows the Vertical grain type.
Mosaic Tiles	Use this filter to redraw the image as if it were made up of mosaic tiles. The filter even adds the grout between the tiles, which you can see in the lower left of Figure 16.31.	Choose the tile size, and the width and darkness of the grout lines.

CHAPTER 16 ▪ FINESSING WITH FILTERS

Filter	How It Works	How to Use It
Patchwork	This filter breaks up an image into squares filled with the predominant color in different areas of the image shown in the bottom center of Figure 16.31	The filter randomly reduces or increases the tile depth to replicate the highlights and shadows. You can set the square size and relief.
Stained Glass	This filter produces cells of different colors outlined in the foreground color. The example at the lower left of Figure 16.31 uses the smallest cell size and thinnest border for the greatest preservation of the original image's appearance.	Before opening this filter, set the foreground color. In the filter's dialog box, set the cell size, border thickness, and light.
Texturizer	This filter allows you to simulate different texture types or select a file to use as a texture. Texture options make images appear as if they are painted onto textures such as canvas and brick or viewed through glass blocks.	Select the texture and its scale, as well as the depth of the texture and direction of light.

The Texturizer lets you choose your own files to use for the filter, or use one of the pre-supplied textures.

Follow these steps to apply and configure a texture to an image:

1. Choose Filter ⇨ Texture ⇨ Texturizer to open the Filter Gallery. If you prefer, choose Filter ⇨ Texture to open the Filter Gallery and choose Texturizer from the Texture category in the filters listing. The options you can customize for the filter are shown in Figure 16.32.

2. Click the Texture drop-down arrow and choose a default texture, or click the arrow next to the field and choose Load Texture. The Open dialog box displays for you to locate and select a file you

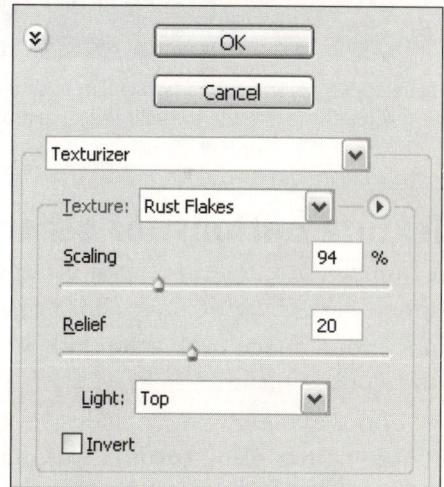

Figure 16.32. Specify characteristics for the pattern you apply as a texture using the Texturizer filter, including the size, depth, and direction of light.

want to use as a texture. Photoshop Elements includes a folder of textures at this hard drive location: C:\Program Files\Adobe\Photoshop Elements 4.0\Presets\Textures.

3. Drag the Scaling slider left to decrease the size of the texture and right to increase its size.
4. Drag the Relief slider left to decrease and right to increase the apparent depth of the texture. A higher Relief value makes the texture look deeper.
5. Click the Light drop-down arrow and choose a light direction.
6. Click OK to close the dialog box and apply the filter.

You can even tailor a type of texture to the image's subject. The left image in Figure 16.33 shows a scene from an industrial park lit at night. The same image at the right uses a pattern simulating rust for the Texturizer filter.

Figure 16.33. Apply imported texture files to an unfiltered image (left) for added interest, such as the rust.psd file (applied to the right image), one of the texture files installed with the program.

Texture options for other filters

A number of filters in several groups such as the Conté Crayon, Glass, Rough Pastels, and Underpainting filters include texturizing settings to make your image look as though it were painted on a surface or seen through a surface.

Choose Filter ⇨ Filter Gallery to open the Filter Gallery window and choose a filter using texture. Customize each filter in the Filter Gallery using the following parameters:

- Specify the texture to apply, or load a custom texture from a Photoshop file.

Bright Idea

Looking for textures to use for brushes, fills, or backgrounds? Use a copy of your image or a selection from the image, apply one of the texture filters, and then use a blur or diffuse type filter. The colors are automatically matched to your original image.

- Adjust the Scaling to increase or decrease the amount of the effect on the surface.
- Choose Invert to reverse an image's light and dark colors.
- Change the Relief value to adjust the surface depth.
- Specify the light source's orientation using the Light Angle value.

Adding Brush Stroke filters

Brush Stroke filters can be used to emphasize objects in your images as well as produce artistic effects. The filters are designed to simulate specific types of brushes or techniques.

The Brush Stroke filters are configured in the Filter Gallery; basic information about the options is listed in Table 16.11.

Table 16.11. Brush Stroke filters

Filter	Characteristics	How to Configure It
Accented Edges	This filter affects the edge appearance in an image. When the edge brightness is high, the edge looks like chalk; when the edge brightness is low, the accented edge looks like black ink.	Set the edge width, edge brightness, and smoothness.
Angled Strokes	This filter uses diagonal strokes to repaint an image with lighter strokes running in the opposite direction to darker strokes.	Set the stroke direction balance, stroke length, and sharpness.
Crosshatch	This filter adds texture and the appearance of pencil hatching.	Set the stroke length, sharpness, and strength, which is the amount of hatching applied.

continued

Table 16.11. *continued*

Filter	Characteristics	How to Configure It
Dark Strokes	This filter paints dark areas in an image with short, dark strokes, and paints lighter areas of the image with long, white strokes.	Set the stroke balance, and black-and-white intensity levels.
Ink Outlines	This filter redraws an image with fine, narrow lines over the original details, in pen-and-ink style.	Set the stroke length, and intensity levels for the dark and light strokes.
Spatter	This filter simulates using a spatter airbrush.	Set the spray radius and smoothness.
Sprayed Strokes	This filter repaints a layer using its dominant colors with angled, sprayed strokes of color.	Set the stroke length, spray radius, and stroke direction.
Sumi-e	This filter simulates a Japanese painting style, using black ink on rice paper.	Set the stroke width, stroke pressure, and contrast for the filter.

Figure 16.34 shows examples of two of the Brush Stroke filters. The left segment of the image uses the Crosshatch filter, the center segment has no applied filter, and the right segment uses Ink Outlines. To apply a Brush Stroke filter, follow these steps:

1. Choose Filter ⇨ Filter Gallery to open the Filter Gallery window, and choose the type of filter from the Brush Stroke category of the filter list.

2. Modify the settings for the brush stroke. The options available vary according to the type of stroke. For example, the Accented Edges filter lets you choose Edge Width, Edge Brightness, and Smoothness because the filter increases the brightness of the image and sharpens the edges. The Ink Outlines filter, shown in the right segment of

Bright Idea

I often use Brush Stroke filters as part of a sequence of filters. Many of the Brush Stroke options decrease contrast, which makes an interesting effect beneath another layer using an enhancing filter or effect.

the image in Figure 16.34, uses the Stroke Length setting, as well as Dark and Light Intensity levels, to define the darkness of the results.

3. Click OK to close the Filter Gallery window and apply the filter.

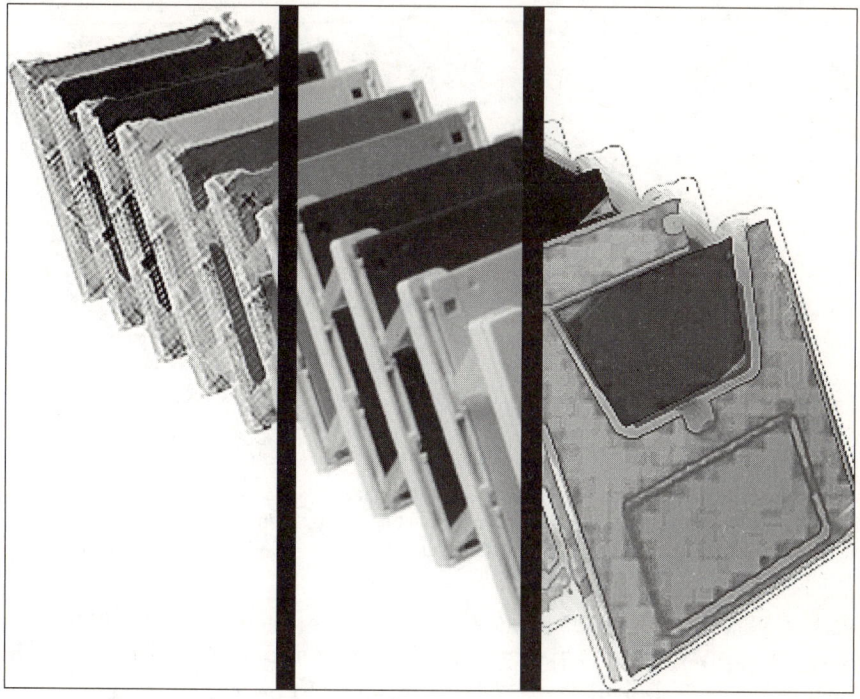

Figure 16.34. The Brush Stroke filters simulate different types of brush techniques and applications such as the Accented Edges technique (left) and the Ink Strokes (right).

Applying Artistic filters

The Artistic filters are one of the collections you work with in the Filter Gallery. As the name suggests, Artistic filters simulate art produced with traditional media such as pastels and colored pencils, or techniques such as smudging or sponging; an example of sponging is shown at the upper left of Figure 16.35. The filters also include other less traditional media effects such as Plastic Wrap shown at the upper right of Figure 16.35. When compared to the original image shown at the bottom of Figure 16.35, you can see the Artistic filters affect both the content and the background of the image.

Figure 16.35. Artistic filters may simulate traditional materials, such as sponging shown at the upper left, or less traditional materials, such as plastic wrap shown at the upper right of the image.

The filters' settings vary according to technique, but in general the filters that apply strokes or patterns specify a size and an intensity or depth for the stroke. Follow these steps to apply a Colored Pencil filter:

1. Choose Filter ⇨ Artistic ⇨ Colored Pencil to open the Filter Gallery and display the Colored Pencil filter's settings.
2. Specify settings for the pencil including the Pencil Width and Stroke Pressure, which together define the appearance of the stroke.
3. Drag the slider to set the Paper Brightness. The lower the value set on the Paper Brightness slider, the darker the background of the image. A Brightness value of 1 is black; a Brightness value of 50 is white.
4. Click OK to close the dialog box and apply the filter.

The stroke filters also offer a third configuration setting in the Filter Gallery that is specific to the filter type. For example, the Colored Pencil filter, shown in the left image in Figure 16.36, offers a Paper Brightness option to define the brightness of the background. The Fresco filter, shown in the right image in Figure 16.36, lets you specify the amount of texture applied, as well as the brush size and detail to define the appearance of the strokes themselves.

Figure 16.36. Artistic filters, such as Colored Pencil (left) and Fresco (right) offer three different settings to configure the look of each.

The Rough Pastels and Underpainting filters have more extensive settings options.

Choose Filter ⇨ Artistic ⇨ Rough Pastels to open the Filter Gallery. The filter's settings are shown in Figure 16.37, and divvied into two categories:

- **Strokes.** Drag the sliders to define the Stroke Length and the amount of Stroke Detail. The higher the Stroke Length value, the longer the strokes applied; the higher the Stroke Detail value, the more detail is shown in the image. In the left image in Figure 16.38, the Stroke Detail is set at a high value of 20 so the clown's features and clothing are identifiable.

- **Texture.** Choose a pattern from the Texture drop-down list, or click the arrow and select a texture file from your hard drive.

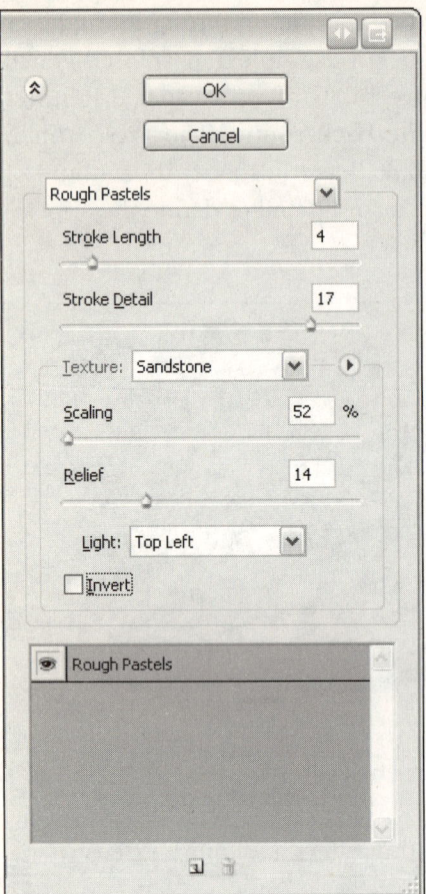

Figure 16.37. The adjustment categories available for the Rough Pastels filter.

The Underpainting filter also lets you specify a texture. In the right image in Figure 16.38, the clown image uses the Underpainting filter, again with the sandstone texture applied. Like its namesake technique, the results of the underpainting are quite indistinct, and need overlying detail to see the subject clearly.

Use the same texture files as those described previously in the Texturizer filter's discussion.

 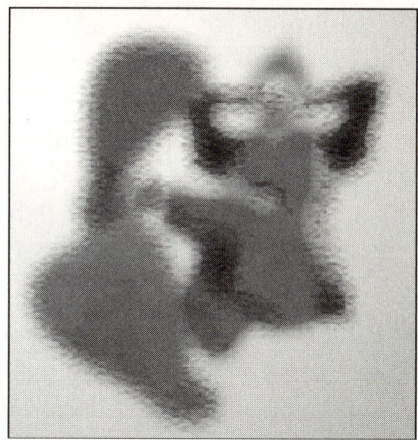

Figure 16.38. Some artistic filters let you configure the texture as well as the strokes or other paint characteristics, including the Rough Pastel filter (left) and the Underpainting filter (right).

Using filters for specific purposes

If you aren't very familiar with the filters and how they work and interrelate to one another, knowing how to achieve a complex, multi-filtered effect can seem overwhelming. But, as long as you understand the filters you want to use and can do some planning when you want to use one or more filters to enhance an image, you shouldn't have a problem.

To get you started and to give you a sense of how to plan and apply the filters, the next few sections describe how to

- Create an artistic image using three filters.
- Add interest to a simple background to coordinate with the subject of your image.
- Unify a group of images by applying the same filters.
- Create a sense of motion where none exists.

Producing a piece of art

You can produce art-like images in many ways, just as you can produce art in many ways. One method lets you use a variety of textures and strokes to simulate an oil-on-canvas painting. For this example, filters are applied in the Filter Gallery window.

The finished painting, shown in the right image in Figure 16.39, uses three filters to achieve the painted appearance. The filters include:

- **Texturizer.** One of the Texture filters, the Texturizer configures and applies one of several different types of surfaces, including the canvas used in the example. Configure the size of the pattern, the depth of the relief, and the light angle. In the example, using a canvas texture simulates the actual painting surface you would use for painting oil.

- **Paint Daubs.** The Paint Daubs filter is one of the Artistic filters, and it creates an appearance of fluid paint applied on a surface. You can choose brush size and sharpness, and you can select from several different brush appearances. The filter is used in the example to create the overall sense of the painting.

- **Angled Strokes.** Angled Strokes, a Brush Stroke filter, simulates strokes on the image using customized stroke length, sharpness, and direction. In the example, the filter's applied strokes are used to emphasize the shapes and detail in the flower.

Figure 16.39. The original image (left) has a much more hand-painted appearance after applying several filters (right).

CHAPTER 16 ■ FINESSING WITH FILTERS

Adding quick (and cool) backgrounds

Instead of searching for image files to use for backgrounds in your projects, create your own using a solid color layer. Here's a simple way to add a useful background to a simple image using an adjustment layer and a couple of filters. The source image used in this example is a PSD file with a transparent background.

1. Open the image you want to use.
2. Click Create Adjustment Layer on the Layers palette to open the drop-down menu, and choose Solid Color. A layer is added to the image and the Color Picker opens.
3. Select a color for the background layer, and click OK.
4. If necessary, move the background layer below the image layer in the Layers palette.
5. Click the background layer in the Layers palette to make it active.
6. In the Styles and Effects palette, click the left drop-down arrow and choose Filters from the menu; click the right drop-down arrow, and choose Pixelate from the menu.
7. Drag the Pointillize thumbnail from the palette to the document window, and release it over the image to apply the filter to the background. You see that the layer is broken into little blobs of color like the Pointillism style of painting, shown in the upper image in Figure 16.40.
8. Drag the Color Halftone thumbnail from the pixelate thumbnails in the Styles and Effects palette to the image, and release it. The Color Halftone dialog box opens; leave the default settings, and click OK to close the dialog box. Now you see that the dots on the background layer are given uniform shapes, shown in the middle image on Figure 16.40.
9. In the Styles and Effects palette, click the right drop-down arrow and choose stylize from the menu.

Bright Idea
If you want to change the background color, double-click the Adjustment layer's thumbnail to reopen the Color Picker and either choose a different color or sample a color from your image to use as the background color.

10. Drag the Emboss effect's thumbnail from the palette to the image, and release it over the background layer. The Emboss dialog box opens; leave the default settings, and click OK to close the dialog box. The dots on the background are given uniform shadow and highlight areas, shown in the lower image on Figure 16.40.

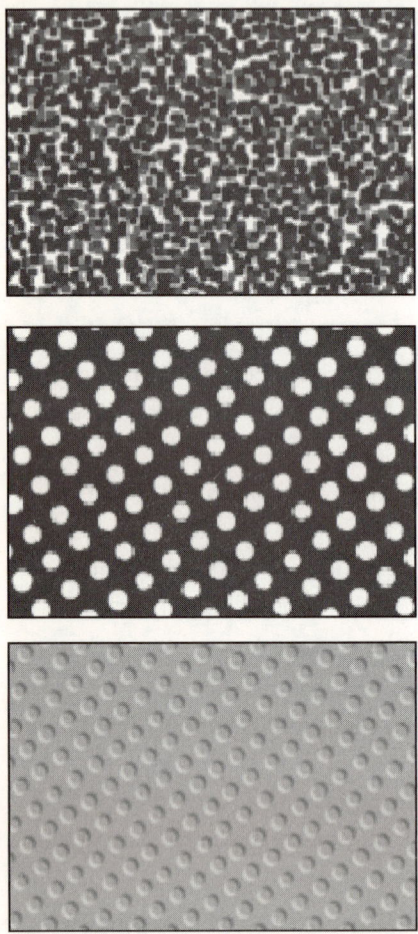

Figure 16.40. Filters can create an interesting background from a solid color layer, such as the Pointillize filter (top), the Color Halftone filter (center), and the Emboss filter applied over the Color Halftone (bottom).

The final image is shown in Figure 16.41. The background, which started as a solid color, now has an interesting graphic appearance.

Figure 16.41. Create a coordinating background for your image using filters.

Stacking filters

Often, I work with filters by applying them to separate copies of the image. As described in the previous set of steps, you can apply filters to individual layers; you can also apply multiple filters to more than one layer.

Choose different blending modes in the Layers palette to blend the effects of multiple filters. Restack the copies in the Layers palette to see the effect of one filter on underlying layers and filters.

Inside Scoop

Because the most recent filter you used is shown at the top of the Filter menu, you can easily reapply the same filter or the Filter Gallery settings a second time just by choosing it from the Filter menu. The same settings are applied again or to another image.

Unifying a number of images

If you have a sequence of images that are quite different, you can create a sense of consistency by using the same filters on each image. For example, Figure 16.42 shows several seashells. Each is different, but because the same background is used, as well as the same filter treatment, they appear unified.

Each image's seashell layer has a Poster Edges filter applied, which is one of the filters in the Artistic filters category. The backgrounds are also made using filters. A background was created for one seashell image and then simply copied and resized for each of the other images, saving time in reproducing the background each time.

The background started out as a solid ochre yellow background. First, a Mezzotint filter (one of the Pixelate filters), was applied using the long strokes option to produce a network of long dark strokes on a yellow background. Then a Radial Blur filter was applied to create the swirling shape from the mezzotint's lines around the central seashell.

Figure 16.42 Use the same filters to unify a collection of images; using the same background further unifies the images.

> **Emphasizing your message**
>
> One way you can emphasize a message in your image, or make the subject more important, is by decreasing distractions in the background. Sometimes, this means removing content altogether. Chapter 14 includes information on how to use a blur to de-emphasize the background of an image; Chapter 15 gives you details of all the available Blur filters.

Creating a sense of motion

You can add a sense of motion to an image where none exists. Although the finished image isn't photorealistic, the filters add to the story. The windup man shown in Figure 16.43 uses three layers and two filters to give Mr. Roboto a sense of motion.

The layers in the image include:

- A gradient adjustment layer used as the background.
- The middle layer is the image of the man.
- The upper layer is a copy of the man's image. The layer's blend mode is set to Overlay at 100% opacity.

There are two filters applied to create the effect:

Figure 16.43. Use filters to provide a sense of motion, enhancing the image's message.

- The Motion Blur filter, one of the Blur filters, is applied to the middle layer (man's image) using the settings shown in Figure 16.44. The angle is set at 0 degrees so the blur is horizontal, and the distance is 13 pixels. The filter is applied to a selection, including the man's back, legs, and the clockwork key. This way the man appears to be moving forward.

- The Find Edges filter, one of the Stylize filters, is applied to the upper layer, which is a copy of the man's image. Blending the copy of the image with the underlying image creates a cartoon quality.

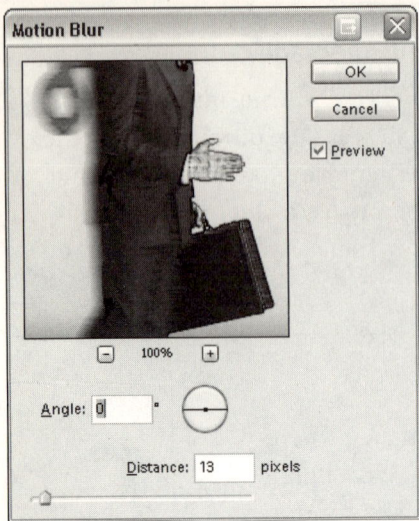

Figure 16.44. Selected areas of one layer use a Motion Blur filter.

Just the facts

- Images can be distorted by using a group of filters that modify the image's geometry.
- Displacement maps are image files that control the application of different effects.
- Many of the filter groups in Photoshop Elements produce an artistic effect through simulating various techniques, materials, and modes of application.
- A wide number of filters can be used to produce backgrounds and textures.
- Use filters in combination for a variety of purposes such as producing very artistic pieces or emphasizing different parts of an image.
- Different filters can be used to create or enhance a sense of motion in an image.

GET THE SCOOP ON...
■ Adding text and text blocks ■ Configuring text ■ Using fonts ■ Masking text ■ Warping and liquifying text

Say It with Words *and* a Picture

The finishing touch in many projects is text. Just as the right background element or graphic can enhance your masterpiece, so too can carefully designed and placed text.

Pay attention to the text, and look through some presentations, projects, and other compilations of images and text that you or others put together. I sometimes find that the text can really make or break the professionalism of a project.

Text is one of two types of vector objects you use in Photoshop Elements; the other vector object is a shape, discussed in Chapter 5. When you apply text to an image, it is placed on its own layer automatically.

Type is either vertical or horizontal in orientation, with horizontal text as the default. Instead of adding text to an image, you can add vertical or horizontal type masks to create some interesting filled layers.

Type tool options

The Type tool gives you a large number of configuration options that display on the options bar when you select the Type tool in the toolbox.

The Type tool's options from left to right, as well as their functions, are listed in Table 17.1.

>  **Inside Scoop**
> You don't have to display the Type tool's submenu in the toolbox; when you select the tool, the four Type tools appear at the left of the tool options. Choose a different tool. When you click the image, the tools disappear from the tool options.

Table 17.1. Type tool options

Tool Group	Tool	Tool Name	How It's Used
Font	Elephant	Font Family	Select a font from the drop-down menu.
	Regular	Font Style	Select a font style for a font family that includes additional typefaces such as bold and italic.
	72 pt	Font Size	Click the drop-down arrow and choose a pre-configured font size, or click the field and type a value.
Anti-aliasing	a̲a̲	Anti-aliased	Use to smooth the text appearance.
Face	T	Faux Bold	Use to apply a simulated bold appearance to text.
	T	Faux Italic	Use to apply a simulated italic or oblique appearance to text.
	T̲	Underline	Use to underline text.
	T̶	Strikethrough	Use to apply a strikethrough to text.
Alignment and Spacing	≡	Left Align Text	Align paragraphs or blocks of text left.
	≡	Center Text	Align paragraphs or blocks of text center.
	≡	Right Align Text	Align paragraphs or blocks of text right.

Tool Group	Tool	Tool Name	How It's Used
	(Auto)	Leading menu	Click the drop-down arrow and choose a value from the menu to specify the space between lines of text.
Color	Color:	Color menu	Click the drop-down arrow to select a color from the swatches or open the Color Picker.
Warp		Warp Text	Use to warp text on different paths.
Orientation		Text Orientation	Change text from vertical to horizontal and vice versa.
Apply text		Cancel	Use to cancel the current text operation.
		Commit	Use to commit the current text operation.

Typing text

You can use text as a single line, such as in a caption or title, or as configured paragraphs in text blocks. The only difference is the way you start the process. Before you start working on a project's text, check the unit of measure set in the program.

Photoshop Elements sets points as the default unit of measurement for type. If you are working with material destined for Web use, for example, you may want to change the default to pixels. To do so, follow these steps:

1. Choose Edit ➪ Preferences ➪ Units & Rulers to open the Preferences dialog box.
2. Click the Type drop-down arrow, and then choose points, mm, or pixels from the menu.
3. Click OK to close the Preferences dialog box.

> **Hack**
> Change the measurement for the font size without changing the preferences. Type a number for the font size in the tool options bar, and then type the unit after the value, such as mm, pt, or px.

Adding a line of text

You can add text to an image by using the Type tool. Follow these steps:

1. Click the tool in the toolbox, and move it over the image to the location where you want to start the text.
2. Click the image with the tool to activate a vertical I-beam, shown in Figure 17.1.
3. Start typing the line of text, and press Enter to wrap text to another line.

Figure 17.1. The active Type tool shows a blinking vertical cursor in the text.

Adding text blocks

Each block of text displayed on an image is a separate object. Instead of clicking the image with the Type tool to activate the cursor and then typing text, click and drag with the tool and create a text box.

With a defined text box, you don't have to add manual returns to break lines of text. Instead, you can use the paragraph alignment options, and resizing the text box automatically wraps the text correctly.

Inside Scoop

Horizontal text uses left, center, and right alignment. Orienting the text vertically renames the alignment options to top, center, and bottom.

Drawing a text block with the Type tool looks different than typed text using manual line breaks. Figure 17.2 shows a text block in its bounding box. You see the resize handles at the sides and corners to use for transforming the text block. A text block also shows a vertical cursor, the same as that shown in Figure 17.1. The difference is that in a block of text wrapped manually, the characters are underlined; a text block in a bounding box isn't underlined.

Figure 17.2. Draw a text block on an image to use a bounding box for containing the text.

Committing text

Text is just a concept until you commit what you have entered to a Type layer in your image in one of these ways:

- Click the Commit button on the options bar.
- Click outside the text box.
- Select a different tool in the toolbox.
- Press Enter on the numeric keypad.

> **Bright Idea**
> You can rename the layer from the shortcut menu and the Layers palette's menu in other ways, but each way involves a couple of mouse clicks to get to the same point where you actually type the new name.

Figure 17.3. The committed text is shown in an active bounding box, and the Select tool is active.

When the text is committed, the actual characters are deselected, and the text displays a bounding box around the content as long as the Type layer is active, shown in Figure 17.3.

The layer is named in the Layers palette using the text you typed by default. You can change the name by double-clicking the existing name in the Layers palette to activate a text box and typing the new name. Click off the Layers palette anywhere to make the change to the layer's name.

Selecting text and text blocks

If you are new to the program, it can take a while to get the hang of selecting text versus selecting the text bounding box or resizing the text box.

You can sort out your selections with time, experimentation, and sometimes a little frustration thrown in for good measure. Keep these thoughts in mind:

- Select the Type tool in the toolbox, and click existing text to activate the cursor in the line of text if you want to add or change the text. The insertion point blinks at the point you clicked.
- Select the Type tool, and drag to select existing text that you want to change. Or click in the text, and then Shift-click to select a range.
- Unless you select existing text first, you can't apply any alternate settings, such as a different font size or color, nor can you delete the text.

Watch Out!
If you select the Type tool and click anywhere on the image except for within the boundaries of existing text, a new layer is added.

- You can delete a text layer in the Layers palette without making any selections on the image.
- Select the Type tool, and double-click a word to select the whole word; triple-click to select a line of text.
- Double-click the text layer's icon in the Layers palette to select all the text in the text block.
- Click the Select tool on the toolbar, and click a text block to select it. If you click the Select tool with an active piece of text, that is, you finish typing text and then immediately click the Select tool, you don't have to select the text block — that's done automatically.
- If you have the Select tool selected in the toolbox and click the type layer in the Layers palette, the text block is selected automatically.
- If you have some text active with the Type tool, when you click another layer in the Layers palette, the text is deselected automatically.

Resizing a text block

One activity that is guaranteed to make you crazy until you figure it out is resizing a text block versus resizing the text.

When you click an existing text block with the Type tool, you see a bounding box surround the text. The bounding box shows whether you used the Type tool and drew a text block, typed text on a single line, or typed text and manually wrapped it by pressing the Enter key.

If you want to resize the text box and automatically wrap the text differently on the image, move the Type tool over a resize handle on one side of the bounding box. When you see the tool change to a straight, double-ended arrow, drag to resize the text box, as shown in Figure 17.4. The text behaves differently depending on whether you wrapped the text manually or typed it in to a text block. The upper image in Figure 17.4 shows manually wrapped text. As the text block is resized, the text doesn't change from the original number of characters per line. In the lower image, showing a drawn text block, the text wraps automatically as the block is resized, either larger as in the image, or smaller.

Figure 17.4. Use the Type tool to resize the text bounding box.

Don't try to resize the text box using the Select tool. Instead of wrapping the text differently within the bounding box, you resize the text vertically and horizontally, depending on your adjustments, as in Figure 17.5.

Inside Scoop

All tools activate the text box in different ways. The Type tool's bounding box is bordered by dashes, while the Select tool's bounding box is bordered by dots. But, if you're like me, you'll think the difference is too close to call.

Figure 17.5. The Select tool resizes the text as you resize the bounding box.

Finding fonts

How many fonts do you have? For some people, fonts are like expensive shoes — you can never have too many. Until recently, however, fonts could be far too much of a good thing if you had to try to figure out which was which.

Photoshop Elements 4 introduces a groovy new feature for font fanatics. After you click the Type tool and activate its options, click the Font drop-down arrow on the options bar and take a look. Rather than seeing multiple columns of font names, you now see the name and a sample of the font, as shown in Figure 17.6. The samples make finding the perfect font simpler.

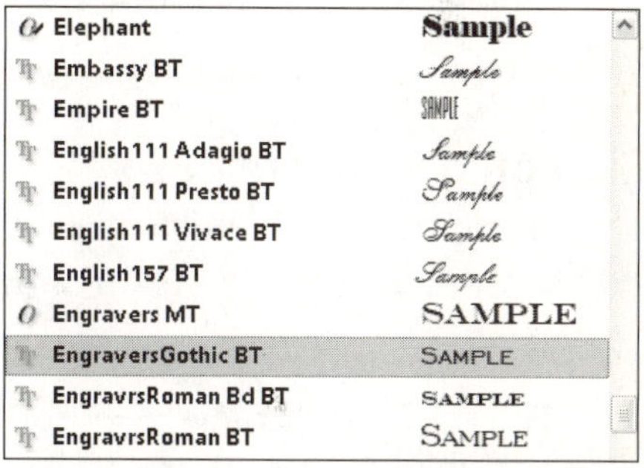

Figure 17.6. The font samples make finding your perfect font easier and more fun.

> **Fonts and faux treatments**
>
> Photoshop Elements lets you apply a faux finish to your fonts. Just like you can apply a faux treatment to make a wall look like leather, you can use a faux bold style to thicken a font and make it appear bold, or faux italic to make the text appear slanted.
>
> The faux appearance looks similar to an actual font face, but if the font you are using has a Bold or Italic variant, use that instead of the faux treatment. If you need to exchange documents in PDF format and need the content of the image to be precisely, you can't use faux font faces.
>
> Faux font faces cannot be embedded or subset. In some types of work, such as creating PDF files, the fonts are embedded, meaning the information about the font is stored in the document properties and transported with the file. Fonts can also be subset, which means the actual characters used in the image are described in the document properties. PDF files exported from Photoshop Elements are in an image PDF format, which automatically retains the appearance of the fonts.

Changing font previews

To take things one step further, you can give your eyes a rest by specifying the size of the sample preview. Follow these steps:

1. Choose Edit ⇨ Preferences ⇨ Type.
2. Click the Font Preview Size drop-down arrow, and choose a size from the list—Small, Medium, or Large.
3. Click OK to close the Preferences dialog box and apply the change. The font menu in Figure 17.6 shows the Large previews preference.

Hack

There are many useful and low-cost (or free!) utilities that let you filter by font style and create collections, including my favorite font utility. Check online for font utilities; check out X-Fonter at www.blacksunsoftware.com.

Using multiple fonts

Suppose you are adding a title to an image and want to use more than one font in the title. No problem. You can add multiple types of text in the same Type layer.

Follow these steps to add and then modify text in the same Type layer, shown in Figure 17.7:

1. Click the Type tool, and choose the settings for your first font.
2. Click the image, and type the text.
3. Drag to select the first word or characters you want to change.
4. Make selections in the options bar, such as using a different font, size, or color.
5. Continue making changes as necessary.
6. Select another tool in the toolbox, or press Enter on the numeric keypad to commit the text to the Type layer.

Figure 17.7. Combine fonts and use different settings in the same Type layer.

Bright Idea

If you have trouble finding a coordinating color for your text, type your text on the image, and then click the Color Swatch on the options bar to open the Color Picker. Use the eyedropper to sample a color from your image. Drag the slider up or down to find a more or less saturated version of the sampled color. Click OK when you've found the color you want.

Multiple spacing

In addition to using multiple fonts, styles, colors, and so on in the same Type layer, you can also use multiple spacing. That is, the spacing between two lines of text, called leading, can be different from that of the rest of the text.

To adjust leading for individual rows follow these steps:

1. Drag to select the line above and below the spacing that you want to adjust.
2. Click the Set the leading drop-down arrow on the type options bar to display the size list.
3. Choose a value from the menu. You can also click the field, and type a value.

The text shown in Figure 17.7 uses different leading between the lines of text.

Masking text

One of the neatest ways to bring a sense of style to a piece is to use text masking, in which you use selections in the shape of letters without any color fill. You can use masked text as titles, within other elements of your image, or as standalone pieces.

Creating the selection

Photoshop Elements offers Horizontal Type Mask and Vertical Type Mask tools that create a selection in the shape of text. They work in the same way as adding text to an image, saving a selection, and then loading the selection separately on another layer. Isn't that convenient?

Follow these steps to create a type mask:

1. Select the layer in the Layers palette on which you want to use the mask.
2. Select the Horizontal Type Mask tool or the Vertical Type Mask tool from the Type tool's submenu; or click the displayed tool in the toolbox, and select the appropriate mask tool in the tool options.
3. Choose options such as font and size from the options bar.
4. Click the image where you want to place the text, and type. You see a red mask overlaying the active layer, shown in Figure 17.8.

>  **Watch Out!**
> Don't try to add a Type mask to an existing Type layer. Instead of typing the selected outline for the text, you simply add more text to the layer.

5. Click another tool to commit the text mask.

6. Fill the mask or apply it to a layer.

Figure 17.8. The selection is typed on a mask layer.

Unmasking your mask

Suppose you have created a mask, but you would like to fill it with an image, rather than cut out the image from the layer on which you applied the mask, like the left image in Figure 17.9.

You can't select the inverse of the mask as with other types of selections. Instead, follow these steps:

1. With the text selection still active on the layer, press Ctrl+X to cut the selection and its fill to the clipboard.

2. In the Layers palette, click New to add a new layer.

3. Press Ctrl+V to paste the content to the new layer.

4. Hide or delete the original layer you used for the fill to achieve the final filled layer, shown in the right image of Figure 17.9.

Figure 17.9. Copy the selection to another layer for an overlaid look. The original masked text is shown in the left image; follow the steps to use the mask on another image (right image).

Warping type

Warping type is one of those effects that can look very good or really, really bad. It's also one of those effects where a little can go a long way.

Getting warped

Photoshop Elements provides a whole palette of options for warping text, ranging from flags to fisheyes. If I use warped text, which isn't very often, I usually restrict it to an arc or an arch that mimics the curvature of another element in the piece.

In Figure 17.10, for example, I applied a slight arch to the heading text that mimics the curvature of the background shape underlying the text.

Figure 17.10. A text warp can enhance text in a composite image, such as a title.

Inside Scoop

The distortion from most warping options misaligns your text. While the Warp Text dialog box is open, you can drag the text object on your image to reposition it.

To apply a text warp, right-click the text layer in the Layer palette and choose Warp Text, or you can click Create Warped Text on the Type tool's options bar. Either action opens the Warp Text dialog box. Follow these steps to warp text in your image:

1. Click the Style drop-down arrow, and choose an option from the menu. Each style has pre-configured settings that display in the dialog box.
2. Click the Horizontal or Vertical button to specify the axis for the effect.
3. Drag the sliders or type a value to define the Bend, Horizontal Distortion, and Vertical Distortion applied to the text.
4. Watch the text in your image as the settings are applied, and adjust as necessary.
5. When you are satisfied with the effect, click OK to close the dialog box.

Getting extremely warped

Save dramatic text warping for extreme purposes. For example, if you are creating a very graphical image, you may want to use the warping of the text as part of the graphics, rather than as instructional or informative text.

In the example shown in Figure 17.11, the angle of the highway is emphasized by a distorted shape layer below the rider and behind the text. In an image like this, it makes sense to change the text substantially to give it a sense of motion as in the rest of the image's elements. The text warp used in the image is the Rise Style, using a +35 percent bend, –70 percent horizontal distortion, and –44 percent vertical distortion.

Figure 17.11. A text warp can be used as a strong graphical element.

Converting text

Text is an interesting thing. As you apply it in layers in the program, it remains a vector object and can be manipulated like a vector object. That is, you can select the text bounding box and apply transformations, resize it, rotate it, and so on.

Text also behaves like text in that you can select it, add or change the content, or modify its characteristics, such as the color or font. You will find, however, that there are some things you can't do with text in Photoshop Elements while it is in vector format. For example, you can't apply some filters and effects to text in vector format like the Liquify filter.

To convert text to a raster image from a vector layer, you can do the following:

- Right-click the layer in the Layers palette, and choose Rasterize Type.
- Choose Layer ⇨ Simplify Layer.
- Click the Layers palette's MORE label to open its menu, and choose Simplify Layer.

Watch Out!
Make sure you have completed edits on the text before converting it. After the text is rasterized, you can no longer modify the text content or characteristics.

You can see in the Layers palette whether a layer is text or not, based on its icon. In Figure 17.12, for example, the upper layer is rasterized, while the lower layer is warped text.

Figure 17.12. Identify the status of a Type layer based on its thumbnail in the Layers palette.

Liquifying type

If simply warping text isn't enough, you can take your experimentation to the next level with liquified text. On the surface, it sounds sort of gruesome, doesn't it? I always visualize dropping a bunch of letters into a blender, and watching them spin and splatter.

Follow these steps to make liquid magic happen to your text:

1. Select the simplified text layer.
2. Choose Filter ⇨ Distort ⇨ Liquify to open the Liquify dialog box and show the text layer.
3. Zoom in or out to size the preview appropriately using the preconfigured Zoom values at the lower left of the dialog box, or click the Zoom tool on the Liquify toolbar and adjust the magnification.
4. Select a tool from the toolbox. The various tools' effects and their icons are identified and explained in Table 16.3, which is located in Chapter 16.

> **Bright Idea**
> In addition to creating very dramatic effects using Liquify tools, you can also enhance and tweak changes made using other filters and commands, such as Transform settings.

5. Configure the tool using the Tool Options. You can set these options:
   - Brush Size from 1 to 600 pixels
   - Brush Pressure from 1 to 100
   - Turbulent Jitter from 1 to 100 for the Turbulence tool
6. Drag with the tool on the preview image to make the changes over a certain area of the image, or click and hold the mouse to make changes only within the perimeter of the brush.
7. When the image has been liquefied to perfection, click OK to close the dialog box and apply the changes in the image, like the one shown in Figure 17.13. In this example, the text was flattened and strung out giving a greater sense of motion, using liberal applications of the Warp, Turbulence, and Bloat tools.

Figure 17.13. The warped text is given more sense of motion using Liquify edits.

> **Inside Scoop**
> The Liquify dialog box is a great place to use a stylus tablet because you are essentially painting the distortions. Use stylus pressure for effect by clicking the Stylus Pressure check box in the Tool Options.

While you are working on an effect in the Liquify dialog box, you can revert to previous states. Here are several ways:

- Click the Reconstruct tool, and drag the brush over the area you want to correct; more of the change happens at the center of the brush.
- Click a point and then Shift+click a second point with the Reconstruct tool to reverse the change in a straight line between the points.
- Press Alt and click Reset to revert to the state of the layer when you opened the Liquify dialog box; the tool settings will stay as you have set them during the session.
- Go back to the start by clicking Revert. The image is restored, and the tools are reset.

If you close the dialog box and then decide you want to revise some aspect of your work, use Ctrl+F to reopen the Liquify dialog box, or choose Filter ⇨ Liquify. In the dialog box, your tool settings are as you left them, but you can't reverse any of the changes you previously made to the layer. For more in-depth information on the Liquify filter, check out Chapter 16.

Just the facts

- Photoshop Elements offers a broad selection of tools and options for adding and configuring text for your images and projects.
- You can add single lines of text or text blocks that can be aligned like paragraphs.
- You can use one or more fonts in the same Type layer, and configure the appearance of each separately.
- Use a Type Mask to create an interesting layered effect in your image.
- Use text warping to add interest or emphasize a message in your image.
- Text can be maintained in the image as a Type layer, or it can be converted to a raster layer.
- Text can use the Liquify filter to configure the content in very elastic and gooey ways.

GET THE SCOOP ON...
■ Painting with brushes ■ Managing brush libraries ■
Customizing and creating brushes ■ Using pattern
stamps ■ Erasing pixels

Are You the Next Picasso?

When you think of working with images, you may not immediately think of painting or of brushes. I know people who have used Photoshop or Photoshop Elements regularly for years without using brushes because they weren't interested in "artwork."

Brushes in Photoshop Elements are used for much more than artistic work, as has been described in other chapters. For example, Chapters 13 and 14 describe different ways of manually editing images and performing visual and conceptual touchups. Many of these different types of manipulation involve using tools that work like brushes, and some use brush settings and values.

Sampling image content

One interesting and timesaving feature in Photoshop Elements is the ability to use one *sample* with different tools. This means that you can save an image or a selected sample from an image, like the selected area in the image at the top left of Figure 18.1. (I've highlighted the selected area in the original image to make it visible in the figure.)

The same pattern can be used as a pattern fill, shown in the upper-right image in the figure; for use with the Pattern Stamp tool, shown in the left lower image in the figure or you can store it a Brush tip. The lower-right image in Figure 18.1 uses the same pattern as the other images for the brush, which is applied by clicking and dragging to paint the stroke. A single copy of the pattern is applied at the lower left of the stroke by clicking the image once with the Brush tool.

Figure 18.1. Use the same pattern with different tools and in multiple ways. The selected area (upper left) can be saved as a pattern fill for filling other selections (upper right), as a pattern for the Pattern Stamp tool (lower left), or as a custom brush stroke (lower right).

The option you choose depends on the follow criteria:

- Whether you want to preserve the pattern for long-term use. If you have a pattern that you like, and can see reusing it in the future, take the time to save the pattern.
- Whether the pattern is discrete enough to use as a brush. Some patterns are very difficult to identify as a brush if they are too indistinct, or there is not enough contrast to make the contents discernible.
- Whether the pattern scales to fit the requirements of your image. A brush tip can be resized to virtually any dimensions. If you produce a brush tip from a very large pattern, it won't be usable at a small size.
- The characteristics of the area you want to fill. If your image has a number of elements that could use the pattern, such as repeating objects used in a background for a collage, saving the pattern will save time when creating the elements.

Types of brush strokes

The painting tools in Photoshop Elements share some common features and options, although each tool produces a different effect on the image. Figure 18.2 shows the paint tools' icons and examples of the various brush strokes including:

- The Brush tool, which paints strokes of smooth, antialiased color

- The Impressionist Brush tool, which applies stylized brush strokes to existing color in your image

- The Pencil tool, which paints hard-edged strokes

- The Impressionist Brush tool, which applies stylized brush strokes to existing color in your image

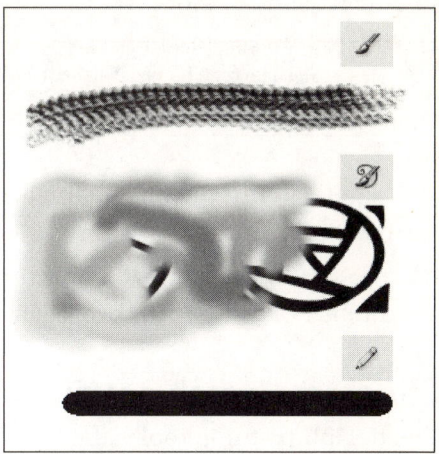

Figure 18.2. Different painting tools produce different effects on the image. From top to bottom, the strokes are applied using the Brush tool, Impressionist Brush tool, and Pencil tool.

Along with tools that you would think of as traditional types of painting, Photoshop Elements offers more tools that affect color in brush strokes. The tools' icons and examples of these tools in action are shown in Figure 18.3 and include the following:

- The Pattern Stamp tool, which paints with a selected pattern

- The Color Replacement Brush tool, which replaces a

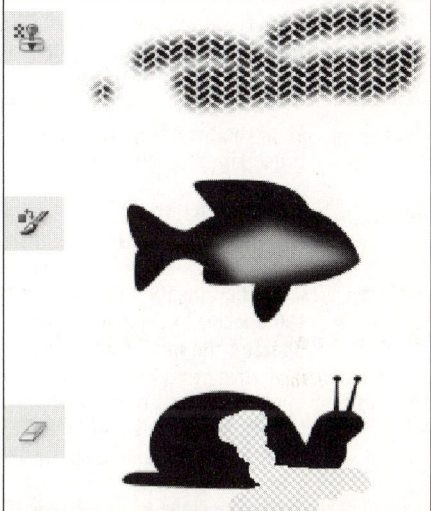

Figure 18.3. Other tools can apply paint to your image. The upper example is a pattern applied with the Pattern Stamp tool, the center example shows color replaced using the Color Replacement Brush tool, and the lower example shows the image and background being erased with the Eraser tool.

Inside Scoop

A number of other tools apply color in other ways than painting strokes, such as the Paint Bucket and Gradient tools, which are described in Chapter 6. The Smudge tool in finger-paint mode applies color as well. Read about using the Smudge tool in Chapter 14.

target color in the image with a different color without affecting the rest of the image

- The Eraser tools, which apply the background color specified in the toolbox or erase color pixels leaving transparent areas

Choosing brush settings

The default painting tool is the Brush tool. When you select a Brush tool in the toolbox, the options bar displays the choices listed in Table 18.1.

Table 18.1. Paint tool options

Option	How to Configure
Brushes palette	Click the drop-down arrow to open the Brushes palette, and choose the brush you want to use; select a category from the Brushes palette's menu to load additional brushes for selection.
Size	Click the Size drop-down arrow to display the slider, and drag to size the brush tip in pixels or type a value in the Size field.
Mode	Blend the painted strokes you apply with the existing image in numerous ways. See Chapter 11 for a discussion on Blend modes.
Opacity	Click the Opacity drop-down arrow to display the slider, and drag to change the opacity in percent or type a value in the Opacity field. The lower the opacity, the more transparent the brush stroke is.
Airbrush	Click the Airbrush check box to use and configure paint characteristics like traditional airbrushing by building more paint up as you apply more pressure, like the example shown in Figure 18.4.
Tablet options	Choose options for the stylus if you are painting with a pressure-sensitive drawing tablet instead of a mouse.

Painting using the Airbrush setting applies the paint gradually in an image when you are using a graphic tablet. Adjusting the opacity and stroking the image repeatedly produces the same effect if you aren't using a tablet. Figure 18.4 shows examples of strokes applied with the same brush tip. The lower stroke uses the Airbrush option, while the upper stroke is applied without using the Airbrush.

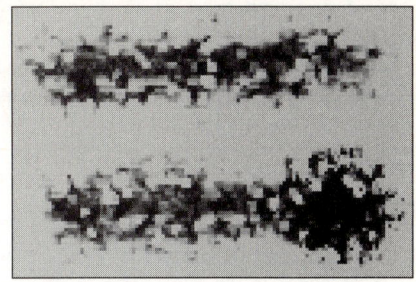

Figure 18.4. The two strokes use the same brush tip; paint builds up when using the Airbrush option, shown in the lower stroke.

Selecting a brush library

The Brushes palette shows you the available brushes in the program in different ways. You can display a brush library as text labels, lists, or thumbnails. The Stroke Thumbnail view is probably the most useful view, especially if you aren't very familiar with the brushes. In that view, shown in Figure 18.5, you see the brush's appearance and its default size in pixels, as well as a representation of how the brush stroke looks using the brush tip.

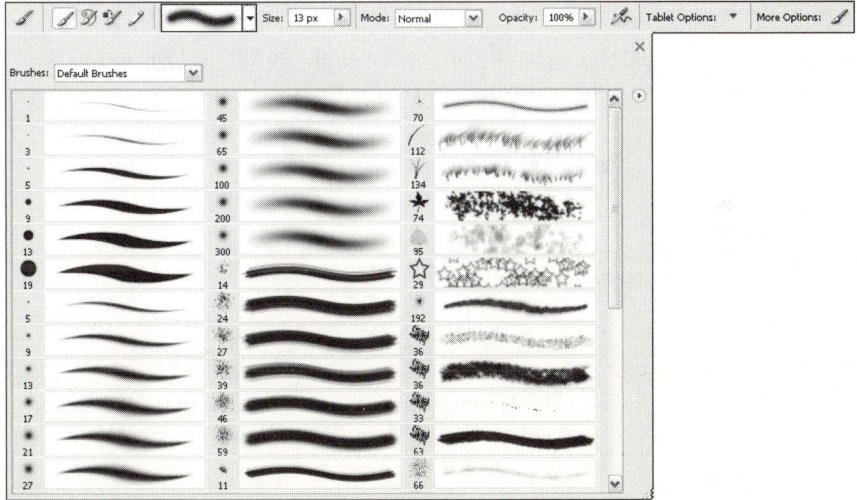

Figure 18.5. See both the brush's tip and how it draws a stroke in the Stroke Thumbnail view.

Inside Scoop

If you are looking at brushes, move your mouse over a thumbnail of the brush and pause to show the brush's name in a tooltip.

Viewing brushes

Click the visible brush in the options bar to open the Brushes palette, and then click the Brushes drop-down arrow to open the listing of brush categories. Information about the different categories of brushes you can use in Photoshop Elements is listed in Table 18.2.

If the Brushes palette isn't sized to your liking, it, like other palettes that open from the options bar, can be resized to show you a larger view than the default single column. Drag the bottom-right corner of the palette to resize it.

Table 18.2. Available types of paint brushes

Brush Category	Characteristics
Default Brushes	The Default brushes include a variety of brushes from different categories, such as round soft and hard brushes, wet media, and faux finish brushes.
Assorted Brushes	The Assorted brushes include a variety of brushes based on a simple shape, such as an open circle, a star, or a set of dots.
Basic Brushes	The Basic brushes contain a selection of hard and soft round brush tips in varying sizes.
Calligraphic Brushes	The Calligraphic brushes are brushes of different hardnesses and angles that produce varying line widths simulating drawing with a calligraphy pen.
Drop Shadow Brushes	The Drop Shadow brushes include varying sizes of round and square brushes; the shadow appears as a blurred margin.
Dry Media Brushes	The Dry Media brushes include different sizes and shapes of brush simulating media such as charcoal and chalk.
Faux Finish Brushes	Faux Finish brushes produce effects similar to those achieved using different decorative painting techniques, such as sponging and feathering.

Brush Category	Characteristics
Natural Brushes and Natural Brushes 2	The Natural brushes produce brushstrokes that look like tree bark, stones, shells, and other natural materials.
Pen Pressure	The Pen Pressure collection of brushes includes a variety of shapes, configurations, and patterns, all of which are sensitive to pen pressure and suited for using a pressure-sensitive tablet.
Special Effect Brushes	The Special Effect brushes use images as the brush tips, letting you draw strokes composed of flowers, butterflies, or a rubber ducky.
Square Brushes	The Square brushes offer a selection of hard-edged, square-tipped brushes in varying sizes.
Thick Heavy Brushes	The Thick Heavy brushes produce brush strokes like those made with different types of bristle brushes.
Wet Media Brushes	Wet Media brushes simulate brushstrokes made using oil, ink, or watercolor on varying surfaces.

Painting with a Drop Shadow brush doesn't produce the same appearance as adding a drop shadow to the stroke on a layer, as you can see in Figure 18.6.

Specifying a default brush category

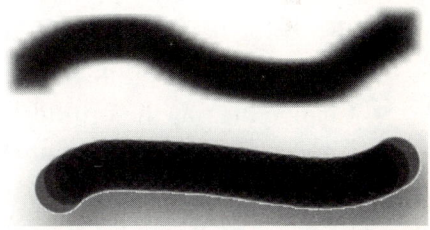

Figure 18.6. A Drop Shadow brushstroke (upper) produces a subtler effect than applying a drop shadow to a brushstroke on a layer (lower).

When you choose a Brush tool, the Default brushes are active in the Brushes palette. You can leave the selection as is or change the displayed brushes in the Preset Manager. Setting a different default brush library is one of the small ways you can increase your efficiency with a few seconds of configuration time.

Follow these steps to manage the brushes:

1. Choose Edit ⇨ Preset Manager to open the dialog box, shown in Figure 18.7.

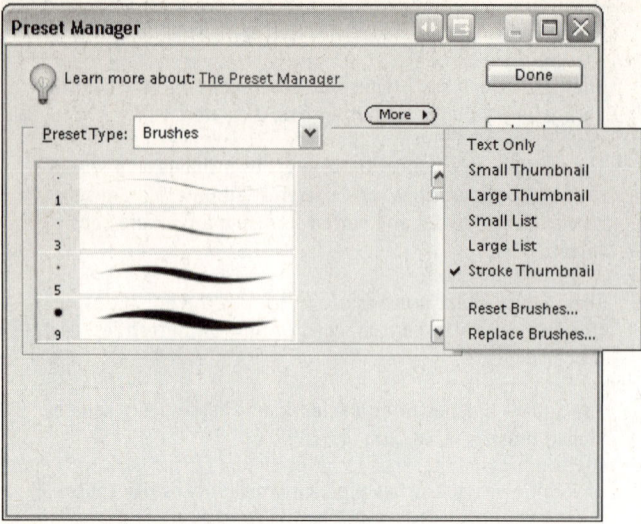

Figure 18.7. Specify the collection of brushes you want to use as the default set in the Preset Manager.

2. Click the Preset Type drop-down arrow, and choose Brushes to load them into the dialog box.

3. In the dialog box, click the More button to open a submenu, where you can do the following:

   - Change the way the brushes are shown in the Preset Manager. Choose options such as thumbnails, lists, and text only.
   - Reset the Brushes palette and the brush libraries to their defaults by choosing Reset Brushes.
   - Change the brushes displayed in the program as the default. Choose Replace Brushes to open the Load Brushes dialog box. Select the brush file, and click Load to close the dialog box.

4. Click Close to dismiss the Preset Manager dialog box.

Hack

Want to bring in a whole collection of brushes from a colleague for a project? Instead of working through Photoshop Elements, work through the Explorer. Ask for the brushes file, which uses the ABR extension. Store the file in this folder: C:\Program Files\Adobe\Photoshop Elements 4.0\Presets\Brushes.

When you select a Brush tool and click the drop-down arrow to open the Brushes palette, the brush file you chose in the Preset Manager is displayed as the default brush library.

Painting with a brush

You can use the Brush tool to paint strokes of color or airbrush color in the image. Follow these steps to use the Brush tools:

1. Specify the foreground color in the toolbox to use as the paint color.
2. Select the Brush tool in the toolbox.
3. Select the Brush type in the options bar from the Brushes palette.
4. Specify options for the tool in the options bar, listed previously in Table 18.1.
5. Click and drag to paint a line.

Customizing brush tips

At first glance, the two brushstrokes shown in Figure 18.8 look as though they are made using different brush tips. In fact, they are the same brush using different customizations.

Figure 18.8. Customizing a brush tip can produce a very different appearance (lower) from the default (upper).

If you want to take the process a step beyond specifying the brush tip's size and blend mode, modify how the brush performs as it is used by setting dynamic options. Dynamic options change as the brush stroke is being applied, producing a more painterly effect.

Click the More Options button on the options bar to open the menu shown in Figure 18.9. For most of the settings, either drag the slider bar or type a value for the setting in the field.

Inside Scoop

Draw a straight line by clicking a starting point, pressing Shift, and clicking the ending point.

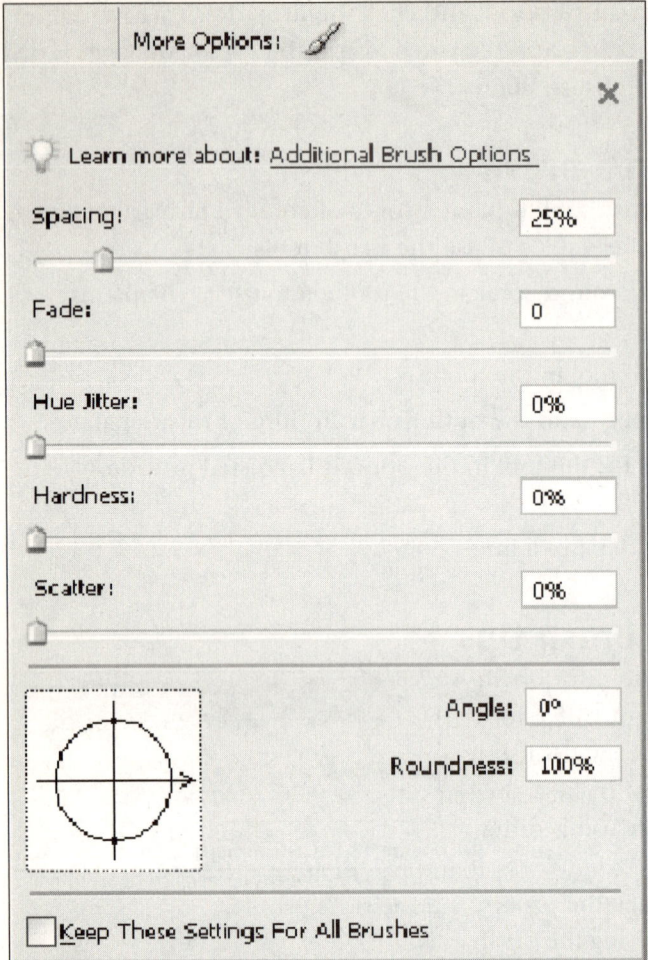

Figure 18.9. Configure additional options for brush tips for a custom look.

You can make adjustments to these settings:

- **Spacing.** Control the distance between applications of the brush marks in a stroke. Increasing the spacing spreads out the brush marks. The brush shown in Figure 18.8 is adjusted from the default 25 percent by setting the spacing for the lower example to 100 percent.

- **Fade.** Specify the number of steps to gradually decrease the paint flow and fade it entirely. At 0, the brush has no fade, like the top image in Figure 18.10. Low values make the paint stroke fade quickly, while increasing the value makes the paint's fade slower. In Figure 18.10, the middle example uses a fade value of 25, and the lower example uses a fade value of 300. The fade range can be 0 to 9999.

Figure 18.10. Specify the number of steps required to fade the paint flow from a brush tip. The upper stroke has no fade, the middle example uses a value of 25, and the lower example a fade value of 300.

- **Hue Jitter.** Specify a rate for switching the stroke color between foreground and background colors set in the toolbox. The higher the value, the faster the switch occurs. Figure 18.11 shows the default brush at the top, which paints with the foreground color only. Contrast that with the lower brush stroke, using a 100 percent Hue Jitter value. The color swaps frequently between variations of both foreground and background color.

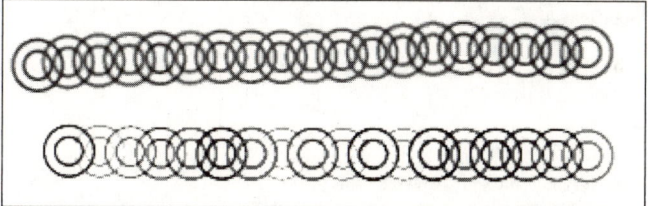

Figure 18.11. Use the Hue Jitter value to define whether to have the paint switch between foreground and background colors and how fast to make the change.

- **Hardness.** Drag the Hardness slider to control the size of the brush's center, which is "harder" and therefore paints darker than the edges of the stroke. The higher the Hardness value as a percentage, the

>  **Inside Scoop**
> You can't specify a Hardness value for all brushes. The basic types of brush, such as round and square brushes, can be modified, while more decorative brushes, such as the Special Effects brushes, can't be modified.

more of the total diameter of the brush is designated as the hard center, up to 100 percent.

If you aren't sure what kind of changes your settings will make on a brush, as you adjust the settings keep an eye on the brush's thumbnail in the options bar. The preview of the brush tip changes with your modifications.

- **Scatter.** Specify how the brush marks are spread in a stroke. The lower the value is, the less scattering and the denser the stroke. For example, the upper stroke in Figure 18.12 uses a Scatter value of 0. The higher the value is, the greater the scattering and dispersal of the brush marks. The lower stroke in Figure 18.12 uses a Scatter value of 300.

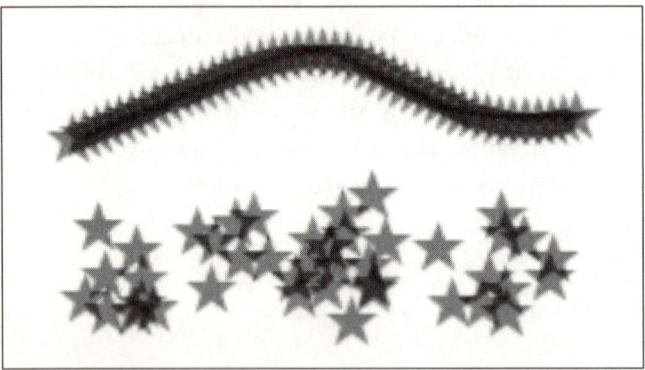

Figure 18.12. Control the density of the stroke and how widely the brush marks are dispersed by setting the Scatter value; the lower image shows the effect of increasing the value.

- **Angle.** Specify an angle for the brush tip by typing a value in degrees or clicking the thumbnail to indicate the correct angle. The upper row of ducks painted in Figure 18.13 uses the default 0 degree angle; the lower paint stroke shows the ducks at –90 degrees.

> ### Setting up a tablet
>
> Wacom and other pressure-sensitive tablets can be configured for drawing and painting in Photoshop Elements. In the Editor, select the Brush tool in the toolbox and then set Tablet Option in the options bar that you want to control with pen pressure. You can use pen pressure to control a brush's Size, Opacity, Hue Jitter, Scatter, and Roundness.

- **Roundness.** Define the ratio between the short and long axes of the brush as a percentage. Type a value in the field or click in the thumbnail to specify the value. At 100 percent, the brush is round, like that used for the upper row of ducks in Figure 18.13. At 0 percent the brush is linear. Between the two extremes, the brush tip is elliptical, such as the lower paint stroke that uses a Roundness value of 45.

Figure 18.13. Both the angle and the roundness of a brush can be modified for a custom brush stroke.

Managing brushes

You don't have to leave the existing brush libraries as is. Add new brushes, or delete existing ones. You can't save more than 8,000 different brush tips, but that isn't likely to be a problem for many of us!

Saving a custom brush

You can save any brush you reconfigure in the Brushes libraries — a terrific feature if you configure and use a brush today and then want to return to the image next week to make edits, or you'd like to use the same brush in another project.

Follow these steps to store a new brush in your library:

1. Modify the brush as desired for your project.
2. Click the drop-down arrow next to the brush sample in the options bar to open the Brushes palette.
3. Click the Brushes drop-down arrow to open the list of brush libraries and choose the brush library in which you want to save your new brush tip.
4. Click the menu arrow to open the palette's menu, and choose Save Brush.
5. Type a name for the new brush in the Brush Name dialog box, and click OK to close the dialog box. Your new brush is added to the Brushes palette — complete with a preview — as you can see in Figure 18.14.

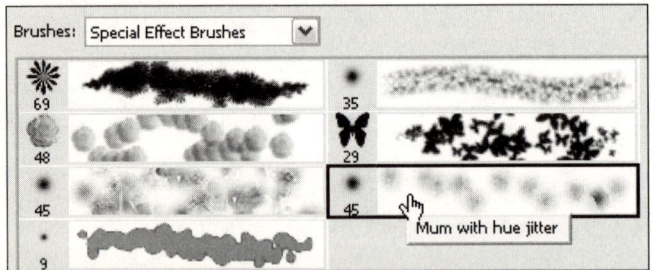

Figure 18.14. New custom brushes and a preview thumbnail are included in the Brush palette.

Watch Out!
If you make changes to an existing brush tip and then save it as custom brush without renaming it, you've permanently changed that brush tip.

> **Bright Idea**
> It's much faster to simply use the Alt key to change the cursor to scissors to delete a brush. Try it a few times, and you won't go back to using menus to select the command.

Deleting brushes

You can easily delete brushes — either existing brushes or custom brushes you have added to a library. Follow these steps:

1. Click the arrow next to the brush sample on the options bar to open the Brushes palette.
2. Click the Brushes drop-down list, and choose the library containing the brush you want to delete.
3. Move the mouse over the brush you want to delete, press Alt to change the mouse cursor to a scissors cursor, and click the brush to delete it.

You can also delete the brush in one of these ways:

- Select the brush in the palette, and click the arrow to open the palette menu. Choose Delete Brush from the palette menu.
- Open the Preset Manager, either from the palette menu or by choosing Edit ⇨ Preset Manager, select Brushes from the Preset Type menu, select the brush from the library, and click Delete.

If you delete a brush by mistake, all is not lost. The brush files are stored at this location on your hard drive: C:\Program Files\Adobe\Photoshop Elements 4.0\Presets\Brushes. You can import the default brush files, which use the ABR file format, from the program's installation CD.

Using images as brushes

You can create a custom brush from anything ranging from drawn or painted content to a section of an existing image to an entire image layer. You can see examples of each of these options in Figure 18.15.

The brush you create is stored as a grayscale object and uses the foreground color selected in the toolbox, just as with other brushes. Custom brushes can be as large as 2500 pixels by 2500 pixels.

Follow these steps to create a new custom brush:

1. Use the painting tools to draw a shape or pattern you want to use as the source for the brush.
2. In the Brushes palette, select the library where you want to store your new brush. You don't have to select a specific brush from the library.
3. Select the content you want to convert to a brush. If you want to use the entire image as a brush, you don't have to make a selection. In the example shown in Figure 18.15, the brush is defined by an elliptical selection around the oval shape.

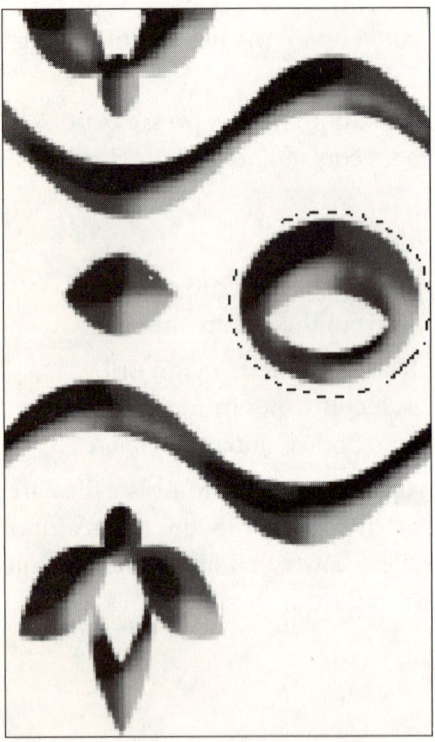

Figure 18.15. Create a custom brush from different forms of existing content like the oval object that is part of a pattern.

4. Choose an option from the Edit menu depending on your source image for the brush, defined in the previous step:
   - Choose Edit ⇨ Define Brush if the entire image is to be used as the brush.

- Choose Edit ⇨ Define Brush From Selection if you have selected content on the image to use for the brush, as in the example shown in Figure 18.15.

5. Type the name for the new brush in the New Brush dialog box shown in Figure 18.16.

Figure 18.16. Name your new brush using a descriptive name.

6. Click OK to save the brush and close the dialog box.
7. Test your brush. Like other brushes you can change the options, as shown in Figure 18.17, such as size, opacity, and other features such as scatter and hue jitter.

Figure 18.17. Modify custom brushes in the same ways as brushes included in the Photoshop Elements brush libraries.

Painting in specialized modes

The Brush and Pencil tools offer two additional blending modes that can both save time and create interesting effects. Selecting either the Brush or Pencil tools activates the Mode setting in the options bar.

Click the Mode drop-down arrow to open the list, which includes Behind and Clear options. Examples of the two specialized blend modes are shown in Figure 18.18, along with an example of the paint applied at the left of the figure using Normal mode for reference. These modes work as follows:

- **Behind mode.** The Behind mode paints only on transparent areas of a layer, such as the leaf and stem areas shown at the center area on the figure. If there are no transparent areas, you don't see any change in your image.

- **Clear mode.** The Clear mode paints each pixel transparent rather than with a color, like the right example in Figure 18.18.

You may find situations where painting in these modes can save you time, so be sure to take a few minutes to experiment with them.

Figure 18.18. In addition to normal application of paint (left), both the Brush and Pencil tools let you paint behind existing content in your image (center) or delete existing content by painting transparent pixels (right).

Watch Out!
If the Clear or Behind modes don't seem to be working, make sure that the layers you are trying to work with aren't locked.

Drawing with a pencil

When is a pencil not a pencil? Answer: when it's a brush. In Photoshop Elements, the Pencil tool is included in the Brush tool group. You don't always want to draw soft, fluid strokes on your images. Use the Pencil tool when you need a hard-edged line or stroke.

Select the Pencil tool from the toolbox, and then choose the options you need in the options bar, shown in Figure 18.19.

Figure 18.19. Configure settings for the Pencil tool in the options bar.

The options you can adjust for the Pencil tool are:

- **Choosing a brush tip.** Click the drop-down arrow on the options bar to open the Brushes palette. Select a brush category and a brush thumbnail. The two upper strokes in Figure 18.20 use a calligraphy brush tip, which draws an angled stroke.

- **Setting the size.** Type a value in the Size field or drag the slider. The strokes shown in Figure 18.20 are 15 pixels wide.

Figure 18.20. Painting with the pencil lets you replace areas of foreground color with background color.

- **Setting a blending mode.** Click the drop-down arrow and choose a blend option for the pencil.
- **Specifying transparency.** Drag the slider or type a value in the Opacity field to define how transparent the pencil strokes are. In the lower strokes in Figure 18.20 that are drawn over the rectangle shape, the Opacity is decreased to 60 percent.
- **Painting with background color.** Click the Auto Erase check box to activate this feature, letting you paint background color over areas containing foreground color, as shown by the two strokes drawn

over the rectangle shape in Figure 18.20. If you start drawing from an area not displaying the foreground color, like the bottom most stroke, the Pencil tool paints with the foreground color instead. How efficient!

Creating an impression

Regardless of the techniques and tools used to create an image, the Impressionist Brush tool can change its appearance to look like it was painted using different types of brush strokes.

Select the Impressionist Brush tool from the toolbox or by clicking its icon on the options bar if another painting tool is active. As with other painting tools, choose options including brush tip, size, and opacity. The Mode choices include only Normal, Darken/Lighten, and Hue/Saturation/Color/Luminosity choices, shown in Figure 18.21.

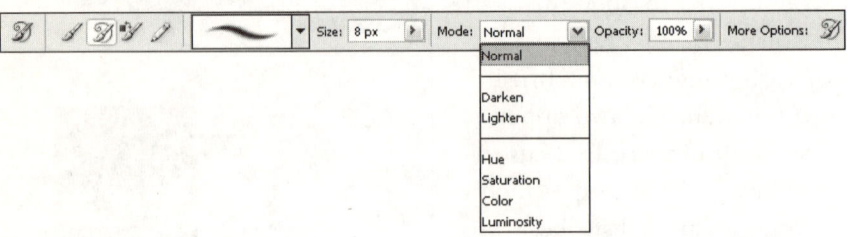

Figure 18.21. Options for the Impressionist Brush tool are similar to other brushes, except there are fewer Mode choices.

The Impressionist Brush includes additional settings for styling the brush stroke. Click More Options on the options bar to display a small dialog box, shown in Figure 18.22.

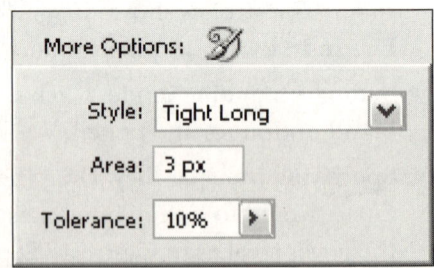

Figure 18.22. Choose additional ways to configure the Impressionist Brush tool.

You can customize the brush stroke by choosing from these options:

- **Style.** Click Style to open a list of different types of brush strokes, ranging from Tight to Loose, Straight to Curly strokes.

> **Inside Scoop**
> The Mode options are restricted for the Impressionist Brush because it doesn't add color pixels itself; it merely acts on the existing pixels using settings that you specify.

- **Area.** Specify the size of the brush stroke as well as the number of strokes applied. Type a value in pixels. Both examples in Figure 18.23 use an area of 3 pixels.

Figure 18.23. Customize an area painted with the Impressionist Brush using different styles, like the Tight Short style (left) or the Tight Curl style (right).

- **Tolerance.** Drag the slider to specify how similar the color values must be between adjacent pixels in percent before they are modified by the brush stroke. The higher the tolerance value, the wider the range of color affected by the brush stroke; the lower the tolerance value the narrower the range of color affected by the brush stroke. In the example shown in Figure 18.23, both samples use a Tolerance value of 10 percent.

Figure 18.23 shows examples of two different brush tips: the Tight Short style is shown at the left, and the Tight Curl style is shown at the right.

Replacing image colors

Another tool offered in the Brush group of tools is used for painting replacement color in an image. The Color Replacement Brush tool is a convenient way to make specific changes, such as changing or correcting the color of an object or changing a background color. The options bar for the Color Replacement Brush tool is shown in Figure 18.24.

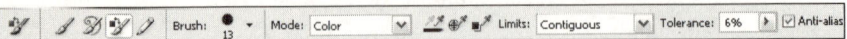

Figure 18.24. Options for the Color Replacement Brush tool to allow you to sample colors in the image and replace them with other colors.

Sampling color

You can use several methods for sampling the color in an image using the Color Replacement tool's features. Each changes the color in different ways, as shown in Figure 18.25.

Figure 18.25. Sample the image according to the color areas that you are replacing.

Bright Idea
For the most control over the brush strokes, use the Dab style and a low area value.

Inside Scoop

Photoshop Elements also includes the Color Replace command that lets you select a range of colors for replacement. Read about using the Color Replace method in Chapter 14.

Your choices include:

- **Continuous.** As you drag in the image with the Color Replacement tool, the color is continuously sampled. The left brim of the hat in Figure 18.25 is sampled using the Continuous method. The color is replaced consistently as each pixel is defined as the replacement color.

- **Sample Once.** Click a color to identify it for replacement. As you drag the tool over the image, only the pixels using the sampled color are replaced. In Figure 18.25, the flowers on the brim are used for the Sample Once example. The sample it taken from the left flower, and only those pixels in the flowers that are within the tolerance range are colored.

- **Background Swatch.** This choice erases only areas containing the current background color. The color in the right brim and background at the right edge of the hat are both replaced in Figure 18.25 as the background color set in the toolbox is within the color range of the modified areas in the image.

The color replacement process can be customized by setting a limit and specifying the tolerance. Select one of two replacement types in the options bar:

- **Discontiguous.** The sample color is replaced wherever it occurs under the brush tip cursor.

- **Contiguous.** This option limits the color replacement to only those pixels that are adjacent to the target color pixel under the cursor.

Check the Tolerance value if you find that too many colors are being replaced as you paint with the tool. If you want only colors very similar to the sampled color to be replaced, use a low percentage value for the Tolerance; to increase the range of color, use a higher percentage value. The tolerance level for the example at the right side of the hat in Figure 18.25 is set very high at a value of 50 percent. As a result, both the dark area of the brim and the light area of the background are within the tolerance range and replaced.

Replacing color

Follow these steps to use the Color Replacement tool:

1. Select the Color Replacement tool from the Brush flyout menu on the toolbox, or select it in the options bar if the active tool is one of the Brush tools.
2. Choose a brush tip from the Brush palette in the options bar.
3. Specify the Mode setting. For replacing color, use the Color option; other choices include Hue, Saturation, and Luminosity. The examples shown in Figure 18.25 use the Luminosity Mode to show the paint effect in a grayscale image.
4. Choose other settings depending on the characteristics of your image and the color you want to replace. The Anti-alias check box is selected by default and smooths the edge of your corrected area.
5. Specify the foreground color to use for replacement.
6. Sample the color you want to replace in the image.
7. Drag in the image to make the color changes.

Stamping patterns

The Pattern Stamp tool paints with a pattern defined from your active image, another image, or an existing pattern. The Pattern Stamp tool is paired with the Clone Stamp tool in the toolbar. The Clone Stamp tool is discussed in Chapter 14.

Creating a new stamp

Draw or open an image in Photoshop Elements that you want to use as the source for your stamp pattern. Creating a pattern for a stamp is similar to creating a brush tip in that you can use new or existing material as the source for the brush or stamp. A stamp pattern, however, can only be defined as a rectangle because the program uses the pattern to tile a fill.

Create your stamping pattern following these steps:

1. Using the Rectangular Marquee tool, select the entire image layer or the area on the image that you want to use as a pattern, like the example shown in Figure 18.26.

> ### Building a logo stamp
>
> If you have a company logo in an illustration format, such as an EPS or AI file, use the information in this section to convert it to a rasterized image, and then save it as a pattern stamp in Photoshop Elements. Be sure to keep in mind that if you are printing the logo you need a file using a resolution about 300dpi. If your logo is already an image format, like a TIFF or a JPEG file, open it and save it as a pattern. When you need a copy for a document or project, just apply it as a stamp to save time locating the file, opening it, copying it, and pasting it as a layer into your current project.

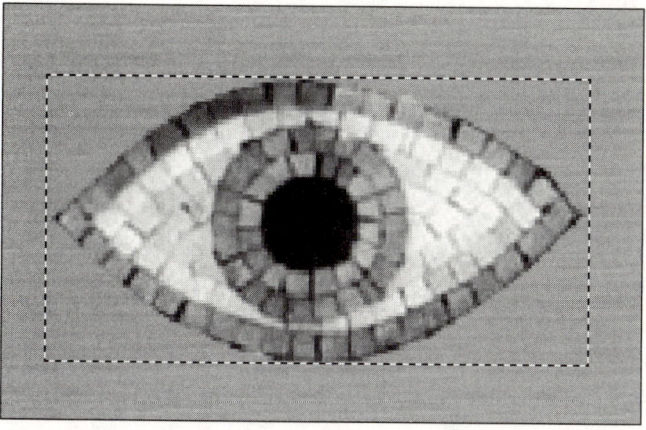

Figure 18.26. Use the Rectangular Marquee tool to select an area to define and save as a pattern.

2. Set the Feather value to 0 in the options bar to produce a consistent pattern.
3. Choose Edit ⇨ Define Pattern from Selection to open the Pattern Name dialog box.
4. Type a name for the pattern, and click OK to close the dialog box and save the pattern.

You can see the pattern displayed in the options bar when you select a tool that uses patterns, such as the Brush tools or the Pattern Stamp tool. Click the Pattern drop-down arrow on the options bar to open the pattern list, shown in Figure 18.27. Your new pattern is added to the end of the list.

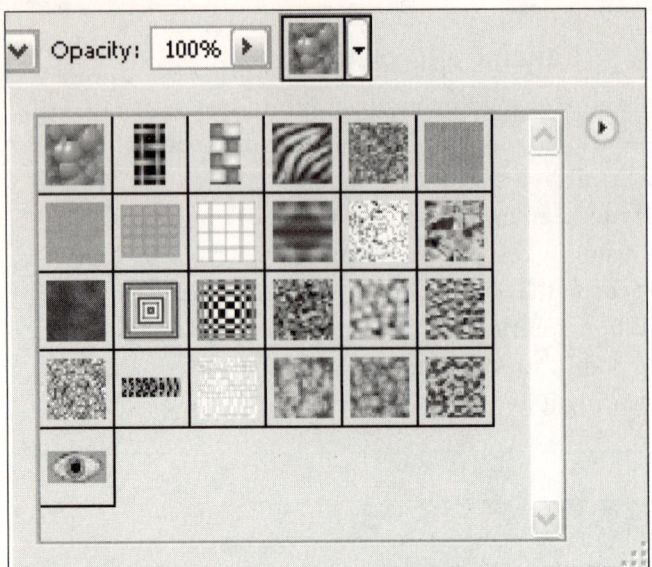

Figure 18.27. Use the Rectangular Marquee tool to select an area to define and save as a pattern.

Applying a Pattern Stamp

The Pattern Stamp and Clone Stamp tools are grouped in the toolbox. Select the visible tool and in the options bar click the Pattern Stamp tool if it isn't the active tool.

Follow these steps to paint with the Pattern Stamp tool on an image:

1. Select options for the Pattern Stamp tool in the options bar shown in Figure 18.28. Your painting characteristics are based on the same features as those used by other brushes described earlier in the chapter, including the brush tip and its size, blend mode, and opacity.

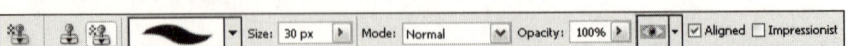

Figure 18.28. Specify options for the Pattern Stamp, including whether to align the pattern or use Impressionist strokes.

2. Define how the pattern is repeated by selecting or deselecting the Aligned check box on the options bar:

Bright Idea

For an extra artistic touch, click the Impressionist check box in the Pattern Stamp's options bar. The pattern is painted using a soft, paint-dabbed effect.

- Click the Aligned check box in the options bar to align the pattern from one paint stroke to the next, making it simple to fill an area with a pattern. The Aligned check box was selected to produce the pattern at the upper left in Figure 18.29.

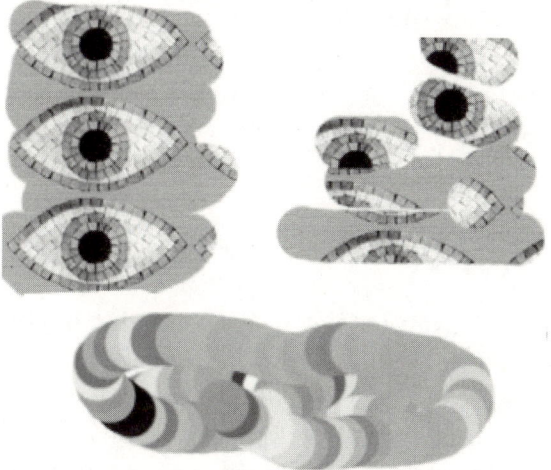

Figure 18.29. A pattern can be aligned as it is applied with the Pattern Stamp (left) or restarted with each mouse click (right). The Impressionist setting blurs and blends the content of the stamp as it is applied (bottom).

- Deselect the Aligned check box to restart the pattern with each brush stroke. Each time you click and drag, the pattern is centered on the cursor's location, like the pattern shown at the upper right in Figure 18.29.

3. Click the Impressionist check box to create a soft blurring of the stamp's contents, shown in the lower image in Figure 18.29.
4. Click or click and drag in the image to paint the pattern.

> ### Working with PostScript patterns
>
> Photoshop Elements includes a folder of PostScript drawings in Adobe Illustrator format that you can use for stamping patterns. The files are stored at this location on your hard drive: ...Program Files/Adobe/Photoshop Elements 4/Presets/Patterns/PostScript Patterns.
>
> When you select a file to open in Photoshop Elements, it is converted automatically from its native PostScript format to a raster format that you can save in an image format, such as TIFF or PSD.
>
> The PostScript patterns are anti-aliased RGB images at 72ppi resolution, but you can change the settings to suit your purpose. If you expect to use the pattern for print work, for example, change the resolution. Modify the size if you want to change the default repeat for the pattern.

Erasing pixels

In addition to adding colored pixels to your image using the different painting tools, you can erase colored pixels from your image using different eraser tools. When erasing pixels from a Background layer or other layer having locked transparency, erased pixels take on the background color specified in the toolbox, like the dark gray area at the left of the image in Figure 18.30. In an unlocked layer, erasing pixels leaves transparent areas, like that at the right of the image in Figure 18.30.

Figure 18.30. Erasing pixels on a locked layer replaces the erased content with the background color (left), while erasing on an unlocked area leaves areas of transparency (right).

Select the Eraser tool in the toolbox, and choose its settings in the options bar shown in Figure 18.31. Like the Brush tools, you can customize the brush tip and size, mode, and opacity for the Eraser tool.

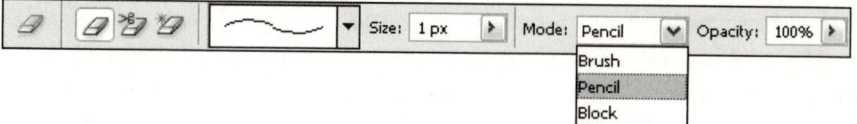

Figure 18.31. Specify settings for the Eraser tools in the options bar.

These modes are available for the Eraser from the Modes drop-down list, shown in Figure 18.31:

- **Brush.** The Brush mode erases content, leaving soft edges that can blend easily with the remaining content.
- **Pencil.** The Pencil mode erases content with hard edges, which is good for working in linear or geometric images.
- **Block.** Use the Block mode when you want to erase in hard-edged squares. The default size of the block is 16 pixels square.

After you have selected the options for the Eraser tool, drag it across the area of the image you want to erase. Figure 18.32 shows the three modes for the Eraser. From left to right, the Eraser uses the Brush, Pencil, and Block modes. For both the Brush and Pencil, the Opacity is set to 50 percent. Both the left and center erasures are soft-edged and semi-transparent; the right erasure is sharp-edged and fully transparent.

Figure 18.32. Erasing modes produce different results on the image based on the transparency and the hardness or configuration of the mode.

Erasing pixels magically

For those of you who aren't the pixel-by-pixel correction type, the Magic Eraser tool is for you. The Magic Eraser tool changes all the pixels that are similar when you drag it through an image.

The way in which the image's appearance changes when you use the tool depends on the layer's status. If the layer is locked, as is the case with either the default Background or a manually locked layer, the erased pixels take on the background color, while in a regular layer the pixels are erased to show the transparent background.

Figure 18.33 shows examples using both locked and unlocked layers. In both the upper and lower images the Magic Eraser tool is used with the same settings. When the Magic Eraser is used on a locked layer, like the example at the top of the figure, the erased content is replaced by the background color set in the toolbox; in the example the background color is black. In the lower erasure, which uses the Magic Eraser tool on a regular layer, erasing pixels leaves transparent areas.

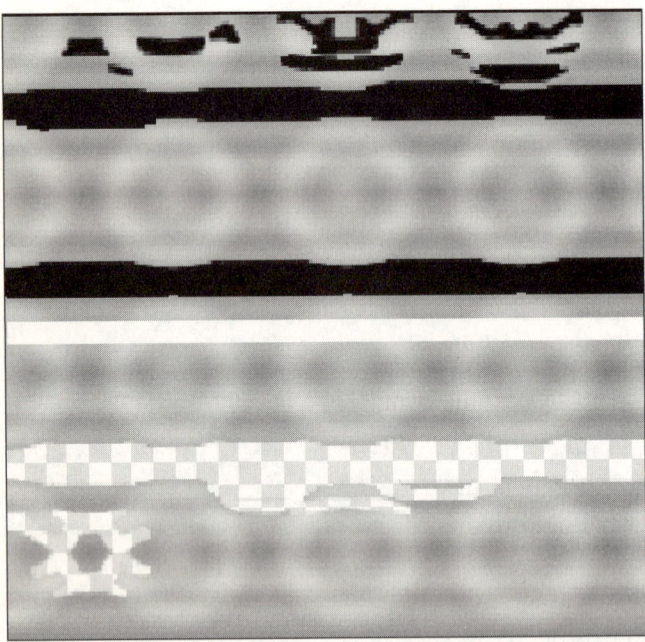

Figure 18.33. The Magic Eraser produces different results depending on whether it is used on a locked layer (upper image) or a regular layer (lower image).

Inside Scoop

If you select the Background in the Layers palette, it automatically becomes a layer when you use the Magic Eraser. Read about Background and regular layers in Chapters 11 and 12.

Customize how the Magic Eraser works by choosing different options. You can specify the following:

- **Tolerance.** Choose a range of colors that the Magic Eraser will remove. The higher the tolerance is, the wider the range of color erased when the tool is applied, as shown in Figure 18.34. In the image, the left erasure uses a low tolerance of 10, while the right uses a high tolerance level of 70. The image is magnified to show you the extent of the selection based on tolerance. In the left image, using a low tolerance requires numerous clicks to erase a range of colors. In the right image, using the higher tolerance erases the transparent areas with a single click of the Magic Eraser tool.

- **Anti-aliased.** Make the edge of the erased area smoother by choosing the Anti-aliased option.

- **Contiguous.** When the Contiguous setting is selected, pixels adjacent to the area you click are affected. If you deselect the Contiguous option, all pixels within the tolerance range of the pixel you click are erased.

- **Sample All Layers.** If you are working on a single layer, deselect the Sample All Layers option to erase pixels only from the selected layer. When the option is active, the eraser removes color from all visible layers.

- **Opacity.** Type a value for the eraser's Opacity. At 100 percent transparency, affected pixels become completely transparent on a layer or completely replaced by the background color on a locked layer,

---

Using erasers as blending tools?

If you want to make content blend, try using the Eraser or Magic Eraser tool. Either may be the right tool for the job, except the Block mode for the Eraser tool, which can't change opacity to allow for blending. Set the Opacity value to a low percentage, and drag on the image to make the pixels partially transparent. Drag repeatedly in the same area to increase the transparency.

> **Watch Out!**
> The Magic Eraser tool has no effect on hidden layers. So, if you are trying to erase from multiple layers with no success, then check the visibility.

shown in Figure 18.34. When the transparency is partial, the pixels are erased to the specified transparency level on a layer or replaced partially with the background color on a locked layer.

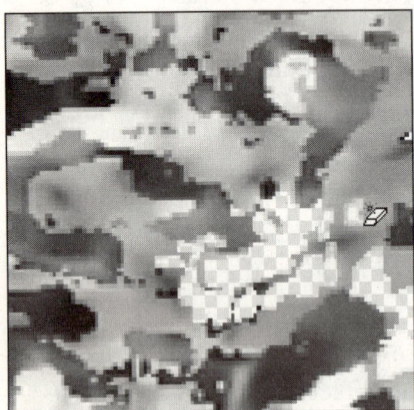

Figure 18.34. Changing the tolerance modifies the range of colors erased by the tool.

Follow these steps to use the Magic Eraser tool:

1. In the Layers palette, select the layer containing the areas you want to erase.
2. Select the Magic Eraser tool in the toolbox.
3. Choose options for the tool in the options bar.
4. Click the area on the image you want to erase; click and drag to apply erasure strokes to the image.

Erasing backgrounds

One of the tools you can use to manually remove an object from an image's background is the Background Eraser tool. This tool chooses color pixels in the background area you select and erases them transparent, allowing you to remove the foreground object.

The Background Eraser tool shows a cursor as a circle with crosshairs identifying the "hot spot" or sampling area, shown in Figure 18.35. The Background Eraser tool evaluates the pixels being sampled by the cursor, and either erases them or leaves them intact, depending on how they match the sampled pixel according to the settings chosen. In Figure 18.35, for example, the difference in the transparency is based on the Tolerance settings. The left area uses a Tolerance of 4 and the right area a Tolerance of 25. The same number of strokes was applied to each area of the sky. The higher tolerance wiped out the sky with few strokes, compared to using the lower tolerance as in the left example.

Figure 18.35. Changing the tolerance defines how large an area of the background is erased. A low tolerance erases smaller areas (left) while a higher tolerance erases a greater area (right).

Select the layer in the Layers palette; if it is a Background, it converts to a layer automatically when you click it with the Background Eraser tool. Specify the options for the tool, and drag through the area you want erased.

 **Bright Idea**
In images where you are trying to remove a distracting background or focus attention on your subject, you can remove the background with the Background Eraser and then paste in another background using a fill tool or the Clone Stamp tool's process.

>  **Watch Out!**
> If you are using a stylus and notice that the characteristics of the tool seem to be changing, check the Brush settings. Separate settings allow you to specify that both Size and Tolerance can be controlled by pen pressure.

You can specify these options:

- Brush settings are listed in the Brush drop-down palette. Select the brush's diameter, hardness, spacing, angle, and roundness.
- Specify Limits by choosing Contiguous to erase connected areas containing the hot spot color; choose Discontiguous to erase any pixels in the tool's cursor circle that are similar to the hot spot color.
- Define how similar a pixel's color must be to the hot spot color in order to be erased using the Tolerance level. Examples are shown in Figure 18.35.

Just the facts

- Painting with brushes can take a number of forms, including paintbrushes, airbrushes, pencils, and even stamps.
- The painting tools can be configured extensively to provide custom brushstrokes.
- Save modified brushes or create original brushes that are stored in the brush libraries.
- Instead of using color with your brush, choose an image to be the brush.
- Create interesting and unique effects using other types of brushes, including the Pencil and Impressionist Brush tools.
- Replace image colors by painting with the Replace Color tool instead of using selection tools and substituting color in the image.
- Use one of several different erasers to remove color from your images.

PART VI

Now That the Images Look Great . . .

GET THE SCOOP ON...
■ Printing photos ■ Assembling and printing multiple images ■ Creating picture packages and labels ■ Ordering prints automatically ■ Configuring and e-mailing images ■ Sharing collections online

I'll Take a Dozen Copies

Sometimes, there's nothing like flipping through the pages of a photo album, checking out the goofy hair-dos and old-fashioned clothes. Just because you're using a digital camera doesn't mean that you can't create pages to flip through. For those who prefer to have their images on paper, Photoshop Elements provides a number of simple printing methods.

With the advent of accurate and low-cost printing technology in the last few years, printing has come a long way from sending rolls of film to a processor for developing. If you prefer not to configure images and printer setups yourself, you can transfer files to an online printing service.

Speaking of online options, you can actually share your collections online using the provided Kodak photo service, or easily connect to one of many other photo services, or you can e-mail photos directly from the Photo Browser, letting your recipients print their own copies.

Printing photos

You have several printing options in Photoshop Elements. The option you choose depends on whether you want to print one image or more than one image, including:

- Printing from the Editor mode, which defaults to a single print of the active image.

- Printing more than a single copy of an image, or printing multiple images (choose File ⇨ Print Multiple Photos to open Photo Browser in the Organizer window).
- Printing from the Photo Browser defaults to the Print Selected Photos dialog box, which can be used for a number of different types of printing.

You can choose from these printing options:

- Printing individual images
- Creating contact sheets or sets of thumbnail images
- Printing a picture package, similar to school photo packages
- Using images as labels printed on specialized label stock

Printing from Editor mode

You can print an image directly from either the Quick Fix or Standard Edit modes.

Follow these steps to print a single image:

1. Click the Print button on the shortcuts bar, or choose File ⇨ Print to open the Print Preview dialog box, shown in Figure 19.1.
2. Select options from the Print Preview dialog box. The options for configuring a printed image and details are listed in Table 19.1.
3. Click Print to close the Print Preview dialog box and open the Print dialog box.
4. Select your printer from the Name drop-down menu. If necessary, click Properties to check your printer's configuration.
5. Click OK to close the Print dialog box and print the image.

Inside Scoop

Images can be combined into different creations that can be printed, such as photo albums and calendars, which are described in Chapter 20. If you prefer to view images onscreen, see Chapter 21 for the scoop on creating slide shows.

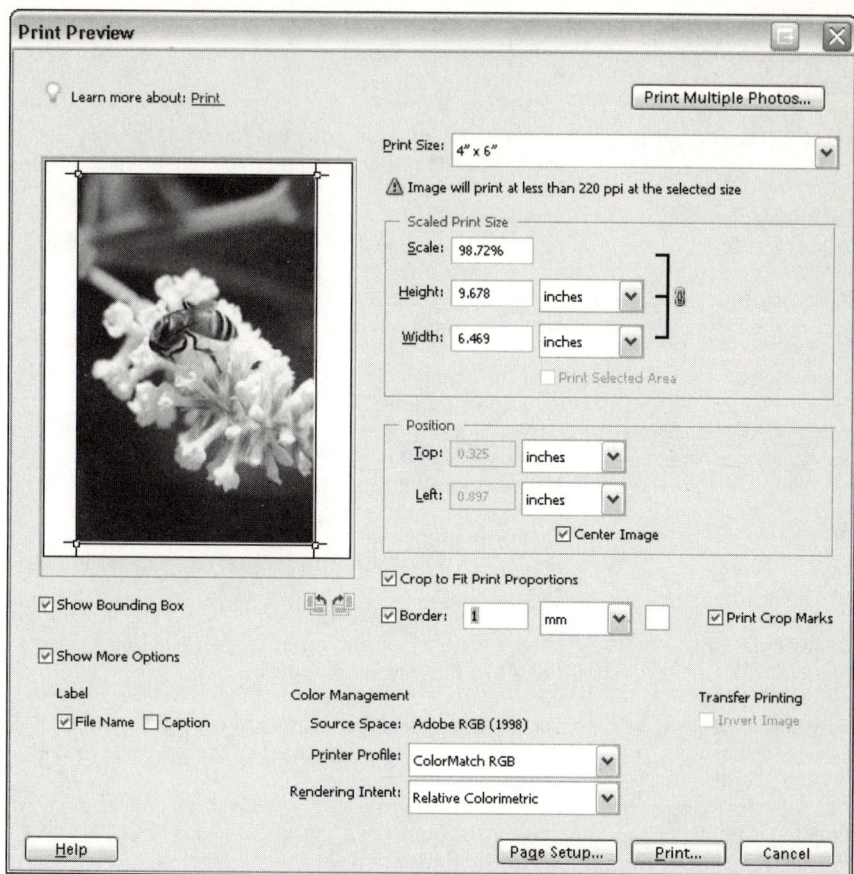

Figure 19.1. Choose options for printing a single image in the Print Preview dialog box.

Table 19.1. Configuring print settings	
Setting	**Comment or Effect**
Show Bounding Box	This displays an outline around the image in the preview area. The outline is for reference and doesn't print.
Show More Options	Click to expand the dialog box to display label and color management options.

continued

Table 19.1. *continued*

Setting	Comment or Effect
Label File Name/Caption	Choose either or both of the File Name and Caption options to add text to the image before printing.
Color Management Printer Profile	Choose a profile from the drop-down menu to specify printer settings (see the Resolution and printing sidebar).
Rendering Intent	Choose from one of four intents from the drop-down menu (see the Resolution and printing sidebar).
Preview area	Drag the bounding box margins to rescale the image proportionally. Print Size displays as Custom Size.
Rotate buttons	Click to rotate an image 90 degrees clockwise or counterclockwise.
Print Size	Choose an image size from the drop-down menu. Choices include the actual size, custom size, common image sizes, and full page size.
Scaled Print Size	Enter a scale in percentage, or type a Height or Width value to adjust the other values.
Position	Specify a location for the image in relation to the page from the top or left edges, or click Center Image to center the print on the page.
Crop to Fit Print Proportions	This option crops the edges of the image to fit the specified print size.
Border	Check this to add a border. Type a value and choose a unit of measure from the drop-down menu. Click the color swatch to open the Color Picker, and choose a border color.
Print Crop Marks	Click to display crop marks at the corners of the image, as shown in the preview area in Figure 19.1.
Transfer Printing	If you are printing a t-shirt transfer, click this setting to flip the print horizontally.
Page Setup	Click to open the system Page Setup dialog box to choose paper size, source, and page orientation. Click OK to close; click Printer to open your printer's dialog box.

> **Inside Scoop**
> Chapter 9 describes using and embedding color profiles, which define the range of colors used for viewing and printing an image.

Color managing printing

As described in Table 19.1, you can specify a Printer Profile as part of the image's print settings to minimize color discrepancies between the image and your printer.

Depending on your system and other available and installed software and printer drivers, you may have a long list of printer profiles. Profiles can match operating systems, monitors, printers, different gamma settings, cameras, and even types of paper. If your printer and paper combination has a specific profile, select it from the menu, like the example shown in Figure 19.2. Select a Rendering Intent from the drop-down menu. As described in Chapter 9, monitors and printers use different ranges of color, or *color gamuts*. To reproduce color, a *rendering intent* specifies how colors are translated from a source color space you can see on a monitor to the closest equivalent color in a printed version of the image.

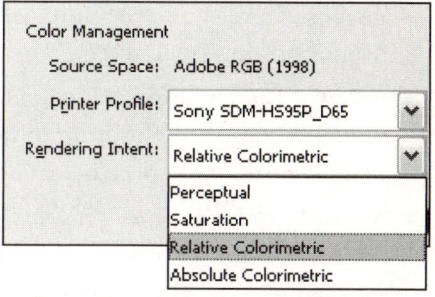

Figure 19.2. The Rendering Intents available depend on the chosen Printer Profile.

Resolution and printing

When printed, an image with a high resolution contains more, and therefore smaller, pixels than an image with a low resolution. Higher-resolution images can reproduce greater detail and subtler color transitions than lower-resolution images because of the density of the pixels in the images.

Choose one of four intents:

- **Perceptual.** The monitor's color gamut is compressed slightly so there are fewer colors that can't be reproduced. Use this intent for accurate hue, although the color may be slightly desaturated. This method reduces artifacts like banding in blue skies.
- **Saturation.** Perceptual rendering intent can desaturate color slightly to compress the color gamut. Saturation intent shifts other factors such as the color hue while preserving the intensity of the color. Use Saturation rendering intent for screen captures, graphs, and other images where the perception of the color is less important than an overall bright appearance.
- **Relative Colorimetric.** All colors that are reproducible are reproduced. Use this method for an image that contains a narrow range of colors, such as a blue ocean against a blue sky.
- **Absolute Colorimetric.** The Absolute Colorimetric intent reproduces the exact color recorded in the image without modifying colors based on light source. This rendering intent often produces color shift, but it's the best one to use for reproducing specific colors like those used in logos.

Printing multiple images

Let's face it: Photo printing paper isn't cheap, nor is printing images especially fast. Save yourself time and paper by maximizing the number of prints you can place on a single page.

Fortunately, you don't have to do the image manipulation, flipping and rotating, manually — Photoshop Elements does it for you.

Follow these steps to set up and configure a specialized print job:

1. In the Photo Browser, select the images you want to print.

Hack
If you need to print images included in a stack, don't bother to unstack first. Instead, right-click and choose Stack ⇨ Reveal Photos in Stack to display the images in a subwindow. Select the images, click Order Prints in the shortcuts bar, and choose Print.

2. Choose File ⇨ Print, or click the Order Prints button on the shortcut bar and choose Print Selected Photos to open the Print Preview dialog box.

3. You can add or remove images from the selected group by clicking the image in the column at the left of the dialog box and clicking either the Add button or the Delete button, shown in Figure 19.3.

4. Choose your printer from the Select Printer drop-down menu. If necessary, click Show Printer Preferences to open your printer's dialog box and configure the settings.

5. Click the Select Type of Print drop-down arrow, and choose a Contact Sheet, Picture Package, or Label configuration — the options are described shortly. The default is Individual Prints.

6. Choose layout options according to the selected type of print job.

7. Click the image thumbnails shown on the Print Selected Photos dialog box to see a larger version in the preview area, or click the left and right arrows to show one page at a time when there are two or more pages.

8. Click More Options to open the More Options dialog box if you want to choose a print space setting.

9. Click Print to print the photos.

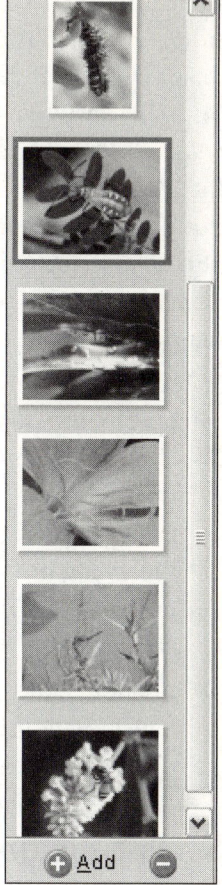

Figure 19.3. Add or remove images from the list in the dialog box.

 **Bright Idea**
If you are in the Editor, choose File ⇨ Print Multiple Photos to open the Print Selected Photos dialog box. If you have the Print Preview dialog box open, click Print Multiple Photos at the top right of the dialog box to open the Print Selected Photos dialog box.

Creating contact sheets

A *contact sheet* is a set of thumbnail images printed on one page for previewing. In the Print Selected Photos dialog box, click the Select Type of Print drop-down arrow and choose Contact Sheet from the list to display the Select a Layout settings on the dialog box. Choose a setting to do the following:

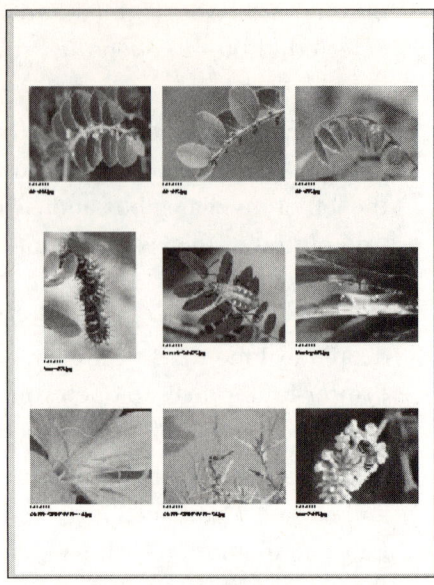

Figure 19.4. Specify the layout and labeling for a contact sheet.

- Specify the number of columns of thumbnails, ranging from 1 to 9. The example preview area from the dialog box, shown in Figure 19.4, shows three columns.

- Add and configure a Text Label including the date, a caption, and/or a file name. The example in the figure uses the date and file name.

Using a picture package

Using the *picture package* option lets you print multiple images in different sizes on the same page. The layout is similar to what you have probably seen in school photo packages, with a few extras.

In the Print Selected Photos dialog box, click the Select Type of Print drop-down arrow and choose Picture Package from the list. In the Select a Layout settings that are listed on the Print Selected Photo dialog box when you choose the picture package option, you have the following choices:

- Click the Select a Layout drop-down arrow, and choose a configuration from the list. In Figure 19.5, the left image shows one preview page using the Letter (1) 5×7 (4) 2.5×3.5 option. The right image shows a page of a preview using the Letter (3) 4×6 option.

Changing page sizes

By default, all the layout choices in the Picture Package option are based on a letter-sized page. You see in the menu that each option starts with "Letter."

To use a different size of paper, click Page Setup in the Print Selected Photos dialog box to open the Page Setup dialog box. Choose an alternate paper size from the Size drop-down menu. Also, specify the page orientation and margins. Click OK.

The Select a Layout menu options change to reflect your selected page size, and they may also change the unit of measure, depending on the paper size selected.

Figure 19.5. Configure images in a picture package for efficient use of photo paper.

- Choose a frame for the images from the Select a Frame drop-down menu. In Figure 19.5, the left image shows a preview using the Antique Rectangle frame; the right image shows a preview using the Red Blue frame.

- Select Fill Page With First Photo to create the quintessential school photo look, like that shown in Figure 19.6. The figure shows the Letter (2) 4×5 (2) 2.5×3.5 (4) 2×2.5 layout.

- Specify Crop to Fit to remove any space between the images in the layout.

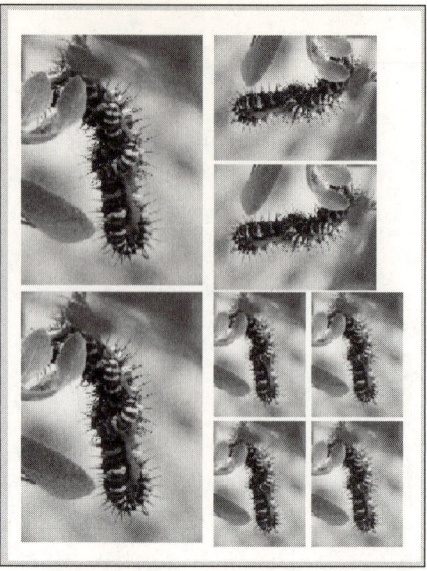

Figure 19.6. You can duplicate the school photo layout familiar from your past, although it isn't likely your classmates were literally worms.

Printing specialized labels

The final specialized print job configures a print layout to use Avery labels. In the Print Selected Photos dialog box, click the Select Type of Print drop-down arrow and choose Labels from the list. The choices for configuring the labels display on the Print Selected Photos dialog box in the Select a Layout settings. You can:

- Click the Select a Layout drop-down arrow, and choose a label option from the list. Figure 19.7 shows one page of a preview using the Avery 53265 (2) 7.00×4.875 option.

- Choose a frame for the images from the Select a Frame drop-down menu. The figure shows the Painted Edge frame, a wildly exotic cutout that accents the images' content very well.

> **Watch Out!**
> If you have to reset the Offset for your labels, check that your printer doesn't have the Borderless option selected — check your printer's documentation for information.

- Click Fill Page With First Photo to duplicate the same image for the entire sheet of labels on each page.
- Specify Crop to Fit to crop each component image to fit the chosen layout.
- Type a value or use the arrows to specify a print offset if the output is misaligned. Adjust the print positions in increments of 0.1mm; the available range is –50mm to 50mm.

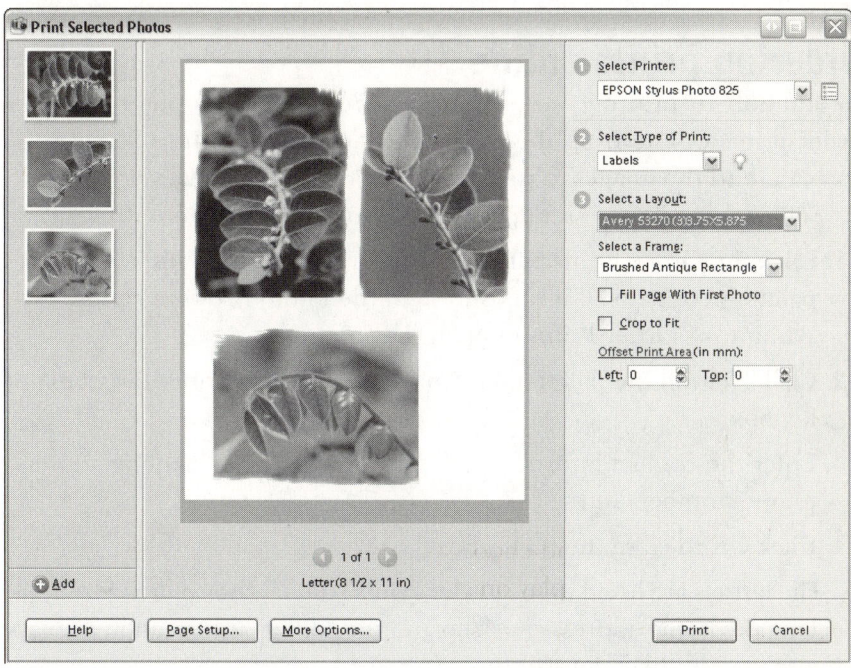

Figure 19.7. Print different images or multiple copies of the same image on a sheet of labels.

Modifying image order

If you aren't pleased with the arrangement of the images on a page in either the Picture Package or Labels print jobs, or if one image is shown in a smaller size than you'd like in a combination Picture Package layout, you can swap the images directly on the preview.

Drag an image from the thumbnails column at the left of the dialog box, and drop it at the location you'd like it placed. The image changes size, depending on the size of the underlying image.

>
> **Inside Scoop**
> You can specify the image used in a location on a page, but you can't adjust how the page is laid out with different-sized images.

If you make any changes to the Picture Package settings or add or delete images, the layout changes are removed. Make sure you have the images and layout you want before modifying the locations of images on the pages.

Ordering prints online

In addition to printing various formats from your computer, you can order prints online from the embedded Adobe Photoshop Services, or you can send the images to your preferred online image developer.

Follow these steps to set up a target account in the Photo Browser:

1. Click the Order Prints palette in the Organize Bin to display the palette's contents. If it isn't shown in the Photo Browser, choose Window ⇨ Order Prints to open the palette.
2. Click New on the palette to open the New Order Prints Target dialog box.
3. Enter the contact information for ordering, such as mailing address, phone number, and so on.
4. Click OK to close the dialog box.

The targets are listed in the Order Prints palette, shown in Figure 19.8. Clicking the home address check box on the contact information displays a house icon in the palette.

Figure 19.8. Create a list of targets for quickly uploading images to an online image processing company.

If you want to edit settings for an existing target, click the Pencil icon on the Order Prints palette to open the details for the target for a target. When you are ready to order, follow these steps:

1. Drag an image from the Photo Browser to the appropriate target in the Order Prints palette.
2. Continue to add images as required.
3. To check the files you have chosen, click the View Photos in Order for Recipient icon on the Order Prints palette. The icon is at the far right of the palette, and shows a stack of images and eyeglasses.
4. In the Order Prints dialog, view the thumbnails for the selected images. You can delete any of the images by selecting it and clicking Remove Selected Photo(s) from Order.
5. Click Close to close the dialog box and return to the Photo Browser or click Confirm Order and proceed with Step 7 (see Figure 19.9).

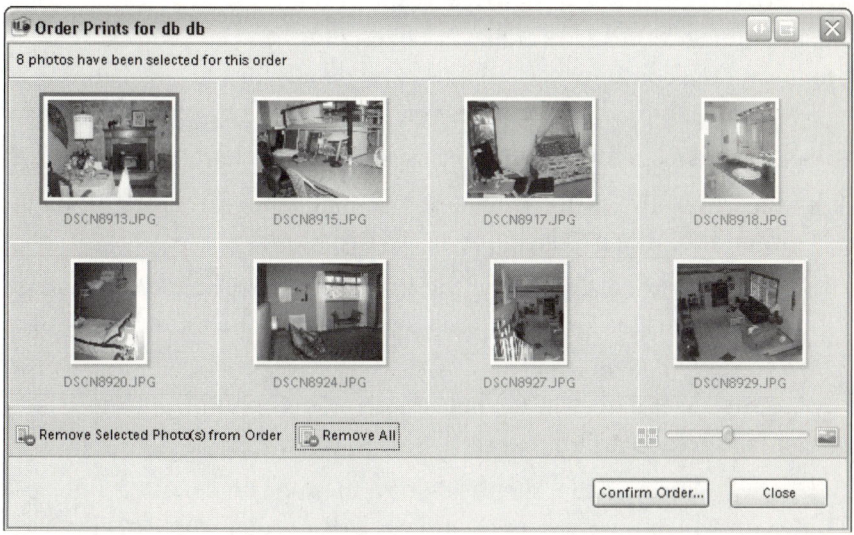

Figure 19.9. Create a list of targets for quickly uploading images to an online image processing company.

Inside Scoop
Choose Edit ⇨ Preferences ⇨ Services from the Photo Browser to update services, find new services, and reset or clear online accounts.

6. Click Confirm Order next to the contact's listing on the Order Prints palette, or from the Order Prints dialog box to launch your Web browser and view a list of the selected images in the Adobe Photoshop Services, provided by Kodak EasyShare Gallery dialog box. that you have selected for ordering.

7. Proceed with your order, and click Checkout to pay for your images; click Cancel to close the dialog box and return to Photoshop Elements.

Sending e-mail images

Any picture can be attached to an e-mail like any other sort of file. In Photoshop Elements, you can go one step further and create e-mails with the images embedded, attached as JPEG images, or attached as a simple PDF slide show.

Configuring message contents

E-mailing images uses several dialog boxes and wizards. The first stage is configuring the contents, recipient list, and details for the e-mail message.

Follow these steps to set up the e-mail message:

1. Select the images in the Photo Browser that you want to send.

2. In the Photo Browser, click Share ⇨ E-mail from the shortcuts bar to open the Attach Selected Items to E-mail dialog box.

3. Selected images are shown in the Items column. Click Add to add additional images, or select an image and click the minus key (−) to remove an image.

4. Click to select names in the Select Recipients column; click Edit Contacts to add additional recipients to the list.

5. Choose a Format from the drop-down menu. The default is Photo Mail, in which messages are sent in HTML format. You can also select PDF slide show or individual attachments, like those sent with a regular e-mail message.

6. Select other content, such as captions, and type a message for the e-mail message.

7. Click Next to process the files and open the subsequent wizard, you configure the appearance of the e-mail message next.

Specifying the layout

After the e-mail message particulars are chosen in the Attach to E-mail or Attached Selected Items to E-mail dialog box, click Next to open the Stationery & Layouts Wizard dialog box. Follow these steps to finish the e-mail message preparation:

1. On the first pane of the wizard, choose a category such as Family, Fun Stuff, or Outdoors, and then choose a specific option such as Birthday. Click Next Step to show the second pane of the wizard.

2. Select a stationery or background from the column at the left of the dialog box. You can choose from simple frames or decorative borders and backgrounds displaying anything from champagne to baseballs, depending on your selections in the initial pane of the wizard.

3. Click the default captions below the images, and type your own captions.

4. Click Next Step to show the third pane of the wizard.

5. On this pane, customize the e-mail message by choosing a background color, image size and configuration, font and color for the text, and customizing options for the selected stationery, shown in Figure 19.10.

6. Check the final e-mail message; you can modify the message and image captions from this pane of the wizard.

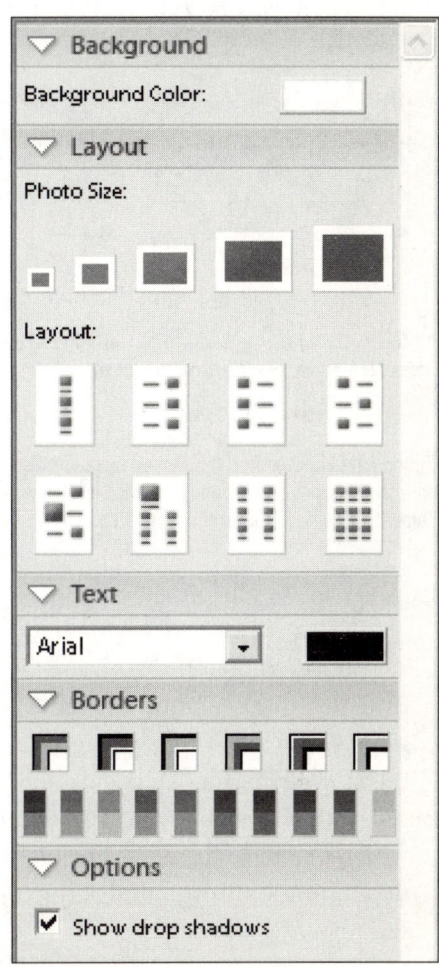

Figure 19.10. Use this dialog box to create a custom background, among other things, for your e-mail message.

7. Click Next. The wizard and dialog box close, and your e-mail program sends the message. The received message is shown in Figure 19.11.

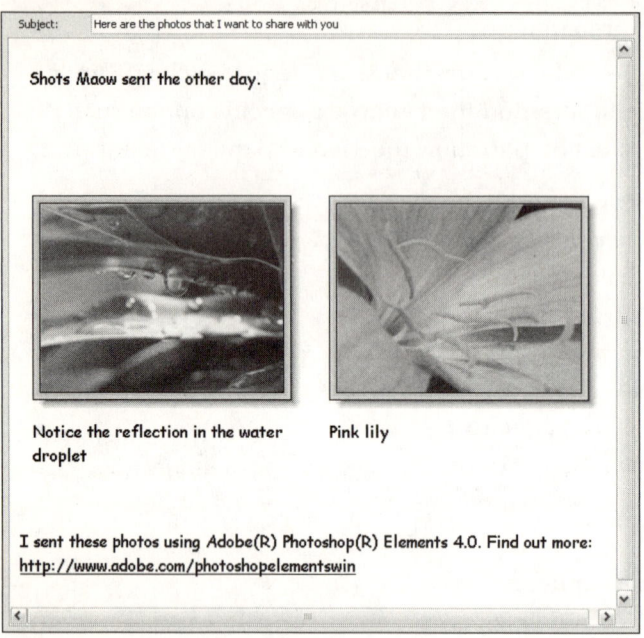

Figure 19.11. Send an HTML e-mail message displaying your images against a custom background. The information and link to the Photoshop Elements Web site is part of the default text.

File attachment options

Choose one of three options for e-mailing images, including the format, image quality, and image size. Remember to balance the impact you are trying create with your image presentation against the size of the file. Don't send an unnecessarily large file to someone with a slow dial-up connection.

The same images can result in different e-mail message sizes, depending on the quality of the image, the image size, and the chosen format.

> **Watch Out!**
> If you aren't using Outlook as your e-mail client, you can't use the Stationery & Layouts Wizard. Check the Sharing option in the Photo Browser. Choose Edit ⇨ Preferences ⇨ Sharing. You'll see a drop-down list named E-mail Client. Click the arrow and choose a client program; click OK to close the Preferences dialog box.

Shared collections

Collections are groups of images collected under a common name in the Photo Browser for keeping track of images from a specific occasion or project. You can also define *shared collections* to share them online with others.

Use a shared collection to distribute images to family and friends, or to upload content for a client to view samples or proofs. Sharing image collections online from Photoshop Elements using the gallery system is one of the slickest, most pain-free methods of distributing content I have ever experienced. You aren't restricted to using the default Kodak EasyShare Gallery. It's easy to configure and use alternate image sharing services.

Creating a shared collection

Start by selecting an existing collection, or create a new collection, described in detail in Chapter 3. Briefly, to build a new collection for online distribution, follow these steps:

1. Select the images you want for the online collection in the Photo Browser.
2. Click the Collections tab in the Organize Bin to display its contents, and then click New and select New Collection.
3. Name the new collection in the Create Collection dialog box, and click OK to close the dialog box and assign the collection name to the images.

> **Inside Scoop**
> I seldom use a layout for sending images. But there's no question that HTML e-mail messages are attractive, and the wizard lets you customize your messages considerably.

> **Hack**
> There is no way to indicate whether a collection is shared or not. You may want to attach a tag to the content of a collection identifying its purpose.

Uploading the collection

After the collection is created, use the wizard to upload the images to a shared server.

Follow these steps to distribute a collection of images:

1. In the Photo Browser, click Shared ⇨ Share Online from the shortcuts bar to open the Adobe Photoshop Services, provided by Kodak Easy Share Gallery wizard. The wizard is composed of three panes. The Recipients pane, shown in Figure 19.12, appears when the wizard opens. On this pane, you can do the following:

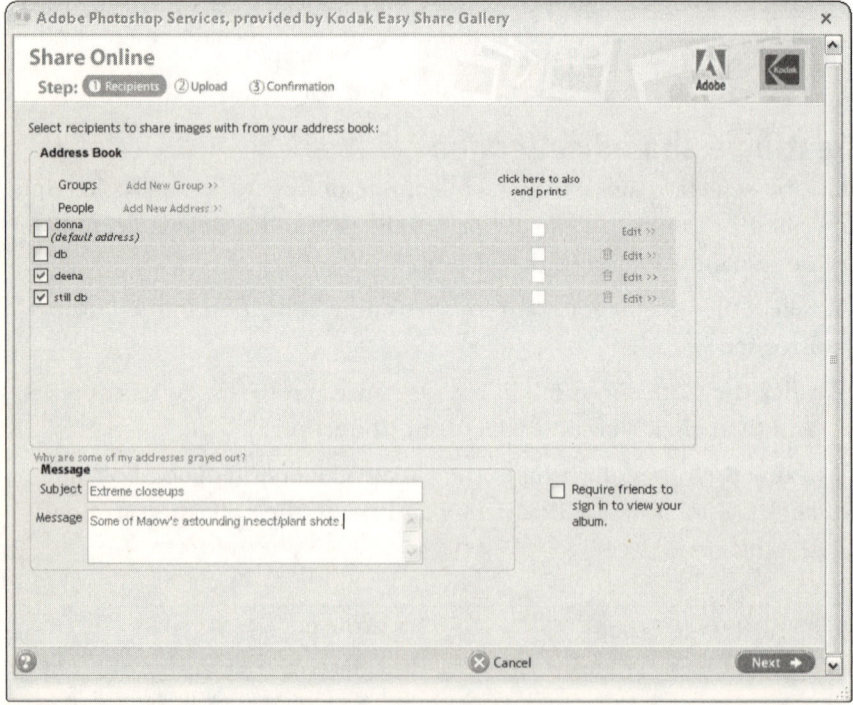

Figure 19.12. Manage recipient information and specify sharing characteristics in the wizard.

> **Sharing preferences**
>
> You have only a couple of choices for sharing preferences. In the Photo Browser, choose Edit ⇨ Preferences ⇨ Sharing. Select a program from the E-mail Client drop-down menu, which shows your default e-mail program as its default. In the Sharing Settings, click the check box to specify that you want e-mail captions written to the catalog. Click OK to close the Preferences dialog box.

- Select recipients for notification of the collection. The recipients can be groups of names, individuals, or both.
- Add or edit names and groups by clicking appropriate links on the wizard.
- Click Send Prints to send printed copies of the images automatically to the specified recipients. Of course, nothing is free — if you choose this command, your recipients get printed copies of the images in their physical mail, and you get to pay for them!
- Type a subject and text for the e-mail message used to notify your recipient list of the collection.
- Add a level of security by clicking Require friends to sign in to view your album. Be aware that anyone on your notification list must create a login and password to view the images if you require them to sign in.

2. Click Next on the wizard dialog box to start the file upload process. You see a progress bar as the images are uploaded.
3. The wizard displays the Confirmation pane automatically. On the final pane of the wizard, you find the following:
   - A list of the names or groups you notified of the new image collection
   - A link to open the gallery in your browser
   - A link to order prints directly from the wizard
4. Click Done to exit the wizard.

Inside Scoop

If you are working in the Edit modes, choose File ⇨ Order Prints to start the wizard process.

Notifying and viewing

The list of people or groups of people you specify for notification in the wizard receive an e-mail message including links to the online gallery. As the sender, you also receive a copy of the notice. Click the View Photos button in the e-mail message to open the gallery.

The images are included in an album and presented as a slide show, shown in Figure 19.13. You and your recipients can share the slide show or individual images, or order prints in different sizes directly from the slide show. Use the controls to play the slide show.

Figure 19.13. View the uploaded slide show in the online gallery.

Bright Idea

If you use an online sharing gallery for business clients, make a group for each client company. That way, you won't have to remember who works for which company, nor will you omit someone from a list — never a smart business move.

Gallery details

The Kodak EasyShare Gallery memberships are free to use and can be upgraded to a premium membership for a fee. You can use the Kodak EasyShare Gallery free online storage for the first 12 months after you upload the first image. The images you have stored are usually deleted after 12 months if you haven't made any purchases on your account. You can store any number of image files, and can also store video files in the same gallery. Video file size is restricted to 15MB per file, and 150MB total video file storage space. Video files are usually deleted after 30 days.

Working in the gallery

You don't have to be working in Photoshop Elements to use the gallery and its features. Access your galleries and manage photos online at http://adobe.kodakgallery.com.

Follow the prompts and online wizards to upload images into an existing or new gallery, view images, delete collections, and share or print photos.

Just the facts

- A single image can be configured and printed from the Organizer or Editor windows.
- Use multiple images for printing in several ways. Thumbnail contact sheets are good for previewing, and picture packages save photo paper. You can produce labels that correspond with popular label media.

- Configure print shop and customer information, and send a job right from the Photo Browser.
- Set up and customize e-mail messages containing images in a number of ways.
- Share image collections online. Upload images through a wizard, and manage online content through an account.

GET THE SCOOP ON...
- Producing paper creations such as cards and calendars
- Assembling and organizing photo albums
- Ordering content online
- Designing Web photo galleries
- Stitching together panoramic images

Creating Fun Stuff

Suppose someone buys you a new camera for your birthday, or you buy yourself one. For the next while, the camera is always in tow, and you dutifully download the images into the Organizer on a regular basis.

After a time, viewing, editing, and printing your shots starts to lose some of its interest. When that happens, you know you have reached the creation zone.

You can use your photos and video clips in photo albums, cards, postcards, wall calendars, and HTML photo galleries. These items are called *creations*. A strong feature in Photoshop Elements is the ease with which you can create these different products. Another type of creation is a slide show, which is covered in Chapter 21.

Photoshop Elements offers a range of wizard-driven creation options, which makes it simple to create output.

For many, using different creations is a more expressive way of sharing your photos than simply attaching them to e-mails. On the other hand, if you are starting out in a new business, consider using the different creation options to prepare a suite of products for marketing and sales.

Managing creations in the Organizer

Before looking at the particulars of creations, let me give you a few words on how the program handles creations. Photoshop Elements includes any creations you have saved in the Photo Browser, identified with a uniform icon, shown in Figure 20.1.

> **Mysterious disappearing creations**
>
> If you can't see your creations and are sure you haven't hidden them from the Photo Browser view, check how the content is sorted in the field at the bottom left of the Photo Browser. If you have specified a sort by Import Batch or Folder Location, the creations are excluded from those sorts because they aren't imported or stored in folders. You can find them using a date sort option.

Figure 20.1. Look for the uniform icon used to identify a creation.

Use these tips to maximize access to your work in the Photo Browser:

- Hide the creations from the Photo Browser if you don't need to access them regularly. Choose View ➪ Media Types from the menu, and deselect Creations from the list.
- To find an existing creation easily, choose File ➪ Open Creation to open a list of the creations within your system. Select the creation, and click OK to open it.

Setting up a creation

You can set up a creation from either the Editor or the Photo Browser by following these steps:

1. Click the Create button to open the Creation Setup window, or choose File ⇨ Create and select an option from the submenu to open the Creation Setup window.
2. Click a creation type in the list at the left of the window; a sample and a short description of the creation appears on the Creation Setup window. The different creation types are listed in Table 20.1 along with the file formats you can use for distributing the finished product.

Table 20.1. Photoshop Elements creations

Creation Type	Description	Export Formats
Slide Show	This creation type offers a presentation using motion, music, transitions, text, and audio narration (see Chapter 21).	View onscreen, export to Video Compact Disc (VCD) for television viewing
VCD with Menu	Burn content onto a CD that can play back on television using most DVD players.	Export to VCD for television viewing
Album Pages	Create page layouts using multiple images, graphical elements, and text.	Save pages as a PDF file, print them, or send via e-mail
Bound Photo Book	Design album pages for professional printing.	Save pages as a PDF file, print, send to an online print company, or send via e-mail
4-Fold Greeting Card	Produce professional-looking four-fold occasion cards.	Save pages as a PDF file, print the card, or send via e-mail
Photo Greeting Card	Print as a postcard using images and graphics, or send to an online company for production.	Save pages as a PDF file, print the card, or send via e-mail
Calendar Pages	Produce a monthly calendar using your images.	Save the calendar pages as a PDF file, print the calendar, or send via e-mail
Bound Calendar	Produce calendar pages and send to an online company for printing and binding.	Save pages as a PDF file, print the calendar, send it to an online print company, or send via e-mail
HTML Photo Gallery	Create Web pages to display photos on your Web site.	View the gallery pages on your computer

Watch Out!
The quest for designing the perfect creation can lead to loss of sleep and bad dreams. After you see you can distribute your images there's no turning back. Please remember that most people don't need more than one calendar a year showing the best of your annual fishing trip.

3. Work through the wizard dialog box to choose and configure the images and other files you want to use in the creation.
4. Choose an export format for the creation and save it according to the options listed in Table 20.2 — none of the creation types offer all output formats. The available export types and samples of their icons are listed in Table 20.2.

Table 20.2. Formats for saving creations

Icon	Export Type
	PDF file
	Print
	Upload file to Web
	E-mail file
	View file onscreen
	Create Video Compact Disc (VCD) file

Bright Idea

Consider using photos that you've cut into shapes using the Cookie Cutter tool for more interest, such as cutting out pictures of the kids at the beach using toy pail and shovel shapes. The images are placed against the template's background.

Creating photo albums

You can create any of the paper-based products, such as album pages, using similar wizards. The photo albums created in Photoshop Elements are tailor-made for all you scrapbookers, and anyone who wants to assemble a collection of prints in a formatted layout.

Follow these steps to create a photo album:

1. Select the photos you'd like to use in the Photo Browser.
2. Click the Create button in the shortcuts bar to open the Creation Setup window.
3. Select Album Pages from the list at the left of the window and click OK to start the wizard.
4. Select a style for your pages from the list of options on the right. Choose customization options such as number of photos per page, captions, headers and footers, and so on. Click Next Step.
5. Reorganize the photos in the next page of the wizard. You see page numbers at the upper-left corner of the thumbnails, shown in Figure 20.2. The numbering is revised automatically as you reorder, add, or remove pages. You can add more than one image on a page or include pages without images. Click Next Step.

Figure 20.2. Images are included as selected in the Photo Browser; reorganize them according to your project's flow. You can add more than one image on a page, or include pages without images that you might want to use for text or a title page.

6. Click Add Text in the Customize panel of the wizard to activate a text box and a Text dialog box, shown in Figure 20.3. Type the text and configure its appearance in the dialog box.

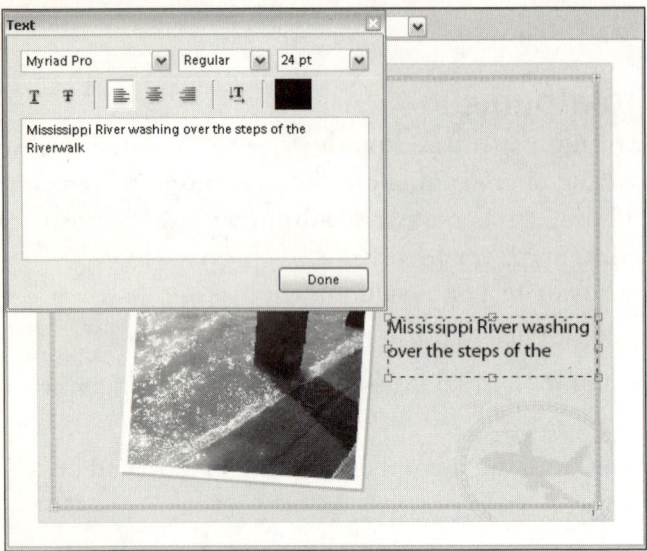

Figure 20.3. Add and configure text headings and captions for the album pages.

7. Drag the text box to position it as desired on the album page. Click Done to finish the text block and close the Text dialog box.

8. Click Next Page to display the next album page, and add the text. Continue with subsequent pages; when you are finished, click Next Step.

9. In the next pane of the wizard, type a name for the creation in the Album Pages Name field at the top right of the wizard and click Save.

10. On the final pane of the wizard, choose an output option, or click Done to close the wizard and process the file.

Read about e-mailing images and creations in Chapter 19.

Online ordering

For a really professional job, or if you don't have the quality of printer you'd like, consider purchasing a photo book. Photo books are a type of album ordered online and delivered as a finished product, as are bound calendars. It's an interesting concept, isn't it?

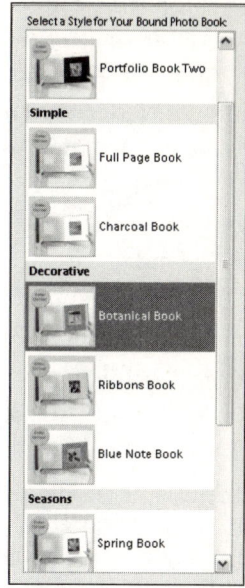

Follow the same wizard as that for other paper-based creations. In the first pane of the wizard, select a style for your book or calendar from the list on the right of the wizard dialog box, shown in Figure 20.4. Styles you can order online show an icon over the style's thumbnail. Customize the style with headings, headers and footers, and so on.

Continue with the rest of the wizard as described earlier. Because both the photo book and bound calendar formats are intended for professional printing, the wizard checks the images for resolution and displays a caution icon over the bottom right of the thumbnail, as shown

Figure 20.4. Choose a style in the wizard; an icon shows styles that can be ordered online.

Why order online?

Ordering online isn't very useful if you are constrained for time, or need only a few copies of a few pages. I would consider having a photo book created using an online service in the following situations:

- I want a bunch of copies of the same collection of photos to give as gifts, such as wedding albums or graduation photos.
- I don't have the time to print and assemble the material.
- I don't have the time or equipment to produce the quality of product that I need.
- I want to prepare a special customer gift, such as calendars, and don't need a large quantity.

in Figure 20.5, if the image resolution is too low. Substitute a higher-resolution image if possible.

After the pages are assembled and checked, name and save the creation. On the final pane of the wizard, click Order Online. The contents of the photo book or calendar are converted to PDF format automatically, and the Adobe Photoshop Services browser window opens. The program defaults to using Kodak's EasyShare Gallery, an online service provider. Step through the ordering wizard to order your photo book or calendar.

Figure 20.5. The wizard identifies the thumbnail images that may not print properly.

Making greeting cards or calendars

How many of us have kids that grew up creating and printing their own cards by computer, never having had the experience of designing a birthday card from paper, glue, and glitter? To rephrase that question: How many of you reading this page have never had that experience either?

Photoshop Elements gives you two options for creating cards; one example is shown in Figure 20.6. You can design a simple postcard-type card or a four-fold greeting card. Either type of card allows for only one photo. Follow through the wizard to design and customize

Figure 20.6. Create greeting cards or wall calendars using wizards.

>  **Hack**
> Use stacks in the Photo Browser to organize your images. When preparing a creation, right-click a stack and choose Stack ⇨ Reveal Photos in Stack. The stacked images are shown in a subwindow of the Photo Browser; select the images, and proceed with the creation process.

the card, and then save it. Cards can be printed, e-mailed, or stored in PDF format.

Finally, you can also build wall calendars — an example of which is shown at the bottom of Figure 20.6 — using any of a number of provided templates to print at home or in the office.

Designing a photo gallery for the Web

One of the creation designs offered by Photoshop Elements is a photo gallery you can use in a Web page that shows a collection of thumbnail images. Click a thumbnail image to view a full-size version of the image.

In the "old" days, you'd have to create both thumbnail and full-size versions of each image, design a page to hold the thumbnails, add links to individual pages to show the full-size images, and provide navigation for the user to return to the thumbnail directory. It sounds like lots of work, and sometimes it certainly was!

Creating an HTML Photo Gallery

The HTML Photo Gallery creation generates the Web page using one of dozens of styles. It creates versions of the images automatically and places all the files into a folder. If you like, you can use video clips in addition to still images in the HTML Photo Gallery.

Follow these steps to create an HTML Photo Gallery:

1. Select the images and video clips you want to use in the gallery in the Photo Browser.
2. Click the Create button, and choose HTML Photo Gallery from the list in the Creation Setup window. Click OK to open the Adobe HTML

>  **Watch Out!**
> Images and clips are shown according to their order in the File Browser. Make changes to the order before building the gallery creation.

Photo Gallery dialog box. You see a list of your selected photos at the left of the dialog box, and a number of tabs on the right.

3. Click the Gallery Style drop-down arrow, and choose a style from the menu. The available styles range from kitsch to country, to special occasions, and framed or single-page styles.

4. In the Destination area at the bottom of the dialog box, click Browse to locate and select the folder in which the finished product is stored.

5. Specify settings on the four tabs of the dialog box; the Custom Colors tab is shown in Figure 20.7.

6. When you are finished, click Save to save the images, pages, and code in the designated folders.

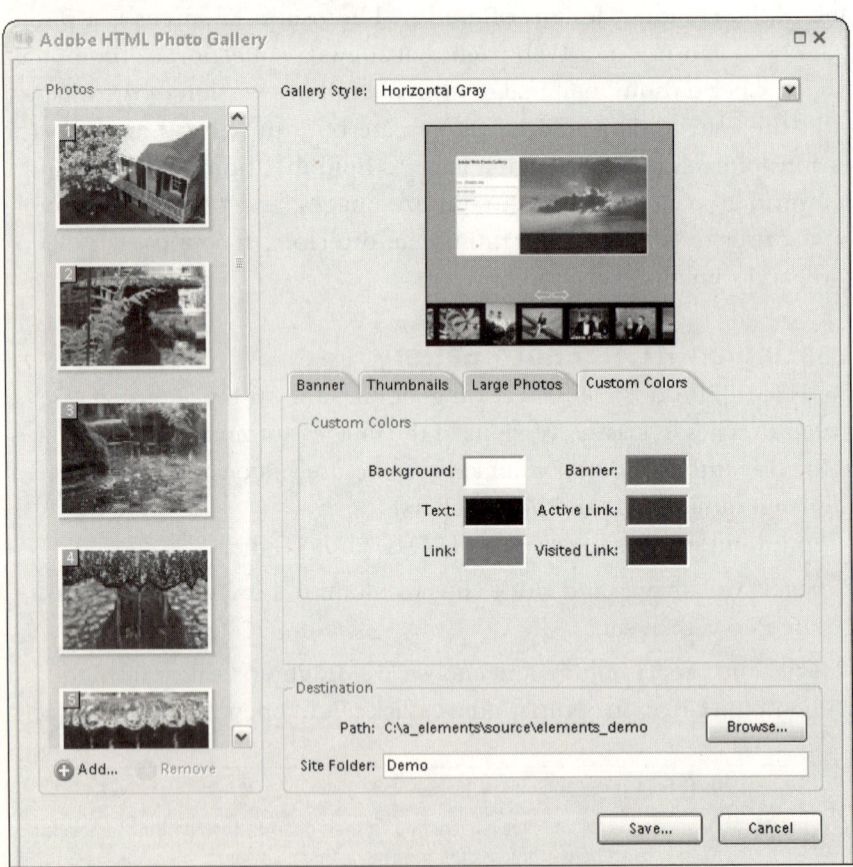

Figure 20.7. Choose and customize settings for the Web page that houses your photo gallery.

Customizing the HTML Photo Gallery Web page

The Adobe HTML Photo Gallery dialog box lets you customize the content using a set of four tabs. You can configure several aspects of the selected gallery page, including the following:

- **Banner.** The first tab of the dialog box contains basic information included on the page and in its Web page. Specify a title, font, and e-mail address.

- **Thumbnails.** On this tab, select a size for the thumbnails, specify whether to use captions, and choose text characteristics such as font and size.

- **Large Photos.** On the Large Photos tab, define how you want photos resized, as well as their quality. Drag the Photo Quality slider left to decrease the quality of the images, or right to increase image quality, shown in Figure 20.8. Also select caption settings and options.

- **Custom Colors.** The HTML Photo Gallery produces a Web page using default Web colors, such as medium blue links and maroon visited links. Click any of the color swatches to open a Color Picker, where you can choose a custom color for the page element.

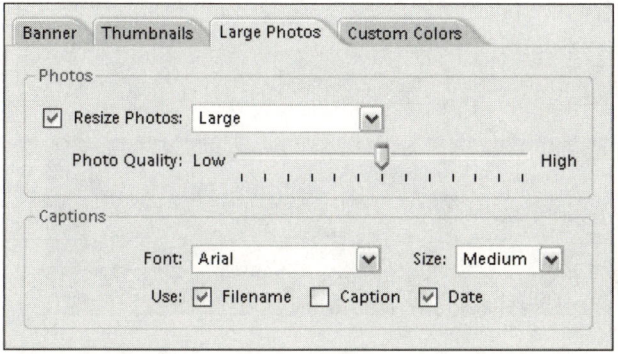

Figure 20.8. Specify the quality of the images in the Large Photos tab of the dialog box.

Inside Scoop
If you know that viewers are looking at your images using a slow Internet connection, set the quality of the images toward the Low end of the Photo Quality slider. The file size of the finished photos is smaller and the images will display faster.

Saving the site

When you are finished and click Save, the files are processed and a preview is displayed in the HTML Photo Gallery Browser dialog box, shown in Figure 20.9. Test your photo gallery by clicking through the arrows. The creation process doesn't include uploading your files to a Web server for online use — that's up to you.

Figure 20.9. Check out the preview of the finished photo gallery.

>
> **Hack**
> Open the HTML pages in any Web-editing program or in Notepad to tweak code if you like.

The photo gallery produces a number of pre-configured folders, including the following:

- A page named index.html, which is the home page for the photo gallery
- An Images subfolder, containing the JPEG images
- A Pages subfolder containing the gallery's HTML pages
- A Thumbnails subfolder containing the JPEG thumbnails

Building panoramic images

Sometimes, you would like to capture a sweeping vista in a single shot. The way to achieve this lofty goal is to shoot a set of images showing a segment of the shot and then stitch them together.

Preplanning tips

If you can, plan ahead for the best outcome with the least problems to save lots of editing time later. Keep these tips in mind:

- Make sure the component images overlap; 15 to 40 percent is recommended, as shown in Figure 20.10. In the figure, the first and second images in a series are shown separately from one another to show you the amount of overlap used.
- Use consistent camera settings. Make sure the focal length is the same throughout, and use the same exposure.
- Use a tripod to prevent inconsistencies in level and positioning.

>
> **Watch Out!**
> The amount of overlap is important to using the automatic Photomoerge Panorama feature. If the overlap is less than 15 percent, the assembly may be patchy; if it is more than 70 percent, the images may not blend well.

Figure 20.10. A single panoramic image is created by overlapping the component images.

Creating the panorama

You don't have to try to assemble images manually in Photoshop Elements. Instead, use the Photomerge Panorama command to stitch several images together into a single image.

You can start the assembly process from the Organizer using the File command, or you can start from the Editor. Follow these steps to create a panorama from the Editor:

1. In the Editor, choose File ⇨ New ⇨ Photomerge Panorama to open the Photomerge dialog box.
2. Files that are open in the Editor are listed on the dialog box in the Source Files list. Click Browse to select other files, or select a listed image and click Remove to delete it from the Source Files list.

3. Click OK to create the composite image. The source files are opened and processed, and the stitched image is displayed in the Photomerge dialog box, shown in Figure 20.11. If any component images can't be placed, they are shown in the Lightbox and you have to add them manually.

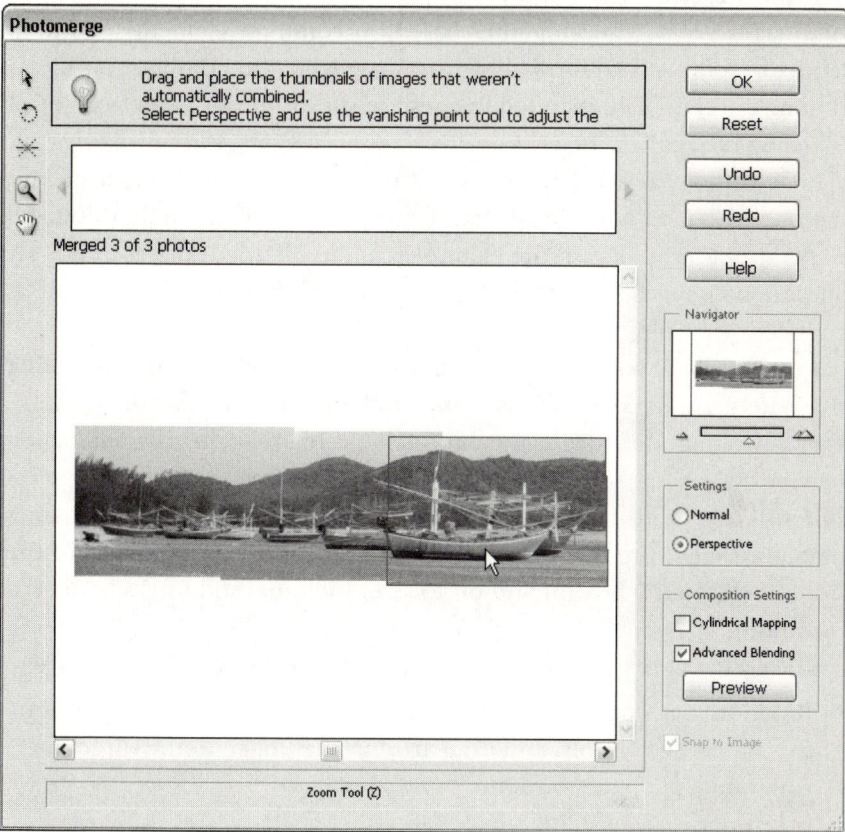

Figure 20.11. Stitch several shots together to produce a panoramic image in the Photomerge dialog box.

4. Review the merged images, and make any necessary adjustments.
5. Click OK to close the dialog box and create the finished panorama.
6. Save the new image file.

Watch Out!
If significant light or color inconsistencies exist among your images, adjust the source images in the Editor before combining them. You may need to adjust further in the Photomerge dialog box.

Adjusting the images

The images are stitched together based on common elements and then blended. Figure 20.11 shows how the images in the composition blend into one another. The blended images are shown in the lower portion of the dialog box, called the *work area*.

Images that can't be included in the composition automatically are shown in the *light box*, the white area at the top of the dialog box. All the component images in the example can be blended; there aren't any component images left in the light box when the panoramic image is produced.

You can make some types of adjustments in the Photomerge dialog box. When you make an adjustment, click Preview to show the changes in a preview mode; toggle the button to return to the regular dialog box view.

If you are adjusting the positions and perspectives of your images manually, toggle the Snap to Image check box at the lower right of the Photomerge dialog box on and off to see which method works better for positioning.

The adjustments you can make include the following:

- **Rotation.** Select the image on the work area, click the Rotate tool in the dialog box's tools, and drag around the image in the direction you want the image to rotate.

- **Vanishing Point.** Correct the panorama's perspective by redefining the default perspective. Click Perspective in the Settings area at the bottom right of the dialog box if the perspective correction is less than 120 degrees. Then select the Vanishing Point tool, and click an image to make it the vanishing point image and establish perspective for the other images. By default, the middle image in a panorama is the vanishing point image.

Inside Scoop

I usually leave the Snap to Image option selected to have the images match automatically, based on common content.

- **Cylindrical Mapping.** Click the Perspective setting, and then click Cylindrical Mapping to correct distortion that often occurs when you adjust perspective. Adjusting perspective produces a winged distortion — similar in appearance to a bow tie — that is corrected by remapping the image.
- **Advanced Blending.** If your source images are shot with different exposures, you are sure to see color differences. Click the Advanced Blending check box at the lower right of the Photomerge dialog box, shown in Figure 20.11. Advanced Blending adjusts color blending by differentiating the amount of blending based on whether the content is detail or main color blocks. For example, in the finished example shown in Figure 20.12, the rigging on the boats is detail, while the color in the hills and beach are main color blocks.

Figure 20.12. Use Advanced Blending and other techniques to produce a seamless panoramic image.

Bright Idea

Not sure which is which in an image you are adjusting? A panorama can have only one vanishing point image to establish perspective. The image you click with the Vanishing Point tool shows a blue frame if it is the vanishing point image; otherwise, it has a red frame.

Just the facts

- Set up the appearance, layout, and content of photo albums using the wizard options.
- Order printed photo albums and calendars online.
- Design different styles of cards and calendars using wizards.
- Create and customize a Web photo gallery, complete with the necessary Web files.
- Produce panoramic images using Photomerge to stitch several images into one.

GET THE SCOOP ON...
■ Setting slide preferences ■ Modifying slide contents ■ Adding features including sound, music, graphics, and text ■ Choosing transitions ■ Using pan and zoom effects ■ Burning slide shows for TV playback

On with the Show

Slide shows are extremely customizable, lots of fun, and a great way to impress friends, family, and clients with your technical skill. Along with images and clips, you can add music, narration, clip art, text, and special effects to enhance your slide show.

Before you create a slide show, consider assembling the images, music, and other clips you want to use in a separate collection in the Photo Browser. By doing so, you make finding the content, adding or changing elements, and keeping track of what you have available for the slide show much easier.

Slide show basics

Although customizations galore are available in a slide show, the basic construction process remains the same.

Follow these steps to create a basic slide show:

1. In the Photo Browser, select the photos you want to use in your slide show.
2. Click the Create button in the shortcuts bar to open the Creation Setup dialog box.
3. Click Slide Show from the list at the left of the dialog box, and then click OK.
4. Check the preferences in the Slide Show Preferences dialog, which opens by default each time you begin a new slide show.

>  **Watch Out!**
> You probably won't think of the amount of effort that goes into building a spectacular slide show until something happens to your computer and your work is lost. Prevent sadness and lost time: Save the project on a regular basis.

5. Click OK to close the preferences and open the Slide Show Editor window.
6. Enhance the images in the slide show with other features, such as music and narration.
7. Click the Preview button to run the slide show; click Edit Slide Show to return to the Slide Show Editor window.
8. Click Save Project to save your work.
9. Click Output, and choose a method of distributing the finished slide show.

Setting slide show preferences

The Photoshop Elements program default is to display the Slide Show Preferences dialog box, seen in Figure 21.1, when starting a new slide show.

It's usually best to leave the "Show this dialog each time a new Slide Show is created" option active. That way, whenever you start a new slide show, you choose settings for different aspects of the slides, saving construction time. On the other hand, if you always prepare slide shows the same way — such as using the same transition, duration, or background color — deselect the option to save mouse clicks. Each time you start a new slide show; the same slide features are used.

If you deselect the Slide Show Preferences dialog box display for new slide shows and then change your mind, choose Edit ⇨ Preferences from the Slide Show Editor menu. In the Preferences dialog box, click Show this dialog each time a new Slide Show is created. Click OK to close the Preferences dialog box. Now each time the Slide Show editor opens, you see the options displayed.

Figure 21.1. Choose common settings before starting a new slide show.

You can specify numerous settings in the Slide Show Preferences dialog box, as described in Table 21.1.

Table 21.1. Specifying slide show preferences

Preference	Explanation and Tips
Static Duration	Click the drop-down arrow, and choose a time in seconds that each slide is displayed onscreen.
Transition	Click the drop-down arrow and choose a transition from the menu. You see how the slides' images change from one to the next in the preview area at the upper right of the dialog box.
Transition Duration	This preference sets the length of time for transitions. If you choose a more striking transition, you may want a longer duration.
Background Color	The default color is black; click the color swatch to open the Color Picker and choose a custom color. The background is shown behind the content of each slide.

continued

Table 21.1. *continued*

Preference	Explanation and Tips
Apply Pan And Zoom To All Slides	This preference applies the pan and zoom of the selected slide to all the slides in a slide show.
Include Photo Captions As Text	If your photos have captions in the Organizer, this option carries the captions into the slide show as slide captions.
Include Audio Captions As Narration	If you added audio captions to your images in the Organizer, the caption is carried into the slide show as narration.
Repeat Soundtrack Until Last Slide	If you use a soundtrack for your slide show and its length is shorter than the time it takes to run the slide show based on the duration, transition, and number of slides, the music loops — or repeats — automatically.
Crop To Fit Slide	If you have some inconsistently sized images in a slide show, specify whether you want to crop those having landscape orientation, portrait orientation, or both to fit the slide show screen.
Preview Playback Options	Select the quality of the playback. Higher quality requires more processing — you see the content of the slides better, but the animation and transition may experience processing delays depending on the computer's resources.

Getting around the Slide Show Editor

The Slide Show Editor is a program window that has its own menu, tools, commands, and controls. Figure 21.2 shows the window and its component areas. The selected slide is highlighted in the Storyboard at the bottom of the window, and shown in the window's display area.

Hack

You can't sample colors from images within the Slide Show Editor. Open the image in the Editor first and sample the color. Make a note of the color values, and refer to the numbers when choosing custom colors in the Slide Show Editor for items such as backgrounds or text.

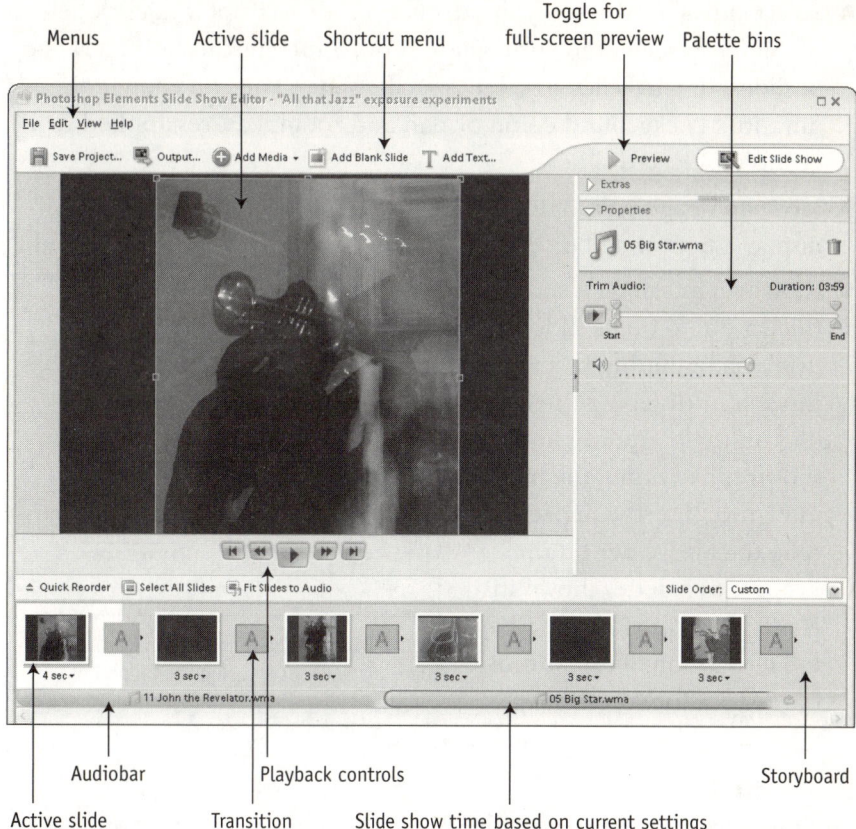

Figure 21.2. Design, configure, and test a slide show in the Slide Show Editor window.

Making common edits

You can manipulate content in the slide show in many ways, most of which are quite intuitive. Here are some of the most common actions:

- **Cut, Copy, Paste, Undo, and Delete.** Use any of the common editing features from the Edit menu or use shortcut keys. Apply the commands to a selected image or to a slide.

- **Add content.** Click Add Media in the shortcuts bar and select additional images, video, or audio content; click Add Blank Slide in the shortcuts bar to place a blank slide after the active slide.

- **Select slides.** In the Storyboard, click a slide to display it, click Select All Slides to select the entire slide show, Shift+click to select a range of slides, or Ctrl+click to select specific slides. You can change the duration, background color, or pan and zoom features applied to a group of selected slides.

- **Move an image on a slide.** Click a photo on its slide to select it and display a bounding box. Drag the image to reposition it on the slide.

- **Resize an image on a slide.** Click a photo on its slide to display a bounding box and resize it by dragging the handles on the bounding box, shown surrounding the image in Figure 21.2. If you prefer, drag the Size slider on the Properties palette, shown in Figure 21.3, or click the Crop to Fit or Fit on Slide buttons to resize automatically.

Figure 21.3. Resize or modify images on the slides manually or by using the Properties palette's options.

Quick edits

You don't have to cancel the slide show production process if you realize an image needs some editing. Instead, you can make edits right from the Slide Show window.

Select the image and choose one of these options from the Properties palette:

- Click Auto Smart Fix or Auto Red Eye Fix to make common adjustments.

- Select the Click to set photo effect to Black and White or the Click to set photo effect to Sepia buttons to modify the image's colors.

- If your image needs more work, click More Editing to open the photo in the Editor. After corrections, save the image and close it. You automatically return to the Slide Show Editor and can finish the project.

Inside Scoop

The thumbnail view for your slides works the same way as a subwindow in the Photo Browser to show you the contents of a version set or a stack.

Reordering the slide show

The images are added to a slide show in the order in which they appear in the Organizer, but you can reorder them as you like. Drag a slide in the Storyboard and move it to a new location. A vertical line between two existing slides identifies the location the slide is placed when you release the mouse.

You can set the slide order according to a specific arrangement by clicking the Slide Order drop-down arrow and choosing an ordering method, such as by date or folder location. If you have made any adjustments to the order manually, the Custom option is shown as the Slide Order method.

Scrolling through lots of slide thumbnails can be confusing and time-consuming, especially if you want to revise the order. If you have many slides, click Quick Reorder — located just above the Storyboard — to expand the Storyboard view into a thumbnail window. Make the changes and reorder as you like, and click Close to return to the main Slide Show Editor window.

Adding sound and music

Whether you are preparing a slide show to play in your display booth at a business tradeshow or assembling vacation slides from the lake last summer, music is a finishing touch. You can use one or more music clips in your slide show and adjust the audio to fit the parameters of your slide show's time frame.

Click Add Media on the Slide Show Editor's shortcuts bar and select either of the following:

- Audio From Organizer to pick a clip you have already added to the catalog
- Audio From Folder to locate and select a music clip from your computer

Save some time, and click the Audio bar at the bottom of the Slide Show Editor window to locate and select audio files. As you can see in Figure 21.4, more than one sound file or music clip can be added to the soundtrack in the Audio bar.

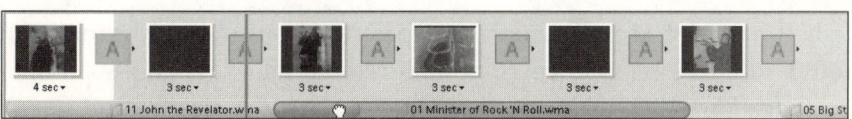

Figure 21.4. Add and reorder music clips in the Audio bar.

If you want to adjust the slide show's pace to match your soundtrack, click Fit Slides to Audio. The length of each slide's duration is adjusted automatically.

Adjusting music clips

Music can be trimmed for length in the slide show, or the slide show's duration can be modified to correlate with the music. Here's how:

1. Click the music clip's label on the Audio bar at the bottom of the window to display the Trim Audio palette in the Properties palette. The controls are shown back in Figure 21.2.
2. Drag the Start tab to change when the music clip starts; drag the End tab to change when the music clip ends.
3. Click the Play/Stop button to the left of the Timeline to preview your clip segment. Drag the volume slider to adjust the volume of the soundtrack segment.

Narrating a slide show

Remember listening to your ol' Uncle Joe ramble on for hours about his vacation, showing you hundreds of slides of the truck stops, gas stations, and other points of interest along his route? Slides developed from film and loaded into a slide projector may be disappearing, but isn't it nice to know that Uncle Joe can now do the same thing digitally?

Most newer computer systems come with sound recording features and a microphone installed. Follow your operating system's instructions to install and configure a microphone if necessary.

When the system is ready, give Uncle Joe a microphone, and let him loose in the Slide Show Editor, following these steps:

1. Click the Narration button in the Extras palette to display the recorder.
2. Use the Record, Stop, and Play buttons to control recording and playback.
3. Click Next Slide to record the narration for the next slide.
4. Continue until the production is complete.

If you prefer, record narration separately from the slide show and store it in individual files corresponding to the slides. When assembling the slide show, click the folder icon in the Narration palette and select the audio file.

Bright Idea
If you can't decide among several clips until you have the slides assembled, move the group of music clips into the catalog. When you select clips in the Organizer, you can click Play in the Browse dialog box to listen first before selecting the music.

Adding graphic enhancements

Photoshop Elements includes dozens of pieces of clip art in the Extras palette. The clip art is divided into categories to make it simpler to track down the perfect piece.

Follow these steps to add clip art:

1. Click Graphics in the Extras palette to load the clip art listings.
2. Browse to find the graphic you want to use.
3. Drag the clip art to the slide.
4. Adjust the graphic as desired by moving or resizing it, using the controls in the bin shown in Figure 21.5.

Figure 21.5. Modify the graphic's characteristics.

If you add several pieces of clip art and text, you may need to change the stacking order to be sure the images overlap correctly. Right-click the object you want to reorder, and select an option from the shortcut menu, shown in Figure 21.6.

Figure 21.6. Reorder objects added to the slides, if necessary.

Bright Idea
If you want to add clip art to a number of slides, select the slides first in the Storyboard and then drag the clip art to the visible slide. The clip art is copied to all selected slides. Resizing or repositioning must be done on the individual slides.

Attaching labels and text

Add labels to your slides, captions for your images, headings, and other information using the Text tools in the Slide Show Editor. You can work with plain text or use a sample from the Extras palette.

Follow these steps to add text to your slide show from the Extras palette:

1. Click Text in the Extras palette to display the text effect samples.
2. Scroll through the options to find the text you want to apply to the slide.
3. Drag the text example from the palette to the slide and drop it.
4. The default text "Your text here" displays on the slide. Double-click the text to open an Edit Text dialog box.
5. Type your text and click OK to close the dialog box.
6. The text on the slide is changed, and you see your text on the Properties palette, shown in Figure 21.7. If you want to change any text, click Edit Text to reopen the Edit Text dialog box.
7. Configure the text as desired.

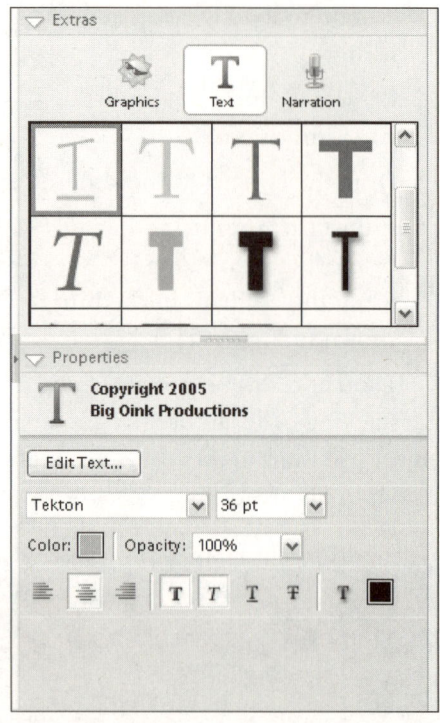
Figure 21.7. Add pre-configured text, and customize it as you like.

Customizing text appearance

Although there are only 16 text style samples, appearances can be deceptive. Regardless of the text sample you start with, you can configure the text in a number of ways, including these:

- Select a font family from the drop-down menu at the left of the palette.
- Choose a font size from the drop-down menu, or type a custom value in the field.
- Change text orientation from horizontal to vertical by clicking the Change Text Orientation button.
- Use a custom text color by clicking the color swatch and selecting a custom color in the Color Picker dialog box.
- Set the opacity of the text by choosing a setting from the Opacity drop-down menu or typing a custom value in the field.
- Specify an alignment for the text by clicking an alignment option.
- Apply a font style or decoration to the text such as bold or strikethrough.
- Use a drop shadow by clicking the Drop Shadow button and setting the color for the shadow via the shadow's color swatch.

Fun with text

You may be surprised by how elaborate a slide show can become in Photoshop Elements! Here are some things to try the next time you have an hour or two to experiment:

- Select groups of slides before adding text. That way, you can add the same text using the same configurations to a number of slides, like the copyright notice shown in Figure 21.8. You save lots of time applying the same thing to multiple slides, although you have to remove it from slides individually.
- Don't bother with the style examples in the Extras palette if you plan to make lots of changes. Just click the Add Text button on the shortcuts bar to open the Text Edit dialog box. Type the text, and carry on as with the styled text.
- If you want to use some bullets on your slides, use symbol fonts like Zapf Dingbats as separate text blocks; the letter "m" is shown as the bullet in Figure 21.8. You can paste several copies of the same text on the same slide; look for pasted copies in the extreme upper left of the slide. Align the bullet and word text blocks manually.
- Don't try to nudge text on a slide using the keyboard arrows. They take you to another slide instead.

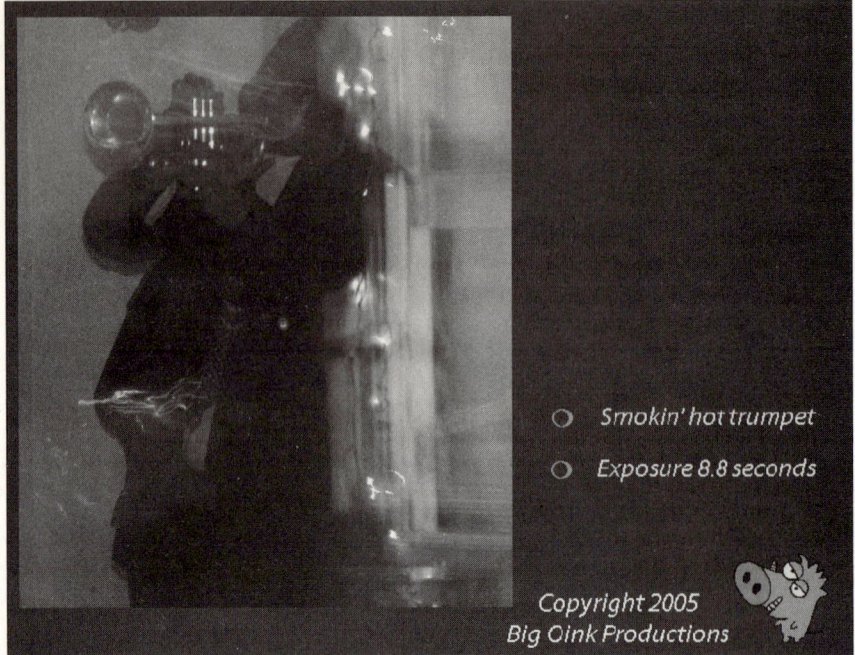

Figure 21.8. Add simulated bulleted text; check the alignment in Preview mode.

- To get a good look at your slide, click Preview to view it in Preview mode; the quality is better than viewing in the Slide Show Editor window.
- Create a sense of animation for the bullets using pan and zoom effects (coming up shortly).

Transitioning slides

Transition effects are techniques used to blend two slides' contents as the slide show progresses from slide to slide. A transition is applied to the whole project when it is created using the transition specified in the Slide Show Preferences dialog box.

When you are working in a slide show, you can change the transition effect, its duration, and the slide's display time.

Here are your options:

- Click the transition icon between two slides on the Storyboard to select it, and choose another transition from the drop-down menu in the Properties palette.
- Ctrl+click transition icons to select multiple transitions and change the transition using the Properties palette's drop-down menu.

CHAPTER 21 ■ ON WITH THE SHOW

- Choose Edit ⇨ Select All Transitions to select your entire slide show's set of transitions and make changes to the entire slide show at once.

- Click the arrow to the right of the transition's icon on the Storyboard to open the menu, shown in Figure 21.9.

- Change the duration of a transition — how long it takes to change from one slide to the next — by selecting the transition or transitions and clicking the drop-down arrow on the Properties palette to open the list of transition times. Click Custom to open the Set Transition Duration dialog box. Type a time in seconds in the field, and click OK to close the dialog box and set the transition.

- You may need to change the display time for your slides as well. Click the duration shown below each slide's thumbnail in the Storyboard to open a shortcut menu, shown in Figure 21.9. Choose a new slide duration, or click Custom and set the time in seconds in the Set Slide Duration dialog box.

- Watch the transitions using the playback controls under the slide in the preview area. The Wedge Wipe transition is shown in Figure 21.10.

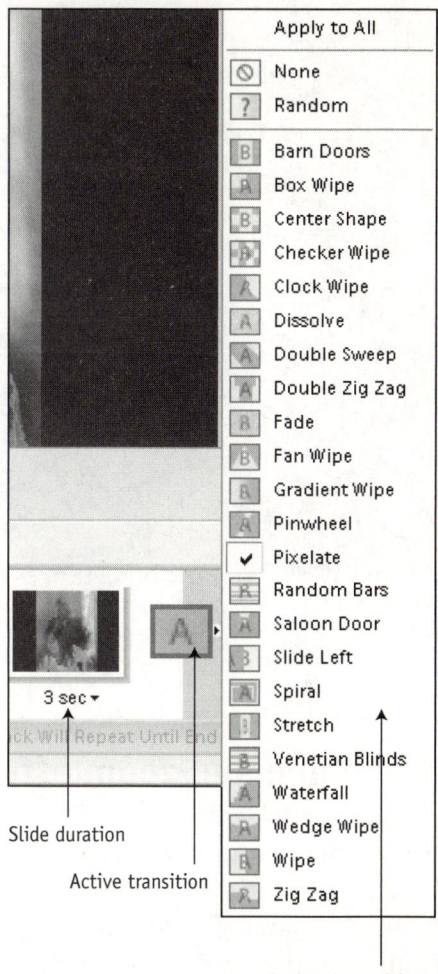

Slide duration

Active transition

Optional transitions

Figure 21.9. Change or remove transitions between slides in your slide show using choices from the menu or the Properties palette.

 **Inside Scoop**
You can also click a slide and set the time in the Properties palette from the drop-down menu. It's much quicker to use the shortcut menu from the Storyboard.

Figure 21.10. Preview transitions in the Preview area of the Slide Show Editor window. In the image you see the current slide being replaced by the following slide by opening wedges along the sides of the image.

Using pan and zoom effects

A tried-and-true video effect that provides lots of impact to a slide show or presentation is a *pan and zoom*. Panning refers to a display of different areas of the slide over time from a specified start point to a specified end point. Zooming refers to changes in the slide's magnification over time. By the way, you don't specify each effect separately. The motion and the change in magnification are based solely on the location and area of the slide you specify for the starting and ending positions.

Applying a pan and zoom

In the Slide Show Editor, you can apply pan and zoom to all slides or to selected slides, and you can add more than one pan and zoom to the same slide.

Follow these steps to add a pan and zoom to a slide:

1. Select the slide in the Storyboard; it appears in the preview area.
2. Click Enable Pan & Zoom in the Properties palette.

3. The green bounding box identifying the Start position overlays the image. Drag the box to overlay the area where you want the animation to start, and resize the box if you like. The box is resized proportionally automatically. The smaller the box, the more dramatic the effect is.

4. Click the End thumbnail in the Properties palette. Now the slide displays a red bounding box. Resize and move the bounding box to define where the effect should end.

5. Use the playback controls under the slide in the preview area to watch the effect.

Adding a second effect

There's no need to stop at one pan and zoom per slide! Click Add Another Pan & Zoom to this slide in the Properties palette. You see that a duplicate of the slide is added to the Storyboard, and a link shows between the two slides rather than a transition, indicating that there are two animation processes. An example is shown in Figure 21.11.

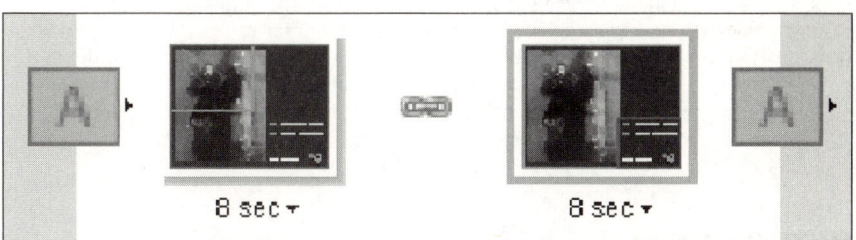

Figure 21.11. Multiple animations show a duplicate slide and a link in the Storyboard.

Position the end bounding box on the second copy of the slide to identify where you want the animation to end. If you look carefully at the thumbnails, you see that the end point on the first slide is duplicated as the start point on the second copy of the slide, which results in a smooth animation effect.

Use the playback controls under the slide in the preview area to watch the effect.

Watch Out!
Be careful working with pan and zoom effects. They can take lots of processing power and sometimes aren't worth the wait. On the other hand, they can be very dramatic.

Sharing a slide show

You can distribute and share slide shows in a number of ways. The different output options, and when to use them, are listed in Table 21.2.

Table 21.2. Slide show outputs

Option	Use This Option When...
Save As a File	The slide show is processed and saved as a WMV file on your hard drive. If you aren't sure how you need to distribute the file, or want to use it from your hard drive only, use this option.
Burn To Disc	The slide show is processed and burned to a VCD or DVD. Use this option to distribute content that can be viewed on television. Also good for mailing when a slide show is too large to send by e-mail.
E-mail Slide Show	You want to send an e-mail with the slide show attached for convenient sharing. Check the size of the file before sending; if it's too large to send in a reasonable time to recipients using dial-up service, consider burning and mailing a Video Compact Disc (VCD) or DVD.
Share Online	You plan to use an online sharing service. Using such a service can be very practical for exchanging content with clients, friends, or family. All users must be able to access the online account.
Send To TV	You want to view your show on TV. Your slide show is output directly to TV if you are running Windows XP Media Center Edition. If you aren't using that operating system, burn to a disc for TV playback.

Burning discs

You can burn your slide shows to a CD in Video Compact Disc (VCD) format or Digital Video Disc (DVD) format that can be viewed using most DVD players. Burning content to CD or DVD is also a good way to safely archive your slide show material.

Insert a writable CD in your CD-RW or DVD-RW drive, and then follow these steps from the Organizer window:

1. Select the slide show or shows you want to burn from the Photo Browser.
2. Click Create to open the Creation Setup dialog box.
3. Choose VCD with Menu in the list at the left of the dialog box, and click OK to open the Create a VCD with Menu dialog box.

> **Choosing a video option**
>
> Your VCD uses either NTSC or PAL video. But what are they? NTSC is named after the National Television Standards Committee, a national committee that established the U.S. color TV standard in 1953. The NTSC standard is the current analog television standard in North and South America, Japan, and other Asian countries.
>
> Phase-alternating line, or PAL, is another color-encoding system introduced in Europe in 1967 and is used in much of Europe and some of the Middle East.

4. The selected slide show or slide shows are listed in the dialog box. You can rearrange the slide shows by dragging them to a different order. Click Add Slide Shows to add more content; select an existing slide show and click Remove Slide show to delete it.
5. Select a video system, either NTSC or PAL.
6. Click Burn. Windows Media Video (WMV) versions of each slide show are produced. You will receive prompts and option dialog boxes depending on your system's configuration as the files are processed.

Just the facts

- Set slide show preferences before starting a project for convenience.
- After images are added to the slide show window, reorder and organize them as desired.
- Add narration, music, and graphics to enhance your presentation.
- Use text in different ways for labels and headings.
- Apply transitions to animate slide replacements onscreen.
- Pan and zoom effects add interesting animation to your slide show.
- Share a slide show in several ways, including burning to a CD or DVD for television playback.

GET THE SCOOP ON...
■ Creating indexed color images ■ Saving and previewing images for Web use ■ Batch processing files ■ Using metadata ■ Copyrighting

Managing Image Distribution

You may think this chapter includes quite a diversity in topics and you'd be right. Essentially there are some important features of Photoshop Elements that are rather specialized, and while you may not use them often, they are nevertheless powerful features.

What ties these different features together, along with being specialized, is that each feature is used for managing the information in an image in some specific way.

When you think of image management you may think only of naming, storing, and e-mailing your files. There's more to it, as you see in this chapter. For example, did you know there are methods of configuring images to make them the best image possible for Web use? Or that instead of manually changing the names or file formats of a group of images; you can use a batch process in Photoshop Elements that makes the changes for you?

Displaying your work online

Photoshop Elements can easily handle the job of creating and preparing images for use on a Web page. You can select and configure graphic file formats, prepare the files for use on the Web, and test how they look on a Web page all from within the program.

The process of considering and responding to all the design and compression issues is called *optimization*. The goal is to create the smallest file using the most appropriate format that shows the right amount of detail and downloads at the most reasonable speed.

Preparing images

Consider these factors when preparing images for use on a Web page:

- **File format.** Different types of images should be converted to appropriate file formats. For example, a line drawing or a logo can often be a compact GIF file, while a photo is usually better saved as a JPEG file, like the examples shown in Figure 22.1.
- **Image quality.** The quality of an image can vary depending on the file format chosen. You don't always need to use high-quality images, which have a larger file size and longer download time.
- **Image size.** Make sure the dimensions of the image are the same as the size you intend to display on your Web page. When the image is larger than its assigned space on a page, your viewers have to wait for the image to be downloaded and then resized by their browser.
- **File size.** The smaller and more compact the file, the faster it will download and display for your viewer in their browser.

Figure 22.1. Different types of images are better suited for different formats. The image of the logo is a compact GIF file, while the photo's range of color is preserved in a JPEG image.

Watch Out!

How an image appears on a Web page depends on the color display capabilities of the operating system, monitor, browser, and platform. If color is a concern, test images on different browsers and platforms.

Choosing a file format

Photoshop Elements provides four file formats that you can use for Web images. These are the options:

- **GIF.** This format is usually best for illustrations, images with large blocks of solid color, and text. GIF is the only animation format supported in the program.

- **PNG-8.** This format is a good alternative to GIF format that supports transparency, but doesn't support animation.

- **JPEG.** This format is most useful for displaying and distributing photographs as it shows gradations of color normally seen in photographs.

- **PNG-24.** This format is another good photograph format that also supports transparency. It supports the use of color gradations and variations like JPEG images.

Optimizing Web images

Photoshop Elements provides the Save For Web dialog box you can use to prepare images for use on Web pages. You can see the results of modifying your settings in the dialog box, and even have the program choose the best settings automatically.

The Save For Web dialog box is divided into several areas:

- A small toolbox contains the Hand, Zoom, and Eyedropper tools, and a color swatch for opening the Color Picker to select a matte color, shown in Figure 22.2.

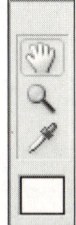

- You see two image windows: The left window shows the original image, while the right shows an export preview of the image using the settings currently selected in the dialog box, shown in Figure 22.3.

Figure 22.2. Choose common tools in the Save For Web dialog box's toolbox.

Inside Scoop

Although the discussion revolves around images for Web pages, the same advice and considerations apply to images you plan to e-mail.

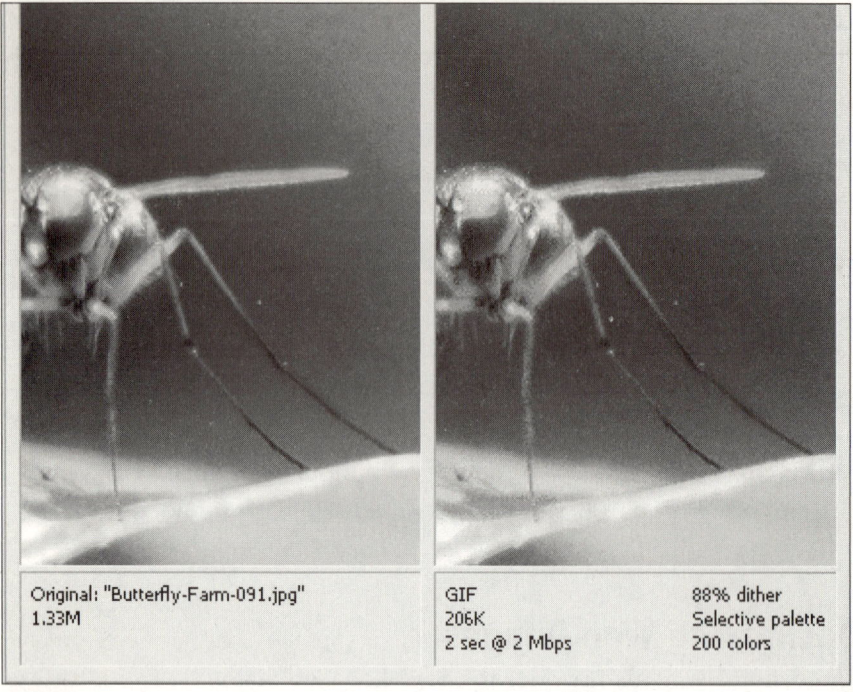

Figure 22.3. View the original image and preview optimized images in the Save For Web dialog box.

- Information about each image display is shown below the image, including the name, format, size of the file, and an estimated download time, as shown in Figure 22.4. Making adjustments to the image revises the data displayed for the export preview.

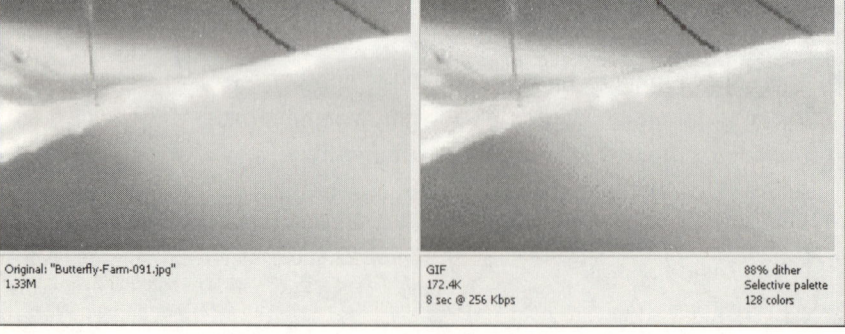

Figure 22.4. The "after" details of the image's configuration are changed as you alter settings.

- You have access to a menu with alternate access speeds to calculate download time, shown in Figure 22.5, ranging from modem to cable and DSL options, as well as color and display options to select for previewing images and data.

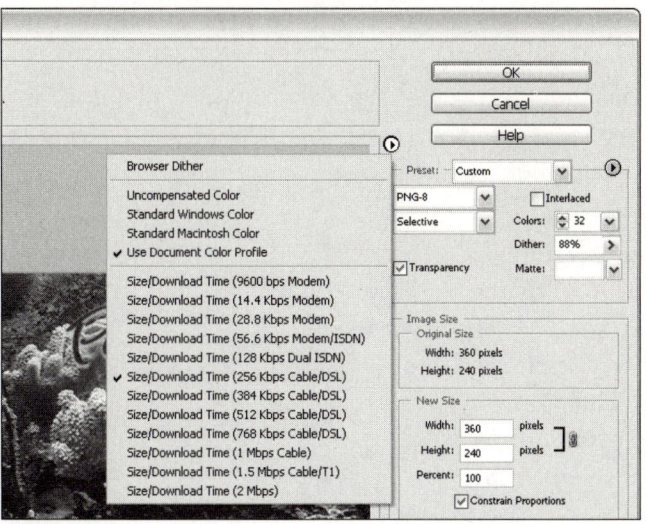

Figure 22.5. Choose options for calculating download time for the image.

- Preset options as well as menus and fields for configuring custom settings are included in the Preset area on the dialog box, shown in Figure 22.6.

- You have access to a dialog box for optimizing based on file size.

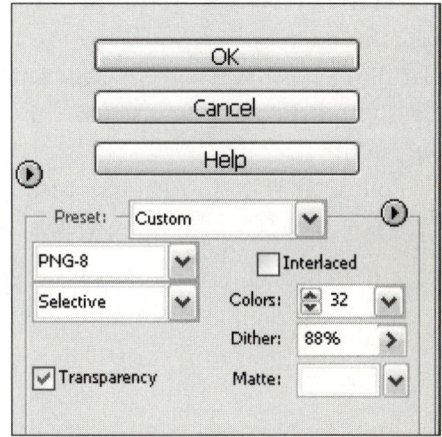

Figure 22.6. Configure settings for the image in the Preset area of the Save For Web dialog box.

> **Watch Out!**
> Pay attention to the download times using different settings. If your images are destined for a corporate intranet, you don't have to worry as much about the file size or download time as you would if you were working with one of a few hundred images for an online catalog.

- Image size information about the original and any modified sizes are shown at the right of the dialog box, shown in Figure 22.7.

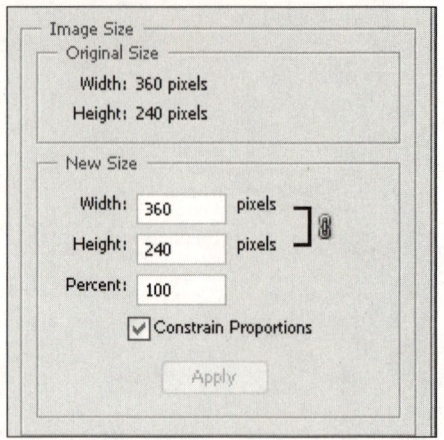

The Animation section at the lower right of the dialog box controls animation playback and speed for configuring animated GIF files. The controls are only active when the appropriate type of file is open in the dialog box.

Figure 22.7. View information about original and modified image sizes in the dialog box.

Optimizing an image automatically

Sometimes, you may not know the best settings to use for an image, or you don't have the time to experiment with different options. Instead, have Photoshop Elements make the best settings for you based on an output file size.

Follow these steps to automatically optimize an image:

1. Open the image in the Save For Web dialog box.

2. Click the Optimize to File Size arrow next to the Preset drop-down list at the right of the dialog box, shown in Figure 22.8. Click Optimize To File Size, which is the only available command.

CHAPTER 22 ■ MANAGING IMAGE DISTRIBUTION

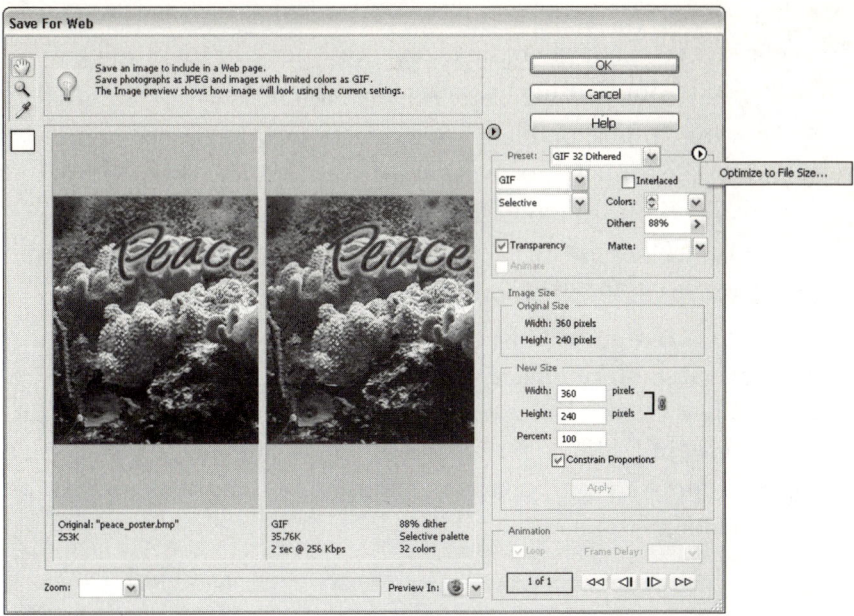

Figure 22.8. Let Photoshop Elements help you create an optimized image for Web use.

3. Type a target size for the finished image file in the Desired File Size field in the Optimize To File Size dialog box, shown in Figure 22.9. The file size you specify depends on your Web page requirements, as well as the original image. For example, trying to optimize an 8×10 photograph to a 30KB file won't produce a usable image as the file size is simply too small to display sufficient image information. On the other hand, a simple logo using a few colors can likely be optimized to produce a usable image at a 30KB file size.

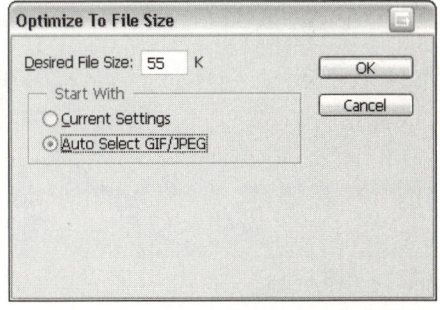

Figure 22.9. Specify the size of the finished file and the program will optimize the image to meet your size and starting requirements.

4. Define which option you want the optimization to start with. These are your choices:

- The settings currently in use, which are either the settings displayed by default when the dialog box opens, or those you have selected prior to using the automatic optimizing feature.

- Allowing Photoshop Elements to auto-select the best configuration of file format, quality, number of colors, and other settings available to the different file types.

5. Click OK to close the dialog box. You see a progress bar below the preview areas as the file is processed.

The right image preview in the Save For Web dialog box shows the optimized version of the image using the settings you specified. As you can see in Figure 22.10, the optimized file is under 54K in size, and the target value set in the dialog box value is 55K. If the image quality isn't appropriate for your purposes, try different optimization settings or change the image size.

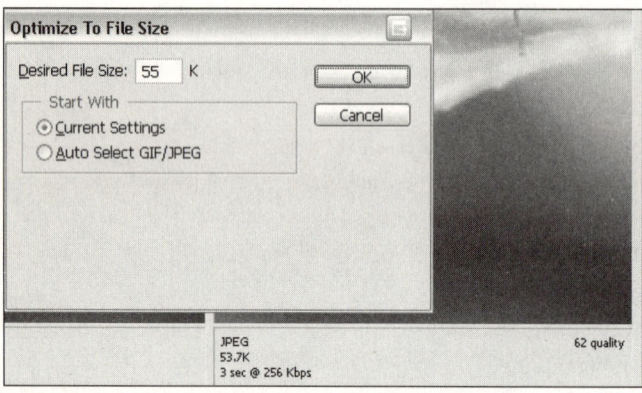

Figure 22.10. Optimize an image automatically based on file size.

Understanding 24-bit color files

Two of the Web image formats, JPEG and PNG-24, support 24-bit color and can display as many as 16 million colors, which is ideal for viewing photographs online, as you can see in the two examples in Figure 22.11. In the figure, a maximum quality JPEG image is shown at the left, and the same image is shown as a PNG-24 image at the right. Both are very high quality and display a photo's subtle color gradations and shading very well.

Read about color and bit depths in Chapter 9.

CHAPTER 22 ▪ MANAGING IMAGE DISTRIBUTION

More optimizing shortcuts

Instead of optimizing an image based on file size, you can apply a preset that automatically configures the settings in the Save For Web dialog box. Click the Preset drop-down arrow at the upper right of the Save For Web dialog box, and choose an option.

All the presets are named according to their action, making it simple to find what you want. For example, use the JPEG Low setting to reformat the image as a low-quality, small-sized JPEG image. If you make changes to the options in the dialog box, the name of the preset changes to Custom. Although you can't save the custom presets, the next time you open the dialog box, the custom settings are shown.

Inside Scoop

In Figure 22.10, the optimization was completed first, and then the dialog box reopened to capture the screenshot for the figure so you could see the comparison of file sizes.

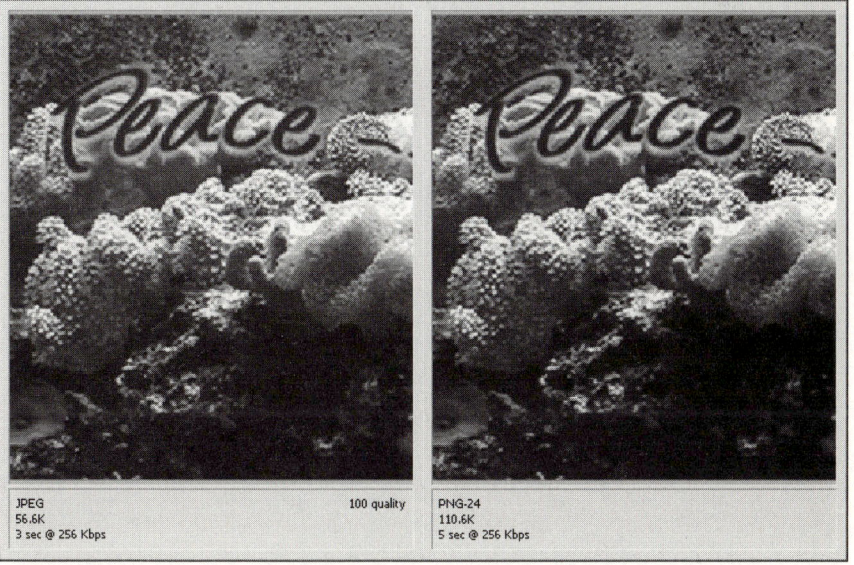

Figure 22.11. Both a maximum quality JPEG image (left) and a PNG-24 image (right) are ideal formats for displaying photographs.

A list of the features and comparisons between JPEG and PNG-24 image formats is included in Table 22.1.

Table 22.1. Comparison of 24-bit color formats

Feature	JPEG	PNG-24
Colors supported	More than 16 million	More than 16 million
Image quality	Five quality levels from Low to Maximum	One quality level
Background transparency	Not supported	Allows for 256 levels of background transparency
Compression	Lossy; can specify quality	Method 0 lossless compression
Download settings	Use progressive download to download in several passes	Select Interlaced to download the image in several passes
Browser support	Widespread	Not all browsers support format's features

Experimenting with formats

Try saving a high-resolution image downsampled for Web use in various formats, and you may find that the results aren't what you always expect.

Both GIF and PNG-8 formats use lossless compression, but optimizing a 24-bit image as an 8-bit file in either format may subtract colors from the image.

Try the same image saved as GIF and PNG-8 files or JPEG and PNG-24 files, and you may see image quality or file size variations. For example, the image shown in the dialog box in Figure 22.12 is 181KB as a PNG-8 file, and 206KB as a GIF file; the image shown in Figure 22.15 is twice the size as a PNG-24 image than it is as a maximum-quality JPEG image.

Managing transparency in 24-bit images

GIF and PNG files support transparency, while JPEG images do not. The PNG-8 and GIF formats both support one level of transparency, and both use the same features for applying a *matte*, or solid background.

Only a PNG-24 image uses more than one transparency level, which means you can have areas that are 50 percent or 38 percent transparent, if you like.

And, what of the JPEG? Well, you can simulate transparency in a JPEG. Why bother if you can get actual transparency from a PNG file? There are two reasons, both based on the image's distribution:

- A PNG-24 image is usually a larger file, which can be an issue for distribution and downloading.

- The JPEG image is more widespread and supported in virtually all browsers, while a PNG-24 image isn't universally supported.

Simulating matting in a JPEG image

Although the JPEG format does not support transparency, you can specify a matte color to simulate the appearance of transparency in the original image.

In the Save For Web dialog box, select a color from the Matte menu. If you show the JPEG image on a Web page using the same background color as the matte color, you see that the image appears to have areas of transparency.

In Figure 22.12 for example, the original image is shown at the left against the Web page background — there's nothing transparent about it. Filling the image's background areas with the matte color, as in the right image in Figure 22.12, blends the image into the page's background.

Hack
Need to match a background color using background matting? Check the HTML for the Web page. The color is listed in the stylesheet attached to the page, which is usually stored with the other Web pages and is a Cascading Style Sheet (CSS) file or included in the opening <Body> tag in HTML.

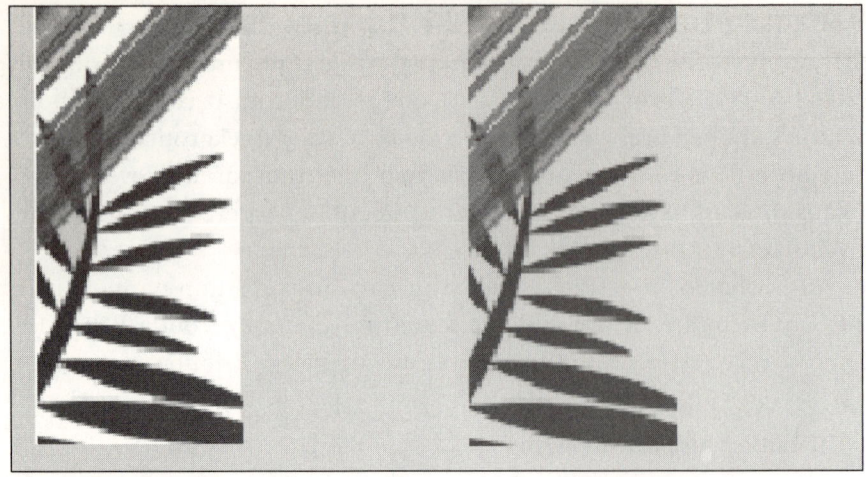

Figure 22.12. JPEG images don't support transparency, but you can specify a matte color to simulate transparency to help the image blend with a Web page background.

Matting a PNG-24 image

A PNG-24 image applies a matte background based on the opacity of the color in the image, which lets you have varying amounts of transparency shown in the same image. In Figure 22.13, for example, the three bands of color in the image use three levels of opacity as indicated in percentages.

To apply a colored matte to a PNG-24 image, follow these steps:

1. Open the image in the Save For Web dialog box.
2. Choose PNG-24 from the Preset drop-down menu.

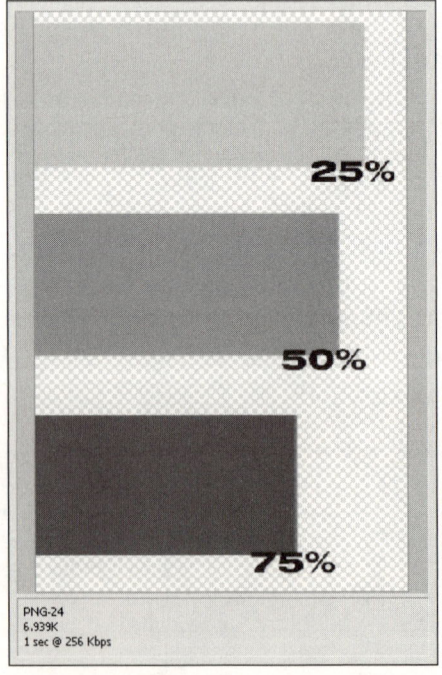

Figure 22.13. PNG-24 images support varying levels of transparency in the same image.

Watch Out!
If your transparent pixels aren't blending with the matte color, check that the Transparency check box is deselected in the Save For Web dialog box.

3. Deselect the Transparency check box in the Preset area of the dialog box, activating the Matte field, shown in Figure 22.14.

4. Click the space shown in the Matte field to open the Color Picker and select a custom color. Click OK to close the Color Picker and apply the matte. The selected color displays in the Matte field.

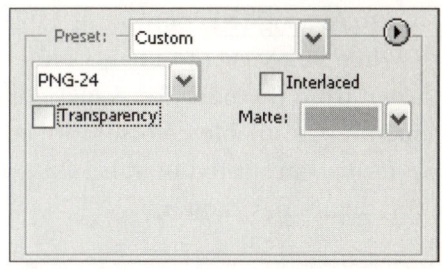

Figure 22.14. Removing the transparency lets you apply a colored matte that blends with the various bands of color according to their opacity levels.

You see in the image shown in Figure 22.15 that transparent and partially transparent pixels blend with the matte color. You see variations in the background because the levels of transparency are blended with the chosen matte color.

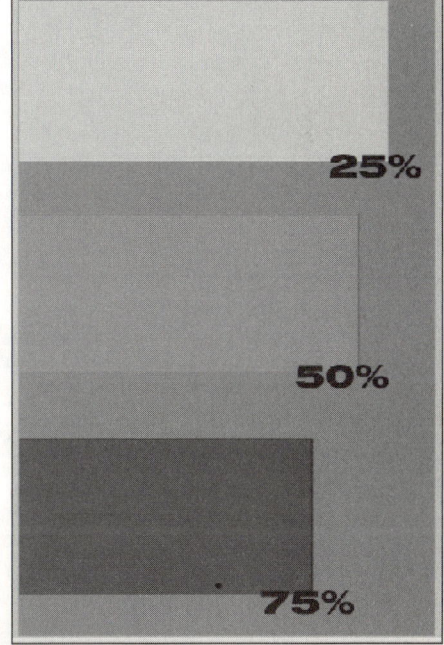

Figure 22.15. The matte blends with the contents in the image according to the existing levels of transparency.

Indexed color images

Both GIF and PNG-8 formats are indexed color images, and use 8-bit color to allow the display of up to 256 colors. In either format, the pixels in the image are colored according to a color lookup table, like the one shown in Figure 22.16. The name *indexed color* derives from matching the pixel to its assigned color in the table.

When you view the image, either the closest color to the original is chosen from the table for display, or the color is simulated using a combination of available colors. More comparisons between GIF and PNG-8 file formats are listed in Table 22.2. Read more about color issues, such as bit depth, in Chapter 9.

Figure 22.16. A color lookup table is created for each indexed image and stored within the image file.

Table 22.2. Comparing GIF and PNG-8 images

Feature	GIF	PNG-8
Color characteristics	8-bit color, 256 colors	8-bit color, 256 colors
Transparency	Supported	Supported
Background matting	Supported	Supported
Dithering	Supported	Supported
Compression	LZW lossless compression	Method 0 lossless compression
Browser support	Widespread	Not all browsers support format

Checking the image's features

You can configure an image as a GIF file by converting its mode using program commands, or through the Save For Web dialog box prior to exporting and saving the image for a Web page.

Before you make any changes to a file's format, check the image's resolution and size. For example, if you use a print quality 300dpi image for a Web page, download time is much longer than necessary. Reducing the resolution also reduces the file size.

Be sure to use a copy of your original image for converting to a GIF file, because after you have decreased the resolution trying to increase it again produces a poor-quality image. So, prior to converting a copy of your print-quality image to a GIF image in Photoshop Elements, follow these steps to change the resolution:

1. Choose Image ⇨ Resize ⇨ Image Size to open the Image Size dialog box.
2. Click the Resolution field, and type either **72** or **96** if your file size is larger than this. Windows monitors are capable of displaying 96dpi; Mac OS monitors display at 72dpi.
3. Note the difference in the Pixel Dimensions when you adjust the Resolution. In the image used as the source for the Image Size dialog box shown in Figure 22.17, its original dimensions were 900×900 pixels at a resolution of 300dpi. After changing the resolution to 96dpi, the dimensions drop to 288×288 pixels.
4. Click OK to close the dialog box.

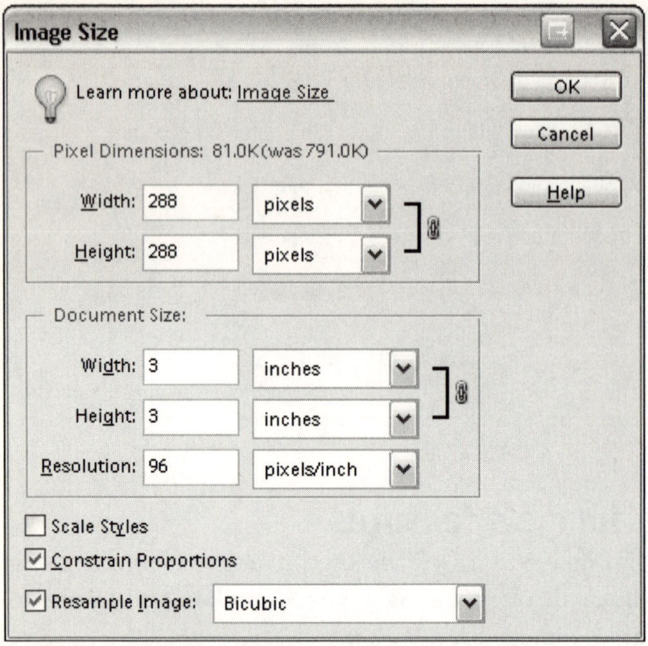

Figure 22.17. Reduce the resolution of an image if necessary to use online.

Now that the image has a lowered resolution, check the dimensions of the image to be sure it is appropriate for your online use. Press and hold the bottom border of the document window to the right of the magnification value to open the document information, shown in the left image in Figure 22.18. You can see the image is 3×3 inches in size.

To use it as a 1-inch wide logo on a Web page, it needs both cropping and resizing. Reducing the resolution and the physical size of the image also has a large impact on the file size, of course. The right image in Figure 22.18 dropped from a file size of more than 80KB to a very small, 7KB file.

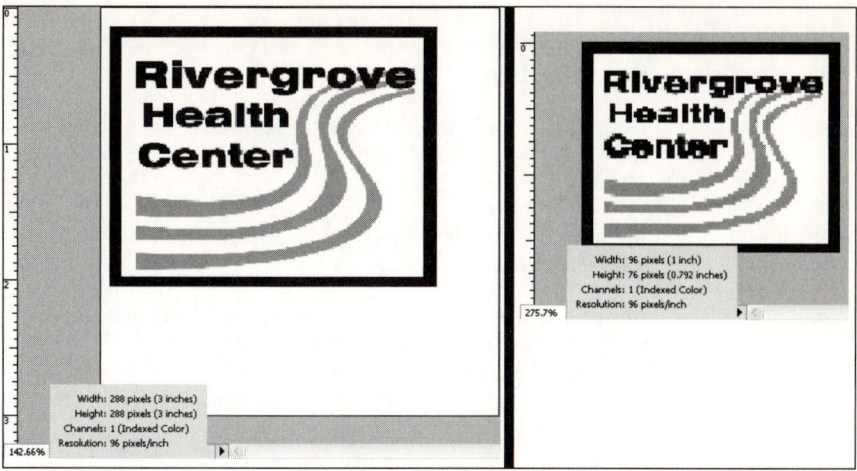

Figure 22.18. Check that your image is the right size and dimensions for your purposes.

Choosing color palettes

Next up, now that your image is a Web-friendly size, choose settings for the indexed color. Indexed color can use one of several color palettes, described in Table 22.3. When you are deciding on a color palette for an image, experiment with the various options. The differences can be very dramatic, or quite subtle.

Table 22.3. Indexed color palettes

Palette or Group	How It Is Used
Exact	The palette uses the exact colors from the original image if the image uses less than 256 colors. When the image contains more than 256 colors, the Exact option is disabled. Image color isn't approximated by combining colors when using an exact palette.
System	Mac OS and Windows palettes use their respective system's default 8-bit palettes.

continued

Table 22.3. continued

Palette or Group	How It Is Used
Web	This palette uses the uniform 216 colors that all Web browsers can display, regardless of platform. Web palettes aren't necessary with newer browsers and monitors.
Uniform	The palette is built on uniform color samples from a standardized matrix of colors.
Perceptual	This palette uses Local or Master palettes based on human color recognition: Local Perceptual applies the palette to a single image, and Master Perceptual applies the palette to multiple images such as an animated GIF which combines numerous images into a single file.
Selective	This palette uses Local or Master palettes based on preserving Web colors. Local Selective applies the palette to a single image; Master Selective applies the palette to multiple images.
Adaptive	This palette uses Local or Master palettes based on the color spectrum that is most frequent in the image, such as the example shown in Figure 22.19. An underwater palette has more blue; an image of molten lava has a predominantly red/orange palette. Local Adaptive applies the palette to a single image; use Master Selective to apply the palette to a number of images like those you might combine as an animated GIF file.
Custom	This palette creates a custom palette in the Color Table dialog box; the existing color table can be edited or a saved table can be loaded.
Previous	If you create a custom palette, select Previous when working on subsequent images. The same custom palette is applied for uniform conversions.

CHAPTER 22 ■ MANAGING IMAGE DISTRIBUTION

Figure 22.19. A predominantly blue image using a 24-color palette can look remarkably different when the palette is Adaptive (as in lower image) from one that uses another palette such as the Uniform palette (as in upper image).

Customizing an indexed image

You can create an indexed image either by converting the image's mode using program commands, or working in the Save For Web dialog box. To use the program commands, follow these steps to create an indexed image:

1. Choose Image ⇨ Mode ⇨ Indexed Color.

2. If your original image is layered, you see the dialog box shown in Figure 22.20. The dialog asks if the image's layers can be flattened. As in the example which has hidden layers, the dialog box also asks if they can be discarded. Click OK to close the dialog box, flatten the image, and discard hidden layers if applicable. The Indexed Color dialog box opens.

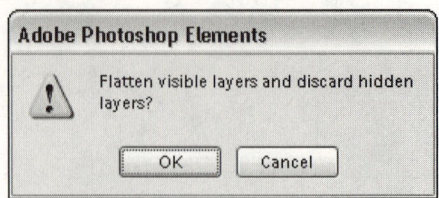

Figure 22.20. Photoshop Elements asks how you want to handle layers before converting the image to an indexed file.

3. Click the Palette drop-down arrow to display the list of Palettes (described in Table 22.3), and select a palette option, such as the Local (Perceptual) option shown in Figure 22.21.

4. Type the number of colors that you want to use in the image in the Colors field. The maximum number of colors is 256. The example in Figure 22.22 compares the same image using 256 colors with 16 colors.

5. Choose an option from the Forced drop-down list to make sure certain colors are included in the color table. These are the options:

   - Choose Black and White to add pure black and pure white to the color table. The Black and White Forced option is selected by default and used in the examples shown in Figure 22.21.

   - Choose Primaries to add red, green, blue, cyan, magenta, yellow, black, and white to the color table.

Inside Scoop
If you choose the Exact palette option, the number of colors in the image is shown in the Colors field automatically.

CHAPTER 22 ■ MANAGING IMAGE DISTRIBUTION

- Choose Web to add the 216 Web-safe colors.
- Choose Custom to define and add custom colors.

6. Click the Transparency check box to define whether transparent areas in the image are preserved in the exported file. If selected, one swatch in the color table is established for the transparent color.

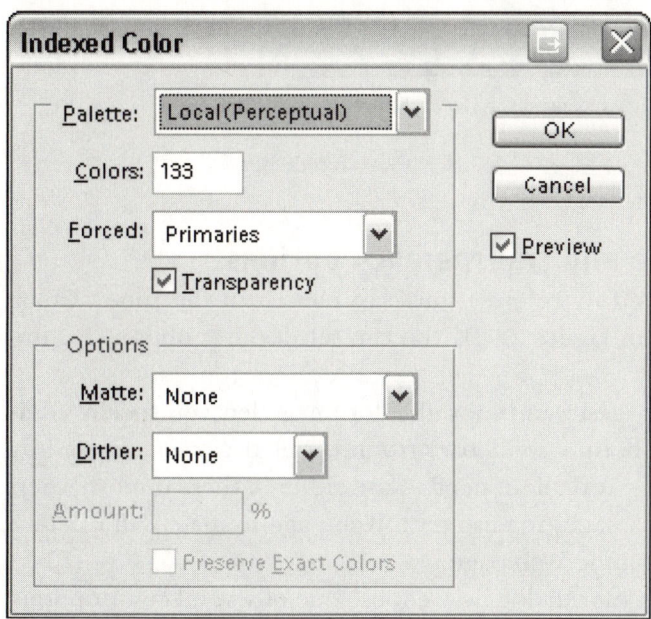

Figure 22.21. Configure the settings for the indexed color image in the dialog box.

Figure 22.22. The number of colors in an image may or may not affect the appearance. The left image uses 256 colors, and the right uses 16 colors — there is a significant loss of detail with fewer colors.

7. If you don't need to use any Options, click OK to close the dialog box. You see the information at the top of the image is changed to reflect the image mode, shown in Figure 22.23.

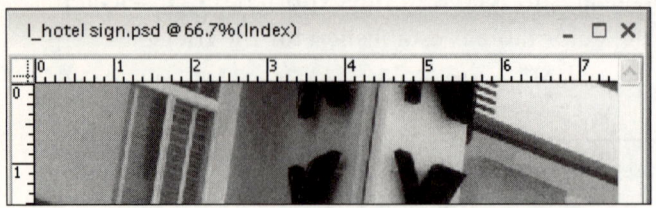

Figure 22.23. Check the color mode at the top of the image's dialog box.

8. Save your file.

Choosing matte and transparency options

After the palette and its color settings are chosen in the Index Color dialog box, shown in Figure 22.21, you can select other options for the background.

Changing an image to an indexed color image lets you specify additional options for both a solid background, called a *matte*, as well as adding transparency. You might need to use either of these options when you are converting images for use on a Web page to match an existing background color on the Web page.

In the Indexed Color dialog box, choose one of several color options for a *matte* (solid background) that fills anti-aliased edges adjacent to transparent areas of the image. The matte can be one of these choices:

- Foreground or background colors as set in the toolbox
- White or black
- Gray
- A custom color selected from the Color Picker

Watch Out!
Of course, you need transparency in the image to start with. A flattened image or one containing a flattened Background layer won't have transparency.

The matte works in conjunction with the Transparency setting. When Transparency is active, the matte is applied to the edges of the image to blend them with a Web background using the same color, like the example shown at the left of Figure 22.24. When Transparency is deselected, the matte is applied to the transparent areas of the image, shown in the right image in Figure 22.24.

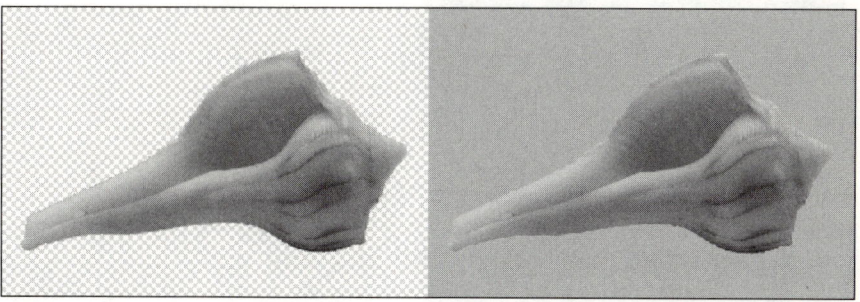

Figure 22.24. When transparency is active, the background is hidden (left). A solid background (right) is displayed when the Transparency check box is deselected in the Indexed Color dialog box.

Choosing None for the matte creates hard-edged non-aliased transparency, like that shown in Figure 22.25, when the Transparency check box is selected.

If Transparency isn't active, all transparent areas are filled with white at 100 percent opacity. Any pixels that are more than 50 percent transparent in the original image become fully transparent, while those less than 50 percent transparent become fully opaque.

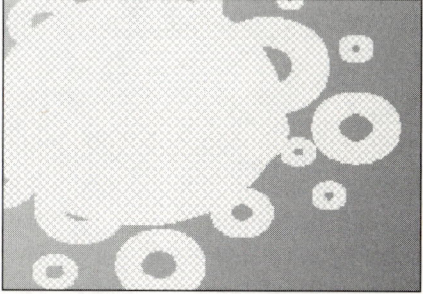

Figure 22.25. The transparent areas remain transparent and show hard, jagged edges when the no matte is used and Transparency is active.

Creating color with dithering

Only an Exact color table shows all the colors in the image, provided there are less than 256 colors in total. In the example shown in Figure 22.26, the image contains 207 colors; the Indexed Color dialog box shows the Colors value as one more (208) if the Transparency check box is selected.

Bright Idea
When your image is destined for a Web page but you don't know the background color (or the background is patterned), use hard-edged transparency.

Figure 22.26. The color table shows the number of colors automatically when the Exact color table option is selected.

What if your image has more than 256 colors? You can use one of several methods to create colors not included in the color table using a dither pattern. *Dithering* mixes the pixels of different colors in the color table using one of several patterns to approximate missing colors.

Click the Dither drop-down arrow in the Indexed Color dialog box, shown in Figure 22.27, and choose an option.

CHAPTER 22 ▪ MANAGING IMAGE DISTRIBUTION   659

Inside Scoop

If your image has less than 256 colors, you won't have access to the Dither options as each color in the image is already represented and there's no need for dithering.

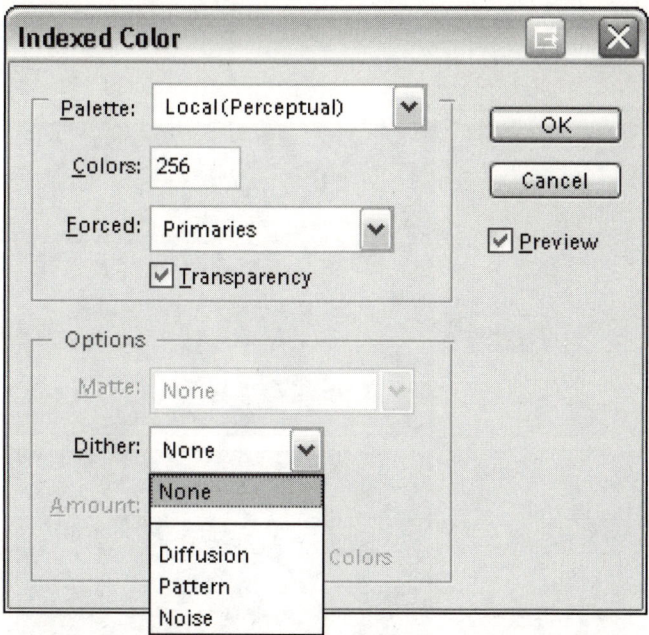

Figure 22.27. Choose a dithering option to approximate missing colors in an indexed image.

The available dither choices are shown in Figure 22.28:

- **None.** Shown in the top left of Figure 22.28, when None is selected, the image uses the color from the color table that is closest to that of the missing color. As a result, the image colors tend to become more blocky and posterized. In images having a low number of colors, posterizing effects aren't visible.

- **Diffusion.** Diffusion dithering, shown in the top right of Figure 22.28, applies an error-diffusion formula to produce a smoother appearance than the Pattern dither, which is in the lower left of the figure. When you choose the Diffusion dither, you can also specify the amount of dithering as a percentage. If you have some colors in the image that must be maintained as is, selecting the Preserve Exact Colors check box prevents dithering colors listed in the table.

- **Pattern.** The Pattern dither (lower left of Figure 22.28) applies a regular square pattern to simulate colors missing from the color table.
- **Noise.** Choose the Noise option, which is shown in the lower right of Figure 22.28, to reduce edge patterns when you are building a composite image from several image slices.

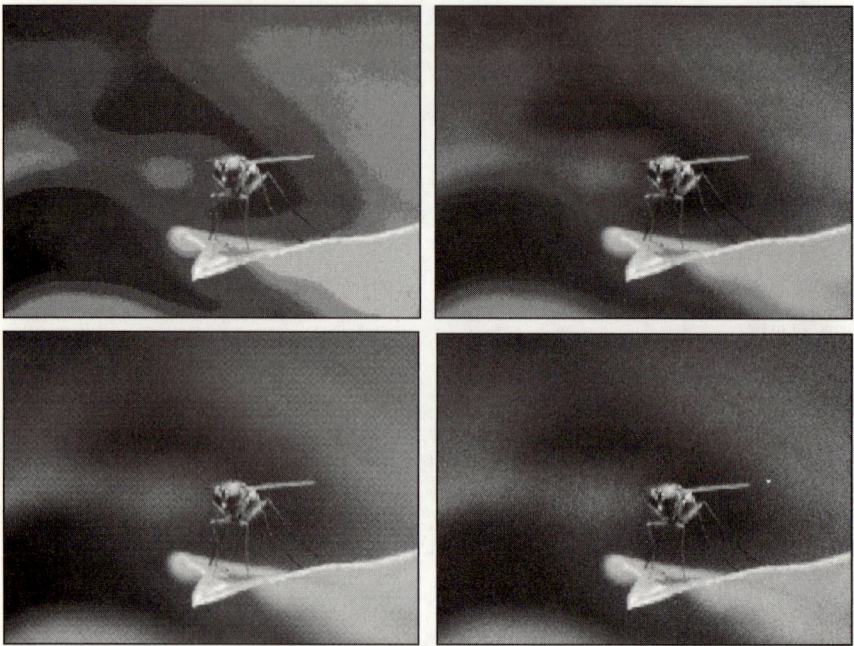

Figure 22.28. Test the appearance of different dither patterns.

Adjust the amount of the Diffusion dither in percentage, with the goal of using the minimum amount that produced the effect you want. More colors are dithered as the value increases, but the file size can increase as well.

Inside Scoop

Dithering also can be caused by browser issues. You can experiment with browser dither in the Save For Web dialog box, coming up later in the chapter.

When you have made your choices, click OK to close the Indexed Color dialog box. Save the finished file as a CompuServe GIF file, and it is ready to add to your Web page.

Editing a color table

After an indexed image is saved, regardless of whether you create it in Photoshop Elements, you can edit its colors in the color table. You might want to edit a color range if you are assembling a number of images that have to be compact, low-resolution images; creating an edited color table lets you apply the most common colors across the range of images.

Open your indexed color image in the Editor, and choose Image ⇨ Mode ⇨ Color Table, shown in Figure 22.29.

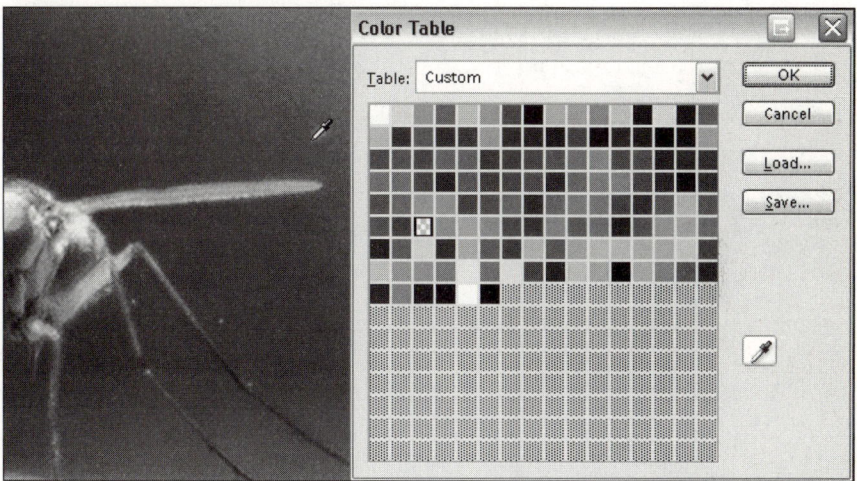

Figure 22.29. Sample a color in the image to find its location in the color table.

In the color table, you can change a single color or range of colors. For a single color, click a color swatch in the table or sample the image with the Color Table dialog box's eyedropper. Release the mouse to open the Color Picker, and choose a replacement color.

If you aren't sure where a color is used in your image, click the Eyedropper tool on the Color Table dialog box and click your image. Its location is framed in the color table. In Figure 22.29, for example, a medium green tone was clicked, and you can see a frame around its location on the color table.

Hack

If you customize a color table for an image in a series of similarly colored images, choose Save in the Color Table dialog box and then name and store the file. For the next images, choose Load, locate the file, and select it, instantly applying the set of custom colors.

If you are changing a range of colors, follow these steps to select and change the color:

1. Click the first color in your range, and drag to select the colors for replacing in the table. The selected colors are outlined with a black border, as shown in Figure 22.30. Release the mouse to open the Color Picker automatically.

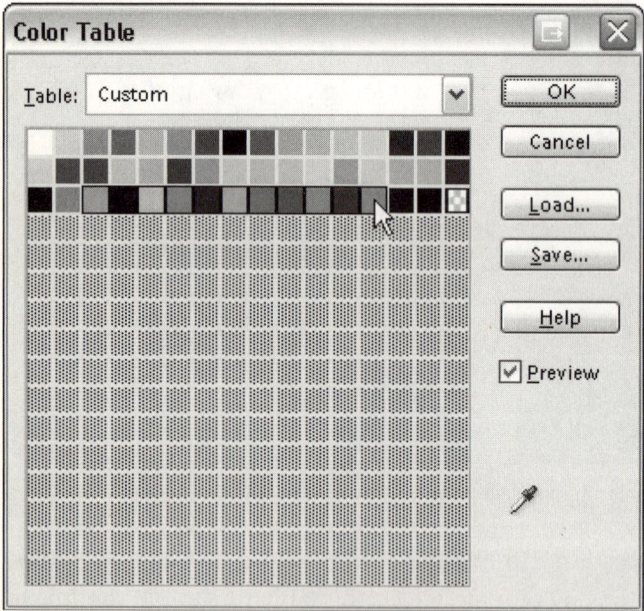

Figure 22.30. Select a single color or range of colors for replacement.

Bright Idea

Not sure an image has indexed color? If you can't select the Color Table command from the menu when the image is open, then it doesn't use indexed color.

2. In the Color Picker, select a color, which is set as the first color in your range, and click OK.

3. The Color Picker closes and automatically reopens for you to choose the last color in the range. Select the color, and click OK again to close the Color Picker. The colors you selected in the Color Picker are placed in the range you selected in the Color Table dialog box. Photoshop Elements creates a gradient of color between the two colors you pick as first and last in the range, like the gradient shown in the table in Figure 22.31.

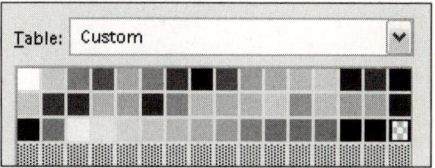

Figure 22.31. The new colors you select replace the selected range in the color table.

4. Check the Preview to see results of your changes.

5. Click OK to close the dialog box and apply the new colors.

Previewing Web images

The Save For Web process offers a number of testing and previewing options that you can perform in the dialog box. Along with previewing the appearance of an image using different formats and settings, you can also preview the following:

- How the image appears using different browsers.
- How an image appears using different color displays.
- The effects of browser dither on an image.

Previewing an image in a browser

A handy feature of the Save For Web dialog box is the option to test an image in a Web browser. After the file is open in the Save For Web dialog box and has been optimized, it can be previewed in any Web browser installed on your computer.

Click the Preview In drop-down arrow below the optimized image preview in the Save For Web dialog box to open a small menu, shown in Figure 22.32.

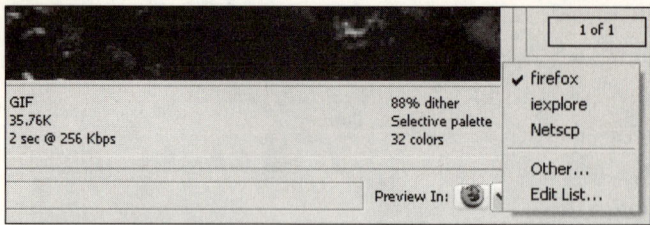

Figure 22.32. The Preview In menu varies according to your installed software and which browsers you have attached to the command.

The contents of the menu vary according to the browsers installed on your computer and which browsers you have included in the menu for testing. The icon for the browser specified as the default appears next to the drop-down arrow; in Figure 22.32, you see my default browser is Firefox.

In the Preview In menu, you can choose two commands for managing the browser list:

- **Other.** Click Other to open the Preview In Other Browser dialog box. Locate a browser program file and select it, then click Open to dismiss the dialog box and display the image.
- **Edit List.** Click Edit List to open the Browsers dialog box, shown in Figure 22.33. Here you can add and remove browsers for testing, specify a default browser, or search your computer for other browsers to include them in your list. Click OK to close the dialog box.

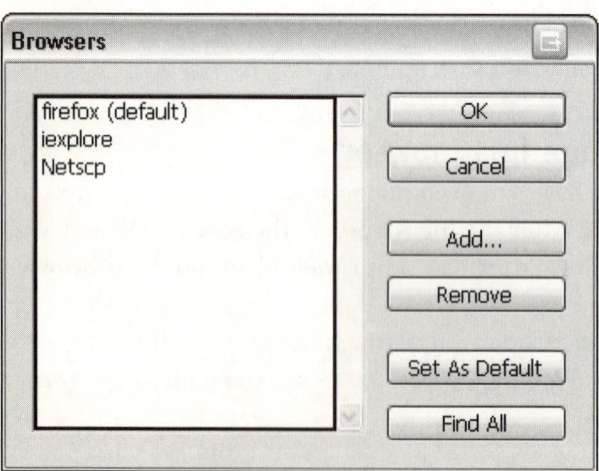

Figure 22.33. Manage the browsers shown in the Preview In list in the Browsers dialog box.

>  **Inside Scoop**
>
> I usually add browsers to the list rather than searching for them using the Other menu option. If you prefer to keep the list short, use the Other command when you want to preview in a browser you don't use often.

To test your image in the browser, click the Preview In icon to choose a browser from the drop-down menu, or click the icon to launch the browser and display your image in your default browser.

The browser window opens and automatically displays a Web page containing your image as shown in Figure 22.34. Other information shown on the page includes the file type, pixel dimensions, file size, compression specifications, and the HTML code required to build the Web page.

```
Format: GIF
Dimensions: 360w x 240h
Size: 35.76K
Settings: Selective, 32 Colors, 88% Diffusion Dither, Transparency on, No Transparency Dither,
Non-Interlaced, 0% Web Snap


<html>
<head>
<title>peace_poster</title>
<meta http-equiv="Content-Type" content="text/html; charset=iso-8859-1">
</head>
<body bgcolor="#FFFFFF" leftmargin="0" topmargin="0" marginwidth="0" marginheight="0">
<!-- ImageReady Slices (peace_poster.bmp) -->
<img src="peace_poster.gif" width="360" height="240" alt="">
<!-- End ImageReady Slices -->
</body>
</html>
```

Figure 22.34. The browser preview lists information along with showing the image.

Bright Idea

If you are starting with images using a matte color and intend to make matching Web pages, check out the HTML for the page in the preview, shown in Figure 22.34. Look for the <body bgcolor = "#xxxxxx"> tag. The characters following the # sign represent the hexadecimal value for the matte color.

Previewing different color displays

Different monitors display images differently. If you are working in an intranet environment where you know everyone is working on the same operating system with similar monitors, you can be fairly confident that the color is close to what you are seeing.

The Save For Web dialog box lets you test your image's color in different color displays. Click the triangle to the upper right of the preview image to open a menu, and choose a display type. The simulated displays are only seen in the Save For Web dialog box and don't affect the actual image.

These color display settings are available:

- **Uncompensated Color.** The default option shows the image without any color adjustment.
- **Standard Windows Color.** The preview simulates the colors as they appear in a standard Windows monitor.
- **Standard Macintosh Color.** The preview simulates the color as they appear in a standard Macintosh monitor.
- **Use Document Color Profile.** If a color profile is attached to the image, the preview shows the colors as specified by the color profile.

Previewing dither

The discussion of building GIF color tables and applying dithering earlier in this chapter showed examples of how different types of dithering affect the appearance of the image. In the Save For Web dialog box, you can test how dithering affects both GIF and PNG-8 image formats, and also how browsers themselves can dither your images.

Watch Out!

It doesn't matter how carefully you process images, if your viewers don't have current monitor calibration, their display may be quite different. Read about calibrating monitors and using color profiles in Chapter 9.

Inside Scoop

Unlike using the Indexed Color dialog box, the Save For Web process doesn't let you choose the type of dithering, only the percentage to apply.

The examples shown in Figure 22.35 are the same PNG-8 image. The left image is shown in PNG-8 format without any added dithering. The right image showing the browser dither preview doesn't have any dithering applied to it either, yet it is very pixilated. Browser dither occurs when the monitor is using an 8-bit color display.

Figure 22.35. Preview dithering in an image, such as this PNG-8 image, using application dither (left) or browser dither (right).

Follow these steps to check your images in a low-quality browser preview:

1. Click the arrow at the top right of the optimized image preview area in the Save For Web dialog box to open the menu.
2. Choose Browser Dither from the shortcut menu.
3. Check the image in the optimized pane of the preview area.

After you are in the Browser preview mode, you can test other settings to see if you can decrease the amount of dithering. Here are some options you can try:

- Increase the number of colors in the image. The more colors available for the image, the less dithering is required to simulate the color — up to 256 colors.

- Decrease the percentage of dither used for the image. Forcing the color to a near match rather than letting the program simulate color by dithering lessens the amount of dither that the browser has to interpret.

- Choose a different palette preset when your image already contains 256 colors. In Figure 22.36, the same PNG-8 image is shown using browser dither. In the left example, the Perceptual palette is used. In the right example, the Web palette is used. The color is flatter, but the image has less noise.

Figure 22.36. Changing palettes can influence the amount of dithering displayed by an image.

Inside Scoop

Whether or not dithering is a problem depends on your material's distribution. If you know the audience and the type of monitor they are likely using, browser dither won't be an issue.

CHAPTER 22 ■ MANAGING IMAGE DISTRIBUTION

The browser dither preview affects any Web image format you are using, including high resolution JPEG or PNG-24 images, like the JPEG example shown in Figure 22.37. If you have tested an image using the option, be sure to reopen the menu and deselect it when you are working with another image.

Building an animated GIF

Although it's not a Web animation design program, Photoshop Elements gives you a handy way to create and export an animated GIF file.

To create an animated GIF, you need to add a set of layers in the image, like those shown in the Layers palette in Figure 22.38. The images can be anything you draw, paint, or import, such as the variety of drawn star shapes shown in the figure, or a series of images of a flower in movement, or text positioned along a document page.

The animation begins with the image that you place on the bottom layer of the image. Each layer becomes a frame when the animation is exported. The animated GIF file creates the illusion of movement by displaying the sequence of images having different visual attributes over time.

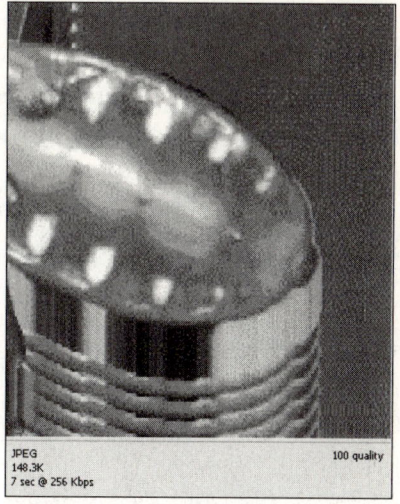

Figure 22.37. Deselect the Browser Dither setting to prevent false image previews, as in this high-resolution JPEG image.

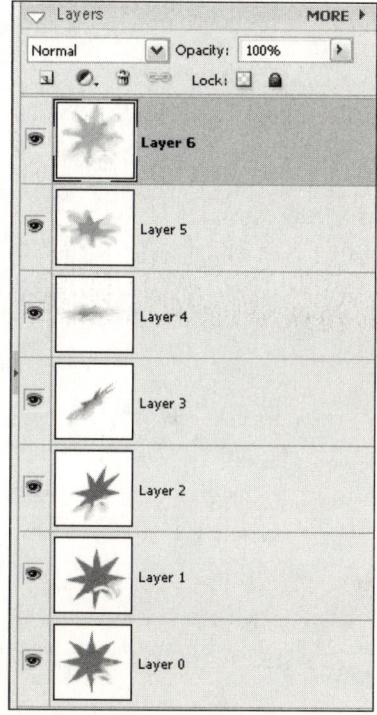

Figure 22.38. Each layer becomes a separate frame in the exported animation.

After you are satisfied with the order and the contents of each layer, follow these steps to prepare and save the animation:

1. Choose File ⇨ Save As to open the Save As dialog box.

2. Name the file, and choose CompuServe GIF from the Format drop-down list.

3. Choose the Layers As Frames check box in the Save Options on the dialog box, shown in Figure 22.39.

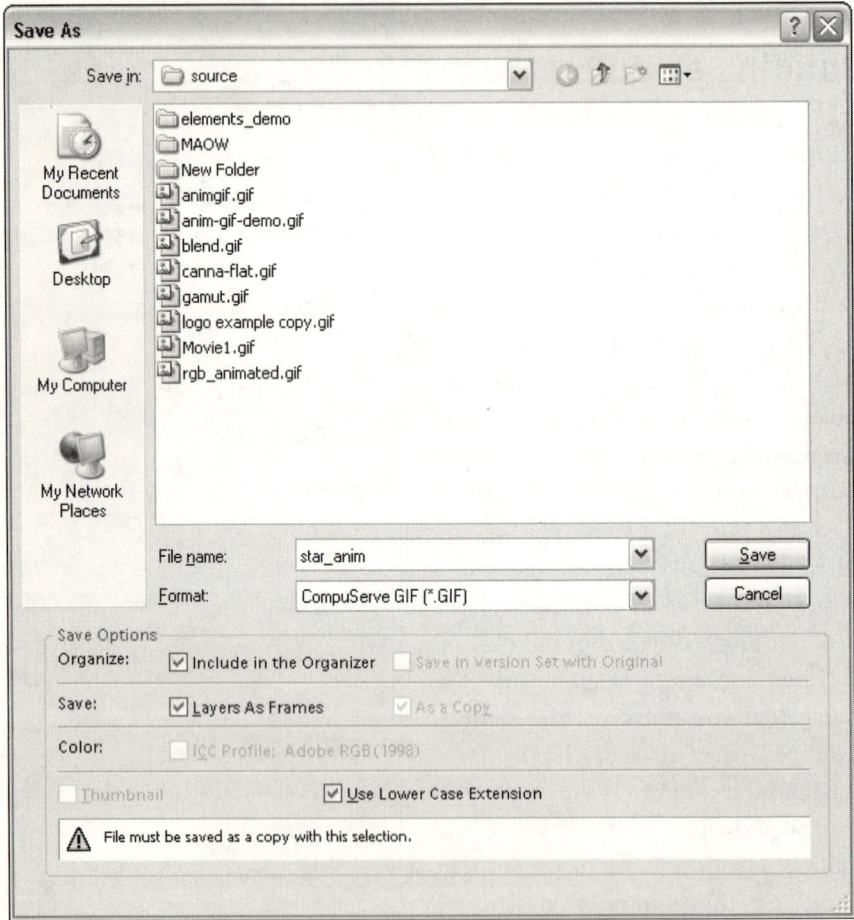

Figure 22.39. Be sure to specify that the image's layers are saved as frames to produce the animation.

CHAPTER 22 ▪ MANAGING IMAGE DISTRIBUTION

4. Click Save to save the file; the image opens in the Save For Web dialog box.
5. Optimize the images' GIF format.
6. Click the Animate check box on the Preset area of the dialog box shown in Figure 22.40. The sequence of layers and the Animation settings at the bottom of the dialog box are activated.

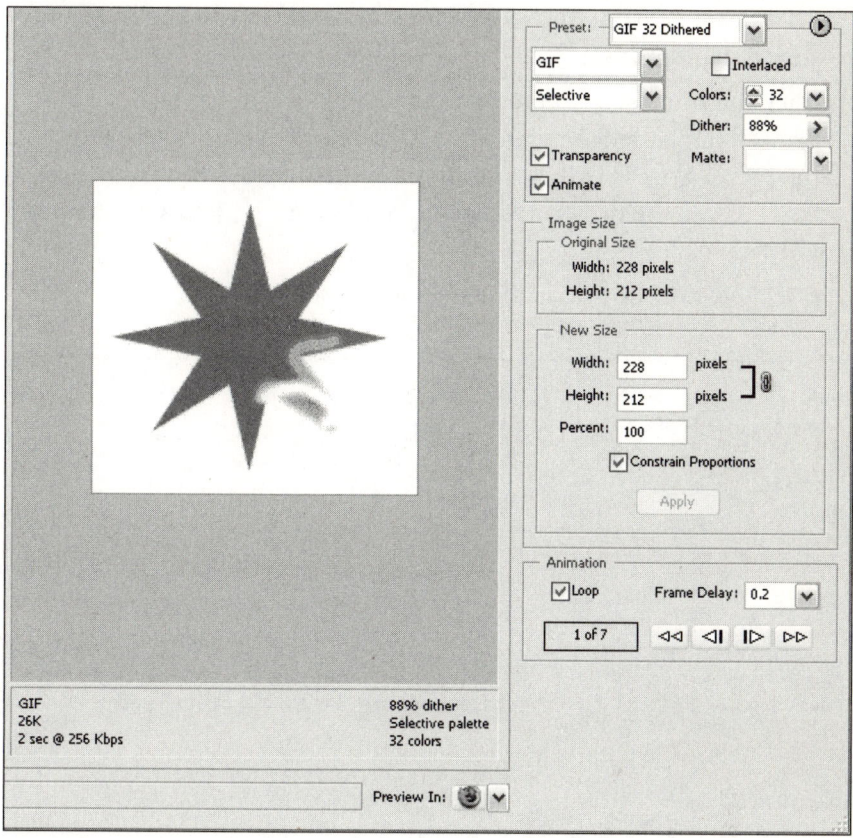

Figure 22.40. Specify basic settings for the animation before testing and exporting the file.

7. Click the Loop Continuously check box if you want the animation to repeat in the Web browser.
8. Type a Frame Delay value, or click the drop-down arrow and choose a value from the list in seconds or fractions of a second. In the

example shown in Figure 22.40, the Frame Delay is set at 0.2 seconds, which means the animation moves from frame to frame at a speed of slightly less than ¼ second.

9. Check the images in the animation by clicking the appropriate icons in the controller at the bottom right of the dialog box. You can move from frame to frame, or to the start or end of the animation.

10. Test the animation in your target browsers. Click the Preview In drop-down arrow, and choose a browser if you don't want to test in your default browser.

11. Click the browser's icon to open the animation in the browser and preview it. You see the animation as well as the settings selected for the file and the HTML required to run the page, shown in Figure 22.41. Close the browser when you have seen it to return to the Save For Web dialog box.

12. Click OK to close the dialog box and save the file.

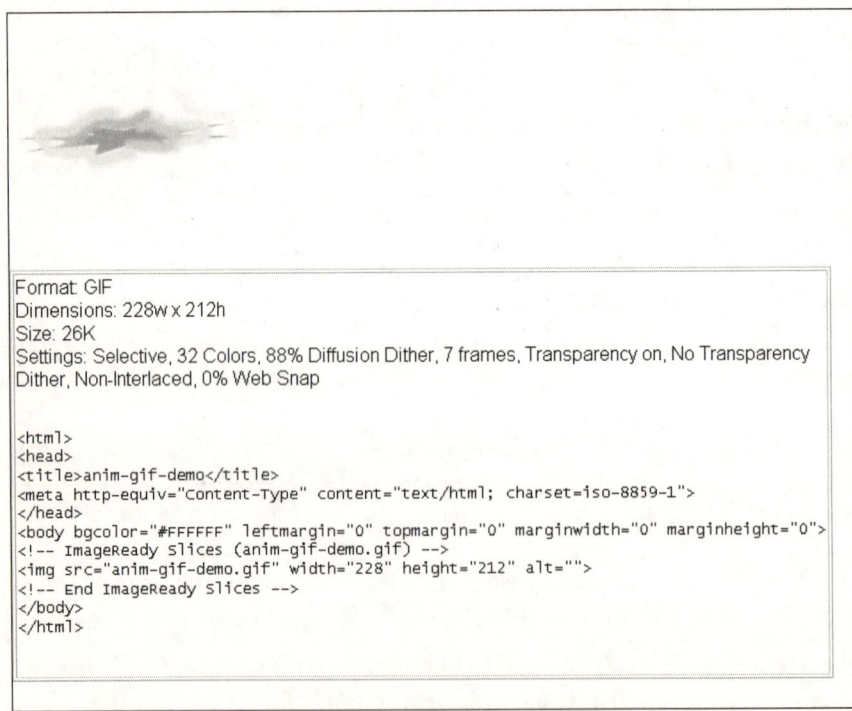

Figure 22.41. The animation test also shows the settings and HTML needed to add and run the animation in a Web page.

>  **Bright Idea**
>
> Choose File ➪ Open in the Editor, and select an animated GIF created in another program that opens in Photoshop Elements as a series of layers that you can paint or use other tools to add some pizzazz.

Batch processing files

What is almost as boring as watching paint dry? Your answers may vary, but one option is repeating the same sequence of steps over and over for a bunch of images. Instead of succumbing to mind-numbing boredom, spark up your neurons by building a batch file that you can then run to make repetitious file processing a thing of the past.

Photoshop Elements lets you apply some common actions such as renaming or resizing images to files in batches. The basic workflow consists of these steps:

1. Specify the source of the files.
2. Define the destination for the processed files.
3. Choose the processing options, such as renaming, resizing, and changing file types.
4. Apply edits or changes such as making Quick Fix corrections.
5. Add watermark or caption labels.
6. Save the selected features, and run the batch.

Specifying file locations

File management for batch processing includes specifying the source of the files and where they are saved. So, to get started, choose File ➪ Process Multiple Files from the Editor's File menu; see Figure 22.42. The first decisions to make are about the source of the files for processing, specified at the upper left of the Process Multiple Files dialog box.

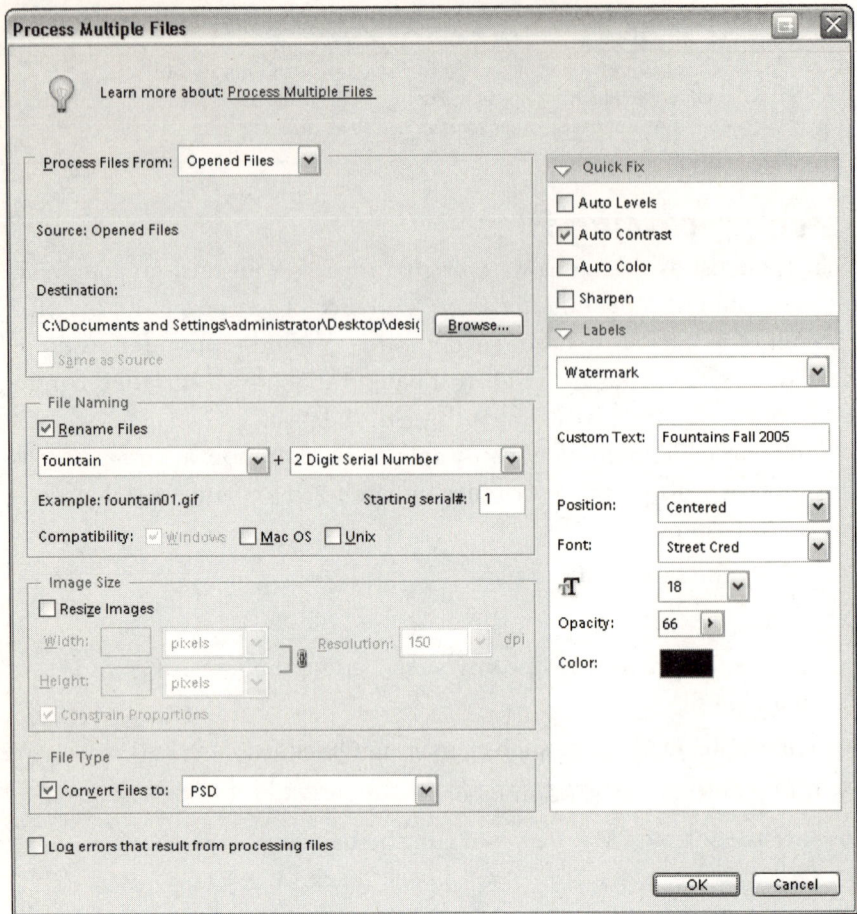

Figure 22.42. Use the Process Multiple Files feature to work with a number of files simultaneously.

Click the Process Files From drop-down arrow to open a list. The options available vary, but can include the following:

- **Folder.** This option is the default and is always available. If you choose Folder, the remaining fields in the upper left of the dialog box are active. Click the Include All Subfolders check box if you want nested files processed as well.

- **Opened Files.** If you have one or more files open in the program, this option is available. Selecting Opened Files changes the available fields in the dialog box. The source is defined as the opened files by default, leaving the Destination field active to specify a storage location.

Hack

The batch processing method can be used with a camera or scanner that has a document feeder. You may need a plug-in for your scanner or camera to use the processing feature; check your device's documentation.

- **Import.** If you have a scanner or camera installed that has a configured document feeder, this option is available. The fields change to show a From field, listing any configured devices in a drop-down menu, shown in Figure 22.43. The Destination field remains to define the location for storing the images after processing.

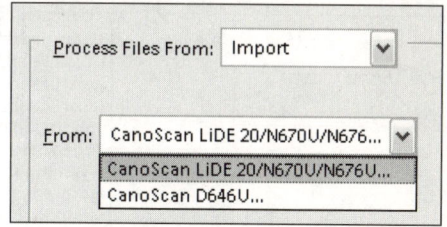

Figure 22.43. Configured devices that use document feeders can be chosen as the source for the batch process.

After you have specified the source files, choose a Destination folder. The default folder is shown in the Destination field on the Process Multiple Files dialog box. To choose another location, click Browse to open the Browse For Folder dialog box and select the storage file. Click OK to close the dialog box; your selected folder is now shown in the Destination field.

Processing images

The next activity is choosing the types of changes you want to make to the images' characteristics. The change categories include the following:

- **Rename Files.** Click the Rename Files check box to activate the fields. The renaming process allows you to use a two-part name for your images. Each of the two drop-down menus contains the same choices. Click a drop-down arrow and choose an option from the list, or type text in the fields to build custom names as shown in Figure 22.44. To create custom naming, as in the example, specify a starting serial number by typing it in the field. Specify a system compatibility setting if you plan to use the files cross-platform.

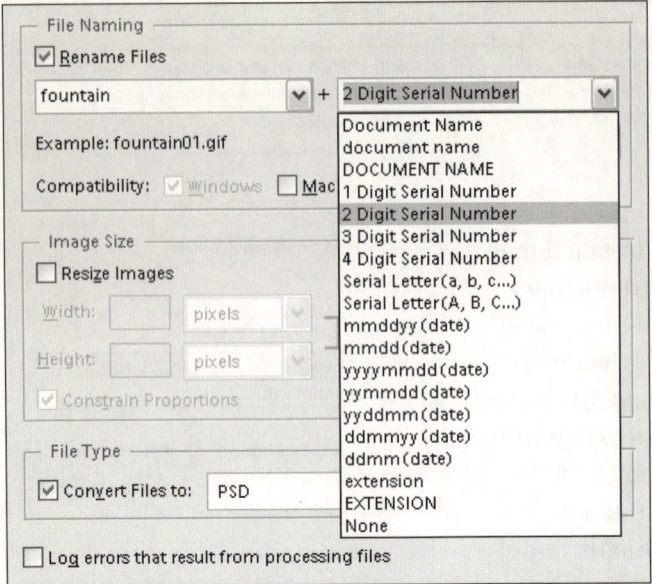

Figure 22.44. Rename the files using meaningful names for your image files such as the batch of files in the image that are shots of different garden fountains.

- **Image Size.** Click the Resize Images check box to activate the fields. Type a value for the Width and Height, and choose a unit of measure from the drop-down lists. If you want the image proportions to vary, deselect the Constrain Proportions check box. Finally, type a resolution in the Resolution field, or choose a preset from the drop-down list.

- **File Type.** Click the Convert Files to check box to activate the selections, and choose a different file type from the drop-down list. You can select from any file format that is supported in Photoshop Elements.

Watch Out!

How you name the images depends on your usual workflow or project requirements, but you must use a unique name for each image file. If you don't, the file is overwritten each time an image is processed and saved.

> **File compatibility**
>
> The Process Multiple Files dialog box includes the option to specify an operating system compatibility for file naming. If you don't anticipate sharing files with another person using a different operating system, don't worry about the setting. By default, Photoshop Elements makes the file naming compatible with Windows.
>
> Directory and file names are capital letter sensitive in UNIX and Macintosh systems; Boo Hoo and Boo_Hoo are defined as different files. Unix and Mac systems are also sensitive to spaces whereas Windows file names allow spaces. A Windows system wouldn't have a problem with a file named *my big adventure*.
>
> Regardless of the operating system you are using, the longer the file name length, the more likely it is to cause problems. Because many of us archive images to CD-R, keep in mind that CD-R software accepts 64 characters or less as a file name. My solution is to never use caps in a name as much as possible, and to always use underscores instead of spaces.

Applying edits

Suppose you have numerous files of your child's last soccer game, and each image is too dark. Fortunately, you can correct each image's levels or other settings as part of the batch process.

There are several Quick Fix options to include in a batch process. As shown in Figure 22.45, options include:

- **Auto Levels.** Adjusts the overall contrast of an image by mapping the lightest and darkest pixels in each of the Red, Green, and Blue color channels to black and white.

Figure 22.45. Automatically correct images in a batch using Quick Fix edit options.

- **Auto Contrast.** Adjusts the overall contrast of an image mapping the lightest and darkest pixels in the image to white and black, making highlights lighter and shadows darker.
- **Auto Color.** Adjusts the image's contrast and color by identifying shadows, midtones, and highlights in the overall image rather than in individual color channels.
- **Sharpen.** Focuses soft edges in an image to increase their clarity.

You can automatically correct the batch of images using the same methods as those used in the Quick Fix editing mode, which you read about in Chapter 7.

Labeling images

The final action is to choose Labels. Select either a Watermark or Label option from the drop-down list. Use a watermark if you want to identify an image's contents or list a copyright holder. You may have seen examples of a simple watermark on the Web. Many sites that offer images or video clips for sale provide low-resolution versions for you to download for testing; often these files include a visual watermark.

After you make a choice, type the text in the Custom Text field. Specify the text characteristics including its position, font, size, opacity, and color as shown in Figure 22.46.

In the example shown in Figure 22.47, a watermark is shown overlaying an image file.

Click OK to process and save the files when you are finished.

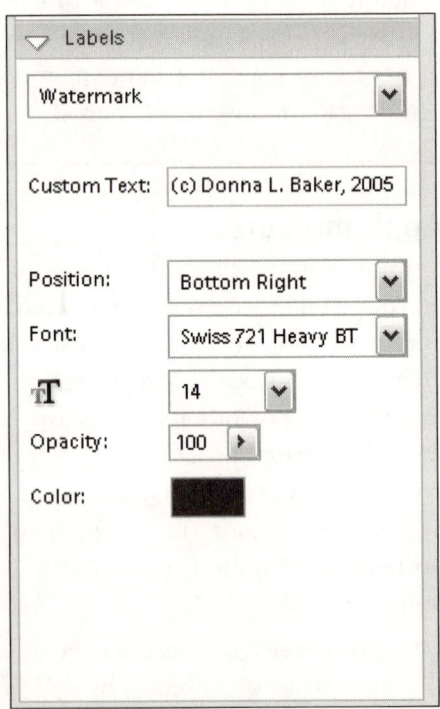

Figure 22.46. Add text to a batch of images as a watermark or a caption.

> **Watch Out!**
> Don't confuse a visual watermark applied as a text layer with an embedded watermark, which is a piece of code included in the image file. Read more about embedded watermarks later in the chapter.

Figure 22.47. The watermark names the copyright holder of the image.

Looking at embedded data

Photoshop Elements lets you use data embedded within your images to define their characteristics, track their editing history, and store details about the settings used to capture an image. The embedded data can sometimes be very important, such as when visually recording damage to your house after a flood or making a catalog of your possessions as a record in case of damage or theft.

> **Inside Scoop**
> If you need to control the image processing carefully, click the Log errors that result from processing files check box at the bottom of the dialog box. Any error that occurs is stored in a text file and doesn't stop the file processing. When an error occurs, a message displays after the files are processed.

When you take a photo with a digital camera, each image file includes information such as the date and time the photo was taken, the shutter speed and aperture, and so forth. Imported video and audio clips also contain file information.

All this information is *metadata*, and you can add even more metadata content in the Editor. Choose File ⇨ File Info to open the dialog box; the dialog box bears the name of the opened file.

If you are in the Organizer, you can find metadata listings in the Properties palette, as shown in Figure 22.48.

Figure 22.48. Read information about the image in the Properties palette of the Organizer.

Importing and exporting tags

The type of metadata you are most likely to come in contact with is tags. Tags are personalized keywords you attach to photos and other items in the Photo Browser to help you organize and search for images — you can read about creating tags in Chapter 3.

The advantage of tagging a file is that the tags are included with the rest of the image's metadata, like the colors of the pixels and the file format. You don't have to leave tags with an image though; you can export them and import them independently of the rest of the image. Your suite of tags, including the hierarchy structure, can be exported as an XML (eXtensible Markup Language) file for sharing.

Tags can be exported either as groups, such as a category or subcategory, or you can export all the tags in your catalog. Follow these steps to export a group of tags:

Bright Idea

If you are sharing files, being able to provide a complete set of tags helps get the other person underway with fewer errors and less time lost than having to re-create the tagging system.

CHAPTER 22 ■ MANAGING IMAGE DISTRIBUTION   681

1. In the Organizer, select a collection, category, or subcategory of tags if you want to export a specific group of tags. As shown in Figure 22.49, the Realtor shots category of tags is selected.

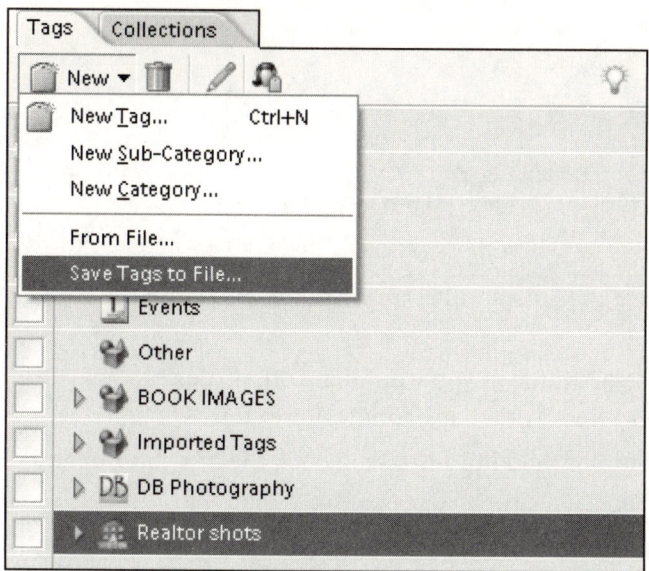

Figure 22.49. Select the collection or category of tags you want to export; if not, all tags in your catalog are exported.

2. Click the New button in the Tags palette, and choose Save Tags to File to open the Save Tags to File dialog box.
3. In the Save Tags to File dialog box, choose one of two options, shown in Figure 22.50:
   - **Export All Tags.** The entire set of tags and the hierarchy are exported as a single XMP file that you can save on your hard drive.
   - **Export Specified Tags.** The tags and subcategories within a selected category are exported. In the image the Realtor shots category of tags is selected as it was selected initially in the Tags palette in Step 1.
4. Click OK to close the dialog box; a Save dialog box — also named Save Tags to File — opens automatically.
5. Type a name for the collection in the File name field, and specify the folder location. The only file format available is the default XML format.

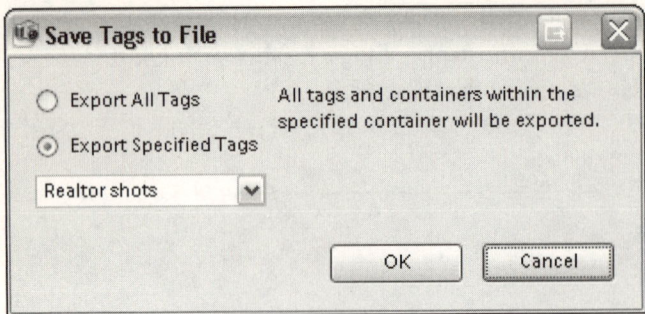

Figure 22.50. Choose whether to export selected tags or all tags from the catalog.

6. Click Save to save the collection as an XML file and close the dialog box.

Send or store the XML file as you would any other file.
When you want to import the tags, follow these steps:

1. In the Tags palette of the Photo Browser, click the New button and choose From File.
2. The Import Tags from File dialog box opens. Locate and select the XML file containing the tags, categories, and subcategories.
3. Click Open to close the dialog box and add the tags to your Organizer.

Importing tags with a photo

If you don't always work with images on the same computer or don't have synchronized catalogs on every workstation you use, you can import tags with images. Tags can be removed, retained, renamed, or mapped to existing tags.

In the Organizer, import photos into the Photo Browser using any command path you prefer. When an image contains tags or keywords, the Import Attached Tags dialog box opens. At the bottom of the dialog box, click Advanced to open the version of the dialog box shown in Figure 22.51.

- Click the check boxes to select the tags you want to import; you can omit tags that aren't relevant to the catalog in which the images are being imported.

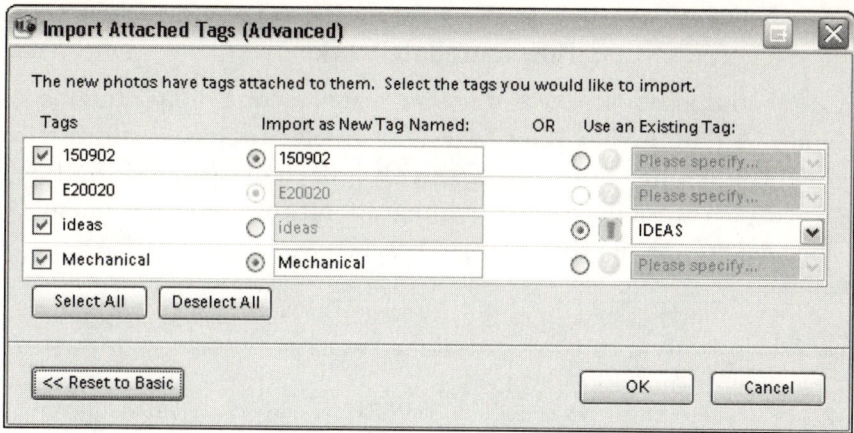

Figure 22.51. Define how tags are imported and mapped to existing tags.

- Click the Import as New Tag Named radio button. You can use the imported name for the tag such as "Mechanical" or type a new name more in keeping with your catalog system.

- Click the Use an Existing Tag radio button, and choose a tag from the drop-down menu of existing tags to map a tag to one of your existing tags. In Figure 22.51, the Ideas tag that was imported has been associated with an existing tag named IDEAS.

Click OK to close the dialog box. Photoshop Elements imports the photos including the selected tags. New tags appear in the Organizer in the Tags palette under a new heading named Imported Tags. The tags use their parent image as the icon, shown in Figure 22.52.

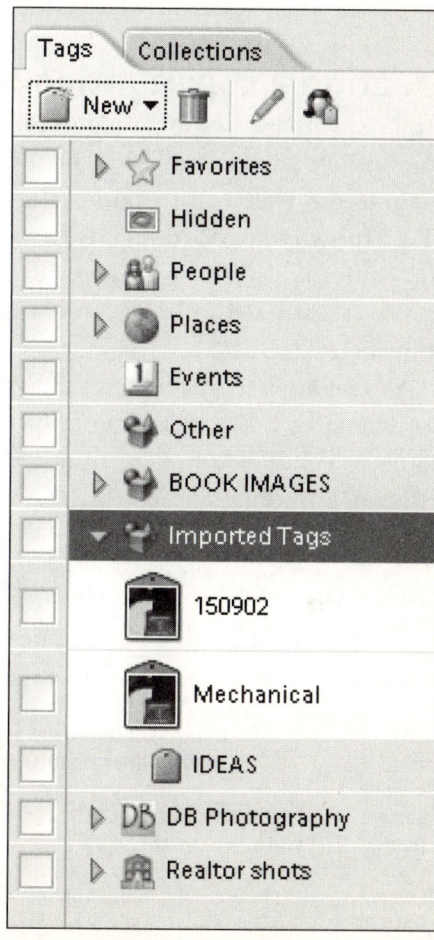

Figure 22.52. New tags are imported, configured, and listed in a new category.

> **How metadata works**
>
> The information you add, either manually or by importing, is embedded in the file using XMP (eXtensible Metadata Platform). Adobe and other applications with an XML framework use XMP-based data to standardize communications, including document metadata creation, processing, and exchange.

Hack
If you import a new tag, it is listed in the Tags palette and you can use it to tag other photos. You can transfer a simple tag hierarchy from one computer to another using a few representative images.

Creating a copyrighting template

Suppose you are making a name for yourself as a photographer in your community. You probably add a copyright to your images before posting them to the Web or distributing them in any form. And, if you take lots of pictures, you are doing this manually for each image. Wouldn't you rather add your metadata with just a few clicks of the mouse? You can. You just need to build a metadata template that can be applied to your image.

You create a template in an image's File Info dialog box. That dialog box contains a significant amount of information about the file. The panes in the dialog box and the types of data stored in each pane are listed in Table 22.4.

Table 22.4. File Info dialog box contents listed by pane

Pane Name	Information Provided	Editable
Description	Basic information about the image such as its title, keywords, and copyright information. Adding keywords on the IPTC Content pane adds them to the Keywords field in the Description pane as well.	Yes
Camera Data 1	Information about the camera and its settings used to capture the image.	No
Camera Data 2	Information about the image file such as its resolution, dimensions, and color space.	No
Categories	Choose or type category and subcategory names.	Yes

Pane Name	Information Provided	Editable
History	Record of changes and alterations made to image.	No
IPTC Contact	Formal photographer contact information.	Yes
IPTC Content	Formal descriptions of the visual content in the image, including a headline, subject code, and keywords.	Yes
IPTC Image	Enter formal descriptions according to IPTC values.	Yes
IPTC Status	Used for formal copyright information and workflow descriptions. Copyright data added to the Description pane is copied to the Copyright Notice field on this pane as well.	Yes
Adobe Stock Photos	If an Adobe Stock Photo is used, this includes the type of image, provider, license, and other details.	Yes
Advanced	Lists information about file programming, such as file format properties and XMP properties.	No

Configuring the template

Metadata templates are stored on your hard drive and are accessible from the Editor window. You can create a template for any purpose, of course, but a copyright template is a common and fairly generic example.

Follow these steps to create a new template:

1. Open an image that doesn't already have all the file information for metadata added to use as an example. You start from an existing image to build the template.

2. Choose File ⇨ File Info to open the File Info dialog box. The dialog box has the name of the file you opened in Step 1.

3. Add information to the fields on the panes that you want to repeat. Make sure you don't add image-specific details such as the image's title. For example, if you are building a copyright template, add your name, the copyright status, the copyright notice, and other generic information on the Description tab.

Watch Out!
Don't hunt for a listing called "Tags" in an image's File Info dialog box accessible from the Editor window, because you won't find one. Tags added to a file in the Photo Browser are listed as keywords in the File Info dialog box. PDF and BMP don't support tags as keywords.

4. If you have added information to other files through the File Info dialog box, clicking any of the active drop-down arrows to the right of the fields opens lists of previous content added to the field, shown in Figure 22.53.

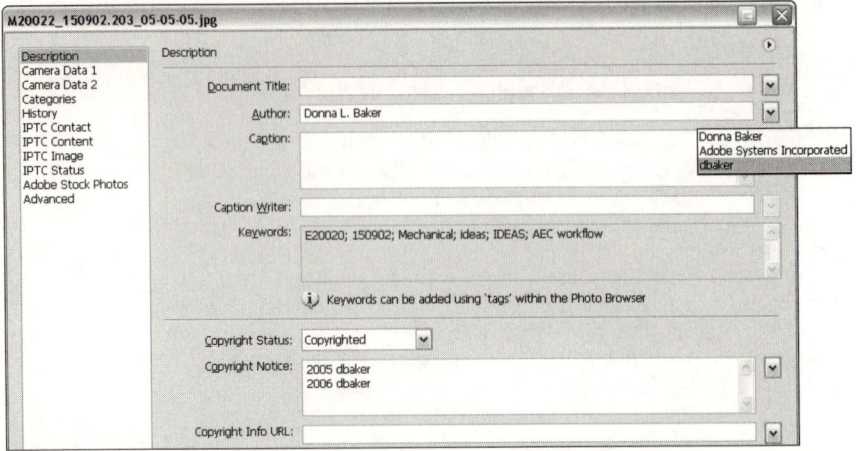

Figure 22.53. Add generic information to the template file, including content used as File Info for other files.

5. Click the arrow at the upper right of the dialog box to open a menu, and choose Save Metadata Template.
6. In the Save Metadata Template dialog box shown in Figure 22.54, type a name for the template and click Save to close the dialog box and store the template file on your hard drive.
7. Click OK to close the dialog box and apply the configured information to the active image file.

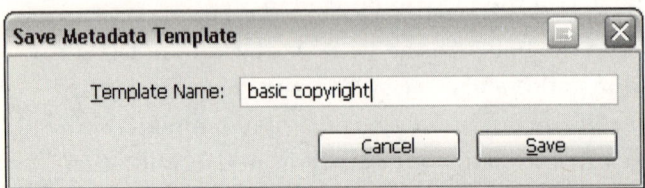

Figure 22.54. Content that can be repeated in numerous files is saved as a metadata template.

> **Inside Scoop**
>
> The International Press Telecommunications Council (IPTC) maintains and develops publishing industry standards for news data. Read about using news codes at www.newscodes.org. You probably don't need to use newscodes unless you are a journalist, but it is interesting information.

Applying the template

When you want to apply the template to another image file, follow these steps:

1. Open the file in the Editor.
2. Choose File ⇨ File Info to open the File Info dialog box and show the active image's name.
3. Click the arrow at the upper right of the dialog box to open the menu and select the new template's name, as shown in Figure 22.55.

Figure 22.55. The new template is included with other previously stored templates.

4. The template is loaded into the active image's File Info listings. Add other information specific to the individual image.
5. Click OK to close the dialog box.
6. Save the image with the new copyright and other information stored in its metadata.

> **Bright Idea**
>
> Adding copyright information isn't the only common use for metadata templates. In many government and other regulated projects, images need to comply with a variety of naming conventions; set up templates for each convention to save time.

> **Hack**
> The XMP files are stored on the hard drive at this location: C:\Documents and Settings\User_name\Application Data\Adobe\XMP\Metadata Templates. Delete a template directly from the hard drive folder.

Watermarking

Watermarks were used originally to identify a type of paper and the papermaker. A watermark is embossed into the paper and is rarely seen unless the paper is held up to light. A digital watermark embeds information about the image and the image maker within the file's code. Depending on the watermarking system in use, images may be simply protected using the mark, or tracked online to identify file locations and users.

Photoshop Elements includes a filter used to scan images for a Digimarc watermark. In a file containing a watermark or other copyrighting process, the image name in the title bar includes a Copyright symbol, as you can see in Figure 22.56.

Figure 22.56. The copyright symbol is included with the image's name and other information on the dialog box.

For any image, you can check for copyright particulars in the File Info dialog box as described in Table 22.4. An example is shown in Figure 22.57. If you see a URL in the File Info dialog box, click Go To URL to open the site and find more information about the copyright holder.

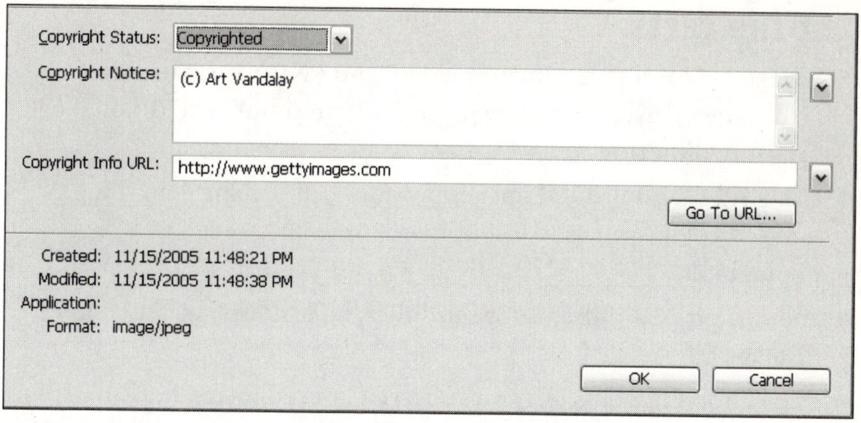

Figure 22.57. Some copyrighting methods include a link to a Web site providing more information.

Securing files

Protecting a file is done for one of two reasons: either to maintain artistic control of the visual appearance of the work, or to maintain the integrity and accuracy of the image's content.

Photoshop Elements doesn't include a method for securing your image files. Although you can add all sorts of data explaining who owns the content, you can't encrypt or protect the file using passwords or apply mathematical algorithms to secure or protect the contents from being changed.

You may consider some alternatives, depending on what software you have available and your needs:

- If you have Adobe Acrobat, you can secure PDF versions of your image files using password encryption or digital certificate security. Specify whether a user needs a password to open the file or if they need a Public-Private Key (PPK) system to view your file.

- Use other file and disk encryption software, such as Cryptainer LE, to protect your files. Encryption programs offer features such as securing files and e-mail, and encrypting files on your hard drive or on removable media.

- If you are working in Windows XP, you can use the Encrypting File System (EFS).

- If you have a Web site, you can password-protect access to your photo gallery files.

Just the facts

- Indexed color images, including GIF and PNG-8 formats, use a color table to assign color to pixels and can simulate additional colors using dithering.
- Using JPEG and PNG-24 images provides better color than using indexed color formats in a continuous tone image such as a photograph.
- You can preview dither, browser dither, image displays, and color displays.
- Photoshop Elements lets you convert a layered image into an animated GIF file.
- Images can be batch processed to take care of common changes such as naming, simple editing, and labeling.
- The tags for an image can be imported and exported.
- A metadata template is a quick way to add the same content to images on an ongoing basis, such as copyright information.

GET THE SCOOP ON...
■ Working with camera sensor information ■ Opening raw images ■ Identifying and removing color casts ■ Adjusting image tone and detail ■ Using digital negative files

Cooking with Raw Images

When you shoot images with your digital camera, the captured data often is processed by your camera depending on your capture settings, such as removing red eye or adjusting contrast.

One format used by some cameras is called *raw*. A raw file contains unprocessed image data that you capture with your camera, and then open and process in a special window in Photoshop Elements. Unlike camera controls that you set to adjust features such as white balance or sharpening that are applied automatically when the image is captured, in a raw file you have full control over the image content because the camera doesn't alter any of the data.

A raw file is simply a digital record of the data captured by the sensors in your camera. Digital cameras use a number of different types of technology, but for the most part, those that can capture raw files are *color filter array* (*CFA*) cameras.

A key feature of raw files is that the original image file is never changed. Instead, the file works like a digital negative and your processing settings are saved and applied to the image. After the image is processed in the Camera Raw dialog box, you can open it and modify it like any other image in Photoshop Elements and save it in a traditional image format.

Inside Scoop

Not all cameras are capable of capturing raw data. See Appendix B for the Adobe Web page address containing current camera models that can capture raw images, or check your camera's manual.

Working with a raw file

When you download images from cameras that can save image data as a raw file to Photoshop Elements, the files have extensions that vary according to the type of camera used. For example, Nikon cameras capture raw files using the NEF format, Canon cameras capture raw files using the CRW format, and so on.

After you download the images to your computer, you can open a raw file in your camera's proprietary application, check your camera's installation guide to see how to install and use the software.

In Photoshop Elements, you can open a raw file like any other image file — from either the Organizer or Editor:

- In the Organizer, select the image in the Photo Browser, click the Edit drop-down arrow, and choose Standard Edit.
- In the Editor, choose File ⇨ Open, locate and select your file in the Open dialog box, and then click Open to dismiss the dialog box and open the image file in the Camera Raw dialog box.

The Camera Raw dialog box

At first glance, the Camera Raw dialog box looks fairly complex. Because it is replacing all the settings you may choose in your camera, it's not that surprising.

But, first things first — figure out what's what in the dialog box. Figure 23.1 shows a sample image taken with a Nikon camera open in the Camera Raw dialog box. Take a look at these settings in the left section of the dialog box:

- **Tools and Rotate options.** Use these options to inspect or select content on the image preview or to rotate the image.
- **Preview.** The effects you add and settings you change show here as they are applied. By default, the Preview check box is selected so you automatically see the image you are working with.
- **View options.** Choose what you want to view, including the preview, identify highlighted areas, or view shadow clipping areas.
- **Zoom levels.** Here, you can change the magnification of the image.

CHAPTER 23 ▪ COOKING WITH RAW IMAGES

> **Inside Scoop**
>
> Sometimes, your camera shoots "perfect" pictures, and no adjustments are necessary. Shooting in raw format allows you to make adjustments to a less-than-perfect image without affecting the original file. It's not necessary to adjust white balance, temperature, shadow values, and brightness for every image, but these controls are available in case you need them.

- **Bit Depth options.** Choose from either 8-bit or 16-bit color information. A raw file captured by your camera uses 16-bit color by default, compared to a JPEG file that uses 8-bit color by default. Check out Chapter 9 for more information on bit depth.

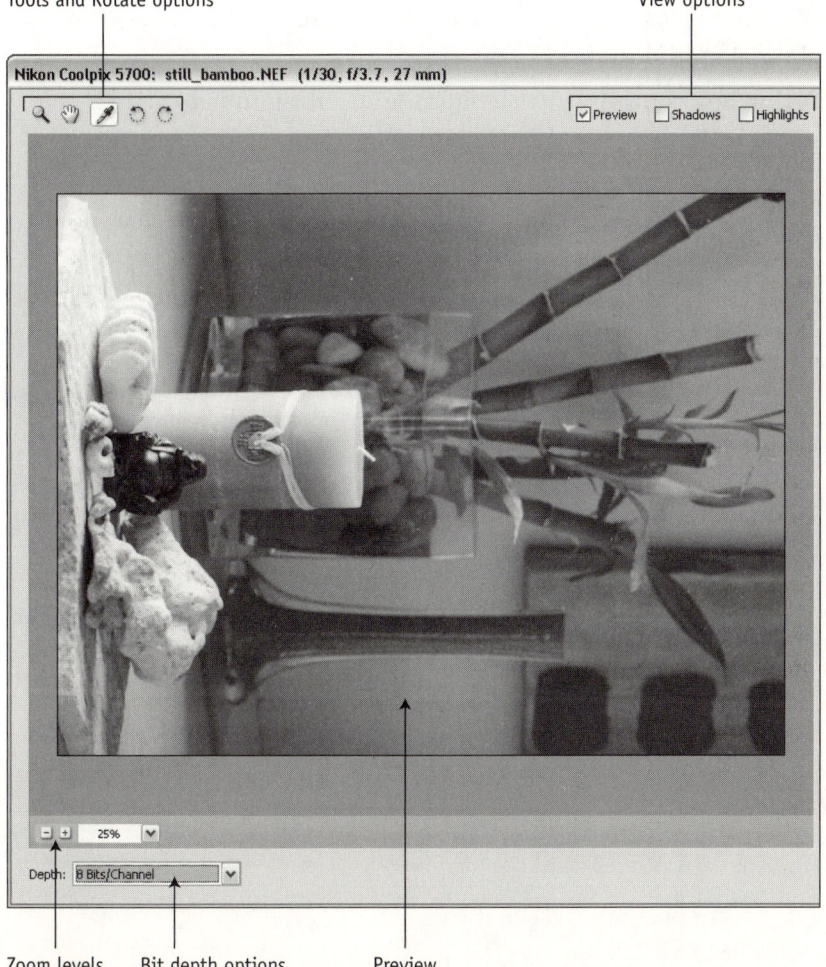

Figure 23.1. The Camera Raw dialog box includes a preview window as well as tools for manipulating the view.

Figure 23.2 shows the right side of the Camera Raw dialog box, containing collections of settings and buttons. The areas include:

- **RGB values.** Monitor the RGB values of pixels in the image by sampling them with a tool.
- **Histogram.** The histogram shows the range of color with the current group of settings. As you make changes to the tonal range in the image, the histogram is automatically updated.
- **Settings menu.** Select and apply settings used in a previous camera raw image, or apply your camera's default settings. If you make changes the settings are renamed "Custom" automatically.
- **Control settings.** These settings consist of two tabs that contain sliders, entry fields, and check boxes to select and modify an assortment of tonal modifications.
- **Dialog box controls.** Click a button to perform functions such as saving settings or showing Help file contents.

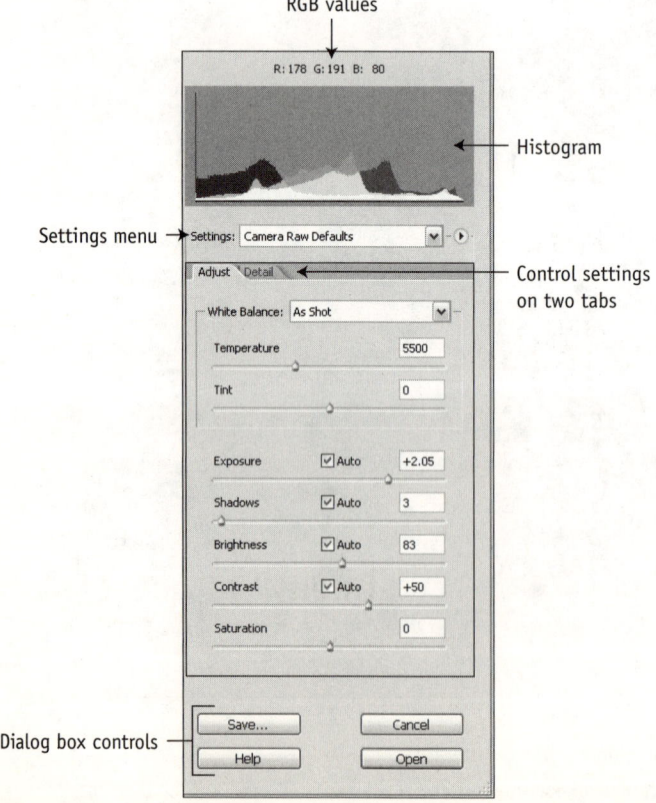

Figure 23.2. The Camera Raw dialog box is made up of several functional areas.

> **Bright Idea**
> The Auto check boxes are selected in the Camera Raw dialog box by default. You can change the selections by modifying the defaults or selecting Use Auto Adjustments from the Camera Raw menu.

Check it out

The best way to see how things work in the Camera Raw dialog box is to experiment. Drag sliders left and right; choose different White Balance settings from the menu; watch how the image's appearance changes as the values for the settings are changed. Many values that you adjust in a raw file have reactions — that is, making a change in one value or choosing one option produces a change in another setting or value. For example, choosing the Daylight setting in the White Balance menu changes the color cast in the image, making it appear warmer. Read more about the temperature of light in Chapter 7.

When you are finished experimenting, choose Camera Raw Defaults from the Settings drop-down menu and you are back where you started. You can also press Alt to show the alternate buttons on the dialog box, and then click Reset.

Finally, there are secondary dialog box controls at your disposal. Press Alt to toggle the set of buttons at the lower-right corner of the Camera Raw dialog box. As shown in Figure 23.3, the Cancel button toggles to a Reset button, and the Open button toggles to an Open Copy button. When you release the Alt key, the default buttons, shown in Figure 23.2, display again.

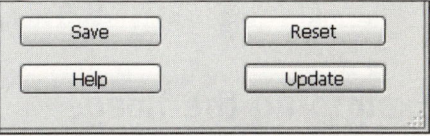

Figure 23.3. Toggle additional command buttons on the dialog box.

Developing an image adjustment plan

The method you use to modify an image depends on its existing appearance, lighting, and other camera settings. Each step in the plan is covered in detail further in the chapter. Of course, keep in mind that not all raw files need adjustment.

Bright Idea

If you are adjusting a value manually by dragging the slider and you discover you aren't on the right track, click the Auto check box to undo your manual adjustment and restore the default setting to start again.

Here's a general approach that you can use as a starting point for working with images in the Camera Raw dialog box:

1. Set the image's view. Use the Zoom settings at the lower left of the preview area to select an option; rotate the image using the Rotate tools, if necessary.
2. Toggle the Shadows and Highlights check boxes, and check for clipped areas in the image.
3. Adjust the White Balance by using an option from the drop-down list.
4. Make further adjustments using the tonal correction sliders or typing values in the fields on the Adjust tab. Modify settings for Exposure, Shadow, Brightness, Contrast, or Saturation according to the lightness and darkness of your image and your correction requirements.
5. Adjust noise using the settings on the Detail tab; zoom in and out of the image to see changes more clearly.
6. Click Save to save the file as a Digital Negative (DNG) image, or click Open to move the image to the Editor window for further editing and saving in a standard image file format, such as PSD or TIFF.

Examining the image

The first parts of the plan outlined for working in the Camera Raw dialog box deal with the image's display. Set the view, check the preview, and then check out other preview options.

Position and zoom

Magnification is managed in the Camera Raw dialog box using the same controls as those found in other dialog boxes and windows in Photoshop Elements.

Rotate your image if necessary using the Rotate tools on the dialog box's toolbar, and then use the Zoom tool from the dialog box's toolbar or the zoom controls at the lower left of the dialog box to control the magnification. Be sure to zoom in and out to see detail and to select color more precisely when setting values.

> **Watch Out!**
> Don't look for scrollbars when the image is zoomed in larger than the preview area — there aren't any! Instead, click the Hand tool and drag the image to view the desired area, or use the Zoom tool or settings to adjust the view.

Viewing clipping in your image

The sample image used in this discussion was shot using daylight from a window to the left of the foreground subject grouping as a light source. The natural light produces an interesting play of light and shadow. Without being a professional photographer, you can assess an image and whether its levels of shadow and highlight are appropriate by showing clipping.

Clipping identifies areas that are uniform with no detail. Clipped shadows are black areas with no detail, and clipped highlights are white areas with no detail. To see any clipping that might exist in the image, click the Shadows and Highlights check boxes at the top of the dialog box. In the example shown in Figure 23.4, several areas of clipped highlights are shown in red along the left side of the candle and the rock and identified with arrows on the image; there are no areas of clipped shadow.

Figure 23.4. Show areas that are over-exposed using the clipping check boxes.

> **Bright Idea**
> Reset the view to 100 percent size by double-clicking the Zoom tool. Press Alt and click with the Zoom tool to decrease the zoom level by one value. Reset the preview to fit in the dialog box by double-clicking the Hand tool.

Taking out color casts

A *color cast* is a color shift in an image that can occur when different forms of lighting are used. For example, indoor photos may have a yellow cast, images taken in an office under fluorescent light may have a blue or pink cast, and so on. Although your brain interprets the color correctly in spite of the light source, a camera can't do the same thing, and the differences in the light source are seen as color casts.

In the Camera Raw dialog box, you can remove a color cast using three related methods: White Balance, Temperature, and Tint.

Balance the white

The *White Balance* option shows the amount of light and the lighting conditions present when the image was shot using the camera's automatic White Balance setting. Your digital camera records the white balance, and the information is applied when the image is opened in the Camera Raw dialog box.

You can manually adjust the White Balance on your camera as well. Suppose you manually set the white balance for some shots of dogs playing frisbee in a park, then went indoors to take more shots. An indoor shot needs tungsten-type or electric lighting — if you forgot to change the white point to one suitable for indoor shots, you find a significant problem with the white point. Fortunately, the Camera Raw dialog box provides ways to correct the image.

Click the White Balance drop-down arrow, and choose from a list of pre-configured lighting conditions that simulate different light sources (see Figure 23.5). Your choices are listed in Table 23.1.

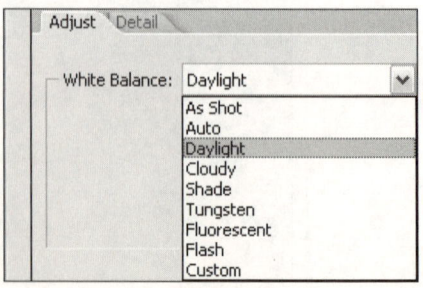

Figure 23.5. Choose a White Balance setting to simulate different types of light.

Table 23.1. Pre-configured lighting options

White Balance Type	Effect on the Image
As Shot	The As Shot option uses the color temperature set by your camera when the image was captured.
Auto	The Auto option lets Photoshop Elements automatically adjust the white balance to a correct level.
Daylight	The Daylight option adds a soft yellow cast to the image simulating ambient daylight.
Cloudy	The Cloudy option adds a soft dark yellow cast to the image simulating cloud-covered daylight. The Cloudy option uses less exposure than the Daylight option.
Shade	The Shade option is similar to the Cloudy light, except the automatic Exposure, Shadows, and Contrast values are set lower, contributing to a darker image with less distinct detail in the darkest areas.
Tungsten	Tungsten whitens the image by simulating a type of white light like that created by ordinary electric bulbs.
Fluorescent	The Fluorescent option adds a cool blue tint to the image, as well as more Exposure and Shadows to simulate the lighting in a typical office.
Flash	The Flash option simulates the bright white of a camera flash; it brightens the image.
Custom	When you choose a lighting option and then adjust the sliders the Custom value is automatically selected.

Sometimes, choosing an option from the White Balance menu produces good results, but more often you have to customize the white balance using the Temperature and Tint adjustments. Some of the types of light produce similar effects, while others are very different.

When you choose a lighting condition from the White Balance menu, the Temperature and Tint are adjusted automatically. If you make adjustments to the sliders or values on the Adjust tab, the White Balance menu automatically displays the Custom setting.

Watch Out!
While you often want to remove a color cast when the lighting conditions are off, be careful when the image is shot at sunrise or sunset. Removing the soft golden glow from the sun defeats much of the purpose of shooting at that time of day.

> **Check your temperature**
>
> If you weren't aware that your colors have temperatures, you aren't alone: But colors do have different temperatures. *Color temperature* is a measurement indicating the *hue*, or color, of a specific type of light source.
>
> Make adjustments to the color temperature if you see a shift in the color — either more blue or more yellow than the actual color should be. Move the slider to the left to shift the image colors to display more blue light and compensate for the lower yellow color temperature of the light. Move the slider to the right to correct a photo taken with a higher color temperature of light, such as a picture taken outside on a very sunny day. The image colors become warmer — more yellow — to compensate for the higher, blue color temperature of the light.

> **Inside Scoop**
>
> If you experiment with the white balance settings and find the Auto and As Shot settings are the same, your camera read and recorded white balance as part of the file's information.

Tint it

While temperature adjusts an image's appearance based on the color of the light between yellow and blue, *tint* adjusts the white balance based on the amount of green or magenta in the image.

To add green to the photo, drag the Tint slider to the left or type a negative value in the field. To add magenta to the photo, drag the Tint slider to the right or type a positive value in the field.

One-click adjustments

Perhaps all the available sliders and choices are a bit overwhelming, but you'd still like to experiment with the raw files. Instead of trying to coordinate change in a number of settings, use the White Balance tool to make a quick adjustment.

The value you select with the tool defines the white balance point for your image, and adjusts all the other colors in the image based on the selection.

Identify an area of your image that appears to be pure white. Zoom in on that area to be sure there is detail in the white area, rather than being a highlight. In my sample image, a good selection area is the stone and rock in the foreground object group, shown in Figure 23.6.

Follow these steps to adjust the image based on a selected point:

1. Click the White Balance tool (the Eyedropper tool) in the Camera Raw dialog box's tools.

Figure 23.6. Magnify an area on your image to use as a starting point for automatic adjustments.

2. Move the tool over the magnified section of the image, and watch the values in the RGB listing at the upper-right corner of the dialog box.

3. Click when you are over an area that should be a neutral white color. That is, an area that is as close to an RGB value of 255/255/255 as possible.

4. Check out the Temperature and Tint sliders, which adjust automatically to make the selected color neutral white.

5. Zoom out for a view of your entire image. The selected neutral white point automatically draws the other colors in the image to a better light balance, like the right image in Figure 23.7.

Figure 23.7. Specifying a neutral white area on the image moves the color temperature and tint from too dark (left) to balanced color and tint (right).

Modifying an image's tone

After you have your image's lighting adjusted properly, you may have to modify the tone of the image further using the other sliders on the Adjust tab of the Camera Raw dialog box.

I hope that you have experimented with the sliders and with choosing different White Balance lighting options. If so, you've seen how choosing a type of light can affect the settings for the image. Adjust the Exposure and Shadows first, and then tweak your image using the remaining settings.

Set exposure and shadows

Exposure is the brightness or darkness of your image. In the Camera Raw dialog box, clipped highlights are shown in red, like those identified in Figure 23.4. Use Exposure and Shadows sliders to take care of those areas in these ways:

- Drag the Exposure slider on the Adjust tab to the right to brighten the image, or drag it to the left to darken the image.

- Drag the Shadows slider on the Adjust tab to the right to darken the image, or drag it to the left to lighten the image.

Previewing the clipped areas

You may find the colored Shadows and Highlights clipping colors distracting you as you work with your image. It's important to check for the clipping in your image to make sure you are using the best range of color in your image.

You can preview the clipped areas directly on the image without using the Shadows or Highlights clipping indicator colors.

Follow these steps to adjust the exposure:

1. Deselect the Shadows and Highlights check boxes at the top of the preview area in the Camera Raw dialog box.

2. Press the Alt key, and begin to drag the Exposure slider.
   The image is replaced by a clipping image as shown in

Inside Scoop
The values used for the exposure are the same as f-stops in your camera. Adjusting the exposure +1 is the same as widening the camera's aperture one stop; adjusting the exposure −1 is the same as narrowing the aperture one stop.

Figure 23.8. In the figure, you see that much of the image is black, indicating unclipped areas. The colored areas indicate clipped highlights.

3. Drag the slider until the colored areas disappear.
4. Reverse the adjustment slightly until you have set the exposure to just below its clipping value.
5. Release the Alt key to view the image.

That takes care of the exposure. Follow the same method to adjust the shadows, this time dragging the Shadows slider. Moving the slider to the right increases the amount of shadow by mapping more areas of the image to black, which appears as more contrast in the image. Press the Alt key as you drag the Shadows slider to see the Shadows clipping preview, like that seen in Figure 23.9. The preview is opposite of that for the Exposure setting — color indicates areas of shadow that are clipped, and white indicates unclipped areas.

Figure 23.8. Show clipping areas as you adjust the Exposure to ensure accurate editing.

Figure 23.9. Preview the effect of adjusting the Shadows setting in the image.

Brightness and contrast adjustments

The Brightness and Contrast sliders work in similar ways to the Exposure and Shadows settings, but they use compression and expansion rather than clipping. Use the Brightness slider to adjust highlight and shadow, and the Contrast slider to adjust midtones.

> **Watch Out!**
> Use the Brightness value to tweak the brightness in an image after you have adjusted clipping using Exposure and Shadows settings to be sure your image is using its full range of color.

Decrease the brightness in an image by dragging the Brightness slider to the left to both compress the highlights and expand the shadows, shown in the left image in Figure 23.10. The reverse is true if you drag the slider to the left to expand the highlights and compress the shadows, as shown in the right figure in 23.10.

What about the midtones — those parts of the image whose color is neither highlight nor shadow, but instead midrange color? Adjust the Contrast slider to decrease the midtone contrast by dragging the slider left, as seen in the left image in Figure 23.11. Increase the midtone contrast by dragging the slider right, as shown in the right image in Figure 23.11.

Figure 23.10. Decrease image brightness by expanding shadows and compressing highlights (left) or increase brightness by compressing shadows and expanding highlights (right).

Saturation adjustments

The last adjustment in the Adjust tab that you can make to an image's tone is the saturation. Drag the Saturation slider right to increase the color saturation. A value of +100 is double-saturated. Drag the Saturation slider left to decrease the color saturation — a value of −100 is a desaturated, or grayscale, image.

Figure 23.11. Change contrast in the midrange colors in the image. Decrease the contrast for less emphasis on the midtones (left) or increase the contrast for sharper emphasis on the midtones (right).

Taking care of the details

The Detail tab of the Camera Raw dialog box has controls for reducing image noise. Noise — the gray or colored dots that make an image look grainy or indistinct — exists to some extent in all images captured by a digital camera which are. Grainy gray dots can be improved using the Luminance Smoothing slider, while colored dots or noise can be corrected using the Color Noise Reduction slider, shown in Figure 23.12.

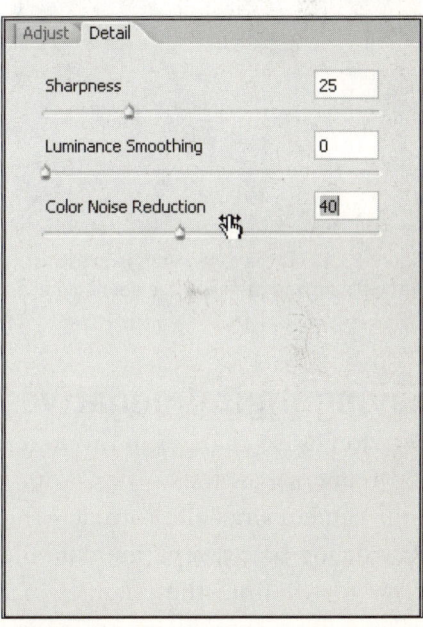

Figure 23.12. When the image's color balance is correct, tweak noise in the Detail tab of the dialog box.

> **Hack**
> If you are planning to do more editing of an image in Photoshop Elements, use the Sharpening filters within the program instead of those in the Camera Raw window after all your other edits are finished. Your finished image will be clearer.

You often find more noise in images shot with high-ISO speeds and those captured by lower-quality cameras. You can adjust both luminance and color noise directly from the Camera Raw dialog box. For each value, drag the slider to increase the amount of correction applied, or click the fields and type a value. Before you make the adjustments, zoom into the image for a clear look at the changes as you make them.

Sometimes, the edge detail in an image isn't as defined as it should be, like the detail in the piece of pumice stone shown in the left image of Figure 23.13. In that case, you can use the Sharpness slider to increase contrast in your image, as used in the right image in Figure 23.13. Drag the Sharpness slider to the right to increase sharpening and to the left to decrease it.

Figure 23.13. If the edge detail is indistinct, as in the left image, increasing the Sharpness in the Details tab can make the detail more distinct, as in the right image.

Saving digital negatives

You don't save changes in the source raw file when you make changes in the Camera Raw dialog box. Your original raw file stays as captured in your camera's raw file format. When you save an image in the Camera Raw dialog box, a separate data file is created and stored on your hard drive that defines the changes made to your original file. The format used in Photoshop Elements is Digital Negative, or DNG format.

Inside Scoop
For me, storing both source and processed files in the same folder is the best way to keep track of my files as I can see instantly which files have been processed. Some prefer to store processed and source files in separate folders. The key is to be consistent.

When you are finished making adjustments to the raw file in the Camera Raw dialog box, follow these steps to save the changes in a new file for future use:

1. Click the Save button to open the Save Options dialog box, shown in Figure 23.14.
2. Specify the storage location, file naming features, and digital negative format details.
3. Click Save to save the image in the digital negative file (DNG) format.

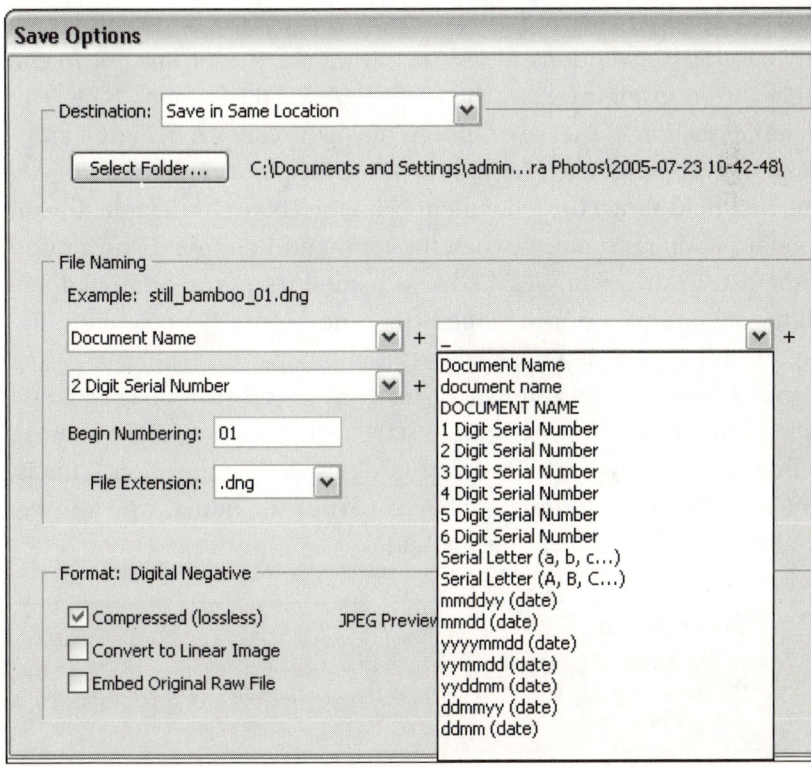

Figure 23.14. Specify details for saving the digital negative version of your raw file complete with adjustments.

Bright Idea

Naming conventions can be complicated. As you are selecting content for the fields, look at the file name in the Example line below the File Naming title on the Save Options dialog box.

Choosing the storage location

If you are working with numerous raw files, take a few minutes and plan how you want to name and save the files. When you have processed the first file, specify the destination in the Save Options dialog box that you can apply for each image you are working with.

The default setting stores the new file in the same folder as the original raw file. Click the Destination drop-down arrow and choose Save in New Location, or click Select Folder and locate the folder you want to use for storage.

Defining image names

Specify naming conventions to use for saving a series of images. In the example shown in Figure 23.1, the file is named still_bamboo.NEF. The File Naming section of the Save Options dialog box shown in Figure 23.14 contains several fields, each having the same drop-down menu.

The first field shows the Document Name selection by default. To add additional naming structures, click the menu and choose a convention from the list. In the example, the file is named using the original document; the second part of the name is the underscore (_) character; the third part of the name is a two-digit serial number.

If you choose a serial number or letter as part of the image's name type the number or letter you want to start with in the Begin Numbering field. Be sure to use the same number of digits as your selection. That is, if you choose a 3 Digit Serial Number as part of the name, type a three-digit value in the Begin Numbering field.

Inside Scoop

To add custom content to a File Naming field, click the drop-down arrow, click the blank row at the bottom of the menu to add a blank field, and then type the text you want to use.

About DNG files

The Digital Negative format is a proposed standard for camera raw files being developed by Adobe and is supported by several Adobe programs. A DNG file is made up of image data and the metadata that describes it. The image data is based on the TIFF format and designed to hold the image data captured by the camera's sensors. The metadata component contains all the information that a raw converter needs to convert the file.

You can find links to the format's specifications and other information in Appendix B.

Choosing digital negative options

The last decisions to make are about the options to include with the Digital Negative file. These options are available:

- **Compressed (lossless).** The data in the file is not altered or degraded in any way. This is a default option in the Save Options dialog box.

- **Convert to Linear Image.** The data in the original raw image file is processed, interpolated, and converted from the raw format's "mosaic" format. If you choose this setting, the image can't be reversed back to its original mosaic format after it's converted to a linear image.

- **Embed Original Raw File.** Embeds the original raw file data from your camera into the DNG file to allow you to extract it at a later time. Use this option if you need long-term storage of your files.

- **JPEG preview.** You can also specify the size of the JPEG preview image by clicking the drop-down arrow and choosing from None, Medium, and Full Size. The default Medium size preview is big enough to clearly see your image.

Watch Out!
You can change settings for different camera models, but you can't store more than one group of settings for a single camera model.

Using your own settings

Photoshop Elements uses the information in the file to determine what camera settings to apply to the image. If you are working with lots of images from the same camera, pay attention to the changes you have to make. If you are always making the same adjustments in the Camera Raw dialog box, change the default setting for your camera instead of making the same changes over and over.

Follow these steps to change the default settings and save yourself time:

1. Open a raw file from either the Editor or Organizer window, which loads the image in the Camera Raw dialog box.
2. Make your series of adjustments.
3. Click the triangle next to the Settings menu, and choose Save New Camera Raw Default from the flyout menu. Now those settings will be used for all images opened in the Camera Raw dialog box, regardless of their camera source.

If you work with several cameras, establish different collections of settings for each camera. When you open files from different cameras, select your custom setting for the applicable camera, and the adjustments are made.

At any time, you can return to the program defaults. Click the triangle next to the Settings menu again, and choose Reset Camera Raw Default.

Just the facts

- Develop a plan for modifying a raw image to save time and produce more accurate results.
- Use the features in the Camera Raw dialog box to show different aspects of your image, such as detail and clipping.
- Adjust color casts to remove extra color using different adjustments.
- Adjust the tone of your image using adjustments that modify lightness and darkness in different ways.
- Smooth detail in several ways to make the image clearer.
- Save raw files as digital negatives for long-term safe storage of your image's information.

Glossary

active layer The selected layer in the Layers palette is the active layer. The active layer's listing in the Layers palette is highlighted.

active window The image window that has been selected by clicking anywhere on the window with the mouse. Actions or commands are applied to the active window.

additive primaries The colors red, green, and blue are used to create all the colors our eyes see. Computer monitors also use combinations of these three colors to produce other color. At full intensity of all three colors, you see white.

Adjustment layer A specialized type of layer used in Photoshop Elements to work with the underlying layer's color and other features. In addition, Adjustment layers can be used to hold gradients or color fills.

Adobe Color Engine (ACE) Color processed in Photoshop Elements is managed by the ACE for screen and print display and processing.

Adobe Color Picker A dialog box used to specify colors in Photoshop Elements. Use different color spaces for selecting the color, including HSB, RGB, and Web colors.

Adobe RGB The default RGB color space used in Photoshop Elements is Adobe RGB.

airbrushing A setting that simulates the effect of spray-painting an image. Holding the mouse button depressed increases the volume of paint applied.

algorithm Mathematical formulas used to perform functions and processes such as resampling and application of effects.

aliasing The jagged edges seen at non-linear edges of shapes resulting from a saw tooth pixel pattern.

alpha channel An alpha channel is a mask used to identify transparent versus opaque areas of an image or layer. The mask is used to manipulate or protect areas on the image. An alpha channel can be created, stored, and managed as a selection.

anchor The center point of a bounding box shown overlaying a selected object. Transformations such as rotation use the anchor position as a point of reference.

animated GIF A sequence of images in GIF format that are displayed at several frames per second simulating motion.

anti-alias A method used to smooth an image. Pixels produce a jagged edge; using anti-aliasing attempts to decrease the jagged appearance by applying a formula that evaluates the color information in pixels surrounding edges and replaces the color.

artifact Unusual and unexpected changes in an image that result from processing errors or camera setting errors. Some common types of artifacts include blooming, moiré, sharpening, and noise.

aspect ratio The width-to-height ratio that defines how an image or frame displays on a monitor or a page.

auto levels One of the Photoshop Elements automatic color correction processes that adjusts the contrast in an image to optimize the levels of dark, medium, and light pixels for displaying maximum detail.

Background layer The bottom-most layer in an image, which is locked and flattened by default. To modify the stacking order, opacity, or blending mode, the Background has to be converted to a generic layer.

backlight Backlighting is a light source or sources occurring naturally, such as the sun, or placed behind the subject of an image like an additional light source, to reduce shadow.

base layer The lowest layer in the stacking order of a group of layers is the base layer. The base layer defines the visible image.

batch processing Tasks can be processed in a defined sequence using specified parameters. The sequence can be applied to one or multiple files.

GLOSSARY

bevel A bevel is an effect showing either a raised or depressed 3D edge around an image or object simulated by highlights and shadows applied to the inside and outside borders.

bicubic An interpolation algorithm that uses the values of surrounding pixels to produce smoother color gradations than Nearest Neighbor or Bilinear methods.

bicubic sharper An interpolation algorithm that applies Bicubic interpolation and then enhances the detail in the image with sharpening.

bicubic smoother An interpolation algorithm that uses the values of surrounding pixels to produce color gradations and then calculates pixels' color further to enhance tonal gradation in the image.

bilinear An interpolation algorithm that adds pixels by averaging color values of surrounding pixels.

bit depth The number of colors that represent a pixel in an image. Black and white is 1-bit color, while 32-bit color can show billions of colors. Other common bit depths are 8-bit, which displays 256 colors or shades of gray, and 16-bit, which displays 65,536 colors.

bitmap An image that is made of a matrix of (usually) square pixels. Bitmaps are resolution-dependent; the size of the pixels and their color determine the clarity of the image onscreen and in print. A bitmap is a standard file format in Windows using the BMP file extension.

bits per channel A measurement that specifies how many tones each color channel contains. Each channel uses a multiple of 4 or 8 to define the number of bits, such as 4, 8, 16, or 32-bit color.

black point A reference point used to represent black.

blending mode Blending modes define how color pixels in one layer interact with the pixels in underlying layers. Blending also refers to the outcome of applying a color to a base color to produce a new color using different editing or painting tools.

blur Decreasing the contrast between pixels in an image to soften the detail results in a blur. Different methods exist for controlling and defining the amount, direction, and other characteristics of the blur.

bounding box The rectangular shape that identifies the margins of a selected object on a layer.

brightness The relative lightness or darkness of a color or an entire image. Brightness defines the intensity of colors. Brightness is expressed as a percentage with black at 0 percent and white at 100 percent.

burning Darkening a specific part in an image. The term arises from traditional photographic techniques where an area on an image that is too light after exposure can be corrected by adding additional light, or burning, the white area.

cache file A virtual memory file that speeds program performance.

camera raw A photo file containing raw sensor data that is not processed in the camera, but instead is transferred to Photoshop Elements and processed in the program.

canvas The workspace on which an image is manipulated. The canvas by default is the same size as its image, but it can be increased in size to provide a larger workspace to accommodate dimension or content changes, or decreased in size to crop content from the image.

channel Color information in an image can be described on the basis of channels. RGB color has three channels, one for each of Red/Green/Blue; CMYK color has four channels; a black-and-white grayscale image has one channel.

chroma The saturation of a color is its chroma. The strength of the color is based on how much black or white is added to the color. Color without any gray is fully saturated.

chromatic aberration An error of color that occurs when the camera lens can't focus the different wavelengths of light onto the same spot on the image. The most common type is fringing, seen as patches of other colors such as purple or blue-green.

Clipboard The holding area on the operating system that stores copied data temporarily.

clipping group A set of layers that use a mask. The lowest layer in the stacking order, the base layer, defines the visible image; the remaining layers are shown through the masked area.

clone Duplicating content in an image using the Clone Stamp tool as a painting tool. The origin of the content used for painting is based on a sampling point specified on the active layer before using the tool.

closed shape A shape that has no definable start or end point and encloses space.

CMYK The CMYK color space is used to print images, often using color separated plates each printing one of cyan, magenta, yellow, and black. Photoshop Elements doesn't support CMYK color.

color cast A color shift in an image that can occur when different forms of lighting are used.

color channels The component colors from which all colors in an image are created. Usually refers to red, green, and blue (RGB).

color depth The amount of color information in a pixel that can be used to display or print. The greater the color depth, the more accurate the color representation.

color gamut The range of colors that a device can reproduce is its color gamut. A computer monitor has a much broader color gamut than a television monitor.

color management The process of adjusting different devices such as scanners, monitors, printers, and cameras to minimize misinterpretation of the color information as it is transferred from one device to another.

color model A structure that specifies the attributes of a color in a systematic way. The common color models include RGB, HSB, and CMYK.

color mode Similar to a color model, a color mode specifies how colors are defined. Color modes include RGB and CMYK.

color separation The reinterpretation of an image's RGB color information into CMYK color information is called color separation. The term also refers to printing color images in separated plates, where each plate prints one color.

color space Different programs and devices use different color spaces, which are color modes designed for a device that may use different identifying structures. A computer monitor can use a wide variety of different color spaces. Two of the most common are Adobe RGB, the color space used by Adobe applications including Photoshop Elements, and sRGB, the color space used by most monitors.

color swatch Color samples used to specify foreground, background, fill, and stroke colors in an image. Colors can be named and stored in the program.

color table A method used to reference colors in an image having a low bit depth that can't represent all colors in the image. Different methods can be used to define the color in the color table, also called a color lookup table (CLUT). A system used to index or reference colors when the bit depth is insufficient to represent all colors.

color value The color of a pixel based on calculating the color components.

color wheel A method of displaying visible color in a wheel showing complementary colors at opposite sides of the wheel with color gradually desaturating as it moves inward toward the center of the wheel.

colorizing A method for enhancing grayscale images by coloring specific areas to draw attention to them, such as a face or an article of clothing.

complementary colors Pairs of colors found on opposite sides of a color wheel. For example, orange and blue are complementary colors.

compression Reducing the file size of a bitmap image is called compression. Compression may be lossless or lossy. Lossless compression, such as that used for saving PNG files, maintains the file's information. In lossy compression, such as JPEG compression, image information is deleted from the file as part of the process.

contrast The difference in the amount of brightness between light and dark areas in an image. The amount of contrast defines the number of shades in an image.

Cookie Cutter A tool used to apply a shape as a cropping template to an image or a layer. Content from the image or layer outside the margins of the selected shape are removed.

Creations Products you can create in Photoshop Elements such as photo albums, cards, postcards, wall calendars, and HTML photo galleries.

crop A process of removing content from an image by decreasing its dimensions. Cropping can be linear and applied using the Crop tool or by decreasing the size of the canvas, or based on shapes applied using the Cookie Cutter tool.

curves A line connecting two points on a path. The appearance of a curve is dependent on the characteristics of the adjoining points at each end of the curve, which define whether the curve is straight, angled, or an arc.

cutout The remaining content in an image after applying a Cookie Cutter shape.

defringing Removing the outer pixels from an image to correct a color artifact called a fringe. Fringing occurs when you remove an image from one background (including some color from the original background) and place it on another background.

desaturate A color or an image that has its color removed, leaving only shades of gray, is referred to as desaturated.

displacement map A flattened Photoshop file or bitmap used by the Displace filter to precisely control how a layer or selection is displaced or shifted on the image.

distorting Changing the relationships among the curves and points in a shape. The Distort tool is used to move points on a shape and alter the appearance of the connecting curves.

dithering In an image where there are more colors than are displayed in the allowed palette, the color can be approximated using a process called dithering. Colors of pixels adjacent to the missing color are changed to simulate the color.

dodging Brightening a part of an image is called dodging. The term originated with photographic development where areas that are too dark are shielded using a hand or paper as the image is exposed.

dot The basic unit of a raster image is a dot.

dots per inch (dpi) The resolution of an image is measured in dots per inch. The higher the dpi, the finer the image detail and the larger the file size.

downsample Decreasing the amount of color information in an image by applying an algorithm. Pixels are removed from the image.

dynamic brush options A set of options you can specify that define how a brush tip behaves as it is in use. You can specify numerous options, including spacing, fading, hue jitter, hardness, angle, and roundness.

embedded profile   An ICC color profile attached to an image file that defines the color space used to interpret the image's color.

Encapsulated PostScript (EPS)   A file format based on the PostScript language used to save images for page layout and illustration programs. An EPS file can store both vector and bitmap data.

Exchangeable Image File Format (EXIF)   A data format used for exchanging data between cameras and software. EXIF data can include camera settings, the camera model, date and time of the photo, and other information.

fade   When painting, the fade controls the number of steps until the paint density decreases to zero; when referring to editing tools, fading controls the amount of adjustment applied by the tool to the image.

faux font   A version of a font generated by a program that simulates the appearance of a style applied to a font where the style isn't available. Faux fonts include faux bold, faux oblique, and faux italic.

Favorites   Tags or collections stored in a subcategory that allow for quick access; content stored within Favorites are not relocated from their original locations.

feathering   The softening of an edge of a selection by fading the color in the pixels or blurring the edge pixels.

fill layer   A fill layer is a type of Adjustment layer that contains a single color, gradient, or pattern fill.

filters   Mathematical formulas or algorithms that can usually be customized before applying to an image to modify its appearance. Filters can create artistic effects, such as brush strokes or media, modify the geometry, or adjust color or contrast.

Find Faces   A feature in the Photo Browser that searches for and locates faces that can be searched and accessed quickly. The Find Faces feature can't distinguish between a human face and a mask or puppet.

flatten   Replacing a version set with a single representative image in the Photo Browser of the Organizer window.

flattening   Merging all visible layers into the Background layer to reduce file size.

font   A file of information describing a set of letters, numbers, punctuation marks, and symbols using common features such as their weight, height, and width.

font family A group of fonts using the same name and basic characteristics but having different styles. The Arial family includes Arial Bold, Arial Italic, and Arial Bold Italic.

font style Versions of a font in the same family are font or type styles. Common font styles are italic, bold, or condensed.

fringing A type of artifact that sometimes occurs after you have selected and removed an object from one background and placed it on another, where the bordering pixels in the cut object include color from the original image's background, called a fringe. Fringing can be removed using the defringing process.

fuzziness A setting used for sampling and selecting that defines the number of shades similar to the point sampled. The lower the number, the fewer similar shades are selected; the higher the number, the more shades are selected with your sample. Fuzziness also refers to a jagged effect at the edges of a selection caused by anti-aliasing.

gamma The brightness of midtone values in an image.

gamma adjustment Changing the contrast in an image by darkening or lightening the midtones of the image. Adjusting the gamma doesn't have much effect on highlights and shadows.

gamut The range of color values in a color system that represents the colors a device can reproduce in a given color space.

Gaussian blur A Gaussian type of blur that uses a mathematical distribution of color and tones along a bell curve to soften an image.

gradient A method used to produce a smooth transition between two adjacent colors or transparency. Gradients follow different patterns, such as radial or linear.

Graphics Interchange Format (GIF) A file format suitable for simple illustrations, line art, and text images used for Web pages and animations. GIF files are small in size, and use a resolution limited to 8-bits, or 256 colors. GIF89a is a more recent format that supports interlacing.

gray point A reference point used to represent a mid-gray point that is composed of equal amounts of black and white.

grayscale An image mode that displays color as shades of gray. Grayscale images can be saved in different file formats.

grid lines   The pattern of horizontal and vertical nonprinting lines displayed over an image window. The lines can be customized for style, size, color, and number of subdivisions.

halo   An artifact that occurs when contrast is increased too much in an image. Over-sharpening results in bright rings or lines at an object's edges.

highlights   The brightest elements in an image.

histogram   A visual display of the relative intensity of color in an image or sample displayed in a graph. The horizontal axis represents levels from 0 (darkest) to 255 (lightest), and the vertical axis represents the numbers of pixels at each level.

History state   An image state listed in the Undo History palette.

HSB   Hue/Saturation/Brightness is a color mode that is based on the human perception of color. All colors can be defined by expressing their levels of hue, saturation, and brightness in percentages.

hue   A perception of color that is reflected from or transmitted through objects. What is perceived as red or blue, for example, is the hue property of a color.

hue jitter   A dynamic brush option that defines how a stroke color switches between the foreground and background colors set in the toolbox. The higher the value, the faster the switch occurs.

image cache   A section of hard disk space used as virtual memory. The image cache speeds the onscreen redraw of high-resolution images.

image mode   The color mode of an image, such as CMYK or RGB.

image tiling   A method of displaying two or more images in the program window by resizing and arranging the windows evenly. Image tiling can be automatic, resizing and arranging images throughout a work session.

Indexed color   A format for coloring images using a limited number of colors, ranging from 2 to 256, where the pixels are indexed to colors in a color table.

interpolation   The formulas applied to the resampling process for adding or removing pixel information from an image.

jitter   The randomness of a brush stroke is referred to as its jitter. Jitter can also refer to direction, color, or other characteristics.

Joint Photographic Experts Group (JPEG) The committee of industry experts that developed algorithms for compressing image files. The JPEG format is used with continuous tone images like photographs and can use specified qualities. The higher the quality, the lower the amount of compression and the larger the file size. Higher levels of compression result in higher loss of image data. JPEG 2000 is a newer version of the format that supports transparency, but is not usable by all images.

JPEG compression The process of compressing a JPEG image reduces the amount of data in an image and its file size used for the image. Compression is lossy because data is lost from the image file and can't be restored.

Kelvin color temperature scale The measurement of light exhibited by color is measured in degrees Kelvin. As a general rule, indoor color is about 3200 degrees K, and outdoor color is about 5500 degrees K. The white point on a computer monitor is 6500 degrees K; a candle flame is about 1850 degrees K.

Lasso tool Image-editing tools used to select areas of an image for moving or cropping.

layer Extra content superimposed over the background of an image. Layers can be manipulated to modify the underlying image. Layers can hold text, image components, drawings, fills, and specialized content for adjusting image characteristics such as brightness and contrast.

layer mask A layer mask is a structure used to define areas of opacity and transparency in an image layer based on areas of black and white. A protected area in an Adjustment layer is a layer mask that prevents content below the mask from editing.

Levels Functionality for adjusting color and tone. With a Levels adjustment, you can set shadow and highlight values to use a full tonal range, adjust middle tones only, correct color casts, and so on.

locked file A file that is set as Read Only. In the Photo Browser, files that are open in the Editor are locked and display a Lock icon.

locked layer A layer in the Layers palette that has the Lock icon active; or the Background layer, which is always locked. Locked layers can't be modified.

lossless compression   A method of image compression in which there is no loss in quality when the image is uncompressed such as ZIP or LZW compression. The uncompressed image is mathematically identical to its original. Lossless compression is usually lower in compression ratio than lossy compression.

lossy compression   A method of image compression in which some image quality is sacrificed in exchange for higher compression ratios, such as a JPEG image. The amount of quality degradation depends on the compression algorithm used and a user selected quality variable.

luminance   Lightness calculated by using the highest of the individual RGB values plus the lowest of the individual RGB values, divided by two.

LZW compression (Lemple-Zif-Welch)   A lossless technique especially suited for compressing images that contain large areas of a single color. LZW compression is often used with TIFF files.

marquee   A hatched outline drawn over an image using one of many tools. Click the image with the tool and drag to form the shape. Release the mouse to complete the marquee, indicating the area selected on the image.

mask mode   A method of working in a layered image where only a layer's mask is active and all layers are inaccessible. Press Alt+-Shift and click the layer thumbnail in the Layers palette to activate its mask mode.

Match Location   A command used to display the same locations in two or more images. Use the Match Zoom command as well to compare two or more images.

Match Zoom   A command used to display the same magnification in two or more images. Use the Match Location command as well to compare two or more images.

matting   A method for simulating transparency in images displayed on Web pages by using a matte color matching the Web page's background color.

metadata   Information about an image is stored within the image file as metadata. The information can include a wide range of common and custom values, such as the file name or type, tags, collections, and capture date. Other common metadata includes camera details such as the model and shutter speed. View and add custom metadata in the Properties palette of the Organizer or the File Info dialog box in the Editor.

midtone An area that falls between the brightest highlight and the darkest shadow.

moiré A common artifact that occurs from scanning images is a wavy tone on tone pattern, called a moiré pattern.

monitor profile A file of information on how color is generated by your monitor and video card that is stored on your computer. The profile contains values for brightness, contrast, gamma, the monitor's white point, and information about the monitor's phosphors.

monitor resolution Pixel dimensions defining the size of the monitor's image display capabilities. The size of an image displayed on a monitor depends on the size of the monitor, its resolution, and the pixel dimensions of the image.

Navigator palette Used to change the view of your active image window by setting the size of a thumbnail image. The Navigator shows a colored box corresponding to the area shown in the image window.

Nearest Neighbor An interpolation algorithm that replicates the pixels in the image. This method is best used for illustrations with hard edges.

noise The most common artifact is noise, caused either by a camera problem or compression errors. Noise is seen as extra pixels in either color or grayscale that give the image a grainy appearance.

nudging Repositioning a selected area or layer on an image one pixel at a time by nudging. Use the keyboard arrow keys to nudge the selected content one pixel in the arrow's direction. Press Shift and an arrow key to nudge 10 pixels at a time in the arrow's direction.

opacity Opacity can be changed in layers, filters, effects, and tools to allow more or less of the underlying pixels to show. This is the opposite of transparency.

open shape A shape that has definite start and end points and doesn't enclose space is an open shape.

Options bar A collection of tools displays across the program window in a toolbar when a tool is selected in the toolbox. The available tools vary depending on the active tool.

origins The point on the ruler displayed at the top and left sides of an image that identifies where the 0, 0 measurements are displayed horizontally and vertically.

output dimensions The size of the printed image; output dimensions are based on the total number of pixels and the pixels-per-inch value.

palette A series of dialog boxes used in Photoshop Elements used to display and control settings for a variety of purposes, such as showing information about selected content or the image in the Info palette, or listing layers, blending modes, and opacities in the Layers palette.

Palette Bin A spot at the right of the program window used to organize and manage palettes. Dock, or store, the palettes you are using to display them away from the work area.

pan and zoom A common video effect often used with slide shows or presentations. Panning displays different areas of the slide over time between start and end points; zooming changes magnification of the slide over time.

panorama A picture or pictures of a scene made by overlapping segments of the scene and then merging them to form a single image.

path A geometric description of a drawn object. A path may be open, such as a line or arc, or closed, such as a circle or a banana. Paths are made up of curves and points.

pattern Repeating graphics or images that are provided by Photoshop Elements or custom creations. Patterns can be used as fills and with fill layers, and the Paint Bucket and Pattern Stamp tools.

perspective The way in which objects appear to the eye based on their dimensions and the position of the eye relative to the objects. For example, the parallel lines of a train track are perceived by the eye as meeting at a distant point at the horizon.

Perspective tool Both vertical and horizontal perspectives can be applied using the Perspective tool. Increase or decrease the dimension of the bounding box side to simulate the appearance of an object shown in relation to the vanishing point or horizon.

Photo Browser The Photoshop Elements component that serves as the controlling window for collecting, organizing, and managing files.

PICT A file format for storing digital images in Mac OS.

pixel A term that comes from picture and element. A pixel represents a point of color in a computer image. Its size depends on the resolution of the display screen.

pixel dimensions   The number of pixels in your image. Pixel dimensions are equal to the document output size times the resolution.

pixelization   The stair-stepped appearance of a curved or angled line in digital imaging. The lower the image resolution, the more apparent the image's pixelization.

point   The default unit of measurement for type. The most common point sizes in books are 10-point and 11-point type.

Polygon tool   A drawing tool used to create a 5-sided shape by default. Configure the drawn shape by changing the number of sides or the indents, which lets you change a 3-sided triangle to a 10-pointed star, for example.

Portable Document Format (PDF)   A file format developed by Adobe that maintains the integrity of an image or document as an image. PDF files can be highly structured, containing a set of tags and content elements, or a single image. PDF files open in Adobe Acrobat or Adobe Reader.

Portable Document Format (PDP)   Image forms of PDF files that open in Photoshop Elements.

Portable Network Graphics (PNG)   Bitmap image formats that use different color depths. PNG-8 uses 8-bit color and compresses areas of solid color while preserving sharp detail in line art or type. PNG-24 supports 24-bit color. The format preserves photographic detail and also supports 24-bit transparency.

posterize   A reduction in the number of continuous tones in an image producing larger blocks of color.

PostScript   A sophisticated page description language developed by Adobe used for printing high-quality text and graphics on PostScript printers and other high-resolution printing devices.

ppi (pixels per inch)   A term used to identify image dimensions displayed onscreen. The higher the ppi is, the smaller the pixel size.

printer profiles   For color printers, a profile is a software file that describes how ink interacts with a specific type of paper using a specific printing system. The print driver uses the profile to adjust the output of ink to match the colors, contrast, and brightness in the picture file.

printer resolution   The level of detail a printer can produce is measured in ink dots per inks (dpi). The higher the resolution is, the finer the level of detail.

PSD   The native file format of Adobe Photoshop and Adobe Photoshop Elements.

Quick Fix mode   One of the interfaces available in Photoshop Elements. The Quick Fix screen lets you apply basic types of color and lighting corrections to an image or images. The Quick Fix mode offers a limited number of the tools and features found in the more extensive Standard Edit mode.

QuickTime   Cross-platform software from Apple Computers widely used for editing, Web video, CD-ROM, and other multi-media.

radius   A setting used by many filters and tools to refer to the distance from the target pixel that is affected by program actions. The larger the radius, the more pixels that are affected.

raster image   Bitmap images created from bits that form pixels. The edges of the pixels are seen as a saw-tooth pattern. Common raster file formats include PSD, BMP, TIFF, GIF, JPEG, and PICT.

raw format   Data that is captured by a camera and preserved without any camera processing. Raw format files can be processed in Photoshop Elements.

red eye   In flash photography, the red glow that results from the reflection of the camera flash from the eye's retina. Photoshop Elements and many cameras have red eye reduction tools.

remapping   Adjusting the relative intensity of pixels by modifying their relationships using sliders in a visual display such as a histogram graph.

rendering   A process that uses geometric lighting, camera, or other models to create images. Rendering also refers to converting a shape or type layer to a normal image layer.

resampling   A process used to redefine the pixel information of an image. An algorithm is applied that determines how the program adds pixels to or removes pixels from the image.

resize handles   Small squares on the corners and sides of a bounding box used as handles for changing the dimensions of the contents of the bounding box. Dragging the corner resize handles changes the contents' size proportionally; dragging the resize handles on the sides of the bounding box changes the contents' size either horizontally or vertically.

resolution The number of pixels per inch that describe the amount of physical space an image uses onscreen or in print. An image's resolution determines the clarity of the content.

RGB The default color model for representing colors on a computer display is RGB color, composed of red, green, and blue in different proportions to represent any color. RGB color can display about 16.7 million colors.

rotate Revolving an object uniformly along an axis clockwise or counterclockwise around its center point. Rotation is defined in degrees and applied to an object using the Rotate tool.

ruler Horizontal and vertical segmented bars that display at the top and left sides of an image window. Select the type of measurement to use, such as pixels or inches, which are displayed in numbers and regularly spaced ticks on the rulers.

sample Clicking an image pixel or pixels with an Eyedropper tool to select the color is sampling the color.

saturation The strength of a color expressed as a percentage of hue to gray. Fully saturated color has no gray and 100 percent color; pure gray is 100 percent gray and no color. Saturation is also known as chroma.

scanning Processing and converting an image of a slide or print into a digital image.

scatter The appearance of brush mark distribution is called its scatter. The spacing and other characteristics of scatter can usually be customized.

scratch disk An area on a hard drive designated as spare processing areas when your system doesn't have enough RAM.

screen resolution The dimensions of the pixel grid used by a monitor. Windows-based computers usually have monitors with a screen resolution of 96 pixels per inch (ppi); Mac monitors have 72ppi resolution.

shadow The darkest elements in an image.

shape Drawn vector-based objects in an image. A shape may be created using any of the Shape tools, including basic shapes, or custom shapes offered in the Shapes palette. Shapes are placed on their own layers.

sharpening Locating pixels that differ from surrounding pixels based on a specified threshold and increasing contrast by a specified amount results in sharpened edges in the image.

simplifying Converting layer types including type, shape, solid color, gradient fill, or pattern fill layers to a regular image layer. The layer types have to be simplified before using filters or painting the layer.

single channel images Several types of images use only a single channel of information, including bitmaps, grayscale, indexed-color, and duotone images.

skew Moving an object along an axis counterclockwise or clockwise in one dimension. One side of the bounding box surrounding an object is affected by using skew. Skew may occur as an artifact, or by applying it to an object using the Skew tool.

smoothing Reducing contrast in an image. Smoothing averages the values of neighboring pixels to create a blurry effect. Smoothing is the opposite of sharpening.

sRGB The standard Web color space is sRGB, a calibrated RGB color space.

Standard Edit mode One of the interface options available in Photoshop Elements. You can access all of the Photoshop Elements actions and commands through the Standard Edit mode.

straighten Making the appearance of an image more parallel to the image's axes. Straightening can be done using Straighten or Rotation tools.

stroke An outline surrounding objects, text, or images.

Tagged Image File Format (TIFF) A digital image format widely used for images that are to be printed or published. TIFF images can be compressed losslessly using different compression algorithms.

Targa (TGA) format A file format used with the Truevision video board.

target colors The colors are defined for highlights, midtones, and shadows when correcting an image.

target layer The selected layer in the Layers palette. Also called the target, or active layer.

text layer An image layer that contains vector-based text, also called a type layer.

threshold A specified distance in pixels at which other pixels are affected by a command or filter.

thumbnail A scaled-down, low-resolution representation of an image. Change the size of thumbnails in the Photo Editor to help locate images.

tint Adding various amounts of white to a color produces tints. The more white that's added, the lower the saturation and the greater the lightness.

tonal correction An adjustment made in the tones of an image: shadows, highlights, or midtones. Increasing the highlight and shadow ranges increases the total tonal range.

toolbar The area below the program menus stretching across the program window is the toolbar area. The toolbar area contains static tools such as File Open and Create tool icons, as well as buttons to toggle different views and modes.

toolbox The set of tools available in Photoshop Elements. Some tools, such as the Hand tool or Eyedropper tool, are singular tools, while others contain a number of tools on a subtoolbar, such as the Healing Brush and Spot Healing Brush tools. The selected tool's icon shows on the toolbox.

transform Using one of several tools and processes to modify the geometry of a layer, selection, or shape. Transform options include scale, skew, distort, and rotate.

transparency Transparent areas in an image or a layer. Some image formats, such as JPEG, do not support transparency.

TWAIN A standard software protocol and application programming interface (API) for communicating between imaging devices such as cameras and scanners and software applications.

type mask A selection outline in the shape of a letter added to an image using either the horizontal or vertical Type Mask tool.

unit of measure The values used to express locations and relative values in Photoshop Elements. The unit of measure can be modified in the program preferences, and are displayed in numerous program locations, such as the image window's rulers, in the Info palette, and the Image Size and Canvas Size dialog boxes.

upsample Increasing the amount of color information in an image by applying an algorithm. Pixels are added to the image.

vanishing point In 3D constructs and the Photomerge dialog box, the vanishing point defines the default perspective.

vector Geometric expressions that define the relationship among an object composed of points and curves. Vector images are resolution-independent and can be scaled and manipulated without quality degradation.

version set A collection of images stacked in the Photo Browser as edited versions of the original image.

vignette A technique of focusing on an image's subject by gradually fading out the edges of the image.

warping A type of distortion that conforms to custom or common shapes. Warps can be multi-peaked or shaped as an arc or another simple shape.

watched folder A folder on the hard drive designated in Photoshop Elements that is automatically scanned and monitored for incoming files, such as downloaded telephone images.

Web-safe color Any of the 216 colors that are displayed consistently on the Web regardless of browser or computer platform.

white balance The amount of light and existing lighting conditions present when an image is captured. White balance can be adjusted to compensate for different displays of identical colors that occur with different sources of light, such as incandescent, fluorescent, sunlight, and so on.

white point A reference point used to represent white. This reference point is used to calculate all other colors in the image.

ZIP encoding A form of lossless compression used for images with large areas of single color.

zoom The level of magnification applied to the image in the active window. An image showing Actual Pixels shows the image at 100 percent, with one screen pixel displaying one pixel of the image. A higher zoom shows less than one image pixel per screen pixel; a lower zoom shows more than one image pixel per screen pixel.

Zoom tool A program tool used to change the level of magnification of the image in the active window. The tool magnifies by default, pressing the Alt key switches the tool to the Zoom Out mode; clicking the image with the tool increases or decreases magnification using preset levels. You can drag a marquee with the Zoom tool to focus on the selected area only using a custom magnification level.

Resource Guide

There are as many Web sites online with useful information as there are Photoshop Elements users. Read about some useful sites (including those from Adobe), as well as a variety of sites about color, photo sharing, all things photo editing, and scrapbooking.

This appendix contains a very small, but useful sampling of the many fine Web sites and resources available.

Adobe sites

Find access to the most extensive collection of information on how, why, when, and what to do with Photoshop Elements at Adobe's Web sites.

Print Resource Center

www.adobe.com/studio/print/main.html This site is devoted to tools, guides, white papers, and other documentation about printing for Adobe products in general. Some content isn't applicable in Photoshop Elements; many papers about printing and color are useful.

Studio

www.adobe.com/studio/main.html This is Adobe's main portal for tools, tips, and resources. Read short tutorials on using specific features or access technical papers and other information resources.

Studio Exchange
http://share.studio.adobe.com   On the Studio Exchange site you find many types of downloads for Photoshop that also work with Photoshop Elements, such as brushes and patterns.

Updates and downloads
www.adobe.com/support/downloads/main.html   Check this page at Adobe periodically for the release of upgrades and other downloads for Adobe products, including Photoshop Elements.

Proxy magazine
www.adobeproxy.com   Adobe's new quarterly design magazine lives here. Proxy shows you cutting edge ways in which Adobe products are used. Register and download the magazine as an e-mail PDF file.

Specifications and color information
Make sure your colors jive by controlling color management for digital devices including cameras, monitors, and printers. Each device has its own color management method, and you won't have correct color if you can't get your equipment to speak the same language!

International Color Consortium (ICC)
www.color.org   This organization encourages the standardization and evolution of an open, vendor-neutral, cross-platform color management system.

Image color management start page
www.microsoft.com/whdc/device/display/color/default.mspx   This site contains Microsoft's library of color management information for Windows systems.

Hot Topic: Color
www.apple.com/pro/color   This site contains Apple's information on color proofing and using color.

Photo sharing online
These sources offer photo storage and albums online that you use to upload, manage, and share photos. Photoshop Elements uses the Kodak EasyShare system as a default, but there are numerous other options. In addition to those listed here, check your favorite camera maker's main Web site to see if sharing services are available.

Imagestation
www.imagestation.com   This is Sony's online photo storage, sharing, and printing service.

Kodak EasyShare
http://adobe.kodakgallery.com   This system is integrated into Photoshop Elements as an online storage and sharing system.

Nikon PictureProject in Touch
www.nikonnet.com/share.html   This is Nikon's free online photo storage and sharing system.

Flickr
www.flickr.com   Here's a great online photo management and sharing application. Free basic accounts let you upload pictures, set access, upload images from camera phones and e-mail, and blog photos.

Online resource sites
Of the tens of thousands of Web sites about design, cameras, Photoshop Elements, and other related topics, here are a few favorites.

bytephoto
www.bytephoto.com   This online site offers information on cameras, editing, photo sharing, and other areas of interest. The site appeals to many levels of expertise.

creativepro
www.creativepro.com   One of the preeminent graphics and design sites, creativepro includes Photoshop Elements information, as well as lots of information on type, color, image editing, correction, and so on.

Photoshop Elements Techniques
www.photoshopelementsuser.com   This huge site is full of tips, tutorials, forums, and information. It's a companion site to Photoshop Elements Techniques magazine.

PhotoshopSupport
www.photoshopsupport.com   The PhotoshopSupport.com site provides information on image editing, and includes a large Photoshop Elements section.

PlanetPhotoshop

www.planetphotoshop.com   This Web site contains tutorials, forums, tips, and information on working with digital cameras. Much of the content applies to both Photoshop and Photoshop Elements.

Retouchpro

www.retouchpro.com   Here you'll find information and forums about photo retouching, restoration, and other image editing questions. It is a terrific resource for finding help with a tricky restoration job.

Wacom tablet user tips

www.wacom.com/tips/index.cfm?category=Photoshop   Wacom offers a collection of tutorials for using their tablets in Photoshop; the tutorials work equally well in Photoshop Elements.

Scrapbooking and memory management

Photoshop Elements is the powerhouse program for scrapbookers. The number of sites devoted to the topic of digital work in scrapbooking is growing by leaps and bounds.

Digital Scrapbook Place

www.digitalscrapbookplace.com   This large site offers contests, forums, and information. Check out the galleries for inspiration.

scrapbook-bytes

www.scrapbook-bytes.com   Read tutorials, view galleries, and learn about digital scrapbooking.

two peas in a bucket

www.twopeasinabucket.com   This site is a good source for information about digital scrapbooking and techniques surrounding the process, such as stamping and layouts.

UK scrappers

www.ukscrappers.co.uk   This site is a veritable smorgasbord of scrapbooking resources, information, and forums.

Appendix B

Useful Real-World Worksheets

Checklist 1
Evaluating an image for correction

Decide on a standard routine to use for checking images after you import them into the Organizer. Using a standard workflow — such as the example here — speeds up your editing and decreases error or omissions. Experiment with the checklist and customize it to suit your needs and how you work best.

- ☐ **Evaluate the highlights and shadows in the image.** Make corrections with one or more of these commands from the Editor's Enhance menu: Auto Smart Fix, Auto Levels, Auto Contrast, Adjust Highlights and Shadows, or Levels.

- ☐ **Adjust the color balance.** Look for unnatural color tints and incorrect skin coloring. Adjust color balance using one or more of these Enhance menu commands: Remove Color Cast, Auto Smart Fix, or Adjust Color for Skin Tone.

- ☐ **Make other changes according to your image.** Changes may include fixing over saturation or faded color using Enhance menu commands: Adjust Hue/Saturation or Auto Smart Fix.

☐ **Make changes in the Color Variations dialog box.** With settings in this dialog box, found in the Enhance menu, you can tweak highlights, shadow, midrange, saturation, and color tones.

Checklist 2
Preparing to create a presentation

Organize and prepare the content that goes into a presentation to see what you have to work with and what needs to be modified. In the midst of your presentation's development frenzy, you won't be distracted by missing images or required edits.

First, collect your material in the Organizer. Use the information in this checklist to bring your images and audio together in a single location:

☐ **Check for the images you want to use in the Photo Browser.**

☐ **Import any missing images into the Photo Browser.**

☐ **Locate and preview the music clips you may want to use in the presentation.** Having more than one gives you the opportunity to test them against the presentation.

☐ **Import the music clips into the Photo Browser.**

☐ **If you are using narration, you can record and save it now or after assembling the presentation's elements.**

Next, assemble the files in the Organizer:

☐ **Create a new collection in the Photo Browser.**

☐ **Attach the collection to the image and audio files for the presentation.**

Now that all the files are together in a collection, check the images you are going to use. When you are collecting images you usually have an idea in your mind as to their editing requirements. Be sure to save each image file as a layered and flattened versions. For each image, check the following:

☐ **The image is the correct resolution.** For onscreen use, you need only 72-96ppi resolution.

☐ **The image is corrected.** Check for proper coloring, contrast, highlights, and shadows.

☐ **Crop the images if necessary.** If you intend to use lots of similar images that use common sizes, consider setting a specific ratio or size for the Crop tool.

- ☐ **Flatten image files.** Flattened files are smaller. If you have flattened the image, be sure to save an original copy of the unflattened image for possible editing in the future.
- ☐ **Make other adjustments or corrections as required.**
- ☐ **Save all files.**

Checklist 3
Things to check before printing

Although paper and printer ink have come down in price, and printers are faster all the time, an image that doesn't print correctly is inconvenient and wastes time and resources. This next checklist assumes that you have tweaked your image to perfection already.

First, check the image's settings in the Editor:

- ☐ **Check the image resolution.** If the resolution is higher than your printer's capabilities, decrease it. If the resolution is lower than your printer's range, decrease the print size.
- ☐ **Check the image's print size.** If it is larger than the print area for your paper, decrease the print size.

Second, check other image characteristics in the Editor:

- ☐ **Check the color profile.** You may not have a color profile attached; having a source space defined is important to color management.
- ☐ **Check the mode.** Full-color printing should use an RGB color space.

Third, check the settings in the Layers palette:

- ☐ **Make sure that all layers you intend to print are visible.**
- ☐ **Make sure that layers you don't want to print are hidden.**

Next, check out the page layout and settings in the Print Preview. The checklist is designed for a single print per page:

- ☐ **Choose a print size, and scale it if necessary for the page.**
- ☐ **Set the position for the print on the page, or center it.**
- ☐ **Add other options if your image needs them, such as a border, file name/caption, or crop marks.**
- ☐ **If you have a custom profile, attach the profile to the image.**

> **Inside Scoop**
>
> Increasing print resolution makes the pixels larger, and your image can show blocky, coarse pixels; your only alternative is to decrease the size of the image to increase the clarity of the image.

Next, check out the printer settings. The settings for your printer vary according to the type, manufacturer, and model:

- ☐ **Check the Page Setup in the File menu.** See that the paper size, orientation, and source are correct for your printer.
- ☐ **Choose a print quality.**
- ☐ **Choose a paper type.** Make sure you are using the correct paper for the type of image you are printing.
- ☐ **Check the color management option for your printer (if you have one).** Use the method recommended by your printer's manufacturer.

Finally, if you are printing a number of images using the same settings, or are printing a large, high-resolution image, print a preview to save time and check your settings:

- ☐ **Print a draft-quality print if you need to check placement on the page.**
- ☐ **Print a single copy of a print if you need a batch of the same image to check the quality and settings.**
- ☐ **Make a copy of a high-resolution color print and crop to a small section of the full image.** Print to test your settings before printing the entire image.

Checklist 4

Preparing images for storage

Editing and working with files can increase the number of images in the Organizer by leaps and bounds. Searching for an image takes longer, and keeping track of what you have is more complicated. When you finish a project, check your images and do some quick cleanup and filing. Start in the Organizer, and finish up in the Editor.

First, check for duplicates of your files in the Organizer and decide what to do with them:

- ☐ **Keep a copy of the layered file in TIF or PSD format for reuse.** This is important especially if you have done extensive correction and editing.

- ☐ **Check for versions of a file.** Delete those from the Photo Browser that you won't be using again, such as those saved in formats you don't need.
- ☐ **Delete extra versions of files.** This includes cropped versions and other manipulated copies that you don't need.

Next, open the files in the Editor to check their contents. You want to store images that are small in size, and fewer layers means smaller file size:

- ☐ **Open the Layers palette, and check through the list of layers.**
- ☐ **Delete any layers that aren't required for future use of the file.**
- ☐ **Merge or combine layers if it is practical.**
- ☐ **Resave the reconfigured files.** Save using the original name otherwise you add more copies to the Organizer!

Sort and organize the images next. Back in the Organizer, check through your files to see how they stack up, so to speak:

- ☐ **Create a version set for any image that you have saved in multiple versions.** It's far simpler to look through the Organizer when you can view one example of several files.
- ☐ **Use stacks where possible, such as stacking several unedited shots of the same subject.** Stacks, like version sets, make searching easier and more efficient.

Finally, tag your images and add other data about the files if you haven't done so. Searching on tags or via collections saves lots of time and jogs your memory:

- ☐ **Make a collection for the images.** You can save the collection or collections within existing headings or build your own organization structure.
- ☐ **Add the images to the collections.**
- ☐ **Assign tags to the images.** Again, use either existing tags or ones you are creating for the new work.
- ☐ **Add information in the Properties.** Add captions or notes in the General tab of the Properties palette.
- ☐ **For future reference, list how you edited an image in the Notes area.** You may think you'll remember, but it's just as likely that you will forget.
- ☐ **Add other data you want for maintaining consistency and storing information.** For example, add copyright information in the metadata for files you are sharing.

Checklist 5

Knowing which file format to use

It isn't always easy to figure out how to best save your images. Table B.1 describes each of the file formats you can use from Photoshop Elements, as well as a description of the format's structure or features.

Table B.1. Choosing a file format

File Extension	Format	Description
BMP	Bitmap	The basic Windows raster image format, represented as a grid of dots.
EPS	Encapsulated PostScript	A vector-based format used for illustration and page-layout programs.
GIF	Graphic Image File Format	A file format often used on the Web. Best for images with large blocks of color or line art.
JPEG	Joint Photographic Experts Group	A graphic format using an algorithm that compresses the information. Best for photographs used online. JPEG uses lossy compression, meaning data is lost permanently when the file is compressed (each time the file is saved).
PDF	Portable Document Format	A file format that maintains the integrity of an image in an electronic format. PDF files are opened in Adobe Acrobat or Adobe Reader.
PDP	Photoshop Portable Document Format	PDP is the same file type as PDF, except files are opened in Photoshop Elements.
RAW	Photoshop Raw Format	A Photoshop format used for uncompressed data.
PICT	Picture	The basic Mac OS raster image format, represented as a grid of dots.
PNG-8	Portable Network Graphics, 8-bit	A raster image format using 8-bit color. Good for simple images such as line art or logos, which often are in a GIF format.
PSD	Photoshop Document	The native file format of Adobe Photoshop and Adobe Photoshop Elements.

File extension	Format	Description
RAW	Raw format or camera raw	A format based on unprocessed camera data.
TGA	Targa	Format compatible with systems using the Truevision video board.
TIFF	Tagged Image File Format	Widely used image format, particularly for printing. Compression is lossless.

Determine your camera needs

Answer each question in Worksheet B.1 according to your needs and habits. At the end, you will have a better idea of how you are likely to use a new camera. Although the worksheet is intended more for a first-time camera buyer (or for the first "real" digital camera you buy), these are basic questions that you should consider regardless of your experience level. Decide how relevant each choice is; in Worksheet B.2 read how your plans influence camera features.

Worksheet B.1. Determining your camera needs

1. How will you distribute and share your photos?

a For online posting.

b Use various ways after editing.

c As 5×7 or larger images from camera or computer files.

2. Where do you plan to edit the images?

a In the camera using its editing options.

b Through a program such as Photoshop Elements.

3. How will you export the images from your camera?

a I am not technically inclined. I need my camera to print directly into the printer.

b Take the memory card to the photo printer.

c Take the memory card from the camera and plug it into a card reader on my hard drive.

d Transfer the images to computer by cable.

4. How much portable power do you need? Are you likely to:

a Be away from a regular source of power for days at a time, wandering through a steamy wet jungle with only the sound of your voice and the wild beasts waiting for nightfall to keep you company?

b Not stray far from the backyard?

c Take the camera on day trips and capture dozens of images of prize roses and peach pies at the fair?

5. How much portable storage do you need? Are you likely to:

a Take your camera on trips and adventures where you can't delete images from your memory for days (see jungle reference in previous question)?

b Never be away from your computer for more than a few hours at a time because you can't bear to be away from it for long.

c Take the camera on day trips and capture lots of images?

6. What sort of pictures do you usually take or plan to take?

a I am a homebody and intend to take indoor photos.

b I like action and would like to shoot action shots such as sports.

c As a creature of the night, I plan to shoot images at night.

7. Is zoom photography in your future?

a Yes, and I plan on sending captured images for third-party printing.

b Yes, and I do my own image editing.

c No, I don't need lots of zoom capabilities. My subjects aren't technically wild animals!

8. Do you use a flash often? Do you want to control the flash yourself?

a I use whatever the camera decides. That's too much detail.

b Yes, when it is needed; my shots are mixed day and night.

c I would like to learn how to create effects such as using long exposure times.

9. Are you interested in other neat stuff?

a Nope. A camera is a camera.

b I use my camera for still images only.

c I want my camera to do everything: Can it walk the dog?

10. Are you intending to capture different image formats for different purposes?

a Not very likely. Point and shoot — it says so right on the box.

b Maybe. I'd like to have the choice between images for online and printing use.

c I know beforehand how I am likely to use an image and would like to control those options.

Choosing your camera's features

What you can have in a camera is basically determined only by your budget. What you need in a camera is another story. Use the answers from Worksheet B.1 to determine what you should look for in a camera's feature set. Each topic in Worksheet B.2 corresponds to the same numbered question in Worksheet B.1.

Worksheet B.2. Buying a digital camera

1. Megapixel requirements

Choice:	Consider these ideas:
a	You would be fine with a 3-megapixel camera.
b	Your needs will vary depending on what you end up doing with the images. To be able to print high-quality prints and e-mail low-quality images or make presentations, look for 5 megapixels or more.
c	For high-quality prints, look for 5 or more megapixels.

2. Editing features

Choice:	Consider these ideas:
a	Buy a camera containing editing features if you think you would actually do the editing.
b	Don't spend money on editing capabilities for your camera.

3. Exporting options

Choice:	Consider these ideas:
a	Look for a camera that docks directly into a printer.
b	Look for a camera with a removable memory card. Be sure the card is upgradeable so you can substitute cards.

Choice:	Consider these ideas:
c	Look for a card reader capability for your computer; be sure your computer has a way to read the memory card, either by inserting the memory card into a card reader, or into a device that plugs into one of your existing drives.
d	Look for Firewire (IEEE 1333) or USB capabilities; check for cabling included with the camera; be sure your computer has the correct cards to connect the cables.

4. Batteries and power

Choice:	Consider these ideas:
a	You need to have upgradeable battery packs, spare batteries, and a charger unit. You need a universal converter to operate the charger in some parts of the world.
b	Look for a camera that has a dock you can set the camera on between uses to automatically charge the battery.
c	Use a battery with a charger to recharge the unit between sessions. You may or may not have use for spare batteries.

5. Portable storage

Choice:	Consider these ideas:
a	Look for high-volume memory cards and a safe storage pack for the filled cards. If you travel and have an opportunity to download images from your cards to an online repository, look for a camera that lets you work with common online services.
b	Card storage volume isn't a big requirement. If you use a third-party photo printer where you drive to the store, insert your card into a machine, and print the images yourself, you may want to have a spare card for interim storage between trips.
c	Consider a spare card or a high-volume card, such as one that holds 1GB or more.

6. Exposure and reaction time

Choice:	Consider these ideas:
a	Look for auto-exposure settings. If you are most comfortable with point-and-click photography, you don't need customization features.
b	Digital cameras need time to set themselves before capturing a shot.
c	If you intend to do lots of action photography, look for a camera with a low reaction time.

7. Zoom features

Choice: Consider these ideas:

a	You may find a digital zoom useful because you aren't editing images yourself. If you do lots of zooming, make sure your power supply is large enough to handle the mechanical load of an optical zoom.
b	Digital zoom features on a camera can be duplicated in Photoshop Elements, so you don't really need the zoom capabilities.
c	Don't spend lots of money for zoom capabilities, either optical or digital.

8. Flash and lighting control features

Choice: Consider these ideas:

a	Use a camera with auto-flash options and perhaps a feature to enable/disable the auto-flash.
b	Look for a camera with several auto-flash options. Consider a tripod for adding stability when using a long exposure time.
c	How fast or slow you can set the shutter speed can determine the type of sports and night photography you can take. Look for advanced features such as manual white-balance control, aperture settings, and the like. Make sure to also invest in a tripod to prevent hand jitter.

9. Capture features

Choice: Consider these ideas:

a	Save your money: Concentrate on the memory card and battery life.
b	Look for a camera that offers a range of camera options for capturing stills, such as a range of resolutions and image sizes.
c	If you must, look for a camera that can also capture video and sound. You need lots of memory and battery power.

10. File format features

Choice: Consider these ideas:

a	There's no value spending money on formatting options if you use the same settings for every shot every time.
b	Look for a camera that lets you choose image sizes and resolutions.
c	You need a camera that lets you establish a number of camera profiles that you can choose as required. Depending on your control issues, consider a camera that captures in RAW format.

Test driving cameras

Now that you have determined both how you plan to use your camera and the features you need, you have to try out different models. Your best bet is to find a camera that you can experiment with in a store, even if you then decide to purchase it online. Examine the camera, and arrange with the salesperson to take some shots and export images from the camera if possible.

The camera's hand feel

How the camera actually feels when you carry it and hold it to take a picture are more important that you might think because camera body styles are all so different. So, here are few things to consider when actually examining the physical camera body:

- Can you get to the camera controls easily?
- Can your fingers manipulate the controls easily? You won't be familiar with them at first, of course, but will you be able to use the controls effectively with experience?
- Is taking a shot simple and not a multi-phased process? If it is complex, can you handle the method?
- Is the camera in a comfortable size? Smaller cameras can be cuter, but more difficult to handle.

The camera's operations

Check that your interaction with the camera and its function is simple and straightforward. Consider the ease of these functions:

- Is it easy to insert/remove the memory card and battery?
- How are the images stored and previewed in the camera?
- How easy is it to extract images from the memory card by using a card reader or photo printer?
- If you intend to use a cable for exporting images to your computer, ask to test the feature using the demo camera. How fast is the transfer? Is the connection process simple to operate?

Index

3D Transform filter
    bending images, 455–459
    introduction, 454–455
    lens flares, 460–461
    lighting effects and, 462–467
    texture and, 467–468
    tools, 454–455
    wireframe reshape, 459–460
24-bit color files
    format comparison, 644
    introduction, 642–643
    transparency, 645

A

A-sized pages, presets, 17
ACE (Adobe Color Engine)
  definition, 711
active layer, 711
active window, 711
additive primaries, 142, 711
Adjustment filters, 429, 434–436
adjustment layers
    applying, 327–328
    definition, 711
    layer mask application, 331–333
    names, 325–327
    shortcuts, 329–330
    targeting, 328–329
    types, 324–325
adjustments, altering, 182–183
Adobe Color Picker, 711
Adobe RGB, 711
airbrushing, 711
algorithms, 711
aliasing, 712
alignment
    arrow keys, 99
    gridlines, 99, 100–101
    rulers, 99, 100

alpha channels, 712
anchors, 712
animated GIFs
    building, 669–673
    definition, 712
anti-aliasing, 712
artifacts
    correction and, 362–363
    definition, 712
    JPEG, 369–370
Artistic filters, 429, 509–513
aspect ratio, 712
Audio icon, 38
auto levels, 712
Auto Red Eye Fix, 178–179

B

background
    erasing, 572–574
    layer, converting, 283–284
    selections, deleting, 281–282
background color, setting, 140–141
Background Eraser tool, 572–574
Background layer, 712
backlight, 712
base layer, 712
batch processing
    definition, 712
    edits, applying, 677–678
    file locations, 673–675
    images, 675–677
    labeling images, 678–379
bevels, 713
bicubic sharpener, 713
bicubic smoother, 713
bilinear, 713
bit depth, 221, 713

bitmap, 713
bitmap images
    color and, 223–225
    pixels and, 107
    vector images comparison, 110
bits per channel, 713
black point, 713
blending mode, 304–305
    color settings, 315–319
    darken, 305–307
    definition, 713
    light, 310–313
    lighten, 307–309
    Overlay blend, 309–310
    subtracting, 313–314
blocks, text, 524–529
blooming, correcting, 363–364
Blur filters, 429, 436–440
blurs, 713
bounding boxes, 713
brightness
    adjusting, 193–194
    definition, 714
    introduction, 142
    raw files, 703–704
browsers, Web image preview and, 663–669
Brush Stroke filters, 430, 507–509
brush strokes
    Brush tool, 543
    Color Replacement Brush tool, 543–544
    Impressionist Brush tool, 543
    Pattern Stamp tool, 543
    Pencil tool, 543
Brush tool
    categories, default, 547–548
    custom brush, saving, 554
    deleting brushes, 554
    description, 543
    images as brushes, 555–558
    library, 545–546
    options, 544
    tips, custom, 549–553
    types of brushes, 546–547
Brushes palette, 544

B-sized pages, presets, 17
burning
    definition, 714
    discs, 632–633

C

cache file, 714
calendars, 606–607
calibrating monitor, 212–215
camera
    downloading images, 7–9
    needs worksheet, 741–743
    preferences, Organizer and, 6–7
camera raw, 714
Camera Raw dialog box, 692–695
cameras, selection tips, 746
canvas
    clipping and, 117–118
    definition, 714
    size, modifying, 116–117
    straightening and, 121–122
card reader, Organizer preferences, 6–7
cascading windows, command, 96
catalog (Organizer)
    deleting files, 32–33
    moving files, 31–32
    new, 30–31
categories
    creating, 75–76
    filters, 429–430
CDs, burning, 632–633
channels
    color, individual, 207–208
    definition, 714
checklists
    file formats, 740–741
    image correction, 735–736
    image storage preparation, 738–739
    presentation creation, 736–737
    printing, 737–738
chroma, 714
chromatic aberration, 714
Clipboard
    definition, 714
    presets, overview, 17

clipping
    previewing clipped areas, 206–207
    raw files, 697
    raw files, previewing, 702–703
clipping groups
    definition, 714
    introduction, 337–338
clipping images, 337–338
clones, 714
cloning pixels, retouching and, 406–408
closed shapes, 715
CMYK color definition, 715
Collection icon, 38
collections
    creating, 56–57, 593–594
    deleting, 62
    deleting images, 62
    groups, defining, 59–60
    icons, 57–58
    images, adding, 58–59
    merging, 62
    notifying recipients, 596–597
    numbering photos, 61
    removing from group, 62
    reorganizing palette, 62–63
    structure, 61
    uploading, 594–596
    viewing, 60–61, 596–597
Collections palette, Organizer, 29, 62–63
color
    additive primaries, 142
    adjustments, 227–229
    background, 140–141
    bit depth, 221
    blending mode, 315–319
    brightness, 142
    channels, 221
    channels, individual, 207–208
    dithering and, 657–661
    exact, specifying, 204–207
    fixes, 185–186
    foreground, 140–141
    graphs and, 195–198
    grayscale, 222–223
    hue, 142
    from image, 149–150
    indexed, 225–227, 654–663
    indexed, image features, 649–651
    indexed, images, 648–649
    information, reading, 235–237
    introduction, 139
    monitor and, 142–143
    out-of-gamut, 212
    previewing for Web distribution, 666
    profiles, embedding in image, 216–217
    replacing, 416–420
    retouching and, 415–420
    saturation, 142
    selecting from Color Picker, 145–146
    skin tone, 228–229
    toolbox and, 140–141
    values, defining, 144–145
    variations and, 231–233
    Web sites for, 732
    Web-safe color, 730
color cast
    changing automatically, 230–231
    corrections, 208–209
    definition, 715
    identification, 230
    raw files, removing, 698–700
color channels, 715
color depth, 715
color gamut, 715
color management
    definition, 715
    overview, 211–212
color mode
    definition, 715
    introduction, 220–221
color models, 141–143, 715
color palettes, indexed color images, 651–654
Color Picker
    color choices, 143–144
    custom colors, 147
    selecting color, 145–146
    Web colors, 148–149
    Windows, 146–148
Color Replacement Brush tool
    replacing color, 564
    sampling color and, 562–563

Color Replacement tool, 543–544
color sampling, overview, 194–195
color separation, 715
color space
    assigning, 217–219
    definition, 715
color swatches
    changing, 140
    definition, 716
    deleting color, 153
    libraries, 150–155
color table
    definition, 716
    editing, 661–663
color value, 716
color wheel, 716
colorizing, 716
commands, transformations, 132–134
complementary colors, 716
compression
    definition, 716
    lossless, 722
    lossy, 722
confusing content, correcting, 387–389
connecting files, Photo Browser, 49–53
contact sheets, creating, 584
contrast
    adjusting, 193–194
    definition, 716
    raw files, 703–704
Cookie Cutter
    definition, 716
    settings, 126
    shapes and, 122–123
copy operations. *See also* duplication
    selections, 268–269
copyright template, creating, 684–688
corrections. *See also* retouching
    artifacts and, 362–363
    automatic enhancement, 179–181
    blooming, 363–364
    checklist, 735–736
    color fixes, 185–186
    color fixes, retouching and, 401–403
    confusing content, 387–389
    fringing, 370–380
    general fixes, 183
    hot spots, 380–383
    lighting fixes, 184–185
    manual, 361–389
    moiré patterns, 365
    Quick Fix, 174–178
    sharpening, 186–187, 383–386
    workflow, 361–362
Creation icon, 38
creations
    definition, 716
    saving, 602–603
    types, 601
Crop tool, quick crops and, 114–115
cropping
    definition, 716
    quick crops, 114–115
    resolution and, 115–116
    into shapes, 125–126
    visually, 113–114
curves, 717
Custom preset, 17
cutouts, 717

D

Date view (Photo Browser)
    days and months, 46–47
    introduction, 44–45
    new events, 47–48
    set date/time, 48–49
    year by year, 45–46
defringing
    definition, 717
    selections, 378–380
De-Interlace filter, 442
desaturate, 717
details
    brightness, 193–194
    contrast, 193–194
    highlight, 190–193
    shadow, 190–193
Digimarc filters, 429
digital camera. *See* camera
Digital Negatives, saving, 706–709
dimensions, presets, 17
Disc icon, 38
discs, burning, 632–633
displacement map, 481–485, 717
Distort filters, 430, 469–485

distorting, 717
distribution
    slide shows, 632
    Web, 635–637
dithering
    color creation and, 657–661
    definition, 717
    previewing for Web distribution, 666–669
dodging, 717
dots, 717
downloading
    from camera, 7–9
    images from video clips, 20–23
    Photo Downloader and, 8–9
    sorting afterward, 10–11
downsampling
    definition, 717
    upsampling and, 111
dpi (dots per inch), 717
drawing
    Pencil tool, 559–560
    shapes and, 128–131
duplication. *See also* copy operations
    layers, 284–285
dynamic brush options, 717

E

Edit and Enhance Photos task, Welcome Screen, 5
editing, versions, 68–69
Editor window, new files, 15
edits, Slide Show Editor, 621–622
effects
    applying, 356–357
    categories, 354–356
Elliptical Marquee tool, 242
e-mail
    collections, 593–597
    contents, 590
    layout, 591–593
embedded data
    introduction, 679–680
    watermarks, 688–689
embedded profiles, 718
EPS (encapsulated PostScript)
    definition, 718

erasing backgrounds, 572–574
erasing pixels
    introduction, 568–569
    Magic Eraser tool, 569–572
EXIF (Exchangeable Image File Format) definition, 718
exporting, tags, 680–684
exposure, raw files, 702
eye enhancements, 408–411

F

faces, tagging, 82–83
fades, 718
faux font, 718
Favorites, 718
Favorites category, tags, 73
feathering
    definition, 718
    selections, 271–272
file formats
    24-bit color files, 644
    checklist, 740–741
    Web page and, 637
File Info dialog box, 684–685
files
    importing, 18
    size, 106
fill layer, 718
fills
    gradients, 164–172
    Paint Bucket and, 160–161
    patterns, 158–160
    properties, 156–157
    shapes, 156–157
    strokes, 163–164
Filter Gallery
    adding filters, 431
    introduction, 430
    working in, 431–434
filters
    3D Transform, 454–468
    Adjustment filters, 434–436
    applying, 426–429
    Artistic, 509–513
    Blur filters, 436–440
    Brush Stroke, 507–509
    categories, 429–430

filters *(cont.)*
  combining, 485
  custom, 447–449
  definition, 718
  De-Interlace, 442
  Distort, 469–485
  High Pass, 444–445
  introduction, 425–426
  Liquify, 486–489
  noise and, 440–441
  NTSC Colors, 442
  Offset, 446–447
  pixel brightness and, 445–446
  pixelation and, 490–492
  Render filters, 450–454
  Sharpen, 441
  Shear, 476–478
  Sketch, 492–498
  specific purposes, 513–520
  Spherize, 471–476
  Stylize, 499–503
  texture, 503–507
  video, 442
  Wave, 478–481
Find bar, Organizer, 27
Find Faces, 718
fixes. *See* corrections
flattening, 300–302, 718
Flickr Web site, 733
folders, watched, 19
font families, 719
font styles, 719
fonts. *See also* text
  definition, 718
  locating, 529–530
  multiple, 531
  previews, 530
foreground color, setting, 140–141
fringing
  definition, 719
  introduction, 370–372
  layers and, 372–376
fuzziness, 719

G

gallery, online management, 597
gamma, 719
gamma adjustment, 719

gamut
  definition, 719
  monitor and, 212
  out-of-gamut colors, 212
Gaussian blue, 719
GB (gigabytes), 106
General Fixes palette, Auto Red Eye Fix, 178–179
geometric selections, 243–244
Get Photos dialog box, 13
GIF (Graphics Interchange Format)
  animated, building, 669–673
  definition, 719
  PNG-8 comparison, 649
  Web page, 637
gigabytes (GB), 106
gradients
  defining, 168–170
  definition, 719
  introduction, 164–165
  noise, 170–171
  path, 166–168
  tips for using, 171–172
  types, 165
graphic enhancements, slide shows, 625–626
gray point, 719
grayscale
  converting to, 222–223
  definition, 719
greeting cards, 606–607
grid
  alignment and, 100–101
  settings, 101–102
grid lines, 720
groups, collections, 59–60

H

halos, 720
healing images, 404–406
Hidden category, tags, 73
High Pass filter, 444–445
highlights
  adjusting, 190–193
  definition, 720
histograms
  definition, 720
  Histogram palette, 235

History state, 720
hotspots
    information on, 381
    removing, 380–383
    Unsharp Mask and, 386
HSB (Hue/Saturation/Brightness)
    definition, 720
HTML Photo Gallery creation, 607–609
hue, 142, 720
hue jitter, 720

I

ICC (International Color Consortium)
    Web site, 732
icons
    collections, 57–58
    Photo Browser, 37–38
image cache, 720
image mode, 720
image tiling, 720
images
    as brushes, 555–558
    color from, 149–150
    cropping visually, 113–114
    document size, 111
    resizing, dimensions, 108–110
    stacking, 64–66
    statistics, 237
    straightening, 118–122
    straightening automatically, 120–121
    tags, removing, 80
Imagestation Web site, 733
importing
    files, 18
    from mobile phone, 20
    tags, 680–684
Impressionist Brush tool
    description, 543
    overview, 560–562
indexed color, 225–227, 720
indexed color images
    color palettes, 651–654
    custom, 654–663
    features, 649–651
    introduction, 648–649
    matte options, 656
    transparency, 656

interpolation
    Bicubic option, 112
    Bicubic Sharpener option, 113
    Bicubic Smoother option, 113
    Bilinear option, 112
    definition, 720
    Nearest Neighbor option, 112

J

jitter, 720
JPEG (Joint Photograph Experts Group)
    artifacts, 369–370
    compression, 721
    definition, 721
    matting simulation, 645–646
    Web page, 637

K

KB (kilobytes), 106
Kelvin color temperature scale, 721
kilobytes (KB), 106
Kodak EasyShare Web site, 733

L

labeling images, batch processing and, 678–679
labels
    printing, 586–587
    slide shows, 626
Lasso tool, 242, 248–250, 721
layer masks
    applying to adjustment layer, 331–333
    definition, 721
    text, 334–337
layers
    active layer, 711
    adding, 285–286
    adjustment, 321–330
    arranging, 289
    background, deleting selections, 281–282
    Background layer, 712
    base layer, 712
    blending modes, 304–319

layers *(cont.)*
    characteristics, 291–292
    clipping images and, 337–338
    complex styles, 347–350
    definition, 721
    duplicating, 284–285
    fringing and, 372–376
    introduction, 277–278
    linking/unlinking, 296–297
    locks, 292–296
    merging, 297–299
    naming, 288–289
    opacity, 302–303
    organization, 288–289
    purposes, 286
    settings, new, 286–287
    shapes, multiple in one layer, 135–137
    simple styles, 346
    styles, 339–345
    target layer, 728
    text, 728
    thumbnails, 279
    transparency appearance, 289–291
    types, 280
Layers palette, 277–278
Layers Styles menu, 346–347
Levels, 198–200, 721
libraries, color swatches, 150–155
lighting
    3D Transform filter and, 462–467
    raw files, 699
links, layers, 296–297
Liquify filter, 486–489
liquifying type, 537–539
locked files, 721
locked layers, 292–296, 721
lossless compression, 722
lossy compression, 722
luminance, 722
LZW compression definition, 722

M

Magic Eraser tool, pixels, erasing, 569–572
Magic Extractor, 262–266
Magic Selection Brush tool, 243, 261–262
Magic Wand tool, 243, 255

Magnetic Lasso tool, 242, 251–254
magnification
    custom settings, 93–94
    default settings, 93
Make Photo Creations Photos task, Welcome Screen, 5
marquee
    definition, 722
    sizing, 247–248
mask mode, 722
masking, text, 532–534
masks, painting, 259–260
matadata, 722
Match Location, 96, 722
Match Zoom, 96, 722
matte options, indexed color images, 656–657
matting
    definition, 722
    JPEG images, 645–646
    PNG images, 646–647
MB (megabytes), 106
megabytes (MB), 106
menus
    filter application and, 428–429
    Organizer, 27
merging, layers, 297–299
midtones
    adjusting, 204
    definition, 723
mobile phone, image capture, 19–20
moiré pattern, 365, 723
monitor
    calibration, 212–215
    color and, 142–143
    profile, 723
    profile, calibration and, 214
    resolution, 723
Move tool, 266–268

N

named image files, 17
naming, layers, 288–289
narration, slide shows, 624–625
Navigator palette
    definition, 723
    docking, 95
Nearest Neighbor, 723

New dialog box, new documents and, 15–16
noise
  correcting, 366–368
  definition, 723
  filters and, 440–441
Noise filters, 429
NTSC Colors filter, 442
nudging, 723

O

Offset filter, 446–447
one-click adjustment, raw files, 700–701
online ordering, 588–590, 605–606
opacity
  Brush tool, 544
  definition, 723
  settings, 302–303
open shape, 723
optimization, Web images, 637–642
Options bar, 723
ordering prints online, 588–590
organization
  layers, 288–289
  Match Location and, 96
  Match Zoom and, 96
  orientation and, 98–99
Organizer
  Arrangement menu, 27
  camera preferences, 6–7
  card reader preferences, 6–7
  catalog, 30–33
  collections, 64
  Collections palette, 29
  creation setup, 600–603
  creation types, 601
  creations, saving, 602–603
  Find bar, 27
  Full Screen View button, 29
  introduction, 599–600
  menu, 27
  methods of organization, 64
  opening, 26
  Organize Bin, 26, 29
  photo album creation, 603–604
  properties, 86–87

  Properties button, 29
  Rotate thumbnails, 29
  Shortcuts bar, 27
  starting Elements, 3
  tags, 64
  Tags palette, 29
  Thumbnail size slider, 27
  Thumbnails view, 27
  Timeline, 27, 35–37
  window, 27
Organizer window, as opening view, 5–6
origins, 723
Other filters, 429
out-of-gamut colors, 212
output dimensions
  definition, 724
  file size and, 106
Overlay blend, 309–310

P

Paint Bucket
  fills and, 160–161
  options, 161–163
painting
  with brush, 549
  contrast, 412
  masks, 259–260
  modes, 558
  selection tools, 258–259
Palette Bin
  definition, 724
  Navigator palette, docking, 95
pan and zoom
  definition, 724
  slide shows, 630–631
panoramas
  creating, 612–616
  definition, 724
  preplanning, 611–312
paper, size, presets, 17
paste operations, selections, 269–271
paths, 724
Pattern Stamp tool
  applying stamps, 566–568
  description, 543
  stamp creation, 564–566

patterns
  definition, 724
  fills, 158–160
PDF (Portable Document Format)
  definition, 725
PDP (Portable Document Format)
  definition, 725
Pencil tool
  description, 543
  drawing, 559–560
perspective, 724
Perspective tool, 724
photo album, creating, 603–604
Photo Browser
  connecting files, 49–53
  Date view, 44–48
  definition, 724
  details, hiding, 38–39
  icons, 37–38
  introduction, 26
  opening automatically, 26–27
  sorting, by batch, 34
  sorting, by date, 33–34
  sorting, by folder, 34–35
  special views control bar, 41–42
  video and, 43–44
  views, 39–43
Photo Downloader, downloading images and, 8–9
Photo Filters, 233–235
photo gallery, Web, 607–611
Photoshop Elements, starting, 3
Photoshop Elements Techniques Web site, 733
PhotoshopSupport Web site, 733
PICT format definition, 724
pixel dimensions
  bitmap images and, 107
  file size and, 106
pixel resolution, file size and, 106
Pixelate filters, 430
pixelation
  definition, 725
  filters and, 490–492
pixels
  brightness, filters and, 445–446
  calculating, 107
  cloning, retouching and, 406–408
  definition, 724

dimensions, 725
  erasing, 568–574
PlanetPhotoshop Web site, 734
Plug-in filters, 429
PNG (Portable Network Graphics)
  definition, 725
  matting simulation, 646–647
  PNG compared to GIF, 649
  Web page, 637
points, 725
Polygon Lasso tool, 250–251
Polygon tool, 725
Polygonal Lasso tool, 242
posterization, 725
PostScript, 725
ppi (pixels per inch)
  calculating, 107
  definition, 725
preferences, slide shows, 618–620
presentation, creation checklist, 736–737
previewing Web images, 663–669
printer, resolution, 725
printer package, 584–586
printers, profiles, 725
printing
  checklist, 737–738
  color management and, 581–582
  contact sheets, 584
  Editor mode, 578–580
  image order, 587–588
  labels, 586–587
  marking images, 42–43
  multiple images, 582–583
  options, 577–578
  ordering prints online, 588–590
  printer package, 584–586
  rendering intent, 581–582
  settings, 579–580
  Web site for, 731
Product Overview task, Welcome Screen, 4
profiles, color, embedding in images, 216–217
properties, Organizer, 29, 86–87
Properties palette, Organizer, 29
Proxy magazine Web site, 732
PSD files definition, 726
purchase considerations worksheet, 743–745

Q

quick crops, 114–115
Quick Fix mode
  definition, 726
  introduction, 174–178
  printing from, 578–580
Quickly Fix Photos task, Welcome Screen, 5
QuickTime, 726

R

radius, 726
raster images, 726
raw files
  adjustment, 695–696
  adjustment, one-click, 700–701
  brightness, 703–704
  clipping, 697
  clipping, previewing, 702–703
  color cast, removing, 698–700
  contrast, 703–704
  details, 705–706
  exposure, 702
  introduction, 691
  lighting options, 699
  positioning, 696
  saturation, 704–705
  saving negatives, 706–709
  shadows, 702
  tint, 700
  white balance, 698–699
  zoom, 696
raw format
  definition, 726
  rotating, 12
Rectangular Marquee tool, 242
red eye
  Auto Red Eye Fix, 178–179
  definition, 726
Red Eye Removal tool, 397–399
remapping, 726
Render filters, 429, 450–454
rendering, 726
rendering intents, 581–582
resampling
  definition, 726
  options, 111–112

resize handles, 726
resizing images, dimensions, 108–110
resolution
  cropping and, 115–116
  definition, 727
  pixel resolution, 106
  screen, presets, 17
  video, presets, 17
resources
  Adobe Web sites, 731–732
  color information Web sites, 732
  online resources, 733–734
  photo sharing online, 732–733
  scrapbooking Web sites, 734
  specifications Web sites, 732
retouching. *See also* corrections
  color and, 415–420
  correction color, defining, 401–403
  darkening and, 414–415
  eye enhancements, 408–411
  healing images, 404–406
  introduction, 391
  lightening and, 414–415
  pixel cloning, 406–408
  Red Eye Removal tool, 397–399
  Spot Healing Brush tool, 399–401
  tools, 411
  weight reduction, 391–397
RGB definition, 727
rotation
  definition, 727
  raw files, 12
rulers
  alignment and, 100
  definition, 727
  settings, 101–102

S

samples, 727
sampling, 541–542
saturation, 142, 704–705, 727
saving, selections, 273–274
scanning
  definition, 727
  overview, 12–14
  TWAIN scans, 14
· scatter, 727

scrapbook Web sites, 734
scratch desk, 727
screen, resolution, 727
screen resolution, presets, 17
searches, tags and, 85–86
security, 689
Select menu, 256–257
Selection Brush tool, 243, 257–260
selection tools, 241–243
selections
    composition, 244–246
    copying, 268–269
    defringing, 378–380
    edge treatments and, 246
    edges, modifying, 272–273
    geometric, 243–244
    Lasso too, 248–250
    Magic Extractor and, 262–266
    Magic Selection Brush tool, 261–262
    Magic Wand tool, 255
    Move tool, 266–268
    painting, 258–259
    pasting, 269–271
    Polygon Lasso tool, 250–251
    reselecting selections, 271–273
    revising, 274–276
    saving, 273–274
    Selection Brush tool, 257–260
    text, 526–527
    text blocks, 526–527
shadows
    adjusting, 190–193
    definition, 727
    raw files, 702
shapes
    cropping into, 125–126
    cutting out, 125–126
    definition, 727
    drawing and, 128–131
    fills, 156–157
    Magnetic Lasso tool and, 251–254
    multiple in one layer, 135–137
    selecting, 124
    tools, options, 130–131
    transforming, 131–134
    viewing, 122–124

Shapes palette, 128–131
sharing photos, Web sites for, 732–733
sharing slide shows, 632
Sharpen filters, 429, 441
sharpening
    correction and, 186–187, 383–386
    definition, 728
Shear filter, 476–478
Shortcuts bar, Organizer, 27
simplifying, 728
single channel images, 728
size
    Brush tool, 544
    marquee, 247–248
    presets, 17
Sketch filters, 430, 492–498
skew, 728
skin tone color adjustment, 228–229
Slide Show Editor
    navigating, 620–623
    reordering slide show, 623
Slide Show Preferences dialog box, 619–620
slide shows
    distributing, 632
    edits, 621–622
    graphic enhancements, 625–626
    labels, 626
    music, 623–624
    narration, 624–625
    overview, 617–618
    panning, 630–631
    preferences, 618–620
    reordering, 623
    sound, 623–624
    text, 626
    text appearance, 626–627
    text effects, 627–628
    transitions, 628–630
    zooming, 630–631
smoothing, 728
smudging, retouching and, 413
sorting
    by batch (Photo Browser), 34
    by date (Photo Browser), 33–34
    by folder (Photo Browser), 34–35
spacing, multiple spaces, 532

special views control bar, Photo Browser, buttons, 41–42
Spherize filter, 471–476
Spot Healing Brush tool, 399–401
sRGB, 728
Stack icon, 38
stacking images
    flattening stack, 65
    introduction, 64–65
    merging stacks, 65
    unstacking, 65
    versions, 67–71
Standard Edit mode
    definition, 728
    printing from, 578–580
Start From Scratch Photos task, Welcome Screen, 5
starting Photoshop Elements, 3
startup, Quick Fix window, 175
Straighten tool, 119–122
straightening
    automatically, 120–121
    canvas adjustments and, 121–122
    definition, 728
    introduction, 118–119
strokes, 163–164, 728
styles
    layers, 339–345
    layers, complex, 347–350
    layers, simple, 346
    reusing, 351–352
Styles and Effect palette, filter application and, 427
Stylize filters, 430, 499–503

T

Tag icon, 38
tags
    categories, 72–73
    categories, creating, 75–76
    creating, 77–78
    editing, 78–80
    exceptions, 73–75
    exporting, 680–684
    faces, 82–83
    images, attaching to, 78
    images, removing, 80
    importing, 680–684
    instant, 80–81
    overview, 71–72
    searches and, 85–86
Tags palette, Organizer, 29, 72–73, 79–80
target colors, 728
target layer, 728
tasks, Welcome Screen, 4–5
templates
    applying, 687
    configuration, 685–687
text. *See also* fonts
    appearance, slide shows, 626–627
    committing, 525–526
    converting, 536–537
    layers and, 334–337
    liquifying, 537–539
    masking, 532–534
    selecting, 526–527
    slide shows, 626, 627–628
    typing, 523–524
    warping, 534–535
text blocks
    introduction, 524–525
    resizing, 527–529
    selecting, 526–527
text layer, 728
Texture filters, 430, 503–507
TGA (Targa) format definition, 728
threshold, 729
thumbnails
    definition, 729
    layers, 279
TIFF (Tagged Image File Format) definition, 728
tiling windows
    automatically, 96
    command, 96
Timeline, Organizer
    introduction, 27
    overview, 35
    toggling on/off, 36
tint
    definition, 729
    raw files, 700

tonal corrections, 729
tones
    automatic adjustment, 201–204
    manual adjustment, 201
    midrange, adjusting, 204
Tool Options bar, Zoom, 92
toolbar, 729
toolbox
    color and, 140–141
    definition, 729
tools
    Quick Fix, 177–178
    Zoom, 92
transformations
    commands, 132–134
    definition, 729
    shapes, 131–134
transitions, slide shows, overview, 628–630
transparency
    24-bit images, 645
    appearance, 289–291
    definition, 729
    indexed color images, 656–657
Tutorials Photos task, Welcome Screen, 5
TWAIN
    definition, 729
    scans, 14
type
    liquifying, 537–539
    warping, 534–535
type mask, 729
Type tool
    introduction, 521–523
    options, 522–523
typing text, 523–524

U

Units & Rulers option, 101–102
units of measure, 729
Unsharp Mask, hotspots and, 386
uploading, collections, 594–596
upsampling
    definition, 729
    downsampling and, 111

V

vanishing point, 730
vector images, bitmap image comparison, 110
vectors, 730
version set, 730
Version Set icon, 38
versions
    contents, viewing, 69–70
    editing, 68–69
    stacking and, 67–71
video
    downloading images from, 20–23
    Photo Browser and, 43–44
video filters, 429, 442
Video icon, 38
View and Organize Photos task, Welcome Screen, 4
View menu, Zoom tools and, 96
views, Photo Browser, 39–43
vignetting, 730

W

warping
    definition, 730
    type, 534–535
watched folders
    creating, 19
    definition, 730
watermarks
    creating, 688–689
    detecting, 449
Wave filter, 478–481
Web distribution
    file formats, 637
    image quality, 636
Web pages
    24-bit color files, 642–645
    image optimization, 637–642
    image preview, 663–669
Web sites
    Adobe, 731–732
    color information, 732
    memory management, 734
    online resources, 733–734
    photo sharing, 732–733

scrapbooking, 734
specifications, 732
Web-safe color, 730
weight reduction retouch, 391–397
Welcome Screen, 3–5
white balance
    definition, 730
    raw files, 698–699
white point, 730
windows
    active, 711
    cascading, 96
    Match Location, 96
    Match Zoom, 96
    Organizer, 27
    resizing, automatic, 95
    tiling, 96

workflow, image correction and, 361–362
worksheets
    camera needs, 741–743
    purchase considerations, 743–745

X–Y–Z

ZIP encoding definition, 730
zoom
    definition, 730
    raw files, 696
    slide shows, 630–631
    Zoom tool, 92
Zoom tool
    definition, 730
    options, 94–95
    toggling, 92

Get it straight.

Straight from the experts — authoritative, must-know information on today's hottest technologies. Each *Unofficial Guide* presents unbiased information based on the author's real-world experience, giving you more than the official line.

For a complete list of *Unofficial Guides* on technology, travel, real estate, business, health, and lifestyle topics, go to wiley.com. Available wherever books are sold.

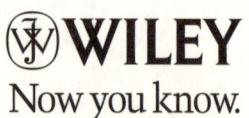

Now you know.